W9-CTU-083

A Community of Readers

A Thematic Approach to Reading

©2007 Pearson Education, Inc.

A Community of Readers

A Thematic Approach to Reading

Fourth Edition

Roberta Alexander
San Diego City College

Jan Lombardi
San Diego City College

PEARSON
Longman

New York   San Francisco   Boston
London   Toronto   Sydney   Tokyo   Singapore   Madrid
Mexico City   Munich   Paris   Cape Town   Hong Kong   Montreal

Acquisitions Editor: Melanie Craig
Development Editor: Ann Grogg
Marketing Manager: Thomas DeMarco
Senior Supplements Editor: Donna Campion
Production Manager: Stacey Kulig
Project Coordination, TextDesign, and Electronic Page Make-up:
   Pre-Press Company, Inc.
Senior Cover Design Manager: Nancy Danahy
Cover Illustration/Photo: ©Getty Images/PhotoDisc Inc. and
   ©Photos.com/Jupiterimages Corporation
Photo Researcher: Vivette Porges
Senior Manufacturing Buyer: Dennis Para
Printer and Binder: R. R. Donnelley and Sons
Cover Printer: Coral Graphic Services

For permission to use copyrighted material, grateful acknowledgment is
made to the copyright holders on pp. 580–583, which are hereby made
part of this copyright page.

Library of Congress Cataloging-in-Publication Data

Alexander, Roberta, 1946–
   A community of readers: a thematic approach to reading / Roberta
Alexander, Jan Lombardi.--4th ed.
      p. cm.
   Includes bibliographical references and index.
   ISBN 0-321-41883-2 (annotated instructor's ed.)
   1. College readers. 2. Reading comprehension. I. Lombardi, Jan.
   II. Title.

PE1122.A35 2006
428.6--dc22

                                                            2006041661

Copyright © 2007 by Pearson Education, Inc.

All rights reserved. No part of this publication may be reproduced, stored
in a retrieval system, or transmitted, in any form or by any means, electronic, mechanical, photocopying, recording, or otherwise, without the
prior written permission of the publisher. Printed in the United States.

Please visit us at www.ablongman.com/alexander

ISBN 0-321-38763-5 (Student edition)
ISBN 0-321-41883-2 (Instructors annotated edition)
1 2 3 4 5 6 7 8 9 10—DOC—09 08 07 06

8/05

We would like to dedicate this text to
Ethel and Hursel Alexander
and
Veronica and Francis Ryan

©2007 Pearson Education, Inc.

BRIEF CONTENTS

Part I   *Skills Instruction and Thematic Readings*   *1*

Part II   *A Reader's Toolkit*   *529*

©2007 Pearson Education, Inc.

DETAILED CONTENTS

©2007 Pearson Education, Inc.

©2007 Pearson Education, Inc.

©2007 Pearson Education, Inc.

©2007 Pearson Education, Inc.

Cumulative Mastery Tests 509

Part II A Reader's Toolkit 529

©2007 Pearson Education, Inc.

READINGS BY DISCIPLINE

In addition to the following readings, examples in the text and excerpts in exercises draw from a variety of disciplines that students will encounter in college.

Biology

Hursel, "Food Pyramids: For Profit or Health"
Insel et al., "Wellness"
Kotulak, "Cyberthought"
Macionis, "Ethical Issues Surrounding Death"
McKay et al., "Pathology of the Black Death"
Williams and Knight, "How Stress Works"

Business

Barlow and Kauzlarich, "Criminals at Work"
Frammolino, "Workers Feel Like Suckers"
Mooney, "Making Well People Better"
Mueller, "As Sick As It Gets"
Mueller, "Emergency Rooms and the Uninsured"
Schlosser, "Behind the Counter"
Schlosser, "Oh, the Flavor of Your Fries"

Computers and Technology

Beekman, "Social and Ethical Issues of Computer Technology"
Beekman, "Living with Computers"
Beekman, "Living Without Computers"
Beekman, "No Secrets"
Kotulak, "Cyberthought"
Weiner, "Robot Soldiers Are Coming"

Economics

Barlow and Kauzlarich, "Criminals at Work"
Frammolino, "Workers Feel Like Suckers"
Hursel, "Food Pyramids: For Profit or Health?"

Education

Cunningham, "Use the Tools for College Success!"
Gregory, "Shame"
Haring-Smith, "What Is Collaborative Learning?"

©2007 Pearson Education, Inc.

Jordan, "Becoming a Student"
Linksman, "How We Learn"
Peifer, "Suburb High, USA"

Ethics

Beekman, "Social and Ethical Issues of Computer Technology"
Beekman, "No Secrets"
Carter and Carter, "Working with Our Hands"
The Economist, "AIDS: The Long War"
Eudy, "Signing for a Revolution: Gallaudet University and Deaf Culture"
Kotulak, "Cyberthought"
Macionis, "Ethical Issues Surrounding Death"
Mooney, "Making Well People 'Better'"
Mueller, "As Sick As It Gets"
Mueller, "Emergency Rooms and the Uninsured"
Twain, "The War Prayer"
Weiner, "Robot Soldiers Are Coming"

Ethnic Studies

Ahmed, "Identity in Transformation"
Espada, "Rage"
Eudy, "Signing for a Revolution: Gallaudet University and Deaf Culture"
Jordan, "Becoming a Student"
Kotlowitz, "Colorblind: When Blacks and Whites Can See No Gray"
Martínez, "Can We All Get Along?"
Staples, "Black Men and Public Space"

Gender Studies

Ahmed, "Identity in Transformation"
Brady, "Why I Want a Wife"
Espada, "Rage"
Gregory, "Shame"
Mayhew, "Easy Bake Ovens and Fashion Magazines"
Moravia, "The Chase"
Sanders, "The Men We Carry in Our Minds"
Staples, "Black Men and Public Space"
Tannen, "Sex, Lies, and Conversation"

Health

Cousins, "Creativity and Longevity"
The Economist, "AIDS: The Long War"
Eudy, "Signing for a Revolution: Gallaudet University and Deaf Culture"
Hales, "A Personal Stress Survival Guide"

©2007 Pearson Education, Inc.

TO THE INSTRUCTOR

A Community of Readers, fourth edition, provides college students with guided, in-depth instruction in all segments of the reading and learning processes: reading, discussing, writing, and critical thinking. Organized around high-interest, motivational, and contemporary themes, *A Community of Readers* is a reading text that emphasizes student involvement in the entire reading process—prereading activities, active reading, postreading activities, and critical reflection. Each chapter presents an essential reading skill and challenges students to master it through readings and exercises with a unifying theme. The first chapter focuses on the reading process and on joining a community of readers in a college setting. Each of the following chapters presents a reading skill, such as building vocabulary, identifying main ideas, understanding inferences, reading literature, and thinking critically.

As students progress through each chapter, they learn, practice, and review all the reading skills they need to succeed in their college courses. Because each chapter of the text builds on a single theme, students have the time to develop schema and exchange knowledge on a particular concept or issue, including computer technology and beyond; food and culture; staying well; where we live; dealing with gender; living in a diverse society; and science, society, and disease. With its emphasis on collaborative learning, *A Community of Readers* is accessible to students from various language and academic backgrounds.

The fourth edition of *A Community of Readers* has a new emphasis—on student participation in the classroom community and on self-motivated learning. A new set of cumulative mastery tests allows students to test themselves on all the skills covered in the text. In addition, recognizing the importance of student motivation and engagement, "A Reader's Toolkit" has been converted from an appendix into Part II of the book, with new opportunities for students to work in their classrooms and by themselves to supplement in-class instruction. New to the "Toolkit" is a focused section on "Reading Visual Aids," where students can inform and test themselves on their visual interpretive skills. An enhanced section on "Evaluating and Navigating Web Sites" gives instruction in the increasingly important skill of using the Internet. And two new sections describe reading circles and poster sessions as means for student-directed learning.

New to the Fourth Edition

- *Fourteen new readings.* The new readings chosen for this edition build on the high-interest themes and relevant topics that are the hallmarks of the book. More than one-fourth of the readings are new, drawn from both academic and popular sources. Some have

©2007 Pearson Education, Inc.

been written especially for *A Community of Readers* to reinforce skills practice within the context of the thematic format. Altogether, the book has 18 readings from textbooks to acquaint students with the content of college courses in a variety of disciplines and to help them build their reading skills in the academic material they will need to master for success in college. All the readings encourage students to learn and practice their skills in the context of the ideas and issues presented in each chapter.

- *Up-to-date topics.* Chapter 2, "Computer Technology and Beyond," focusing on vocabulary acquisition, has two new readings on some of the latest technological developments. Chapter 5 has four new readings and one updated reading on patterns of migration and urban development that maintain the currency of the chapter theme and facilitate mastery of the patterns of organization.

- *Integration of visual aids.* Instruction for "reading visual aids" has now been integrated throughout the text and highlighted in a condensed section in "A Reader's Toolkit," where students may inform and test themselves on their skills. The reduction in the number of chapters thus achieved recognizes the limits of instruction time and concentrates students' efforts on the most necessary skills.

- *Original and meaningful Web-based activities.* Each chapter includes an entirely new Web activity. These activities direct students to do interesting and relevant research on the Web throughout the text. With this practice, students will be more prepared for research tasks required in other disciplines and in freshman composition.

- *Cumulative mastery tests.* The two new cumulative mastery tests give students the opportunity to test themselves on all the skills covered in the text. They can be used for review at the end of the term or even as pre- and posttest instruments to measure student progress.

- *Reading circles for working together in a collaborative community.* The new section on reading circles in "A Reader's Toolkit" guides students through the process of successfully working as a *community.* It establishes a sustained, student-centered collaborative setting while providing the instructor with the necessary tools to effectively facilitate the process and monitor student progress and participation.

- *Poster sessions.* The new section on poster sessions in "A Reader's Toolkit" walks students through the process of developing oral presentations with visual aids. This technique reduces stress for shy students and ensures that the presentations are interactive and participatory. At the same time, students with diverse learning styles and strengths are recognized and rewarded.

- *Improved pedagogy and exercises.* The explanations and practice exercises for understanding inferences, reading literature, the scientific method, and critical thinking have been strengthened and made more accessible for student mastery.

Continuing Features

The fourth edition of *A Community of Readers* continues to offer a number of innovative features to enhance students' learning experience:

- *Focus on the reading process.* The essential steps to reading—prereading activities, active reading, postreading tasks, and critical thinking—are built into each chapter. Students are led to apply the new skills within the context of the reading process.
- *Thematic organization.* Because each chapter focuses on one theme, students can work with the ideas long enough to begin to understand and use complex material. Readings, as well as the examples used for skills, explanations and exercises, further explore the chapter theme.
- *Topics that are current and relevant to students.* The readings reflect some of the most recent concerns of American society, addressing issues of gender, diversity, health care, advances in technology, and the nature and consequences of eating habits and the fast-food industry.
- *Integration of reading, vocabulary, and learning strategies.* Chapter 2 focuses on vocabulary skills, and those skills are reinforced throughout the text. Learning strategies (including outlining, summarizing, and mapping) are introduced in Chapter 4, with ample practice material presented throughout the text.
- *Critical thinking skills.* By concentrating on one theme at a time, students have the opportunity to apply sustained critical thinking skills in class discussions and assigned writings. Chapter exercises consistently encourage students to use their background knowledge and to evaluate ideas, reflect, and make connections among various approaches and viewpoints.
- *Preparation for freshman composition.* Because the theme-based approach corresponds closely to the organization of a wide range of freshman composition texts, students become better prepared for the material in their composition classes. Emphasis is given to the writing and thinking skills essential for composition: paraphrasing; summarizing; recognizing organizational patterns; and evaluating bias, point of view, purpose, opinion, and arguments.
- *Collaborative work.* Exercises throughout the text encourage students to collaborate with their peers. Group problem-solving skills help students in their academic work as well as in their future careers.

Also available in this series is *Joining a Community of Readers,* which includes these same features but is intended for students in the first reading course.

Organization

The fourth edition of *A Community of Readers* introduces a new, two-part organization. Part I, "Skills Instruction and Thematic Readings," includes the skills-based chapters as well as the "Extend Your Thinking" readings

©2007 Pearson Education, Inc.

and the cumulative mastery tests. Part II, "A Reader's Toolkit," provides additional instruction in related skills and activities (note taking, test taking, writing tips, reading response journals, evaluating and navigating Web sites) that can be assigned to complement classroom activities or can be worked on individually by students. In addition, Part II includes instructions for students on working collaboratively in reading circles and making presentations in poster sessions. Finally, "A Reader's Toolkit" offers an updated list of suggested readings for book reports.

Each chapter in *A Community of Readers* is designed to teach specific reading and study skills within the context of learning about and reflecting on an issue and generating informed reactions, opinions, and possible solutions to that issue. To accomplish this progression, each chapter contains the following features:

- *An opening illustration and quotation* introduce the theme of the chapter and provide prereading questions asking students to explore their background knowledge and opinions on the topic.
- *Skills instruction* is carefully interwoven with readings about the topic of the chapter. Examples, readings, and exercises all focus on the chapter theme.
- A *chapter review* summarizes the issues and skills of the chapter and suggests postreading extension activities for collaborative group work and writing assignments.
- Two *mastery tests* at the end of each chapter give students further opportunities to demonstrate their proficiency in the skills they have learned.

An exciting collection of *additional readings* complement the themes and skills found in the text in the "Extending Your Thinking" section of Part I.

The Ancillary Package

The **instructor's manual** offers teaching tips, sample syllabi, and assignment schedules, as well as a transparency–ready answer key for mapping, outlining, and summarizing assignments. It also includes suggestions for how to use the text to prepare students for state proficiency tests. Please ask your Longman sales representative for ISBN 0-321-41948-0.

A separate **test bank** with reproducible, easily graded quizzes is also available. Please ask your Longman sales representative for ISBN 0-321-41373-3.

Also be sure to visit *A Community of Readers* online at http://www.ablongman.com/alexander. This Companion Web site offers a wealth of resources for instructors and students, including chapter quizzes, additional readings, PowerPoint presentations, and Web-based activities.

In addition to these book-specific supplements, many other skills-based supplements and testing packages are available for both instructors and students. All these supplements are available either at no additional cost or at greatly reduced prices.

The Longman Developmental English Package

Longman is pleased to offer a variety of support materials to help make teaching reading easier on teachers and to help students excel in their coursework. Many of our student supplements are available free or at a greatly reduced price when packaged with *A Community of Readers*, 4e. Contact your local Longman sales representative for more information on pricing and how to create a package.

Support Materials for Reading and Study Skills Instructors:

Printed Test Bank for Developmental Reading (Instructor / 0-321-08596-5) Offers more than 3,000 questions in all areas of reading, including vocabulary, main idea, supporting details, patterns of organization, critical thinking, analytical reasoning, inference, point of view, visual aides, and textbook reading. (Electronic also available; see CDs)

Electronic Test Bank for Developmental Reading (Instructor / CD 0-321-08179-X) Offers more than 3,000 questions in all areas of reading, including vocabulary, main idea, supporting details, patterns of organization, critical thinking, analytical reasoning, inference, point of view, visual aides, and textbook reading. Instructors simply choose questions, then print out the completed test for distribution OR offer the test online.

The Longman Guide to Classroom Management (Instructor / 0-321-09246-5) This guide is designed as a helpful resource for instructors who have classroom management problems. It includes helpful strategies for dealing with disruptive students in the classroom and the "do's and don'ts" of discipline.

The Longman Guide to Community Service-Learning in the English Classroom and Beyond (Instructor / 0-321-12749-8) Written by Elizabeth Rodriguez Kessler of California State University–Northridge, this monograph provides a definition and history of service-learning, as well as an overview of how service-learning can be integrated effectively into the college classroom.

The Longman Instructor's Planner (Instructor / 0-321-09247-3) This planner includes weekly and monthly calendars, student attendance and grading rosters, space for contact information, Web references, an almanac, and blank pages for notes. Available

©2007 Pearson Education, Inc.

For Students:

Vocabulary Skills Study Cards (Student / 0-321-31802-1) Colorful, affordable, and packed with useful information, Longman's Vocabulary Study Card is a concise, 8 page reference guide to developing key vocabulary skills, such as learning to recognize context clues, reading a dictionary entry, and recognizing key root words, suffixes, and prefixes. Laminated for durability, students can keep this Study Card for years to come and pull it out whenever they need a quick review.

Reading Skills Study Card (Student / 0-321-33833-2) Colorful, affordable, and packed with useful information, Longman's Reading Skills Study Card is a concise, 8 page reference guide to help students develop basic reading skills, such as concept skills, structural skills, language skills, and reasoning skills. Laminated for durability, students can keep this Study Card for years to come and pull it out whenever they need a quick review.

The Longman Textbook Reader, Revised Edition (with answers Student /0-321-11895-2 or without answers Student / 0-321-12223-2) Offers five complete chapters from our textbooks: computer science, biology, psychology, communications, and business. Each chapter includes additional comprehension quizzes, critical thinking questions, and group activities.

The Longman Reader's Portfolio and Student Planner (Student / 0-321-29610-9) This unique supplement provides students with a space to plan, think about, and present their work. The portfolio includes a diagnostic area (including a learning style questionnaire), a working area (including calendars, vocabulary logs, reading response sheets, book club tips, and other valuable materials), and a display area (including a progress chart, a final table of contents, and a final assessment), as well as a daily planner for students including daily, weekly, and monthly calendars.

The Longman Reader's Journal, by Kathleen McWhorter (Student / 0-321-08843-3) The first journal for readers, The Longman Reader's Journal offers a place for students to record their reactions to and questions about any reading.

The Longman Planner (Student / 0-321-04573-4) Ideal for organizing a busy college life! Included are hour-by-hour schedules, monthly and weekly calendars, an address book, and an almanac of tips and useful information.

10 Practices of Highly Effective students (Student / 0-205-30769-8) This study skills supplement includes topics such as time management, test taking, reading critically, stress, and motivation.

Newsweek Discount Subscription Coupon (12 weeks) (Student / 0-321-08895-6) Newsweek gets students reading, writing, and thinking about what's going on in the world around them. The price of the subscription is added to the cost of the book. Instructors receive weekly lesson plans, quizzes, and curriculum guides as well as a complimentary Newsweek subscription. The price of the subscription is .59 cents per issue (a total of $7.08 for the subscription). *Package item only.*

Interactive Guide to *Newsweek* (Student / 0-321-05528-4) Available with the 12-week subscription to *Newsweek,* this guide serves as a workbook for students who are using the magazine.

Research Navigator Guide for English, H. Eric Branscomb & Doug Gotthoffer (Student / 0-321-20277-5) Designed to teach students how to conduct high-quality online research and to document it properly, Research Navigator guides provide discipline-specific academic resources; in addition to helpful tips on the writing process, online research, and finding and citing valid sources. Research Navigator guides include an access code to Research Navigator™-providing access to thousands of academic journals and periodicals, the NY Times Search by Subject Archive, Link Library, Library Guides, and more.

Penguin Discount Novel Program In cooperation with Penguin Putnam, Inc., Longman is proud to offer a variety of Penguin paperbacks at a significant discount when packaged with any Longman title. Excellent additions to any developmental reading course, Penguin titles give students the opportunity to explore contemporary and classical fiction and drama. The available titles include works by authors as diverse as Toni Morrison, Julia Alvarez, Mary Shelley, and Shakespeare. To review the complete list of titles available, visit the Longman-Penguin-Putnam Web site: http://www.ablongman.com/penguin.

Oxford American College Dictionary (Student / 0-399-14415-3) Drawing on Oxford's unparalleled language resources, including a 200-million-word database, this college dictionary contains more than 175,000 entries and more than 1000 illustrations, including line drawings, photographs and maps. *Available at a significant discount when packaged with a Longman textbook—only $15.*

The New American Webster Handy College Dictionary (Student / 0-451-18166-2) A paperback reference text with more than 100,000 entries.

Multimedia Offerings:

Interested in incorporating online materials into your course? Longman is happy to help. Our regional technology specialists provide training on all of our multimedia offerings.

MyReadingLab (www.myreadinglab.com) This exciting new website houses all the media tools any developmental English student will need to improve their reading and study skills, and all in one easy to use place. Resources for reading and study skills include:

©2007 Pearson Education, Inc.

- **Reading Roadtrip 5.0 Website.** The best selling reading software available, Reading Roadtrip takes students on a tour of 16 cities and landmarks throughout the United States, with each of the 16 modules corresponding to a reading or study skill. The topics include main idea, vocabulary, understanding patterns of organization, thinking critically, reading rate, notetaking and highlighting, graphics and visual aids, and more. Students can begin their trip by taking a brand new diagnostics test that provides immediate feedback, guiding them to specific modules for additional help with reading skills. New version 5.0 includes a brand new design, a new Pioneer Level (4th–6th grade level), and new readings.

- **Longman Vocabulary Website.** The Longman Vocabulary Website component of MySkillsLab features hundreds of exercises in ten topic areas to strengthen vocabulary skills. Students will also benefit from "100 Words That All High School Graduates Should Know," a useful resource that provides definitions for each of the words on this list, vocabulary flashcards and audio clips to help facilitate pronunciation skills.

- **Longman Study Skills Website.** The site offers hundreds of review strategies for college success, time and stress management skills, study strategies, and more. Students can take a variety of assessment tests to learn about their organizational skills and learning styles, with follow-up quizzes to reinforce the strategies they have learned.

- **Research Navigator.** In addition to providing valuable help to any college student on how to conduct high-quality online research and to document it properly, Research Navigator provides access to thousands of academic journals and periodicals (including the NY *Times* Archive), allowing reading students to practice with authentic readings from college level primary sources.

State Specific Supplements

For Florida Adopters:

Thinking Through the Test: A Student Guide for the Florida College Basic Skills Exit Test, by D.J. Henry FOR FLORIDA ADOPTIONS ONLY. This workbook helps students strengthen their reading skills in preparation for the Florida College Basic Skills Exit Test. It features both diagnostic tests to help assess areas that may need improvement and exit tests to help test skill mastery. Detailed explanatory answers have been provided for almost all of the questions. *Package item only-not available for sale.*

Available Versions:

- Thinking Through the Test A Study Guide for the Florida College Basic Skills Exit Tests: Reading and Writing, 2/e 0-321-27660-4

- Thinking Through the Test A Study Guide for the Florida College Basic Skills Exit Tests: Reading and Writing, w/Answers, 2/e 0-321-27756-2

- Thinking Through the Test A Study Guide for the Florida College Basic Skills Exit Tests: Reading 0-321-27746-5

- Thinking Through the Test A Study Guide for the Florida College Basic Skills Exit Tests: Reading, With Answers 0-321-27751-1

Reading Skills Summary for the Florida State Exit Exam, by D.J. Henry (Student / 0-321-08478-0) FOR FLORIDA ADOPTIONS ONLY. An excellent study tool for students preparing to take Florida College Basic Skills Exit Test for Reading, this laminated reading grid summarizes all the skills tested on the Exit Exam. *Package item only—not available for sale.*

CLAST Test Package, 4/e (Instructor/Print ISBN 0-321-01950-4) These two, 40-item objective tests evaluate students' readiness for the Florida CLAST exams. Strategies for teaching CLAST preparedness are included.

For Texas Adopters:

The Longman THEA Study Guide, by Jeannette Harris (Student / 0-321-27240-0) Created specifically for students in Texas, this study guide includes straightforward explanations and numerous practice exercises to help students prepare for the reading and writing sections of THEA Test. *Package item only—not available for sale.*

TASP Test Package, 3/e (Instructor / Print ISBN 0-321-01959-8) These 12 practice pre-tests and post-tests assess the same reading and writing skills covered in the Texas TASP examination.

For New York/CUNY Adopters:

Preparing for the CUNY-ACT Reading and Writing Test, edited by Patricia Licklider (Student / 0-321-19608-2) This booklet, prepared by reading and writing faculty from across the CUNY system, is designed to help students prepare for the CUNY-ACT exit test. It includes test-taking tips, reading passages, typical exam questions, and sample writing prompts to help students become familiar with each portion of the test.

©2007 Pearson Education, Inc.

ACKNOWLEDGMENTS

We are grateful to our families—Laura, Christina, Paul-Vincent, and Chuck; and Elena, Paul, Aasiya, and Marley—for their patience and assistance. We would also like to thank all our reading students and our colleagues and friends for their help and positive support, especially Enrique Dávalos, Heather Eudy, María Figueroa, Kelly Mayhew, Jim Miller, and Elva Salinas.

A special thank you to Susan Kunchandy for her continued support and enthusiasm for this project. Thank you to Ann Hofstra Grogg, whose good ideas, diligence, perseverance, and editorial insights were invaluable to our successfully completing the text.

Thank you to our reviewers across the country:

Roberta Alexander
Jan Lombardi

TO THE STUDENT

Welcome to *A Community of Readers*

You have probably bought this book because you need to strengthen your reading skills and strategies to be ready for the demands of college reading. If you are prepared to take responsibility for your own learning, and if you are ready to commit yourself to the work involved, you will learn the strategies and skills that you need to become an effective, thoughtful reader. You need these skills not only to pass this course but also to succeed in college and, even more important, in the workplace of the twenty-first century.

Why Is Reading So Important?

Read any newspaper today or talk to any employer or human resources manager and you will realize that the demands of today's society—not only of college study—require that you be a literate person, that you be able to learn new skills and even new jobs or professions. During your lifetime, you will probably face the need to change jobs or professions three, four, or more times. And even if you are one of the lucky few who stays in one position or is successful at creating your own business, you will constantly face the need to upgrade your skills. Professionals of all kinds must stay current in their fields. This is true of office professionals, medical professionals, teachers, engineers, auto mechanics, managers, computer programmers, and industrial workers.

Learning is a lifelong endeavor that doesn't stop when you get your degree. The ability to learn and grow never becomes outdated and will serve you for the rest of your life. This textbook addresses the basics that will help you become a strong reader and student, acquire the skills necessary to be successful in your composition classes, be prepared for the challenges of lifelong learning for the workplace, and be an effective, fulfilled adult and citizen of the twenty-first century.

The skills and strategies you need to become a proficient reader and successful student are the same skills you will need in the workplace. A Department of Labor survey concluded that students should learn these workplace basics:

1. *Learning to learn. A Community of Readers* shows you how to become active in your own reading and learning processes (Chapter 1 and "A Reader's Toolkit"). You learn how you study best and whether you are putting your study time to good use.

2. *Listening and oral communications.* As a college reader, you will learn that the act of reading is reinforced and made more meaningful when you listen to other people's ideas about a subject and when

©2007 Pearson Education, Inc.

you orally express your own ideas to your peers. All chapters of the text emphasize these skills.

3. *Competence in reading, writing, and computation.* As you work through this course, your reading competence will constantly improve. You will learn, review, and practice all the basic skills necessary to be a strong reader: prereading (Chapter 1); active reading (Chapter 1); building your vocabulary (Chapter 2); monitoring your comprehension and recognizing main ideas and supporting details (Chapters 3 and 4); reviewing and remembering what you have read (Chapters 4 and 5); making connections between what you know and what you read (all chapters); and organizing what you read so you can retain information and understanding for tests and future needs (Chapters 3 through 8).

4. *Adaptability based on creative thinking and problem solving.* As a member of your classroom and a community of readers, you will be involved in bringing what you already know and what you learn through reading and discussion to a variety of issues, and you will practice thinking creatively and solving problems (all chapters). You will learn how to take notes ("A Reader's Toolkit"), how to interpret what an author is saying and how to make inferences (Chapter 6), and how to think critically to evaluate an author's position (Chapters 7 and 8 and in the Reflect exercises throughout the text).

5. *Group effectiveness characterized by interpersonal skills, negotiation skills, and teamwork.* You will learn to work with your peers—other students—sharing your strengths and learning from each other (all chapters and "A Reader's Toolkit").

6. *Organizational effectiveness and leadership.* You will develop your organizational and leadership skills in the process of working with classmates toward a common goal.

If you are ready to tackle the material of this course, you are taking a big step toward a successful college career. Can you answer "yes" to the following key questions?

- Are learning and practicing college reading skills priorities for you at this time?
- Are you willing to make the effort to be actively involved in your own learning?
- Have you decided that you can and will succeed, one small step at a time?
- Do you have the time to commit to being a student? Remember that as a student, you have a job. The payoff may seem to come with passing grades and a degree, but most important, the payoff of developing your reading and learning skills is for yourself and your future.

- Are you willing to share ideas and to work together with other students to reach your goals?
- Are you willing to learn new reading strategies, not just to pass this class but to use whenever you must learn something new?
- Are you willing to open your mind to new ideas and ways of thinking?
- Are you willing to reflect on ideas and arguments, and to make conclusions and form opinions for yourself and with others?
- Did you answer "yes" to all or most of the questions? If so, this book will help you reach your goals by assisting you to become a lifelong reader and learner. Welcome to *A Community of Readers!*

©2007 Pearson Education, Inc.

PART 1

Skills Instruction and Thematic Readings

Chapter 1

The Reading Process
Joining a Community of Readers

My first semester at college was painful and frustrating until I realized that studying hard was important but not enough. When I got to know other students in my classes, made friends, and formed study groups with them, everything got better—my learning, my grades, and my feelings about being a student.

—CARLOS MARTÍNEZ

● What do you think the people in this picture are discussing?

● Can you imagine yourself in a picture like this?

● What advice do you think Carlos Martínez would give to new college students based on this quotation?

©2007 Pearson Education, Inc.

PREPARE TO READ

When we chose the title of this book, *A Community of Readers*, we were thinking about the word *community* in a lot of ways. One is the community of learners you have joined by enrolling in college. More specifically, we had in mind the community of readers in your class. It is important for you to be an active member of your classroom community. If you try to do everything on your own, you may end up feeling isolated and depressed. When you learn to work with other students or friends, to help them and to be helped by them, your chances of success in college (and in life) are much greater. When your classroom community is a friendly one, when you trust and respect each other, you feel comfortable and can participate in your own learning.

Purpose

In this chapter, you will read about becoming a successful student and learn
- The PRO reading system:
  Preparing to read
  Reading actively and Reflecting
  Organizing and using what you have read
- The importance of working with other students

In the process of acquiring these skills, you will read about joining a community of students, important habits to become a successful learner, college and school environments, and memory techniques.

Previous Knowledge

Answer these questions and prepare to discuss them in class.

1. What do you need to do to become a successful college student?

   _____

2. How do you think family and friends, fellow students, and resources in the college community can help you be successful?

   _____

Preview and Predict

Take a quick look at the rest of Chapter 1. Based on your preview, list three things you think you will learn in this chapter.

1. _____

2. _____

3. _____

Reading 1   *Becoming a Student: Joining a Study Group*

Barbara Jordan

Barbara Jordan (1936–1996), an African-American congresswoman and lawyer, was also named one of the ten most influential women in Texas. In the following passage from her autobiography, she describes her struggle to succeed in law school. She had already completed her undergraduate education, during which she was a member of the debate team, but she found that she still needed to work on her reading and study skills to keep up with her classmates. Most importantly, she describes how studying together with a group helped her really understand the issues.

1   So I was at Boston University in this new and strange and different world, and it occurred to me that if I was going to succeed at this strange new adventure, I would have to read longer and more thoroughly than my colleagues at law school had to read. I felt that in order to compensate for what I had missed in earlier years, I would have to work harder, and study longer, than anybody else. I still had this feeling that I did not want my colleagues to know what a tough time I was having understanding the concepts, the words, the ideas, the process. I didn't want them to know that. So I did my reading not in the law library, but in a library at the graduate dorm, upstairs where it was very quiet, because apparently nobody else studied there. So I would go there at night after dinner. I would load my books under my arm and go to the library, and I would read until the wee hours of the morning and then go to bed. I didn't get much sleep during those years. I was lucky if I got three or four hours a night, because I had to stay up. I had to. The professors would assign cases for the next day, and these cases had to be read and understood or I would be behind, further behind than I was.

2   I was always delighted when I would get called upon to recite in class. But the professors did not call on the "ladies" very much. There were certain favored people who always got called on, and then on some rare occasions a professor would come in and would announce: "We're going to have Ladies Day today." And he would call on the ladies. We were just tolerated. We weren't considered really top drawer when it came to the study of the law.

3   At some time in the spring, Bill Gibson, who was dating my new roommate, Norma Walker, organized a black study group, as we blacks had to form our own. This was because we were not invited into any of the other study groups. There were six or seven in our group—Bill, and Issie, and I think Maynard Jackson—and we would just gather and talk it out and hear ourselves do that. One thing I learned was that you had to talk out the issues, the facts, the cases, the decisions, the process. You couldn't just read the cases and study alone in your library as I had been doing; and you couldn't get it all in the classroom. But once you had talked it out in the study group, it flowed more easily and made a lot more sense. . . .

4   Finally I felt I was really learning things, really going to school. I felt that I was getting educated, whatever that was. I became familiar with the

©2007 Pearson Education, Inc.

process of thinking. I learned to think things out and reach conclusions and defend what I had said.

5   In the past I had got along by spouting off. Whether you talked about debates or oratory, you dealt with speechifying. Even in debate it was pretty much canned because you had, in your little three-by-five box, a response for whatever issue might be raised by the opposition. The format was structured so that there was no opportunity for independent thinking. (I really had not had my ideas challenged ever.) But I could no longer orate and let that pass for reasoning. Because there was not any demand for an orator in Boston University Law School. You had to think and read and understand and reason. I had learned at twenty-one that you couldn't just say a thing is so because it might not be so, and somebody brighter, smarter, and more thoughtful would come out and tell you it wasn't so. Then, if you still thought it was, you had to prove it. Well, that was a new thing for me. I cannot, I really cannot describe what that did to my insides and to my head. I thought: I'm being educated finally.

JORDAN AND HEARON, *BARBARA JORDAN: A SELF-PORTRAIT*

Exercise 1   ## Recall and Discuss

Based on Reading 1, Jordan's "Becoming a Student," answer the following questions and prepare to discuss them with your classmates.

1. What did Barbara Jordan do at first in her attempts to keep up with her fellow students?

_____

_____

2. What activity did she say made all the difference in her being successful in her studies? Why do you think this was so?

_____

_____

3. Why might it be important for you to understand the activity that made all the difference for Barbara Jordan?

_____

_____

Exercise 2   ## Reflect: Introduce Yourself

To begin building your classroom community, you first need to do a little thinking about yourself and how you can become a part of this community. Answer the following questions about who you are and what your expectations are for this class. Be prepared to share your answers with other students.

1. What is your name, and how might we easily remember it? (Does your name have a special meaning? Is it readily associated with someone famous you admire? Does it sound like a word that might be used to describe you?)

   _____

   _____

2. What accomplishment are you most proud of?

   _____

   _____

3. Why are you going to college?

   _____

   _____

4. What kinds of things do you like to read for enjoyment?

   _____

   _____

THE READING PROCESS: PRO

Reading is a *process;* that means reading is a series of small steps. We've divided the process into three basic steps. All good readers follow these steps, even though they may do so automatically. Depending on your purpose for reading and the type of material you are reading, you will vary your strategies for the three basic steps. You may find that you use some steps more than once in completing a reading task. Eventually, the reading process and the basic steps involved will become automatic: You won't even have to think about them most of the time. Until you form these good habits, you will need to be conscious of your reading strategies and to apply them deliberately as you read and study.

PRO reading system
A process to follow for developing effective reading habits

The **PRO reading system** makes it easy for you to understand and remember the steps of the reading process so that you can approach your reading assignments more confidently and complete them more successfully. Each letter stands for an activity in the system.

P = <u>**P**</u>**reparing to read**
R = <u>**R**</u>**eading actively and** <u>**R**</u>**eflecting**
O = <u>**O**</u>**rganizing and using what you have read**

When you've mastered this system, you will be a reading pro!

©2007 Pearson Education, Inc.

Preparing to Read

prepare to read
Determine a
purpose, preview,
recognize previous
knowledge, and
predict what you
will learn

The first step is preparing to read. Master readers **prepare to read**. They don't take a lot of time to prepare, but they are in the habit of completing certain activities as they begin the process of reading. Taking the time to get yourself ready to read is essential to understanding what you read. By preparing yourself to read, you can figure out what information will be coming and get ready to receive it. You can also develop curiosity about a subject, so that you will already be thinking as you begin to read. Have you ever read something and then not known what you had just read? One possible reason for this lack of focus is failure to prepare.

The first step in the PRO reading system, **P,** actually includes four p's, all of which are easy to understand and do. You may already include some of these in your reading approach. Preparing to read includes

- Determining a **purpose** for your reading
- **Previewing** what you are about to read
- Recognizing **previous knowledge** (what you already know about this topic)
- **Predicting** what you will learn from the reading

purpose   Your
reading goals

Determining Your Purpose   Your **purpose** as a reader determines how carefully you will read, how much time you will need, and what reading strategies you will use. For example, you read the sports section of your daily newspaper very differently from the way you read a portion of your anatomy textbook, especially if you are preparing to take the state nursing exam. Your purpose in reading the sports page may be to find out the score in a particular game. You can scan the page quickly to find this information. If you are reading about anatomy, you have to read more slowly and methodically to understand, and you want to use strategies to help you remember the material.

As a college student, you will often have an obvious purpose: to learn as much as you possibly can about Native American poetry, about computer programming, or about the mechanics of laser graphics, for instance. At the same time, your purpose may be to master enough to do well on your exams. For example, in a reading class, you may need to demonstrate how well you can use your reading skills on a timed test. Whatever your immediate purpose, remember that the pleasure of learning should also influence how you read.

previewing   Briefly
looking over a
section to find key
points

Previewing   **Previewing** is exactly what the word suggests. When you prepare to read, you should begin by "pre-viewing" the material you intend to read. In other words, look at what you're going to read before you read it. Get an overview of the material, and notice how interesting, as well as how difficult, it may be for you. Once you have done this, you can predict what topics the reading will cover and choose the most effective reading strategies for that particular piece.

Previewing can be done on many levels. You can preview an entire text, a chapter of a text, or a section of a chapter that you are about to read.

Previewing a Textbook   When previewing a new textbook, look for the features that are common to textbooks:

- Title page—title of the book, name of the author(s), place of publication; usually the first page of a book
- Copyright page—number of editions, date of publication, ordering information; located on the back of the title page
- Preface or foreword—information about the book's purpose, special features, student aids; located before the first chapter
- Table of contents—a list of the book's major topics and subtopics in the order they'll be presented; organized in chapters, sections, or units, with page numbers
- Epigraphs—appropriate quotations, often from well-known writers and thinkers; usually found at the beginning of a book or as a regular feature at the beginning of each chapter
- Footnotes—extra explanations, data, sources of information; may be at the bottom of the page, at the end of the chapter, or listed by chapter at the end of the book
- Appendix—additional useful information, such as maps, lists, charts, and tables; located at the end of a book
- Glossary—a list of important terms and their definitions; usually located in a special section at the end of a book
- Bibliography or references—a list of additional information on a topic, including books, journals, audiovisual materials, and Web sites; located at the end of each chapter or in a special section at the end of a book
- Answer keys—sometimes included in a special section at the end of a book, or in an appendix, to assist students
- Index—usually an alphabetical list of all important topics and terms found in the text, with page numbers for each; located at the end of a book

Your purpose in looking at all these features is to figure out as much as you can about the book. Who wrote it? When was it published? What are the contents? How are the chapters organized? Does the material look difficult? easy? interesting? Are there any elements at the end of chapters, or at the end of the book, that you should know about, such as a glossary of new terms, appendixes that give special information, or answer keys that you can use to check your work?

Exercise 3   ### Preview *A Community of Readers*

Now apply these previewing skills to familiarize yourself with *A Community of Readers*. Then answer the following questions. After your answer, write the page number where you found it.

©2007 Pearson Education, Inc.

1. Who are the authors of this book?

   _____

2. When was this book published? Which edition of the book is this?

   _____

3. What is the epigraph for Chapter 4?

   _____

4. In which chapter do you learn how to identify important supporting points?

   _____

5. Where do you find which skills you will be studying in each chapter?

   _____

   _____

6. In which chapter will you be studying about health and well-being?

   _____

7. In which chapter will you be thinking about questions related to gender?

   _____

8. Where will you find instructions on how to write a summary?

   _____

9. Which chapter looks most interesting to you?

   _____

10. Which skill or reading strategy covered in this book do you think you need the most?

    _____

    ◆

Previewing a Chapter   Once you have previewed a book and are familiar with its format, you should be able to locate the information you need easily. Most of your assignments in college will direct you to read a chapter of a textbook or sections of chapters. To preview a chapter, look for the following information:

- Title and subtitle—the subject and important sections of the chapter, usually in larger print and in boldface type
- Objectives—goals to be accomplished in the chapter
- Introduction—background information and main ideas to be covered in the chapter

- Headings, subheadings, and sub-subheadings—indicate the subject being covered
- Pictures—visual aids for understanding the focus and content of the chapter
- Charts and graphs—visual interpretations of information in the text that sometimes present additional facts and figures
- *Italicized* and **boldfaced** words—important terms the author wants to emphasize. Sometimes terms are defined in the margins, as they are in this book. Other times they are defined in a glossary at the end of a book.
- Review or summary—a brief overview of the essential information covered in the chapter. Located at the end of the chapter, it is an aid for study and retaining what you have learned.

Exercise 4   ## Preview a Chapter

Look at Chapter 7 and answer the following questions.

1. What can you learn about the chapter from the first page, which has the title, subtitle, a quotation, and picture?

   _____

   _____

2. What are the main headings of the chapter?

   _____

   _____

3. What skills will you learn?

   _____

   _____

4. What subjects will you be reading about as you practice these skills?

   _____

   _____

5. What kinds of charts and photos are there?

   _____

   _____   ◆

Previewing a Section   When you begin to study for a specific class assignment, you should preview short sections as you are about to read them. Most people can deal with only one small block of reading material at a time. For each assignment, determine how much material to

©2007 Pearson Education, Inc.

cover in your preview based on the level of difficulty of the material and your level of expertise as a reader.

For each section, read titles and headings, the introduction, the first sentences under the headings or the first sentence of each paragraph, italicized and boldfaced words, and the conclusion. Briefly study pictures, charts, graphs, picture captions, and any other unusual visual effects meant to "catch your eye." Keep in mind how this section fits with the information before and after it.

| Exercise 5 | **Preview a Section** |

Preview the material from here to Reading 2 on page 15. This section covers the next steps in preparing to read. Fill in the following information as you preview.

1. List the headings in this section:

_____

_____

2. Read the first sentence under each heading. Briefly write what you learned from each.

_____

_____

3. What words are written in the margins with their definitions (glossed)?

_____

◆

Using Previous Knowledge   Part of preparing to read is considering what you already know about the topic. As you preview a section, you will probably recognize information about which you have some **previous knowledge.** This knowledge may come from your studies or your life experiences. If you already know a great deal about the subject of a reading, prepare to add any new information you find in this reading to your storehouse. Your brain has an extraordinary filing system, more sophisticated than those of the most advanced computers. Sometimes you know as much as, or even more than, some authors about a given subject. In that case, prepare to compare your information and interpretation with theirs; you may even want to argue some points with them. At other times, you may know little about a topic. In that case, you can still relate the information to similar facts you already know. For example, when you read an article about health problems among preschool children in Rwanda, you may know nothing specific about Rwanda and its problems, but you probably do know—from your own experience, reading, and tele-

previous knowledge
What you already know about a topic from prior reading and experience

vision—something about young children and about health problems. So you can relate the new information to what you already know.

Make thinking about your previously acquired knowledge part of preparing to read. You'll soon find you do it almost automatically, and your confidence in approaching new material will certainly increase. Also, it's easier to remember the new knowledge when you recognize its relationship to what you already know.

predicting
Considering what you expect to learn from a reading

Predicting What You Will Learn   **Predicting** what you think you will learn in the reading is the last step in preparing to read. Based on your preview of the reading and previous knowledge of the subject, you should have a good idea of what new information you will acquire. The preview gave you the framework or outline of the content. Now raise some questions that you think will be answered in the selection you are preparing to read. Asking questions will prepare you to read actively, to be engaged with the material as you go through it. Actively seeking the answers to your questions will keep you alert and attentive and will help you understand what you are reading.

One simple way to create questions is to use the topics and concepts you noticed in your preview. For example, a section from a physical science textbook might have the following title and headings:

Atomic Structure
The Electron
The Atomic Nucleus
Protons and Neutrons

The title and headings give you clues to the content, and each subheading is about the makeup of an atom. In predicting what you will learn, you might come up with these reader's questions first:

1. What is an electron? What is an atomic nucleus? What is a proton? What is a neutron?

The text includes a diagram of an atom. So your second question might combine the headings and the diagram:

2. What role does each part have in the functioning of the atom?

Besides these questions, which are fairly obvious, questions might arise from your previous knowledge and reading. You might ask a question like the following:

3. What does the structure of an atom have to do with the creation of the atomic bomb?

Thoughtful questions like this may not be answered in the text, but they can prepare you for the class lecture and discussion. Looking beyond the literal content to its implications can prepare you for critical thinking about the material you read.

©2007 Pearson Education, Inc.

In general, ask questions specifically related to the information in the textbook. Let the headings, objectives, and other features you noticed in your preview suggest the questions you think the reading will answer. If the reading you are previewing doesn't have headings or lists of objectives, quickly read the first sentences of each paragraph; if you are reading a long passage, you will also want to read the first and last paragraphs. The more closely your questions are related to the actual content of the reading, the more useful they will be in helping you achieve your goal for the reading assignment.

Besides your preview, there are several other good ways to predict what you will be expected to learn from a reading. Watch for questions your professors raise. They may say something like, "Be sure you know the components of an atom for Wednesday's class." They are assuming you'll find that information in your assigned reading and then be well prepared to comprehend the upcoming lecture on the topic. Some teachers even provide study guides for difficult chapters. These are a great resource. Another excellent source of prediction questions is a list of questions, which may appear at the end of the chapter, that the authors feel test readers on the essential information in the chapter. Read these questions before you read a chapter or a section of the chapter, and you'll know what you need to learn from the material you're about to read.

Exercise 6   ## Prepare to Read a Textbook Section

Preview Reading 2, which was written for this edition of *A Community of Readers*, and answer the following questions.

1. What is the title of this reading?

   _____

2. What is your purpose for reading this piece?

   _____

   _____

3. What *previous knowledge* do you have about this topic? That is, what do you already know about it?

   _____

   _____

4. From your preview, write three questions that you predict the reading will answer.

   a. _____

   b. _____

   c. _____

©2007 Pearson Education, Inc.

Reading 2   *Use the Tools for College Success!*

Jesse Cunningham

The following reading provides you with some very important tips on how to be a successful college student. Notice that the author has tried to make the material as accessible as possible by using subheads, italics, and bulleted lists to call your attention to important points. Look for them as you preview the reading.

1   Many students have struggled when making the transition from high school to college or the university. Perhaps even more difficult is the plight of those students who find themselves returning to college or attending for the first time after years spent away from the academic environment. The challenge of meeting the high expectations of college is often met with confusion by those students who, for whatever reason, find themselves unprepared to succeed in their college experience. In fact, some studies show that many students don't do their homework or even read their textbooks, thinking that they can pass without doing so. Are you one of those students? Do you often find yourself struggling to keep up with your schoolwork? Do you ever feel lost during the professor's lecture or fall behind on the readings? Are you insufficiently prepared for tests, or unaware of the instructor's expectations for your assignments? A "yes" answer to any of these questions is a danger signal. So, what can you do to correct this situation? The answer is to change your approach and work habits. A good start would be to pay attention to the following three keys to college success.

- *Be organized.*
- *Stay motivated.*
- *Develop responsible study habits.*

Be Organized

2   Being organized is essential to success in college. Without organization, you will likely find it impossible to meet the demands of college and your life outside of school. Some methods for good organization include the following important techniques:

3   • Good *time management* is essential, for if you do not set aside time to study and complete assignments, then the college experience may prove discouraging or even disastrous. Many students have to work at least part-time in order to supplement their income; others have to work even longer hours because they are responsible for supporting themselves or their families. Walking the tightrope between school and work can be a precarious balancing act. To ensure academic success while working, take a job that offers flexible hours that don't interfere with assignments or conflict with class schedules. Success at the college level is almost impossible with poor class attendance. If faced with a decision between school and work, do not sacrifice your long-term goal

in favor of a short-term necessity. A good tool for managing your time is to use a calendar or daily planner to note your appointments, class times, work schedule, and other responsibilities. Build in time for home-work and study.

4 • Another important way to stay organized is to set *priorities*. In college, tasks that need to be completed have a way of piling up, and some-times it becomes difficult to keep track of them all. A great way to en-sure that you stay on top of these tasks is to keep a *things-to-do* list. After noting all of your assignments, readings, and study needs, give priority to those tasks that are most important, time sensitive, or diffi-cult. By completing the most urgent tasks first and checking them off, you will find that the other tasks become easier as you proceed down your list.

5 • In order to fulfill your expectations and meet your goals, remember this: *do not procrastinate*. Your day planner and *things-to-do* list can help you to complete your goals in a timely manner. Any project will seem doable if you start early, but if you wait until the last minute to begin even an easy project will seem daunting. The longer you wait to begin, the more likely the chance of failure. Try to establish a time frame that you can meet. Err on the side of caution: if you set the com-pletion of your class project early enough, then, even if you are late in meeting your personal time frame, you can still finish the project by the time it is due. You can avoid the pitfall of procrastination altogether by sticking to your time frame.

Stay Motivated

6 Another key to college success is to keep yourself motivated. Without the proper motivation, you may find your dreams of college success slipping away from you.

7 • Of course, a classic motivational technique is to set, maintain, and keep *goals*, or objectives. The most effective goals are specific and well defined. For example, a goal to get a score of 90 or better on your next anthropology test is far more effective than a vague goal simply to do well or to learn the subject. Challenging yourself with your goals is preferable to setting objectives that are too easy, but make sure, too, that your goals are achievable. Have realistic expectations and avoid setting yourself up for failure with goals that are nearly impossible to meet.

8 • An important element in staying motivated is *thinking positively.* Re-member to value your effort. You've made an important and responsi-ble decision to start college, and you should take some healthy pride in what you've already done to get here. Shut out doubt and negative thinking. If you doubt yourself by thinking that you won't be able to ful-fill your goals and responsibilities, then you're setting yourself up for failure. Use the technique of *visualization* to envision success. Mentally

see yourself scoring that A or receiving that degree. Thinking positively is a great way to begin turning your desires into reality; it is also crucial for having good self-esteem.

Develop Responsible Study Habits

9 Certainly one of the most important keys to success in college is to develop responsible study habits. With a strong work ethic and good study habits, you can go very far on your academic journey. In some of your classes, you will learn the importance of *active reading* and *critical thinking*. Internalizing these practices will greatly aid you in your studies. In the meantime, don't forget some of the basics for good study habits:

10 • *Use the materials!* This idea may seem obvious, but it is surprising how many students think that they can "get by" without referring to their notes from class or even cracking open their textbooks. The sloppy, passive approach may have worked in high school, but with the rigors of college come greater expectations for, and demands on, the student. Do your assigned reading, and you will find yourself keeping up better in class.

11 • *Be involved in the learning process.* College often requires you to think in-depth about the material. Your view of what you're learning becomes important and is a good starting point for your work. While many professors are humorous, exciting, or enthusiastic in class and lecture, they are not there to entertain you. Engage in class discussion with your professors and classmates. Listen hard and take notes, even if a professor or class is not entertaining.

12 • *Find a study partner or study group.* You would be surprised at how effective studying with others can be. Reviewing class notes and textbook assignments with a classmate or two and discussing the material will help make sure you understand it completely. The very act of stating or explaining something to another person can help you learn it. Not only does a study partner or study group provide you with a ready-made support group, it may also invigorate the social aspect of your college experience and make learning fun.

13 • *Take advantage of learning resources.* Almost every college campus has computer labs, libraries, resource and media centers, and often tutoring facilities. Their services are usually provided to students for free. Unfortunately, many students don't utilize them, or sometimes aren't even aware of them. Don't be one of those students. Ask your teachers, other students, or a counselor where you can find them. Don't be intimidated or shy about getting tutoring. The notion that tutoring is for remedial students is an outdated misconception—all students have much to gain from tutors. Enhance your learning experience by taking advantage of all the help your college offers.

14 Overall, these tips and suggestions are just some of the ways you can prepare yourself to succeed in your college experience. They will give you a

©2007 Pearson Education, Inc.

good start and provide a foundation for you to build on. And really, that is the most important key for college success—you. Ultimately, it's up to you to find solutions, use resources, and build on what you've accomplished. Getting here and reading this article are important steps you've already taken to succeed in college, so congratulations. Now, enable yourself to achieve your goals. Good luck!

CUNNINGHAM, "Use the Tools"

Exercise 7 Check Your Understanding

Based on Reading 2, Cunningham's "Use the Tools for College Success!" choose the best answer to each of the following multiple-choice questions.

1. According to the author, if you have to work, it's best to get work
   a. that pays the most.
   b. where you can study while on the job.
   c. that doesn't interfere with your college responsibilities.

2. The most effective goals are
   a. ambitious.
   b. specific and well defined.
   c. cautious.

3. Procrastinate means
   a. put off doing things for another time.
   b. prioritize your work.
   c. eliminate one assignment at a time.

4. Some of the techniques that can help you stay motivated are
   a. studying hard and long.
   b. keeping goals, not procrastinating, and thinking positively.
   c. surrounding yourself with other people who also think positively.

5. Visualization in this reading means
   a. seeing things.
   b. using your glasses.
   c. imagining your success.

Exercise 8 Reflect

Think about what you read in Reading 2 and what you already know about this topic. Answer the following questions, and prepare to discuss them with your classmates.

1. How did preparing to read help you while you were reading this selection?

   _____

   _____

   _____

2. Do you read your book and do the exercises if the instructor doesn't collect the work? Explain why or why not.

_____

_____

_____

3. What do you think motivates most students to do well in their classes?

_____

_____

_____

4. Write three specific goals that you would like to achieve as a student this semester.

_____

_____

_____

◆

Reading Actively and Reflecting

Successful readers are actively involved in the process of reading. They interact with the text and think about what they are reading. These activities are part of the next step in the PRO system.

Reading Actively The second major step in the PRO reading system is **R,** which stands for reading. Probably the most important advice we can give you about reading is that you must be an active reader. To remind you of this, we'll usually refer to reading in this text as **active reading.** Active reading is involved reading. What are you involved in doing? You are searching for the meaning of the author's words.

active reading An involved, focused search for meaning while reading

Reading is an act of **communication.** Reading allows you to share the thoughts and feelings of people you've never met, even people who lived hundreds or thousands of years ago or in a country you've never visited. Reading the printed word—in a book or magazine, or on the computer—is a remarkably efficient way to communicate ideas across time and distance. Remember that there is a real human being on the other end—the writer—who is trying to share facts, ideas, and feelings with you. You are trying to decode his or her words and discover their meaning. When you understand the writer's message, the communication is complete.

communication The art of sharing thoughts and feelings between people

So what do you need to do to be an active reader? First, you must become _involved_ in what you are reading. Preparing to read, as you have

©2007 Pearson Education, Inc.

learned in this chapter, will make that easier. In fact, careful preparation for reading may make active reading almost automatic. Once you have a purpose, previewing provides a framework for what you are about to read. Thinking about your previous knowledge of the subject helps you make connections between new and old information. Predicting helps you anticipate what you will learn as you read.

Second, you must be *interested* in what you are reading. It is not always easy to be interested in a topic, particularly if you know nothing about it. Allow yourself to be endlessly curious, to be open-minded about all kinds of information and all viewpoints. Books are a bit like people—the ones who seem unexciting at first may someday become your best friends. Also, keep your reading purpose in mind. Pleasure may sometimes have to take second place to necessity. What initially appears to be an uninspiring book may be required reading for the career you are pursuing. You may have to motivate yourself to stay attentive. Set yourself a goal of reading attentively for 50 minutes, and then reward yourself by doing something different for 10 or 15 minutes (i.e., shooting hoops, calling a friend, or exercising). With a positive outlook, you can stay interested enough to profit from even the dullest books.

Third, you must be *alert and attentive* while reading. Choose a time and a place that allow you to concentrate. Most people try to establish a special setting where the habit of focusing becomes natural and is not a constant struggle. Your brain must have a chance to work uninterrupted for you to interpret the meaning of what you are reading. If you're too tired or distracted, you can't concentrate on reading.

monitor comprehension Regular checks for involvement in and understanding of what you read

Lastly, you should **monitor,** or check, your involvement and **comprehension** periodically. Does your attention wander? How soon or how often does your attention wander? Can you determine why your attention wanders? Ask yourself, "Am I understanding what I'm reading?" Test yourself at intervals by asking, "What have I just read?" and "What seems to be important?" Or stop and try to answer the predicting questions you asked while you were preparing to read. Some people mark their texts—by underlining, highlighting, numbering, or checkmarking—to help their understanding. It's usually best to mark a section of a text during a second reading, when you are organizing to learn. Otherwise, you may mark too much. You'll practice techniques for marking texts in Chapter 4.

reflecting Thinking about the concepts, ideas, interpretations, and emotions you've read about

Reflecting When you read actively, you also reflect as you read. **Reflecting** is thinking about the concepts, ideas, interpretations, and emotions you've read about. At times, we may become so involved in a reading that we stop to think about what we've just discovered. Reading is a *discovery process*. Certainly one of the greatest pleasures in reading comes from these discoveries. We are constantly learning new information about our world and gaining insight and understanding about ourselves and other people through our reading. It's not surprising that these insights make us stop and think. Every author hopes that will happen when we read his or her work. If a reading provides a lot of discovery stops for you, remember to allow yourself enough time to complete the work—and then enjoy your reading!

Reflecting on what you read does happen naturally, but it's often necessary to consciously plan to reflect on what you've been reading. You need to think not only about what you're learning now but also about how these ideas *connect* or relate to what you already know. People understand and learn new information best by connecting it with what they already know. Placing new knowledge in the context of what you already know requires time and thoughtful analysis.

There are a number of ways to actively organize your reflections. You might first ask yourself, "How does this information fit with what I've already learned and experienced?" If the information is new, you might simply insert it in the appropriate category in your "idea files." For example, if you recently learned the location of Dubuque, Iowa, you can place that information in your category of current information on U.S. geography. Sometimes, though, it's not so simple to add new information to your files. When you reflect on the new information, you will also have to decide how it connects with your previous knowledge. Reflecting on the relationships between old and new knowledge will help you to develop greater depth as a thinker. As you move forward in your college and work careers, reflection will be an invaluable tool for dealing with increasingly complex ideas, concepts, and problems.

critical thinking
Analyzing, synthesizing, and evaluating the significance and usefulness of what you've read

Reflecting is also known as **critical thinking.** Critical thinking requires you to do more than collect large masses of data on a topic. It challenges you to synthesize, or combine, what you learn in meaningful ways, to weigh facts against opinions, and to evaluate the significance and usefulness of ideas and solutions to problems. You'll get plenty of chances in the following chapters to develop and practice your critical reading and thinking skills.

Exercise 9 Prepare to Read, Read Actively, and Reflect

Preview the following passage about self-esteem from a health textbook, and complete items 1 through 4. Then follow the instructions in item 5 as you read. Finally, answer questions 6 and 7.

1. Preview the reading and list two or more things that you noted in your preview.

   a. _____

   b. _____

   c. _____

2. What do you already know about self-esteem?

   _____

©2007 Pearson Education, Inc.

3. What might be your purpose for reading textbook material like this?

_____

4. Write three questions you predict this selection will answer.

a. _____

b. _____

c. _____

5. To monitor your active reading, write two reflections (thoughts, comments, or questions) in the margins as you read.

Self-Esteem

Self-esteem refers to one's sense of self-respect or self-worth. It can be defined as how one evaluates oneself and values one's own personal worth as an individual. People with high self-esteem tend to feel good about themselves and have a positive outlook on life. People with low self-esteem often do not like themselves, constantly demean themselves, and doubt their ability to succeed.

Tips for Improving Your Self-Esteem

- **Finding a Support Group.** The best way to maintain self-esteem is through a support group—peers who share your values and offer the nurturing that your family can no longer provide. The prime prerequisite for a support group is that it makes you feel good about yourself and forces you to take an honest look at your actions and choices. Although the idea of finding a support group seems to imply establishing a wholly new group, remember that old ties are often among the strongest. Keeping in contact with old friends and with important family members can provide a foundation of unconditional love that may help you through the many life transitions ahead.

  Try to be a support for others, too. Join a discussion, political action, or recreational group. Write more postcards and "thinking of you" notes to people who matter. This will build both your own self-esteem and that of your friends.

- **Completing Required Tasks.** A way to boost your self-efficacy is to learn how to complete required tasks successfully and develop a history of success. You are not likely to succeed in your studies if you leave term papers until the last minute, fail to keep up with the reading for your courses, and do not ask for clarification of points that are confusing to you. Most college campuses provide study groups and learning centers for various content areas. These groups offer tips for managing time, understanding assignments, dealing with professors, and preparing for test taking. Poor grades, or grades that do not meet expectations, are major contributors to diminished self-esteem and self-efficacy and to emotional distress among college students.

- **Forming Realistic Expectations.** Having realistic expectations of yourself is another method of boosting self-esteem. College is a time to explore your potential. The stresses of college life may make your expectations for success difficult to meet. If you expect perfect grades, a steady stream of Saturday-night dates and a soap-opera-type romantic involvement, and the perfect job, you may be setting yourself up for failure. Assess your current resources and the direction in which you are heading. Set small, incremental goals that are possible to meet.

- **Taking and Making Time for You.** Taking time to enjoy yourself is another way to boost your self-esteem and psychosocial health. Viewing each new activity as something to look forward to and an opportunity to have fun is an important part of keeping the excitement in your life. Wake up focusing on the fun things you have to look forward to each day, and try to make this anticipation a natural part of your day.

- **Maintaining Physical Health.** Maintaining physical health also contributes to self-esteem and self-efficacy. Regular exercise fosters a sense of well-being. Nourishing meals can help you avoid the weight gain experienced by many college students.

- **Examining Problems and Seeking Help.** Knowing when to seek help from friends, support groups, family, or professionals is another important factor in boosting self-esteem. Sometimes life's problems are insurmountable; sometimes you can handle them alone. Recognizing your strengths and acting appropriately are keys to psychosocial health.

DONATELLE, *ACCESS TO HEALTH*

6. Answer your questions from question 4 on page 22.

    a. _____

    b. _____

    c. _____

7. How well were you able to read actively and reflect? Did the two reflections that you wrote down during your preview of the reading help you read actively? Explain your answer.

_____

_____

©2007 Pearson Education, Inc.

Organizing and Using What You Have Read

organizing what you have read
Selecting, using, reciting, and examining yourself on what you have learned from your reading so you will retain it for tests and work applications in the future

Once you have successfully completed the **P** and **R** steps of the PRO system, you will be ready for **O, organizing and using what you have read.** You will have already prepared to read, read actively, and reflected on what you read. Actually, you will probably have done some organizing of your new knowledge already. All of the steps in the reading process are interrelated and sometimes overlap, so it is a pleasant surprise when you arrive at the next step to find that you may have already done some of the work.

The purpose of organizing what you've read is to be sure that you can use your new information for exams and future assignments. The following steps, which spell the word *SURE*, will provide many ways to organize your material. Once you've practiced the different methods, you can decide which ones work best for you.

S: Selecting the Facts and Concepts You Need to Know   You need a great deal of skill to *select* the important points to study. You must first understand what you've read. You must also be flexible in applying your skills to the expectations of different fields of study—such as biology, math, and sociology—and to the different approaches of individual instructors. This text provides you with reading experience in many subject areas. The following skills will help you select the facts and concepts you need to know. Each of these skills is explained in greater detail in later chapters, and you will practice each of them, some of them many times.

- Identifying the topic, main ideas, and important supporting points.
- Identifying thought patterns and relationships between ideas.
- Recognizing the author's purpose.
- Understanding inferences.
- Evaluating fact versus opinion.

U: Using the Material You've Selected   To understand the new ideas you're learning, you must use the material in some way. Good readers know that it's easy to be overconfident. It's tempting to stop after you've read something and feel you understand it, but really mastering new information requires that you do something with it. You might use any of the following activities. You'll have plenty of chances in this book to practice these methods with readings from different content areas. You'll probably find that some methods are more effective for you than others.

- Summarizing and paraphrasing
- Underlining and annotating texts
- Answering questions (your preview questions, questions you write in the margins as you actively read, instructor questions, questions at the end of each chapter, and others)
- Outlining
- Concept mapping
- Completing charts, graphs, and timelines

- Discussing (in your classroom, in a study group, with a tutor, or with a friend)

You will learn these skills in Chapters 3, 4, and 5.

R: Reciting the Information

Once you have selected what you need to know and you've organized the information in a manageable format, you need to *recite*. Reciting is self-testing. Ask yourself the following questions:

- Do I really know the material? Have I memorized the essential concepts, definitions, and facts?
- Do I understand the important relationships and interpretations?
- Could I explain the information to someone else?
- Could I apply what I've learned in similar situations?
- Can I analyze, synthesize, and evaluate what I've learned?
- Can I use this knowledge to propose solutions to problems?

To help you, each chapter in this text ends with a self-testing Reader's Checklist.

E: Examining Your Learning Periodically

This is where the real work of being a student happens. You must recite, or self-test, periodically to remember what you need to know for exams and/or your future career. You need to *examine* yourself at regular intervals to reinforce what you have learned. A nursing student, for example, needs to know the names of muscles and bones in the body to pass exams—and to practice nursing in the years to come. Examining yourself helps you memorize the material and usually helps you to keep it in your long-term memory, not just to pass exams. To help you examine how well you've learned the skills and concepts in this textbook, there are two mastery tests at the end of the chapter.

Educational psychologists know that regular reviews are the key to long-term retention of what we have learned. Most forgetting occurs immediately. That is, what you read today and what you learn in class lectures today will be almost totally forgotten within 24 hours, unless you review it. When you learn new information, try reviewing it on a schedule like this:

- Immediately
- Within 24 hours
- In two or three days
- In a week
- In two or three weeks
- In a month
- In increasingly wider-spaced intervals

After the first review, you can spread your reviews further and further apart and still remember what you need to know. Keep in mind that, as Barbara Jordan came to realize (see Reading 1), probably the most enjoyable and effective way to review is in study groups. Study groups can be your key to success as a student.

©2007 Pearson Education, Inc.

Use Table 1.1 to review what you learned about the reading process in this chapter. You will use this process throughout the text.

Table 1.1	The PRO Reading System

P = Prepare to Read
Purpose (know what your purpose is)
Preview
Previous knowledge (recognize your previous knowledge)
Predict (ask questions about what you will learn)

R = Read Actively
Become involved
Be interested
Be alert and attentive
Monitor your involvement and comprehension

R = Reflect
Discover new ideas
Connect new knowledge to previous knowledge
Use critical thinking skills to evaluate your new knowledge

O = Organize: SURE
S = Select the facts and concepts you need to know
U = Use the material you've selected
R = Recite the information (self-test)
E = Examine yourself periodically (review)

Exercise 10   Prepare to Read

Preview Reading 3 and complete items 1 through 4. Then follow the instructions in item 5 as you read.

1. List three or more things that you noted in your preview.

a. _____

b. _____

c. _____

2. What do you already know about how public high schools function?

_____

_____

3. What might be your purpose for reading material like this?

_____

_____

4. Write three reader's questions you predict this selection will answer. Remember that in this essay, Peifer will be giving his opinions about high schools, so your questions might be about Peifer's ideas.

   a. _____

   b. _____

   c. _____

5. Write two reflections (thoughts, comments, or questions) in the margins as you read, using what you know about schools and the atmosphere that helps people learn. You can base these reflections on your own experiences or on the experiences of people you know.

Reading 3 *Suburb High, USA: School or Prison?*

Marley Peifer

The following reading, written by a high school senior, presents his opinions about the deterioration of the learning environment in suburban high schools in the United States. Prepare yourself to read actively and to reflect on what you read. As you read, make connections to what you already know about U.S. high schools and about learning situations. Also, to assist yourself in reading actively, think about whether or not you agree with the author's point of view.

1 After eating a quick breakfast, taking a shower, and brushing my teeth, I hoist my 20-pound backpack and leave my house. Living only a few blocks from school, I hear the first bell sound. As the school comes into sight, I see crowds of students walking to their classes. The daily traffic jam in front of the school is as bad as usual. Sixteen-year-olds with fresh licenses in their wallets haphazardly honk and maneuver their way toward the full parking lot. Many live closer to school than I do. Security guards direct cars into the lot. The standard two cop cars are parked on the sidewalk in front of the gates. The two officers stand by their cars, arms crossed, faces stern, and emotionless as statues. The dean, vice principal, and other miscellaneous staff patrol the sidewalk wearing sunglasses and trench coats that make them seem almost inhuman. I stop at the crosswalk, push the button and wait to cross the street. Other kids standing around talk and joke with each other. Then the one-minute bell rings. People start running to their classes. Students carelessly park their cars, jump out, and start running. Just in case the students didn't seem hurried enough, or maybe to make themselves feel important, the previously described staff members whip electronic bullhorns out of their trench coats and remind them. Remarks such as "Get moving!" "Hurry it up, Missy!" and "Come on, one minute!" are how these staff greet the students and welcome them to another day of learning.

©2007 Pearson Education, Inc.

2   The students with me on the other side of the street have stopped talking and now shuffle nervously, eyeing the crosswalk light and the second
hand on their watches. A diminutive freshman next to me whose backpack
is nearly bigger than he is has started a countdown on his digital watch. He
looks at his friend next to him who is tightening his shoe laces. "Forty-five
seconds." He looks up at the crosswalk, which still displays a red hand.
"Thirty-five seconds." Further down the street I see students jaywalking, fa-
voring dodging cars to being late. I look back at the tiny freshman, who's
nearly trembling. "Twenty-five seconds," he stutters. Finally, the light turns
green, and it's as if someone just fired the gun for a race. The top-heavy
freshman sprints off, wobbling precariously. Everyone else is close behind.
The bullhorn-toting staff spur them on. I run across the front lawn of the
school toward the closest building. "Fifteen seconds," I hear from the bull-
horn as I charge through the door, narrowly missing another student. Now,
sprinting down the hallway, I see all the teachers lined up next to their open
doors. My teacher is at the end of the hall. Her eyes make contact with
mine. I'm only twenty yards away. Then the last bell rings. Up and down the
hallway, the teachers shut and lock the doors. Exhausted and defeated, I
walk the last few steps to my class and look in the window. The students
are sitting down, and the teacher is taking roll. I try the doorknob even
though I know it is locked. I look down the hallway and see the other students who didn't make it. A few, who have never been late before, look no-
ticeably scared. Just then, the doors at the end of the hallway swing open
and three security guards come in. They fan out, one coming toward me
and the other students near me. "Let's go! ISS Room," he says, and begins
escorting us out of the building. On our way there, I see other late students
being taken away on golf carts. The staff members lock the gates, take off
their trench coats, and return to their desk jobs. I spend an hour in the In-
School Suspension Room because I was caught in the "Tardy Sweep."

School or Prison?

3   The previous account is of an average morning at my suburban high school.
Much of it could have come from the pages of a prison inmate's journal.
Even though a prison should be the last thing that one thinks of to describe
a school, the school-prison analogy is quite commonly used by my fellow
students these days. Unfortunately, my school is losing qualities of a high
school and gaining more and more qualities of a prison. The administration
increasingly emphasizes controlling students and ignores educational matters. In many cases, quality of education is sacrificed for increased "security."
The administration seems to be more concerned with getting students in
class on time than they are with whether students are learning once they
are inside. This has been a steady trend since I was a freshman, and the future of the school doesn't look too good.

The Erosion of Freedoms

4   When I was in eighth grade I was amazed at how much freedom the high
school students had. I saw how they had "open campus" and could leave

school for lunch. Many seniors who had jobs or were studying at a community college weren't even required to stay at school for all six periods. For these reasons I couldn't wait to go to high school. I wanted to be treated more like an adult. All the restrictions of middle school made me long for the new responsibilities and freedoms of high school. However, during the summer before I started high school, the administration got rid of the "open campus" system, saying it was causing too many truancies. So I wouldn't be able to eat my lunch at local fast food restaurants as I had dreamed of in eighth grade. That same summer, the lockers were removed, which meant that students had to carry absurdly heavy backpacks. Since I have been at the school, I have watched the number of security guards double, and I have seen how the nice ones have been replaced with stern ones. At the same time, I have witnessed the increased presence of uniformed police. Currently, two officers are assigned to our school, and on occasion there are more. They make no attempt to interact positively with the students or even to smile. The officers are in fact very intimidating. They wear dark glasses and walk around the school with scowls on their faces. They don't seem to realize they are at a school, or at least they don't show it. Instead, they walk around looking like prison guards with guns in their holsters. In my four years at the high school, I have watched countless new rules put into place as well as numerous regulations. Not only have most of these regulations been unnecessary, but many have in fact been detrimental to students' learning.

Overreacting

5   In light of the recent shootings at high schools across the United States, it's easy to see why parents and school officials might be interested in increased security. They obviously want to prevent more shooting incidents. However, many of the measures being taken at my school would not help prevent a shooting, but they do slow the learning process and make students feel uncomfortable. Penalizing students who are ten seconds late by sending them to spend an hour doing nothing in the In-School Suspension Room is not going to prevent a school shooting or make the school safer. In fact, it creates more disruption to learning than being a little late. Not letting students wear hats on campus is not going to stop the next shooting; nor will not letting students go to the bathroom during a class period. Since the wave of school shootings, parents and teachers have been afraid to question new regulations imposed in the name of "security." I feel a few administrators have taken advantage of this to make the school as bureaucratically efficient and easy to manage as possible, regardless of the effects on education.

6   One of the adverse effects of these changes is psychological. Students are like sponges: we pick up what the staff are feeling and what the environment is like. If the school is an open, happy place where we feel like we can just walk up to the staff and talk to them, we will feel comfortable and probably even enjoy going to school and be enthusiastic about learning. If the school is a place where all the doors lock at the sound of a bell, and our interactions with the staff are limited to the times they yell at us through

©2007 Pearson Education, Inc.

bullhorns, we will be unenthusiastic, sullen, and withdrawn. If the school is run like a school, students will act like students; but if the school is run like a prison, students will act like prisoners.

7   I need to say that I have had some teachers who know what school is about. They treat us like young people who will soon be making our way in life, either working or continuing our studies. They teach us to think critically and also to take responsibility for our actions, not simply to follow rules. They see that the way that our school is trying to provide order and security for students is frequently, or even most of the time, detrimental to learning. Most students know that if we are treated with respect rather than like prisoners, we will be better learners and thinkers.

8   Making our schools more like prisons negates what schools are supposed to be all about.

PEIFER, "Suburb High, USA"

Exercise 11   ## Read Actively

Briefly answer the following questions about how you applied the active reading process as you read Reading 3.

1. Did your attention wander as you read this short selection? When? Why?

_____

2. If you were distracted, how could you have avoided this interruption to your reading?

_____

3. How did you continue predicting and asking questions as you read?

_____

4. How well did you monitor your comprehension?

_____

5. Did your reflections trigger other connections and ideas? Explain.

_____

Exercise 12   ## Check Your Understanding

Based on Reading 3, Peifer's "Suburb High, USA: School or Prison?" write your answers to the following questions.

1. What do you learn about Peifer's school in paragraphs 1 and 2?

_____

_____

2. Why do you think Peifer says his school is like a prison?

_____

_____

_____

3. List at least three events or situations at Peifer's school that he doesn't like. (par. 4)

a. _____

b. _____

c. _____

d. _____

e. _____

4. Why have so many new security measures been put into place? (par. 5)

_____

_____

5. Why does Peifer say the students will act like prisoners?

_____

_____

| Exercise 13 | **Reflect**

Think about what you read in Reading 3 and what you already know about this topic. Answer the following questions, and prepare to discuss them with your classmates.

1. What was high school like when you attended?

_____

_____

2. Do you think Peifer's description of schools becoming more like prisons is accurate? Explain.

_____

_____

©2007 Pearson Education, Inc.

3. What do you think is most important in shaping students' attitudes about learning?

_____

_____

4. What kinds of things do you think can be done to make high schools healthy places to learn and safe places for young people?

_____

_____

5. What do you think schools could do to create a learning community where all students feel comfortable?

_____

_____

CHAPTER REVIEW

✔ Reader's Checklist

Check (✓) the concepts and skills introduced in this chapter that you are confident you understand and can now use in your reading strategy. If you are not sure about any items (1) go back to the explanations in the text, (2) study and review with other members of your college learning community, (3) ask your instructor for help, (4) check out the Web site for this textbook at **www.ablongman.com/alexandercommunity4e** for additional exercises on the reading process and to take the chapter quiz, or (5) complete additional practices in the *Reading Road Trip.*

The PRO reading system
  ❏ Reading is a process

Prepare to read
  ❏ Determine your purpose
  ❏ Preview a textbook
  ❏ Preview a chapter
  ❏ Preview a section
  ❏ Use previous knowledge
  ❏ Predict what you will learn

Read Actively
  ❏ Become involved
  ❏ Be interested
  ❏ Be alert and attentive
  ❏ Monitor your comprehension

Reflect
  ❏ Discover new ideas
  ❏ Connect new knowledge to previous knowledge
  ❏ Use critical thinking skills

Organize what you have read (SURE)
- ❏ Select facts and concepts
- ❏ Use material you've selected
- ❏ Recite the information
- ❏ Examine yourself periodically

The importance of working with other students
- ❏ Classroom community/ study groups

When you are confident that you have mastered these concepts and skills, test yourself with Mastery Tests 1A and 1B (pp. 35–49).

Critical Reflections

Answer the following questions, and prepare to discuss them with your classmates.

1. In Reading 2, "Use the Tools for College Success!" Cunningham states that having goals is one of the most important sources of motivation. However, your goals must be specific, have a time frame, and be challenging but achievable. Write three academic goals for yourself for this semester that follow these recommendations.

   a. _____

   b. _____

   c. _____

Writing Activity

1. What are some steps you can take to ensure that you can accomplish your goals this semester?

   a. _____

   b. _____

   c. _____

   d. _____

2. Write a paragraph or short essay that answers the question, "How can I be successful as a student this semester?" Be specific, and give examples of what you will do. Some things to consider include making sure you set up study times when you can concentrate, making friends with other students in the class and studying with them, and using techniques for remembering, such as reviewing regularly.

3. Go visit at least two learning resources on your campus (tutoring centers, academic advising or counseling centers, computer labs, library,

©2007 Pearson Education, Inc.

etc.). Find out what services they offer and their hours of operation. Using this information, write up a short blurb to explain these resources to other students.

Classroom Community

Discuss as a group the following questions.

1. What can you and your classmates do to set up a study environment in which you support each other, like Barbara Jordan did in law school?

2. In what ways was the learning atmosphere in your high school similar to and different from the learning atmosphere you are now experiencing in college?

Extend Your Thinking

For another reading related to learning and memory, see "How We Learn," by Ricki Linksman, in the "Extend Your Thinking" section at the end of Part I (pp. 460–465).

Work the Web

College Web sites usually have a section devoted to skills students need to succeed. After completing the exercise below you may want to check out your own college's Web site or the Web site of any colleges you are interested in, and find out which tips and support services these schools provide.

Go to Dartmouth College's Academic Skills Center Web page at http://www.dartmouth.edu/~acskills/success. At the Dartmouth site, complete the following task about listening habits—an essential skill for success in college—that was not covered in Chapter 1 of *A Community of Readers*.

1. Click on the link "Taking Lecture and Class Notes."

2. Then scroll down to the section on Listening. Read "Ten Bad Listening Habits."

3. Make a list of four listening habits that you will change based on this reading.

_____

_____

_____

_____

Go to www.ablongman.com/alexandercommunity4e for additional Web-based activities.

Mastery Test

1A

©2007 Pearson Education, Inc.

Exercise 1   **Prepare to Read and Read Actively**

Answer the following questions. They will help you prepare to read "How to Remember," which begins on page 36.

1. Which of the following might you do as you prepare to read? (Circle all that apply.)
   a. Determine your purpose for reading.
   b. Carefully start reading, beginning with the first sentence.
   c. Preview the reading.
   d. Ask questions the reading might answer.
   e. Try to determine what words you need to know and look them up in the dictionary.
   f. Consider your previous knowledge about the subject.

2. What is your purpose for reading this text? (Circle all that apply.)

   _____

   a. To complete a homework assignment
   b. To answer your questions about remembering material better
   c. To demonstrate that you can read and understand a textbook excerpt and respond to questions within a limited time
   d. To remember the information for a future test
   e. To get some information because you are interested in the subject

3. What previous knowledge do you have about memory? Write what you already know about how memory works.

   _____

4. Very quickly, preview the reading. What did you notice in your preview?

   _____

   _____

   _____

5. Write two reader's questions you predict might be answered in this reading.

   a. _____

   b. _____

6. As you read, write two questions or comments in the margins that you might have as an active reader.

   _____

How to Remember Carole Wade and Carol Tavris

The following reading, from the textbook Invitation to Psychology *by Carole Wade and Carol Tavris, offers some good ways to remember what you study. As you read, consider what you learned about this topic as you prepared to read.*

1 Someday, drugs may help people with memory deficiencies and may increase normal memory performance. For the time being, however, those of us who hope to improve our memories must rely on mental strategies.

2 • *Pay attention!* It seems obvious, but often we fail to remember because we never encoded the information in the first place. For example, which of these is the real Lincoln penny? (See Figure 1.1.)

Figure 1.1

3 • Most Americans have trouble recognizing the real penny because they have never <u>attended to</u> the details of a penny's design (Nickerson & Adams, 1979). We are not advising you to do so, unless you happen to be a coin collector or a counterfeiting expert. Just keep in mind that when you do have something to remember, such as the material in this book, you will do better if you encode it well. (The real penny, by the way, is the left one in the bottom row.)

4 • *Encode information in more than one way.* The more elaborate the encoding of information, the more memorable it will be. Use your imagination! For instance, in addition to remembering a telephone number by the sound of the individual digits, you might note the spatial pattern they make as you punch them in on a touch-tone phone.

5 • *Add meaning.* The more meaningful the material, the more likely it is to link up with information already in long-term memory. Meaningfulness also reduces the number of chunks of information you have to learn. Common ways of adding meaning include making up a story about the material (fitting the material into a cognitive schema) and forming visual images. (Some people find that the odder the image, the better.) If your license plate happens to be 236MPL, you might think of 236 maples. If you are trying to remember the concept of procedural memory . . . you might make the concept meaningful by thinking of an example from your own life, such as your ability to ride a mountain bike, and then imagine a "P" <u>superimposed</u> on an image of yourself on your bike.

6 • *Aim for a moderate arousal level.* Hormones released by the adrenal glands during stress and emotional arousal, including epinephrine (adrenaline) and certain steroids, appear to enhance memory—but only if the hormones remain at moderate levels (Cahill et al., 1994; McGaugh, 1990). Thus, if you want to remember information well, you should try not to be too worked up *or* too relaxed.

7 • *Take your time.* Just as concrete takes time to set, the neural and synaptic changes in the brain that underlie long-term memory take time to develop. . . . Memories, therefore, require a period of consolidation, or stabilization, before they solidify. That fact may help explain why leisurely learning, spread out over several sessions, usually produces better results than harried cramming (although *reviewing* material just before a test can be helpful). In terms of hours spent, "distributed" (spaced) learning sessions are more efficient than "massed" ones; in other words, three separate one-hour study sessions may result in more retention than one session of three hours.

8 • *Take time out.* If possible, minimize interference by using study breaks for rest or recreation. Sleep is the ultimate way to reduce interference. In a classic study, students who slept for eight hours after learning lists of nonsense syllables retained them better than students who went about their usual business (Jenkins & Dallenbach, 1924). Sleep is not always possible, of course, but periodic mental relaxation usually is.

9 • *Overlearn.* You can't remember something you never learned well in the first place. Overlearning—studying information even after you think you already know it—is one of the best ways to ensure that you'll remember it.

10 • *Monitor your learning.* By testing yourself frequently, rehearsing thoroughly, and reviewing periodically, you will have a better idea of how you are doing. Don't just evaluate your learning immediately after reading the material, though; because the information is still in short-term memory, you are likely to feel a false sense of confidence about your ability to recall it later. If you delay making a judgment for at least a few minutes, your evaluation will probably be more accurate (Nelson & Dunlosky, 1991).

11   Whatever strategies you use, you will find that active learning produces more comprehension and better retention than does passive reading or listening. The mind does not gobble up information automatically; you must make the material digestible. Even then, you should not expect to remember everything you read or hear. Nor should you want to. Piling up facts without distinguishing the important from the trivial is just confusing. Popular books and tapes that promise a "perfect," "photographic" memory, or "instant recall" of everything you learn, fly in the face of what psychologists know about how the mind operates. Our advice: Forget them.

WADE AND TAVRIS, *INVITATION TO PSYCHOLOGY*

©2007 Pearson Education, Inc.

| Exercise 2 | Check Your "Prepare to Read and Read Actively"

Briefly answer the following questions about how you applied the active reading process as you read "How to Remember."

1. Which of your reader's questions were answered?

_____

2. What strategies did you use to be an active reader? In what ways did these strategies help you remain involved, interested, and attentive?

_____

_____

3. List the important information in the reading that was new for you.

_____

| Exercise 3 | Work with Words

Choose the best definition for each of the following words underlined in the reading. The paragraph number is provided in case you want to check the context.

1. *Attended to* (par. 3)
   a. taken care of
   b. paid attention to
   c. had a tendency to

2. *Superimposed* (par. 5)
   a. put on top of a visual image
   b. imposed to the extreme
   c. modeled in a superior way

3. *Arousal* (par. 6)
   a. excitement
   b. indifference
   c. imagination

4. *Epinephrine* (par. 6)
   a. arousal
   b. certain steroids
   c. adrenaline

5. *Consolidation* (par. 7)
   a. solidification
   b. leisure
   c. stabilization

6. *"Distributed" learning* (par. 7)
   a. passed out assignments
   b. spaced learning
   c. reviewed before a test

7. *Overlearning* (par. 9)
   a. studying for long periods at a time
   b. studying information even after you think you already know it
   c. studying information meticulously by reading it over several times

8. *Monitor your learning* (par. 10)
   a. measure your learning
   b. relearn the information
   c. test yourself periodically

9. *Periodically* (par. 10)
   a. from time to time
   b. every few minutes
   c. after you finish reading

10. *Retention* (par. 11)
    a. comprehension
    b. remembering
    c. perfect recall

Exercise 4   Check Your Understanding

Based on the reading "How to Remember" by Wade and Tavris, choose the best answer to each of the following multiple-choice questions.

1. Most people don't remember exactly what a penny looks like because
   a. we all use pennies so often.
   b. we don't pay attention to the details of a penny.
   c. we don't think pennies are very important because they're not worth much.

2. Noticing the spatial pattern as you punch in the digits of a phone number on a touch-tone phone is an example of
   a. adding meaning.
   b. aiming for a moderate arousal level.
   c. encoding information in more than one way.

3. It is a good idea to add meaning to information you want to remember because
   a. you can remember information better if it has meaning for you.
   b. meaning usually doesn't have much to do with your life.
   c. making up a story helps erase cognitive schema.

©2007 Pearson Education, Inc.

4. Leisurely learning, spread out over several sessions, is usually better than harried cramming because
   a. you learn better if you are completely relaxed.
   b. it is not good to be excessively nervous about every aspect of your studies.
   c. memories require a period of consolidation before they solidify.

5. It is helpful to encode information in more than one way because
   a. it will be difficult for someone else to decode the same information.
   b. it will be more memorable, especially if you use your imagination.
   c. it is the least stressful way to remember information.

6. All of the following are ways that the authors give to add meaning to what you are learning except
   a. making up a story.
   b. forming visual images.
   c. paying attention to a high level of detail.

7. Students who slept for eight hours after learning lists of nonsense syllables retained them better than students who went about their usual business because
   a. getting enough sleep is important to you when you are studying.
   b. sleep reduces interference.
   c. students who made time for sleep had good time-management skills.

8. Which of the following is not recommended by the authors as a way to "monitor your learning"?
   a. Review periodically.
   b. Rehearse thoroughly.
   c. Relax so that you're not too nervous.

9. The authors recommend that
   a. you buy some books or tapes that help you perfect your memory.
   b. you accumulate facts because all that information will help you.
   c. you develop your own strategies for active learning.

10. Probably the most important overall idea to remember from this reading is
    a. you should add meaning to what you are trying to learn.
    b. you should be active in a variety of ways when you are trying to learn and remember information.
    c. you should encode information in more than one way.

Exercise 5   Reflect

Think about what you read in "How to Remember" and what you know about this topic. Then answer the following questions.

1. How can this reading help you study more effectively?

   _____

   _____

2. Why do you think that the authors tell you to forget about books or tapes that promise a photographic memory?

   _____

   _____

©2007 Pearson Education, Inc.

Mastery Test

1B

Exercise 1 **Prepare to Read and Read Actively**

Answer the following questions. They will help you prepare to read "What Is Collaborative Learning?" which begins on page 43.

1. Which of the following might you do as you prepare to read? (Circle all that apply.)
   a. Determine your purpose for reading.
   b. Carefully start reading, beginning with the first sentence.
   c. Preview the reading.
   d. Ask questions the reading might answer.
   e. Try to determine what words you need to know and look them up in the dictionary.
   f. Consider your previous knowledge about the subject.

2. What is your purpose for reading this text? (Circle all that apply.)
   a. To complete a homework assignment
   b. To answer your questions about remembering material better
   c. To demonstrate that you can read and understand a textbook excerpt and respond to questions within a limited time
   d. To remember the information for a future test
   e. To get some information because you are interested in the subject

3. What previous knowledge do you have about collaborative learning? Write what you already know about how collaborative learning works.

   _____

4. Very quickly, preview the reading. What did you notice in your preview?

   _____

   _____

   _____

5. Write two reader's questions you predict might be answered in this reading.

   a. _____

   b. _____

6. As you read, write two questions or comments in the margins to monitor your understanding as an active reader.

   _____

What Is Collaborative Learning?

Toni Haring-Smith

The following reading is from a college writing textbook by Toni Haring-Smith. In this section, the author is explaining how group work can benefit the class as a whole and each student individually by helping students become active learners. She explains how writers and readers work together, a process she calls collaborative learning.

We work together, whether together or apart.
ROBERT FROST

1 When you think of writing, what do you visualize? Do you see a solitary individual like Emily Dickinson sitting alone in an attic room? Do you imagine F. Scott Fitzgerald lying drunk in his lonely study? Or, do you see people working together—the early leaders of this country huddled in candlelight, talking, writing, and revising the Declaration of Independence? Do you see a famous novelist like Hemingway leaning over the typescript of a new book with his editor? . . .

2 Although most of our familiar images of writers and students present them as solitary, in fact most writers and thinkers work together to share ideas with one another. Our historical and cultural mythology encourages us to think of great ideas, discoveries, and events as the product of individual effort when they usually result from group effort. We remember Alexander Graham Bell and his telephone, Marie Curie and radium, Aristotle and the definition of tragedy, or Martin Luther King, Jr., and the Civil Rights movement. But none of these people worked alone. Bell developed his invention with his associate, Thomas Watson; Curie performed most of her experiments with her husband or her daughter; Aristotle spent twenty years discussing ideas with thinkers in Plato's Academy and later with his friend Theophrastus; and Martin Luther King, Jr., had a small army of supporters surrounding him as he marched out of Selma. There are, of course, hermits and solitary geniuses in our society, but they are the exceptions—so exceptional, in fact, that we frequently brand them peculiar or even insane.

3 It is not surprising, then, that recent research in education, psychology, and business management shows us that people can accomplish more if they work together. Dozens of studies have revealed that people working as a group to solve mazes or number puzzles can outperform individuals working alone at the same task. And perhaps the most interesting, research demonstrates that groups even solve puzzles more accurately than the brightest individual in them could alone. . . .

4 The classroom in which collaborative learning is used looks quite different from a more traditional lecture or class discussion. You will work in pairs or small groups, you may move about the room rather than sit still, and you will find out answers for yourselves rather than wait for the teacher to give you the answer. In fact, in most of these exercises, there is no "right answer," so you and your groups will be developing and defending your own ideas, not just trying to figure out "what the teacher wants."

©2007 Pearson Education, Inc.

43

5   Have you been asked to work in groups before and thought, "What a waste of time. Why doesn't the teacher just lecture?" Have you ever waited patiently through a class discussion in order to find out what the teacher really thinks? If you have been asked to read and comment on another student's paper, have you wondered what you could possibly have to say? Have you assumed that your classmates wouldn't be able to help you write, and have you wished that the teacher would read your essay drafts? Or maybe most of your teachers have spent class time presenting material to you, while you took notes or worked on homework.

6   If any of these experiences sounds familiar, you will find collaborative learning a new approach. Of course, it is not a new kind of learning—in fact, reading, talking, and learning together was the practice in most schools until the twentieth century. But collaborative learning is not very common in American schools now. The first rules that most students learn in school are

- Be quiet.

- Don't talk to other students.

- Do your own work.

Our school systems have become so concerned with testing individual comprehension of material that they have stopped students from learning together. This has had a very serious effect on how well students learn and it has warped our assumptions about teachers' and students' roles in the classroom. Let's look at how collaborative learning challenges the kind of schooling most Americans now receive.

7   In order to work together with your classmates, you will have to recognize the knowledge and experience that you and your classmates have. Why work with others if you don't think that they have anything worthwhile to share? Why ask someone to respond to your writing if you think that only the teacher can do that? Most students have gradually come to distrust the knowledge they and their classmates have. The American educational system teaches most students that they should listen to the teacher, memorize what she and the textbooks say, and then <u>regurgitate</u> that information on exams and in papers. In many cases, students find it easier to forget or ignore what they think and just concentrate on what the teacher thinks.

8   I know that when I was a student, I was often afraid to speak in class. It seemed safer to be quiet than to be wrong. I remember sitting in English class and thinking, "Where did the teacher get that interpretation of this text? I thought that the poem was about a flower and she says that it is about existentialism." I learned to keep quiet rather than reveal my ignorance. I think many students share my fear of being wrong. Consequently, it is not surprising that American educators today <u>bemoan</u> the fact that their students are <u>passive</u>. . . .

9   In most colleges and universities, teachers and students alike assume that students are empty <u>vessels</u>, waiting to be filled with the knowledge of calculus, Chinese history, modern American architecture, or whatever. The basic definition of a teacher is one who knows a subject, while a student is assumed to be ignorant of the subject. Now to some extent, this is true. You

take a class in organic chemistry because you want to learn organic chemistry. If you already knew the subject, you would probably try to "test out" of the course and take a different one. Of course, you might take a diagnostic test at the beginning of a course to see how much American history or calculus you remember, but these random questions can't really tell teachers what you know about a subject. If you know that Washington was president before Lincoln, does this mean that you also understand different cultural or political climates in which these two men worked? . . .

10   Most of the time, you do know something about the subject of the courses you take. Your courses up to this point have prepared you for organic chemistry. You have learned methods for balancing chemical equations, and you understand the basic structure of chemical compounds. Similarly, although you may never have taken a course in Chinese history, you probably know something about it—that it involves many dynasties, that China was a great silk producer, that Chinese women used to bind their feet, that the Chinese built the Great Wall, that the Communist party has been crushing political dissent, and so on. Some of the things you "know" about a subject may not be "true." For example, based on popular media, you might assume that the Chinese were especially ruthless warriors. You might also have memorized incorrect valences for certain chemical elements. In any case, your mind is not a blank slate.

11   Not only do you come into a course with knowledge and experience that is relevant to it, but, as you go along in the course, you gradually come to understand its content. You will be learning about the subject from the teacher, the texts, and the other students in the class. What you learn will shape the way you hear the teacher, argue with your classmates, or read the texts.

12   If we teachers treat you as if you know nothing about the subject, and if you are afraid to speak for fear of being wrong, then you will become passive. You will wait for us to tell you what you think, and then you will write it down, and tell it back to us in papers and on exams. In this kind of system, there is little reward for thinking on your own. There is also little reward for listening to other, apparently equally ignorant students. This is why students often complain about group work of any kind. They want to know why the teacher does not just give them the answer.

13   Collaborative learning asks that you

- Have the courage to recognize and speak your own ideas.
- Respect the ideas and knowledge that other students bring to the class.
- Trust the teacher to listen to you with respect and to care about your ideas.

Collaborative learning redefines your relationship to your teacher and to the other students in the class. Rather than assume that your mind is a blank slate, waiting to be written on by the teacher, collaborative learning focuses on the knowledge and experience that you bring to a classroom. It works by finding out what you know and then allowing the teacher to respond

©2007 Pearson Education, Inc.

and give you exercises that will let you learn. The teacher does not digest all the knowledge and feed it to you like the predigested food fed to baby birds. The teacher does not report her learning. You learn for yourself, and the teacher is there as a kind of coach to guide your learning, to point you to important ideas and books, to give you exercises that will help you sharpen your skills.

HARING-SMITH, *WRITING TOGETHER*

Exercise 2   **Check Your "Prepare to Read and Reading Actively"**

Briefly answer the following questions about how you applied the active reading process as you read "What Is Collaborative Learning?"

1. Which of your reader's questions were answered?

_____

2. What strategies did you use to be an active reader? In what ways did these strategies help you remain involved, interested, and attentive?

_____

_____

3. List the important information in the excerpt that was new for you.

_____

Exercise 3   **Work with Words**

Choose the best definition for each of the following words underlined in the reading. The paragraph number is provided in case you want to go back to the reading to check the context. Use a dictionary if necessary.

1. *Solitary* (par. 2)
   a. with other people
   b. with one other person
   c. by oneself, alone

2. *Brand* (par. 2)
   a. put a mark on (a person or animal) with a hot piece of metal
   b. put a name brand on (a person or an object)
   c. put a person or object into a category

3. *Regurgitate* (par. 7)
   a. spit something out of your mouth
   b. throw up
   c. give the same information back

4. *Bemoan* (par. 8)
   a. complain about
   b. moan when in pain
   c. groan

5. *Passive* (par. 8)
   a. uninvolved
   b. pacific
   c. involved

6. *Vessels* (par. 9)
   a. ships
   b. containers
   c. tanks

7. *Climates* (par. 9)
   a. temperatures
   b. atmospheres
   c. weather zones

8. *Dissent* (par. 10)
   a. agreement
   b. beliefs
   c. disagreement

9. *Blank slate* (par. 10)
   a. blackboard with nothing on it
   b. empty
   c. full of information already

10. *Redefines* (par. 13)
   a. gives a new definition of
   b. gives the same meaning to
   c. changes the quality of

Exercise 4   Check Your Understanding

Based on the reading "What Is Collaborative Learning?" by Haring-Smith, choose the best answer to each of the multiple-choice questions.

1. The author chose the examples of Alexander Graham Bell, Madame Curie, Aristotle, and Martin Luther King Jr., because
   a. they were all very famous, solitary geniuses.
   b. they were all very famous and they all worked with other people.
   c. they were all a part of history that we are familiar with.

2. According to the author, we frequently say that hermits and solitary geniuses are "peculiar" because
   a. they are strange people.
   b. they are exceptions.
   c. they are smarter than other people.

©2007 Pearson Education, Inc.

3. Research shows that
   a. the smartest person in a group can finish a task faster alone.
   b. groups work faster and more accurately than the brightest person in them could do alone.
   c. groups rarely outperform bright individuals working alone.

4. Research on working together has been done in
   a. education, business management, and psychology.
   b. religious studies.
   c. anthropological studies.

5. The collaborative classroom looks different from regular classrooms because
   a. people frequently move around.
   b. students are quieter and neater than usual.
   c. learning is taking place.

6. According to the author
   a. collaborative learning is not very commonly used in American colleges and universities.
   b. most teachers assume that their students already know a great deal about the subject they are studying.
   c. collaborative learning is a new approach to education that was introduced in the twentieth century.

7. The author believes that our schools
   a. are not concerned enough with testing individual comprehension.
   b. are doing a good job educating generations of Americans and should be supported.
   c. should encourage students to learn together.

8. To work with your classmates, you should
   a. not assert your opinion too strongly, just go along with the group.
   b. recognize that the teacher will give you the correct answers in the end.
   c. recognize that you and your classmates have knowledge and experience to contribute to the discussion.

9. For collaborative learning to work
   a. students need to be more involved in their own learning.
   b. teachers need to prepare their lecture notes more carefully than usual.
   c. teachers do not need to know their subject matter as well.

10. Collaborative learning
   a. relies on the teacher more than on the students themselves.
   b. changes your relationship to your teacher and to other students in the class.
   c. is very difficult for students who study on their own.

Exercise 5   **Reflect**

Think about what you read in "What Is Collaborative Learning?" and what you already know about this topic. Then answer the following questions.

1. What experiences have you had working with groups of people to achieve a common goal?

   _____

   _____

   _____

2. What examples do you know of people who worked together and achieved a better result than they would have by working alone?

   _____

   _____

   _____

3. Why do you think that students do better when they study and work together in groups?

   _____

   _____

   _____

   _____

© 2007 Pearson Education, Inc.

Chapter 2

Working with Words

Computer Technology and Beyond

A grand design is getting grander. A global computer is taking shape and we're all connected to it.

—STEWART BRAND

- What do you think the person in the picture is doing? Where do you think he is?

- How does this quotation from Stewart Brand relate to the picture?

- What are some of the implications of the quotation?

© 2007 Pearson Education, Inc.

PREPARE TO READ

New technological developments affect us in many ways. Information technology and its machines—computers—influence everything from bus schedules, bank statements, and grocery shopping to air traffic control, medical equipment, and weapons of war. When the computers are down, we are all, at the least, inconvenienced. We can't get the information we want, and often we can't do the things we need to do. Computers have changed the way we communicate. Studying computer science texts and reading about new technological developments are good ways of learning about vocabulary because so many technology-related words have been introduced into the language in the last 20 years.

Purpose

In this chapter, you will learn a variety of approaches for learning new vocabulary, such as

- Figuring out the meaning of the word from the context
- Figuring out the meaning of words by using word parts
- Using the dictionary
- Using textbook aids and learning specialized vocabulary

In the process of acquiring these skills, you will read about modern technology and how it influences our lives.

Previous Knowledge

Answer these questions and prepare to discuss them in class.

1. In what ways do computers affect your life now?

   _____

2. How do you think computers will affect your life in the future?

   _____

Preview and Predict

Preview Chapter 2. Remember to look at the section titles.

1. Based on your preview, predict two things you think you will learn in this chapter.

   a. _____

   b. _____

2. Write two questions you think will be answered in this chapter.

   a. _____

   b. _____

©2007 Pearson Education, Inc.

Reading 1 *Living Without Computers* George Beekman

George Beekman is the author of the popular college computer science textbook Computer Confluence. *In the following brief reading, he discusses the many ways that we depend on computers and describes the kinds of problems we would have if computers had all stopped working, as people were afraid they would do, on January 1, 2000.*

1 You wake up with the sun well above the horizon and realize your alarm clock hasn't gone off. You wonder if you've overslept. You have a big research project to finish today. The face of your digital wristwatch stares back at you blankly. The TV and radio are no help; you can't find a station on either one. You can't even get the time by telephone, because it doesn't work either.

2 The morning newspaper is missing from your doorstep. You'll have to guess the weather forecast by looking out the window. No music to dress by this morning—your CD player refuses your requests. How about some breakfast? Your automatic coffeemaker refuses to be programmed; your microwave oven is on strike, too.

3 You decide to go out for breakfast. Your car won't start. In fact, the only cars moving are at least 15 years old. The lines at the subway are unbelievable. People chatter nervously about the failure of the subway's computer-controlled scheduling device.

4 You duck into a fast-food outlet and find long lines of people waiting while cashiers handle transactions by hand. Still, you're hungry, so you decide to wait and join the conversation that's going on around you. People seem more interested in talking to each other since all the usual tools of mass communication have failed.

5 You're down to a couple of dollars in cash, so you stop after breakfast at an automated teller machine. Why bother?

6 You return home to wait for the book you ordered by overnight mail. You soon realize that you're in for a long wait; planes aren't flying because air-traffic-control facilities aren't working. You head for the local library to see if the book is in stock. Of course, it's going to be tough to find since the book catalog is computerized.

7 As you walk home, you speculate on the implications of a worldwide computer failure. How will people function in high-tech, high-rise office buildings that depend on computer systems to control everything from elevators to humidity? Will electric power plants be able to function without computer control? What will happen to patients in computerized medical facilities? What about satellites that are kept in orbit by computer-run control systems? Will the financial infrastructure collapse without computers to process and communicate transactions? Will the world be a safer place if all computer-controlled weapons are grounded?

BEEKMAN, *COMPUTER CONFLUENCE*

| Exercise 1 | **Recall and Discuss**

Based on Reading 1, Beekman's "Living Without Computers," answer the following questions and prepare to discuss them with your classmates.

1. Think about what you do in the course of a day. If all the computers were to stop working, how would your daily life be affected?

_____

_____

_____

_____

2. This reading demonstrates how much we depend on computers. What are the advantages and disadvantages that computers bring into our lives?

_____

_____

_____

_____

WORKING WITH WORDS

Computers are a relatively new invention, and they are even changing our language. We have added words to English such as *hardware, software, e-mail, chat room, listserv, CD-ROM,* and many others because we need them to talk about computers. Everyone in our society today needs to know these words.

As a student, you will encounter new words in your college courses, and it is important for you to have a variety of strategies for dealing with them. In this chapter, you will learn some of the most basic ways of building your vocabulary and dealing with words that you may not know.

Reading and Vocabulary

Probably the one activity that will most improve your vocabulary is reading. The more you read, the more words you will learn. It's as simple as that. The more words you know, the easier it is for you to read and the more you will enjoy reading for its own sake. So maybe instead of watching a rerun of a TV program, try to set aside about half an hour a day to read for fun. Pick anything that you enjoy reading—sports magazines, fashion magazines, mystery novels, the newspaper. It doesn't matter what you read at first, as long as you get into the habit. Then gradually push yourself to read material that is a little more challenging and that expands the type of reading you do. Still, you want to enjoy this reading, so pick things that interest you. You will find that developing the lifelong habit of reading a lot will help you build your general vocabulary. And having a large vocabulary will help you in many ways: in school, at work, and whenever you want to communicate. A strong vocabulary is a powerful tool that you can put to work for you.

Context Clues

When you are reading college textbooks, you may run into many words that you do not know. One important skill you need to develop is figuring out the meaning of those words from the context of the reading itself. **Context** refers to the rest of the statement in which a particular word appears. It may include the entire sentence or even a paragraph or more.

context The sentence or paragraph in which a word appears

For practice in understanding context clues, read the following paragraph, which has some words that you don't know but which you will understand because you understand the context.

> Yesterday, when I went to the *osmotle* to buy some *wattish* for dinner, I saw a *slampfer* I knew when I was 10 years old. He smiled and was very *ovish* to see me, but I was *amvish* to see him because I had some bad *dosilums* from the last time I had seen him.

Of course, the italicized words in this passage are not really words, but they could be. From the context, you know that *osmotle* is probably a store, *wattish* is some kind of food, and *slampfer* is a friend or acquaintance, or at least a person. Why were you able to understand these "words"? Because you understood the meaning of the rest of the sentence and paragraph. You understood the context in which the words appeared. You may not know precisely what each word means, but you have a pretty good idea.

In this next section, you will work on figuring out the approximate meaning of words using context clues. All the examples are either from introductory computer textbooks or from books and articles about computers and modern technology.

The context provides basically four kinds of clues that might help you understand a word. They are

- Definition and synonym clues
- Example clues
- General information clues
- Contrast clues

Definition and Synonym Clues When you first encounter a word that you don't understand, don't immediately go to the dictionary. Often the actual definition of a word is provided for you in what you are reading.

©2007 Pearson Education, Inc.

synonym A word that has a similar meaning to another word

Sometimes the definition is an explanation of the word, and sometimes it is a synonym for the word. A **synonym** is a word that means the same as another word. Sometimes the definition or synonym is provided for you in different ways. Consider the following possibilities and the examples of each.

- **Between or after commas.** Notice how the comma can set off the actual definition of a word in the following sentence:

  Computer output, useable information in the form of text or graphics, is generated by the computer when it processes input data.

  In this example, we know that *computer output* means "useable information in the form of text or graphics." We also know that text or graphics are examples of computer output. The definition, set off by commas, is our clue.

- **After certain words.** The words *is, are, means, consists of, is called,* or *that is* can alert you to a definition. Notice how this kind of clue works in the following sentence:

  The equipment associated with a computer system is called *hardware.*

  We know, then, that *hardware* is "the equipment associated with a computer system" because of the words *is called.*

- **Between dashes.** In the following sentence the synonym of a word appears between dashes:

  Output devices show people the *processed data*—information—in understandable and usable form. (Capron, *Computers*)

  The dashes tell us that *information* is a synonym for *processed data.*

- **In parentheses.** In the following sentence, the synonym of a word appears in parentheses:

  Computers perform millions of instructions per second. To measure computer speed, we use *nanoseconds* (billionths of a second).

  The parentheses tell us that the definition of *nanoseconds* is "billionths of a second."

Exercise 2 ## Definition and Synonym Clues

Read the following sentences and write the definition or synonym of the italicized word or words, using the language used in the sentences themselves. Then write down what definition and synonym clue(s) helped you find the meaning. Be sure to use only the definitions provided in these sentences. Some of these words have a special meaning in computer science. The first one has been done for you.

1. *Data* are the raw material to be processed by a computer, such as grades in a class, baseball batting averages, or light and dark areas in a photograph. (Capron, *Computers*)

   Data: <u>the raw material to be processed by a computer</u>

   Clues: <u>are</u>

2. *Output*—the result produced by the central processing unit—is, of course, a computer's whole reason for being. *Output* is usable information—that is, raw input data that has been processed by the computer into information. (Capron, *Computers*)

   Output: _____

   _____

   Clues: _____

3. Computers are often described in terms of their clock speeds, measured in units called *megahertz (Mhz)*. (Beekman, *Computer Confluence*)

   Megahertz: _____

   Clues: _____

4. In addition, memory holds the *programs* (computer instructions) needed by the central processing unit. (Capron, *Computers*)

   Programs: _____

   Clues: _____

5. *RAM (random access memory)* is the most common type of primary storage, or computer memory. (Beekman, *Computer Confluence*)

   Random access memory: _____

   Clues: _____

6. Before the microcomputer revolution, most information processing was done on *mainframe computers*—room-sized machines with price tags that matched their size. (Beekman, *Computer Confluence*)

   Mainframe computers: _____

   Clues: _____

   ◆

Example Clues   Sometimes you can figure out the meaning of a word because you understand the examples, or because both a definition and examples are provided in the reading. Look for the examples and the definitions for the italicized words in the following paragraph.

©2007 Pearson Education, Inc.

Most computer *applications,* such as word processing, are more convenient to use on a faster machine. Many *applications* that use graphics and computations, such as statistical programs, graphic design programs, and many computer games, require faster machines to produce satisfactory results. (Beekman, *Computer Confluence*)

In this paragraph, the examples the author gives for computer applications are "word processing," "graphics," "statistical programs," "graphic design programs," and "computer games." We know from this list of examples that *applications* means something like "the different kinds of programs that computers can run."

Exercise 3   **Example Clues**

Read the following sentences and write the definition or synonym of the italicized word or words, using language provided in the sentences themselves. Then write down what example clue helped you find the meaning. Be sure to use only the definitions provided in these sentences.

1. Mainframe computers are capable of communicating with several users simultaneously through a technique called *timesharing*. For example, a timesharing system allows travel agents all over the country to make reservations using the same computer and the same information at the same time. (Beekman, *Computer Confluence*)

   Timesharing: _____

   Example clues: _____

2. The 1950s and 1960s represented an era of *institutional computing*. Corporations and government institutions used the large, expensive computers of the time to transform and streamline their operations, and the world changed as a result. (Beekman, *Computer Confluence*)

   Institutional computing: _____

   _____

   Example clues: _____

   ◆

General Information Clues   Often you can understand an unfamiliar word because you already comprehend the rest of the information in the surrounding sentence or group of sentences. It was from this type of context clue that you were able to understand the example using the "words" *osmotle* and *wattish* on page 55. The contexts for the italicized words in the following example are a little more complicated, but you will probably be able to figure out what the words mean because you will understand the context. Sometimes you can understand a new word because the text explains what the word means. Often in the context of technology, the text explains what something does, and that helps you understand the meaning of the new term. Consider the following example:

> *Input devices* accept data or commands in a form that the computer can use; they send the data or commands to the processing unit. (Capron, *Computers*)

From this sentence, we know that input devices accept data and send it to the processing unit. So we can write a definition using this information: "Input devices are the parts of the computer that accept data in a form that the computer can use and send the data to the processing unit." Our clue is the explanation of what input devices do.

Exercise 4   General Information Clues

Read the following examples and write the definition or synonym of the italicized word or words, using language provided by the reading itself. Then write down what general information clue(s) helped you find the meaning. Be sure to use only the definitions provided in these sentences.

1. Not all computers are general-purpose machines. Many are *special-purpose (dedicated) computers* that perform specific tasks, ranging from controlling the temperature and humidity in a high-rise office building to monitoring your heart rate while you work out. (Beekman, *Computer Confluence*)

   Special-purpose (dedicated) computers: _____

   _____

   Clues: _____

2. *Embedded computers* enhance all kinds of consumer goods: wristwatches, game machines, stereos, video cassette recorders, and ovens. Because of embedded computers, a typical new car has more computing power than the salesperson's PC! (Beekman, *Computer Confluence*)

   Embedded computers: _____

   _____

   Clues: _____

3. Anita had a good grasp of computer basics and could perform such tasks as preparing memos on the computer. But her greatest reward was learning how to use *spreadsheets,* which let her enter, revise, and print numerical data in rows and columns. (Capron, *Computers*)

   Spreadsheets: _____

   Clues: _____

◆

©2007 Pearson Education, Inc.

Contrast Clues   Sometimes you can figure out the meaning of a word by understanding what it is *not*. Occasionally a context indicates that a word is different from or the opposite of another word. These words can be clues that there is a contrast:

but	on the other hand
in contrast to	however
although	unlike

Consider the following example. Using the contrast clue, we can determine the meaning of *public domain software*.

> Unlike *public domain software,* copyrighted software must be purchased and cannot be copied.

We know that public domain software is different from copyrighted software. The information given about copyrighted software is that it must be purchased and cannot be copied. We can conclude, then, that the definition of *public domain software* is "software that is free and can be copied."

Exercise 5   **Contrast Clues**

Use contrast clues to explain the meanings of the italicized words.

1. Although many of the early software packages were *cumbersome,* software packages today are quite easy to use.

   Cumbersome: _____

   Clues: _____

2. Today's personal computers are small, fast, and cheap. However, it is important to remember that the computers of the 1940s such as the *ENIAC (Electronic Numerical Integrator and Computer)* were in total contrast to the computers of today.

   ENIAC (Electronic Numerical Integrator and Computer): _____

   _____

   Clues: _____

Exercise 6   **Context Clues**

The following excerpt is from *Computers: Tools for an Information Age,* an introductory computer science textbook by H. L. Capron. It describes the Internet to students. As you read, you will notice that most of this excerpt is dedicated to the special vocabulary of the Internet. When you are done reading, define the vocabulary terms listed in the exercises using the context clues in the excerpt itself. Explain which type of context clues helped you, such as *definition, synonym, example, general information,* or *contrast.*

The *Internet,* sometimes called simply the Net, is the largest and most far-flung network system of them all, connecting users worldwide. Surprisingly, the Internet is not really a network at all but a loosely organized collection of about 25,000 networks. Many people are astonished to discover that no one owns the Internet; it is run by volunteers. It has no central headquarters, no centrally offered services, and no comprehensive index to tell you what information is available.

Originally developed and still subsidized by the United States government, the Internet connects libraries, college campuses, research labs, businesses, and any other organization or individual who has the capacity to hook up.

Getting Connected

How are all kinds of different computers able to communicate with one another? To access the Internet, a user's computer must connect to a computer called a *server.* Each server uses the same special software called TCP/IP (for Transmission Control Protocol/Internet Protocol); it is this consistency that allows different types of computers to communicate. . . . The supplier of the server computer, often called an *Internet service provider (ISP),* charges a fee, usually monthly, based on the amount of service provided. Once a user has chosen a service provider, he or she will be furnished with the information needed to connect to the server and, from there, to the Internet.

Getting Around

Since the Internet did not begin as a commercial customer-pleasing package, it did not *initially* offer attractive options for finding information. The arcane commands were invoked only by a hardy and determined few. Furthermore, the vast sea of information, including news and trivia, can seem an overwhelming challenge to navigate. As both the Internet user population and the available information grew, new ways were developed to tour the Internet.

The most attractive method used to move around the Internet is called browsing. Using a program called a browser, you can use a mouse to point and click on screen icons to explore the Internet, particularly the World Wide Web (WWW or the Web), an Internet subset of text, images, and sounds linked together to allow users to peruse related topics. Each different location on the Web is called a *web site* or, more commonly, just a site. You may have heard the term *home page*; this is just the first page of a web site.

©2007 Pearson Education, Inc.

The Internet is an important and complex topic. Although it is easy to use once you know how, there is much to learn about its use and its place in the world of computers. (Capron, *Computers*)

1. *Internet*: _____

   Clues: _____

2. *Server*: _____

   _____

   Clues: _____

3. *Internet service provider*: _____

   _____

   Clues: _____

4. *Initially*: _____

   Clues: _____

5. *Web site*: _____

   Clues: _____

6. *Home page*: _____

   Clues: _____

Reading 2   *Living with Computers*   George Beekman

The following reading from the textbook Computer Confluence *introduces some basic concepts we need to understand about computers as well as some of the things that we need to think about as we consider how computers affect our lives. As you read, notice how frequently the meanings of words are made clear by the context in which they appear.*

1   The proliferation of computers and networks today is transforming the world rapidly and irreversibly. More than any other recent technological breakthrough, the development of the computer is responsible for profound changes in society. Of course, computer scientists and computer engineers aren't responsible for all the technological turbulence. Developments in fields as diverse as telecommunications, genetic engineering, medicine, and atomic physics contribute to the ever-increasing rate of social change. But researchers in all of these fields depend on computers to produce their work.

2   In less than a human lifetime computers have evolved from massive, expensive, error-prone calculators like the Mark I and ENIAC into a myriad

of dependable, versatile machines that have worked their way into just about every nook and cranny of modern society. The pioneers who created and marketed the first computers didn't foresee the spectacular advances in computer technology that came about in the decades that followed. Thomas Watson, Sr., the founding father of IBM, declared in 1953 that the world wouldn't need more than five computers! And the early pioneers certainly couldn't have predicted the extraordinary social changes that resulted from the computer's rapid evolution. In the time of UNIVAC who could have imagined Nintendo and Netscape?

3   Technological breakthroughs encourage further technological change, so we can expect the *rate* of change to continue to increase in coming decades. In other words the technological and social transformations of the past five decades may be dwarfed by the changes that occur over the next half century. It's just a matter of time, and not very much time, before today's state-of-the-art computers look as primitive as ENIAC looks to us today. Similarly, today's high-tech society just hints at a future world that we haven't begun to imagine. . . .

Explanations

4 You don't need to be a computer scientist to coexist with computers. But your encounters with technology will make more sense if you understand a few basic computer concepts. Computers are evolving at an incredible pace, so many of the details of hardware and software change every few years. But most of the underlying concepts remain constant as computers evolve. If you understand the basics, you'll find that it's a lot easier to keep up with the changes.

Applications

5 Many people define *computer literacy* as the ability to use computers. But because computers are so versatile, there's no one set of skills that you can learn to become computer literate in every situation. *Application programs*, also known simply as *applications*, are the software tools that allow a computer to be used for specific purposes. Many computer applications in science, government, business, and the arts are far too specialized and technical to be of use or of interest to people outside the field. On the other hand, some applications are so flexible that they can be used by all kinds of people. Regardless of your background or aspirations, you can almost certainly benefit from knowing a little about these applications.

6 • *Word processing and desktop publishing. Word processing* is a critical skill for anyone who communicates in writing. It's far and away the number one application used by students. *Desktop publishing* uses the personal computer to transform written words into polished, visually exciting publications.

7 • *Spreadsheets and other number-crunching applications.* In business the electronic *spreadsheet* is the personal computer application that

©2007 Pearson Education, Inc.

pays the rent, or at least calculates it. If you work with numbers of any kind, spreadsheets and statistical software can help you turn those numbers into insights.

8 • *Databases for information storage and retrieval.* If word processors and spreadsheets are the most popular PC applications, *databases* reign supreme in the world of mainframes. Of course, databases are widely used on PCs, too. As libraries, banks, and other institutions turn to databases for information storage, the average person has more reasons to learn the basics of databases.

9 • *Computer graphics.* Computers aren't limited to working with text and numbers; they're capable of producing all kinds of graphics, from the charts and graphs produced by spreadsheets to realistic 3-D animation. As graphics tools become more accessible, visual communication skills become more important for all of us.

10 • *Multimedia and hypermedia.* Many of the computing industry's visionaries have their sights focused on these two related technologies. *Multimedia* tools for PCs make it possible to combine audio and video with traditional text and graphics, adding new dimensions to computer communication. *Hypermedia* tools focus on the interactive capabilities of computers. Unlike books, videos, and other linear media, which are designed to be experienced from beginning to end, hypermedia allow users to explore a variety of paths through information sources. The combination of multimedia and hypermedia has an almost unimaginable potential for transforming the way we see and work with information.

11 • *Telecommunication and networking.* A network connection is a door into a world of electronic mail, on-line discussion groups, hypermedia publishing ventures, database sharing, and other new forms of communication. If current trends continue, *telecommunication*—long-distance communication—may soon be the single most important function of computers. The multipurpose global communication web known as the Internet may become as important in our lives as the telephone system, the postal service, and broadcast television are today.

12 • *Artificial intelligence. Artificial intelligence* is the branch of computer science that explores the use of computers in tasks that require intelligence, imagination, and insight—tasks that have traditionally been performed by people rather than machines. Until recently, artificial intelligence was mostly an academic discipline—a field of study reserved for researchers and philosophers. But that research is paying off today with commercial applications that exhibit intelligence—applications that you may be using soon.

13 • *General problem solving.* People use computers to solve problems. Most people use software applications written by professional programmers. But some kinds of problems can't easily be solved with off-the-shelf applications; they require at least some custom programming.

Programming languages aren't applications; they're tools that allow you to build and customize applications. Many computer users find their machines become more versatile, and valuable, when they learn a little about programming.

Implications

14 Even if you never touch a personal computer, computer technology will continue to have a growing impact on your life and your world. People all around you use PCs to manage finances and schedules, to write letters and novels, to draw maps and illustrations, to publish newspapers and political manifestos, to store addresses and musical scores, to send messages across town and around the world. Computers routinely save lives in hospitals, keep space flights on course, and predict the weekend weather.

15 The future is rushing toward you, and computer technology is a big part of it. It's exciting to consider the opportunities arising from advances in artificial intelligence, multimedia, robotics, and other cutting-edge technologies of the electronic revolution—opportunities in the workplace, the school, and the home. But it's just as important to pay attention to the potential risks, including:

- the threat to personal privacy posed by large databases and computer networks
- the hazards of high-tech crime and the difficulty of keeping data secure
- the risks of failure of computer systems
- the threat of automation and the dehumanization of work
- the abuse of information as a tool of political and economic power
- the dangers of dependence on complex technology

16 For better *and* for worse, we'll be coexisting with computers till death do us part. As with any relationship, a little understanding can go a long way.

BEEKMAN, *COMPUTER CONFLUENCE*

Exercise 7 ## Work with Words: Vocabulary in Context

The following sentences appear in Reading 2, Beekman's "Living with Computers." Use context clues to choose the best definition or synonym of each italicized word in the sentences. The paragraph number is provided in case you want to check the context.

1. In less than a human lifetime computers have *evolved* from massive, expensive, error-prone calculators like the Mark I and ENIAC into a *myriad* of dependable, versatile machines that have worked their way into just about every nook and cranny of modern society. (par. 2)

Evolved
a. splintered
b. developed
c. combined

©2007 Pearson Education, Inc.

2. *Myriad*
   a. large number
   b. pyramid
   c. combination

3. It's just a matter of time, and not very much time, before today's *state-of-the-art* computers look as primitive as the ENIAC looks to us today. (par. 3)

   State-of-the-art
   a. most speedy
   b. most out of date
   c. most modern

4. *Application programs*, also known simply as applications, are the software tools that allow a computer to be used for specific purposes. (par. 5)

   Application programs
   a. applications
   b. software tools that allow a computer to be used for a specific purpose
   c. computer programs that make filling out applications easier

5. *Desktop publishing* uses the personal computer to transform written words into polished, visually exciting publications. (par. 6)

   Desktop publishing
   a. a tool to transform written words into polished, visually exciting publications
   b. finished documents, ready for publication
   c. publications that are put together on the top of a desk exclusively

Exercise 8   Work with Words: More Vocabulary in Context

For the following italicized words, write the definitions on the lines provided. Write the context clue(s) you used to find the definition *(definition, synonym, example, general information, contrast)*.

1. *Multimedia* tools for **PCs** make it possible to combine audio and video with traditional text and graphics, adding new dimensions to computer communication. (par. 10)

   Multimedia: _____

   _____

   Clues: _____

2. *Hypermedia* tools focus on the interactive capabilities of computers. Unlike books, videos, and other linear media, which are designed to be experienced from beginning to end, *hypermedia* allow users to explore a variety of paths through information sources. (par. 10)

Hypermedia: _____

_____

Clues: _____

3. If current trends continue, *telecommunication*—long-distance communication—may soon be the single most important function of
computers. The multipurpose global communication web known as
the Internet may become as important in our lives as the telephone
system, the postal service, and broadcast television are today. (par. 11)

Telecommunication: _____

Clues: _____

4. *Artificial intelligence* is the branch of computer science that explores
the use of computers in tasks that require intelligence, imagination,
and insight—tasks that have traditionally been performed by people
rather than machines. (par. 12)

Artificial intelligence: _____

_____

Clues: _____

Exercise 9   Check Your Understanding

Based on Reading 2, choose the best answer to each of the following
multiple-choice questions.

1. Which of the following statements would the author consider true?
   a. It is not easy, but it is possible to live your life without being
   affected by computers.
   b. Even the most modern computers today will be useless and
   obsolete in a few years.
   c. Computers have little or no impact on health and public
   safety.

2. According to the author,
   a. it will be helpful to understand a few basic computer concepts.
   b. you need to be a computer scientist to be able to coexist with
   computers.
   c. you shouldn't worry about understanding computer concepts because they're far too complex to grasp.

3. "Computer literacy"
   a. is simply the ability to use computers.
   b. is the set of skills that will make you computer literate in every
   situation.
   c. almost always requires extreme specialization.

©2007 Pearson Education, Inc.

4. Which of the following is not identified as a risk of computer technology today?
   a. Threat to personal privacy
   b. Hazards of high-tech crime and data security
   c. Increasing dependence on scarce natural resources

5. The author believes
   a. computers are a positive influence on our lives.
   b. computers are a negative influence on our lives.
   c. computers provide opportunities, but also risks.

Exercise 10   Reflect

Think about what you read in Reading 2 and what you already know about computers in everyday life. Answer the following questions, and prepare to discuss them with your classmates.

1. Do you think computers have made our lives easier? Give some examples. _____

   _____

2. Choose three of the risks listed by Beekman that you think are most serious. Why would you worry about them most? _____

   _____

   ◆

Word Parts

Probably one of the most difficult aspects of studying any new subject is the vocabulary. The specialized vocabulary of a college discipline, for example, may be new to you. While you are often going to have to learn a lot of new words for certain subjects, certain techniques can help you. In addition to using the clues to understand the meaning of words from the context, recognizing word parts can make this job much easier for you.

word parts
Prefixes, roots, and suffixes

Many thousands of words in the English language are made up of **word parts.** As a reader, you can greatly increase your vocabulary simply by learning some of the most common word parts. Knowing them will help you "take apart" a word to figure out its meaning. There are three types of word parts:

1. *Prefixes*, which appear at the beginning of a word
2. *Roots*, which can be at the beginning, middle, or end of a word
3. *Suffixes*, which appear at the end of a word

Each of these parts contributes to the meaning of a word. For example, *concurrent*, from *concurrent processing*, is actually a combination of two word parts, *con* (meaning *with*) and *current* (meaning *in progress*). So, *concurrent processing* means processing more than one thing at the same time—a large computer works on several jobs at one time.

You can add a suffix to *concurrent* to get *concurrently*. The *ly* on the end turns the word into an adverb, which describes how something is done; in this case, it describes how the processing is done. You could say, "A large computer can process several jobs *concurrently*." This means that the computer can do several jobs at the same time.

Tables 2.1, 2.2, and 2.3 list some of the most common Greek and Latin word parts used in English words and some more specialized word parts used in this chapter.

prefix An addition at the beginning of a word that changes the word's meaning

Prefixes   A **prefix** is an addition at the beginning of a word that changes the word's meaning. Look at the list of prefixes in Table 2.1. Notice the meaning and example word given for each prefix, and then write an example of your own on the line provided.

Table 2.1	**Prefixes**		
Prefix	**Meaning**	**Example 1**	**Example 2**
ab-	away from, from	abnormal	_____
bene-	good, well	beneficial	_____
bi-	two, or twice	biweekly	_____
bio-	life	biology	_____
com-, con-, col-	with, together, jointly	command	_____
		connect	_____
		collaborate	_____
contra-	against	contradict	_____
de-	reverse, undo	deactivate	_____
dis-	apart from, reversal of	disapprove	_____
ex-, e-	out	excrete	_____
		evade	_____
hyper-	excessive, over	hyperactive	_____
in-, im-	not	incomplete	_____
		immortal	_____
inter-	between, among	international	_____
mal-	bad, wrong	malfunction	_____
mis-	wrong	mistake	_____

©2007 Pearson Education, Inc.

Table 2.1	Prefixes (continued)		
Prefix	**Meaning**	**Example1**	**Example 2**
mono-	one	monotonous	_____
multi-	many	multiparty	_____
peri-	around	perimeter	_____
poly-	many	polygamy	_____
post-	after	postpone	_____
pre-	before	prefix	_____
pro-	in favor of, forward	progress	_____
quad-	four	quadratic	_____
re-	again	rewrite	_____
sym-, syn-	together, with, similar	sympathetic	_____
		synthetic	_____
sub-	follow, under	submarine	_____
tele-	distance	telepathy	_____
trans-	across, over	transfer	_____
tri-	three	triangle	_____
uni-	one	unify	_____

Exercise 11   Prefixes

Using Table 2.1 as well as context, define each italicized word in the following sentences. Then identify the prefix and its meaning. The first one has been done for you.

1. By donating millions of dollars to charities, Bill Gates is hoping to be remembered as a *beneficent* man.

   Beneficent: _doing good (charitable)_____

   Prefix and its meaning: _bene, "good"_____

2. The *binary* number system uses two symbols, the digits 0 and 1.

   Binary: _____

   Prefix and its meaning: _____

3. Some security systems use *biometrics*, the science of measuring individual body characteristics. (Capron, *Computers*)

   Biometrics: _____ _____

   Prefix and its meaning: _____

4. If you make an error on the computer, you can *delete* it, so documents are really very easy to correct.

   Delete: _____

   Prefix and its meaning: _____

5. *Hypermedia* is an exciting new combination of text, numbers, music, sound, and visuals.

   Hypermedia: _____

   Prefix and its meaning: _____

6. Computerized programs for translating languages are very likely to *misinterpret* the meanings of some words.

   Misinterpret: _____

   Prefix and its meaning: _____

7. Using *multimedia* presentations in the classroom really helps the lessons come alive for the students.

   Multimedia: _____

   Prefix and its meaning: _____

8. Since they are not limited to black and white images, *polychromatic* screens are especially important for visual artists.

   Polychromatic: _____

   Prefix and its meaning: _____

9. Today computer *synthesizers* are used to put the sounds of many instruments together to get the effect the composer wants.

   Synthesizers: _____

   Prefix and its meaning: _____

10. *Telecommunication* through computers could well be one of the most important ways we link up with the outside world in the future.

    Telecommunication: _____

    Prefix and its meaning: _____

©2007 Pearson Education, Inc.

root The core part of a word to which prefixes and suffixes may be added

Roots   The **root** is the core part of a word. It provides the essential meaning that prefixes and suffixes modify. Look at the list of roots in Table 2.2. Notice the meaning and example word given for each root, and then write an example of your own on the line provided.

Table 2.2	Roots		
Root	**Meaning**	**Example1**	**Example 2**
auto	self-propelled, acting from within	automobile	_____
cede, ceed	go	proceed	_____
cept	receive	intercept	_____
chrom	color	monochromatic	_____
chron	time	chronicle	_____
cyber	having to do with computers	cyberspace	_____
data	numerical information in the form a computer can read	data processing	_____
digit	a single Arabic numeral, such as 1, or 2, or 0, or 3	digital clock	_____
duct	lead	conduct	_____
equi	equal	equidistant	_____
gen	kinds, types	generalization	_____
homo	same	homogeneous	_____
log[y]	study of, reason, thought	psychology	_____
mit, mis	let go, send	missile	_____
mort	death	mortality	_____
neuro	nerve	neurosis	_____
peri	around	perimeter	_____
phobia	fear	acrophobia	_____
port	harbor, a place to come to; having to do with carry	portable	_____

Table 2.2	**Roots (continued)**		
psych	mind, soul	psychological	_____
sequi, seque	follow	sequence	_____
vis	see	vision	_____

| Exercise 12 | ## Roots and Prefixes |

Using Tables 2.1 and 2.2, on prefixes and roots, as well as the context, define each italicized word in the following sentences. Then identify the word part and its meaning. The first one has been done for you.

1. *Automated* factories require very little human input; instead they use robots for the assembly-line jobs, and computers for keeping inventory and taking care of the machines.

   Automated: _Automated means something that works with little human input._

   Word part and its meaning: _auto, "acting from within" or "self-propelled"_

2. Online *databases* that give you access to updated encyclopedias or university libraries are a rich source of information when you are doing research.

   Databases: _____

   Word part and its meaning: _____

   _____

3. Before information can be input into a computer, it must be in a *digital* form.

   Digital: _____

   Word part and its meaning: _____

4. You have to be careful not to buy computer software that is *incompatible* with your specific computer system. You cannot use Macintosh software on an IBM computer.

   Incompatible: _____

   Word part and its meaning: _____

5. The *Internet* is an incredible resource that millions of people use to connect with each other and with a vast quantity of information.

   Internet: _____

   Word part and its meaning: _____

©2007 Pearson Education, Inc.

6. Keyboards, printers, and fax machines are essential computer *peripherals*. Without them, we would not be able to do much with the computer itself.

   Peripherals: _____

   Word part and its meaning: _____

7. The beginning of the twenty-first century is going to see incredibly fast technological advances. It is not a good time to be *technophobic*.

   Technophobic: _____

   Word part and its meaning: _____

8. Early computers that could "speak" only did so in *monotone* so they sounded very strange.

   Monotone: _____

   Word part and its meaning: _____

9. *Sociologists* are very interested in analyzing the impact of computers on social interactions, and on society in general.

   Sociologists: _____

   Word part and its meaning: _____

10. *Portable* laptop computers have become increasingly popular with people who frequently need to travel and work.

    Portable: _____

    Word part and its meaning: _____

◆

suffix An addition to the end of a word that often indicates the part of speech

part of speech Designation of the function of a word— i.e., noun, verb, adjective, adverb

Suffixes   A **suffix** is the ending of a word. Suffixes frequently tell us what **part of speech** the word is—that is, whether it is a noun, a verb, an adjective, or an adverb. Parts of speech tell you how words work in a sentence. Dictionaries identify the part of speech for a word and each of the word's various forms. For example, consider the word *conspire*; it has many forms, and each is used in a different way, depending on its function in a sentence:

- *To conspire* is a verb. *The students* conspired *against their teacher.* (It tells you what the students *did*.) A verb is an action word.
- *Conspiracy* is a noun. *There was a* conspiracy *to overthrow the president.* (It tells you what something is.) A noun names a person, place, thing, or concept.
- *Conspirator* is another noun, meaning someone who conspires. *The police estimated that there were at least four* conspirators *involved in the crime.* (It tells you what someone is.)

- *Conspiratorial* is an adjective. *The atmosphere in the room was* conspiratorial. (It *describes* something for you.) An adjective modifies a noun. It usually answers the questions "What kind?" or "How many?"
- *Conspiratorially* is an adverb. *The boys discussed their plans* conspiratorially *in the bathroom.* (It tells you *how* the boys discussed their plans.) An adverb describes how, when, or where an action occurs.

Look at the list of suffixes in Table 2.3. Notice the meaning and example given for each suffix, and then write an example of your own on the line provided.

Table 2.3	**Suffixes**		
Suffix	**Meaning**	**Example1**	**Example 2**
-or, -er, -ist, -ee, -ian	a person	conspirator	_____
		teacher	_____
		futurist	_____
		referee	_____
		physician	_____
-acy	an act, form of	conspiracy	_____
	government	democracy	_____
-ance, -ation, -tion,	an act, a state,	attendance	_____
-sion, -ment	a condition	computation	_____
		restriction	_____
		tension	_____
		resentment	_____
-ism	a belief, form of government	socialism	
-ship, -hood, -ness	having to do with,	relationship	_____
	referring to	neighborhood	_____
		friendliness	_____
Adjective suffixes			
-able, -ible, -al, -ic,	having a characteristic	reliable	_____
-ing, -ive, -ous, -orial,		responsible	_____

©2007 Pearson Education, Inc.

Table 2.3	**Suffixes (continued)**		
Suffix	**Meaning**	**Example1**	**Example 2**
-ant, -an		practical	_____
		antagonistic	_____
		insulting	_____
		inventive	_____
		serious	_____
		dictatorial	_____
		deviant	_____
		authoritarian	_____
Adverb suffixes			
-ly	describes how something is done (sometimes added to the endings of adjectives)	efficiently, responsibly, insultingly	_____

Exercise 13   Suffixes

Read the following two paragraphs from Beekman's *Computer Confluence*. Circle all the words with suffixes you recognize. Then list ten of those words in the space provided and identify the part of speech of each. Two have been done for you.

1   In George Orwell's *1984*, information about every citizen was stored in a massive database controlled by the ever-vigilant Big Brother. As it turns out, this kind of central computer is no longer necessary for producing computerized dossiers of private citizens. With networked computers it's easy to compile profiles by combining information from different database files. As long as the files share a single unique field, like Social Security number, record matching is trivial and quick. And when database information is combined, the whole is often far greater than the sum of its parts.

2   Sometimes the results are beneficial. Record matching is used by government enforcement agencies to locate criminals ranging from tax evaders to mass murderers. Because credit bureaus collect data about us, we can use credit cards to borrow money wherever we go. But these benefits come with at least three problems:

- *Data errors are common.* A study of 1,500 reports from the three big credit bureaus found errors in 43 percent of the files.

- *Data can become nearly immortal.* Because files are commonly sold and copied, it's impossible to delete or correct erroneous records with absolute certainty.

- *Data aren't secure. A Business Week* reporter demonstrated this in 1989 by using his computer to obtain then Vice President Dan Quayle's credit report. Had he been a skilled criminal, he might have been able to change that report. (Beekman, *Computer Confluence*)

Word	Part of Speech
1. *information*	*noun*
2. *massive*	*adjective*
3. _____	_____
4. _____	_____
5. _____	_____
6. _____	_____
7. _____	_____
8. _____	_____
9. _____	_____
10. _____	_____

Exercise 14   ## Word Parts

Based on the reading in Exercise 13, define each italicized word, using the word part and context clues. Then identify the word part and its meaning.

1. With networked computers it's easy to *compile* profiles combining information from different *database* files. (par. 1)

   Compile: _____

   Word part and its meaning: _____

2. *Database*: _____

   Word part and its meaning: _____

   _____

3. Sometimes the results are *beneficial*. Record matching is used by government enforcement agencies to locate criminals ranging from tax evaders to mass murderers. Because credit bureaus collect data about us, we can use credit cards to borrow money wherever we go. But these *benefits* come with at least three problems: (par. 2)

   Beneficial: _____

   Word part and its meaning: _____

©2007 Pearson Education, Inc.

4. *Benefit*: _____

   Word part and its meaning: _____

5. Data can become nearly *immortal*. Because files are commonly sold and copied, it's impossible to delete or correct erroneous records with absolute certainty. (par. 2)

   Immortal: _____

   Word part and its meaning: _____

◆

The Dictionary

As a reader and as a student, you will find that the dictionary is a valuable tool to use when you don't understand a word. However, before you go to the dictionary, ask yourself these questions.

- Is it essential to understand the exact meaning of the word to understand the reading? You should consider your purpose as a reader: Do you need to understand the term completely because you will be tested on it or because you need it for your work?
- Is the word important? Is it key to understanding the subject or material you are reading?
- Have you tried to figure out the meaning from the context clues and from using what you know about word parts, but you are still not sure about the meaning?

If you answered "yes" to all three of these questions, then go to the dictionary.

Parts of a Dictionary Entry   In your reading about computer science, you may encounter sentences like this:

> E-mail can be a dangerous time bomb because litigators argue that, more than any other kind of written communication, e-mail reflects the real, unedited thoughts of the writer. This candid form of corporate communication increasingly has provided the most incriminating evidence used against companies in litigation.

In the first sentence, you find the word *litigators*. When you look it up in the dictionary (*American Heritage Talking Dictionary*, CD-ROM, 1998), you notice that *litigator* doesn't appear as an independent entry. So you will have to find another form of the word—in this case, by dropping the suffix to get *litigate*.

Notice that the dictionary entry gives you some very specific information. There are many different dictionaries, even dictionaries on CD-ROM, like the one we used here. CD-ROM versions also have audio portions to help you with the pronunciation of the word. With some variations, most dictionaries list the following information:

Source: American Heritage Dictionary of the English Language, 3d ed., Talking Dictionary CD (Boston: Houghton Mifflin, 1998). Learning Company Properties © 1995 by Inso Corporation.

pronunciation   *part of speech*

definition

lit·i·gate (lĭt′ĭ-gāt′) *v.* **lit·i·gated, lit·i·gating, lit·i·gates.** *Law.*
—*tr.* **1.** To subject to legal proceeding. —*intr.* To engage in legal proceedings. [Latin *lītigāre*, lītigāt,- : *līs*, līt-, lawsuit + *agere*, to drive; see **ag-** below.] —**lit′i·ga·ble** (-gə-bəl) adj. —**lit′i·ga′tion** *n.*— **lit′i·ga′tor** *n.*

other forms of the word

- Pronunciation (in parentheses after the word).
- Part of speech (after each form given for the word). Notice how the suffixes work in helping you understand the part of speech.
- Definition(s)—usually numbered. Often there is more than one meaning for a word. The dictionary shows this by giving additional definitions using both numbers and letters (for example, *1a* and *1b*).
- Other forms of the word.
- Origins of the word (in brackets after the definition). Frequently, you will find explanations of the Latin or Greek word parts that form the word.
- Examples of how the word has been used. Some dictionaries provide a quotation in which the word has been used by a famous author. Some simply include a sentence that illustrates how to use the word.

Altogether, there are four forms of *litigate* in the dictionary:

1. *litigate* is the base form of the word, and it is a verb.
2. *litigable* has the suffix *-able,* which forms the adjective meaning "can be litigated."
3. *litigation* has the suffix *-tion,* which forms the noun meaning "the act of litigating."
4. *litigator* has the suffix *-or,* which forms the noun meaning "someone who litigates."

Exercise 15   **Dictionary Entries**

Look at the following dictionary entries for two additional words, and answer the questions.

can·did (kan-dəd) *adj.* **1.** Free from prejudice; impartial. **2.** Characterized by openness and sincerity of expression; unreservedly straightforward: *In private, I gave them my candid opinion.* See Synonyms at **frank**[1]. **3.** Not posed or rehearsed: *a candid snapshot.* —**can·did** *n.* An unposed informal photograph. [Latin *candidus*, glowing, white, pure, guileless, from *candēre*, to shine. See **kand-** below.] —**can·did·ly** *adv.* —**can·did·ness** *n.*

(American Heritage Dictionary)

©2007 Pearson Education, Inc.

in·crim·i·nate (ĭn-krĭm′ə-nāt′) *tr.v.* **in·crim·i·nat·ed, in·crim·i·nat·ing, in·crim·i·nates. 1.** To accuse of a crime or other wrongful act. **2.** To cause to appear guilty of a crime or fault; implicate: *testimony that incriminated the defendant.* [Late Latin *incrīmināre,* incrīmināt- : Latin *in-,* causative pref.; see IN-² + Latin *crīmen,* crīmin-, crime; see CRIME.] —**in·crim′i·na′tion** *n.* —**in·crim′i·na·to′ry** (-nə-tôr′ē, -tor′e) *adj.*

(American Heritage Dictionary)

1. What is the adverb form of *candid*? _____

2. What are the definitions of *candid* and what part of speech is it?

   _____

   _____

3. How many noun forms of *candid* are in this entry? _____

4. What are the definitions of *incriminate* and what part of speech is it?

   _____

5. What other forms of *incriminate* are provided? What part of speech is each? _____

   _____

◆

Choosing the Correct Meaning from the Dictionary   Dictionaries frequently list several meanings for words. Learning to use a dictionary and to find the definition for the word that you need as it is used in the context of your reading is a very important skill. If you are reading a college textbook, you should first look to see whether your text has a **glossary** at the end of the book. If it does, this is definitely the best place to look up the meanings of words that you don't know, because the definitions will correspond to the meanings of the words as they are used in the discipline you are studying. However, if your textbook does not come with a glossary of terms, you will need to use a dictionary.

glossary A dictionary of important words, frequently found in the back of college textbooks

Read the following sentence, taken from a computer science textbook, and think about the word *convey.*

> Companies may fail to convey the message that e-mail, as a company conduit, is not private. (Capron, *Computers*)

When you look up the word *convey* in the dictionary, you cannot just pick the first definition that you find. You must look through all the definitions to find the one that matches the way your text uses the word. Study this dictionary entry:

con·vey (kən-vā′) *tr.v.* **con·veyed, con·vey·ing, con·veys. 1.** To take or carry from one place to another; transport. **2.** To serve as a medium of transmission for; transmit: *wires that convey electricity.* **3.** To communicate or make known; impart: *"a look intended to convey sympathetic comprehen-sion"* (Saki). **4.** *Law.* To transfer ownership of or title to. **5.** *Archaic.* To steal. [Middle English *conveien,* from Old French *conviār,* from Medieval Latin *conviare,* to escort : Latin *com-,* com- + *via,* way; see **wegh-** below.] —con·vey′a·ble *adj.*

(American Heritage Dictionary)

Note that *convey* has five definitions. The first definition has to do with transporting something from one place to another. The second has to do with serving as a medium for transmission. The third means to communicate or make known. The fourth refers to a legal transfer of ownership, and the fifth means to steal. Notice that the fourth and fifth definitions have italicized words in front of them. *Law* before the fourth definition gives the legal meaning of *convey. Archaic* before the fifth definition means that "to steal" is an old use of the word, and something written to-day would probably not be using that meaning. So which is the best def-inition for *convey* as it is used in the sentence?

> Companies may fail to *convey* the message that e-mail, as a company conduit, is not private.

Clearly the only meaning from the list of definitions that works is the third, "to communicate or make known."

Exercise 16 | Choose the Correct Dictionary Definitions

Read the following excerpt from a computer science textbook, paying special attention to the *italicized* words. Then find the correct definition for each italicized word using the dictionary definitions that follow. Write the definition and the part of speech (noun, verb, adjective, ad-verb) on the lines provided. As you do this exercise, take the time to look at the origins of the word (in brackets); you may notice some of the word parts that you learned earlier.

1 You have no privacy whatsoever. No privacy on the company e-mail, that is. Your employer can snoop into messages you send or receive even if you think you erased them. You have only erased them from their *current* hard drive location; copies are still in the company computer files. In fact, most companies *archive* all such files on tape and store them for the foreseeable future. Companies may fail to convey the message that e-mail, as a company *conduit,* is not private. Employees are often startled, after the fact, to discover that their messages have been invaded.

2 Furthermore, some people specialize in *extracting* deleted messages for use as evidence in court. E-mail can be a dangerous time bomb be-cause litigators argue that, more than any other kind of written commu-nication, e-mail *reflects* the real, unedited thoughts of the writer. This candid form of corporate communication increasingly is providing the most incriminating evidence used against companies in litigation.

3 What to do? It is certainly *degrading* to have something you thought was private waved in front of you as evidence of *malingering.* As one

©2007 Pearson Education, Inc.

computer expert put it, if nothing is private, just say so. Companies have begun doing exactly that. The company policy on e-mail is—or should be—expressed in a clear, written document and routinely *disseminated* to all employees. However, even that step is probably insufficient. People tend to forget or get *complacent*. Reminders should be given through the usual company conduits—bulletin boards, posters, and so forth.

4   What about the e-mail you send and receive at home—do you at least have privacy in your own home? Maybe not. You certainly cannot count on it if the computer of the party at the other end is in an office. Further, keep in mind that messages sent across the Internet hop from computer to computer, with (depending on the service used) the sender having little say about its route. There are many *vulnerable* spots along the way. (Capron, *Computers*)

Definition	**Part of Speech**
1. *Current:* _____	_____
2. *Archive:* _____	_____
3. *Conduit:* _____	_____
4. *Extracting:* _____	_____
5. *Reflects:* _____	_____
6. *Degrading:* _____	_____
7. *Malingering:* _____	_____
8. *Disseminated:* _____	_____
9. *Complacent:* _____	_____
10. *Vulnerable:* _____	_____

ar·chive (är′kīv′) *n.* **1.** Often **archives.** A place or collection containing records, documents, or other materials of historical interest: *old land deeds in the municipal archives; the studio archives, a vast repository of silent-film prints and outtakes.* **2.** A repository for stored memories or information: *the archive of the mind.* [From French *archives*, from Latin *archīva*, from Greek *arkheia*, pl. of *arkheion*, town hall, from *arkhē*, government, from *arkhein*, to rule.] —**ar′chive′** *v.*

com·pla·cent (kəm-plā′sənt) *adj.* **1.** Contented to a fault; self-satisfied and unconcerned: *He had become complacent after years of success.* **2.** Eager to please; complaisant. [Latin *complacēns*, complacent-, present participle of *complacēre*, to please : *com-*, intensive pref.; see COM- + *placēre*, to please; see **plāk-1** below.] —**com·pla′cent·ly** *adv.*

con·duit (kŏn′doo-ĭt, -dĭt) *n.* **1.** A pipe or channel for conveying fluids, such as water. **2.** A tube or duct for enclosing electric wires or cable. **3.** A means by which something is transmitted: *an arms dealer who served as a conduit* *for intelligence data.* **4.** *Archaic.* A fountain. [Middle English, from Old French, from Medieval Latin *conductus*, from Latin, past participle of *cond cere*, to lead together. See CONDUCE.]

cur·rent (kûr′ ənt, kur′-) *adj.* **1.** *Abbr.* **cur. a.** Belonging to the present time: *current events; current leaders.* **b.** Being in progress now: *current negotiations.* **2.** Passing from one to another; circulating: *current bills and coins.* **3.** Prevalent, especially at the present time: *current fashions.* See Synonyms at **prevailing. 4.** Running; flowing. **—cur·rent** *n.* **1.** A steady, smooth onward movement: *a current of air from a fan; a current of spoken words.* See Synonyms at **flow. 2.** The part of a body of liquid or gas that has a continuous onward movement: *rowed out into the river's swift current.* **3.** A general tendency, movement, or course. See Synonyms at **tendency. 4.** *Symbol* **i, I** *Electricity.* **a.** A flow of electric charge. **b.** The amount of electric charge flowing past a specified circuit point per unit time. [Middle English *curraunt,* from Old French *corant,* present participle of *courre,* to run, from Latin *currere.* See **kers-** below.] **—cur′rent·ly** *adv.* **—cur′rent·ness** *n.*

de·grade (dĭ-grād′) *tr.v.* **de·grad·ed, de·grad·ing, de·grades. 1.** To reduce in grade, rank, or status; demote. **2.** To lower in dignity; dishonor or disgrace: *a scandal that degraded the participants.* **3.** To lower in moral or intellectual character; debase. **4.** To reduce in worth or value: *degrade a currency.* **5.** To impair in physical structure or function. **6.** *Geology.* To lower or wear by erosion or weathering. **7.** To cause (an organic compound) to undergo degradation. [Middle English *degraden,* from Old French *degrader,* from Late Latin *dēgradāre* : Latin *dē-,* de- + Latin *gradus,* step; see **ghredh-** below.] **—de·grad′er** *n.*

de·grad·ing (dĭ-grā′dĭng) *adj.* Tending or intended to degrade: *"There is nothing so degrading as the constant anxiety about one's means of livelihood"* (W. Somerset Maugham). **—de·grad′ing·ly** *adv.*

dis·sem·i·nate (dĭ-sĕm′ə-nāt′) *v.* **dis·sem·i·nat·ed, dis·sem·i·nat·ing, dis·sem·i·nates. —***tr.* **1.** To scatter widely, as in sowing seed. **2.** To spread abroad; promulgate: *disseminate information.* **—***intr.* To become diffused; spread. [Latin *dissēmināre,* dissēmināt- : *dis-,* dis- + *sēmināre,* to sow (from *sēmen,* sēmin-, seed; see **sē-** below).] **—dis·sem′i·na′tion** *n.* **—dis·sem′i·na′tor** *n.*

dis·sem·i·nat·ed (dĭ-sĕm′ə-nā′tĭd) *adj.* Spread over a large area of a body, a tissue, or an organ.

ex·tract (ĭk-străkt′) *tr.v.* **ex·tract·ed, ex·tract·ing, ex·tracts. 1.** To draw or pull out, using great force or effort: *extract a wisdom tooth.* **2.** To obtain despite resistance: *extract a promise.* **3.** To obtain from a substance by chemical or mechanical action, as by pressure, distillation, or evaporation. **4.** To remove for separate consideration or publication; excerpt. **5.a.** To derive or obtain (information, for example) from a source. **b.** To deduce (a principle or doctrine); construe (a meaning). **c.** To derive (pleasure or comfort) from an experience. **6.** *Mathematics.* To determine or calculate (the root of a number). **—ex·tract** (ĕk′străkt′) *n.* **ext. 1.** A passage from a literary work; an excerpt. **2.** A concentrated preparation of the essential constituents of a

©2007 Pearson Education, Inc.

food, a flavoring, or another substance; a concentrate: *maple extract.* [Middle English *extracten*, from Latin *extrahere*, extract- : *ex-*, ex- + *trahere*, to draw.] —**ex·tract′a·ble** or **ex·tract′i·ble** *adj.* —**ex·trac′tor** *n.*

ma·lin·ger (mə-lĭng′gər) *intr.v.* **ma·lin·gered, ma·lin·ger·ing, ma·lin·gers.** To feign illness or other incapacity in order to avoid duty or work. [From French *malingre*, sickly.] —**ma·lin′ger·er** *n.*

re·flect (rĭ-flĕkt′) *v.* **re·flect·ed, re·flect·ing, re·flects.** —*tr.* **1.** To throw or bend back (light, for example) from a surface. See Synonyms at **echo**. **2.** To form an image of (an object); mirror: *"Baseball reflects America's history"* (Roslyn A. Mazer). **3.** To manifest as a result of one's actions: *Her work reflects intelligence.* **4.** *Archaic.* To bend back. —*intr.* **1.** To be bent back. **2.** To give back a likeness. **3.a.** To think seriously. See Synonyms at **think. b.** To express carefully considered thoughts. —**phrasal verb. reflect on. 1.** To form or express carefully considered thoughts about: *reflects on her country's place in history.* **2.** To give evidence of the qualities of (one): *The hasty preparation of this report reflects on you.* **3.** To give evidence that (one) has acted in a given way: *The excuses you gave reflect disappointingly on you.* [Middle English *reflecten*, from Old French *reflecter*, from Latin *reflectere*, to bend back : *re-*, re- + *flectere*, to bend.]

vul·ner·a·ble (vŭl′nər-ə-bəl) *adj.* **1.a.** Susceptible to physical injury. **b.** Susceptible to attack: *"We are vulnerable both by water and land, without either fleet or army"* (Alexander Hamilton). **c.** Open to censure or criticism; assailable. **2.a.** Liable to succumb, as to persuasion or temptation. **b.** *Games.* In a position to receive greater penalties or bonuses as a result of having won one game of a rubber. Used of bridge partners. [Late Latin *vulnerābilis*, wounding, from Latin *vulnerāre*, to wound, from *vulnus*, vulner-, wound. See **welə-** below.] —**vul′ner·a·bil′i·ty** or **vul′ner·a·ble·ness** *n.* —**vul′ner·a·bly** *adv.*

(American Heritage Dictionary)

Reading 3 *The Robot Soldiers Are Coming*   Tim Weiner

The following reading from a February 2005 New York Times article explains the plans of the U.S. government to rely in the future on robots to perform some of the functions of soldiers. As you read, think about what this could mean for the U.S. military as well as what it would mean for countries the United States goes to war against. Weiner is a respected journalist who frequently writes articles about military matters and war for the New York Times and the International Herald Tribune.

1 The American military is working on a new generation of soldiers, far different from the army it has.

2   "They don't get hungry," said Gordon Johnson of the Joint Forces Command at the Pentagon. "They're not afraid. They don't forget their orders.

They don't care if the guy next to them has just been shot. Will they do a better job than humans? Yes."

3 The robot soldiers are coming. The Pentagon predicts that robots will be a major fighting force in the American military in less than a decade, hunting and killing enemies in combat. Robots are a crucial part of the Army's effort to rebuild itself as a 21st-century fighting force, and a $127 billion project called Future Combat Systems is the biggest military contract in American history.

4 The military plans to invest tens of billions of dollars in automated armed forces. The costs of that transformation will help drive the Defense Department's budget up almost 20 percent, from a requested $419.3 billion for next year [2006] to $502.3 billion in 2010, excluding the costs of war. The annual costs of buying new weapons is scheduled to rise 52 percent, from $78 billion to $118.6 billion.

5 Military planners say robot soldiers will think, see and react increasingly like humans. In the beginning, they will be remote-controlled, looking and acting like lethal toy trucks. As the technology develops, they may take many shapes. And as their intelligence grows, so will their autonomy.

6 The robot soldier has been a dream at the Pentagon for 30 years. And some involved in the work say it may take at least 30 more years to realize in full. Well before then, they say, the military will have to answer tough questions if it intends to trust robots with the responsibility of distinguishing friend from foe, combatant from bystander. . . .

7 Robots in battle, as envisioned by their builders, may look and move like humans or hummingbirds, tractors or tanks, cockroaches or crickets. With the development of nanotechnology—the science of very small structures—they may become swarms of "smart dust." The Pentagon intends for robots to haul munitions, gather intelligence, search buildings or blow them up.

8 All these are in the works, but not yet in battle. Already, however, several hundred robots are digging up roadside bombs in Iraq, scouring caves in Afghanistan and serving as armed sentries at weapons depots.

Firing 1,000 Rounds a Minute

9 By April [2005], an armed version of the bomb-disposal robot will be in Baghdad, capable of firing 1,000 rounds a minute. Though controlled by a soldier with a laptop, the robot will be the first thinking machine of its kind to take up a front-line infantry position, ready to kill enemies. . . .

10 Congress ordered in 2000 that a third of the ground vehicles and a third of deep-strike aircraft in the military must become robotic within a decade. If that mandate is to be met, the United States will spend many billions of dollars on military robots by 2010.

11 As the first lethal robots head for Iraq, the role of the robot soldier as a killing machine has barely been debated. The history of warfare suggests that every new technological leap—the longbow, the tank, the atomic bomb—outraces the strategy and doctrine to control it. "The lawyers tell me there are no prohibitions against robots making life-or-death decisions," said Mr. Johnson, who leads robotics efforts at the Joint Forces Command

©2007 Pearson Education, Inc.

research center in Suffolk, Va. "I have been asked what happens if the robot destroys a school bus rather than a tank parked nearby. We will not entrust a robot with that decision until we are confident they can make it." Trusting robots with potentially lethal decision-making may require a leap of faith in technology not everyone is ready to make. Bill Joy, a co-founder of Sun Microsystems, has worried aloud that 21st-century robotics and nanotechnology may become "so powerful that they can spawn whole new classes of accidents and abuses." . . .

12   Pentagon officials and military contractors say the ultimate ideal of unmanned warfare is combat without casualties. Failing that, their goal is to give as many difficult, dull or dangerous missions as possible to the robots, conserving American minds and protecting American bodies in battle. "Anyone who's a decision maker doesn't want American lives at risk," Mr. Brooks [the director of Computer Science and Artificial Intelligence Laboratory at M.I.T. and a co-founder of the iRobot Corporation] said. "It's the same question as, Should soldiers be given body armor? It's a moral issue. And cost comes in."

Money or Morals

13   Money, in fact, may matter more than morals. The Pentagon today owes its soldiers $653 billion in future retirement benefits that it cannot presently pay. Robots, unlike old soldiers, do not fade away. The median lifetime cost of a soldier is about $4 million today and growing, according to a Pentagon study. Robot soldiers could cost a tenth of that or less. "It's more than just a dream now," Mr. Johnson said. "Today we have an infantry soldier" as the prototype of a military robot, he added. "We give him a set of instructions: if you find the enemy, this is what you do. We give the infantry soldier enough information to recognize the enemy when he's fired upon. He is autonomous, but he has to operate under certain controls. It's supervised autonomy. By 2015, we think we can do many infantry missions. . . ."

14   The hunter-killer at the Space and Naval Warfare Systems Center is one of five broad categories of military robots under development. Another scouts buildings, tunnels and caves. A third hauls tons of weapons and gear and performs searches and reconnaissance. A fourth is a drone in flight; last April, an unmanned aircraft made military history by hitting a ground target with a small smart bomb in a test from 35,000 feet. A fifth, originally designed as a security guard, will soon be able to launch drones to conduct surveillance, psychological warfare and other missions.

15   For all five, the ability to perceive is paramount. "We've seen pretty dramatic progress in the area of robot perception," said Charles M. Shoemaker, chief of the Army Research Laboratory's robotics program office at Aberdeen Proving Grounds in Maryland. That progress may soon allow the Army to eliminate the driver of many military vehicles in favor of a robot. "There's been almost a universal clamor for the automation of the driving task," he said. "We have developed the ability for the robot to see the world, to see a road map of the surrounding environment," and to drive from point to point without human intervention. Within 10 years, he said, convoys of robots should be

able to wend their way through deep woods or dense cities. But the results of a road test for robot vehicles last March [2004] were vexing: 15 prototypes took off across the Mojave Desert in a 142-mile race, competing for a $1 million prize in a Pentagon-sponsored contest to see if they could navigate the rough terrain. Four hours later, every vehicle had crashed or had failed.

16   All this raises questions about how realistic the Army's timetable is for the Future Combat Systems, currently in the first stages of development. These elaborate networks of weapons, robots, drone aircraft and computers are still evolving in fits and starts; a typical unit is intended to include, say, 2,245 soldiers and 151 military robots. The technology still runs ahead of robot rules of engagement. "There is a lag between technology and doctrine," said Mr. Finkelstein of Robotic Technology, who has been in the military robotics field for 28 years. "If you could invade other countries bloodlessly, would this lead to a greater temptation to invade?"

WEINER, "A New Model Army Soldier"

Exercise 17   Work with Words

The following sentences appear in Reading 3, Tim Weiner's "The Robot Soldiers Are Coming." Use context clues, dictionary skills, and your knowledge of word parts to choose the best definition of each italicized word in the sentences. The paragraph number is provided in case you want to check the context.

1. The costs of that *transformation* will help drive the Defense Department's budget up almost 20 percent, from a requested $419.3 billion for next year [2006] to $502.3 billion in 2010, excluding the costs of war. (par. 4)
   a. change in form
   b. campaign
   c. movement

2. And as their intelligence grows, so will their *autonomy*. (par. 5)
   a. anxiety
   b. independence
   c. rebellion

3. The robot soldier has been a dream at the Pentagon for 30 years. And some involved in the work say it may take at least 30 more years to *realize* in full. (par. 6)
   a. understand
   b. achieve
   c. become aware of

4. With the development of *nanotechnology*—the science of very small structures—they may become swarms of "smart dust." (par. 7)
   a. swarms of smart dust
   b. advanced technology
   c. science of very small structures

©2007 Pearson Education, Inc.

5. Congress ordered in 2000 that a third of the ground vehicles and a third of deep-strike aircraft in the military must become robotic within a decade. If that *mandate* is to be met, the United States will spend many billions of dollars on military robots by 2010. (par. 10)
   a. order
   b. promise
   c. expense

6. As the first *lethal* robots head for Iraq, the role of the robot soldier as a killing machine has barely been debated. (par. 11)
   a. innocent
   b. deadly
   c. intelligent

7. "Today we have an infantry soldier" as the *prototype* of a military robot, he added. (par. 13)
   a. duplication
   b. copy
   c. first example

8. A fourth is a *drone* in flight; last April, an unmanned aircraft made military history by hitting a ground target with a small smart bomb in a test from 35,000 feet. (par. 14)
   a. pilotless aircraft
   b. type of bird
   c. ground target

9. For all five, the ability to perceive is *paramount*. "We've seen pretty dramatic progress in the area of robot perception," said Charles M. Shoemaker, chief of the Army Research Laboratory's robotics program office. (par. 15)
   a. extremely different
   b. completely impossible
   c. extremely important

10. But the results of a road test for robot vehicles last March [2004] were *vexing*: 15 prototypes took off across the Mojave Desert in a 142-mile race, competing for a $1 million prize in a Pentagon-sponsored contest to see if they could navigate the rough terrain. Four hours later, every vehicle had crashed or had failed. (par. 15)
    a. convincing
    b. encouraging
    c. disturbing

| Exercise 18 | **Check Your Understanding** |

Based on Reading 3, choose the best answer to each of the following multiple-choice questions.

1. The new generation of soldiers that the military is working on will be
   a. soldiers who are better trained.
   b. soldiers who can look forward to better benefits.
   c. robots that will do some of the work of human soldiers.

2. How much money does the military plan to invest for automated armed forces?
   a. billions of dollars
   b. tens of billions of dollars
   c. $419.3 billion

3. The more "intelligent" the robots become, the more they will be able to
   a. have emotions like human soldiers.
   b. act on their own.
   c. follow directions through a remote control.

4. The armed version of the bomb-disposal robot can
   a. explode bombs more easily than the original version.
   b. fire 1,000 rounds a minute.
   c. operate independently.

5. The author is concerned that while the United States has already committed to using robot soldiers as killing machines,
   a. there has not been much discussion about how to control this new technology.
   b. human soldiers will lose their jobs.
   c. the Pentagon might change its commitment to using the robots.

6. The main reason behind unmanned warfare is to
   a. stop spending so much money on veterans' benefits.
   b. avoid casualties and save money.
   c. guarantee that the United States gets involved only in just wars.

7. The infantry soldier is considered a prototype of a military robot because he or she
   a. follows a set of instructions.
   b. is essentially unsupervised.
   c. is a hunter-killer.

8. The robot that was originally designed as a security guard will soon be able to
   a. hunt and kill enemy personnel.
   b. conduct surveillance and psychological warfare.
   c. completely replace human soldiers.

9. There are indications that there will be problems developing robot vehicles because
   a. no one is really interested in their research and development.
   b. they are likely to be too costly to manufacture.
   c. none of the prototypes were able to finish a road test in 2004.

10. The author questions whether
    a. the army's timetable is realistic.
    b. the robots will ever be developed.
    c. the United States will have the billions of dollars necessary for realizing the robot soldier plan.

©2007 Pearson Education, Inc.

| Exercise 19 | ## Reflect

Think about what you read in Reading 3 and what you already know about the military, wars, and robots. Answer the following questions, and prepare to discuss them with your classmates.

1. An expert on robot soldiers quoted in the article said, "Anyone who's a decision maker doesn't want American lives at risk." Explain why politicians might support having robot soldiers.

   _____

   _____

   _____

2. What do you think about the statement that another expert made: "If you could invade other countries bloodlessly, would this lead to a greater temptation to invade?" Do you think it's possible to invade another country "bloodlessly"? Would robots make warfare more frequent or less frequent? Explain your answers.

   _____

   _____

   _____

3. What is your opinion about robot soldiers? Explain your answer.

   _____

   _____

◆

Textbook Aids and Specialized Vocabulary

Most academic disciplines have specialized vocabularies, and when you take courses in math, sociology, psychology, biology, business, computer science, and others, you will need to learn terms that are unique to those subjects. Textbooks usually explain these special terms when they are introduced. They also contain other aids for learning them.

boldface A typeface that is extra wide and dark for emphasis

italics A typeface that is sloped to the right for emphasis

- The use of **boldface** or *italics* to emphasize specialized or important words
- Definitions of specialized words in the margins
- "Key words and concepts" sections, often at the ends of chapters
- Vocabulary questions in chapter reviews
- Glossaries at the ends of chapters or the back of the book

Notice that this textbook, *A Community of Readers,* highlights reading skill terms by printing them in boldface, defining them in the text, repeating them with definitions in the margins, and reminding you about them in the Chapter Review.

When you come across a term in your reading that is crucial for understanding a chapter or a reading assignment, be sure to look in the text itself for the author's definition or explanation. If, after checking the vocabulary aids in your textbook you still can't find the meaning of a new term, you may have to look it up in a dictionary.

To help you learn specialized terms, it is a good idea to keep an ongoing list of them in your notebook. You will eventually figure out a system that works for you, but when you make your list or start a file of three-by-five cards, you might want to use a format like this:

Word: **databases**

Appropriate definition for computer science: computerized information storage

Sentence: Libraries, banks, and other institutions use databases to store information.

Your sentence: I wonder if I need to learn how to use database software in order to increase my chances of getting a good job.

Exercise 20   Textbook Vocabulary Aids

Review two textbooks that you are using this semester or have used in the past. What kinds of vocabulary aids do they have?

Textbook Title   **Vocabulary Aids**

1. _____   _____

2. _____   _____

Exercise 21   Your System for Specialized Vocabulary

Choose ten words that you think are important to learn from *A Community of Readers* or from another textbook. On a separate piece of paper or on three-by-five cards, write each word, its appropriate definition, the original sentence in which it appeared, and your own sentence using the word. Follow the model above.

©2007 Pearson Education, Inc.

CHAPTER REVIEW

✔ Reader's Checklist

Check (✔) the concepts and skills introduced in this chapter that you are confident you understand and can now use as vocabulary-learning strategies. If you are not sure about any items, (1) go back to the explanations in the text, (2) study and review the words with other members of your college learning community, (3) ask your instructor for help, (4) check out the Web site for this textbook at **www.ablongman.com/alexandercommunity4e** for additional vocabulary exercises and to take the chapter quiz, or (5) complete additional practices in the *Reading Road Trip.*

Vocabulary in context
❑ Definition and synonym clues   ❑ General information clues
❑ Example clues   ❑ Contrast clues

Word parts
❑ Prefixes
❑ Roots
❑ Suffixes

Dictionary
❑ Parts of dictionary entries
❑ Finding the correct dictionary meaning from the context of the reading

Textbook aids and specialized vocabulary
❑ Recognizing textbook vocabulary aids
❑ Organizing a system for learning specialized vocabulary

When you are confident that you have mastered these concepts and skills, test yourself with Mastery Tests 2A and 2B (pp. 94–108).

Critical Reflections

Answer the following questions, and prepare to discuss them with your classmates.

1. What are some technologies that were rare or unheard of 15 years ago but are common today?

   _____

   _____

2. Have you experienced any negative effects from the increased use of computers? Explain.

   _____

   _____

   _____

Writing Activity

Write the answers to the following questions on your own paper.

1. List three to five new ways you imagine computers and other forms of technology will be used in your life ten years from now.

2. Using your list, write a paragraph or short essay titled "Technology in Our Future."

Classroom Community

Share your predictions for the future with your class group. Make one list, eliminate duplications, and then discuss the implications of the innovations. Will the effects be positive, negative, or both? Why?

Extend Your Thinking

For another reading related to computer technology, see "Social and Ethical Issues of Computer Technology," by George Beekman, in "Extend Your Thinking" (pp. 468–470).

Work the Web

A Web site devoted to technology, HowStuffWorks, explores in depth how a number of new and old technologies actually function. With a spirit of curiosity and attention to new vocabulary, complete the following tasks.

1. Go to the home page of HowStuffWorks at http://www.howstuffworks.com.

2. After previewing the home page, notice a bar with a number of categories. Choose either Computer Stuff, Auto Stuff, Electronics Stuff, or Science Stuff, whichever you are more interested in, and find one particular technology you would like to learn about. (Avoid going to the many shopping links.) Click on the article and then the printable version so you won't be too distracted by the many advertisements. Read about how the technology you've chosen works. Using your vocabulary skills—context clues, word parts, and dictionary usage—choose five new words that are important to your understanding of this technology. On a piece of paper, identify which technology you chose and write down at least five new words you learned. Also provide the sentences in which they were written on the Web site.

Go to **www.ablongman.com/alexandercommunity4e** for additional Web-based exercises.

©2007 Pearson Education, Inc.

Mastery Test   2A

Cyberthought   Ronald Kotulak

The following reading, from a March 2004 article in the Chicago Tribune, *discusses how a man's mind can control a machine. This field of medicine is called neural engineering, which means training neurons—the impulse-conducting cells of the nervous system and the brain—to control artificial limbs. As you read, consider the possible implications and consequences of this new technology. Also, notice that some of the words used in this article are so new that they do not appear in dictionaries yet.*

1   Jesse Sullivan doesn't know exactly how his brain liberated itself from his armless body and began doing things for him on its own. But he has become a pioneer in a new field of medicine called <u>neural engineering</u>, whose practitioners are proving that there is such a thing as mind over matter. Sullivan, a Tennessee power company worker who lost both arms in a job-related accident, has been outfitted by Rehabilitation Institute of Chicago researchers with a kind of <u>bionic arm</u>, which is controlled directly by his thoughts. This extraordinary achievement—just one of several breakthroughs nationally in linking mental activity with machines—signifies an <u>impending</u> step of immense proportions: The human brain is poised to make its biggest evolutionary leap since the appearance of early man eons ago.

2   The first direct brain-computer hookups have already been achieved in paralyzed patients, with limited success. Building on that, Cyberkinetics, a Massachusetts <u>biotech</u> company, has government approval to implant chips containing 100 tiny electrodes into the brains of five quadriplegics this year [2004] to see if their thoughts can operate computers. At least two other research teams are planning similar brain-machine experiments in people.

3   "I think what we're going to find is that we can help people who are disabled become super-able in a new sense," says Cyberkinetics chief executive Timothy Surgenor. "These people may be able to do things we can't do, like operate a computer faster or do very precise tasks. That's what we're really trying to accomplish. We're not trying to make an <u>incremental</u> change for these people. We're trying to do something that's a breakthrough."

Thought Control or Controlling Thoughts?

4   These experiments have ushered science into a new era, the age of the cyborg, where the melding of brain and machine, long envisioned by the masters of science fiction, is now possible. And the research is not just aimed at the handicapped. Able-bodied people may also be able to greatly expand the capacity of their minds.

5   "We're getting into sort of a scary field, in a way, that of cyborgs, where relatively healthy people are going to control machines (with their

thoughts)," says Dr. Philip Kennedy of Neural Signals Inc., in Atlanta. In 1998, Kennedy, a former Emory University neurologist, was the first researcher to implant an electrode into the brain of a totally paralyzed patient, who was then empowered to use his mind to slowly spell out words on a computer. If it works the way Kennedy and many other scientists now believe, the two-way brain-machine interface could give people expanded memory banks and super calculating power. Implanted computer chips, for example, could enable people to quickly learn a foreign language and master other tough subjects.

6   "We do dream about that, of enhancing functionality, just like the Six Million Dollar Man," says University of Chicago neuroscientist Nicholas Hatsopoulous, who worked with Brown University's John Donoghue to show that the Cyberkinetics chip enabled monkeys to move a computer cursor with their brains. "It would actually improve your capabilities beyond what a normal person could do. You could see better, hear better, move better and think faster." . . .

Super-able

7   Are such things possible?

8   Not now, but very likely soon.

9   "I have no doubt that that is the future of those technologies," says Arthur Caplan, director of the University of Pennsylvania's Center for Bioethics.

10   The technology raises disturbing questions: Who would have access to electronic mind-enhancers? Would companies and other institutions coerce employees to have chips implanted in their brains to gain a competitive edge? Would chips be given to children? Would they be used to control the behavior of sex offenders and others? Would it change our notion of what it means to be human?

11   Says Caplan, "If you really started to change your memory speed, or clearly started to be able to do things that you weren't able to do before, like learn languages in a day, or had infrared vision, you do start to get to questions about, 'Is that still me?'

12   My answer to that is, I'm not sure. But that won't stop people."

Second Chance

13   Sullivan, 57, of Dayton, Tennessee, entered this dazzling new world three years ago when his arms were incinerated on the job as a lineman for a Tennessee power company. Somehow he accidentally grabbed a high-tension wire carrying 7,400 volts of electricity. His arms took the full fury of the charge. When it came time to rebuild Sullivan, doctors first fitted him with a standard plastic-and-metal prosthesis. But it moved clumsily and demanded arduous shoulder gyrations. Last year, Sullivan received an experimental myoelectric arm, a device designed by Dr. Todd Kuiken that transmits instructions from the brain via unused nerves to points outside the body. . . . Sullivan was a good candidate because the memory of his

©2007 Pearson Education, Inc.

arms and hands remained fresh in his mind, while the neural circuits that controlled those parts were still powered up as they had been before the accident.

14   "That was probably one of the best feelings I'd had since I had my accident, when they first put it on and told me to close my hand," Sullivan says. "When I did, this grasper on the end of the arm closed up."

15   Sullivan's robotic arm has given him a new sense of independence. He can do things he couldn't just a year ago, like shave, put on socks, weed the garden, water the yard, open small jars, use a pair of handicapped scissors and throw a ball to his grandson.

16   "It gave me part of my dignity back," he says.

KOTULAK, "Cyberthought"

Exercise 1   Work with Words

Use context, dictionary skills, and your knowledge of word parts to choose the best definition for each of the following words underlined in the reading. The paragraph number is provided in case you want to check the context.

1. *Neural engineering* (par. 1)
   a. designing links between mental activity and machines
   b. designing machines that have feelings
   c. designing restrictions on the mental activities of individuals

2. *Bionic arm* (par. 1)
   a. excessively strong arm
   b. artificial arm, controlled by thoughts
   c. arm that can think independently

3. *Impending* (par. 1)
   a. unfortunate
   b. already accomplished
   c. about to happen

4. *Biotech* (par. 2)
   a. applications combining bionic with other characteristics
   b. applications combining biology and technology
   c. applications for biological restrictions on technology

5. *Incremental* (par. 3)
   a. huge, major
   b. small, gradual
   c. insignificant

6. *Interface* (par. 5)
   a. point of connection
   b. line
   c. point of division

7. *Enhancing* (par. 6)
  a. reducing
  b. confusing
  c. improving

8. *Edge* (par. 10)
  a. border
  b. advantage
  c. slight movement

9. *Incinerated* (par. 13)
  a. strengthened
  b. lost due to tension
  c. burned to ashes

10. *Prosthesis* (par. 13)
  a. artificial limb
  b. shoulder gyrations
  c. arms and legs

Exercise 2   **Check Your Understanding**

Based on the reading "Cyberthought" by Ronald Kotulak, choose the best answer to each of the following multiple-choice questions.

1. The author writes that Jesse Sullivan "has become a pioneer in a new field of medicine called neural engineering," because Sullivan
  a. lost his arms in a work-related accident.
  b. succeeded in sending mental messages to his prosthetic arms.
  c. invented the bionic arm.

2. Cyberkinetics, a Massachusetts biotech company, has government approval to
  a. genetically engineer a bionic person.
  b. patent any discoveries it makes in the field of bioengineering.
  c. implant chips into the brains of five quadriplegics.

3. Timothy Surgenor of Cyberkinetics believes that the firm will be able to
  a. give people superhuman abilities.
  b. make significant profits from their groundbreaking scientific work.
  c. make incremental changes for people with handicaps.

4. Some people, such as Dr. Philip Kennedy, have expressed
  a. some concerns about the implications of controlling machines with thoughts.
  b. complete confidence in a future in which people's lives can be improved through biotechnology.
  c. uncertainty about being able to finish the bioengineering project.

©2007 Pearson Education, Inc.

5. What are some examples given in the reading of things people could conceivably do with a two-way brain-machine interface?
   a. People could run faster than any of today's athletes.
   b. People could learn a foreign language and master difficult subjects much faster.
   c. People could analyze the psychological makeup of anyone they meet.

6. Experiments have already succeeded in
   a. creating humanoid cyborgs.
   b. enabling monkeys to control an unattached arm with their minds.
   c. enabling a totally paralyzed patient to use his mind to spell words on a computer.

7. Arthur Caplan, from the University of Pennsylvania's Center for Bioethics, is
   a. concerned with the many moral and ethical problems that implanting chips in people's brains will create.
   b. convinced that people will not use bioengineering, in particular implanting chips in people's brains, for selfish reasons.
   c. convinced that corporations are researching electronic mind-enhancers only because there are profits to be made.

8. Sullivan was a good candidate for an experimental myoelectric arm because
   a. he volunteered to be a subject in the experiment without financial compensation.
   b. the memory of his arms and hands remained fresh in his mind and the neural circuits were still capable of functioning.
   c. he was hoping to become stronger.

9. Sullivan's robotic arm has
   a. allowed him to return to work.
   b. not worked all that well in the time that he's had it.
   c. given him a new sense of independence.

10. The article is titled "Cyberthought" because it
    a. is about how computers think.
    b. demonstrates the potential of computers that can think like people.
    c. is about people being able to mentally send messages to computers.

| Exercise 3 | Reflect |

Think about what you read in "Cyberthought" and what you already know about this topic to answer the following questions.

1. Why do you think some people believe there are problems with implanting chips into people's brains to make them smarter or able to learn things more easily? Explain what some of the problems would be.

_____

_____

_____

_____

2. Do you think there should be some kind of control over the use of this kind of technology? If yes, explain why, and what kind of control you would recommend. If no, explain your reasoning.

_____

_____

_____

_____

©2007 Pearson Education, Inc.

Mastery Test

2B

No Secrets   George Beekman

The following reading is from a computer textbook. In it the author presents some of the threats to personal privacy, such as the selling of personal information and the monitoring and surveillance of individuals, that have been accelerated by advances in computer technology. As you read, consider what the loss of personal privacy can mean and how it can affect you personally.

1   Instant airline reservations, all-night automated banking, overnight mail, instant library searches, Web shopping—databases provide us with conveniences that were unthinkable a generation ago. But convenience isn't free. In the case of databases the price we pay is our privacy.

Personal Data: All About You

2   We live in an information age, and data is one of the currencies of our time. Businesses and government agencies spend billions of dollars every year to collect and exchange information about you and me. More than 15,000 specialized marketing databases contain 2 billion consumer names, along with a surprising amount of personal information. The typical American consumer is on at least 25 marketing lists. Many of these lists are organized by characteristics like age, income, religion, political affiliation, and even sexual preference—and they're bought and sold every day.

3   Marketing databases are only the tip of the iceberg. Credit and banking information, tax records, health data, insurance records, political contributions, voter registration, credit card purchases, warranty registrations, magazine and newsletter subscriptions, phone calls, passport registration, airline reservations, automobile registrations, arrests, Internet explorations—they're all recorded in computers, and we have little or no control over what happens to most of those records once they're collected.

4   For most of us this data is out of sight and out of mind. But lives are changed because of these databases. Here are some representative stories: . . .

- When a credit bureau mistakenly placed a bankruptcy filing in the file of a St. Louis couple, banks responded by shutting off loans for their struggling construction business, forcing them into real bankruptcy. They sued but lost because credit bureaus are protected by law from financial responsibility for "honest" mistakes!

- A Los Angeles thief stole a wallet and used its contents to establish an artificial identity. When the thief was arrested for a robbery involving murder, the crime was recorded under the wallet owner's name in police databases. The legitimate owner of the wallet was arrested five times in the following 14 months and spent several days in jail before a protracted court battle resulted in the deletion of the record.

- In a more recent, more typical example of *identity theft*, an <u>impostor</u> had the mail of an innocent individual temporarily forwarded to a post office box so he could easily collect credit card numbers and other personal data. By the time the victim discovered an overdue Visa bill, the thief had racked up $42,000 in bogus charges. The victim wasn't liable for the charges, but it took the better part of a year to correct all of the credit bureau errors.

5   As these examples indicate, there are many ways that abuse and misuse of databases can take away personal privacy. Sometimes privacy violations are due to government surveillance activities. Sometimes they're the result of the work of private corporations. Privacy <u>breaches</u> may be innocent mistakes, strategic actions, or malicious mischief. The explosive growth of identity theft—which claims millions of victims each year—makes it clear that database technology can be a powerful criminal tool. . . .

The Privacy Problem

6   In George Orwell's *1984,* information about every citizen was stored in a massive database controlled by the ever-vigilant Big Brother. Today's data warehouses in many ways resemble Big Brother's database. Data-mining techniques can be used to extract information about individuals and groups without their knowledge or consent. And databases can be easily sold or used for purposes other than those for which they were collected. Most of the time this kind of activity goes unnoticed by the public. . . .

7   Centralized data warehouses aren't necessary for producing computerized <u>dossiers</u> of private citizens. With networked computers, it's easy to compile profiles by combining information from different databases. As long as the tables in the databases share a single unique field, such as a Social Security number field, *record matching* is trivial and quick. And when database information is combined, the whole is often far greater than the sum of its parts.

8   Sometimes the results are beneficial. Record matching is used by government enforcement agencies to locate criminals ranging from tax evaders to mass murderers. Because credit bureaus collect data about us, we can use credit cards to borrow money wherever we go. But these benefits come with at least three problems:

- *Data errors are common.* A study of 1,500 reports from the three big credit bureaus found errors in 43 percent of the files.

- *Data can become nearly immortal.* Because files are commonly sold and copied, it's impossible to delete or correct erroneous records with absolute certainty.

- *Data isn't secure.* A *Business Week* reporter demonstrated this in 1989 by using his computer to obtain then Vice President Dan Quayle's credit report. Had he been a skilled criminal, he might have been able to change that report.

101

9   Protection against invasion of privacy is not explicitly guaranteed by the U.S. Constitution. Legal scholars agree that the *right to privacy*—freedom from interference in the private sphere of a person's affairs—is implied by other constitutional guarantees, although debates rage about what this means. Federal and state laws provide forms of privacy protection, but most of those laws were written years ago. Most European countries have had strong privacy protection laws for years. The 1998 European Data Protection Directive guarantees a basic set of privacy rights to citizens of all countries in the European Union—rights that go far beyond those of American citizens. The directive allows citizens to have access to all personal data, to know where that data originated, to have inaccurate data rectified, to seek recourse in the event of unlawful processing, and to withhold permission to use their data for direct marketing. The American legislatures have refused to pass similar laws because of intense lobbying by business interests. When it comes to privacy violation in America, technology is far ahead of the law.

Big Brother and Big Business

10 Database technology clearly poses a threat to personal privacy, but other information technologies amplify that threat:

- Networks make it possible for personal data to be transmitted almost anywhere instantly. The Internet is particularly fertile ground for collecting personal information about you. And the Web makes it alarmingly easy for anyone with a connected computer to examine your personal information. . . .

- Workplace monitoring technology enables managers to learn more than ever before about the work habits and patterns of workers. Supervisors can (and do) count keystrokes, monitor Web activity, screen email, and remotely view what's on the screens of employees.

- Surveillance cameras, increasingly used for nabbing routine traffic violations and detecting security violators, can be combined with picture databases to locate criminals—and others. Florida law enforcement officials came under fire from privacy groups because they used cameras, face-recognition software, and criminal databases to find and arrest several attendees of the 2001 Super Bowl. After the terrorist attacks of September 11, 2001, surveillance cameras were installed in hundreds of businesses and government agencies to guard against future attacks.

- Surveillance satellites can provide permanent peepholes into our lives for anyone willing to pay the price.

- Cell phones are now required by law to include technology to determine and transmit their locations to emergency personnel responding to 911 calls. Privacy advocates point out that the same technology can easily be used for less noble purposes.

11   In George Orwell's *1984* personal privacy was the victim of a centralized Communist police state controlled by Big Brother. Today, our privacy is threatened by many Big Brothers—with new threats emerging almost every

day. As Simson Garfinkel says in *Database Nation,* "Over the next 50 years, we will see new kinds of threats to privacy that don't find their roots in totalitarianism, but in capitalism, the free market, advanced technology, and the <u>unbridled</u> exchange of electronic information."

12 Democracy depends on the free flow of information, but it also depends on the protection of individual rights. Maintaining a balance is not easy, especially when new information technologies are being developed at such a rapid pace.

BEEKMAN, *COMPUTER CONFLUENCE*

Exercise 1 **Work with Words**

Use context clues, dictionary skills, and your knowledge of word parts to choose the best definition for each of the following words underlined in the reading. The paragraph number is provided in case you want to go back to check the context.

1. *Currencies* (par. 2)

    cur·ren·cy (kûr′ən-sē) *n., pl.* **-cies. 1.** *Abbr.* **cur.** Any form of money in actual use as a medium of exchange. **2.** A passing from hand to hand; circulation. **3.** Common acceptance; prevalence. [Medieval Latin *currentia,* "a flowing," from Latin *currēns,* present participle of *currere,* to run. See **current.**]

    (American Heritage Dictionary)

    a. forms of exchange
    b. something passed hand to hand
    c. something that is prevalent

2. *Affiliation* (par. 2)

    af·fil·i·ate (ə-fĭl′ē-āt) *v.* **-ated, -ating, -ates.** —*tr.* **1.** To adopt as a subordinate associate. **2.** To associate (oneself) as a subordinate or subsidiary with. **3.** To admit as one's own child; adopt. **4.** *Law.* **a.** To determine the paternity of (an illegitimate child). Used with *upon.* **b.** To refer an illegitimate child to (its father). —*intr.* To associate or connect oneself: *We decided to affiliate.* —*n.* (ə-fĭl′ē-ĭt). A person or organizaiton associated with another in subordinate relationship. [Medieval Latin *affiliāre,* "to take oneself as a son" : *ad-,* to + *filius,* son (see **dhēi-** in Appendix*).] —**af·fil′i·a′tion** *n.*

    (American Heritage Dictionary)

    a. subordination
    b. admission of parenthood
    c. association

3. *Legitimate* (par. 4)

    le·git·i·mate (lə-jĭt′ə-mĭt) *adj.* **1.** In compliance with the law; lawful. **2.** In accordance with traditional or established patterns and standards. **3.** Based on logical reasoning; reasonable; *a legitimate solution.* **4.** Authentic; genuine. **5.** Born in wedlock. **6.** Of, relating to, or ruling by hereditary right.

© 2007 Pearson Education, Inc.

103

7. *Theater.* **a.** Of or pertaining to drama performed on a stage as opposed to other media, such as motion pictures or television. **b.** Of or pertaining to drama of high professional quality, as opposed to burlesque, vaudeville, and the like. —*tr.v.* (lə-jĭt′ə-māt) **legitimated, -mating, -mates. 1.** To justify as legitimate; authorize. **2.** To make, establish, or declare legitimate. [Middle English, born in wedlock, from Medieval Latin *lēgitimātus,* past participle of *lēgitimāre,* to make lawful, from Latin *legitimus,* lawful, legal, from *lēx* (stem *lēg-*), law. **See leg-** in Appendix.*] —**le·git′i·macy** (-məsē) *n.* —**le·git′i·mate·ly** *adv.*   *(American Heritage Dictionary)*

   a. lawful
   b. traditional
   c. hereditary

4. *Protracted* (par. 4)

pro·tract (prō-trăkt′) *tr.v.* **-tracted, tracting, tracts. 1.** To draw out or lengthen in time; prolong. **2.** *Surveying.* To draw to scale by means of a scale and protractor; to plot. **3.** *Anatomy.* To extend or protrude. —See Synonyms at **prolong.** [Latin *prōtrahere* (past participle *prōtractus*), to drag out, lengthen: *prō-,* out, extending + *trahere,* to drag, pull (see **tragh-** in Appendix*).] —**pro·tract′ed·ly** *adv.* —**pro·tract′ed·ness** *n.* —**pro·trac′tive** *adj.*   *(American Heritage Dictionary)*

   a. prolonged
   b. drawn to scale
   c. protruding

5. *Impostor* (par. 4)

im·pos·tor (im-pŏs′tər) *n.* A person who deceives under an assumed identity. [Old French *imposteur,* from Late Latin *impos(i)tor,* from Latin *impōnere* (past participle *impositus*), IMPOSE.]   *(American Heritage Dictionary)*

   a. a person pretending to be someone else
   b. an imposing figure
   c. a dishonest person

6. *Breaches* (par. 5)

breach (brēch) *n.* **1.** A violation or infraction, as of a law, legal obligation, or promise. **2.** A gap or rift, especially in a solid structure such as a dike or fortification: *"The first breach in . . . the monolith of international communism opened new horizons"* (John C. Bennett). **3.** A breaking up or disruption of friendly relations; an estrangement. **4.** The leaping of a whale from the water. **5.** The breaking of waves or surf. **6.** *Obsolete.* A wound; an injury. —*v.* **breached, breaching, breaches.** —*tr.* To make a hole or gap in; break through. —*intr.* To leap from the water. Used of a whale. [Middle English *breche, brek,* partly from Old French *breche,* from Old High German *brehha,* from *brehhan,* to break, and partly from Old English *brǣc, brēc,* from *brecan,* to break. See **bhreg-** in Appendix.*]   *(American Heritage Dictionary)*

a. violations

b. disruptions

c. gaps

7. *Dossiers* (par. 7)

dos·si·er (dŏs′ē-ā′, dôs′yā′) *n.* A collection of papers or documents pertaining to a particular person or subject; a file. [French, from Old French, bundle of papers having a label on the back, from *dos,* back, from Latin *dorsum.* See **dorsum** in Appendix.*]

(American Heritage Dictionary)

a. collections of papers

b. files

c. bundles of papers with a label on the back

8. *Directive* (par. 9)

di·rec·tive (dĭ-rĕk′tĭv, dī-) *n.* An order or instruction, especially one issued by a government or military unit. —*adj.* Serving to direct, indicate, or point out; directing.

(American Heritage Dictionary)

a. directions

b. request

c. order

9. *Amplify* (par. 10)

am·pli·fy (ăm′plə-fī′) *v.* **-fied, -fying, -fies.** —*tr.* **1.** To make larger or more powerful; extend; increase. **2.** To add to, as by illustrations; make complete. **3.** To exaggerate. **4.** *Physics.* To produce amplification of. —*intr.* To write or discourse at length; expatiate. [Middle English *amplifien,* from Old French *amplifier,* from Latin *amplificāre* : *amplus,* AMPLE + *facere,* to make (see **dhē-**[1] in Appendix*).] —**am′pli·fi·ca′tive** (-fĭ-kā′tĭv), **am·plif′i·ca·to·ry** (ăm-plĭf′ĭ-kə-tôr′ē, -tōr′ē) *adj.*

(American Heritage Dictionary)

a. make complete

b. exaggerate

c. make more powerful

10. *Unbridled* (par. 11)

un·bri·dled (ŭn′brī′dəld) *adj.* **1.** Not wearing or fitted with a bridle. **2.** Unrestrained; uncontrolled. —**un′bri′dled·ly** *adv.*

(American Heritage Dictionary)

a. malicious

b. not wearing a bridle

c. uncontrolled

©2007 Pearson Education, Inc.

Check Your Understanding

Based on the reading "No Secrets" by Beekman, choose the best answer to each of the following multiple-choice questions.

1. Why is data a form of currency?
   a. It is prevalent and up-to-date with our technological times.
   b. It is increasingly available for both good and bad uses.
   c. It is exchanged by those who use it to their benefit.

2. If a credit bureau makes a mistake about your credit that causes you great financial difficulty, you can
   a. sue the credit bureau, but you may lose if the court rules that it was an honest mistake.
   b. do nothing because credit bureaus are not legally responsible for what they do.
   c. explain your situation to a judge to have it straightened out and to get some of your losses paid back.

3. What happened to the man whose wallet was stolen in Los Angeles?
   a. He had a difficult time reestablishing his credit record, which eventually led him to lose his business and go into bankruptcy.
   b. He was never able to find out who stole his wallet because the thief was able to change his identity.
   c. He spent several days in jail and had to fight in court because the crime was recorded under his name in police databases.

4. Which of the following is not mentioned as privacy violators by the author?
   a. educational institutions
   b. government
   c. private corporations

5. Beekman, the author of the reading, talks about George Orwell's novel, *1984*, because
   a. Orwell's prediction of a society in which just about everything about you is known has become a reality.
   b. databases can be easily sold for purposes other than those for which they were collected.
   c. private corporations were already collecting information about individuals when Orwell wrote his book.

6. Data-mining refers to
   a. getting information out of people.
   b. extracting information about people without their consent.
   c. cross-checking to make sure data is accurate.

7. The author believes that record-matching
   a. can be beneficial.
   b. is always used for the wrong purposes.
   c. is safe.

8. People in the United States
   a. can access all personal data, know where it came from, and have it corrected if it's wrong.
   b. have very little real protection of the right of privacy.
   c. can be confident that the legislature will pass laws to protect their privacy.

9. When Beekman writes, "Data errors can become nearly immortal," he means that
   a. once the wrong information is on your record at credit bureaus, it is practically impossible to get it changed.
   b. errors are almost always corrected.
   c. mistakes, as so many of us know from experience, will never die.

10. Beekman is
    a. clearly optimistic about the potential of databases to improve our lives.
    b. not worried about American democracy because it depends on the free flow of information, and databases help guarantee it.
    c. concerned about the misuse of databases by business and government and the lack of protection for American citizens.

Exercise 3   **Reflect**

Think about what you read in "No Secrets" and what you already know about the information gathered about you to answer the following questions.

1. Have you ever gotten mail from an organization or company that you have never had any contact with? How do you think they got your address?

   _____

   _____

   _____

   _____

   _____

©2007 Pearson Education, Inc.

2. What does the European Data Protection Directive guarantee, and why, according to the author, is the European approach to personal privacy different from the U.S. approach?

_____

_____

_____

_____

_____

3. How do you feel about your personal information being so widely available to businesses, the government, and even on the Internet to the general public?

_____

_____

_____

_____

_____

Chapter 3
Topics and Main Ideas
Our Food, Our Culture

You are what you eat.

—*ANONYMOUS*

- When you see the picture, what do you think about?
- What do you think the quotation means?
- How does the quotation relate to the picture?

© 2007 Pearson Education, Inc.

PREPARE TO READ

Most of us take food for granted. We eat every day, usually several times a day. We lead very busy lives and, unlike our ancestors, spend relatively little time gathering, preparing, and even eating food. As a group, Americans eat more processed and "instant" foods than ever before. We eat at fast-food restaurants or on the go with take-out meals. Most children don't even think about where the food in the packages comes from, and often adults don't either. But food is more than nourishment. It is also an important part of our social lives. It plays a role in our get-togethers with friends and family. And although our tastes may be different, people around the world like to eat good food. So how do our eating habits—what and where we eat—affect our relationships with others? How do they affect our nutrition and health? How do they affect our culture?

Purpose

In this chapter, you will learn to
- Recognize topics in readings
- Identify stated and implied main ideas in paragraphs and short passages
- Recognize thesis statements in longer passages
- Put main ideas and thesis statements into your own words

In the process of acquiring these skills, you will read about food: how the foods we eat have changed, how our foods are processed and prepared, what's in the food we eat, and how our eating habits and expectations influence our lives.

Previous Knowledge

Answer these questions and prepare to discuss them in class.

1. List five possible situations for eating food. Think about whom you might eat with, where you might be when you eat, and what kinds of special occasions are celebrated by eating food.

   a. _____   d. _____

   b. _____   e. _____

   c. _____

2. What happy or sad memories or associations do you have about food?

   _____

   _____

Preview and Predict

Preview Chapter 3. Then list two things you think you will learn in this chapter.

1. _____

2. _____

Reading 1 *Oh, the Flavor of Your Fries*   Eric Schlosser

The following reading is from Eric Schlosser's best seller, Fast Food Nation. *This book examines many aspects of the fast-food industry: where the food comes from, how it is processed, what ingredients it contains, what the working conditions are at all stages of producing and serving the food, and how the fast-food culture fits into other parts of our lives. In this reading, Schlosser explains the source of much of the flavor of fast food.*

1 The taste of McDonald's French fries has long been praised by customers, competitors, and even food critics. James Beard loved McDonald's fries. Their distinctive taste does not stem from the type of potatoes that McDonald's buys, the technology that processes them, or the restaurant equipment that fries them. Other chains buy their French fries from the same large processing companies, use Russet Burbanks, and have similar fryers in their restaurant kitchens. The taste of a fast food fry is largely determined by the cooking oil. For decades, McDonald's cooked its French fries in a mixture of about 7 percent cottonseed oil and 93 percent beef tallow. The mix gave the fries their unique flavor—and more saturated beef fat per ounce than a McDonald's hamburger.

2 Amid a barrage of criticism over the amount of cholesterol in their fries, McDonald's switched to pure vegetable oil in 1990. The switch presented the company with an enormous challenge: how to make fries that subtly taste like beef without cooking them in tallow. A look at the ingredients now used in the preparation of McDonald's French fries suggests how the problem was solved. Toward the end of the list is a seemingly innocuous, yet oddly mysterious phrase: "natural flavor." That ingredient helps to explain not only why the fries taste so good, but also why most fast food—indeed, most of the food Americans eat today—tastes the way it does.

3 Open your refrigerator, your freezer, your kitchen cupboards, and look at the labels on your food. You'll find "natural flavor" or "artificial flavor" in just about every list of ingredients. The similarities between these two broad categories of flavor are far more significant than their differences. Both are man-made additives that give most processed food most of its taste. The initial purchase of a food item may be driven by its packaging or appearance, but subsequent purchases are determined mainly by its taste. About 90 percent of the money that Americans spend on food is used to buy processed food. But the canning, freezing, and dehydrating techniques used to process food destroy most of its flavor. Since the end of World War II, a vast industry has arisen in the United States to make processed food palatable. Without this flavor industry, today's fast food industry could not exist. The names of the leading American fast food chains and their best-selling menu items have become famous worldwide, embedded in our popular culture. Few people, however, can name the companies that manufacture fast food's taste.

SCHLOSSER, *FAST FOOD NATION*

©2007 Pearson Education, Inc.

| Exercise 1 | **Recall and Discuss** |

Based on Reading 1, Schlosser's "Oh, the Flavor of Your Fries," answer the following questions and prepare to discuss them with your classmates.

1. What gave McDonald's french fries their unique flavor before 1990?

_____

2. What gives McDonald's french fries their flavor now?

_____

3. What kinds of foods have "natural flavor" or "artificial flavor" listed as ingredients? Check your cabinets and list the foods that you find that have those ingredients.

_____

_____

4. Where do you think the "natural" and "artificial" flavors come from?

_____

_____

5. What is your favorite food? What food do you most dislike?

_____

6. What do you think of fast-food restaurants? How often do you eat fast food? Explain your answer.

_____

7. What are your eating habits? Do you usually eat with other people or alone? Do you eat quickly or slowly? At home or out? Explain your answers.

_____

TOPICS AND MAIN IDEAS

As a college reader, you need to be able to identify topics and main ideas in the information you read. In this chapter, you will practice these skills in a variety of readings and identify topics as well as stated and unstated main ideas in paragraphs and longer passages.

topic Subject of a reading; answers the question "What is it about?"

Topics

When your instructors ask, "What is the **topic**?" of a paragraph or passage, they are asking, "What is it about?" You can usually state the answer in just a few key words. For example, read the following paragraph and decide what the topic is:

> The flavor industry is highly secretive. Its leading companies will not divulge the precise formulas of flavor compounds or the identities of clients. The secrecy is deemed essential for protecting the reputation of beloved brands. The fast food chains, understandably, would like the public to believe that the flavors of their food somehow originate in their restaurant kitchens, not in distant factories run by other firms. (Schlosser, *Fast Food Nation*)

If someone asked you what the topic of this reading was, you would readily say "the flavor industry." If you wanted to be more specific, you might say the topic is "the secrecy of the flavor industry." Usually, you express the topic of a paragraph or passage in a few words rather than a complete sentence.

Main Ideas

main idea Main point of the reading; a general statement about the topic

generalization Broad, general statement that covers all the important points about a topic

To answer the question "What is the **main idea**?" of a paragraph or longer reading, you must decide what **generalization** the writer is making about the topic. The main idea is a general statement that covers all the important points the author makes about the topic. For example, in the paragraph about the flavor industry, Schlosser's topic is the flavor industry—specifically, the secrecy of the flavor industry. What point is the author trying to make? Schlosser presents three facts about the topic:

1. Leading companies will not divulge the formulas of flavor compounds or the names of their clients.
2. Secrecy is deemed essential for protecting the reputation of beloved brands.
3. The fast-food chains would like the public to believe that the flavors of their food somehow originate in their restaurant kitchens, not in distant factories.

These facts support the main idea, which the author stated in the first sentence: "The flavor industry is highly secretive."

assertion Statement of an opinion or an argument for a particular understanding of the topic

The main idea can also be an **assertion** about or an interpretation of the topic, because some authors do more than present generalizations and supporting points. They take a stand, state an opinion, or argue for a particular understanding of their topics. Essays and editorials use main ideas this way. For example, a writer could focus a paragraph on the same topic—the secrecy of the flavor industry—with a much more argumentative edge, such as the following:

> The flavor industry should not be allowed to operate in secret. The formulas of flavor compounds as well as the identities of clients should be made public. People should know that the flavors of their food do not come from the restaurant kitchens but from factories run by other firms.

©2007 Pearson Education, Inc.

In this case, the point that the author wishes to make about the topic is stated in the first sentence: "The flavor industry should not be allowed to operate in secret."

To identify the topic and main idea in a reading, ask yourself the following questions:

1. What is the reading about? (Identify the topic.)
2. What is the general point that is being made about the topic? (Identify the main idea.)
3. Do all or most of the important ideas or information in the reading support the main idea you have identified?

Stated Main Ideas in Paragraphs

stated main idea
Main idea that clearly appears in a reading, often near the beginning

Often you may find a **stated main idea** in a passage. That is, you might find a sentence you can simply identify as the main idea. If a main idea is specifically stated in the paragraph, it is usually located near the beginning or the end. Less often, it appears in the middle of the paragraph. Remember to identify the topic of the reading first. The main idea is simply the point the author is making about the topic. If you have already completed a writing class, it may also help to think about the reading from the writer's viewpoint. Ask yourself which sentence in the paragraph tells you what the author believes about the topic. In your writing classes, you usually call the main idea sentence for a paragraph the **topic**

topic sentence
Name for a main idea sentence usually used in writing classes

sentence.

Read the following paragraph about the policy the federal government has set for labeling foods and its consequences:

> In a policy that's beneficial to flavor companies, the Food and Drug Administration does not require that they reveal all the chemicals in their additives as long as those chemicals are "generally regarded as safe" (GRAS). This policy means companies can keep their chemical flavor formulas secret. The fact that some flavor compounds have more ingredients than the food itself is kept hidden. The familiar phrase "artificial strawberry flavor" doesn't tell us about the chemical "magic" and manufacturing skill that can make a highly processed food taste like a strawberry. (Adapted from Schlosser, *Fast Food Nation*)

1. What is the topic of this paragraph? _____

_____

2. Underline the sentence that you think most clearly states the main idea in this paragraph.

Your answers are probably similar to these:

1. The topic is "policy regarding flavor formulas" or "labeling secrecy of flavor formulas."

2. You probably underlined the first sentence: "In a policy that's beneficial to flavor companies, the Food and Drug Administration does not require that they reveal all the chemicals in their additives as long as those chemicals are 'generally regarded as safe' (GRAS)."

The two examples we've looked at so far both have stated main ideas, and the main ideas are conveniently located at the beginning of the paragraphs. In expository writing—writing that explains—and the typical English essay, the main idea frequently appears at or near the beginning of the paragraph or in the opening paragraph. Sometimes, however, the writer waits until the end of the passage to present the main point. He or she may feel that presenting the details first will draw the reader to the same conclusions as the writer.

Read the following paragraph about International Flavors and Fragrances (IFF):

> In addition to being the world's largest flavor company, IFF manufactures the smell of six of the ten best-selling fine perfumes in the United States, including Estée Lauder's Beautiful, Clinique's Happy, Lancome's Trésor, and Calvin Klein's Eternity. It also makes the smell of household products such as deodorant, dishwashing detergent, bath soap, shampoo, furniture polish, and floor wax. . . . The basic science behind the scent of your shaving cream is the same as that governing the flavor of your TV dinner. (Schlosser, *Fast Food Nation*)

1. What is the topic of this paragraph? _____

_____

2. Underline the sentence that you think most clearly states the main idea in this paragraph.

Your answers are probably similar to these:

1. The topic is "flavors and scents manufactured by IFF" or "the science of scents and flavors."
2. You probably underlined the last sentence: "The basic science behind the scent of your shaving cream is the same as that governing the flavor of your TV dinner." Notice that the first and second sentences are examples that support this main idea.

Exercise 2   ### Identify Topics and Stated Main Ideas

Read the following paragraphs about food issues. For each paragraph, write the topic on the line provided, and then choose the sentence you think most clearly states the main idea.

1. The flavor industry is now huge and extremely profitable. According to Eric Schlosser, "It has annual revenues of about $1.4 billion. Approximately ten thousand new processed food products are introduced

©2007 Pearson Education, Inc.

every year in the United States. Almost all of them require flavor additives. . . . The latest flavor innovations and corporate realignments are heralded in publications such as *Food Chemical News, Food Engineering, Chemical Market Reporter,* and *Food Product Design.* The growth of IFF [International Flavors and Fragrances] has mirrored that of the flavor industry as a whole. IFF was formed in 1958, through the merger of two small companies. Its annual revenues have grown almost fifteen-fold since the early 1970s, and it now has manufacturing facilities in twenty countries." (Adapted from Schlosser, *Fast Food Nation*)

Topic: _____

Main idea:
a. The IFF was formed in 1958, through the merger of two small companies.
b. IFF's annual revenues have grown almost fifteenfold since the early 1970s, and it now has manufacturing facilities in twenty countries.
c. The flavor industry is now huge and extremely profitable.

2. Some of the most important advances in flavor manufacturing are now occurring in the field of biotechnology. Complex flavors are being made through fermentation, enzyme reactions, fungal cultures, and tissue cultures. All of the flavors being created through these methods—including the ones being synthesized by funguses—are considered natural flavors by the FDA. The new enzyme-based processes are responsible for extremely lifelike dairy flavors. One company now offers not just butter flavor, but also fresh creamy butter, cheesy butter, milky butter, savory melted butter, and super-concentrated butter flavor, in liquid or powder form. The development of new fermentation techniques, as well as new techniques for heating mixtures of sugar and amino acids, have led to the creation of much more realistic meat flavors. (Schlosser, *Fast Food Nation*)

Topic: _____

Main idea:
a. The new enzyme-based processes are responsible for extremely lifelike dairy flavors.
b. Some of the most important advances in flavor manufacturing are now occurring in the field of biotechnology.
c. The development of new fermentation techniques, as well as new techniques for heating mixtures of sugar and amino acids, have led to the creation of much more realistic meat flavors.

3. Other popular fast foods derive their flavor from unexpected sources. Wendy's Grilled Chicken Sandwich, for example, contains beef extracts. Burger King's BK Broiler Chicken Breast Patty contains "natural smoke flavor." A firm called Red Arrow Products Company specializes in smoke

flavor, which is added to barbecue sauces and processed meats. Red Arrow manufactures natural smoke flavor by charring sawdust and capturing the aroma chemicals released into the air. The smoke is captured in water and then bottled, so that other companies can sell food which seems to have been cooked over a fire. (Schlosser, *Fast Food Nation*)

Topic: _____

Main idea:
a. Other popular fast foods derive their flavor from unexpected sources.
b. The smoke is captured in water and then bottled, so that other companies can sell food which seems to have been cooked over a fire.
c. Wendy's Grilled Chicken Sandwich, for example, contains beef extracts.

4. The human craving for flavor has been . . . [an extremely important] force in history. Royal empires have been built, unexplored lands have been traversed, great religions and philosophies have been forever changed by the spice trade. In 1492 Christopher Columbus set sail to find seasoning. Today the influence of flavor in the world marketplace is no less decisive. The rise and fall of corporate empires—of soft drink companies, snack food companies, and fast food chains—is frequently determined by how their products taste. (Schlosser, *Fast Food Nation*)

Topic: _____

Main idea:
a. In 1492 Christopher Columbus set sail to find seasoning.
b. The human craving for flavor has been [an extremely important] force in history.
c. The rise and fall of corporate empires is frequently determined by how their products taste.

5. Although flavors usually arise from a mixture of many different volatile chemicals, a single compound often supplies the dominant aroma. Smelled alone, that chemical provides an unmistakable sense of the food. Ethyl-2-methyl butyrate, for example, smells just like an apple. Today's highly processed foods offer a blank palette: whatever chemicals you add to them will give them specific tastes. Adding methyl-2-peridylketone makes something taste like popcorn. Adding ethyl-3-hydroxybutanoate makes it taste like marshmallow. The possibilities are now almost limitless. Without affecting the appearance or nutritional value, processed foods could even be made with aroma chemicals such as hexanal (the smell of freshly cut grass) or 3-methyl butanoic acid (the smell of body odor). (Schlosser, *Fast Food Nation*)

Topic: _____

©2007 Pearson Education, Inc.

Main idea:

a. Although flavors usually arise from a mixture of many different volatile chemicals, a single compound often supplies the dominant aroma and provides an unmistakable sense of the food.

b. Processed foods could even be made with aroma chemicals such as hexanal (the smell of freshly cut grass) or 3-methyl butanoic acid (the smell of body odor).

c. Adding methyl-2-peridylketone makes something taste like popcorn.

Exercise 3   ## Work with Words

Use context clues, dictionary skills, and your knowledge of word parts to determine the meaning of each italicized word in the following sentences from the paragraphs in Exercise 2. Write the meaning of the word on the lines provided. The paragraph number is provided in case you want to check the context.

1. The flavor industry is now huge and extremely profitable. According to Eric Schlosser, "It has annual *revenues* of about $1.4 billion." (par. 1)

   Revenues: _____

2. The latest flavor *innovations* and corporate *realignments* are heralded in publications such as *Food Chemical News, Food Engineering, Chemical Market Reporter, and Food Product Design.* (par. 1)

   Innovation: _____

3. *Realignment:* _____

4. Complex flavors are being made through *fermentation,* enzyme reactions, fungal cultures, and tissue cultures. (par. 2)

   Fermentation: _____

5. All of the flavors being created through these methods—including the ones being *synthesized* by funguses—are considered natural flavors by the FDA. (par. 2)

   Synthesize: _____

6. Wendy's Grilled Chicken Sandwich, for example, contains beef *extracts.* (par. 3)

   Extracts: _____

7. Red Arrow manufactures natural smoke flavor by *charring* sawdust and capturing the aroma chemicals released into the air. (par. 3)

   Charring: _____

8. Royal empires have been built, unexplored lands have been *traversed*, great religions and philosophies have been forever changed by the spice trade. (par. 4)

Traversed: _____

9. *Ethyl-2-methyl butyrate,* for example, smells just like an apple. (par. 5)

Ethyl-2-methyl butyrate: _____

10. Without affecting the appearance or nutritional value, processed foods could even be made with *aroma chemicals* such as hexanal (the smell of freshly cut grass) or 3-methyl butanoic acid (the smell of body odor). (par. 5)

Aroma chemicals: _____

◆

Restating Main Ideas

One valuable way to check your understanding of a main idea is to try to write it in your own words. Can you explain to a friend or fellow student the point the author is trying to make? If the instructor in a history or biology class rewords an important idea in a test question, will you immediately recognize it and be able to answer the question correctly? We retain information more easily if we can "translate" it into terms that connect with what we already know.

Many college assignments in other classes require you to restate main idea sentences in your own words. For example, the stated main idea for paragraph 1 in Exercise 2 was "The flavor industry is now huge and extremely profitable." You could restate it as "The flavor industry makes a lot of money and has grown tremendously."

Notice that the restated main idea is written as a complete sentence. A topic is written in only a few words or a single phrase, but a main idea has to be expressed as a complete thought about the topic.

Exercise 4   ## Restate Main Ideas

Restate the following main idea sentences (from Exercise 2) in your own words.

1. Some of the most important advances in flavor manufacturing are now occurring in the field of biotechnology.

_____

_____

2. Popular fast foods derive their flavor from unexpected sources.

_____

_____

©2007 Pearson Education, Inc.

3. The human craving for flavor has been an extremely important force in history.

_____

_____

4. Although flavors usually arise from a mixture of many different volatile chemicals, a single compound often supplies the dominant aroma and provides an unmistakable sense of the food.

_____

_____

◆

Implied Main Ideas in Paragraphs

Sometimes the main idea is not directly stated in a paragraph. But all of the ideas in the reading add up to a general point that the writer wants you to understand. In this case, the **main idea** is **implied**. Whether the main idea is stated or implied, you can construct a main idea sentence based on the wording of the topic that you have identified.

implied main idea
Main idea that is suggested but not specifically stated by a reading

For example, read the following paragraph about the vegetarian diet:

> Studies show that vegetarians' cholesterol levels are low, and vegetarians are seldom overweight. As a result, they're less apt to be candidates for heart disease than those who consume large quantities of meat. Vegetarians also have lower incidences of breast, colon, and prostate cancer; high blood pressure; and osteoporosis. When combined with exercise and stress reduction, vegetarian diets have led to reductions in the buildup of harmful plaque within the blood vessels of the heart. (Hales, _An Invitation to Health_)

What is the topic? You probably decided "vegetarians' health or the benefits of a vegetarian diet." You need to ask, "What is the point the author is trying to make about this topic? What is the main idea?" You might say that her overall point is, "The vegetarian diet is beneficial." Or, if you wanted to be more specific, you might say, "The vegetarian diet has a variety of proven health benefits."

Exercise 5   ## Identify Implied Main Ideas

Read the following paragraphs about food. For each paragraph, write the topic on the line provided, and then select the best statement of the main idea from the choices given. The first one has been done for you.

1. A meal at a fast-food restaurant may contain one-half of the calories that you should eat in a day. It easily costs twice the price of preparing a meal at home. It usually has an exceedingly high level of additives,

such as salt, sugar, and chemical flavor enhancers. At the same time, it is low in nutritional value. According to Dianne Hales, in the health text *An Invitation to Health*, "A Burger King Whopper with cheese contains 723 calories and 48 grams of fat, 18 grams from saturated fat. A McDonald's Sausage McMuffin with egg has 517 calories and 33 grams of fat, 13 grams from saturated fat." In response to criticisms from the public, many fast-food chains have stopped using beef tallow or lard and now use vegetable oils. The fat content, however, remains the same. (Adapted from Hales, *An Invitation to Health*)

Topic: *disadvantages of fast food*

Main idea:
a. Fast-food chains have stopped using beef tallow or lard and now use vegetable oils.
b. Burger King Whoppers are extremely high in fat content.
ⓒ The food at fast-food restaurants is not healthy.

The best statement of the main idea is c. Although choices a and b state important facts from the paragraph, neither one is general enough to be the main idea.

2. Sodium and calcium propionate, sodium benzoate, potassium sorbate, and sulfur dioxide are food additives that prevent the growth of bacteria, yeast, and mold in baked goods. BHA (butylated hydroxyanisole), BHT (butylated hydroxytoluene), propyl gallate, and vitamin E protect against the oxidation of fats (rancidity). Other helpful additives include leavening agents, emulsifiers, stabilizers, thickeners, dough conditioners, and bleaching agents. (Adapted from Hales, *An Invitation to Health*)

Topic: _____

Main idea:
a. Some helpful additives include leavening agents, emulsifiers, and stabilizers.
b. Many additives are helpful.
c. BHA and BHT protect against fats becoming rancid.

3. Nitrites—additives used in bacon and lunch meats—add color and inhibit spoilage, but they have been identified as contributing to the development of cancer. Sulfites—additives used to prevent food such as dried apricots from turning brown—can cause severe allergic reactions. (Adapted from Hales, *An Invitation to Health*)

Topic: _____

Main idea:
a. Nitrites can cause cancer.
b. Sulfites can cause allergic reactions.
c. Some additives, such as nitrites and sulfites, pose health risks.

©2007 Pearson Education, Inc.

4. From 1859 until 1875, the annual per capita consumption of raw sugar in the United States had varied from a low of 18.6 pounds (during the Civil War) to a high of 42.6 pounds. By 1898, the year of the Spanish-American War, it had risen to 65.4 pounds per person per year. But ten years later, the figure was over 86 pounds or nearly four ounces daily. The consumption of *sucrose*—processed sugar from cane and beet—reached around 115 pounds in the 1920s; but the present-day consumption of *all* processed sugars in the United States is higher than that. In the last three decades, and due as much to political changes as anything else, a corn sweetener called high-fructose corn syrup has captured an important portion of the sweetener market. (Mintz, "Pleasure, Profit, and Satiation")

Topic: _____

Main idea:
a. Because of political pressures, corn sweeteners have captured an important portion of the sweetener market.
b. From 1859 until 1875, the annual per capita consumption of raw sugar in the United States went from a low of 18.6 pounds to a high of 42.6 pounds.
c. The consumption of sugar per person in the United States increased steadily from 1859 to the present.

5. The statistics about food additive consumption in the United States are interesting. The average American consumes over 140 pounds of sweeteners every year. We eat over 15 pounds of table salt. And by eating processed and fast-foods, we also put a number of chemicals in our bodies that we are not at all aware of—between 5 to 10 pounds. (Adapted from Hales, *An Invitation to Health*)

Topic: _____

Main idea:
a. We eat a huge quantity of additives, especially if we include the sugar and salt.
b. We eat between five and ten pounds of chemicals per year that we are not aware of.
c. The average American consumes over 140 pounds of sweeteners every year.

6. Because calcium intake is so important throughout life for maintaining a strong bone structure, it is critical that you consume the minimum required amounts each day. Over half of our calcium intake usually comes from milk, one of the highest sources of dietary calcium. New, calcium-fortified orange juice provides a good way to get calcium if you are not a milk drinker. Many green, leafy vegetables are good sources of calcium, but some contain oxalic acid, which makes their calcium harder to absorb. Spinach, chard, and beet greens are not particularly good sources of calcium, whereas broccoli, cauliflower, and many peas and

beans offer good supplies (pinto beans and soybeans are among the best). Many nuts, particularly almonds, brazil nuts, and hazelnuts, and seeds such as sunflower and sesame contain good amounts of calcium. Molasses is fairly high in calcium. Some fruits—such as citrus fruits, figs, raisins, and dried apricots—have moderate amounts. (Donatelle, *Access to Health*)

Topic: _____

Main idea:
a. Calcium intake is important for maintaining a strong bone structure.
b. Fortified orange juice is a new way to get your calcium.
c. There are many good food sources of calcium.

7. The Spaniards gave the name "pepper" (pimienta) to the hot-tasting capsicums (called chili peppers today) they found in Mexico. But the "pepper" they were looking for was in Asia, not the newly found continent of America. Chili peppers, which can be various sizes, colors, and shapes, are used to flavor foods. They can be blistery hot, used for chili powder or cayenne pepper. They can be an ingredient in mild Tabasco sauce and are frequently added directly to a variety of bean and meat dishes. Bell peppers—green, yellow, or red—are often used in salads. And some types of bell peppers make the mild spice called paprika which is not hot at all. (Johnson, "Peppers")

Topic: _____

Main idea:
a. The Spaniards mistakenly called capsicums peppers, or pimientas, when they discovered them in Mexico.
b. Chili peppers come in a variety of forms and are used in many different ways to flavor food.
c. The "pepper" that the Spaniards were looking for was not in America but in Asia.

8. Food can also bestow powerful feelings of comfort in times of need and create a sense of community and togetherness. In many ways, food is important in our culture. It can be beautiful to look at, have a delicious smell, and offer exquisite tastes—whether the item in hand is a perfectly seared sirloin steak or a carne asada burrito dripping with freshly made guacamole. In our diverse culture, we have special foods for holidays, such as hard-boiled eggs at Easter and turkey with cranberry sauce at Thanksgiving, as well as ethnic specialties like *tamales* (Mexican and Central American), *pasteles* (Puerto Rican), and dishes made with sticky rice (Chinese and Southeast Asian). An important symbolic gesture in times of war can be seen in food drops—with the attacking country showering the civilians, caught between warring interests, with meals (as the United States did in Afghanistan in 2001 and 2002). And one way many people in the United States show their charity is by participating

©2007 Pearson Education, Inc.

in meal programs such as Meals-On-Wheels, which delivers food to housebound folks, or soup kitchens, which provide meals for homeless or hungry people. (Mayhew, "Easy Bake Ovens and Fashion Magazines")

Topic: _____

Main idea:
a. Holiday foods are important to people of all cultures.
b. In many ways, food is important in culture.
c. An important symbolic gesture in times of war can be seen in food drops—with the attacking country showering the civilians, caught between warring interests, with meals.

9. The average American eats fast food or highly processed foods several times a week—an eating habit that in many ways is symptomatic of our lifestyle: we are in a hurry. At the same time, fast-food restaurants are now opening in countries all over the world. Many people, however, are not happy with the trend toward eating quickly and rushing through life. In reaction to this tendency, the Slow Food Movement has begun. The principles of the Slow Food Movement are simple. Its 65,000 members from 42 different countries believe it is important to take the time to enjoy life, and part of that enjoyment comes from spending hours working together preparing family meals and eating together leisurely. They advocate opposing the spread of American fast-food outlets and the growth of supermarkets. They support local farmers and food producers, and they believe that it is healthier to eat organic foods. The movement—perhaps led by their Italian members—advocates the consumption of excellent local wines. (Roberta Alexander)

Topic: _____

Main idea:
a. In response to the growth of the fast-food industry, people around the world have organized the Slow Food Movement, whose principles are to support the local production of food and to take the time to cook and enjoy healthy food together.
b. The Slow Food Movement has demonstrated its importance and its popular success by recruiting 65,000 members in 42 countries.
c. The average American eats fast food or highly processed foods several times a week—an eating habit that in many ways is symptomatic of our lifestyle: We are in a hurry.

10. In 1998, products made of Olean (also known by its generic name, olestra), the first calorie-free fat replacement ingredient that can be used to fry foods, entered the national marketplace. Because the ingredients of Olean are processed in a special way, the body doesn't break them down and so Olean doesn't add fat or calories to foods. On the basis of more than 150 research studies, the FDA [Food and Drug Administration] approved Olean for use in savory snacks, such as chips and crackers, and many medical organizations, including the American

Dietetic Association, have supported its use as one way to reduce fat and calories in the diet. However, some participants in early tests have reported gastrointestinal side effects, and consumer advocacy groups, such as the Center for Science in the Public Interest, have warned that fat replacement products may pose potential risks that could outweigh their benefits. (Hales, *An Invitation to Health*)

Topic: _____

Main idea:
a. There is disagreement about the health benefits and risks of Olean, the calorie-free fat replacement.
b. Olean lets you enjoy the flavor without consuming the calories of fat.
c. Fat replacement products are risky.

Exercise 6   ## Identify Stated and Implied Main Ideas

Read the following paragraphs about eating disorders taken from a variety of college textbooks. For each paragraph, write the topic on the line provided, and then select the best statement of the main idea from the choices given. Finally, to check your understanding, rewrite the main idea in your own words on the lines provided. The first one has been done for you.

1. When I was in high school, female figures that can only be described as well-rounded were in vogue. Beginning in the mid-1960s, however, this standard of beauty changed drastically, shifting toward a much slimmer shape. Puzzling as this is to me personally, the "thin is beautiful" image has persisted and is emphasized over and over again by television, films, and magazines. Despite this fact, a growing proportion of adults in the United States and other countries are actually overweight. . . . Given this increasing gap between physical reality and the image of personal beauty portrayed by the mass media, it is not surprising that feeding and eating disorders—disturbances in eating behavior that involve maladaptive and unhealthy efforts to control body weight—are increasingly common. . . . In addition, the trend in recent decades has been for these disturbing disorders to start at earlier and earlier ages—as young as age eight (Nietzel et al., 1998). (Baron, *Psychology*)

Topic: *beauty standards and eating disorders*

Main idea:
a. When I was in high school, female figures that can only be described as well-rounded were in vogue.
b. While the media sends the "thin is beautiful" message, many adults in the United States are overweight, so it is no surprise that eating disorders are becoming more common.
c. The trend in recent decades has been for disturbing eating disorders to start at earlier and earlier ages.

©2007 Pearson Education, Inc.

The main idea in your own words: *One cause of eating disorders is the difference between increasingly overweight Americans and the "thin is beautiful" image they see in the media.*

2. Anorexia nervosa involves an intense and excessive fear of gaining weight coupled with refusal to maintain a normal body weight. In other words, people with this disorder relentlessly pursue the goal of being thin, no matter what this does to their health. They often have distorted perceptions of their own bodies, believing that they are much heavier than they really are. As a result of such fears and distorted perceptions, they starve themselves to the point where their weight drops to danger- ously low levels. (Baron, *Psychology*)

Topic: _____

Main idea:
a. People with anorexia nervosa have an excessive fear of gaining weight.
b. Because they have distorted perceptions of their own bodies, peo- ple with anorexia nervosa try to be excessively thin, no matter what it does to their health.
c. People with anorexia nervosa often have distorted perceptions of their own bodies, believing that they are much heavier than they really are.

The main idea in your words: _____

_____

3. Why do persons with this disorder have such an intense fear of becom- ing fat? Important clues are provided by the fact that anorexia nervosa is far more common among females than males. This has led re- searchers to propose that because many societies emphasize physical attractiveness for females far more than for males, adolescents and young women feel tremendous pressure to live up to the images of beauty shown in the mass media—to be as thin as the models who are held up as paragons of female desirability. If they are not this thin, they reason, they will be viewed as unattractive. Actually, such assumptions appear to be false: Research findings indicate that few men prefer the extremely thin figures that anorexics believe men admire (e.g., Williamson, Cubic, & Gleaves, 1993); rather, men find a fuller-figured, more rounded appearance much more attractive. (Baron, *Psychology*)

Topic: _____

Main idea:
a. Researchers propose that anorexia is more common among fe- males because many societies emphasize physical attractiveness for women, and the media (television, magazines, etc.) define "at- tractive" as thin.

b. Actually, few men prefer the extremely thin figures that anorexics believe men admire.
c. Anorexics believe that if they are not extremely thin, they will be viewed as unattractive.

The main idea in your own words: _____

_____

_____

4. If you found anorexia nervosa disturbing, you may find a second eating disorder, bulimia nervosa, even more unsettling. In this disorder individuals engage in recurrent episodes of binge eating—eating huge amounts of food within short periods of time—followed by some kind of compensatory behavior designed to prevent weight gain. This can involve self-induced vomiting, the misuse of laxatives, fasting, or exercise so excessive that it is potentially harmful to the person's health. Amazing as it may seem, persons suffering from bulimia nervosa—again, mainly young women—report purging about twelve times per week, and many purge even more often than this. My daughter once had a roommate who was a recovered bulimic. She was no longer trapped in the binge-purge cycle and was of normal weight, as are most bulimics; but her repeated binge-purge cycles had done permanent harm to her digestive system, and she had to stick to a bland diet of boiled or steamed foods. (Baron, *Psychology*)

Topic: _____

Main idea:
a. Bulimia nervosa—an eating disorder that involves binge eating and then purging to prevent weight gain—can lead to permanent health problems.
b. Purging can involve self-induced vomiting, the misuse of laxatives, fasting, or exercise so excessive that it is potentially harmful to the person's health.
c. Persons suffering from bulimia nervosa report purging about twelve times per week or even more often.

The main idea in your own words: _____

_____

_____

5. Does binge eating have a biochemical basis? It has been suggested that both binge eaters—people who go through episodes of overindulgence in food—and bulimics tend to crave and binge on sugars and starchy foods—that is, simple carbohydrates. Laboratory animals have been observed to overeat and become obese when offered highly palatable foods that are high in sugar and fat and low in fiber, and perhaps the same is true with some humans. A possible explanation is that simple

©2007 Pearson Education, Inc.

carbohydrates elevate the level of the brain chemical serotonin, which affects mood and emotion and which may be low in compulsive overeaters and bulimics. In other words, people with eating disorders may be self-medicating themselves against depression by responding to carbohydrate cravings. (Williams and Knight, *Healthy for Life*)

Topic: _____

Main idea:
a. Laboratory animals have been observed to overeat and become obese when offered highly palatable foods that are high in sugar and fat and low in fiber, and perhaps the same is true with some humans.
b. Simple carbohydrates elevate the level of the brain chemical serotonin.
c. Binge eating may have a biochemical basis.

The main idea in your own words: _____

_____

6. Because anorexics frequently deny their symptoms, there is often powerful resistance to treatment. With therapy, about 70% of patients recover or are improved. Unfortunately, the disease may be fatal for those who are not able to seek treatment or don't respond to treatment. Clearly, an important goal of treatment is to improve nutrition. Other therapies include psychotherapy and behavior therapy to control food-consumption behavior. Some drug therapy has been successful, including the use of antidepressants and antipsychotic drugs. (Williams and Knight, *Healthy for Life*)

Topic: _____

Main idea:
a. The goal of treatment for anorexics is to improve nutrition.
b. It is important for anorexics to get treatment, and several options are available, although anorexics often resist treatment.
c. Therapies include psychotherapy and behavior therapy to control food-consumption behavior.

The main idea in your own words: _____

_____

Exercise 7   **Work with Words**

Use context clues, dictionary skills, and your knowledge of word parts to determine the meaning of each italicized word in the following sentences from the paragraphs in Exercise 6. Write the meaning of the word on the lines provided. The paragraph number is provided in case you want to check the context.

1. Puzzling as this is to me personally, the "thin is beautiful" image has *persisted* and is emphasized over and over again by television, films, and magazines. (par. 1)

   Persisted: _____

2. Given this increasing gap between physical reality and the image of personal beauty portrayed by the mass media, it is not surprising that *feeding and eating disorders*—disturbances in eating behavior that involve . . . unhealthy efforts to control body weight—are increasingly common. (par. 1)

   Feeding and eating disorders: _____

   _____

3. In other words, people with this disorder *relentlessly* pursue the goal of being thin, no matter what this does to their health. (par. 2)

   Relentlessly: _____

4. As a result of such fears and *distorted perceptions,* they starve themselves to the point where their weight drops to dangerously low levels. (par. 2)

   Distorted perceptions: _____

   _____

5. This has led researchers to propose that because many societies emphasize physical attractiveness for females far more than for males, adolescents and young women feel tremendous pressure to live up to the images of beauty shown in the mass media—to be as thin as the models who are held up as *paragons* of female desirability. (par. 3)

   Paragons: _____

6. [Bulimia nervosa] can involve self-induced vomiting, the misuse of laxatives, fasting, or exercise so excessive that it is potentially harmful to the person's health. Amazing as it may seem, persons suffering from bulimia nervosa—again, mainly young women—report *purging* about twelve times per week, and many purge even more often than this. (par. 4)

   Purging: _____

7. Laboratory animals have been observed to overeat and become *obese* when offered highly *palatable* foods that are high in sugar and fat and low in fiber, and perhaps the same is true with some humans. (par. 5)

   Obese: _____

8. *Palatable:* _____

©2007 Pearson Education, Inc.

9. A possible explanation is that simple carbohydrates elevate the level of the brain chemical *serotonin,* which affects mood and emotion and which may be low in compulsive overeaters and bulimics. (par. 5)

Serotonin: _____

10. Some drug therapy has been successful, including the use of *antidepressants* and antipsychotic drugs. (par. 6)

Antidepressants: _____

$\blacklozenge$

Main Ideas in Short Passages

Sometimes the main idea is not presented in a single paragraph but across two or more connected paragraphs that are unified around one idea. For short passages, titles and subheads can often help you identify the topic and main idea.

Read the following passage, and then select the best topic and main idea from the choices given. Remember, consider the information in both paragraphs as you make your selections.

Corn
Corn is the staple of the U.S. diet. Most of the American diet is affected by corn, although few Americans fully recognize its pervasiveness. In addition to being a vegetable, corn (in one form or another) appears in soft drinks, canned foods, candy, condensed milk, baby food, jams, instant coffee, instant potatoes, and soup, among other things.

Among the many colors of corn, only the yellow and white varieties are defined as edible in the dominant U.S. culture; the more exotic colors (blue, green, orange, black, and red) are considered fit only for decoration at Thanksgiving time (although blue corn chips and other blue corn products have become available in gourmet food stores and trendy restaurants). One might speculate that this arbitrary preference for some colors of corn reflects the early American immigrants' rejection of the "exotic" elements of Native American cultures. (Ferrante, *Sociology*)

What is the best topic for this passage?

a. corn in the United States
b. colors of corn
c. immigrants and corn

The best choice is "a" because both paragraphs deal with corn in the United States. What is the best main idea for this passage?

a. Americans prefer certain colors of corn because the early settlers rejected "exotic" elements of Native American culture.
b. Corn is pervasive in the American diet, and our preferences in types of corn may reflect the preferences of early American immigrants.
c. Corn is the staple of the U.S. diet.

The best choice is "b" because it covers the information in both paragraphs. The first paragraph deals with how pervasive corn is in the American diet, but the second paragraph is about the types and colors of corn and speculates about why we prefer certain varieties. Both ideas are included in "b."

Exercise 8   ## Identify Topics and Main Ideas in Short Passages

Read the following passages about food. For each passage, choose the best topic and main idea. Then write the main idea in your own words on the lines provided.

1. **Water, an Essential Part of Your Food and Your Body**

Water is the major component in both foods and the human body: You are composed of about 60% water. Your need for other nutrients, in terms of weight, is much less than your need for water. You can live up to 50 days without food, but only a few days without water.

Water is distributed all over the body, among lean and other tissues and in blood and other body fluids. Water is used in the digestion and absorption of food and is the medium in which most of the chemical reactions take place within the body. Some water-based fluids like blood transport substances around the body, while other fluids serve as lubricants or cushions. Water also helps regulate body temperature.

Water is contained in almost all foods, particularly in liquids, fruits, and vegetables. The foods and fluids you consume provide 80-90% of your daily water intake; the remainder is generated through metabolism. You lose water each day in urine, feces, and sweat and through evaporation from your lungs. To maintain a balance between water consumed and water lost, you need to take in about 1 milliliter of water for each calorie you burn—about 2 liters, or 8 cups, of fluid per day—more if you live in a hot climate or engage in vigorous exercise. Many Americans fall short of this recommended intake. (Insel et al., *Core Concepts in Health*)

Topic:
a. water in the human body and in food
b. dehydration
c. water in the human body

Main idea:
a. Water is distributed all over the body, among lean and other tissues and in blood and other body fluids.
b. Water is the major component in foods and the human body, and it is essential to get enough water to be healthy.
c. You are composed of about 60 percent water.

The main idea in your own words: _____

_____

©2007 Pearson Education, Inc.

2. **Immigrants and Food**

Early in the 1900s, as America struggled to digest yet another wave of immigrants, a social worker paid a visit to an Italian family recently settled in Boston. In most ways, the newcomers seemed to have taken to their new home, language, and culture. There was, however, one troubling sign. "Still eating spaghetti," the social worker noted. "Not yet assimilated." Absurd as that conclusion seems now—especially in this era of pasta—it aptly illustrates our long-standing faith in a link between eating and identity. Anxious to Americanize immigrants quickly, U.S. officials saw food as a critical psychological bridge between newcomers and their old culture—and as a barrier to assimilation.

Many immigrants, for example, did not share Americans' faith in large, hearty breakfasts, preferring bread and coffee. Worse, they used garlic and other spices, and mixed their foods, often preparing an entire meal in a single pot. Break these habits, get them to eat like Americans—to partake in the meat-heavy, superabundant U.S. diet—and, the theory confidently held, you'd have them thinking, acting, and feeling like Americans in no time. (Roberts, "How Americans Eat")

Topic:
a. spaghetti and Italian immigrants in the early 1900s
b. immigrants' preferences for breakfast
c. immigrants and food in the early 1900s

Main idea:
a. Italian immigrants were still eating spaghetti and garlic in the early 1900s.
b. It was believed that if you could get immigrants to eat like Americans, you could get them to think, act, and feel like Americans.
c. Many immigrants did not share Americans' faith in large, hearty breakfasts, preferring bread and coffee.

◆

Main Ideas and Thesis Statements in Long Passages

You've already identified main ideas in paragraphs and short passages. You can use the same skills when reading essays, short articles, and long excerpts from textbooks. Essays often have a persuasive, assertive, or even argumentative main idea. In such cases, the main idea is called a **thesis statement**. A thesis statement is the main idea in a longer piece of writing, particularly an essay. Unlike the main idea of an article or a section of a textbook, which is usually based on facts and data, the thesis statement of an essay may be based on arguments and interpretations of information, events, or ideas. A longer piece of writing may contain several paragraphs or combinations of paragraphs, each of which has a main idea. All the main ideas combine to form the thesis statement of the entire article or essay. Whether you are identifying the main idea of a paragraph or looking for the thesis of an essay, the process is the same.

thesis statement
Main idea in a long piece of writing, especially an essay, often intended to state an argument

Remember to consider the title when you are trying to determine the author's thesis. Frequently, the title itself gives you the clues you need to determine the thesis.

Identify Thesis Statements in Long Passages

Read the following article by Rachel Garrett. In it, she discusses the misleading food labeling in the United States compared with the labeling in other countries. Then choose the best topic and thesis statement, and write the thesis statement in your own words on the lines provided.

Reading the Labels

When I shop, I rely on the nutrition information and the list of ingredients to tell me exactly what I'm getting. In certain countries, like Britain and Thailand, manufacturers are required to state the exact percentages of each ingredient.[1] This makes it easier for consumers to determine more accurately what's in the food they're buying. In the United States, on the other hand, food manufacturers are required only to list the ingredients in order from highest to lowest percentage. This sometimes makes it difficult to tell exactly how much of any given ingredient is really in the package. Also, it's easy to form an inaccurate impression of a food's ingredients from the larger design of the label. Sometimes certain words are emphasized, and other words—like "artificially flavored"—are barely visible. Also, pictures often misrepresent what's in the package. During a recent trip to the grocery store, I found a number of examples of this technically accurate but deliberately misleading packaging.

First up was a cup of Maruchan Instant Lunch Ramen Noodles with Vegetables. When I opened it (after paying for and taking it home, of course), I found very few vegetables. The ingredients label says there are carrots, garlic, and onions. But I found less than half a teaspoon of freeze-dried carrots, and the five green flecks are a far cry from the seventeen fresh-looking scallions on the box. "With chili piquin and shrimp," the box says. And indeed, the picture shows five shrimp and colorful red chilies. I found that there were only four shrimp (about half an inch across) in the whole container, and no sign of the chilies. Nissin Cup Noodles with Shrimp does not fare much better. The box features five plump shrimp along with an array of fresh peas and carrots. Inside, there were four freeze-dried shrimp even smaller than Maruchan's (three were less than half an inch across) and five sad-looking peas, split and cracked from the same freeze-drying process. There was also a third of a teaspoon of carrots.

In the same aisle, I found a box of Rice-a-Roni's Chicken and Broccoli. Below the large green box that says "Chicken and Broccoli," I noticed the word "Flavor"—but only because I was looking for it. It is in light brown lettering on a lighter brown background. In other words, I'm not getting a chicken and broccoli meal, I'm getting chicken and broccoli flavor. That is a big difference: There is more chicken fat, MSG, chicken broth, "natural flavors," and gelatin in this box than there is chicken.

In the juice section, Kerns All Nectar seems to be aiming for the "natural" look, with its colorful, fruit-covered cans and clean black and white lettering. I don't know what "All Nectar" means, but the Mango All Nectar says, in tiny lettering above the nutrition label, "Contains 20% Juice." The hummingbird hovering above those fresh mangoes on the can must be in for a nasty surprise. Instead of "nectar," which carries connotations of something naturally sweet, the poor bird will find mango puree concentrate in a solution of water and high fructose corn syrup. In fact, this product is distributed by Nestlé, a company I associate more with chocolate milk than healthy, natural fruit beverages. But it was not easy to find the Nestlé brand anywhere on the label. It's down at the bottom of the tiny print.

I found another healthy-sounding drink a few shelves down. Tropicana Twister Kinetic Kiwi Strawberry is covered with pictures of kiwi fruit and strawberries, which did lead me to believe those were significant ingredients. In fact, this beverage contains only 15 percent juice, most of which is made of pears and grapes. The main ingredients are, once again, water and high fructose corn syrup. The label says, "Now with FruitForce™ Energy Releasing B Vitamins Infused Into Bold Fruit Flavors For An Active Lifestyle!" This is a fancy way of saying that they added two B vitamins: niacin and pantothenic acid (they are the last two ingredients on the list). In the United States, herbal and dietary supplements must tell consumers that their claims are just that, claims. But because Tropicana Twister is a food and not a supplement, the label doesn't have to say, "This statement has not been evaluated by the FDA." I wonder what sort of "energy" is supposed to be released. Perhaps I would feel a "sugar rush" after drinking all that high fructose corn syrup, but medical science has not proved that B vitamins have a similar effect.

Kiwi Strawberry seems to be a popular flavor, and I was curious to see if I could find anything called "Kiwi Strawberry" in which there were real kiwi fruit and strawberries, with no other added flavors. I didn't find anything like that, but I did find TreeTop's Fruit Rocketz: Ztrawberry Kiwi. This is a fruit snack that comes in a tube. It doesn't require refrigeration or a spoon, which might make it appealing for school lunches. A regular apple would be a better—and cheaper—option. The tubes of fruit are covered with strawberries and kiwi fruit. So I expected to find strawberry or kiwi fruit at least among the ingredients. In fact, the three main ingredients are apples, high fructose corn syrup, and water, followed by "natural flavor" and Red 40 (food coloring). Essentially, I'm buying red-colored, artificially flavored applesauce.

Fed up with all the prepared food, I went to the baking aisle to see what sort of options are available if I wanted to step into the kitchen and make something myself. Betty Crocker's Blueberry Muffin Mix seems designed to let me do just that. "Blueberry" is the largest word on the label, but next to "Muffin Mix" I saw (in very thin pink letters on a red background), "Imitation Blueberries Artificially Flavored." Those delicious-looking muffins on the package are, in fact, full of "imitation blueberry nuggets" made of dextrose, soybean and cottonseed oil, bleached flour, cellulose gum, citric acid, and artificial colors and flavors. Among the other muffin ingredients is—surprise—dried corn syrup. (Garrett, "Reading the Labels")

Note

1. "Label Watch," *Nutrition Action Health Letter,* U.S. Edition, July/August 2001, Center for Science in the Public Interest, http://www.cspinet.org/ nah/ 07_01/ingredients.html (accessed September 2, 2005).

Topic:
a. U.S. consumers and labels
b. dishonest and misleading food labeling in the United States
c. more is less

Thesis statement:
a. Processed foods in the United States are of a poorer quality than processed foods in other countries such as Thailand and the United Kingdom.
b. There are many kinds of processed foods such as Maruchan Instant Lunch Ramen Noodles with Vegetables, Nissan Cup Noodles with Shrimp, Rice-a-Roni Chicken and Broccoli, and Kerns All Nectar.
c. The labeling of processed foods in the United States is often deliberately misleading and dishonest.

The thesis statement in your own words: _____

_____

_____

Exercise 10   ## Identify Thesis Statements in Long Passages

Read the following excerpt from an article about chocolate by Jim Spadaccina. In it he discusses some of the side effects of eating chocolate. See if you can identify the topic and the main idea of the reading—that is, the author's thesis statement. Then try writing the thesis statement in your own words.

The Sweet Lure of Chocolate

One of the most pleasant effects of eating chocolate is the "good feeling" that many people experience after indulging. Chocolate contains more than 300 known chemicals. Scientists have been working on isolating specific chemicals and chemical combinations which may explain some of the pleasurable effects of consuming chocolate.

©2007 Pearson Education, Inc.

Caffeine is the most well known of these chemical ingredients, and while it's present in chocolate, it can only be found in small quantities. Theobromine, a weak stimulant, is also present, in slightly higher amounts. The combination of these two chemicals (and possibly others) may provide the "lift" that chocolate eaters experience. Phenylethylamine is also found in chocolate. It's related to amphetamines, which are strong stimulants. All of these stimulants increase the activity of neurotransmitters (brain chemicals) in parts of the brain that control our ability to pay attention and stay alert.

While stimulants contribute to a temporary sense of well-being, there are other chemicals and other theories as to why chocolate makes us feel good. Perhaps the most controversial findings come from researchers at the Neurosciences Institute in San Diego, California. They believe that "chocolate contains pharmacologically active substances that have the same effect on the brain as marijuana, and that these chemicals may be responsible for certain drug-induced psychoses associated with chocolate craving." (Spadaccina, "The Sweet Lure of Chocolate")

Topic:
a. reasons for the good feeling when you eat chocolate
b. chocolate and marijuana
c. chocolate and stimulants

Thesis statement:
a. Chocolate contains more than 300 known chemicals.
b. Researchers say that the good feeling people get when they eat chocolate may be due to the stimulants and other chemicals in chocolate.
c. Stimulants increase the activity of neurotransmitters (brain chemicals) in parts of the brain that control our ability to pay attention and stay alert.

Write the thesis statement in your own words. _____

_____

Reading 2   *Food Pyramids: For Profit or Health?*

Paul Hursel

The following reading explores the background of the guidelines that Americans have been given for the past 30 years for healthy eating, and it presents some new information based on scientific research. As you read, think about the information you have received over the years about what is a healthy diet. Then consider how the new information contradicts some of the beliefs that we have held for so long. Examine the three food pyramids, analyze how they are different, and try to determine the reasons for those differences.

1   We are in the midst of a health-threatening obesity epidemic that started in the early 1980s and has been growing steadily. One out of two Americans is overweight, and one out of four Americans is obese. As a group, we have gained weight, and our rates of heart disease, cancer, and diabetes have continued to rise. We buy more food but eat less healthily than we did 35 years ago, and as our weight increases, our health declines. How did we get here?

Food Industry

2   A major player in our increasingly unhealthy eating habits is none other than the food industry itself. Compounding the general confusion about diets, the food industry spends $33 billion annually to promote its products, and most of this money is spent to get us to buy not just fast food but highly processed and elaborately packaged food. Seventy percent of this amount goes for advertising convenience foods, and only 2.2 percent goes for advertising fruits, grains, and vegetables, including beans. Food companies spend more than $11 billion on advertising in all the major media—newspapers, radio, television, and billboards. The other $22 billion goes toward coupons and discounted promotions.[1] But advertising is not the only trick under the belt of those who influence our eating habits.

3   Responding to the barrage of information about diets and health that we have been subjected to since the 1980s, the food industry has taken up the banner of promoting good health. In supermarket aisles across America, we find low-fat and low-carbohydrate frozen dinners, entire shelves dedicated to diet products, and an array of packaging that screams out, "Eat me. I'm healthy." Almost daily, new products are introduced and touted as "healthy," "low fat," "vitamin fortified," or "providing a day's worth of vitamins and minerals." The idea of adding fortification to products is not new. Iodine has been added to table salt since the 1830s to prevent iodine deficiencies. Vitamin D has been added to milk since 1931. Today, however, spraying vitamins and minerals onto Kellogg's Fruit Loops, Count Chocula Breakfast Cereal, and Gummy Bears candy demonstrates industry promotion gone cynical. Now we are supposed to feel good about giving our children these products—highly sweetened (essentially candy) breakfast cereals and candy itself—because they are "healthy" and a "nutritional part of a healthy diet."[2]

Problems with the USDA Food Guide Pyramid

4   Between 1992 and 1995, we studied and followed the United States Department of Agriculture (USDA) Food Guide Pyramid (see Figure 3.1). It appeared in chapters on nutrition in just about every high school or college textbook. It told us that all fats, oils, and sweets were the bad guys and should be eaten in very small quantities, which had been the official position of the U.S. government since 1977.[3] It also showed us that we should daily eat 2 to 3 servings of milk, yogurt, and cheese; 2 to 3 servings of meat, poultry, fish, dry beans, eggs, and nuts; 3 to 5 servings of vegetables; 2 to 4 servings of fruit; and a whopping 6 to 11 servings of bread, cereal, rice, and pasta.

©2007 Pearson Education, Inc.

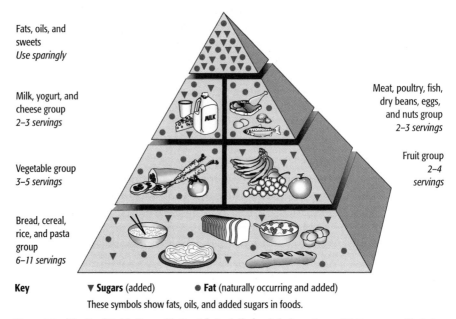

Fats, oils, and sweets
Use sparingly

Milk, yogurt, and cheese group
2–3 servings

Vegetable group
3–5 servings

Bread, cereal, rice, and pasta group
6–11 servings

Meat, poultry, fish, dry beans, eggs, and nuts group
2–3 servings

Fruit group
2–4 servings

Key   ▼ **Sugars** (added)   ● **Fat** (naturally occurring and added)
These symbols show fats, oils, and added sugars in foods.

Figure 3.1   The Food Guide Pyramid: A guide to daily food choices. Source: U.S. Department of Agriculture, Human Nutrition Information Service, "Food Guide Pyramid," *Home and Garden Bulletin* 249 (1992).

5   Some alarming reports started to come out, however. In spite of the hundreds of millions of dollars the government had spent on research trying to prove that a low-fat diet was the healthiest, there was no scientific proof that it worked.[4] Professor Walter C. Willett of Harvard Medical School criticized the old pyramid. He said it was supposed to give us the truth, but it was just plain wrong. He believed it was based on very shaky scientific evidence and that its misinformation actually contributed to "overweight, poor health, and unnecessary early deaths."[5]

Food Industry Lobby

6   Marion Nestle, chair of the Department of Nutrition and Food Studies at New York University, offers some insights. In the 1980s, she was hired to edit the *Surgeon General's Report on Nutrition and Health,* which was published in 1988. "My first day on the job," she reports, "I was given the rules: No matter what the research indicated, the report could not recommend 'eat less meat' as a way to reduce intake of saturated fat, nor could it suggest restrictions on intake of any other category of food. In the industry-friendly climate of the Reagan administration, the producers of foods that might be affected by such advice would complain to their beneficiaries in Congress, and the report would never be published."[6] Adding to the pressures put on policy development, the dietary guidelines are put out by the U.S. Department of Agriculture, whose primary role is to promote American agriculture; it is not a public health agency like the Department of Health and Human Services or the National Institutes of Health. So the problem

lies in an inherent contradiction: what's good for agribusiness isn't necessarily good for people who eat their food products. According to Willett, "Serving two masters is tricky business, especially when one of them includes persuasive and well-connected representatives of the formidable meat, dairy, and sugar industries." [7]

Harvard Medical School Healthy Eating Pyramid

7   As a spokesperson for Harvard Medical School, Willett responded to what he believed was wrong with the old Food Guide Pyramid by creating the Harvard Medical School Healthy Eating Pyramid, which he asserts is based on accumulated evidence, does not oversimplify recommendations, and does not kowtow to the big players in the food industry (see Figure 3.2). The only feature that is the same in both pyramids is the recommendation for vegetables and fruit. Refined carbohydrates (white rice, white bread, pasta), potatoes, and sweets are at the top of the pyramid along with red meat and butter—to be used sparingly. At the base of the pyramid are whole grain foods and plant oils.

The Scoop on Carbs

8   A significant change in the Harvard Medical School Healthy Eating Pyramid was the distinction made among the food groups that make up the

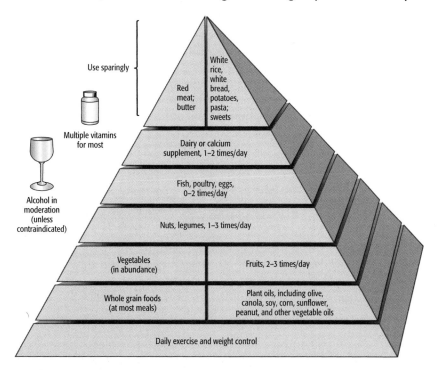

Figure 3.2   Healthy Eating Pyramid. Source: Walter C. Willett, MD, *Eat, Drink, and Be Healthy,* © 2001 by Simon and Schuster.

©2007 Pearson Education, Inc.

carbohydrates: the refined carbohydrates versus whole grains. Following the antifat dietary guidelines, Americans did reduce their intake of fat but replaced it with additional calories of refined carbohydrates. Since the late 1970s, we have increased our consumption of grains (usually refined) by almost 60 pounds per person and caloric sweeteners (primarily high-fructose corn syrup) by 30 pounds.[8] Now scientists hypothesize that the real culprit is not fat but the refined carbohydrates and sugars we have turned to in place of fat. First of all, fat gives us a full feeling, while carbohydrates with little fat in them leave us able to eat more, so we consume more calories just trying to get full. In addition, carbohydrates have an effect on insulin and blood sugar that was not factored into the USDA Food Guide Pyramid.

9   The oversimplification of the carbohydrate category in the Food Guide Pyramid was one example of the oversimplification of the pyramid as a whole. Another important category that needed to be revisited was fat. Research pointed to the need to distinguish between different types of fat. Simply put: (1) plant oils are generally good for you; (2) animal fat from red meat and milk have some disadvantages; but (3) transfats, which are present in most margarines, shortenings, partially hydrogenated vegetable oils, deep-fried chips, many fast foods, and most commercial baked goods, are bad for you in a variety of ways.[9]

The New USDA Pyramid and the Politics of Health Advice

10 Finally, in 2005, the USDA—in response to criticism from the medical community—came out with a new pyramid called "My Pyramid." This new pyramid (see Figure 3.3) is designed to be different for each individual, depending on age, sex, and level of physical activity. To find out what it recommends for you, you can go to the Web site (http://mypyramid.gov). Many of the new recommendations are excellent, especially the recommendations that

Figure 3.3   My Pyramid Plan. For an assessment of your food intake and physical activity, go to the MyPyramid.gov Web site. Source: MyPyramid.gov.

at least half of all the grains we eat should be whole grains, and people should engage in physical activity at least 30 minutes a day. The Web site even has links to the Harvard Medical School and School of Public Health.

11   Despite these improvements, Dr. Willett believes that the new pyramid still recommends too many dairy products and too much red meat. Why did it take so long for the Department of Agriculture to change its recommendations? Why, in the face of so much scientific evidence to the contrary, does its new pyramid still emphasize milk and deemphasize sources of protein other than red meat? The answer is clear: The powerful food industry continues to promote its products to the American consumer through undue influence on government.

Notes

1. Marion Nestle, *Food Politics* (Berkeley: University of California Press, 2002), 22.

2. Dana Canedy, "Is the Box Half-Full or Half-Empty?" *New York Times,* November 28, 1998.

3. This is the year that a Senate committee headed by George McGovern published its "Dietary Goals for the United States," which recommended that Americans drastically reduce their consumption of fat.

4. Gary Taubes, "What If It's All Been a Big Fat Lie?" *New York Times,* July 7, 2002.

5. Walter C. Willett, *Eat, Drink, and Be Healthy: The Harvard Medical School Guide to Healthy Eating* (New York: Simon and Schuster Fireside Books, 2001), 15–16.

6. Nestle, *Food Politics,* 3.

7. Willett, *Eat, Drink, and Be Healthy,* 21.

8. Taubes, "What If It's All Been a Big Fat Lie?" 7.

9. For a full discussion of fats, see Willett, *Eat, Drink, and Be Healthy,* chap. 4: "Surprising News about Fat."

HURSEL, "Food Pyramids"

Exercise 11   Work with Words

The following sentences appear in Reading 2, Hursel's "Food Pyramids: For Profit or Health?" Use context clues, dictionary skills, and your knowledge of word parts to determine the meaning of each italicized word in the sentences. Write the meaning of the word on the lines provided. The paragraph number is provided in case you want to check the context.

1. We are in the midst of a health-threatening obesity epidemic that started in the early 1980s and has been growing steadily. One out of two Americans is overweight, and one out of four Americans is *obese.* (par. 1)

Obese: _____

©2007 Pearson Education, Inc.

2. *Compounding* the general confusion about diets, the food industry spends $33 billion annually to promote its products, and most of this money is spent to get us to buy not just fast food but highly processed and elaborately packaged food. (par. 2)

Compounding: _____

3. Responding to the *barrage* of information about diets and health that we have been subjected to since the 1980s, the food industry has taken up the banner of promoting good health. (par. 3)

Barrage: _____

4. Almost daily, new products are introduced and *touted* as "healthy," "low fat," "vitamin fortified," or "providing a day's worth of vitamins and minerals." (par. 3)

Touted: _____

5. The idea of adding *fortification* to products is not new. Iodine has been added to table salt since the 1830s to prevent iodine deficiencies. (par. 3)

Fortification: _____

6. He believed it was based on very shaky scientific evidence and that its *misinformation* actually contributed to "overweight, poor health, and unnecessary early deaths." (par. 5)

Misinformation: _____

7. "In the industry-friendly climate of the Reagan administration, the producers of foods that might be affected by such advice would complain to their *beneficiaries* in Congress, and the report would never be published." (par. 6)

Beneficiaries: _____

8. So the problem lies in an *inherent* contradiction: what's good for *agribusiness* isn't necessarily good for people who eat their food products. (par. 6)

Inherent: _____

9. *Agribusiness:* _____

10. Willett, a spokesperson for Harvard Medical School, responded to what he believed was wrong with the Food Guide Pyramid by creating the Harvard Medical School Healthy Eating Pyramid, which he asserts is based on accumulated evidence, does not oversimplify recommendations, and does not *kowtow* to the big players in the food industry. (par. 7)

Kowtow: _____

Exercise 12   Identify Topics and Main Ideas

For each of the following paragraphs from Reading 2, choose the best topic and main idea statement. Then write the main idea in your own words on the lines provided.

1. Paragraph 1

   Topic:
   a. obesity epidemic and diets
   b. overwhelming number of diets
   c. obesity epidemic

   Main idea:
   a. One out of two Americans is overweight, and one out of four Americans is obese.
   b. We are in the midst of a health-threatening obesity epidemic.
   c. In recent decades, the incidence of diabetes has continued to rise.

   The main idea in your own words: _____

   _____

2. Paragraph 2

   Topic:
   a. food industry product development
   b. consumer expectations
   c. advertising for food industry products

   Main idea:
   a. Food companies spend more than $11 billion on advertising in newspapers, radio, television, and billboards.
   b. The food industry spends $33 billion annually to promote its products, and most of this money is spent to get us to buy not just fast food but highly processed and elaborately packaged food.
   c. Seventy percent of the advertising budget goes to advertising convenience foods, while only 2.2 percent goes for advertising fruits, grains, and vegetables, including beans.

   The main idea in your own words: _____

   _____

3. Paragraph 3

   Topic:
   a. availability of healthy food alternatives
   b. food industry promotions of so-called healthy food
   c. concern about food additives

©2007 Pearson Education, Inc.

Main idea:

a. The idea of adding fortification to products is not new.

b. Almost daily, new products are introduced and touted as "healthy," "low fat," "vitamin fortified," or "providing a day's worth of vitamins and minerals."

c. In response to a nationwide concern about eating healthily and avoiding fat, the food industry has launched products advertised as low fat, fortified, and healthy.

The main idea in your own words: _____

_____

4. Paragraph 5

Topic:

a. the Food Guide Pyramid

b. the misinformation of the Food Guide Pyramid

c. scientific proof for the Food Guide Pyramid

Main idea:

a. The USDA Food Guide Pyramid is supposed to offer straight talk that rises above the jungle of misinformation and contradictory claims.

b. The USDA Food Guide Pyramid is full of misinformation and scientifically unsound advice on what to eat.

c. Great gaps remain in biochemical knowledge about food safety, especially about the effect on the human body of chemicals interacting with one another.

The main idea in your own words: _____

_____

5. Paragraph 6

Topic:

a. the industry-friendly Reagan administration

b. feel-good dietary recommendations

c. food lobbies and bad government information

Main idea:

a. The powerful food industry pressures government agencies to distribute watered-down and incorrect information.

b. In the industry-friendly climate of the Reagan administration, the food producers that might be affected by nutritional advice would complain to their friends in Congress.

c. The USDA ended up putting out a positive, feel-good set of recommendations.

The main idea in your own words: _____

_____

Exercise 13   ## Check Your Understanding

Based on Reading 2, write your answers to the following questions.

1. What is the thesis statement for Reading 2?

_____

_____

_____

_____

_____

2. What examples does the author give to demonstrate that the food industry falsely claims that some foods are healthy when really they are not?

_____

_____

3. What is the problem with the U.S. Department of Agriculture establishing dietary guidelines?

_____

_____

_____

_____

4. Who is Marion Nestle? Why are her experiences important for this reading?

_____

_____

_____

_____

5. Who is Walter C. Willett? What is his major accusation regarding USDA pyramids?

_____

_____

_____

©2007 Pearson Education, Inc.

Exercise 14 **Reflect**

Think about what you read in Reading 2 and what you already know about dietary guidelines. Answer the following questions, and prepare to discuss them with your classmates.

1. Are your eating habits closer to those in Figure 3.1 or Figure 3.2? What can you do to improve your diet and health? Be specific.

_____

_____

2. Visit the Web site http://mypyramid.gov. Under "My Pyramid Plan," enter your age, sex, and level of physical activity. How close to your current diet is the plan the USDA now recommends for you?

_____

_____

3. Examine the questions Hursel asks in the last paragraph (paragraph 11) of his article. Do you agree with his conclusion? Why or why not?

_____

_____

Reading 3 *Easy Bake Ovens and Fashion Magazines: Women's Complex Relationships to Food and Eating*
Kelly Mayhew

The following reading explores the contradictions between what women are supposed to look like in our society and their role as the providers of food for their families. As you read, think about Mayhew's thesis and the support she provides to persuade us. Within the paragraphs, look for the main ideas.

1 When I was a little girl, I loved to make elaborate messes in my Easy Bake Oven. It never bothered me that the cake and brownie mixes never quite finished "baking" in my little lightbulb-driven oven; I was just as happy to eat the squishy, undercooked products of my labors. But then, I loved to eat all sorts of things (except liver and lima beans).

2 Flash forward to adolescence: I had a subscription to *Seventeen* magazine and was obsessed with how I looked. Food was full of potential dangers because it would most certainly make me fat. Yet I still enjoyed the taste of things: freshly made falafels dripping with tahini sauce; my dad's crisply fried zucchini with garlic and onions; a juicy hamburger with hickory sauce, pickles, and a huge chunk of iceberg lettuce.

3   This was a dilemma: My magazines were telling me that to look good and be successful in love and work, I'd have to be slim and toned. On the other hand, I was also discovering all sorts of new dining experiences, and I was learning how to cook for real. Between the messages of my taste buds and newly found cooking skills and the pressure from the beauty industry and my peers, I was caught in the struggle of femininity in the United States. For women, food is necessary, plentiful (for many), and can provide comfort. Beauty, however, is achieved by denying oneself the pleasures of a full plate.

4   Flash forward one more time to womanhood: An enormous number of fashion magazines appear alongside cooking and food magazines on the newsstands right now. At the same time women are told to be thin and fit, they're also compelled to be fabulous cooks and informed eaters who are up on all the food and health trends. The difficulties with food that begin to emerge in early adolescence become full-fledged problems by the time a woman enters adulthood. Because women are socialized to see themselves as objects to be looked at, how their bodies are shaped has a great deal to do with how they think of themselves. Consider which humans are the targets of the majority of beauty magazines, and which humans have their sexuality on display to sell everything from beer to motorcycles. Although traditionally women have gained a certain amount of power and prestige in the household from being the provider of food and sustenance, they are cut off from enjoying what they produce.

5   Associating women with their bodies has a long history in Western cultures. Dating back to Aristotle and the ancient Greeks, women were viewed in terms of their reproductive abilities and their closeness to nature. They were seen not for their ability to think rationally but for their appearance and ability to bear children. If men were associated with the mental and political spheres, women were aligned with the physical and domestic spheres. Hence, men were seen as rulers, leaders, and providers, and women were ruled, led, and provided for, at least in terms of money and protection.

6   These uneven gender roles have evolved through the ages and have been influenced by various social, political, and economic systems. It's important to note, however, that women have always performed extremely powerful roles in the home. Traditionally, one of those roles is the care and feeding of families. We need to remember that until fairly recently, women were barred from holding any real power in society. They did not have the right to vote, and if they were married, they could not own their own property or hold onto any wages they earned. Privately, however, women have always held a great deal of power. And food preparation and provision was a central avenue through which women could exercise this power in their households. Beginning with pregnancy, when a fetus is directly nourished by its mother, on through breastfeeding and then to meal preparation, women have been intimately connected with food.

7   In fact, my little Easy Bake Oven is part of a whole range of kitchen toys for girls. The tiny kitchen set-ups, the miniature plastic appliances, the

©2007 Pearson Education, Inc.

plethora of pots, pans, utensils, plates, bowls, and cups, are all aimed at conditioning girls into their proper roles as women. The irony, however, is when one gets out of the kitchen and wanders into Barbie-land and sees that even though little girls are supposed to grow up to be the cooks in their households, they're not supposed to eat what they make, much less enjoy food. For Barbie's look (an anatomically rare 36-21-33 body) depends on suppressing one's appetite. In addition, femininity is defined by "lady-like" behavior: An attractive "girl" doesn't finish what's on her plate; she picks daintily at her food; she doesn't order anything messy and difficult to eat, such as pasta; and she eats a lot of salads. She does all this to appear feminine and to keep her shape. Or, at least, this is what she is supposed to do. What is cruel and terrible about Barbie dolls for girls and fashion magazines for women is that they send a message that the ideal shape ranges from a size 0 all the way up to a 4. If we believed the message, then only men would be eating. In reality, the average dress size for women is around a 12 to 14. What's going on?

8   Only about 5 percent of women in the United States actually have the fashion-ideal body. They are born with it, and in interviews, many models talk about having trouble keeping weight on rather than working hard to keep it off. Yet many girls and women exercise and starve themselves trying to achieve this lean (some would say emaciated) body that is the media ideal. Since most women can never attain this extremely thin shape and keep it, we have a society of body-obsessed women, full of self-loathing and disappointment. We also have a society of secret bingers and girls and women with severe eating disorders. This is not to say that a healthy diet and exercise are not good for people but that for women, more is on their minds when they diet than staying fit, maintaining a smoothly functioning cardiovascular system, and reducing stress.

9   Maybe there is a way to solve the dilemma of enjoying food preparation and consumption while being expected to be thin. Some high-profile women in the world of food and cooking (Ruth Reichl, editor of *Gourmet* magazine, and chef Sarah Moulton of The Food Network, for instance) are regular sized and down-to-earth. They are unashamed of their love of cooking and eating and their ability to nurture. They show women that food is not just about sacrifice and denial. These women know—as I did when playing with my Easy Bake Oven, before the influence of Barbie—that you can bake your cake and eat it, too.

MAYHEW, "Easy Bake Ovens and Fashion Magazines"

Exercise 15   Work with Words

The following sentences appear in Reading 3, Mayhew's "Easy Bake Ovens and Fashion Magazines." Use context clues, dictionary skills, and your knowledge of word parts to determine the meaning of each italicized word in the sentences. Write the meaning on the lines provided. The paragraph number is provided in case you want to check the context.

1. This was a *dilemma:* My magazines were telling me that to look good and be successful in love and work, I'd have to be slim and toned. On the other hand, I was also discovering all sorts of new dining experiences, and I was learning how to cook for real. (par. 3)

   Dilemma: _____

2. At the same time women are told to be thin and fit, they're also *compelled* to be fabulous cooks and informed eaters who are up on all the food and health trends. (par. 4)

   Compelled: _____

3. Because women are *socialized* to see themselves as objects to be looked at, how their bodies are shaped has a great deal to do with how they think of themselves. Consider which humans are the targets of the majority of beauty magazines, and which humans have their sexuality on display to sell everything from beer to motorcycles. (par. 4)

   Socialized: _____

4. If men are associated with the mental and political *spheres,* women are aligned with the physical and domestic *spheres*. (par. 5)

   Sphere: _____

5. Hence, men were seen as rulers, leaders, and providers, and women were ruled, led, and provided for, at least in terms of money and protection. These uneven *gender roles* have evolved through the ages and have been influenced by various social, political, and economic systems. It's important to note, however, that women have always performed extremely powerful roles in the home. Traditionally, one of those roles is the care and feeding of families. (pars. 5–6)

   Gender roles: _____

6. We need to remember that until fairly recently, women were *barred* from holding any real power in society. They did not have the right to vote, and if they were married, they could not own their own property or hold onto any wages they earned. Privately, however, women have always held a great deal of power. (par. 6)

   Barred: _____

7. The *irony,* however, is when one gets out of the kitchen and wanders into Barbie-land and sees that even though little girls are supposed to grow up to be the cooks in their households, they're not supposed to eat what they make, much less enjoy food. (par. 7)

   Irony: _____

   _____

©2007 Pearson Education, Inc.

8. Since most women can never *attain* this extremely thin shape and keep it, we have a society of body-obsessed women, full of *self-loathing* and disappointment. (par. 8)

Attain: _____

9. *Self-loathing:* _____

10. This is not to say that a healthy diet and exercise are not good for people but that for women, more is on their minds when they diet than staying fit, maintaining a smoothly functioning *cardiovascular* system, and reducing stress. (par. 8)

Cardiovascular: _____

Exercise 16   ## Identify Topics and Main Ideas

For each of the following paragraphs from Reading 3, choose the best topic and main idea statement. Then write the main idea in your own words on the lines provided.

1. Paragraph 2

Topic:
a. the necessity of food
b. food and body image of adolescent girls
c. the need for adolescent girls to be trim

Main idea:
a. As an adolescent, the author faced the dilemma of enjoying all sorts of food but also thinking she needed to be extremely thin.
b. For women, food is necessary and serves as a source of comfort as well as artistic expression.
c. The magazines were telling the author that to look good and be successful in love and work, she'd have to be slim and toned.

The main idea in your own words: _____

_____

2. Paragraph 5

Topic:
a. the Greek idea of beauty
b. women and their bodies in Western cultures
c. the ability to think rationally

Main idea:
a. Associating women with their bodies has a long history in Western cultures.
b. Dating back to Aristotle and the ancient Greeks, women were viewed in terms of their reproductive abilities and their closeness to nature.

c. Men were associated with the mental and political spheres.

The main idea in your own words: _____

_____

3. Paragraph 6

Topic:
a. meal preparation
b. feeding families
c. women's sphere of power

Main idea:
a. Traditionally, women have had power in the home through their role in caring for and feeding their families.
b. Beginning with pregnancy, when a fetus is directly nourished by its mother, on through breastfeeding, and then to meal preparation, women have been connected with food.
c. Women did not have the right to vote, and if they were married, they could not own their own property or hold onto any wages they earned.

The main idea in your own words: _____

_____

4. Paragraph 8

Topic:
a. the problems caused for women by an impossible ideal body
b. a society of bingeing and eating disorders
c. women with the fashion ideal body

Main idea:
a. Only about 5 percent of women in the United States actually have the fashion-ideal body.
b. We have a society of secret bingers and girls and women with severe eating disorders.
c. Since most women cannot ever attain the "ideal" extremely thin shape and keep it, we have a society of body-obsessed women trying to stay thin through extreme dieting and exercise.

The main idea in your own words: _____

_____

_____

Exercise 17   ## Check Your Understanding

Based on Reading 3, choose the best answer to each of the following multiple-choice questions.

©2007 Pearson Education, Inc.

1. What is the thesis of "Easy Bake Ovens and Fashion Magazines"?
   a. Girls don't enjoy cooking as much after they are given Barbie dolls.
   b. Most women don't have the "ideal body" they see in magazines such as *Seventeen*.
   c. Women struggle under society's conflicting pressures to be good cooks and unrealistically thin.

2. The author lists some of her favorite foods (par. 2), such as fried zucchini and hamburgers so that the reader
   a. can imagine how much she loved to eat.
   b. can experiment with new flavors.
   c. can revisit childhood pleasures

3. The author explains that in the past, women did not have certain rights, such as the right to vote (par. 6), to give an example for her statement that
   a. women have always been powerless in society.
   b. until recently, women were barred from holding power in society.
   c. women have always been connected with food preparation.

4. Why does the author say that women have power in the home (par. 6)?
   a. They can influence what their husbands do.
   b. Behind every important man, there's a woman.
   c. Women are responsible for providing and preparing food.

5. According to the author,
   a. many models talk about having trouble keeping weight on.
   b. many models talk about having trouble keeping weight off.
   c. it is possible to achieve the thin look of models with moderate diet and exercise.

Exercise 18   Reflect

Think about what you read in Reading 3 and what you already know about expectations of women and food. Answer the following questions, and prepare to discuss them with your classmates.

1. What image do you have of how the "ideal woman" should look? Where did you get this idea? Explain your answers.

_____

_____

_____

2. Do you think men are also under pressure to conform to an "ideal" image? Explain your answer.

_____

_____

_____

3. Do you feel that society has conflicting expectations of you? That is, are there things you're expected to do that conflict with other things you're expected to do? (Try to use an example that doesn't involve what you eat or how you look.) Explain your answer.

_____

_____

_____

CHAPTER REVIEW

✔ Reader's Checklist

Check (✔) the concepts and skills introduced in this chapter that you are confident you understand and can now use to identify topics and main ideas in your reading. If you are not sure about any items (1) go back to the explanations in the text, (2) study and review with other members of your college learning community, (3) ask your instructor for help, (4) check out the Web site for this textbook at **www.ablongman.com/alexander community4e** for additional exercises on main ideas and to take the chapter quiz, or (5) complete additional practices in the *Reading Road Trip*.

❏ Topic
❏ Main idea
❏ Stated main idea
❏ Generalization
❏ Assertion
❏ Topic sentence
❏ Implied main idea
❏ Thesis statement

When you are confident that you have mastered these concepts and skills, test yourself with Mastery Tests 3A and 3B (pp. 156 through 170).

Critical Reflections

Answer the following questions, and prepare to discuss them with your classmates.

©2007 Pearson Education, Inc.

1. List at least four ways that convenience foods—fast food and processed food—have affected our lives. You may also want to think about and include how it has affected the way we work.

a. _____

b. _____

c. _____

d. _____

2. List three things that would help women have a comfortable relationship to their appearance and food.

a. _____

b. _____

c. _____

Writing Activity

Find a short article (approximately two pages) from a magazine, newspaper, or Internet source about one of the following topics:

- Food and nutrition
- Eating disorders
- The fast-food industry
- A specific food (e.g., salt, sugar, chocolate, hamburgers)
- American eating habits
- Diets

On a separate sheet of paper and in your own words, answer the following questions about the article you have chosen.

1. What is the title of the article, and who is the author?
2. Where does the article come from? (Write the name of the magazine or Web site and give the date, if possible.)
3. What is the topic of the article?
4. What is the thesis?
5. What points does the author make to help you understand or to convince you of the thesis of the article?
6. What is your reaction to the article? Was the article interesting to you? Why or why not?
7. Would you recommend this article for other students? Explain.
8. What new information did you learn from the article?

Classroom Community

As a group or individually, complete the following activities.

1. List the ingredients in five foods you find on store shelves or in your kitchen at home, and when you come to class, compare lists. Discuss which foods have the most additives and how much you can find out about the food from the label.

2. Go to a fast-food restaurant, find out about, and then write a report on the calories of the meals served, fat content, and price. If you are working with classmates, different students in your group should go to different fast-food restaurants. Present and compare your findings in class.

3. Follow the directions in activity 2, but talk to the workers at the restaurant(s) about how the food is prepared, how much the workers earn, and what benefits they have. If possible, also interview the manager(s).

4. Present the article you chose for the Writing Activity. Explain the article to your class group. After each student has briefly explained his or her article, the group will choose one article to present to the entire class.

Extend Your Thinking

For another reading related to food and culture, see "Table Rituals," by Laurie Tarkan, in "Extend Your Thinking," (pp. 473–474).

Work the Web

Because so many American adults are overweight, researchers are investigating the causes of and possible solutions to the problem. But it is not just adults who are struggling with obesity. Read the article "Childhood Obesity on the Rise" on the National Institutes of Health's Web site (http://www.nih.gov/news/WordonHealth/jun2002/childhoodobesity.htm), and determine the topic and the main idea of the article. On the lines provided, write the main idea statement in your own words.

_____

_____

_____

_____

Go to **www.ablongman.com/alexandercommunity4e** for additional Web-based activities.

©2007 Pearson Education, Inc.

Mastery Test   **3A**

Behind the Counter   Eric Schlosser

The following reading is from Eric Schlosser's best-seller, Fast Food Nation. *Here he explains how work is organized in fast-food restaurants and the historical precedents for organizing work in this way. One of Schlosser's main assertions is that fast-food restaurants are really run like factory assembly lines. As you read, you might think about what it's like to work in one of these restaurants and the way assembly-line preparation affects the food you eat. Also, try to identify his thesis for the reading and the main idea of each paragraph.*

1   The labor practices of the fast food industry have their <u>origins</u> in the assembly line systems adopted by American manufacturers in the early twentieth century. Business historian Alfred D. Chandler has argued that a high rate of "<u>throughput</u>" was the most important aspect of these mass production systems. A factory's throughput is the speed and volume of its flow—a much more crucial measurement, according to Chandler, than the number of workers it employs or the value of its machinery. With innovative technology and the proper organization, a small number of workers can produce an enormous amount of goods cheaply. Throughput is all about increasing the speed of assembly, about doing things faster in order to make more.

2   Although the McDonald brothers had never <u>encountered</u> the term "throughput" or studied "scientific management," they instinctively grasped the underlying principles and applied them in the Speedee Service System. The restaurant operating scheme they developed has been widely adopted and refined over the past half century. The ethos of the assembly line remains at its core. The fast food industry's obsession with throughput has <u>altered</u> the way millions of Americans work, turned commercial kitchens into small factories, and changed familiar foods into commodities that are manufactured.

3   At Burger King restaurants, frozen hamburger patties are placed on a conveyer belt and <u>emerge</u> from a broiler ninety seconds later fully cooked. The ovens at Pizza Hut and at Domino's also use conveyer belts to ensure the standardized cooking times. The ovens at McDonald's look like commercial laundry presses, with big steel hoods that swing down and grill hamburgers on both sides at once. The burgers, chicken, french fries, and buns are all frozen when they arrive at a McDonald's; the shakes and sodas begin as syrup. . . . At Taco Bell restaurants the food is "assembled," not prepared. The guacamole isn't made by workers in the kitchen; it's made at a factory in Michoacán, Mexico, then frozen and shipped north. The chain's taco meat arrives frozen and precooked in vacuum-sealed plastic bags. The beans are dehydrated and look like brownish corn flakes. The cooking process is fairly simple. "Everything's add water," a Taco Bell employee told me. "Just add hot water."

4   Although Richard and Mac McDonald introduced the division of labor to the restaurant business, it was McDonald's executive named Fred Turner who created a production system of unusual thoroughness and attention to detail. In 1958, Turner put together an operations and training manual for the company that was seventy-five pages long, specifying how almost everything should be done. Hamburgers were always to be placed on the grill in six neat rows; french fries had to be exactly 0.28 inches thick. The McDonald's operations manual today has ten times the number of pages and weighs about four pounds. Known within the company as "the Bible," it contains precise instructions on how various appliances should be used, how each item on the menu should look, and how employees should greet customers. Operators who disobey these rules can lose their <u>franchises</u>. Cooking instructions are not only printed in the manual, they are often designed into the machines. A McDonald's kitchen is full of buzzers and flashing lights that tell employees what to do.

5   At the front counter, computerized cash registers issue their own commands. Once an order has been placed, buttons light up and suggest other menu items that can be added. Workers at the counter are told to increase the size of an order by recommending special promotions, pushing dessert, pointing out the financial logic behind the purchase of a larger drink. While doing so, they are instructed to be upbeat and friendly. "Smile with a greeting and make a positive first impression," a Burger King training manual suggests. "Show them you are glad to see them. Include eye contact with the cheerful greeting."

6   The strict <u>regimentation</u> at fast food restaurants creates standardized products. It increases the throughput. And it gives fast food companies an enormous amount of power over their employees. "When management determines exactly how every task is to be done . . . and can impose its own rules about pace, output, quality, and technique," the sociologist Robin Leidner has noted, "[it] makes workers increasingly interchangeable." The management no longer depends upon the talents or skills of its workers—those things are built into the operating system and machines. Jobs that have been "de-skilled" can be filled cheaply. The need to <u>retain</u> any individual worker is greatly reduced by the ease with which he or she can be replaced.

7   Teenagers have long provided the fast food industry with the <u>bulk</u> of its workforce. The industry's rapid growth coincided with the baby-boom expansion of that age group. Teenagers were in many ways the ideal candidates for these low-paying jobs. Since most teenagers still lived at home, they could afford to work for wages too low to support an adult, and until recently, their limited skills attracted few other employers. A job at a fast food restaurant became an American rite of passage, a first job soon left behind for better things. The flexible terms of employment in the fast food industry also attracted housewives who needed extra income. As the number of baby-boom teenagers declined, the fast food chains began to hire other <u>marginalized</u> workers: recent immigrants, the elderly, and the handicapped.

SCHLOSSER, FAST FOOD NATION

©2007 Pearson Education, Inc.

Exercise 1   **Work with Words**

Use context clues, dictionary skills, and your knowledge of word parts to choose the best definition for each of the following words underlined in the reading. For numbers 5 through 10, dictionary definitions have been provided for you. The paragraph number is provided in case you want to check the context.

1. *Origins* (par. 1)
   a. beginnings, precedents
   b. ancestry, family tree
   c. connections

2. *"Throughput"* (par. 1)
   a. crucial measurement
   b. number of workers a factory employs and the value of its machinery
   c. speed and volume of flow in a mass production system

3. *Emerge* (par. 3)
   a. come out
   b. burn
   c. come out of water

4. *Marginalized* (par. 7)
   a. baby-boom teenagers
   b. fast-food workers
   c. recent immigrants, the elderly, the handicapped

5. *Encountered* (par. 2)

   en·coun·ter (ĕn-koun′tər) *n.* **1.** A meeting, especially one that is unplanned, unexpected, or brief: *a chance encounter in the park.* **2.a.** A hostile or ad-versarial confrontation; a contest: *a tense naval encounter.* **b.** An often vio-lent meeting; a clash.—**en·coun·ter** *v.* **en·coun·tered, en·coun·ter·ing, en·coun·ters.**—*tr.* **1.** To meet, especially unexpectedly; come upon: *en-countered an old friend on the street.* **2.** To confront in battle or contention. **3.** To come up against: *encounter numerous obstacles.*—*intr.* To meet, espe-cially unexpectedly. [Middle English *encountre,* from Old French, from *encontrer,* to meet, from Late Latin *incontrāre* : Latin *in-,* in; see EN-[1] + Latin *contrā,* against; see **kom** below.]

   (American Heritage Dictionary)

   a. confronted in battle
   b. met, as in seen or heard
   c. came up against obstacles

6. *Altered* (par. 2)

   al·ter (ôl′tər) *v.* **al·tered, al·ter·ing, al·ters.**—*tr.* **1.** To change or make dif-ferent; modify: *altered my will.* **2.** To adjust (a garment) for a better fit.

3. To castrate or spay (an animal, such as a cat or a dog).—*intr.* To change or become different. [Middle English *alteren*, from Old French *alterer*, from Medieval Latin *alterāre*, from Latin *alter*, other. See **al-¹** below.]

(American Heritage Dictionary)

    a. castrated or spayed
    b. adjusted for a better fit
    c. changed or made different

7. *Franchises* (par. 4)

fran·chise (frăn′chīz′) *n.* **1.** A privilege or right officially granted a person or a group by a government, especially: **a.** The constitutional or statutory right to vote. **b.** The establishment of a corporation's existence. **c.** The granting of certain rights and powers to a corporation. **d.** Legal immunity from servitude, certain burdens, or other restrictions. **2.a.** Authorization granted to someone to sell or distribute a company's goods or services in a certain area. **b.** A business or group of businesses established or operated under such authorization. **3.** The territory or limits within which immunity, a privilege, or a right may be exercised. **4.** *Informal.* A professional sports team.

(American Heritage Dictionary)

    a. a privilege officially granted by a government
    b. authorization granted to someone to sell or distribute a company's goods or services in a certain area
    c. the constitutional right to vote

8. *Regimentation* (par. 6)

reg·i·ment (rĕj′ə-mənt) *n. Abbr.* **reg.**, **regt. 1.** A military unit of ground troops consisting of at least two battalions, usually commanded by a colonel. **2.** A large group of people.—**reg·i·ment** *tr.v.* **reg·i·ment·ed**, **reg·i·ment·ing**, **reg·i·ments** (rĕj′ə-mĕnt′). **1.** To form into a regiment. **2.** To put into systematic order; systematize. **3.** To subject to uniformity and rigid order. [Middle English, government, rule, from Old French, from Late Latin *regimentum*, rule, from Latin *regere*, to rule. See **reg-** below.]—**reg′i·men′tal** (-mĕn′tl) *adj.*—**reg′i·men′tal·ly** *adv.*—**reg′i·men·ta′tion** *n.*

(American Heritage Dictionary)

    a. formation of a military unit
    b. a large group of people
    c. the act of putting into systematic order and making uniform

9. *Retain* (par. 6)

re·tain (rĭ-tān′) *tr.v.* **re·tained**, **re·tain·ing**, **re·tains.** *Abbr.* **ret. 1.** To maintain possession of. See Synonyms at **keep. 2.** To keep or hold in a particular place, condition, or position. **3.** To keep in mind; remember. **4.** To hire (an attorney, for example) by the payment of a fee. **5.** To keep in one's

©2007 Pearson Education, Inc.

service or pay. [Middle English *retainen*, from Old French *retenir*, from Latin *retinēre* : *re-*, re- + *tenēre*, to hold; see **ten-** below.]— **re·tain'a·bil'i·ty** *n.*—**re·tain'a·ble** *adj.*—**re·tain'ment** *n.*

(American Heritage Dictionary)

a. maintain possession of
b. to keep in mind
c. to keep in one's service or pay

10. *Bulk* (par. 7)

bulk (bŭlk) *n.* **1.** Size, mass, or volume, especially when very large. **2.a.** A distinct mass or portion of matter, especially a large one: *the dark bulk of buildings against the sky.* **b.** The body of a human being, especially when large. **3.** The major portion or greater part: *"The great bulk of necessary work can never be anything but painful"* (Bertrand Russell). **4.** See **fiber**. **5.** Thickness of paper or cardboard in relation to weight. **6.** *Abbr.* **blk.** *Nautical.* A ship's cargo.

(American Heritage Dictionary)

a. size, mass, or volume
b. the major portion or greater part
c. thickness of paper or cardboard

| Exercise 2 | **Check Your Understanding** |

Based on the reading, Schlosser's "Behind the Counter," choose the best answer to each of the following multiple-choice questions.

1. "Throughput" is probably
   a. the most important aspect of mass production systems.
   b. organizing work by following instincts.
   c. a term that has become obsolete in the beginning of the twenty-first century.

2. The McDonald brothers used the same ideas as "scientific management," even though
   a. they were never exposed to those ideas.
   b. they knew instinctively the ideas might not work.
   c. the ideas were obsolete.

3. The author argues that the fast-food industry's obsession with throughput has
   a. changed the nutritional value of food.
   b. changed the way millions of Americans work.
   c. improved the working conditions of millions of Americans.

4. Fred Turner was the first person to
   a. introduce a division of labor in the restaurant business.
   b. open a McDonald's restaurant.
   c. put together an operations and training manual for McDonald's.

5. When the author writes, "Hamburgers were always to be placed on the grill in six neat rows," he is giving an example of
   a. the regimentation of fast-food preparation.
   b. the need for longer operations manuals.
   c. the way cooking instructions are designed into the machines.

6. Workers at the counter are told to recommend special promotions to
   a. make the customers happy.
   b. increase the size of an order.
   c. help customers save money.

7. Fast-food workers tend to be upbeat and cheerful because they are
   a. satisfied with their jobs.
   b. chosen because they like to work with people.
   c. instructed to do so.

8. Robin Leidner noted that the organization of work at fast-food restaurants "makes workers increasingly interchangeable." This means that
   a. it is easy to replace a fast-food worker.
   b. managers will value the workers more because it takes time to train them.
   c. workers can use their talents and skills to contribute to the smooth running of the business.

9. Teenagers have provided the fast-food industry with most of its workforce for all the following reasons except
   a. the jobs are low paying.
   b. there are good possibilities for advancement.
   c. they didn't need to have skills and experience.

10. Eric Schlosser, the author of the reading "Behind the Counter," is
    a. very happy about the organization of the fast-food business because of the advantages it brings to the customers.
    b. interested only in analyzing how fast-food businesses work.
    c. critical of the way fast-food restaurants turn food preparation into assembly lines and make workers easily replaceable.

| Exercise 3 | **Identify Topics and Main Ideas** |

For each of the following paragraphs from the reading, choose the best topic and main idea statement.

1. Paragraphs 1 and 2

   Topic:
   a. the fast-food industry
   b. throughput and the fast-food industry
   c. the McDonald brothers and restaurant operating schemes

©2007 Pearson Education, Inc.

Main idea:

a. The fast-food industry bases its practices on throughput, an idea that was developed by American manufacturers in the early twentieth century and is about increasing the speed of assembly.

b. Business historian Alfred D. Chandler has argued that a high rate of "throughput" was the most important aspect of mass production systems.

c. A factory's throughput is the speed and volume of its flow.

2. Paragraph 3

Topic:

a. standardized cooking times

b. how the food is prepared

c. the use of water to prepare food

Main idea:

a. The foods at fast-food restaurants may come from far away.

b. At Taco Bell, the cooking process comes down to just adding water.

c. At fast-food restaurants, food seems to be "assembled" (like putting pieces of something together) rather than prepared.

3. Paragraph 4

Topic:

a. operating instructions at McDonald's

b. the division of labor in the restaurant business

c. McDonald's franchises

Main idea:

a. Operations manuals specify exactly how everything is supposed to be done at McDonald's.

b. Fred Turner created a production system of unusual thoroughness.

c. Cooking instructions are often designed into the machines.

4. Paragraph 6

Topic:

a. workers at fast-food restaurants and the team approach

b. the talents of workers at fast-food restaurants

c. regimentation and easy replacement of employees at fast-food restaurants

Main idea:

a. The need to retain a worker is reduced because it is easy to replace them.

b. The management no longer depends on the talents or skills of its workers.

c. The strict regimentation at fast-food restaurants creates standardized products, increases throughput, and gives fast-food companies an enormous power over their workers.

Topic for the whole reading:
a. source of food at fast-food restaurants
b. organization of work at fast-food restaurants
c. quality of food at fast-food restaurants

Main idea for the whole reading:
a. The regimented organization and de-skilling of tasks at fast-food restaurants have turned the work into very simple assembly and has made the employees easily replaceable and vulnerable.
b. The fast-food industry has gotten most of its techniques of organization from assembly-line systems of the early twentieth century.
c. Fast-food workers are mostly teenagers and other marginalized workers because the jobs are low paying and don't require skill.

| Exercise 4 | **Reflect** |

Think about what you read in "Behind the Counter" and what you already know about different work situations. Then answer the following questions.

1. Why do you think fast-food restaurants have organized their food preparation systems like assembly lines? Explain your answer.

_____

_____

_____

_____

2. Have you or anyone you know ever worked in a fast-food restaurant or in a situation where the work was strictly regimented, as in a factory assembly line? Describe what it's like to work under those conditions. (If you don't have experience, use your imagination.) What kinds of satisfaction might workers get? What kinds of problems might they have? Explain your answers.

_____

_____

_____

_____

©2007 Pearson Education, Inc.

Mastery Test

3B

What's in the Beef? Howard F. Lyman

The following reading is from Howard F. Lyman's book, Mad Cowboy. *After Lyman, a fourth-generation Montana cattle rancher, became critically ill with a spinal tumor, he investigated the effects of eating meat as it is raised and processed in the United States today. Here he discusses the "rendering industry," emphasizing the food that cattle eat. As you read, you will notice that he is passionate about what he writes. Try to identify his thesis and the main ideas of each paragraph.*

1   When a cow is slaughtered, about half of it by weight is not eaten by humans: the intestines and their contents, the head, hooves, and horns, as well as bones and blood. These are dumped into giant grinders at rendering plants, as are the entire bodies of cows and other farm animals known to be diseased. Rendering is a $2.4-billion-a-year industry,[1] processing forty billion pounds of dead animals a year.[2] There is simply no such thing in America as an animal too ravaged by disease, too cancerous, or too putrid to be welcomed by the all-embracing arms of the renderer. Another staple of the renderer's diet, in addition to farm animals, is euthanized pets—the six or seven million dogs and cats that are killed in animal shelters every year. The city of Los Angeles alone, for example, sends some two hundred tons of euthanized cats and dogs to a rendering plant every month.[3] Added to the blend are the euthanized catch of animal control agencies, and road-kill. (Roadkill is not collected daily, and in the summer, the better roadkill collection crews can generally smell it before they can see it.) When this gruesome mix is ground and steam-cooked, the lighter, fatty material floating to the top gets refined for use in such products as cosmetics, lubricants, soaps, candles, and waxes. The heavier protein material is dried and pulverized into a brown powder—about a quarter of which consists of fecal [stool, or waste] material. The powder is used as an additive to almost all pet food as well as to livestock feed. Farmers call it "protein concentrates." In 1995, five million tons of processed slaughterhouse leftovers were sold for animal feed in the United States.[4] I used to feed tons of the stuff to my own livestock. It never concerned me that I was feeding cattle to cattle.

2   In August, 1997, in response to growing concern about the spread of bovine spongiform encephalopathy (or Mad Cow disease), the FDA [Food and Drug Administration] issued a new regulation that bans the feeding of ruminant protein (protein from cud-chewing animals [like cows]) to ruminants; therefore, to the extent that the regulation is actually enforced, cattle are no longer quite the cannibals that we had made them into. They are no longer eating solid parts of other cattle, or sheep, or goats. They still munch, however, on ground-up dead horses, dogs, cats, pigs, chickens, and turkeys, as well as blood and fecal material of their own species and that of chickens. About 75 percent of the ninety million beef cattle in America are rou-

tinely given feed that has been "enriched" with rendered animal parts.[5] The use of <u>animal excrement</u> in feed is common as well, as livestock operators have found it to be an efficient way of disposing of a portion of the 1.6 million tons of livestock wastes generated annually by their industry.[6] In Arkansas, for example, the average farm feeds over fifty tons of chicken litter to cattle every year.[7] One Arkansas cattle farmer was quoted in *U.S. News & World Report* as having recently purchased 745 tons of <u>litter</u> collected from the floors of local chicken-raising operations. After mixing it with small amounts of soybean bran, he then feeds it to his eight hundred head of cattle, making them, in his words, "fat as butterballs." He explained, "If I didn't have chicken litter, I'd have to sell half my herd. Other feeds are too expensive."[8] If you are a meat-eater, understand that this is the food of your food.

3   We don't know all there is to know about the extent to which the <u>consumption</u> of diseased or unhealthy animals causes disease in humans, but we do know that some diseases—rabies, for example—are <u>transmitted</u> from the host animal to humans. We know that the common food poisonings brought on by such organisms as the prevalent E. coli bacteria, which results from fecal contamination of food, causes the death of nine thousand Americans a year[9] and that about 80 percent of food poisonings come from tainted meat.[10] And now we can also be certain, from the tragedy that has already afflicted Britain, that Mad Cow disease can "jump species" and give rise to a new variety of the always fatal, brain-wasting Creutzfeldt-Jakob disease in humans.[11] . . .

4   The American people have been raised to believe that someone is looking out for their food safety. The disturbing truth is that the protection of the quality of our food is the <u>mandate</u> of foot-dragging bureaucrats at the U.S. Department of Agriculture and the Food and Drug Administration who can generally be counted upon to behave not like public servants but like hired hands of the meat and dairy industries.

Notes

1. Sandra Blakeslee, "Fear Prompts Look at Rendering," *New York Times,* March 11, 1997.

2. Ibid.

3. Ibid.

4. Dr. Fred Bisplinghoff, testimony before USDA/APHIS and FDA/CVM symposium on TSEs, May 13 and 14, 1996.

5. Kienan Mulvarey, "Mad Cows and the Colonies," *E: The Environmental Magazine,* vol. VII, no. 4 (July/August 1996), 38.

6. C. Tharp and W. P. Miller, "Poultry Litter Practices of Arkansas Poultry Producers," USDA, 1994 (Sustainable Agriculture Research and Education Project AS92-1), cited in Haapapuro, Eric R., et al., "Animal Waste Used as Livestock Feed: Dangers to Human Health," Physicians Committee for Responsible Medicine review, 1997, 1.

© 2007 Pearson Education, Inc.

7. Ibid., 2.

8. Mitchell Satchell and Stephen J. Hedges, "The Next Bad Beef Scandal," *U.S. News & World Report,* September 1, 1997, 22.

9. Agriculture Department statistic, cited in Nicols Fox, "Safe Food? Not Yet," *New York Times,* January 30, 1997.

10. Amy O'Connor, "8 Nutritional Myths," *Vegetarian Times,* July 1997, 80.

11. John Collinge et al., "Spongiform Encephalopathies: A Common Agent for BSE and vCJD," *Nature,* October 2, 1997, 449–450.

LYMAN, *MAD COWBOY*

Exercise 1   **Work with Words**

Use context, clues, dictionary skills, and your knowledge of word parts to choose the best definition for each of the following words underlined in the reading. The paragraph number is provided in case you want to check the context.

1. *Rendering plants* (par. 1)
   a. profitable factories
   b. factories that process dead animals
   c. grinding factories

2. *Euthanized* (par. 1)
   a. killed for humanitarian reasons
   b. killed on the road by cars
   c. killed by people who don't like animals

3. *Pulverized* (par. 1)
   a. ground up
   b. compressed
   c. moistened

4. *Spongiform encephalopathy* (par. 2)
   a. the Food and Drug Administration
   b. ruminant problems
   c. Mad Cow disease

5. *Ruminant protein* (par. 2)
   a. protein from animals that chew cud like cows
   b. protein from animals that are cannibals
   c. regulation protein

6. *Animal excrement* (par. 2)
   a. animal diseases
   b. animal droppings
   c. animal body parts

7. *Chicken litter* (par. 2)
   a. chicken pellets
   b. what's on the floor of chicken-raising operations
   c. chicken food

8. *Consumption* (par. 3)
   a. eating
   b. purchasing
   c. infecting

9. *Transmitted* (par. 3)
   a. spread
   b. send as a message
   c. joined

10. *Mandate* (par. 4)
   a. concern
   b. opinion
   c. responsibility

Exercise 2 **Check Your Understanding**

Based on the reading, Lyman's "What's in the Beef?" choose the best answer to each of the following multiple-choice questions.

1. When a cow is slaughtered,
   a. the intestines, hooves, head, bones, and blood are eaten by humans.
   b. nothing is done with the intestines and other uneaten parts.
   c. only about half of it is eaten by humans.

2. What happens to the remains of cows at rendering plants?
   a. They are ground up with other dead animals and cooked.
   b. They are euthanized.
   c. They are processed into cosmetics.

3. What part of the "gruesome mix" is turned into cosmetics, soaps, candles, and waxes after it is steam-cooked?
   a. The heavier protein material
   b. The lighter, fatty material floating at the top
   c. The pulverized material

4. What is the material that farmers call "protein concentrates"?
   a. Fatty material
   b. Pulverized protein material
   c. Pet food

5. The FDA issued a regulation that bans feeding ruminant (cow, sheep, or goat) protein to cows in response to
   a. the report in *U.S. News & World Report*.
   b. concern about Mad Cow disease.
   c. public pressure from consumers.

© 2007 Pearson Education, Inc.

6. Which of the following are not mentioned in the reading as a source of cattle food?
   a. Animal excrement
   b. Animal renderings
   c. Grains

7. Chicken excrement—waste—is used to feed cattle because it
   a. is proven to be healthy for the cows.
   b. is cheap and fattens up the cattle.
   c. solves the problem of disposing of all the wastes generated by the chicken industry.

8. According to the author, we don't know
   a. if rabies is spread from animals to humans.
   b. if *E.coli* bacteria come from tainted meat.
   c. the extent to which eating diseased or unhealthy animals causes disease in humans.

9. The author is
   a. critical of the cattle industry.
   b. supportive of the cattle industry.
   c. understanding of the problems the cattle industry faces.

10. The author is
    a. not confident that someone is making sure that our food is safe.
    b. confident that the government is making sure that our food is safe.
    c. supportive of the U.S. Department of Agriculture and the Food and Drug Administration.

| Exercise 3 | Identify Topics and Main Ideas |

For each of the following paragraphs from the reading, choose the best topic and stated or implied main idea.

1. Paragraph 1

   Topic:
   a. the uses of animal carcasses and the rendering industry
   b. the euthanization of animals
   c. animal rendering and the making of cosmetics

   Main idea:
   a. Millions of animals are euthanized every year by animal shelters and animal control agencies.
   b. Cosmetics, lubricants, soaps, candles, and waxes are made with the fatty material produced by the animal-rendering process.
   c. Parts of animal carcasses from many sources are rendered into many products, one of which is food for cattle.

2. Paragraph 2

Topic:
a. cattle food "enriched" with animal parts
b. poultry livestock waste
c. what cattle are fed in the United States

Main idea:
a. In response to concern about Mad Cow disease, the FDA issued a new regulation that bans the feeding of ruminant protein to other ruminants.
b. U.S. cattle are no longer fed processed remains of cattle, sheep, or goats, but they do get feed that is rendered from parts of other animals, including their excrement, and litter from poultry farms.
c. Some cattle ranchers routinely feed their cows chicken excrement.

3. Paragraph 3

Topic:
a. *E. coli* bacteria
b. human diseases
c. the relationship between eating unhealthy animals and human disease

Main idea:
a. We don't know the extent to which the consumption of diseased or unhealthy animals causes disease in humans, but we do know that some diseases are transmitted from the host animal to humans.
b. Common food poisonings result from fecal contamination of food.
c. Mad Cow disease can "jump species" and give rise to a new variety of always fatal, brain-wasting Creutzfeldt-Jakob disease in humans.

4. Paragraph 4

Topic
a. the U.S. Department of Agriculture
b. the lack of food safety enforcement
c. the Food and Drug Administration

Main idea:
a. Americans believe someone is looking out for their food safety.
b. The U.S. Department of Agriculture is looking out for food safety in this country.
c. Although Americans believe someone is looking out for their food safety, in reality, the officials in the USDA and FDA serve the meat and dairy industries, not the American people.

©2007 Pearson Education, Inc.

5. Topic for the whole reading:
   a. what cattle eat and how it affects the health of people who eat beef
   b. food safety
   c. failure to protect public health

   Main idea statement for the whole reading:
   a. There may be serious health consequences to the practice of feeding cattle rendered dead animal parts and chicken excrement.
   b. No sane person should eat beef after finding out what the cattle themselves eat.
   c. Rendering dead animals into useful products is a very important way to turn a potential problem into a helpful and profitable solution.

Exercise 4   Reflect

Think about what you read in "What's in the Beef?" and what you already know about healthy diets. Then answer the following questions.

1. Who is at fault for the health risks to beef eaters? cattle ranchers? meat processors? government regulators? consumers? Explain your answer.

   _____

   _____

   _____

   _____

2. Does reading "What's in the Beef?" change your attitudes about eating beef? Explain. What more would you want to learn before deciding not to eat beef?

   _____

   _____

   _____

   _____

Chapter 4

Support for Main Ideas

Staying Well

A sound mind in a sound body is a short but full description of a happy state in this world.

—*John Locke*

● What do you think the women in the picture are doing?

● What do you think this quotation means, and how does it relate to the women in the picture?

© 2007 Pearson Education, Inc.

PREPARE TO READ

Today, according to health experts, we are living in the age of *wellness*. In the past century, human life expectancy has almost doubled. The average person born a hundred years ago could only expect to live into his or her 40s, while the average baby born now can expect to live well into his or her 70s. How can you take advantage of the information about health and wellness that has become available to all of us? How can you achieve optimal well-being and live a long, productive, and fulfilling life?

Purpose

In this chapter, you will learn to
- Recognize how major and minor points support main ideas
- Organize your understanding of what you have read by
  Marking texts
  Making lists
  Outlining
  Summarizing

In the process of acquiring these skills, you will read about the qualities of wellness and how your health is affected by factors such as exercise, diet, and stress.

Previous Knowledge

Answer these questions and prepare to discuss them in class.

1. List three things you think people need to live a healthy and happy life.

   a. _____

   b. _____

   c. _____

2. What habits do you have that contribute to your health and happiness?

   _____

   _____

   _____

Preview and Predict

Preview Chapter 4. Then list two things you think you will learn in this chapter.

1. _____

2. _____

©2007 Pearson Education, Inc.

Reading 1   *Wellness: The New Health Goal*   Paul M. Insel,
Walton T. Roth, L. McKay Rollins, and Ray A. Peterson

The following reading from the college text Core Concepts in Health
*defines "wellness" as "the ability to live life fully—with vitality and meaning."
The authors identify six dimensions of health and well-being that interact in
all our lives.*

1 *Wellness* is an expanded idea of health. Many people think of health as being just the absence of physical disease. But wellness transcends this
concept of health, as when individuals with serious illnesses or disabilities
rise above their physical or mental limitations to live rich, meaningful, vital
lives. Some aspects of health are determined by your genes, your age, and
other factors that may be beyond your control. But true wellness is largely
determined by the decisions you make about how to live your life. . . . We
will use the terms "health" and "wellness" interchangeably to mean the
ability to live life fully—with vitality and meaning.

The Dimensions of Wellness

2 No matter what your age or health status, you can optimize your health in
each of the following six interrelated dimensions. Wellness in any dimension is not a static goal but a dynamic process of change and growth.

Physical Wellness

3 Optimal physical health requires eating well, exercising, avoiding harmful
habits, making responsible decisions about sex, learning about and
recognizing the symptoms of disease, getting regular medical and dental
checkups, and taking steps to prevent injuries at home, on the road, and on
the job. The habits you develop and the decisions you make today will
largely determine not only how many years you will live, but the quality of
your life during those years.

Emotional Wellness

4 Optimism, trust, self-esteem, self-acceptance, self-confidence, self-control,
satisfying relationships, and an ability to share feelings are just some of the
qualities and aspects of emotional wellness. Emotional health is a dynamic
state that fluctuates with your physical, intellectual, spiritual, interpersonal
and social, and environmental health. Maintaining emotional wellness requires monitoring and exploring your thoughts and feelings, identifying
obstacles to emotional well-being, and finding solutions to emotional problems, with the help of a therapist if necessary.

Intellectual Wellness

5 The hallmarks of intellectual health include an openness to new ideas, a capacity to question and think critically, and the motivation to master new

skills, as well as a sense of humor, creativity, and curiosity. An active mind is essential to overall wellness, for learning about, evaluating, and storing health-related information. Your mind detects problems, finds solutions, and directs behavior. People who enjoy intellectual wellness never stop learning. They relish new experiences and challenges and actively seek them out.

Spiritual Wellness

6   To enjoy spiritual health is to possess a set of guiding beliefs, principles, or values that give meaning and purpose to your life, especially during difficult times. Spiritual wellness involves the capacity for love, compassion, forgiveness, altruism, joy, and fulfillment. It is an antidote to cynicism, anger, fear, anxiety, self-absorption, and pessimism. Spirituality transcends the individual and can be a common bond among people. Organized religions help many people develop spiritual health. Many others find meaning and purpose in their lives on their own—through nature, art, meditation, political action, or good works.

Interpersonal and Social Wellness

7   Satisfying relationships are basic to both physical and emotional health. We need to have mutually loving, supportive people in our lives. Developing interpersonal wellness means learning good communication skills, developing the capacity for intimacy, and cultivating a support network of caring friends and/or family members. Social wellness requires participating in and contributing to your community, country, and world.

Environmental or Planetary Wellness

8   Increasingly, personal health depends on the health of the planet. Examples of environmental threats to health are ultraviolet radiation in sunlight, air and water pollution, secondhand tobacco smoke in indoor air, and violence in our society. Wellness requires learning about and protecting yourself against such hazards—and doing what you can to reduce or eliminate them, either on your own or with others.

9   The six dimensions of wellness interact continuously, influencing and being influenced by one another. Making a change in one dimension often affects some or all of the others. Maintaining good health is a dynamic process, and increasing your level of wellness in one area of life often influences many others.

INSEL ET AL., *CORE CONCEPTS IN HEALTH*

Exercise 1   ## Recall and Discuss

Based on Reading 1, "Wellness," by Insel et al., answer the following questions and prepare to discuss them with your classmates.

1. What are the six dimensions of wellness that the authors identify? Are there others you would add?

a. _____   e. _____

b. _____   f. _____

c. _____   g. _____

d. _____   h. _____

2. The authors state that "true wellness is largely determined by the decisions you make about how to live your life." Do you agree or disagree with the authors? Explain your answer using examples from your own experiences or observations.

_____

_____

_____

_____

3. How do you think the six dimensions of wellness are affected by people's decisions?

_____

_____

_____

_____

SUPPORTING POINTS

Main ideas are explained by *supporting points*. In Chapter 3, when you learned to identify the main idea of a paragraph or longer passage, you were finding the most important idea in the reading. All the rest of the information supported the main idea. Recognizing how to distinguish between main ideas and supporting points is an important reading comprehension skill. This chapter focuses on the support that writers provide to back up their main ideas.

Major Supporting Points

major supporting points Chief ideas or facts that support the main idea

Supporting points explain the writer's main idea in detail. **Major supporting points** are the chief ideas or facts that support the main idea. For example, in Reading 1, "Wellness," the authors' main idea is stated in the first sentence of the second paragraph: "No matter what your age or health status, you can optimize your health in each of the following six interrelated dimensions." The authors are alerting the readers to

©2007 Pearson Education, Inc.

watch for six supporting points. The six subheadings that follow name the major supporting points:

Physical Wellness	Spiritual Wellness
Emotional Wellness	Interpersonal and Social Wellness
Intellectual Wellness	Environmental or Planetary Wellness

For each of these sections, you can identify a major supporting sentence. For example, under "Environmental or Planetary Wellness," the main idea of the paragraph is "Increasingly, personal health depends on the health of the planet." Together, the main ideas of the paragraphs are major supporting points for the main idea of the reading. Identifying main ideas and their major supporting points can help you determine which points you need to know for tests or for work situations.

Minor Supporting Points

minor supporting points Additional explanations, examples, facts, and statistics that develop the major supporting points

Besides major supporting points, readings contain many additional explanations that may be identified as **minor supporting points.** Minor supporting points are simply more detailed explanations, examples, facts, or statistics that back up the major points. For example, after asserting in paragraph 8 of the reading, "Increasingly, personal health depends on the health of the planet," the authors go on to provide examples of environmental threats to health:

- Ultraviolet radiation in sunlight
- Air and water pollution
- Secondhand tobacco smoke in indoor air
- Violence in our society

For each of these examples, the authors could certainly have provided additional layers of details, such as statistics on skin cancer and identification of areas most affected by water pollution. However, writers judge how much detail to include based on their perceptions of readers' needs and purposes. For an introductory health text, they would include a lot less information on this topic than they would for a group of environmental scientists studying the relationship between health and the environment. In that case, several books of detailed information would be needed to discuss the topic thoroughly.

Distinguishing Between Major and Minor Supporting Points

Perhaps one of the most important skills for a reader to acquire is the ability to tell which parts of a reading are most important to remember. Certainly, identifying main ideas is crucial, but distinguishing between major and minor supporting points is also essential. For practice, read the following paragraph and determine the main idea. Then we'll take a look at the major and minor supporting points.

Today, many people are striving for optimal health. A century ago, such a goal was unknown—people counted themselves lucky just to survive. A child born in 1890, for example, could expect to live only about 40 years. Killers such as polio, smallpox, diphtheria, measles, and mumps took the lives of a tragic number of infants and children in the days before vaccinations. Youngsters who escaped these threats still risked death from infectious diseases such as tuberculosis, typhus, or dysentery. In 1918 alone, 20 million people died in a flu epidemic. Millions of others lost their lives to common bacterial infections in the era before antibiotics. Environmental conditions—unrefrigerated food, poor sanitation, and air polluted by coal-burning furnaces and factories—contributed to the spread and the deadliness of these diseases. (Insel et al., *Core Concepts in Health*)

You probably came up with a statement for the main idea of this paragraph that is something like, "A hundred years ago, people were not concerned about optimal health; they felt lucky just to survive the many risks to their health at that time."

How do the authors go on to convince readers that their main idea is valid? First, they present the *major supporting points:* the major risks people faced, such as

- Childhood diseases
- Infectious diseases
- Common bacterial infections
- Environmental conditions

But the authors do not stop with a simple identification of each risk; they go on to give *minor supporting points*—explanations and examples for each. For example, under childhood diseases, the authors identify "killers such as polio, smallpox, diphtheria, measles, and mumps." Obviously, many books could be written on health issues in the early twentieth century, with a great deal more specific detail on this subject. The authors of this health text selected only the details they felt were most important for students to know in an introductory course on the subject.

| Exercise 2 | ## Identify Main Ideas and Major and Minor Supporting Points |

Read the following summary of *Healthy People 2010,* and identify the major and minor supporting points for the entire reading. Then choose the best answer to each of the multiple-choice questions.

1   *Healthy People,* published by the U.S. Department of Health and Human Services (DHHS), sets forth broad public health goals for the United States. Originally published in 1990, it has been updated for the year 2010. There are two main goals proposed in *Healthy People 2010.*

©2007 Pearson Education, Inc.

2 • *Increasing Quality and Years of Healthy Life.* Although life expectancy in the United States has increased since the beginning of the century, there is still room for improvement. Surprisingly, 18 countries have a longer life expectancy than the United States. In Japan, for example, women can expect to live an average of 82.9 years compared with 78.9 years for women in the United States. Japanese men have a life expectancy of 76.4 years compared with 72.5 years for American men.

3   Increasing the number of years of healthy life is another important goal. "Years of healthy life" refers to the time people spend in good health, with no acute or chronic limiting conditions. Although life expectancy increased by a full year from 1990 to 1996, years of healthy life only increased from 64.0 years to 64.2 years during the same time. This meant that although people were living longer, they were spending more time in poor health.

4 • *Eliminating Health Disparities.* Health disparities between different ethnic groups in the American population continue to be a source of concern. Some groups, such as African Americans, Hispanics, American Indians, and Alaska Natives, are disproportionately affected by certain diseases. For example, the death rates for heart disease, all forms of cancer, and HIV/AIDS are higher for African Americans than for whites. Hispanics, who made up 11 percent of the total population in 1996, accounted for 20 percent of the new tuberculosis cases. American Indians and Alaska Natives have a rate of diabetes that is more than twice that of whites.

5   There are also substantial differences in life expectancy among different economic groups in the United States. For example, people from households with an annual income of at least $25,000 live an average of 3 to 7 years longer than people from households with annual incomes of less than $10,000. People with higher income levels generally can afford better care, are able to take time off work for medical reasons, and aren't limited by public transportation.

1. Which of the following is the best thesis statement for *Healthy People 2010*?
   a. There are large health disparities among various ethnic groups in the United States.
   b. A goal of *Healthy People 2010* is to increase life expectancy in the United States.
   c. *Healthy People 2010* proposes to improve the health of all Americans.

2. The line "Japanese men have a life expectancy of 76.4 years compared with 72.5 years for American men" in paragraph 2 is a
   a. major supporting point.
   b. minor supporting point.

3. The line "Increasing the number of years of healthy life is another important goal" in paragraph 3 is a
   a. major supporting point.
   b. minor supporting point.

4. The line "Although life expectancy increased by a full year from 1990 to 1996, years of healthy life only increased from 64.0 years to 64.2 years during the same time" in paragraph 3 is a
   a. major supporting point
   b. minor supporting point.

5. The line "Health disparities between different ethnic groups in the American population continue to be a source of concern" in paragraph 4 is a
   a. major supporting point.
   b. minor supporting point.

6. The line "Hispanics, who made up 11 percent of the total population in 1996, accounted for 20 percent of the new tuberculosis cases" in paragraph 4 is a
   a. major supporting point.
   b. minor supporting point.

7. The line "There are also substantial differences in life expectancy among different economic groups in the United States" in paragraph 5 is a
   a. major supporting point.
   b. minor supporting point.

8. The line "For example, people from households with an annual income of at least $25,000 live an average of 3 to 7 years longer than people from households with annual incomes of less than $10,000" in paragraph 5 is
   a. major supporting point.
   b. minor supporting point.

Exercise 3   **Restate Main Ideas and Major and Minor Supporting Points**

Based on the summary of *Healthy People 2010* on pages 177 through 178, complete the following.

1. Write, in your own words, the thesis of this reading.

_____

_____

_____

©2007 Pearson Education, Inc.

2. List the four major supporting points in this excerpt.

a. _____

_____

b. _____

c. _____

_____

d. _____

_____

3. List the three examples (minor supporting points) used to support the point "There are large disparities between different ethnic groups."

a. _____

_____

b. _____

_____

c. _____

_____

ORGANIZING TO LEARN

organizing to learn
Last portion of the PRO reading system; helps you understand and remember what you learned in a reading

Organizing to learn is the last major step in the PRO reading process. As you learned in Chapter 1, organizing helps you to understand what you read and remember the information for tests and for use in the future. There are a number of ways to organize the information you read, and identifying main ideas, major supporting points, and minor supporting points makes this part of the reading process much easier. In this section, you will practice four different ways to organize what you've read: marking texts, making bulleted lists, outlining, and summarizing.

marking texts
Highlighting and using a system of symbols and annotations on the text itself to make review and retention easier

Marking Texts

Marking texts is probably the quickest way to organize what you have read. People use a variety of methods to mark texts, including the following:

- Highlighting or underlining important points
- Putting check marks beside important points

- Using numbers to identify lists of examples, steps in a process, and so on
- Drawing arrows to "connect" ideas
- Circling essential vocabulary (note that *essential vocabulary* consists of only the important words, not all the words that you don't know)
- Using different colors for different types of information
- Using question marks (???) to identify points where you need to ask questions of the instructor, a tutor, or someone in your study group
- Annotating—writing notes in the margin to draw your attention to a point in a paragraph, noting "causes," "definition," or "examples"
- Writing down your own reactions or comments, such as "good point," or "I don't agree," in the margins

There are probably as many ways to mark texts as there are individual students. You need to choose the ways that work best for you and then use them consistently so you can come back in a month, or three months, and still know what your marks mean. Use the knowledge you've already gained about main ideas and major supporting points to select the material to be marked. Also, be very conscious of what your professor emphasizes in lecture and discussion. If he or she makes a special effort to reinforce some concept or vocabulary in the text, you will probably need to know that material.

You need to mark ideas, concepts, and vocabulary in your text carefully and efficiently. You will return to these items many times for review. When you are studying for an exam about several chapters, you do not want to reread the chapters completely, so careful selection of the significant points to mark is important.

Perhaps the best advice to help you save time in marking texts is this: *When you read new material the first time, do not mark text that you plan to memorize.* During a first reading, almost everything seems important, so you may mark too much. That's why you see so many used textbooks with whole pages "painted" with yellow highlighter.

Many texts have been designed to make the task very easy for you. Bullets, boldfaced print, italics, color changes, charts, graphs, and numerous inserts are already provided in many texts to highlight the concepts and vocabulary you need to learn. Efficient marking of texts is probably most important in books that don't provide as much assistance to the student.

After you have marked your text, you should have a clear understanding of what you have read, and you should have organized it in a way that's easy to learn and to remember.

Now let's take a paragraph about health issues in the United States and see how you might mark it for future review. Notice that the following paragraph is marked in a way that will make reviewing the main points easy. The main idea is underlined twice. The seven major supporting points are numbered and underlined. The annotations in the margin note some points the marker of the text wished to emphasize in her review.

©2007 Pearson Education, Inc.

causes

Is good health just the absence of disease-causing organisms? In many big-city hospitals, <u>a great many health problems have nothing to do with germs</u>, points out medical-ethics consultant Bruce Hilton. Surgeons regularly practice "battlefield medicine," attending to the multiple gunshot and knife wounds of the (1) <u>victims of violence</u>. Or they sew up (2) <u>car-crash survivors</u>, many of whom (a) did not wear seatbelts, many of whose (b) accidents were alcohol-caused. In the psychiatric wing, a high proportion of patients have (3) <u>cocaine or other drug-related problems</u>. In the nursery, (a) undersized crack-cocaine babies fight to survive. Other newborns won't live out the year because their mothers (4) <u>didn't have access to prenatal health care</u>. Elsewhere cigarette (5) <u>smokers</u> await their turn for radiation treatment of their lung cancer or respiratory therapy for their emphysema. Indeed, if you were to walk around the hospital you would turn up many other reasons for poor health, says Hilton: "(6) <u>skin cancer</u> from too many days on the beach, or people whose disease was (7) <u>food—too much, not the right kind, or too little</u>." (Williams and Knight, *Healthy for Life*)

nursery

lack of prevention

bad health habits

Exercise 4   Organize to Learn: Mark a Text

Read the following excerpt from Dianne Hales's *An Invitation to Health*, about maintaining health in sexual relationships. Note that the acronym STD stands for sexually transmitted diseases and HIV for human immunodeficiency virus. Underline main ideas and number major supporting points under each main idea. Use other marking and annotations as you wish. Do not mark too much!

1 Abstinence is the only guarantee of sexual safety—and one that more and more young people are choosing. The choice of an abstinent (or celibate) lifestyle offers many advantages, both in the present and the future. By choosing not to be sexually active with a partner, individuals can safeguard their physical health, their fertility, and their future.

2   For men and women who are sexually active, a mutually faithful sexual relationship with just one healthy partner is the safest option. For those not in such relationships, safer-sex practices are essential for reducing risks. Some experts believe that condom use may be a more effective tactic than any drug or vaccine in preventing STDs.

3   How can you tell if someone you're dating or hope to date has been exposed to an STD? The bad news is, you can't. But the good news is, it doesn't matter—as long as you avoid sexual activity that could put you at risk of infection. Ideally, before engaging in any such behavior, both of you should talk about your prior sexual history (including number of partners and sexually transmitted diseases) and other high-

risk behavior, such as the use of injection drugs. If you know someone well enough to consider having sex with that person, you should be able to talk about STDs. If the person is unwilling to talk, you shouldn't have sex.

4   Even if you do talk openly, you can't be sure a potential partner is telling you the truth. In various surveys of college students, a significant proportion of the men and women said they would lie to a potential partner about having an STD or testing positive for HIV. The only way of knowing for certain that a prospective partner is safe is through laboratory testing. Sex educators and health professionals strongly encourage couples to abstain from any sexual activity that puts them at risk for STDs until they both undergo medical examinations and laboratory testing to rule out STDs. This process greatly reduces the danger of disease transmission and can also help foster a deep sense of mutual trust and commitment. Many campus and public health clinics provide exams or laboratory testing either free of charge or on a sliding scale determined by your income. (Hales, *An Invitation to Health*)

◆

Making Bulleted Lists

bulleted lists Lists accented by symbols called bullets to make supporting points easier to identify

Another way to organize supporting points is to list them. When people make computer-aided presentations in school or at work, they often use **bulleted lists** to reinforce the main ideas and major supporting points. Textbooks very frequently use lists accented by bullets to attract the readers' attention to important supporting points. For example, read the following discussion on smokers' dependence on nicotine. Notice how the author uses bullets to emphasize the list of causes for dependence.

Nicotine has a much more powerful hold on smokers than alcohol does on drinkers. Whereas about 10% of alcohol users lose control of their intake of alcohol and become alcoholics, as many as 80% of all heavy smokers have tried to cut down on or quit smoking but cannot overcome their dependence.

Nicotine causes dependence by at least three means:
- It provides a strong sensation of pleasure.
- It leads to fairly severe discomfort during withdrawal.
- It stimulates cravings long after obvious withdrawal symptoms have passed. (Hales, *An Invitation to Health*)

Exercise 5   Organize to Learn: Make a Bulleted List

Using Reading 1 on pages 173 through 174, list the major supporting points on the bulleted lines provided. The main idea and the first supporting point have already been done for you.

©2007 Pearson Education, Inc.

Wellness: The New Health Goal

No matter what your age or health status, you can optimize your health in each of the following six interrelated dimensions.

- *physical wellness* _____

- _____

- _____

- _____

- _____

- _____

◆

Outlining

outlining A formal strategy for organizing readings by divisions showing the relationships between main ideas and major and minor supporting points

Outlining is another strategy for thinking about and organizing information so that you can remember it for future use. Outlining requires you (1) to select the most important points in what you have read and (2) to decide how the various points are related.

Formal outlining requires you to follow an exact pattern. You may not always want to outline your study materials formally, but even when you are doing an informal outline for your own use, it's helpful to use this format as a basis. Also, you will find that a formal outline is required for many college research writing assignments.

Outlines may be constructed by topic (usually phrases) or in complete sentences. The format includes a title, which names the topic of the outline; a statement of the main idea (called a thesis statement in writing classes), which states the main point about the topic; and divisions of the support for the thesis, which are marked first by Roman numerals (I, II, III, IV, V), then by capital letters (A, B, C, D, E), next by Arabic numerals (1, 2, 3, 4, 5), and then by lowercase letters (a, b, c, d, e). Each division means that the information has been divided into still lower levels of support. Since each indentation and change of number and letter means you are dividing information, you must always have at least a I and II, A and B, 1 and 2, or a and b. If the Roman numerals are major supporting points, then the capital letters are minor supporting points, and numbers and small letters are still more detailed points of support. Traditional topic outline format looks something like the following example:

Title (Topic)

Main Idea: This is the main point about the topic.

  I. Major supporting point
    A. Minor supporting point
      1. More minor supporting point
        a. Still more minor supporting point and details
        b. Still more minor supporting point and details

       2. More minor supporting point

    B. Minor supporting point

II. Major supporting point

    A. Minor supporting point

       1. More minor supporting point

         a. Still more minor supporting point and details

         b. Still more minor supporting point and details

       2. More minor supporting point

    B. Minor supporting point

The following is one example of an outline of the section headed "Physical Stress Reactions: The General Adaptation Syndrome" from Reading 3, pages 194 through 199.

Physical Stress Reactions: The General Adaptation Syndrome

Main Idea: The body's physical reaction to stress, called the general adaptation syndrome, involves the nervous system and three stages of response.

  I. The nervous system

    A. The central nervous system—brain and spinal cord

    B. The peripheral nervous system—nerves that connect from sense organs to central nervous system and from central nervous system to muscles and glands

       1. Somatic nervous system—controls voluntary muscles

       2. Autonomic nervous system—controls involuntary muscles

         a. Parasympathetic nervous system—conserves energy, decreases heart rate, promotes relaxing

         b. Sympathetic nervous system—generates energy, fight-or-flight response

  II. The general adaptation syndrome

    A. Stage I: Alarm—fight-or-flight response

       1. Hypothalamus stimulates pituitary to produce ACTH, which goes to the adrenal glands

       2. Hypothalamus triggered by autonomic nervous system

         a. Sends hormones

         b. Adrenal glands stimulated and send out cortisol and epinephrine (adrenaline)

       3. Effects of cortisol and epinephrine

         a. Make blood ready for brain and muscles

         b. Increase intake of oxygen

         c. Increase heart rate and blood pressure

         d. Release glucose—for energy

         e. Increase perspiration to reduce high temperature

         f. Expand pupils for better visual sensitivity

         g. Break down fat for extra fuel

         h. Produce antibodies if body is fighting a disease

©2007 Pearson Education, Inc.

B. Stage 2: Resistance
  1. Adapt body systems to challenge of stressors
  2. Concentrate on psychological coping mechanisms rather than fight-or-flight response
C. Stage 3: Exhaustion
  1. Body needs to rest
  2. If prolonged, may cause illness or even death

| Exercise 6 | **Organize to Learn: Outline** |

Complete the following outline for *Healthy People 2010*, which appears in Exercise 2 on pages 177 through 178.

Healthy People 2010

Thesis: _____ .

_____

I. Increase years of life and quality of life

    A. _____

      1. _____

      2. _____

    B. _____

II. Eliminate health disparities

    A. _____

      1. _____

      2. _____

      3. _____

    B. _____

      1. _____

      2. _____

Summarizing

summary A concise version of the main idea and major supporting points of a reading in your own words

A fourth important method of organizing information is writing a summary. Once you have identified the topic, the main idea or thesis statement, and the major supporting points in a reading, you are well prepared to write a summary. A **summary** is a condensed version of a reading, much shorter than the original, that includes the main idea and the major supporting points. It must be written *in your own words*, and it should not include your opinions or extra details and examples from the original.

Summaries are useful in organizing information for studying, for answering essay questions on exams, for writing research papers, and for condensing large amounts of data for research assignments.

The Process of Summarizing   To write an effective summary, follow these steps:

1. Carefully read and make sure you understand the material you are going to summarize.

2. Determine the main idea or thesis (for readings that are written to persuade). Write that main idea in a sentence using your own words. (When you write the main idea sentence, you will give credit to the author whose work you are summarizing and will mention the title of the reading, article, or book. Giving information on the source is described in more detail later.)

3. Decide what major supporting details you need to include.

4. Decide whether to include minor supporting details. A summary is supposed to be brief, so you usually do not need to include this level of detail.

5. Write the summary in your own words, beginning with your main idea sentence and including the major supporting details. Use complete sentences.

6. Remember, it is easier to use your own words if you are not looking directly at the passage while you write. *Don't copy!* If you use the author's language, be sure to put quotation marks around those words.

In a summary, you are giving the information or opinion of another writer in an abbreviated form. You are not giving your own opinion. Unless your instructor asks you to do so, do not inject your ideas into your summary.

Writing Main Idea Sentences in Summaries   The first sentence of your summary should include not only the main idea but also some basic information about the source.

1. The name of the author or of the group or institution responsible for the reading

2. The title of the reading or the article

3. The main idea (or thesis statement if the reading is trying to persuade you)

One way to write your first sentence is to start with "According to [author's name], in the article, "[title of article]," [complete main-idea sentence in your own words].

For example, this is the thesis statement for Reading 1, Insel et al.'s "Wellness": "True wellness is largely determined by the decisions you make about how to live your life." So the first sentence of a summary might say this:

According to Paul M. Insel and his coauthors, "Wellness: The New Health Goal,"

"wellness" depends on the decisions each person makes about how to live.

©2007 Pearson Education, Inc.

A full summary of Reading 1 might look like this:

> *According to Paul M. Insel and his coauthors, in the reading "Wellness: The New Health Goal," "wellness" depends on the decisions each person makes about how to live. Wellness is more than not being sick. Included in this concept of health is the ability to live an active, full, and meaningful life. To achieve wellness, people need to address the six dimensions of wellness: (1) physical wellness, (2) emotional wellness, (3) intellectual wellness, (4) spiritual wellness, (5) interpersonal and social wellness, and (6) environmental or planetary wellness.*

Exercise 7   ## Write Main Idea Sentences for Summaries

The following are main idea sentences. Rewrite them in your own words, and give credit to the author and the title of the reading. Use the format "According to. . . ." Other than the sentences from *Healthy People 2010*, these are not real authors or real texts. We've created them to give you practice in writing strong first sentences for summaries.

1. Smoking is a behavior that increases a variety of health risks, including death. (From an article entitled "Break the Habit," by Elizabeth Jones)

   _____

   _____

2. Inequalities in income and education lead to health disparities in the United States. (From *Healthy People 2010*, a publication of the Department of Health and Human Services)

   _____

   _____

3. African Americans are at a greater risk for heart disease and high blood pressure. (From the article "Disparities in Health Care," by Joe Davis)

   _____

   _____

4. Even though more than 50 percent of Americans are overweight, it doesn't mean that we are eating well. (From Nellie Jones's book *Eat Right to Stay Fit*)

   _____

   _____

5. Recent health gains for the U.S. population as a whole appear to reflect achievements among the high socioeconomic groups; low socioeconomic groups continue to lag behind. (From *Healthy People 2010,* a publication of the Department of Health and Human Services)

Exercise 8 **Organize to Learn: Write a Summary**

Using the outline you made in Exercise 6, page 186, write a summary on a separate sheet of paper of the information about the goals of *Healthy People 2010.*

Reading 2 *Exercise for Health and Fitness*   Paul M. Insel,
Walton T. Roth, L. McKay Rollins, and Ray A. Peterson

In the following reading, Paul M. Insel and his coauthors define physical fitness and explain the benefits of exercise. As you read, pay particular attention to how the main ideas are developed and explained with major and minor supporting points.

What Is Physical Fitness?

1 Physical fitness is the ability of the body to adapt to the demands of physical effort—that is, to perform moderate-to-vigorous levels of physical activity without becoming overly tired. Physical fitness has many components, some related to general health and others related more specifically to particular sports or activities. The five components of fitness most important for health are cardiorespiratory endurance, muscular strength, muscular endurance, flexibility, and body composition (proportion of fat to lean body mass).

Cardiorespiratory Endurance

2 *Cardiorespiratory endurance* is the ability to perform prolonged, large-muscle, dynamic exercise at moderate-to-high levels of intensity. It depends on such factors as the ability of the lungs to deliver oxygen from the environment to the bloodstream, the heart's capacity to pump blood, the ability of the nervous system and blood vessels to regulate blood flow, and the capability of the body's chemical systems to use oxygen and process fuels for exercise. When levels of cardiorespiratory fitness are low, the heart has to work very hard during normal daily activities and may not be able to work hard enough to sustain high-intensity physical activity in an emergency. As cardiorespiratory fitness improves, the heart begins to function more effi-

©2007 Pearson Education, Inc.

ciently. It doesn't have to work as hard at rest or during low levels of exercise. A healthy heart can better withstand the strains of everyday life, the stress of occasional emergencies, and the wear and tear of time.

3   Cardiorespiratory endurance is considered the most important component of health-related fitness because the functioning of the heart and lungs is so essential to overall wellness. A person simply cannot live very long or very well without a healthy heart. Low levels of cardiorespiratory fitness are linked with heart disease, the leading cause of death in the United States. Cardiorespiratory endurance is developed by activities that involve continuous rhythmic movements of large muscle groups like those in the legs—for example, walking, jogging, cycling, and aerobic dance. This type of activity is called *cardiorespiratory endurance exercise* or *aerobic exercise.*

Muscular Strength

4   *Muscular strength* is the amount of force a muscle can produce with a single maximum effort. Strong muscles are important for the smooth and easy performance of everyday activities, such as carrying groceries, lifting boxes, and climbing stairs, as well as for emergency situations. They help keep the skeleton in proper alignment, preventing back and leg pain and providing the support necessary for good posture. Muscular strength has obvious importance in recreational activities. Strong people can hit a tennis ball harder, kick a soccer ball farther, and ride a bicycle uphill more easily.

5   Muscle tissue is an important element of overall body composition. Greater muscle mass (or lean body mass) makes possible a higher rate of metabolism and faster energy use. Muscular strength can be developed by training with weights or by using the weight of the body for resistance during calisthenic exercises such as push-ups and sit-ups.

Muscular Endurance

6   *Muscular endurance* is the ability to sustain a given level of muscle tension—that is, to hold a muscle contraction for a long period of time, or to contract a muscle over and over again. Muscular endurance is important for good posture and for injury prevention. For example, if abdominal and back muscles are not strong enough to hold the spine correctly, the chances of low-back pain and back injury are increased. Muscular endurance helps people cope with the physical demands of everyday life and enhances performances in sports and work. It is also important for most leisure and fitness activities. Like muscular strength, muscular endurance is developed by stressing the muscles with a greater load (weight) than they are used to. The degree to which strength or endurance develops depends on the type and amount of stress that is applied.

Flexibility

7   *Flexibility* is the ability to move the joints through their full range of motion. Although range of motion is not a significant factor in everyday activities for most people, inactivity causes the joints to become stiffer with age. Stiffness often causes older people to assume unnatural body postures, and it can

lead to back pain. The majority of Americans experience low-back pain at some time in their lives, often because of stiff joints. Stretching exercises can help ensure a normal range of motion.

Body Composition

8 *Body composition* refers to the relative amounts of lean body tissue (muscle, bone, and water) and fat in the body. Healthy body composition involves a high proportion of lean body tissue and an acceptably low level of body fat, adjusted for age and gender. A person with excessive body fat is more likely to experience a variety of health problems, including heart disease, high blood pressure, stroke, joint problems, diabetes, gallbladder disease, cancer, and back pain. The best way to lose fat is through a lifestyle that includes a sensible diet and exercise. The best way to add lean body tissue is through weight training, also known as strength or resistance training.

The Benefits of Exercise

9 As mentioned above, the human body is very adaptable. The greater the demands made on it, the more it adjusts to meet the demands. Over time, immediate, short-term adjustments translate into long-term changes and improvements. For example, when breathing and heart rate increase during exercise, the heart gradually develops the ability to pump more blood with each beat. Then, during exercise, it doesn't have to beat as fast to meet the body's demand for oxygen. The goal of regular physical activity is to bring about these kinds of long-term changes and improvements in the body's functioning.

10 Exercise is one of the most important things you can do to improve your level of wellness. Regular exercise increases energy levels, improves emotional and psychological well-being, and boosts the immune system. It prevents heart disease, some types of cancer, stroke, high blood pressure, diabetes, obesity, and osteoporosis. At any age, people who exercise are less likely to die from all causes than their sedentary peers.

Improved Cardiorespiratory Functioning

11 Every time you take a breath, some of the oxygen in the air you take into your lungs is picked up by red blood cells and transported to your heart. From there, this oxygenated blood is pumped by the heart throughout the body to organs and tissues that use it. During exercise, the cardiorespiratory system (heart, lungs, and circulatory system) must work harder to meet the body's increased demand for oxygen. Regular endurance exercise improves the functioning of the heart and the ability of the cardiorespiratory system to carry oxygen to body tissue.

More Efficient Metabolism

12 Endurance exercise improves metabolism, the process by which food is converted to energy and tissue is built. This process involves oxygen, nutrients, hormones, and enzymes. A physically fit person is better able to generate en-

©2007 Pearson Education, Inc.

ergy, to use fats for energy, and to regulate hormones. Physical training also protects the body's cells from damage from free radicals, which are produced during normal metabolism. Training activates antioxidant enzymes that prevent free radical damage and maintain the health of the body's cells.

Improved Body Composition

13 Healthy body composition means that the body has a high proportion of lean body mass (primarily composed of muscle) and a relatively small proportion of fat. Too much body fat is linked to a variety of health problems, including heart disease, cancer, and diabetes. Healthy body composition can be difficult to achieve and maintain because a diet that contains all essential nutrients can be relatively high in calories, especially for someone who is sedentary. Excess calories are stored in the body as fat.

14   Exercise can improve body composition in several ways. Endurance exercise significantly increases daily calorie expenditure; it can also raise *metabolic rate,* the rate at which the body burns calories, for several hours after an exercise session. Strength training increases muscle mass, thereby tipping the body composition ratio toward lean body mass and away from fat. It can also help with losing fat because metabolic rate is directly proportional to lean body mass: The more muscle mass, the higher the metabolic rate.

Disease Prevention and Management

15 Regular physical activity lowers your risk of many chronic disabling diseases. It can also help people with those diseases improve their health.

16 **Cardiovascular Disease**   A sedentary lifestyle is one of the four major risk factors for *cardiovascular disease* (CVD). . . . The other factors are smoking, unhealthy cholesterol levels, and high blood pressure. People who are sedentary have CVD death rates significantly higher than fit individuals. There is a dose-response relationship between exercise and CVD: The benefit of physical activity occurs at moderate levels of activity and increases with increasing levels of activity.

17   Many research studies have shown conclusively that exercise not only affects the risk factors for CVD but also directly interferes with the disease process itself. Endurance exercise improves blood fat levels by increasing levels of high-density lipoproteins and decreasing levels of low-density lipoproteins and triglycerides. Endurance exercise reduces high blood pressure and lowers one's risk of coronary heart disease and stroke.

18 **Cancer**   Some studies have shown a relationship between increased physical activity and a reduction in a person's risk of all types of cancer, but these findings are not conclusive. There is strong evidence that exercise reduces the risk of colon cancer, and promising data that it reduces the risk of cancer of the breast and reproductive organs in women.

19 **Osteoporosis**   A special benefit of exercise, especially for women, is protection against osteoporosis, a disease that results in loss of bone density and poor bone strength. Weight-bearing exercise, which includes almost everything except swimming, helps build bone during the teens and twen-

ties. Older people with denser bones can better endure the bone loss that occurs with aging. Strength training can increase bone density throughout life. With stronger bones and muscles and better balance, fit people are less likely to experience debilitating falls and bone fractures. (But too much exercise can depress levels of estrogen, which helps maintain bone density, thereby leading to bone loss, even in young women.)

20 **Diabetes** People with diabetes, a disorder characterized by high blood sugar levels and the inability of cells to take up and use glucose, are prone to heart disease, blindness, and severe problems of the nervous and circulatory systems. Recent studies have shown that exercise actually prevents the development of the most common form of diabetes, called Type 2 diabetes. Exercise burns excess sugar and makes more cells sensitive to insulin. Exercise also helps keep body fat at healthy levels. (Obesity is a key risk factor for Type 2 diabetes.) For people who have diabetes, physical activity is an important part of treatment.

Improved Psychological and Emotional Wellness

21 The joy of a well-hit cross-court backhand, the euphoria of a walk through the park, or the rush of a downhill schuss through deep snow powder provides pleasure that transcends health benefits alone. People who are physically active experience many social, psychological, and emotional benefits. They experience less stress and are buffered against the dangerous physical effects of stress, and are less likely to experience anxiety or depression. People who exercise also tend to have a more positive self-image. Exercise offers an arena for harmonious interaction with other people as well as opportunities to strive and excel. . . .

Improved Immune Function

22 Exercise can have either positive or negative effects on the immune system, the physiological processes that protect us from disease. It appears that moderate endurance exercise boosts immune function, while excessive training depresses it. Physically fit people get fewer colds and upper respiratory tract infections than people who are not fit.

Prevention of Injuries and Low-Back Pain

23 Increased muscle strength provides protection against injury because it helps people maintain good posture and appropriate body mechanics when carrying out everyday activities like walking, lifting, and carrying. Strong muscles in the abdomen, hips, low back, and legs support the back in proper alignment and helps prevent low-back pain, which afflicts over 85% of all Americans at some time in their lives.

Improved Wellness Over the Life Span

24 Although people differ in the maximum levels of fitness they can achieve through exercise, the wellness benefits of exercise are available to everyone. Exercising regularly may be the single most important thing you can do now to improve the quality of your life in the future. All the benefits of exercise

©2007 Pearson Education, Inc.

continue to accrue but gain new importance as the resilience of youth begins to wane. Simply stated, exercising can help you live a longer and healthier life.

INSEL ET AL., *CORE CONCEPTS IN HEALTH*

<hr>

Exercise 9   ## Work with Words

The following sentences appear in Reading 2, Insel et al.'s "Exercise for Health and Fitness." Use context clues, your knowledge of word parts, and if necessary, dictionary skills to determine the meaning of each italicized word in the sentences. Write the meaning on the lines provided. The paragraph number is provided in case you want to check the context.

1. *Greater muscle mass* (or lean body mass) makes possible a higher rate of metabolism and faster energy use. (par. 5)

   Greater muscle mass: _____

2. *Body composition* refers to the relative amounts of lean body tissue (muscle, bone, and water) and fat in the body. (par. 8)

   Body composition: _____

3. Endurance exercise improves *metabolism*, the process by which food is converted to energy and tissue is built. (par. 12)

   Metabolism: _____

4. Endurance exercise significantly increases daily calorie expenditure; it can also raise *metabolic rate*, the rate at which the body burns calories, for several hours after an exercise session. (par. 14)

   Metabolic rate: _____

5. A special benefit of exercise, especially for women, is protection against *osteoporosis*, a disease that results in loss of bone density and poor bone strength. (par. 19)

   Osteoporosis: _____

Exercise 10   ## Check Your Understanding

Based on Reading 2, write your answers to the following questions on the lines provided.

1. Why is cardiorespiratory endurance considered the most important component of health-related fitness?

   _____

2. What is muscular endurance, and why is it important?

   _____

3. What are the benefits of having a more efficient metabolism?

   _____

4. What kind of exercise is best for improving immune function?

_____

5. What percentage of Americans are affected by low back pain? _____

Exercise 11 **Organize to Learn: Outline**

Complete the following outline for Reading 2.

Exercise for Health and Fitness

Main Idea: _Physical fitness, achieved through a variety of regular exercise, has_ _____

many benefits for our well-being. _____

I.   Physical fitness definition: _____

_____

II. Components of physical fitness

A. _____

B. _____

C. _____

D. _____

E. _____

III. Benefits of exercise

A. _____

B. _____

C. _____

D. _____

1. _____

2. _____

3. _____

4. _____

E. _____

F. _____

G. _____

H. _____

©2007 Pearson Education, Inc.

| Exercise 12 | Organize to Learn: Write a Summary |

Based on the outline that you completed in Exercise 11, write a brief summary of Reading 2 on a separate sheet of paper. Be sure to put the main idea sentence in your own words and include the author's name and the title of the reading.

| Exercise 13 | Reflect |

Think about what you read in Reading 2 and what you already know about health and fitness. Answer the following questions, and prepare to discuss them with your classmates.

1. In what ways are you most physically fit?

_____

_____

2. In what ways would you like to improve your physical fitness?

_____

_____

Reading 3   *How Stress Works*

Bryan Williams and Sharon Knight

The following reading is from a chapter of the college health education textbook Healthy for Life. *Read it actively.*

Stress and Stressors

1 Stress is the body's reaction: stressors are the source of stress. Stressors may be small irritating hassles, short-duration crises, or long-duration strong stressors. A source of stress may be negative and cause "distress" or be positive and cause "eustress."

2   *Stress* is the reaction of our bodies to an event. The source of stress is called a *stressor*. Stressors may be specific, ranging from a flat tire to a death in the family, but the physical reaction is nonspecific and generalized, being felt throughout the entire body.

3   Life and health in modern society require that we continually adapt to a variety of events. The human body constantly strives to maintain a state of balance known as *homeostasis*, in which physiological and psychological systems are stable, or in equilibrium. Stressors may disturb this homeostasis by causing one's body to become unbalanced and, if the stress is too great for too long, eventually causing illness and potentially death.

4   Stress has both physical and emotional components. Physically, according to Canadian researcher Hans Selye, a pioneer in this area, stress is "the nonspecific response of the body to any demand made upon it." Emotionally, stress has been defined as the feeling of being overwhelmed, "the perception that events or circumstances have challenged, or exceeded, a person's ability to cope."

Types of Stressors: Hassles, Crises, Strong Stressors

5   There is probably no way to completely escape stress, whether it starts with small daily hassles or with unexpected one-time crises. Such negative sources of stress, when they become too cumulative or too powerful, eventually can lead to illness, depression, and even premature death. Let us consider the types of stressors, ranging in intensity and duration from hassles to crises to strong stressors.

6   **Hassles**   Simply frustrating, *hassles* are irritants, but their cumulative effect can be significant and even hazardous to health. College students, says psychologist Richard Lazarus, are most hassled by (1) anxiety over wasting time, (2) pressure to meet high standards, and (3) feeling lonely.

7   One of the authors took an informal poll: When I asked my students what the principal hassles were in their lives, they reported being worried about finding time to study, having relationship problems with roommates and partners, and conflicts over partying versus studying.

8   Lazarus contends that nearly everyone, regardless of age, complains about three kinds of hassles: (1) misplacing or losing things, (2) physical appearance, and (3) having too many things to do.

9   Of course we all have many other kinds of hassles, but their importance varies with one's age and situation in life. One study found that younger adults experienced significantly more hassles in the domains of finances, work, home maintenance, personal life, and family and friends than did older adults. White, middle-class men and women of middle age had their own specific hassles.

10   **Crises**   A *crisis* is an especially strong source of stress, one that may appear suddenly and be of short duration but have long-lasting effects. For instance, sudden occasions of overwhelming terror—a horrible auto accident, an incident of childhood abuse, a wartime experience—can have a tremendous biological impact. This is so whether the event is a one-time experience or repeated, according to Yale psychiatrist Dennis Charney, director of clinical neuroscience at the National Center for Post-Traumatic Stress Disorder. Brain chemistry changes in response to the stress so that people are more sensitive to adrenaline surges even decades later, and people experience normal events as repetitions of the original trauma. Such people experience troubled sleep, irritability and rages, and recurrent nightmares and flashbacks that repeat the original horror.

©2007 Pearson Education, Inc.

11 **Strong Stressors**   There are also strong sources of stress of continuing duration, called *strong stressors*, which can dramatically strain a person's ability to adapt. A strong stressor can be extreme mental or physical discomfort. For example, two years after Kay Bartlett suffered a neck injury from a fall in her kitchen she wrote that pain had become her constant companion. Pain, she stated, "regulates nearly every moment of my waking life, holding me captive to its savage dictates." Indeed, she said, "Pain has changed my life, narrowing it as old age will eventually do. But, at 49, I'm not old enough to be this old. I feel like in the last two years I have aged 30." For Kay Bartlett, obviously, the stressor of chronic pain has significantly impaired the quality of her life.

12 **Stressors, Good and Bad**   So far, we have mainly dealt with stress as though its sources were negative. However, stress researcher Selye points out that stressors can be *both negative and positive.* He writes: "It is immaterial whether the agent or situation we face is pleasant or unpleasant; all that counts is the intensity of the demand for readjustment and adaptation." Stressors, he says, are of the following types:

- Distressors: When the source of stress is a negative event (for example, being fired, being rejected in love), it is called a *distressor* and its effect is called *distress*. Although distress can be helpful when one is facing a physical threat, too much of this kind of stress may result in illness.

- Eustressors: When the source of stress is a positive event (for example, falling in love, being promoted), it is called a *eustressor*; its effect is called *eustress* (pronounced "*you*-stress"). Eustress can stimulate a person to better coping and adaptation. (Selye coined this word by adding the Greek prefix *eu*, for "good," to the word *stress*.)

13   We can't always prevent distressors, but we can learn to recognize them, understand our reactions to them, and develop ways of managing both the stressors and the stress. Eustressors, on the other hand, are what impel us to do our best—to become the "peak performers."

Physical Stress Reactions: The General Adaptation Syndrome

14 The physical response to stress been described as a three-stage general adaptation syndrome. Stage 1, alarm, is the "fight-or-flight" response, in which the body's nervous system takes over. Stage 2, resistance, gives the body increased strength and endurance. Stage 3, exhaustion, is the wearing down from continuing stress.

15   As we mentioned, stress reactions have both physical and mental components, although the responses are intertwined. In this section, we consider the physical reactions. . . .

16   As you might guess, one key player in stress is the nervous system. . . . The nervous system consists of two principal parts:

- Central nervous system: The *central nervous system* is made up of the brain and the spinal cord.

- Peripheral nervous system: The *peripheral nervous system* consists of the nerves that carry messages from the sense organs to the central nervous system and from the central nervous system to the muscles and glands.

The peripheral nervous system in turn has two parts:

- Somatic nervous system: The *somatic nervous system* controls the voluntary muscles. When you do deep-breathing exercises to control stress, you are using muscles in the somatic nervous system.
- Autonomic nervous system: The *autonomic nervous system* controls the involuntary muscles. When you become frightened and begin to perspire and your heart begins to race, these activities are controlled by the autonomic nervous system.

The autonomic nervous system also has two parts:

- Parasympathetic: The *parasympathetic nervous system* conserves energy, decreases heart rate, increases digestive activities, and promotes body activities that are relaxing.
- Sympathetic: The *sympathetic nervous system generates* energy, increases the heart rate and breathing rate, and prepares the body for either fighting or fleeing when it perceives a threat.

17   Selye described the response to a stressor as a three-stage general adaptation syndrome. The stages are *alarm, resistance,* and *exhaustion.* . . . To various degrees, these reactions can occur whether you meet a mugger in an alley, get a terse "See me immediately!" note from the boss, hear the starting gun in a race, or are called upon to give a toast at a wedding. Before the first stage, there may be a conscious or unconscious evaluation in which a decision is made as to whether or not a threat exists.

Stage 1—Alarm

18 The alarm phase is often called the fight-or-flight response. This is the stage in which the brain rapidly and subconsciously perceives the stressor, which may be either external (real threat) or internal (probably imagined threat). The brain decides that the stressor is a disturbing event and almost instantly mobilizes your body's defensive forces to stand and fight or to turn and flee. Specifically:

- The autonomic nervous system takes over: The autonomic nervous system, which controls your movements and internal functions, operates largely without any conscious thought on your part.
- The hypothalamus causes adrenal glands to release stress-response hormones: The autonomic nervous system triggers the hypothalamus. The *hypothalamus* is a part of the brain that directs the flow of *hormones*, or chemicals, throughout the body. The hypothalamus stimulates the *adrenal glands*—specialized glands located on top of the kidneys. This stimulation comes about when two conditions occur:

©2007 Pearson Education, Inc.

1. The hypothalamus stimulates the *pituitary gland* (the "master gland" of the endocrine system) to produce *ACTH (adrenocorticotropic hormone)*, which is transmitted to the adrenal glands.

2. The hypothalamus sends impulses via the autonomic nervous system. The adrenal glands then release into the bloodstream hormones related to stress responses, among them *cortisol* and *epinephrine (adrenaline)*.

- Cortisol and epinephrine "arm" your body to fight or flee: The hormones cortisol and epinephrine (the "fear hormone") bring about a number of changes to enable your body to meet the stress. These hormones act to:

    1. Reduce blood supply to your kidneys and intestines, making more blood ready for your brain and muscles.

    2. Increase the intake of oxygen by the lungs and increase the supply of oxygen to muscles and brain.

    3. Increase heart rate and blood pressure to increase blood circulation.

    4. Release *glucose*, a type of sugar stored (as glycogen) in the liver, for use as energy for muscular exertion.

    5. Increase perspiration to reduce the high body temperature caused by the speeding up of the body's functions.

    6. Cause the pupils of the eye to expand (dilate), providing increased visual sensitivity.

    7. Break down fat tissue (and, eventually, even muscle tissue) to provide additional fuel for energy, if needed.

    8. Produce *antibodies*, specific chemical compounds to destroy disease-producing microorganisms, if the body is threatened by a specific disease.

19 Clearly, these include several of the reactions—thumping heart, rapid breathing, sweating—that one associates with fear or stress.

Stage 2—Resistance

20 In this second stage of the general adaptation syndrome, your body's systems adapt themselves to the challenge of the stressor, giving the body increased strength and endurance, if necessary, or they return to a level of normal activity. In addition, during this phase, you begin to concentrate more on psychological coping mechanisms and defensive behavior to deal with the stressor rather than continuing the physical fight-or-flight response.

Stage 3—Exhaustion

21 If the stress goes on long enough, your physical and psychological energy will be depleted, and your body will need to rest. When weeks and months pass with no letup in stress—as can happen with a working parent short on

money or a soldier exposed to constant combat—eventually you will show symptoms of exhaustion and may become ill. Indeed, if stressors cause wear and tear over a long period of time, they may even lead to death. It's important, therefore, for you to find ways to counter long-sustained tension.

WILLIAMS AND KNIGHT, *HEALTHY FOR LIFE*

Exercise 14   ## Work with Words

Various parts of the nervous system play specific roles. To master the material in Reading 3, "How Stress Works," by Williams and Knight, you would have to memorize a great deal of specialized vocabulary that was introduced about the nervous system (and the endocrine system). Look at the following lists, A and B. Circle the word parts that you recognize in list B. Then use your knowledge of word parts and the reading itself to match each function or description in list A with the correct nervous system part in list B. You may use a letter from list B more than once.

A. Function/Description

___ 1. Brain and spinal cord
___ 2. Conserves energy
___ 3. Controls involuntary muscles
___ 4. Controls voluntary muscles
___ 5. Decreases heart rate
___ 6. Increases breathing rate
___ 7. Something that causes stress
___ 8. Carries sense organ messages
___ 9. Prepares body for fight or flight
___ 10. Chemical compounds that destroy disease-producing microorganisms

B. Nervous System Part

A. Autonomic nervous system
B. Central nervous system
C. Parasympathetic nervous system
D. Peripheral nervous system
E. Somatic nervous system
F. Sympathetic nervous system
G. Antibodies
H. Stressor.

Exercise 15   ## Check Your Understanding

Based on Reading 3, decide whether each of the following statements is true or false.

_____ 1. The extent of our reaction to stress depends on the intensity of our perception of the source of stress.

_____ 2. Stress is a natural part of our lives.

_____ 3. Stress can produce physical and/or psychological effects.

_____ 4. Time management is only a hassle for people who are going to school.

_____ 5. Selye states that stress is almost always negative.

©2007 Pearson Education, Inc.

_____ 6. During the alarm stage of stress, the somatic nervous system takes over.

_____ 7. Cortisol and epinephrine (adrenaline) are the two hormones that are released into your bloodstream to prepare your body for the fight-or-flight response.

_____ 8. The three stages of the general adaptation syndrome are alarm, resistance, and rest.

_____ 9. The alarm phase of reacting to extreme stress is called the fight-or-flight response.

_____ 10. When people experience too much stress over long periods, they enter the exhaustion phase, which forces them to rest and recover.

Exercise 16   Organize to Learn

1. On pages 196 through 198, mark the text in the section headed "Stress and Stressors." Stop before you begin the "Physical Stress Reactions" section.

2. Now outline the material you marked on pages 196 through 198.

3. Briefly summarize the material. Remember to put the main idea sentence in your own words.

Exercise 17   Write Main Idea Sentences

This section presents 13 strategies for handling stress that came from a health textbook. As you read the explanation for each strategy, decide what the main idea or general rule of that strategy should be. Write it on the line provided. The first two have been done for you.

1. _Adopt a new way of looking at life. Rely on yourself._

Stress management begins with adopting the philosophy that you, as an individual, are basically responsible for your own emotional and physical well-being. You can no longer allow other people to determine whether or not you are happy. You have little control over the behavior of anyone but yourself, and your emotional well-being is too important to trust to anyone but yourself. Your goal should be to develop such positive emotional wellness that nobody can ruin your day.

2. _Keep a positive outlook on life._

This is absolutely essential to successful stress management. Your perception of events, not the events themselves, is what causes stress. Almost any life situation can be perceived as either stressful or nonstressful, depending on your interpretation. A negative view of life guarantees a high stress level. People who habitually view life negatively can recondition themselves to be more positive. One way is by applying a thought stopping technique: whenever you catch yourself thinking negatively, force yourself to think about the positive aspects of your situation. Eventually you will just automatically begin to see life more positively.

3. _____

Exercise is an excellent tension reliever. In addition to the physical benefits, exercise is also good for the mind. Participating in at least three aerobic exercise sessions a week for at least 20 minutes each can greatly reduce stress. Daily stretching exercises provide relaxation and improve flexibility and posture. Participate in leisure activities that keep you physically active.

4. _____

Disorganization, sloppiness, chaos, and procrastination may seem very relaxed, but they are stressful. Set short-term, intermediate-term, and long-term goals for yourself. Every morning list the things you want and need to accomplish that day. Assign each item an A, B, or C priority. Take care of the most urgent matters first. Be realistic; don't expect too much of yourself. Perhaps some C priority items don't really have to be done.

5. _____

Some people accept too many responsibilities. If you spread yourself too thin, not only will you be highly stressed, but important things will be done poorly or not at all. Know your limits and be assertive. If you don't have time to do something or simply don't want to do it, don't. Practice saying no effectively. Try, "I'm flattered that you've asked me, but given my commitments at this time, I won't be able to. . . ."

6. _____

Our culture is extremely goal-oriented. Many of the things we do are directed toward achieving a goal, with no thought or expectation of enjoying the process. We may go to college for a degree, but we should enjoy the process of obtaining that degree. We may go to work for a paycheck, but we should enjoy our work. Happiness can seldom be achieved when pursued as a goal. It is usually a by-product of other activities. In whatever you do, focus on and enjoy the activity itself, rather than on how well you perform the activity or what the activity will bring you.

7. _____

Perfectionists set impossible goals for themselves, because perfection is unattainable. Learn to tolerate and forgive both yourself and others. Intolerance of our own imperfections leads to stress and low self-esteem. Intolerance of others leads to anger, blame, and poor relationships, all of which increase stress.

©2007 Pearson Education, Inc.

8. _____

Find things other than yourself and your own achievements to care about and believe in. Self-esteem and a sense of purpose in life come from dedication to people, relationships, ideas, and values. Learn to see the world and yourself through the eyes of others. Interpersonal relationships are less stressful when we understand others' viewpoints.

9. _____

There are plenty of opportunities for involvement with others, including youth programs, hospices, hospitals, and programs for the homeless or needy. Helping others reduces stress by boosting self-esteem and putting our own problems in a different perspective.

10. _____

Everyone can list things that he or she might have done differently in the past. Other than learning through experience and trying not to make the same mistakes again, there is nothing to be gained by worrying about what we did or didn't do in the past. To focus on the past is nonproductive, stressful, and robs the present of its joy and vitality. An exception to this rule is those forms of psychotherapy that explore one's past in order to understand present behaviors and attitudes. Such directed examination of one's past can be quite productive.

11. _____

How we eat affects our emotions and our ability to cope. When our diet is good we feel better and deal better with difficult situations. Eat more carefully for two weeks and feel the difference it makes.

There is no unique stress reduction diet, despite many claims to the contrary. The same diet that helps prevent heart disease, cancer, obesity, and diabetes (low in sugar, salt, fat, and total calories; adequate in vitamins, minerals, and protein) will also reduce stress.

What about the highly advertised "stress formula" vitamin pills? If your physiology is normal and you eat carefully, you have no need for these or any other vitamin pills. There is no evidence that very large vitamin doses help combat stress and megadoses can be toxic.

12. _____

Sleep is essential for successfully managing stress and maintaining your health. People have varying sleep requirements, but most people function best with seven to eight hours of sleep per day. Some people simply don't allot enough time to sleep, while others find that stress makes it difficult for them to sleep. It is easy to become trapped in a cycle in which stress makes sleep difficult and lack of sleep further increases stress.

13. _____

The use of alcohol and other drugs in an effort to reduce stress levels actually contributes to stress in several ways. As alcohol and other drugs wear off, the rebound effect makes the user feel very uncomfortable and stressed. Also, heavy use of alcohol or other drugs invariably creates problems that further increase stress levels. Eliminating or minimizing alcohol and other drug use is essential in stress management.

Don't overlook the possibility that excess caffeine intake is contributing to your stress. Caffeine is a powerful stimulant that, by itself, produces many of the physiological manifestations of stress. Plus, its effect of increased energy contributes to more stressful, rushed behavior patterns. Remember that not only coffee and tea, but chocolate and many soft drinks contain caffeine.

BYER AND SHAINBERG, *LIVING WELL*

Exercise 18   ## Reflect

Fill out the following questionnaire, "How Stressed Out Are You?" Then read the section, "What Your Scores Mean." Prepare to discuss your results with your classmates.

How Stressed Out Are You?   Lora Elise Ma

Part 1: The Stress in Your Life

How often are the following stressful situations a part of your daily life? Check the number that best describes your experience.

1. *Never*

2. *Rarely*

3. *Sometimes*

4. *Often*

5. *All the time*

I work long hours. ....1☑ 2☐ 3☐ 4☐ 5☐
There are signs my job isn't secure. ....1☐ 2☐ 3☐ 4☐ 5☐
Doing a good job goes unnoticed. ....1☐ 2☐ 3☐ 4☐ 5☐
It takes all my energy just to make it through the day. ....1☐ 2☑ 3☐ 4☐ 5☐
There are severe arguments at home. ....1☐ 2☑ 3☐ 4☐ 5☐
A family member is seriously ill. ....1☐ 2☐ 3☐ 4☐ 5☐
I'm having problems with child care. ....1☐ 2☐ 3☐ 4☐ 5☐
I don't have enough time for fun. ....1☐ 2☐ 3☐ 4☐ 5☐
I'm on a diet. ....1☐ 2☑ 3☐ 4☐ 5☐
My family and friends count on me to solve problems. ....1☐ 2☑ 3☐ 4☐ 5☐
I'm expected to keep up a certain standard of living. ....1☐ 2☐ 3☐ 4☐ 5☐

©2007 Pearson Education, Inc.

My neighborhood is crowded or dangerous. ....1☑ 2☐ 3☐ 4☐ 5☐
My home is a mess. ....1☑ 2☐ 3☐ 4☐ 5☐
I can't pay my bills on time..1☑ 2☐ 3☐ 4☐ 5☐
I'm not saving money. ....1☐ 2☑ 3☐ 4☐ 5☐

Your Total Score _____

Below 38: You have a *Lower-Stress Life.*
38 and Above: You have a *High-Stress Life.*

Part 2: Your Stress Susceptibility

Try to imagine how you would react in these hypothetical situations.

You've been waiting 20 minutes for a table in a crowded restaurant, and the host seats a party that arrived after you. You feel your anger rise as your face gets hot and your heart beats faster.

True or False

Your sister calls out of the blue and starts to tell you how much you mean to her. Uncomfortable, you change the subject without expressing what you feel.

True or False

You come home to find the kitchen looking like a disaster area and your spouse lounging in front of the TV. You tense up and can't seem to shake your anger.

True or False

Faced with a public speaking event, you get keyed up and lose sleep for a day or more, worrying about how you'll do.

True or False

On Thursday your repair shop promises to fix your car in time for a weekend trip. As the hours go by, you become increasingly worried that something will go wrong and your trip will be ruined.

True or False

Total True _____

Total False _____

Two or fewer true: You're a *Cool Reactor,* someone who tends to roll with the punches when a situation is out of control.

Three or more true: Sorry, you're a *Hot Reactor,* someone who responds to mildly stressful situations with a "fight-or-flight" adrenaline rush that drives up blood pressure and can lead to heart rhythm disturbances, accelerated clotting, and damaged blood vessel linings. Some hot reactors can seem cool as a cucumber on the outside, but inside their bodies are silently killing them.

What Your Scores Mean

Combine the results from parts 1 and 2 to get your total stress rating.

Lower-Stress Life   Cool Reactor

Whatever your problems, *stress isn't one of them. Even when stressful events do occur—and they will—your health probably won't suffer.*

Lower-Stress Life   Hot Reactor

You're not under stress—*at least for now. Though you tend to overreact to problems, you've wisely managed your life to avoid the big stressors. Before you honk at the guy who cuts you off in rush hour traffic, remember that getting angry can destroy thousands of heart muscle cells within minutes. Robert S. Eliot, author of* From Stress to Strength, *says hot reactors have no choice but to calm themselves down with rational thought. Ponder the fact that the only thing you'll hasten by reacting is a decline in health. "You have to stop trying to change the world," Eliot advises, "and learn to change your response to it."*

High-Stress Life   Cool Reactor

You're under stress, *but only you know if it's hurting. Even if you normally thrive with a full plate of challenges, now you might be biting off more than you can chew. Note any increases in headaches, backaches, or insomnia; that's your body telling you to lighten your load. If your job is the main source of stress, think about reducing your hours. If that's not possible, find a way to make your job more enjoyable, and stress will become manageable.*

High-Stress Life   Hot Reactor

You're in the danger zone. *Make an extra effort to exercise, get enough sleep, and keep your family and friends close. Unfortunately, even being physically fit does little to protect you if your body is in perpetual stress mode. To survive, you may need to make major changes—walking away from a life-destroying job or relationship, perhaps—as well as to develop a whole new approach to life's hourly obstacles. Such efforts will be rewarded, too. In one experiment, 77 percent of hot reactors were able to cool down—lower their blood pressure and cholesterol levels—training themselves to stay calm.*

(MA, "How Stressed Out Are You?")

CHAPTER REVIEW

Reader's Checklist

Check (✔) the concepts and skills introduced in this chapter that you are confident you understand and can now use to distinguish between main ideas, major supporting points, and minor supporting points. Also check the

©2007 Pearson Education, Inc.

organize-to-learn skills that you can use. If you are not sure about any items, (1) go back to the explanations in the text, (2) study and review with other members of your college learning community, (3) ask your instructor for help, (4) check out the Web site for this textbook at **www.ablongman. com/alexandercommunity4e** for additional exercises on support for main ideas and to take the chapter quiz, or (5) complete additional practices in the *Reading Road Trip*.

- ❏ Major supporting points
- ❏ Minor supporting points
- ❏ Organize to learn
- ❏ Marking texts
- ❏ Making bulleted lists
- ❏ Outlining
- ❏ Summarizing

When you are confident that you have mastered these concepts and skills, test yourself with Mastery Tests 4A and 4B (pp. 210 through 227).

Critical Reflections

Answer the following questions, and prepare to discuss them with your classmates.

1. List at least five positive aspects of your life that enhance the quality of your life and could increase your life expectancy.

   a. _____

   b. _____

   c. _____

   d. _____

   e. _____

2. List three or four sources of stress in your life.

   a. _____

   b. _____

   c. _____

   d. _____

Writing Activity

Choose the stressor that is most important in your life *now*. In a brief composition, (1) explain its causes, (2) describe its impact on your life, and (3) develop and explain a plan for managing this stress. Be sure to include sufficient major and minor supporting points to make your ideas clear and to back up your main idea. Be prepared to share your essay with classmates.

Classroom Community

As a group, choose and discuss one common problem that students share, are likely to find stressful, and might make it difficult for them to be successful at their studies. Choose from the following list or pick your own stressor. Once your group has identified the stressor, discuss what you can do to overcome it or to deal with it successfully. Some possible stressors are

- Parking problems
- Transportation problems
- Finding time to study
- Finding a way to concentrate in required courses that don't interest you
- Transportation and parking problems
- Anxiety over wasting time
- Pressure to meet high standards
- Feeling lonely
- Relationship problems
- Dealing with friends who want to distract you from your studies
- Dealing with family members who might not support your decision to be a student

Prepare to report your list of solutions back to the class.

Extend Your Thinking

For another reading related to wellness, see "Creativity and Longevity," by Norman Cousins, in "Extend Your Thinking," (pp. 477–482).

Work the Web

There are many sites on the Web devoted to health. One site developed by doctors and researchers that provides information on and tools for improving health is that of the Mayo Clinic. The home page is located at http://www.mayoclinic.com/. Go to this site.

1. Once you've arrived at the home page, click on the "Healthy Living" button at the top of the page.
2. There you will find a number of links, such as "Fitness and Sports Medicine," "Food and Nutrition," and "Stress."
3. From the list, pick an aspect of healthy living that interests you, and continue to narrow your search until you find an article you like.
4. Read the article, paying attention to the main idea and supporting details.
5. Using the guidelines for writing summaries presented in this chapter, write a summary of your article.

Go to **www.ablongman.com/alexandercommunity4e** for additional Web-based activities.

©2007 Pearson Education, Inc.

Mastery Test

4A

A Personal Stress Survival Guide Dianne Hales

The following reading from the textbook An Invitation to Health *outlines some of the most important ways that people can deal with the stress in their lives. As you read, pay attention to how the main ideas are explained and developed with supporting points.*

1 Although stress is a very real threat to emotional and physical well-being, its impact depends not just on what happens to you, but on how you handle it. . . .

2   In studying individuals who manage stress so well that they seem "stress-resistant," researchers have observed that these individuals share many of the following <u>traits</u>:

- They respond actively to challenges. If a problem comes up, they look for resources, do some reading or research, and try to find a solution rather than giving up and feeling helpless. Because they've faced numerous challenges, they have confidence in their abilities to cope.
- They have personal goals, such as getting a college degree or becoming a better parent.
- They rely on a combination of planning, goal setting, problem solving, and risk taking to control stress.
- They use a minimum of substances such as nicotine, caffeine, alcohol, or drugs.
- They regularly <u>engage</u> in some form of relaxation, from meditation to exercise to knitting, at least 15 minutes a day.
- They tend to seek out other people and become involved with them.

3   In order to achieve greater control over the stress in your life, start with some self-analysis: If you're feeling overwhelmed, ask yourself: Are you taking an extra course that's draining your last ounce of energy? Are you staying up late studying every night and missing morning classes? Are you living on black coffee and jelly doughnuts? While you may think that you don't have time to reduce the stress in your life, some simple changes can often ease the pressure you're under and help you achieve your long-term goals. . . .

4   Since the small ups and downs of daily life have an enormous <u>impact</u> on psychological and physical well-being, getting a handle on daily hassles will reduce your stress load.

Positive Coping Mechanisms

5 After a perfectly miserable, aggravating day, a teacher comes home and yells at her children for making too much noise. Another individual, after an equally stressful day, jokes about what went wrong during the all-time most

---

Strategies for Change
How to Cope with Stress

6   ✔   Recognize your stress signals. Is your back bothering you more? Do you find yourself speeding or misplacing things? Force yourself to stop whenever you see these early warnings and say, "I'm under stress; I need to do something about it."

✔   Keep a stress journal. Focus on intense emotional experiences and "autopsy" them to try to understand why they affected you the way they did. Re-reading and thinking about your notes may reveal the underlying reasons for your response.

✔   Try "stress-inoculation." Rehearse everyday situations that you find stressful, such as speaking in class. Think of how you might handle the situation, perhaps by breathing deeply before you talk.

✔   Put things in proper perspective. Ask yourself: Will I remember what's made me so upset a month from now? If you had to rank this problem on a scale of 1 to 10, with worldwide catastrophe as 10, where would it rate?

✔   Think of one simple thing that could make your life easier. What if you put up a hook to hold your keys so that you didn't spend five minutes searching for them every morning?

---

miserable moment of the month. Both of these people are using defense mechanisms—actions or behaviors that help protect their sense of self-worth. The first is displacing anger onto someone else; the second uses humor to vent frustration.

7   Under great stress, we all may turn to negative defense mechanisms to alleviate anxiety and eliminate conflict. These can lead to maladaptive behavior, such as rationalizing overeating by explaining to yourself that you need the extra calories to cope with the extra stress in your life. Coping mechanisms are healthier, more mature and adaptive ways of dealing with stressful situations. While they also ward off unpleasant emotions, they usually are helpful rather than harmful. The most common are:

• Sublimation, the redirection of any drives considered unacceptable into socially acceptable channels. For example, someone who is furious with a friend or relative may go for a long run to sublimate anger.

• Religiosity, in which one comes to terms with a painful experience, such as a child's death, by experiencing it as being in accord with God's will.

• Humor, which counters stress by focusing on comic aspects. Medical students, for instance, often make jokes in anatomy lab as a way of dealing with their anxieties about working with cadavers.

- Altruism, which takes a negative experience and turns it into a positive one. For example, an HIV-positive individual may talk to teenagers about AIDS prevention.

Managing Time

8 Every day you make dozens of decisions, and the choices you make about how to use your time directly affect your stress level. If you have a big test on Monday and a term paper due Tuesday, you may plan to study all weekend. Then, when you're invited to a party Saturday night, you go. Although you set the alarm for 7:00 A.M. on Sunday, you don't pull yourself out of bed until noon. By the time you start studying, it's 4:00 P.M., and anxiety is building inside you.

9 How can you tell if you've lost control of your time? The following are telltale symptoms of poor time management:

- Rushing.
- Chronic inability to make choices or decisions.
- Fatigue or listlessness.
- Constantly missed deadlines.
- Not enough time for rest or personal relationships.
- A sense of being overwhelmed by demands and details and having to do what you don't want to do most of the time.

10 One of the hard lessons of being on your own is that your choices and your actions have consequences. Stress is just one of them. But by thinking ahead, being realistic about your workload, and sticking to your plans, you can gain better control over your time and your stress levels.

Overcoming Procrastination

11 Putting off until tomorrow what should be done today is a habit that creates a great deal of stress for many students. The three most common types of procrastination are: putting off unpleasant things, putting off difficult tasks, and putting off tough decisions. Procrastinators are most likely to delay by wishing they didn't have to do what they must or by telling themselves they "just can't get started," which means they never do.

12 People procrastinate, not because they're lazy, but to protect their self-esteem and make a favorable impression. "Procrastinators often perceive their worth as based solely on task ability, and their ability is determined only by how well they perform on completed tasks," notes psychologist Joseph Ferrari, Ph.D. "By never completing the tasks, they are never judged on their ability, thus allowing them to maintain an illusion of competence."[1]

13 To get out of a time trap, keep track of the tasks you're most likely to put off, and try to figure out why you don't want to tackle them. Think of alternative ways to get tasks done. If you put off library readings, for instance, figure out if the problem is getting to the library or the reading itself. If it's the trip to the library, arrange to walk over with a friend whose company you enjoy.

14   Develop daily time-management techniques, such as a "To Do" list. Rank items according to priorities: A, B, C, and schedule your days to make sure the A's get accomplished. Try not to fixate on half-completed projects. Divide large tasks, such as a term paper, into smaller ones, and reward yourself when you complete a part.

15   Do what you like least first. Once you have it out of the way, you can concentrate on the tasks you do enjoy. You also should build time into your schedule for interruptions, <u>unforeseen</u> problems, unexpected events, and so on, so you aren't constantly racing around. Establish ground rules for meeting your own needs (including getting enough sleep and making time for friends) before saying yes to any activity. Learn to live according to a three-word motto: Just do it!

Relaxation Techniques

16 Relaxation is the physical and mental state opposite that of stress. Rather than gearing up for a fight or flight, our bodies and minds grow calmer and work more smoothly. We're less likely to become frazzled and more capable of staying in control. The most effective relaxation techniques include progressive relaxation, visualization, meditation, mindfulness, and biofeedback.

17   *Progressive relaxation* works by intentionally increasing and then decreasing tension in the muscles. While sitting or lying down in a quiet, comfortable setting, you tense and release various muscles, beginning with those of the hand, for instance, and then proceeding to the arms, shoulders, neck, face, scalp, chest, stomach, buttocks, genitals, and so on, down each leg to the toes. Relaxing the muscles can quiet the mind and restore internal balance.[2]

18   *Visualization,* or *guided imagery,* involves creating mental pictures that calm you down and focus your mind. . . . Some people use this technique to promote healing when they are ill. The Glasser study showed that elderly residents of retirement homes in Ohio who learned progressive relaxation and guided imagery <u>enhanced</u> their immune function and reported better health than did the other residents. Visualization skills require practice and, in some cases, instruction by qualified health professionals.[3]

19   *Meditation* has been practiced in many forms over the ages, from the yogic techniques of the Far East to the Quaker silence of more modern times. Meditation helps a person reach a state of relaxation, but with the goal of achieving inner peace and harmony. There is no one right way to meditate, and many people have discovered how to meditate on their own, without even knowing what it is they are doing. Among college students, meditation has proven especially effective in increasing relaxation.[4] Most forms of meditation have common elements: sitting quietly for 15 to 20 minutes once or twice a day, concentrating on a word or image, and breathing slowly and rhythmically. If you wish to try meditation, it often helps to have someone guide you through your first sessions. Or try tape recording your own voice (with or without favorite music in the background) and playing it back to yourself, freeing yourself to concentrate on the goal of turning the attention within.

20   *Mindfulness* is a modern-day form of an ancient Asian technique that involves maintaining awareness in the present moment. You tune into each part of your body, scanning from head to toe, noting the slightest sensation. You allow whatever you experience—an itch, an ache, a feeling of warmth—to enter your awareness. Then you open yourself to focus on all the thoughts, sensations, sounds, and feelings that enter your awareness. Mindfulness keeps you in the here-and-now, thinking about what is rather than about "what if" or "if only."

21   *Biofeedback* . . . is a method of obtaining feedback, or information, about some physiological activity occurring in the body. An electronic monitoring device attached to a person's body detects a change in an internal function and communicates it back to the person through a tone, light, or meter. By paying attention to this feedback, most people can gain some control over functions previously thought to be beyond conscious control, such as body temperature, heart rate, muscle tension, and brain waves. Biofeedback training consists of three stages:

1.   Developing increased awareness of a body state or function.

2.   Gaining control over it.

3.   Transferring this control to everyday living without use of the electronic instrument.

22   The goal of biofeedback for stress reduction is a state of tranquility, usually associated with the brain's production of alpha waves (which are slower and more regular than normal waking waves). After several training sessions, most people can produce alpha waves more or less at will.[5]

Notes

1. Joseph Ferrari, "Self-Destructive Motivation—Personality, Social, and Clinical Perspectives" (paper presented to the American Psychological Association, August 1992).

2. Herbert Benson and Michael McKee, "Relaxation and Other Alternative Therapies," *Patient Care* 27 (December 15, 1993).

3. Janice Kiecolt-Glaser and Ronald Glaser, "Stress and the Immune System: Human Studies," *Review of Psychiatry* 11 (1992).

4. John Janowiak, "The Effects of Meditation on College Students' Self-Actualization and Stress Management," *Dissertation Abstracts International* 53 (April 1993).

5. Benson and McKee, "Relaxation and Other Alternative Therapies."

HALES, *AN INVITATION TO HEALTH*

| Exercise 1 | **Work with Words** |

Use context, clues, dictionary skills, and your knowledge of word parts to choose the best definition for each of the following words underlined in the reading. The paragraph number is provided in case you want to check the context.

1. *Traits* (par. 2)
   a. problems
   b. responses
   c. characteristics

2. *Engage in* (par. 2)
   a. participate in
   b. plan to get married
   c. indulge in

3. *Impact* (par. 4)
   a. collision
   b. increase
   c. effect

4. *Defense mechanisms* (par. 5)
   a. actions to defend oneself from attack
   b. tactics of self-defense
   c. actions or behaviors that help protect one's sense of self-worth

5. *Autopsy* (par. 6)
   a. study or review
   b. examine a body to determine cause of death
   c. reduce

6. *Stress-inoculation* (par. 6)
   a. advance preparation for stress
   b. vaccination for stress
   c. stressful shot

7. *Coping mechanisms* (par. 7)
   a. healthier, more mature, and adaptive ways of dealing with stressful situations
   b. ways of displacing anger onto someone else so that one feels better
   c. some of the most important forms of defense mechanisms

8. *Sublimation* (par. 7)
   a. recognition of the sublime or wonderful aspects of a mental condition
   b. the redirection of any drives considered unacceptable into socially acceptable channels.
   c. going for a run as a way of dealing with anger with a friend

9. *Unforeseen* (par. 15)
   a. seen from before
   b. not expected
   c. seen in the past

10. *Enhanced* (par. 18)
    a. decreased
    b. improved
    c. immunized

Exercise 2   Check Your Understanding

Based on the reading, Hales's "A Personal Stress Survival Guide," choose the best answer to each of the following multiple-choice questions.

1. Although stress is a very real threat to emotional and physical well-being
   a. some individuals manage it better than others.
   b. everyone suffers from it equally.
   c. there is not much that can be done about it.

2. People who manage stress well
   a. abuse drugs.
   b. have personal goals.
   c. respond passively to challenges.

3. All of the following are strategies for coping with stress except
   a. recognizing your stress signals.
   b. putting things in proper perspective.
   c. having a relaxing drink.

4. Yelling at your children after a miserable day at work is an example of
   a. physical child abuse.
   b. a positive defense mechanism.
   c. a negative defense mechanism.

5. Sublimation, religiosity, humor, and altruism are examples of
   a. negative defense mechanisms.
   b. coping mechanisms.
   c. redirecting drives considered unacceptable into socially acceptable channels.

6. If you don't have time for rest or personal relationships, and you feel overwhelmed by demands and details, the chances are
   a. you are using ineffective coping mechanisms.
   b. you are not managing your time well.
   c. you have a mature outlook on life.

7. According to Hales, some people procrastinate because they
   a. are lazy.
   b. don't like to do what they have to do.
   c. want to protect their self-esteem.

8. One suggestion for overcoming procrastination is
   a. do what you like least first.
   b. concentrate on enjoying everything that you do.
   c. fixate on half-completed projects.

9. Progressive relaxation is
   a. a way to progress from one form of relaxation to another.
   b. a method of intentionally increasing and then decreasing tension in the muscles.
   c. one of the ways to best apply visualization.

10. Mindfulness is a technique that helps you
    a. maintain and be aware of the present moment.
    b. get away from the stress of the moment.
    c. meditate for relaxation.

Exercise 3   **Organize to Learn: Outline**

Complete the following outline for the reading. Then, using your outline, write a brief summary of the reading on a separate paper. In the first sentence of your summary, put the main idea in your own words, and be sure to include the title and author of the reading.

A Personal Stress Survival Guide

Main Idea: In "A Personal Sress Survival Guide," Dianne Hales emphasizes that although stress can threaten your emotional and physical health, how it affects you also depends on how you cope with it.

I.   Common traits of people who manage stress well

   A. Respond actively to stress

      1. Look for resources

      2. _____

      3. _____

      4. Have confidence in their ability to cope

   B. _____

   C. Rely on combination of activities to control stress

      1. _____

      2. _____

      3. Problem solving

      4. _____

   D. Use a minimum of substances (nicotine, caffeine, alcohol, drugs)

   E. _____

   F. _____

II. How to cope with stress

   A. _____

   B. _____

   C. Think in advance about how you would handle a stressful situation

   D. _____

   E. _____

III. Positive coping mechanisms

   A. Sublimation (redirection of unacceptable drives into acceptable channels)

   B. _____

   C. _____

   D. _____

IV. Signs of poor time management

   A. _____

   B. Inability to make decisions

   C. _____

   D. _____

   E. _____

   F. Sense of being overwhelmed

V. Overcoming procrastination

   A. Three common forms of procrastination

     1. _____

     2. _____

     3. _____

   B. Reason for procrastination

     1. _____

     2. _____

   C. Ways to stop procrastinating

     1. _____

     2. _____

     3. _____

VI. Relaxation techniques

A. _____

B. _____

C. _____

D. _____

E. _____

Exercise 4 **Reflect**

Think about what you read in "A Personal Stress Survival Guide" and what you already know about stress. Then answer the following questions.

1. Which of the techniques for avoiding stress have you observed other people using? Give an example of someone you know and how that person uses or has used a technique mentioned in the reading.

_____

_____

_____

2. Which of the techniques for avoiding stress do you think are most important for you to master? Explain.

_____

_____

_____

© 2007 Pearson Education, Inc.

Mastery Test

4B

Smoking   Dianne Hales

The following reading from An Invitation to Health *explains why people start smoking and why it is difficult for them to quit. As you read, pay attention to how the main ideas are explained and developed with major and minor supporting points.*

Why People Start Smoking

1 The two main factors linked with the onset of a smoking habit are age and education. The vast majority of white men (93%) with less than a high school education are current or former daily cigarette smokers. White women with similar educational backgrounds are also very likely to smoke or to have smoked every day. Latino men and women without a high school education are less likely to be or become daily smokers.[1]

2 Most Americans are aware that there is a health risk associated with smoking, but many don't know exactly what that risk is or how it might affect them. Other <u>factors</u> associated with starting smoking are discussed in the following sections.

Heredity

3 Researchers <u>speculate</u> that genes may account for about 50% of smoking behavior, with environment playing an equally important role. Studies have shown that identical twins, who have the same genes, are more likely to have matching smoking profiles than fraternal twins. If one identical twin is a heavy smoker, the other is also likely to be; if one smokes only occasionally, so does the other.[2]

Parental Role Models

4 Children who start smoking are 50% more likely than youngsters who don't smoke to have at least one smoker in their families. A mother who smokes seems a particularly strong influence on making smoking seem acceptable. The majority of youngsters who smoke say that their parents also smoke and are aware of their own tobacco use.

Adolescent Experimentation and Rebellion

5 Young people who are trying out various behaviors may take up smoking because they're curious or because they want to defy adults. Others simply want to appear grownup or cool. In a 1998 poll by University of Michigan researchers, about 30% of 2000 high school seniors reported that they had their first cigarettes in or before the sixth grade. The majority of the teens <u>surveyed</u>—88%—said they have at least a few friends who smoke; only 59%

felt that they would definitely not smoke themselves. At least from the teen's perspective, little is done to discourage smoking by young people. Fewer than half reported that teachers and administrators attempted to prevent smoking, while more than half said they believed there are no health consequences from smoking.[3] Whatever the reason for starting may be, teens often <u>misjudge</u> the addictive powers of cigarettes. Many, sure that they'll be able to quit any time they want, figure that smoking for a year or two won't hurt them. But when they do try to quit, they can't.[4] Like older smokers, most young people who smoke have tried to quit at least once. The American Cancer Society has found that young smokers tend to become heavy smokers and that the longer anyone is exposed to smoke, the greater the health dangers.

Limited Education

6 People who have graduated from college are much less likely to smoke than are high school graduates; those with fewer than 12 years of education are most likely to smoke. An individual with 8 years or less of education is 11 times more likely to smoke than someone with <u>post-graduate</u> training.

Weight Control

7 Smokers burn up an extra 100 calories a day compared with nonsmokers— the <u>equivalent</u> of walking a mile—probably because nicotine increases metabolic rate. Once they start smoking, many individuals say they cannot quit because they fear they'll gain weight. The CDC estimates that women who stop smoking gain an average of eight pounds, while men put on an average of six pounds. One in eight women and one in ten men who stop smoking put on 29 pounds or more. The reasons for this weight gain include nicotine's effects on <u>metabolism</u> as well as emotional and behavioral factors, such as the habit of frequently putting something into one's mouth. Yet as a health risk, smoking a pack and a half to two packs a day is a greater danger than carrying 60 pounds in extra weight.

8 Weight gain for smokers who quit is not <u>inevitable</u>, however. Aerobic exercise helps increase metabolic rate; and limiting alcohol and foods high in sugar and fat can help smokers control their weight as they give up cigarettes.[5]

Aggressive Marketing

9 Cigarette companies spend billions each year on advertisements and promotional campaigns, with manufacturers targeting ads especially at women, teens, minorities, and the poor. Most controversial are cigarette advertisements in magazines and media aimed at teenagers and even younger children. As part of a nationwide antismoking campaign, health and government officials have called for restrictions on cigarette ads, and manufacturers have agreed not to aim their sales efforts at children and teens.

© 2007 Pearson Education, Inc.

Stress

10 In studies that have analyzed the impact of life stressors, depression, emotional support, marital status, and income, researchers have concluded that an individual with a high stress level is approximately 15 times as likely to be a smoker than a person with low stress. About half of smokers identify workplace stress as a key factor in their smoking behavior.[6]

Why People Keep Smoking

11 Whatever the reasons for lighting up that first cigarette, very different factors keep cigarettes burning pack after pack, year after year. In national polls, four out of five smokers say that they want to quit but can't. The reason isn't a lack of willpower. Medical scientists have recognized tobacco dependence as an addictive <u>disorder</u> that may be more powerful than heroin dependence and that may affect more than 90% of all smokers.

Pleasure

12 According to the American Cancer Society, 87.5% of regular smokers find smoking pleasurable. Nicotine—the addictive ingredient in tobacco—is the reason. Researchers have shown that nicotine reinforces and strengthens the desire to smoke by acting on brain chemicals that influence feeling of well-being. This drug also can improve memory, help in performing certain tasks, reduce anxiety, dampen hunger, and increase pain tolerance.

Relief of Depression

13 Some people with depression use the mood-altering properties of nicotine to relieve depressive symptoms. According to new research, depressed and nondepressed people who smoke to improve their mood may do so because of their genetic makeup.[7] Previous studies have shown that people with a history of depression are significantly more likely to be smokers and to be diagnosed as nicotine-dependent. Smokers are more likely than nonsmokers to report depressive symptoms—and these symptoms may interfere with quitting. According to researchers, the likelihood of quitting smoking is about 40% lower among depressed than nondepressed smokers.

Dependence

14 Nicotine has a much more powerful hold on smokers than alcohol does on drinkers. Whereas about 10% of alcohol users lose control of their intake of alcohol and become alcoholics, as many as 80% of all heavy smokers have tried to cut down on or quit smoking but cannot overcome their dependence.

15   Nicotine causes dependence by at least three means:

- It provides a strong sensation of pleasure.
- It leads to fairly severe discomfort during withdrawal.

- It stimulates cravings long after obvious withdrawal symptoms have passed. . . .

16   Few drugs act as quickly on the brain as nicotine does. It travels through the bloodstream to the brain in seven seconds—half the time it takes for heroin injected into a blood vessel to reach the brain. And a pack-a-day smoker gets 200 hits of nicotine a day—73,000 a year.

17   After a few years of smoking, the most powerful incentive for continuing to smoke is to avoid the discomfort of withdrawal. Generally, ten cigarettes a day will prevent withdrawal effects. For many who smoke heavily, signs of withdrawal, including changes in mood and performance, occur within two hours after smoking their last cigarette. . . . Smokeless tobacco users also get constant doses of nicotine. However, absorption of nicotine by the lungs is more likely to lead to dependence than absorption through the linings of the nose and mouth. As with other drugs of abuse, continued nicotine intake results in tolerance (the need for more of a drug to maintain the same effect), which is why only 2% of all smokers smoke just a few cigarettes a day, or smoke only occasionally.

Use of Other Substances

18 Many smokers also drink or use drugs. According to the Addiction Research Foundation in Canada, tobacco smokers say cigarettes are harder to abandon than other drugs, even when they find them less pleasurable than their preferred drug of abuse. Individuals who drink excessively also find their cigarette habit a hard one to break. In a study of 3977 men and women, those who drank heavily or in binges were more likely to smoke more—and to find it harder to quit.[8]

Notes

1. Vicki Kemper, "Where the Action Is," *Common Cause Magazine* 21 (Spring 1995); Rosanne Spector, "White Men with Limited Education Almost Certain to Smoke; Hispanics Less Likely," Stanford University Medical Center, August 8, 1995.

2. Neal Benowitz, "The Genetics of Drug Dependence: Tobacco Addiction," *New England Journal of Medicine,* September 17, 1992.

3. Dianne Hales, "Smoking Earlier," *Parade,* March 1, 1998.

4. Centers for Disease Control and Prevention, "Reasons for Tobacco Use and Symptoms of Nicotine Withdrawal Among Adolescent and Young Adult Tobacco Users," *Journal of the American Medical Association* 272 (December 7, 1994). Frederick Gibbons, et al., "Prevalence Estimates and Adolescent Risk Behavior: Cross-Cultural Differences in Social Influence," *Journal of Applied Psychology* 80 (February 1995).

5. Gerald Talcott et al., "Is Weight Gain After Smoking Cessations Inevitable?" *Journal of Consulting & Clinical Psychology* 63, (April 1995).

©2007 Pearson Education, Inc.

6. Sharon Sheahan and Melissa Latimer, "Correlates of Smoking, Stress, and Depression Among Women," *Health Values* 19, (January–February 1995).

7. Caryl Lerman, et al., "Depression and Self-Medication with Nicotine: The Modifying Influence of the Dopamine D4 Receptor Gene," *Health Psychology* 17 (January 1998).

8. Robert Murray et al., "Level of Involvement with Alcohol and Success at Smoking Cessation in the Lung Health Study," *Journal of Studies on Alcohol* 56 (January 1995).

HALES, *An Invitation to Health*

Exercise 1   **Work With Words**

Use context, clues, dictionary skills, and your knowledge of word parts to choose the best definition for each of the following words underlined in the reading. The paragraph number is provided in case you want to check the context.

1. *Factors* (par. 2)
   a. facts
   b. reasons
   c. distinctions

2. *Speculate* (par. 3)
   a. believe based on solid evidence
   b. disagree based on personal opinion
   c. guess with insufficient evidence

3. *Surveyed* (par. 5)
   a. answered
   b. smoked
   c. questioned

4. *Misjudge* (par. 5)
   a. don't understand correctly
   b. come to the correct verdict
   c. are guilty of

5. *Post-graduate* (par. 6)
   a. after graduating from college
   b. before graduating from college
   c. graduating from college

6. *Equivalent* (par. 7)
   a. different from
   b. similar to
   c. same as

7. *Metabolism* (par. 7)
   a. body processes that burn energy (calories)
   b. the equivalent of walking a mile
   c. the cause for weight gain

8. *Inevitable* (par. 8)
   a. controllable
   b. uncontrollable
   c. unavoidable

9. *Disorder* (par. 11)
   a. physical or mental affliction
   b. lack of order
   c. presence of order

10. *Incentive* (par. 17)
    a. reason to do something
    b. something that encourages rebellion
    c. discouragement

Exercise 2 **Check Your Understanding**

Based on the reading "Smoking," by Dianne Hales, choose the best answer to each of the following multiple-choice questions.

1. What is the best main idea statement for the reading "Smoking"?
   a. People begin smoking for a variety of reasons and it is very difficult to quit.
   b. Heredity, adolescent rebellion, aggressive marketing, and stress are the major factors leading people to smoke.
   c. Because people become dependent on smoking, it is difficult for them to quit.

2. What is the best topic for paragraph 1?
   a. Education and lifestyle
   b. Smoking and education
   c. Latinos and smoking habits

3. What is the best main idea statement for paragraph 1?
   a. Latino men and women without a high school education are less likely to become smokers.
   b. More people smoke who have less than a high school education.
   c. White women with similar educational backgrounds are very likely to smoke.

4. What is the best topic for paragraph 3?
   a. Genetic influence on smoking
   b. Smoking habits of twins
   c. Smoking habits of identical and fraternal twins

5. What is the best main idea statement for paragraph 3?
   a. Researchers believe that genes may account for about 50 percent of smoking behavior.
   b. Identical twins are more likely than fraternal twins to have the same smoking habits.
   c. People in the same family are influenced by the habits of their parents.

6. Which of the following statements is *not* accurate, according to this article?
   a. In calculating health risk, how much you smoke is more important than how long you have smoked.
   b. People with high stress levels are more likely to smoke than those with low stress.
   c. People who smoke burn about 100 calories a day more than non-smokers.

7. People continue to smoke for all of the following reasons, except
   a. they get pleasure from smoking.
   b. they are subject to becoming depressed if they smoke.
   c. they are addicted to nicotine that is present in tobacco.

©2007 Pearson Education, Inc.

8. Which of the following is not a cause of nicotine dependence?
   a. It stimulates cravings after withdrawal symptoms have passed.
   b. It leads to discomfort during withdrawal.
   c. It provides a sensation of comfort during withdrawal.

9. Only 2 percent of all smokers smoke just a few cigarettes a day because
   a. ten cigarettes a day will prevent withdrawal effects.
   b. smokeless tobacco doesn't affect how many cigarettes a person smokes.
   c. continued nicotine intake results in tolerance.

10. Teen smokers rarely
    a. also drink or use drugs.
    b. believe that cigarettes are harder to quit than other drugs.
    c. find it easier to quit if they also drink.

| Exercise 3 | Organize to Learn |

Complete the following outline for the reading. Then, using your outline, write a brief summary of the reading on a separate sheet of paper. In your first sentence, put the main idea in your own words, and include the title and the author of the reading.

Smoking

Main Idea: _____

_____

I.   _____

   A. Heredity

   B. _____

   C. _____

   D. _____

   E. _____

   F. _____

   G. _____

II. Reasons people keep smoking

   A. _____

   B. _____

226

C. _____

   1. Pleasure

   2. _____

   3. _____

D. _____

Exercise 4   **Reflect**

Think about what you read in "Smoking" and what you already know from your experience and observations about smoking. Then answer the following questions.

1. Do you smoke? If you do, explain why you became a smoker. If you don't, explain why you chose not to smoke.

   _____

   _____

   _____

   _____

2. Do you know any smokers who have tried to quit? Was that person successful? Explain your answer.

   _____

   _____

   _____

   _____

©2007 Pearson Education, Inc.

Chapter 5

Patterns of Organization

Where We Live

**Little boxes on the hillside,
Little boxes, all the same**

—*Song by Malvina Reynolds*

- What kind of housing is shown in the picture? What might be the advantages and disadvantages in living in a place like this?

- What do you think the lyrics to the song "Little Boxes" mean?

PREPARE TO READ

Americans have always been a people on the move. Our mobility has a profound impact on where and how we live in the twenty-first century. During the nineteenth and early twentieth centuries, we moved from the countryside to the cities. Then, especially after World War II, we moved to the suburbs, where we thought we could escape the hassles, crowds, and crime of the cities. Now more Americans live in suburbs than in the cities themselves. But, a new trend has emerged—toward the far suburbs, or "edge cities," and into gated communities, where more than 7 million Americans live today. Even as urban "sprawl" has intruded on farmlands, the cost of housing has skyrocketed in many parts of the country, making decent housing and home ownership an almost impossible dream for many. And a significant number of Americans experience homelessness at least once in their lives. What are the effects of these trends in where Americans live? How does where we live affect our quality of life?

Purpose

In this chapter, you will learn to
- Recognize a variety of patterns of organization
- Identify transitions and other clues that signal each pattern
- Use patterns to organize what you read into concept maps, outlines, summaries, and other forms to aid your comprehension and retention

In the process of acquiring these skills, you will read about the history of urbanization and trends in the places and spaces in which we live.

Previous Knowledge

Answer these questions and prepare to discuss them in class.

1. Briefly describe the area in which you live—city, suburb, small town, or rural area. _____

    _____

2. Why did you choose to live in the area where you live now?

    _____

    _____

Preview and Predict

Preview Chapter 5. Based on your preview, list two things you think you will learn in this chapter.

1. _____

2. _____

Reading 1 *American Cities One Hundred Years Ago*

Robert A. Divine, T. H. Breen, George M. Fredrickson,
and R. Hal Williams

The following reading from an American history textbook, America, Past and Present, *describes what life was like in American cities at the beginning of the twentieth century. As you read, compare the living conditions of the people described here to how you and your family live today.*

1   One day around 1900, Harriet Vittum, a settlement house worker in Chicago, went to the aid of a young Polish girl who lived in a nearby slum. The girl, aged 15, had discovered she was pregnant and had taken poison. An ambulance was on the way, and Vittum, told of the poisoning, rushed over to do what she could.

2   Quickly, she raced up the three flights of stairs to the floor where the girl and her family lived. Pushing open the door, she found the father, several male boarders, and two or three small boys asleep on the kitchen floor. In the next room, the mother was on the floor among several women boarders and one or two small children. Glancing out the window, Vittum saw the wall of another building so close she could reach out and touch it.

3   There was a third room; in it lay the 15-year-old girl, along with two more small children who were asleep. Looking at the scene, Vittum thought about the girl's life in the crowded tenement. Should she try to save her? Vittum asked herself. Should she even try to bring the girl back "to the misery and hopelessness of the life she was living in that awful place"?

4   The young girl died, and in later years, Vittum often told her story. It was easy to see why. The girl's life in the slum, the children on the floor, the need to take in boarders to make ends meet, the way the mother and father collapsed at the end of a workday that began long before sunup—all reflected the experiences of millions of people living in the nation's cities.

5   People poured into cities in the last part of the nineteenth century, lured by glitter and excitement, by friends and relatives who were already there, and, above all, by the greater opportunities for jobs and higher wages. Between 1860 and 1910, the rural population of the United States almost doubled; the number of people living in cities increased sevenfold.

6   Little of the increase came from natural growth, since urban families had high rates of infant mortality, a declining fertility rate, and a high death rate from injury and disease. Many of the newcomers came from rural America, and many more came from Europe, Latin America, and Asia. In one of the most significant migrations in American history, thousands of African Americans began in the 1880s to move from the rural South to northern cities. By 1900, there were large black communities in New York, Baltimore, Chicago, Washington, DC, and other cities. Yet to come was the even greater black migration during World War I.

7   Two major forces reshaped American society between 1870 and 1920. One was industrialization; the other was urbanization, the headlong rush of people from their rural roots into the modern urban environment. By

©2007 Pearson Education, Inc.

1920, the city had become the center of American economic, social, and cultural life.

DIVINE ET AL., *AMERICA, PAST AND PRESENT*

Recall and Discuss

Based on Reading 1, "American Cities One Hundred Years Ago," by Divine and his coauthors, answer the following questions and prepare to discuss them with your classmates.

1. What story does this reading begin with, and why do you think the authors begin with it? _____

_____

_____

_____

2. How did the rural and urban populations of the United States change between 1860 and 1910? _____

_____

_____

3. Where did the people come from who were moving to the cities?

_____

_____

4. What were the two major forces that reshaped American society between 1870 and 1920? _____

_____

_____

5. Describe the house or apartment you live in. What is each room used for? How many people live together? Are they related? Are they friends? Are they former strangers sharing living space? Does the space feel crowded? Compare and contrast where you live to where the young girl in the story lived.

_____

_____

_____

PATTERNS OF ORGANIZATION

patterns of organization The way a writer chooses to organize his or her material to help us understand the relationships among ideas

As you learned in Chapter 4, separating supporting points from main ideas is an important reading skill. Identifying the different ways writers organize their supporting points is another essential skill for improving reading comprehension. The various arrangements authors use are called **patterns of organization.** Recognizing them helps you to

- *See how the writer thinks* about the topic and understand the relationships among ideas as the writer perceives them
- *Organize to learn,* using the patterns to improve your comprehension and make it easier for you to remember the information for tests and other uses in the future

Some of the most common patterns of organization are

- Chronological order and narration
- Definition and classification
- Exemplification
- Cause and effect
- Comparison and contrast
- Process
- Problem and solution
- Argument

You will be introduced to each one in this chapter. Sometimes one pattern will clearly be dominant in a paragraph or in an essay. But writers often combine patterns of organization to express their ideas. As a reader, you need to decipher the writer's patterns. In composition classes, you will learn to use many of these same patterns for organizing your own writing into effective essays. As a student, you need to recognize patterns used frequently in various disciplines, such as sociology, biology, math, and anthropology. In history, for example, much of the information is organized chronologically. In biology, textbooks often emphasize classifications of plants and animals. Introductory sociology may provide you with many definitions of important terms, and math will require you to analyze and solve problems.

transitions Words or phrases that link ideas and/or identify relationships

The different organizational patterns are easier to identify if you are aware of the transitions and other clues that usually accompany each pattern. **Transitions** are words or phrases that link ideas, such as *for example, second, in contrast, on the other hand, because,* and *therefore.* They establish relationships between clauses, between sentences within a paragraph, and between paragraphs and longer sections. They provide you with clues for identifying which pattern is being used in a selection.

Chronological Order and Narration

chronological order Information organized in time order

Chronological order is a pattern of organization commonly used in history and other disciplines. It answers the questions, "When did it happen?" and "In what order?" This pattern presents information according to the

©2007 Pearson Education, Inc.

order that it occurred in time. For example, in the following excerpt from a sociology textbook, the authors state the main idea in the first sentence: "the United States is becoming increasingly urbanized." Then they explain in chronological order that this urbanization has occurred over a long period. In the following excerpt, italics have been added to emphasize the transitions and clues related to time organization.

> Many Americans have romantic notions of moving to the country to escape the hustle and bustle of city life, but the United States is becoming increasingly urbanized. *In 1790,* only about 5 percent of Americans lived in cities and fewer than 25 cities had a population of more than 25,000. *Two hundred years later* those figures had substantially changed. Over three-fourths of the U.S. population now lives in towns or cities, and another 20 percent live within the sphere of influence of a city. (Thompson and Hickey, *Society in Focus*)

The phrases "in 1790" and "two hundred years later," and the word *now* keep you aware of the movement of Americans over time.

narration
Information organized to tell a story

Narration is a similar pattern that uses chronological or time order. It answers the question "What happened?" It uses a story, or a narrative, to communicate information. In a narrative, the reader is always wondering what will happen next. Narrative is commonly used in short stories and novels, but some textbooks use narrative as well. For example, the history textbook from which Reading 1 was taken used the story of an impoverished pregnant girl and the social worker who tried to rescue her as a way to tell students about the experiences of those who lived in America's cities 100 years ago. Here's a story of a different period of American history: the Depression of the 1930s, when a drought forced tens of thousands of farmers off their land. Having lost everything they had, thousands headed to California, where they had heard jobs were plentiful. This mass migration movement was called the Dust Bowl Migration. The following narrative is told in retrospect: a grown woman now, the narrator tells her story of that period as she experienced it as a young girl.

> The year was 1936 when Daddy set me on his knee, looked me in the eye, and said, "Ruby, you ever heard o' California?" His voice was shaky but sure, if that's possible, and I knew right then we wouldn't be in Gavin County, Oklahoma, much longer. I was born in Gavin County, in a farmhouse, just like the ones you may have seen in the pictures, and so was my three older brothers and two big sisters. At that time—actually, for the five years or so before that—all anybody could talk about was "Black Sunday" and all the wind and dust that had took away our wheat. It took away my granddaddy's entire house, too, and all the while my daddy was clipping out advertisements in the papers saying they needed hands in some place called San Joaquin. We were always hungry, and Mama cried a lot, especially after Aunt Rose died. So I didn't

fuss much when we loaded up the truck with everything we could fit—mattresses, pots, pans, trunks of clothes, you name it—and made our way onto the Mother Road, the street they call U.S. Highway 66.
(Meyer, "Dust Bowl Days")

Many clues in this narrative passage tell you that it is organized in time order. Ruby says father let her know they were leaving Oklahoma when "The year was 1936," and the reader learns how long the troubles had been going on when the author says, "for five years or so." We learn that her father had been considering moving the family when Ruby states, "while my daddy was clipping out advertisements." We know things got worse for the mother "after Aunt Rose died" and the daughter's reaction "when we loaded up the truck . . . and made our way." If you were to read the rest of this story, you would find out what happened on the journey to California and what life was like for migrant farmworkers there.

The narration of a story does not always move forward in a straight line. Stories, novels, and movies sometimes reorganize the time order and employ techniques like flashbacks—narratives that take place in the past—to enhance the effect of the storytelling. Textbooks, on the other hand, are much more likely to use strict chronological order to present information. An American history text, for example, might start at the time before Columbus and continue through the Revolutionary War, westward expansion, the Civil War, and so forth, up to the present time.

Transitions and Clues As you've seen, chronological order and narration often use dates and times to specify when something happened. Besides actual dates and times, transitional words such as *then, when, after, before, while, during, earlier, meanwhile, until, now, immediately, finally, as soon as, next, last*, and *later* signal you to be aware of time relationships between the ideas or events.

Organizing to Learn: Creating a Time Line One way to learn events in the proper chronological order as you study and review for a test is to prepare a **time line.** For example, the information in the following paragraph from *Sociology: A Down-to-Earth Approach* by James Henslin, could be organized in a time line like the one that appears on page 236.

time line A graphic representation that uses lines and dates to illustrate the time order of events

It took all of human history [about 250,000 years] for the world's population to reach its first billion around 1800. It then took about one hundred thirty years (until 1930) to add the second billion. Just thirty years later (1960), the world population hit 3 billion. The time it took to reach the fourth billion was cut in half, to only fifteen years (1975). It then took just twelve more years (1987) for the total to hit 5 billion, and another twelve for it to reach 6 billion (in 1999). (Henslin, *Sociology*).

©2007 Pearson Education, Inc.

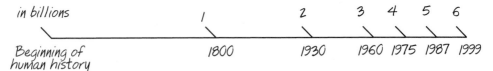

Population Growth in Human History

Exercise 2 Organize to Learn: Create a Time Line

Use the following paragraph from *Cities of the World*, a textbook by Stanley D. Brunn and Jack F. Williams on world urbanization, to complete the time line. Italics have been added to the paragraph to emphasize the transitions and clues related to time organization. Add the correct percentage of urban population for each period. The first entry has been made for you.

Around the year 1800, perhaps 3 percent of the world's population lived in urban places of 5,000 people or more. *By 1900* the proportion had risen to over 13 percent and by 1990 the percentage had increased to over 43. According to statistical data provided by the United Nations, *by the year 2025,* 60 percent of the world's population will live in urban places. *Within the past century* the city has thus become the dominant center of modern civilization. (Brunn and Williams, *Cities of the World*)

Growth in World Urban Population, 1800–2025

Definition and Classification

definition
Information organized to answer the question, "What is it?"

Definition is the pattern of organization that attempts to answer the question, "What is it?" A definition of a term or concept may be short—just a few words—or it may be quite long—a paragraph or more. Textbooks often print key terms in boldface and include definitions in the body of the text, in the margins, and/or in a glossary at the end of the book. In this textbook, we show the definitions in the margins, immediately after the term is introduced in boldface.

A longer definition may also be an extended comparison, which is called an **analogy.** For example, a common analogy used in biology texts compares the workings of the human eye to the workings of a camera. Longer definitions may be dedicated to defining the meaning of a single, complicated term, such as *democracy, black holes,* or *love.*

analogy An extended comparison

Sometimes a definition places an item in a class, or category, and then distinguishes it from the other items in that category. For example, a Siamese is a cat, but *Webster's II New Riverside University Dictionary* does much more than place Siamese in the category of cats. According to *Webster's,* a Siamese cat is "a short-haired cat originally bred in the Orient, having blue eyes and a pale fawn or gray coat with darker ears, face, tail, and feet."

classification
Information organized into categories or groups

As you may have already realized, definition is closely related to another organizational pattern, **classification.** Classification is information organized into categories or groups. This pattern answers the questions, "What kinds or types are there?" and "How can we group items into classes or categories?" It is common to see definition and classification used in combination, because they are closely related. For example, an article might classify all the major breeds of cats and define the characteristics of each specific breed. Here is another example. In this excerpt from a sociology textbook, *Society in Focus,* the authors William E. Thompson and Joseph V. Hickey explain "urbanization" in paragraph 1 and go on to classify urban areas into three types—the metropolis, megalopolis, and suburb—and then they define each type.

The Metropolis, Megalopolis, and Suburbs

From the beginning of the twentieth century through the mid-1960s, urbanization patterns reflected a steady migration from rural to urban areas. Since the mid-1960s, however, while cities have continued to grow, most migration has been into the fringe areas around major cities. The traditional concept of the city grew increasingly inadequate to describe American urbanization, and the newer term *metropolis* was coined to describe the bulging urban areas that were once cities.

The Metropolis

A *metropolis* is a major urban area that includes a large central city surrounded by several smaller incorporated cities and suburbs that join to form one large recognizable municipality. New York City, for example, has a population of over 16 million and includes people who live in the city's five boroughs—Manhattan, the Bronx, Brooklyn, Queens, and Staten Island—as well as surrounding suburbs in Long Island and Westchester Counties and in the states of Connecticut and New Jersey. Similarly, Los Angeles has absorbed the communities of Anaheim, Beverly Hills, and several other satellite cities; today metropolitan Los Angeles includes over nine separate cities and 60 self-governing communities. Even the Dallas metroplex, which cherishes its Western tradition and rural roots, boasts a population of well over 1 million and includes the cities of Garland, Mesquite, Irving, Arlington, Plano, and Las Colinas, to mention only a few, as part of its greater metropolitan area.

The Megalopolis

As major metropolitan areas have continued to absorb smaller surrounding cities, an even larger urban unit has developed. The *megalopolis*

©2007 Pearson Education, Inc.

consists of two or more areas linked politically, economically, socially, and geographically. Along the Eastern Seaboard, a chain of hundreds of cities and suburbs now stretches from Boston through Washington, D.C., to Richmond, Virginia, in an almost continuous urban sprawl. Similarly, much of Florida is almost one continuous city, from Jacksonville through Tampa to Miami. Dallas and Fort Worth, once two distinct cities 30 miles apart, are now linked by an international airport and a nearly unbroken band of suburban communities. Urban sprawl joins Chicago to Pittsburgh. Along the West Coast, a huge megalopolis stretches from San Diego through Los Angeles and up to San Francisco and Oakland, with only a few breaks. Migration patterns reflect a move from older cities in the Northeast (sometimes dubbed the rustbelt because of its decaying factories) to cities in the sun belt of the South and the Southwest. In fact, over half the U.S. population growth during the 1980s and 1990s occurred in three states: California, Texas, and Florida. It is predicted that if those trends continue even more megalopolises or "supercities" will emerge in the sun belt states.

The Suburbs

Prior to World War II, less than one-fifth of the U.S. population lived in *suburbs,* residential areas surrounding cities, which expand urban lifestyles into previously rural areas. By 1990, however, almost half of all Americans could be classified as suburbanites. The rush to the suburbs by urban dwellers and rural residents alike can be explained by several factors. After World War II, Americans wanted to raise the families they had deferred during the Great Depression and the war—and they produced a huge baby boom and a demand for housing. The expansion of interstate highway systems, including loops around major cities, made it easier for disenchanted city dwellers to leave the congestion of the city and move into surrounding neighborhoods, from which they could easily commute to their jobs. The shortage of desirable housing in many cities, combined with rapid economic expansion and the availability of cheap land, government-subsidized loans, and moderately priced housing in outlying areas, made suburban living attractive and economically practical for working-class and middle-class families.

Another important variable was the idyllic stereotype of suburban living promoted by the mass media. According to television, motion pictures, and popular magazines, the suburbs provided all the amenities of urban life yet were far enough from the central city that people could avoid the hassles of the city. (Thompson and Hickey, *Society in Focus*)

Transitions and Clues   Authors frequently use the word *is* to connect a term to a definition. For example, "A metropolis *is* a major urban area." Definitions might also be introduced with commas or with phrases such as *could be defined as, refers to, means, signifies,* or *consists of.* Classifications may use clues like the *first type, second kind, third variety, fourth category,* or *another group* to introduce elements in a classification.

Organizing to Learn: Creating a Vocabulary List   One way to organize definitions for studying is to create a *vocabulary list* or prepare vocabulary cards for terms to be memorized, as you did for specialized vocabulary in Chapter 2, pages 51 through 108. For example, for the previous excerpt, you might make the following list, or vocabulary cards, for terms it introduces and defines.

- *Metropolis:* A major urban area that includes a large central city surrounded by several incorporated cities and suburbs that join to form one large and recognizable municipality
- *Megalopolis:* Two or more major metropolitan areas linked politically, economically, socially, and geographically
- *Suburbs:* Residential areas surrounding cities which expand urban lifestyles into previously rural areas

Outlining is also a good way to study information that has already been organized as a classification. See pages 184 through 186 in Chapter 4 for directions.

Exercise 3   ## Organize to Learn: Identify Definition and Classification

Read the following excerpt from Henslin's college textbook, *Sociology: A Down-to-Earth Approach.* The author begins by defining terms and concepts that are important to understanding the evolution of U.S. cities. Notice that the key terms are printed in italics. When you have finished the reading, complete the two activities that follow.

The U.S. Census Bureau has divided the country into 274 *metropolitan statistical areas (MSAs).* Each MSA consists of a central city of at least 50,000 people and the urbanized areas linked to it. About three of every five Americans live in just fifty or so MSAs. . . .

As Americans migrate, *edge cities* have developed to meet their needs. This term refers to clusters of shopping malls, hotels, office parks, and residential areas that are located near the intersection of major highways. Although these clusters may overlap the boundaries of several cities or towns, they provide a sense of place to those who live, work, or shop there.

Another major U.S. urban pattern is *gentrification,* the movement of middle-class people into rundown areas of a city. They are attracted by the low prices for quality housing that, although deteriorated, can be restored. One consequence is an improvement in the appearance of some urban neighborhoods—freshly painted buildings, well-groomed lawns, and the absence of boarded-up windows. Another consequence is that the poor residents are displaced as the more well-to-do newcomers move in and drive up prices. Tension often arises between these groups. (Henslin, *Sociology*)

©2007 Pearson Education, Inc.

1. Circle two transitions and hints that these paragraphs are organized by definition.

2. Define the following terms and categories from the context of the excerpt.

   a. *Metropolitan statistical area*

   _____

   _____

   b. *Edge cities*

   _____

   _____

   c. *Gentrification*

   _____

   _____

   ◆

Exemplification

exemplification A pattern of examples used to support ideas

One of the most common patterns of organization is **exemplification,** the use of examples to support ideas. It answers the question, "What examples support the main idea?" Examples can support most of the other patterns of organization. Examples are listed in different orders to accomplish distinct purposes; the order might add clarity or emphasis. For example, in a paragraph you read earlier on p. 237, focusing on definition, notice that the authors support their definition of *metropolis* by providing examples of three major American metropolitan areas, which are numbered in the following paragraph. The order moves from America's two largest metropolitan areas—New York and Los Angeles—to a smaller one, Dallas.

> A *metropolis* is a major urban area that includes a large central city surrounded by several smaller incorporated cities and suburbs that join to form one large recognizable municipality. The greater metropolitan area of (1) New York City, for example, has a population of over 16 million and includes people who live in the city's five boroughs—Manhattan, the Bronx, Brooklyn, Queens, and Staten Island—as well as surrounding suburbs in Long Island and Westchester Counties and in the states of Connecticut and New Jersey. Similarly, (2) Los Angeles has absorbed the communities of Anaheim, Beverly Hills, and several other satellite cities; today metropolitan Los Angeles includes over nine separate cities and 60 self-governing communities. Even (3) the Dallas

metroplex, which cherishes its Western tradition and rural roots, boasts a population of well over 1 million and includes the cities of Garland, Mesquite, Irving, Arlington, Plano, and Las Colinas, to mention only a few, as part of its greater metropolitan area. (Thompson and Hickey, *Society in Focus*)

Notice that the authors do not simply name three examples of *metropolis* as major supporting points. They go on to further explain the term with minor supporting points: lists of examples of the satellite cities and suburbs that make up each metropolis. For instance, the Dallas metropolitan area includes Garland, Mesquite, Irving, Arlington, Plano, Las Colinas, and other cities.

Examples support many patterns of organization. In the following portion of a short story, "Up the Coule," Hamlin Garland writes about what he saw on a train ride from the city of Milwaukee to the rural area of Wisconsin, near the Mississippi River, where he grew up. He begins the first paragraph of his story with the main idea: "The ride from Milwaukee to the Mississippi is a fine ride at any time, superb in summer." He then supports this overall idea with many descriptive examples of views that make this ride so "superb" in the summer. We've underlined and numbered them.

The ride from Milwaukee to the Mississippi is a fine ride at any time, superb in summer. To lean back in a reclining-chair and whirl away in a breezy July day, past ① lakes, ② groves of oak, past ③ fields of barley being reaped, past ④ hay fields, where the heavy grass is toppling before the swift sickle, is a panorama of delight, a road full of delicious surprises, ⑤ where down a sudden vista lakes open, or a ⑥ distant wooded hill looms darkly blue, or ⑦ swift streams, foaming deep down the solid rock, send whiffs of cool breezes in at the window. (Garland, "Up the Coule")

Transitions and Clues   Garland has listed seven examples of the beauties of the view to support his generalization. The words *for example, for instance, in fact, in addition, furthermore, moreover,* and *also* are often used to introduce examples. In textbooks, a string of examples may even be numbered to make it easier for you to identify them. The words *and* or *or* are commonly used to link the final examples in a series. The use of *commas* for a *series of items*, as in the paragraph from "Up the Coule," indicates a list of examples.

Organizing to Learn: Creating an Outline and Map   Outlining and mapping help you understand the relative importance of the detailed information that examples provide. For example, the paragraph on the metropolis (p. 237) could be outlined as follows.

©2007 Pearson Education, Inc.

The Metropolis

Main Idea: "A metropolis is a major urban area that includes a large central city surrounded by several smaller incorporated cities and suburbs that join to form one large recognizable municipality."

I.   New York City
   A. Five boroughs
      1. Manhattan
      2. Bronx
      3. Brooklyn
      4. Queens
      5. Staten Island
   B. Surrounding suburbs
      1. Long Island County
      2. Westchester County
      3. Other states
         a. Connecticut
         b. New Jersey

II. Metropolitan Los Angeles
   A. Absorbed communities of Anaheim, Beverly Hills, and other satellite cities
   B. More than 9 separate cities
   C. 60 self-governing communities

III. Dallas
   A. Garland
   B. Mesquite
   C. Irving
   D. Arlington
   E. Plano
   F. Las Colinas
   G. Other cities

mapping
Information organized graphically to show relationships among facts and/or ideas

Mapping is also an excellent choice for organizing examples and other patterns. For some people, this method is more helpful than outlining, marking, or summarizing. Mapping requires that you recognize the relationships among facts and/or ideas and represent these relationships graphically. The type of graphic representation that you choose for material usually reflects the organizational pattern the writer used to organize his or her thoughts. Use whatever shape most clearly represents the relationships of the ideas for you and makes it easiest for you to remember the ideas. Some people use different-colored pens or pencils when mapping to make it easier to visualize the important concepts when they study for a test. Computer software is also available to make the process of mapping easier.

The outlined information from the paragraph "The Metropolis" (p. 237), could be organized in a map like the one shown on the opposite page. Compare the map to the outline. The principles are basically the same. In a map, the topic of the excerpt is placed on the first line. All the

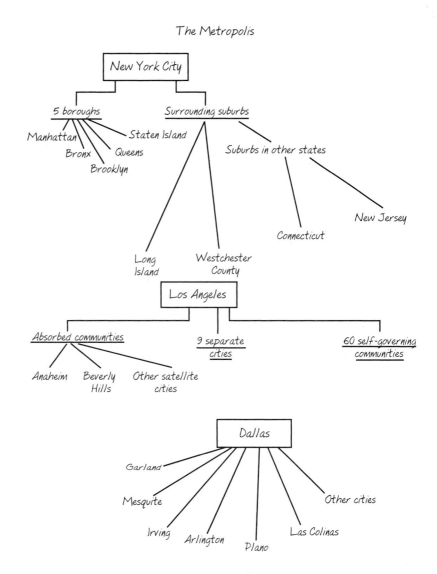

major supporting points are on the first lines drawn away from the topic. Then the minor supporting points are on the lines branching out from the major supporting points.

Exercise 4 ## Organize to Learn: Mark Examples in Text

In the following excerpt about the central downtown park in Tijuana, Mexico, number the examples that support the main idea stated in the first sentence.

> You can get a taste of the more traditional features of Mexican cities if you visit the central downtown park, or *la plaza central.* Usually, this plaza is in the middle of the Mexican city or town. It is a place where

©2007 Pearson Education, Inc.

people go to take a walk, to see friends, or to just enjoy themselves and socialize. The central plaza is home to the government palace and the major church. Frequently, you find many small stores and markets in and around the plaza. Bus and minivan routes often begin and end here as well, so it's easy to get there. (Dávalos, "Tijuana and San Diego")

| Exercise 5 |

Organize to Learn: Create a Map

Reread the following paragraph about the megalopolis that you read earlier. Then create a map of the examples on a separate sheet of paper.

As major metropolitan areas have continued to absorb smaller surrounding cities, an even larger urban unit has developed. The megalopolis consists of two or more areas linked politically, economically, socially, and geographically. Along the Eastern Seaboard, a chain of hundreds of cities and suburbs now stretches from Boston through Washington, D.C., to Richmond, Virginia, in an almost continuous urban sprawl. Similarly, much of Florida is almost one continuous city, from Jacksonville through Tampa to Miami. Dallas and Fort Worth, once two distinct cities 30 miles apart, are now linked by an international airport and a nearly unbroken band of suburban communities. Urban sprawl joins Chicago to Pittsburgh. Along the West Coast, a huge megalopolis stretches from San Diego through Los Angeles and up to San Francisco and Oakland, with only a few breaks. Migration patterns reflect a move from older cities in the Northeast (sometimes dubbed the rustbelt because of its decaying factories) to cities in the sun belt of the South and the Southwest. In fact, over half of the U.S. population growth during the 1980s and 1990s occurred in three states: California, Texas, and Florida. It is predicted that if those trends continue even more megalopolises or "supercities" will emerge in the sun belt states. (Thompson and Hickey, *Society in Focus*)

◆

Cause and Effect

cause Information that answers the question "Why?"

effect Information that explains results or outcomes

causal analysis A lengthy discussion of causes or reasons for an event or trend

Readings organized using the pattern of **cause** and **effect** usually answer the questions, "*Why* did something happen?" and "What were the *results* of a particular event?" For example, a reading on urbanization from a college sociology textbook might try to explain why cities have grown so rapidly and the effects, or results, of that rapid growth. A lengthy discussion of the causes, or reasons, for a particular event or trend is called a causal analysis. **Causal analysis** is a careful examination of all the elements involved; it seeks to break a series of events or a process into its parts and then examine the relationships among the parts. Since cause-and-effect relationships are often very complicated, it's easy to see why analysis is frequently combined with this organizational pattern. Sometimes there is not simply one cause-and-effect relationship to explain a situation. Sometimes there are underlying causes and immediate causes. Sometimes there are immediate effects and long-range effects. All these layers of relationships require considerable analysis by the writer and then by the reader to reach reasonable conclusions.

For example, read the following paragraph about housing from James W. Coleman and Donald R. Cressey's textbook *Social Problems.*

> While the number of poor people has been growing, the supply of affordable housing has been shrinking. Rents for the least expensive apartments are rising much faster than the income of the tenants. The average poor family now spends about 65 percent of its income on housing—more than double the maximum amount the Department of Housing and Urban Development says they should have to spend. An increasing number of people are being forced to move in with relatives and friends or are living in converted garages, old cars and vans, tents, or on the streets. Estimates of the number of homeless people in the United States vary widely, but virtually everyone agrees that their numbers have soared in the last decade. (Coleman and Cressey, *Social Problems*)

This paragraph analyzes one of the basic causes for the increase in homelessness: The cost of housing is increasing much faster than poor people's incomes.

Transitions and Clues   Many transitions are commonly associated with cause-and-effect reasoning, making this pattern easy to identify. Causal relationships are indicated by words such as *the reason why, because,* and *since,* and verbs such as *lead to, cause, result in, influence, give rise to,* and *contribute to,* and verbs that show a trend, such as *accelerate, intensify,* and *increase.* Effects may be introduced by transitions such as *therefore, as a result, subsequently, consequently, so,* and *hence.*

Organizing to Learn: Creating a Chart   One way to organize cause-and-effect relationships among facts and/or ideas is to create a chart. For example, the information in the above paragraph might be organized like this:

Shrinking Supply of Affordable Housing

Cause		Effects on Poor Families
Rent rising faster than income	$\Rightarrow$	Spend 65% of income on housing
	$\Rightarrow$	Forced to move in with relatives
	$\Rightarrow$	Moving into old cars, tents
	$\Rightarrow$	Number of homeless has soared

In this case, only one cause is identified—the rising cost of housing—but it is obvious that that one cause has multiple effects.

©2007 Pearson Education, Inc.

Exercise 6   ### Organize to Learn: Identify Cause and Effect

Read the following paragraph about urbanization from a sociology textbook. Circle all the transitions and other words indicating that the reasoning used here is primarily cause and effect. Then complete the cause-and-effect chart.

> Because cities have tended to grow rapidly, very little planning has gone into their physical shape, and their social structure has also given rise to occasional problems. The large concentration of people in cities requires buildings that are close together and many stories high. Without proper planning, this necessity can lead to ugliness, to lack of green and open spaces, to the often-mentioned "asphalt jungle" look. Modern city planners are much more aware of the need to pay special attention to a pleasing appearance, so that the cities of the future will probably be much more attractive than those of the past. (Perry and Perry, *Contemporary Society*)

Lack of Urban Planning

Cause	**Effect**
1. Cities have grown rapidly	1. _____
2. _____	2. Buildings are close together and many stories high
3. Without proper planning	3. _____
4. _____	4. Cities of the future will probably be more attractive

Exercise 7   ### Organize to Learn: Identify Cause and Effect

Read the following paragraph about urbanization from a sociology textbook. Circle all the transitions and other words indicating that the reasoning used here is primarily cause and effect. Then complete the cause-and-effect chart.

> The stunning increase in the cost of buying a private home has been a major contributor to the growing division between the haves and the have-nots in our society. Those who already own a home have received windfall profits, but first-time home buyers are often shut out of the market. And even though the recent pace of real estate inflation seems to have slowed, the cost of an average home more than doubled in the last decade and a half. And as a result, the average buyer is now older and more likely to need two incomes to make the payments. (Coleman and Cressey, *Social Problems*)

Higher Housing Prices

Cause	Effect
1. _____	a. Growing division between haves and have nots
	b. _____
	c. _____
	_____

◆

Comparison and Contrast

©2007 Pearson Education, Inc.

comparison
Information that explains how two things are similar

contrast
Information that explains how two things are different

Another common pattern of organization is comparison and contrast. **Comparison** answers the question, "How are two items similar?" **Contrast** answers the question, "How are two items different?" The items being compared or contrasted can be almost anything: people, ideas, cities, trees, buildings, processes, and so on. The items being considered usually fit into the same general category or have something in common.

Many times, authors use both comparison and contrast in an article, but usually their examination focuses primarily on either similarities or differences. The term *compare* is sometimes used to mean both comparison and contrast. For example, on an essay test, a professor may ask students to compare the economies of Chicago and Tokyo. A complete answer would need to include the significant similarities and differences between the two cities' economies.

Transitions and Clues   Transitional words and phrases used for comparisons include *similarly, likewise, also, alike, same,* and *in comparison.* For contrasts, *yet, nevertheless, in contrast, on the other hand, however, but,* and *conversely* are some of the transitional words used.

Organizing to Learn: Creating a Circle Diagram   An effective way to organize a comparison and contrast is to use circles to form a diagram sometimes called a Venn diagram. If two items being compared share a common trait, the circles overlap. Read the following excerpt about grocery stores, and then study the accompanying diagram.

> The grocery stores in low-income neighborhoods and those in the better-off sections of cities have a couple of things in common: They sell food, and people shop and spend money in them. But the similarities end there. Big grocery stores in low-income areas are few and far between. Most residents have to take buses or drive at least 10 miles to get to one. The few stores in the "hood" are stark contrasts to those found in more affluent areas. Only people who have no choice go to "poor stores" because their prices are generally higher, the quality of the food is usually poorer, and the selection is meager.

The conveniently located "rich stores" frequently have bright lights highlighting delicious-looking produce, beautiful refrigerated cases of freshly cooked "homemade" foods that can be picked up for the evening dinner, and cheery folks all around the store offering the shoppers samples of tasty tidbits. In contrast, the poor stores have fluorescent bulbs that don't do much to make the wilted produce look very appetizing, no display areas offering freshly prepared foods, and certainly no samples for shoppers to take.

The poor stores do have at least one feature not found in their upscale counterparts across town: they accept WIC (Women-Infants-Children) coupons for poor families. Many low-income shoppers use WIC coupons, and the program has excessively complicated rules, so checkout lines are almost always painfully long. The result is more restless children, more frustration, and more humiliation for the shoppers. (Roberta Alexander)

Notice that in the diagram, there are many differences and only two similarities. Sometimes you might map two elements that are completely different, completely contrasting. In that case, the circles would be completely separate.

Exercise 8   ## Organize to Learn: Create a Circle Diagram

Read Yi-Fu Tuan's contrast of American and Chinese attitudes toward where we live. Then, on a separate sheet of paper, create circles that identify the main points of comparison and contrast. According to the author, are there any points where the attitudes of the two cultures are similar? If so, you can allow the circles to overlap at that point.

> Americans have a sense of space, not of place. Go to an American home in exurbia, and almost the first thing you do is drift toward the picture window. How curious that the first compliment you pay your host inside his house is to say how lovely it is outside his house! He is pleased that you should admire his vistas. The distant horizon is not merely a line separating earth from sky, it is a symbol of the future. The American is not rooted in his place, however lovely: his eyes are drawn by the expanding space to a point on the horizon, which is his future.
>
> By contrast, consider the traditional Chinese home. Blank walls enclose it. Step behind the spirit wall and you are in a courtyard with perhaps a miniature garden around the corner. Once inside the private compound you are wrapped in an ambiance of calm beauty, an ordered world of buildings, pavement, rock, and decorative vegetation. But you have no distant view: nowhere does space open out before you. Raw nature in such a home is experienced only as weather, and the only open space is the sky above. The Chinese is rooted in his place. When he has to leave, it is not for the promised land on the terrestrial horizon, but for another world all together along the vertical, religious axis of his imagination. (Tuan, "American Space, Chinese Place")

◆

Process

process
Information organized to show how something is done step-by-step

Process is the organizational pattern that answers the questions "How?" and "In what sequence?" For example, a reading organized around process might explain how to write an essay, how to replace brake shoes, or how to earn money on the stock market. A process is usually explained in steps. If you are learning to bake a cake, you will follow the recipe directions in order, step by step. Often success depends on completing each step in the proper sequence; thus, the steps in a process are often labeled *first, second, third,* and so on. Frequently, the process for doing something is written as a numbered list. For instance, a cookie recipe might start like this:

1. Heat the oven to 350 degrees.
2. Mix together the flour, baking powder, salt, and sugar.
3. Melt the butter.

The recipe would continue to list the steps the cook would follow to make the final product.

©2007 Pearson Education, Inc.

Another kind of writing that involves process is a description of how something takes place. You will encounter this kind of organizational pattern in many college courses, including sociology, biology, physics, and history. Read the following paragraph, which explains the gentrification process that was defined in the excerpt on page 239. Once you understand the process of gentrification, you will understand the meaning of the word if it's not familiar to you.

> The gentrification of a neighborhood is usually a gradual process. Some recent examples of neighborhoods in different stages of the gentrification process are Harlem in New York and the Mission District in San Francisco. The process begins in a neighborhood where low-income and blue-collar people have lived for years. Slowly, the area becomes interesting and desirable to people with extra money to spend. The neighborhood is usually convenient, close to downtown and entertainment districts. It has beautiful, old homes, some divided up into apartments. The homes are cheap, and young professional people with lots of money and energy for renovation are attracted to them.
>
> As the gentrification process continues, more people buy and remodel homes or rent upscale space in these areas, and prices go up. A natural part of the process is that the residents who do not make a lot of money eventually are forced to move out because they can no longer afford to stay in the neighborhood. Homeowners decide to move because they can no longer afford the property taxes and selling their houses for substantially more than they paid for them seems like a good idea. Throughout the process, services that cater to the upper-middle class begin to appear: fancy coffee shops, upscale restaurants, and specialty stores such as bakeries, bistros, and delicatessens. In the end, the neighborhood is completely transformed. People whose families may have lived there for generations are no longer there. (Roberta Alexander)

Transitions and Clues   The transitions commonly used to identify process as an organizational pattern include *how to, in the process of, the steps to follow, stages,* and terms that identify steps, such as *begin, continue,* and *end* or *first, second,* and *third.* Some of these transitions overlap with those used in chronological order because both patterns of organization arrange points in time, although for different purposes.

Organizing to Learn: Creating a Flowchart   Because a process consists of clearly defined steps, making a numbered list of them is one way to organize ideas to be sure you understand them. Another way is to create a **flowchart,** which is a graphic organizer popular among businesses and computer applications. A flowchart uses arrows to show sequence, or directions. For example, the stages of the gentrification process could be represented in a simple flowchart like the one shown on the next page.

flowchart A graphic representation of a process, usually using arrows

The Gentrification Process

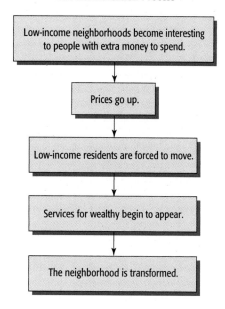

Low-income neighborhoods become interesting to people with extra money to spend.

↓

Prices go up.

↓

Low-income residents are forced to move.

↓

Services for wealthy begin to appear.

↓

The neighborhood is transformed.

Exercise 9   ## Organize to Learn: Create a Flowchart

Read the following excerpt. Watch for the stages in the process of migration that help to explain the ethnic concentrations in some urban and rural neighborhoods. Then, on a separate sheet of paper, create a flowchart that illustrates the process of chain migration and the growth of ethnic groups.

Chain Migration

In the United States, people are considered ethnic if they are not part of the majority. Mexicans in Mexico are generally not part of an ethnic group, but when they immigrate to the United States, they become part of an ethnic group. Chain migration describes the process by which people migrate to a specific community of a foreign country and become members of an ethnic group.

First, usually one person or a few people decide to move in search of a better life. Then, after establishing themselves in a new place, these people write letters and make phone calls back home telling people they should move too. Eventually, the idea catches on, and many people from the same area decide to migrate. Finally, large numbers of people move from one village or from neighboring villages to join the first pioneers in their new home. In this way, neighbors in the old country become neighbors in a new country. And each person who moves encourages other people from back home to follow. Thus the process of chain migration continues, and the ethnic groups grow. (Adapted from Jordan-Bychkov and Domosh, *Human Mosaic*)

©2007 Pearson Education, Inc.

Exercise 10   ## Organize to Learn: Write a Summary

In your own words, *briefly* summarize "Chain Migration." Start with a sentence that states the main idea and gives credit to the source (the author and title of the excerpt). Then list, in sentence form, the steps in the process. _____

_____

_____

_____

_____

Exercise 11   ## Organize to Learn: Create a Vocabulary List

Define the following terms from the context of the excerpt.

1. *Ethnic* _____

2. *Chain migration* _____

_____

Exercise 12   ## Reflect

Think about what you read in "Chain Migration" and what you already know about the topic. Answer the following questions, and prepare to discuss them with your classmates.

1. How long have you lived where you are now? Where does your immediate family live? _____

_____

2. Has your family migrated from one state to another or from one country to another? Did your grandparents or great-grandparents migrate here from somewhere else? _____

_____

3. How did the members of your family end up living where they are now? What were the steps in the *process* of their migration?

_____

_____

4. Why did your family migrate? If you don't know, interview a family member. If there is no one in your family who migrated, interview a neighbor or a classmate. _____

_____

Reading 2   *Gated Developments: Fortresses or Communities?*

Heather Eudy

The following reading studies the upsurge in what are known as gated communities—their characteristics and history as well as the reasons why they appeal to a growing number of people. As you read, think about the gated communities in your area, and notice the patterns of organization that Eudy uses.

1   A sea-breeze-kissed, Italian-style, 2,500-square-foot home at the Royal Palm Yacht and Country Club in Boca Raton, Florida, will provide you with a waterfront villa, yacht dockage, and a private lap pool for approximately $29.5 million. Also in Italian style, a home in Beverly Park in Los Angeles, California, can be had for between $10 million and $26 million, where you can bask in the "privacy" and "prestige" of 24-hour security, your own park, and a golf course. Or perhaps you would prefer to live in Cobblestone, also known as "The Toughest Gate," in Tucson, Arizona, for $13.5 million and enjoy your very own indoor gun and archery range fortressed from the outside world.

2   Gated communities such as these are not all that new to America; however, their numbers are rising, and not just as ostentatious and elaborate walled cities—hideouts for the affluent—but also as planned developments for the middle class. In fact, people of all economic standing are seeking closed communities with controlled access—entry available only to residents usually requiring a key, code, or electronic device—and the protection of walls or fences. Where did this propensity for restricted-entry neighborhoods begin?

3   Walled cities could first be found in ancient Rome and areas occupied by the Romans. In particular, walled settlements built by Roman soldiers around 300 BC guarded the Roman families in England. In the Middle Ages, English kings followed the Roman example by creating barriers to protect their castles against invaders. Later, Spanish fort towns were built in the Caribbean, and as early as the 1850s, gated developments could be found in major U.S. cities like New York and St. Louis. These communities functioned as solace for the very wealthy well into the twentieth century. In the 1960s and 1970s, the appeal of protected communities grew as retirement developments arose, and increased rapidly for prestige, leisure, and safety reasons in the 1980s. The majority of these developments are in the Sun belt states (the Southeast and Southwest), where most resort and retirement areas are located because of the weather. California, Florida, and Texas have particularly high numbers of gated communities. But these exclusive neighborhoods have now sprung up everywhere, except in rural states. And although in the past they were restricted to the elite, they are now primarily settled by the middle and upper-middle classes.

4   The types of gated communities vary depending on the economic status of the residents and the purpose the residents have for living there. In their book entitled, *Fortress America: Gated Communities in the United States,* Edward J. Blakely and Mary Gail Snyder categorize gated communi-

©2007 Pearson Education, Inc.

ties according to people's reasons for moving into them. The three categories are Lifestyle Communities, Prestige Communities, and the Security Zone. Lifestyle Communities are those centered around leisure activities. Here you find private golf courses, athletic clubs, riding trails, parks, rivers, and sometimes beaches. A planned community in Las Vegas, Nevada, known as Green Valley, for example, centers around swimming pools, a cinema, restaurants, and an upscale athletic club where made-to-order smoothies come fresh from the bartender's blender. Prestige Communities, the second category, exist for distinction and status—a place where the rich and famous can separate themselves from the less rich and less famous. Finally, Security Zone communities are marketed as havens from crime, with gates, guards, and barricades to keep out uninvited people. In all of the communities, walls serve as dividers from the outside. Most have round-the-clock security, private guards, surveillance, controlled access, video monitors, and streets and parks for residents only.

5   Demographers and sociologists—scientists who study the characteristics of populations and those who study social developments and institutions—are scrutinizing the causes for the rise in popularity of gated communities. They are finding that many people move to homes within gates in order to feel safe. Some enjoy the cleanliness, the shared values, status, exclusiveness, seclusion, and quiet. They also appreciate the high property values gated communities ensure and the private access to leisure areas such as beaches and parks.

6   To fully understand this trend toward gated communities in the United States, one must study the country's history of suburbanization. Suburbanization—the development of areas just outside of city boundaries—began when transportation improvements, such as rail lines and automobiles, allowed upper-class and middle-class people to escape city life. At that time, suburbia seemed to be a utopia—a harmonious environment free of the tensions of the city. Even the names of the suburban developments suggest features of the natural landscape, such as River Forest and Forest Park, both suburbs of Chicago. Middle-class Americans relocated to the suburbs to get away from real and perceived urban problems. The suburbs, they thought, were safe and clean, had good schools, and were inhabited by like-minded people. But then the suburbs began to get crowded and run down, and racial minorities and immigrants began moving in. So now new communities are being built with gates to provide privacy and safety, once and for all.

7   But, safety from what? There seem to be growing fears in America about the future, fears about physical and economic security. Fulbright scholar Renaud Le Goix claims that urban fear and social paranoia have pushed Americans inside the gates. According to the U.S. Census Bureau's 2001 American Housing Survey, more than 7 million households live in walled or fenced developments, and 4 million of those have controlled access. Homeowners (predominantly white) and renters (more ethnically diverse and less affluent) alike are living behind gates. But are gated communities really safer? Research has uncovered very little evidence that gating reduces crime. There have been cases in which gated communities have

been deliberately, and successfully, targeted for burglary, and cases in which the residents of gated communities have themselves been the criminals. In fact, firefighters and police officers even question gated developments' efficiency during emergencies, since access to the properties is difficult.

8   Even if the illusion of safety is enough to ease residents' fears, there is a negative impact on the individual and society. Many demographers and sociologists have concluded that controlled-access living accelerates socioeconomic segregation, even isolation. For example, in "Gates and Ghettoes," Anita Rice asserts that gating increases the polarization of social classes and highlights inequality. People living inside gated communities are, on average, wealthier and more likely to be property owners than the general population. Additionally, gated communities intensify exclusion. That means there is less public space available to people on the outside. When public resources like beaches, parks, and nature trails are private spaces, not public places, those who are excluded lose. And while those in gated communities find their property values rising, people outside the gates find theirs dwindling. Finally, the social segregation that comes with gated communities breeds a culture of distrust. People of different backgrounds are less likely to interact. Fellow citizens become intruders. If we don't know each other and trust each other, if we continue to isolate ourselves from one another, will we ever be able to genuinely solve social problems? At what cost do the barriers rise?

Sources

Blakely, Edward J., and Mary Gail Snyder. *Fortress America: Gated Communities in the United States.* Washington, DC: Brookings Institution Press, 1999.

El Nasser, Haya. "Gated Communities More Popular, and Not Just for the Rich." *USA Today,* December 15, 2002.

Le Goix, Renaud. "The Suburban Paradise or the Parceling of Cities?" *UCLA International Institute.* http://www.international.ucla.edu/article.asp?parentid=4664 (accessed September 7, 2005).

Rice, Anita. "Gates and Ghettoes: A Tale of Two Britains?" *BBC News.* March 18, 2004. http://news.bbc.co.uk/I/hi/programmes/if/3513980.stm.

U.S. Census Bureau. *American Housing Survey for the United States: 2001.* http://www.huduser.org/datasets/ahs.html (accessed September 25, 2005).

EUDY, "Gated Developments"

Exercise 13   ## Work with Words

The following sentences appear in Reading 2, Eudy's "Gated Developments." Use context clues, your knowledge of word parts, and if necessary, your dictionary skills to determine the meaning of each italicized word in the sentences. Write the meaning of the word in the lines provided. The paragraph number is provided in case you want to check the context.

©2007 Pearson Education, Inc.

1. Gated communities such as these are not all that new to America; however, their numbers are rising, and not just as *ostentatious* and elaborate walled cities—hideouts for the affluent—but also as planned developments for the middle class. (par. 2)

   Ostentatious: _____

2. Where did this *propensity* for restricted-entry neighborhoods begin? (par. 2)

   Propensity: _____

3. These communities functioned as *solace* for the very wealthy well into the twentieth century. (par. 3)

   Solace: _____

4. *Demographers and sociologists*—scientists who study the characteristics of populations and those who study social developments and institutions—are *scrutinizing* the causes for the rise in popularity of gated communities. (par. 5)

   Demographers: _____

5. *Sociologists:* _____

6. *Scrutinizing:* _____

7. *Suburbanization*—the development of areas just outside the city boundaries—began when transportation improvements, such as rail lines and automobiles, allowed upper-class and middle-class people to escape city life. (par. 6)

   Suburbanization: _____

8. Indeed, suburbia has served as a *utopia*—a harmonious environment free of the tensions that the city represents. (par. 6)

   Utopia: _____

9. Fulbright scholar Renaud Le Goix claims that urban fear and social *paranoia* have pushed Americans inside the gates. (par. 7)

   Paranoia: _____

10. For example, in "Gates and Ghettoes," Anita Rice asserts that gating increases the *polarization* of social classes and highlights inequality. (par. 8)

    Polarization: _____

Exercise 14   ## Check Your Understanding

Based on Reading 2, write your answers to the following questions on the lines provided.

1. What is the topic of Reading 2?

_____

2. What is the main idea of the reading?

_____

_____

3. Where and when did gated communities begin, and where in the United States are they most popular today?

_____

_____

4. What are the three categories of gated communities Blakely and Snyder discuss in their book?

_____

_____

5. What is the topic of paragraph 5?

_____

_____

6. What is the main idea of paragraph 5?

_____

_____

_____

7. What connection between suburbia and gated communities does the author make in paragraph 6?

_____

_____

8. What has research shown about the safety of gated communities?

_____

_____

9. What is the main idea of paragraph 8?

_____

_____

_____

©2007 Pearson Education, Inc.

10. List three ways that gated communities intensify the divisions between classes.

1. _____

2. _____

3. _____

Exercise 15   ## Identify Patterns of Organization

Based on Reading 2, choose the best answer to each of the following multiple-choice questions. Then write the transitions or clues that helped you select the pattern of organization.

1. What is the dominant pattern of organization for paragraph 1?
   a. Cause and effect
   b. Process
   c. Exemplification

   Transitions and clues: _____

2. What is the dominant pattern of organization for paragraph 3?
   a. Problem and solution
   b. Chronological order
   c. Comparison and contrast

   Transitions and clues: _____

   _____

3. What is the dominant pattern of organization for paragraph 4?
   a. Classification
   b. Narration
   c. Chronological order

   Transitions and clues: _____

4. What is the dominant pattern of organization for paragraph 5?
   a. Process
   b. Comparison and contrast
   c. Cause and effect

   Transitions and clues: _____

5. What are the dominant patterns of organization for paragraph 6?
   a. Definition and chronological order
   b. Narration, comparison and contrast
   c. Exemplification and classification

   Transitions and clues: _____

   _____

| Exercise 16 | ### Organize to Learn: Create an Outline, Map or Flowchart |

On a separate sheet of paper, organize what you read in Reading 2 to help you learn it.

1. Create a map or flowchart of the information in paragraph 4.

2. Prepare an outline or map of the information in paragraph 8.

| Exercise 17 | ### Reflect |

Think about what you read in Reading 2 and what you already know about the topic. Then answer the following questions.

1. Were you aware that some homes cost millions of dollars, like the ones mentioned in paragraph 1 of the reading? Describe the wealthy homes you have seen in your region.

   _____

   _____

   _____

2. What is your opinion of gated communities? Do you believe that, for communities, they are positive, negative, or both? Why?

   _____

   _____

   _____

COMBINED PATTERNS OF ORGANIZATION

Most of the time, an author uses a combination of organizational patterns to express ideas, rather than just one pattern. There may be one primary pattern, but to explain an idea or concept thoroughly, the author may need to use other patterns, too. A paragraph can have almost any combination of organizational patterns. For example, you might find comparison and contrast combined with exemplification and cause and effect. Two more patterns of organization that you should be able to recognize and analyze are *problem and solution* and *argumentation*. Authors of essays and editorials frequently use these patterns when they write about controversial topics.

Problem and Solution

problem An issue that needs to be resolved

In problem-and-solution organization, a writer first presents a significant **problem** and explains in detail the issue that needs to be resolved. Often, the writer uses a cause-and-effect approach to explain the problem. But other patterns of organization can also be used effectively

©2007 Pearson Education, Inc.

within the problem-and-solution organization. The following paragraph from *America and Its Peoples,* a U.S. history textbook by James Kirby Martin and coauthors, uses exemplification and cause and effect to list the problems made worse by the growth of cities.

> The growth of urban areas exacerbated many problems, including the absence of clean drinking water, the lack of cheap public transportation, and most importantly, poor sanitation. Sanitation problems led to heavy urban mortality rates and frequent epidemics of typhoid, dysentery, typhus, cholera, and yellow fever. (Martin et al., *America and Its Peoples*)

solution   a way of resolving issues or solving problems

A textbook in sociology or a government analysis of urban problems might conclude a discussion of urban problems with a series of possible **solutions,** or ways that the problems can be solved. Here is a paragraph from the U.S. Department of Housing and Urban Development's publication *The State of the Cities 1999.* Notice that it uses the exemplification and comparison-and-contrast patterns of organization to explain both problems and solutions.

> *St. Louis, MO.* The East-West Gateway Coordinating Council—the planning body for the St. Louis metropolitan area—is engaged in a variety of regional efforts to address the economic, social, and environmental issues facing the region. A major concern is the mismatch between where unemployed workers in the central city live and where jobs are proliferating in the metro area. The Council launched the St. Louis Regional Jobs Initiative to try to address these imbalances and better align the region's workforce development, economic development, transportation, and social service programs to help low-income jobseekers. The initiative provides funding and support for community-based initiatives that help the workers, especially young people, find meaningful jobs that can support a family. The council also coordinates the local HUD-funded *Bridges to Work* demonstration, which is testing the effectiveness of jobs initiatives that coordinate placement, transportation, and career-building services that connect inner-city neighborhoods to job-rich suburbs. (U.S. Department of Housing and Urban Development, *The State of the Cities, 1999*)

Transitions and Clues   To identify a problem, writers use terms like *problem, need, difficulty, dilemma, challenge,* and *issue.* When they present possible solutions, writers use terms like *propose, suggest, indicate, solve, resolve, improve, rectify, plan,* and *respond to a need.*

Organizing to Learn: Creating a Chart   One way to organize problem-and-solution relationships is to create a chart. Study how the information in the paragraph from *The State of the Cities* has been organized into a chart.

Solving Problems in St. Louis

Problem	Solution
Mismatch between where unemployed workers live and where the jobs are	Formation of St. Louis Regional Jobs Initiative to better align • Workforce development • Economic development • Transportation • Social services and help low-income job seekers find meaningful jobs that can support a family
Need to connect inner-city neighborhoods to job-rich suburbs	*Bridges to Work* demonstration—testing effectiveness of job initiatives that coordinate • Placement • Transportation • Career-building services

Exercise 18   Organize to Learn: Create a Chart or Map and Write a Summary

Read the following paragraphs from a cultural geography textbook about the problems caused by the movement from the cities to the suburbs and some of the solutions that are being implemented. Then complete the activities that follow.

Decentralization

Unfortunately, decentralization has taken its toll. Many of the urban problems now burdening North American cities are direct products of the rapid decentralization that has taken place in the last 40 years. Those people who cannot afford to live in the suburbs are forced to live in inadequate and run-down housing in the inner city, areas that currently do not provide good jobs. Vacant storefronts, empty offices, and deserted factories testify to the movement of commercial functions from central cities to suburbs. Retail sales in North American central cities have steadily declined, losing business to suburban shopping centers. Even offices are finding advantages to suburban locations. Like industry, offices capitalize on lower costs and easier access to new transportation networks.

Decentralization has also cost society millions of dollars in problems brought to the suburbs. Where rapid suburbanization has been the case, sprawl has usually resulted. A common pattern is leapfrog or *checkerboard development,* where housing tracts jump over parcels of farmland resulting in a mixture of open lands with built-up areas. This pattern results because developers buy cheaper land farther away from built-up areas, thereby cutting their costs. Furthermore, home buyers often pay premium prices for homes in subdivisions surrounded by farmlands. . . .

©2007 Pearson Education, Inc.

This form of development is costly because it is more expensive to provide city services, such as police, fire protection, sewers, and electrical lines, to those areas laying beyond open, unbuilt-up parcels. Obviously, the most cost-efficient form of development is adding new housing directly adjacent to built-up areas. That way the costs of providing new services are minimal.

Furthermore, sprawl extracts high costs because of increased use of cars. Public transportation is extremely costly and inefficient when it must serve a low-density checkerboard development pattern—so costly that many cities and transit firms cannot extend lines into those areas. This means that the automobile is the only form of transportation there. More energy is consumed for fuel, more air pollution is created by exhaust, and more time is spent in commuting and everyday activities in a sprawling urban area than in a centralized city.

We should not overlook the costs of losing valuable agricultural land to urban development. Farmers cultivating the remaining checkerboard parcels have a hard time making ends meet. They are usually taxed at extremely high rates because their land has high potential for development, and few can make a profit when taxes eat up all their resources. Often the only recourse is to sell out to subdividers. So the cycle of leapfrog development goes on.

Many cities are now taking strong measures to curb this kind of sprawling growth. San Jose, California, for example, one of the fastest-growing cities of the 1960s, is now focusing new development on empty parcels of the checkerboard pattern. This is called *in-filling*. New growth takes place not by extending the sprawling outer edge of the city, but by developing the existing urban area, where services are already available and can be provided at lower costs.

Other cities are tying the number of building permits granted each year to the availability of urban services. If schools are already crowded, water supplies inadequate, and sewer plants overburdened, the number of new dwelling units approved for an area will reflect this lower carrying capacity. . . .

In summary, the costs of decentralization range from decayed and moribund downtowns to costly and inefficient public transportation. While inner-city poverty and ghettoization can be partially blamed on decentralization, so can the loss of farmland, increased auto air pollution, and higher energy consumption. Though planning measures have alleviated some of these problems, many of these ills will multiply as our cities continue to decentralize. (Jordan-Bychkov and Domosh, *Human Mosaic*)

1. On a separate sheet of paper, make a chart or map in which you show the problems caused by decentralization and the solutions that are being tried.

2. On separate sheet of paper, write a summary of the excerpt. Use your chart or map to help you.

◆

Argument

©2007 Pearson Education, Inc.

argument
Information intended to convince a reader through logical reasoning

Argument is a pattern of organization writers often use to convince you to believe or act in a certain way. As an extension of the problem-and-solution pattern, the argument pattern presents evidence that a problem exists or is serious. Sometimes a writer wants to persuade you that one or more of the proposed solutions is the best. Writers whose intention is to persuade often incorporate emotional appeals into the argument. On the other hand, some writers rely on logic alone. They don't want to persuade you that one solution is better than any other. Instead, they present facts to help you draw your own conclusions, which they hope match their own. The passage in Exercise 18 on pages 261 through 262 relies on logic to make the point that decentralization creates problems. Notice that all the supporting evidence focuses on high costs: the expense of providing city services, the costs and consequences associated with the increased use of cars, the costs of losing valuable agricultural land. The writers want to show that the effects of decentralization are costly and to explain some solutions that cities have implemented. In Chapter 8, you will study ways to evaluate arguments and persuasion essays.

Transitions and Clues   Arguments use terms like *argue, strongly recommend, in support of, therefore, thus, convince,* and *persuade.*

Organizing to Learn: Using Many Options   Since an argument can be used in combination with any organizational pattern as a way to support its points, you will need to decide, based on the nature of the argument, which is the best way to organize to learn. Like the problem-and-solution pattern of organization, an argument is well organized in a chart.

Exercise 19   Identify Combined Patterns of Organization

The following excerpt is primarily organized as a process, but two other patterns are used as well. Identify the combination of organizational patterns used by answering the questions that follow. For ease of reference, the sentences are numbered.

(1) The process of chain migration continues even after the first emigrants have departed. (2) From their new home, they write letters back to their native place, extolling the virtues of their new life and imploring others to join them. (3) Such letters written from the United States became known as *American letters.*

(4) Chain migration caused the movement of people to become *channellized,* linking a specific source region to a particular destination, so that neighbors in the old country became neighbors in the new country as well. (5) It was at work three centuries ago and still operates today. (6) The recent mass migration of Latin Americans to Anglo-America provides an example. (7) Research by geographer Richard C.

Jones revealed that different parts of the southwestern United States draw upon different source regions in Mexico. (Jordan-Bychkov and Domosh, *Human Mosaic*)

1. The primary pattern used to organize this excerpt is
   _____ .

2. The words *known as American letters* in sentence 3 indicate that the _____ pattern is being used.

3. The transition word *caused* in sentence 4 indicates that the _____ pattern is also being used here.

4. In sentence 6, the word *example* signals that the _____ pattern is also being used.

◆

| **Table 5.1** | **Patterns of Organization** |

Patterns	Transitions and Clues
Chronological order and narration	*then, when, after, before, while, during, earlier, meanwhile, until, now, immediately, finally, as soon as, next, last, later,* plus *dates* and *times*
Definition and classification	Definition: *is, could be defined as, refers to, means, signifies, denotes, consists of*
	Classification: *kinds, types, varieties, categories, groups*
Exemplification	*and, or, for example, for instance, in fact, in addition, furthermore, moreover, also,* plus a series of items, set off by many commas
Cause and effect	Cause: *the reason why, because, since, lead to, cause, result in, influence, give rise to, contribute to, accelerate, intensify, increase*
	Effect: *therefore, as a result, subsequently, consequently, so, hence*
Comparison and contrast	Comparison: *similarly, likewise, also, alike, same, in comparison*
	Contrast: *yet, nevertheless, in contrast, on the other hand, however, but, conversely*
Process	*how to, in the process of, the steps to follow, stages, begin, continue, end, first, second, third*
Problem and solution	Problem: *problem, need, difficulty, dilemma, challenge, issue*
	Solution: *propose, suggest, indicate, solve, resolve, improve, rectify, plan, respond to a need*
Argument	*argue, strongly recommend, in support of, therefore, thus, convince, persuade*

©2007 Pearson Education, Inc.

Reading 3   *Why Are People Homeless?*

National Coalition for the Homeless
_____

Unfortunately, many Americans are homeless. The following reading, written in 2000, analyzes the causes of homelessness. It concludes with a brief summary of social problems that need to be remedied if homelessness is to be eliminated. As you read, think about the connections between homelessness and other social problems. Notice the main ideas and patterns of organization the authors use to present their supporting points.

1 Two trends are largely responsible for the rise in homelessness over the past 20–25 years: a growing shortage of affordable rental housing and a simultaneous increase in poverty. Below is an overview of current poverty and housing statistics. . . .

Poverty

2 Homelessness and poverty are inextricably linked. Poor people are frequently unable to pay for housing, food, child care, health care, and education. Difficult choices must be made when limited resources cover only some of the necessities. Often it is housing, which absorbs a high proportion of income, that must be dropped. Being poor means being an illness, an accident, or a paycheck away from living on the streets.

3 In 2000, 11.3% of the U.S. population, or 31.1 million people, lived in poverty (U.S. Bureau of the Census, 2001). While the number of poor people has decreased a bit in recent years, the number of people living in extreme poverty has increased. In 2000, 39% of all people living in poverty had incomes of less than half the poverty level. This statistic remains unchaged from the 1999 level. Forty percent of persons living in poverty are children; in fact, the 2000 poverty rate of 16.2% for children is significantly higher than the poverty rate for any other age group.

4 Two factors help account for increasing poverty: eroding employment opportunities for large segments of the workforce, and the declining value and availability of public assistance.

Eroding Work Opportunities

5 Media reports of a growing economy and low unemployment mask a number of important reasons why homelessness persists, and, in some areas of the country, is worsening. These reasons include stagnant or falling incomes and less secure jobs which offer fewer benefits.

6 While the last few years have seen growth in real wages at all levels, these increases have not been enough to counteract a long pattern of stagnant and declining wages. Low-wage workers have been particularly hard hit by wage trends and have been left behind as the disparity between rich and poor has mushroomed. To compound the problem, the real value of the minimum wage in 1997 was 18.1% less than in 1979 (Mishel, Bernstein, and Schmitt, 1999). Although incomes appear to be rising, this growth is largely

due to more hours worked—which in turn can be attributed to welfare reform and the tight labor markets. Factors contributing to wage declines include a steep drop in the number and bargaining power of unionized workers; erosion in the value of the minimum wage; a decline in manufacturing jobs and the corresponding expansion of lower-paying service-sector employment; globalization; and increased nonstandard work, such as temporary and part-time employment (Mishel, Bernstein, and Schmitt, 1999).

7   Declining wages, in turn, have put housing out of reach for many workers: in every state, more than the minimum wage is required to afford a one- or two-bedroom apartment at Fair Market Rent.[1] In fact, in the median state a minimum-wage worker would have to work 89 hours each week to afford a two-bedroom apartment at 30% of his or her income, which is the federal definition of affordable housing (National Low Income Housing Coalition, 2001). Currently, 5 million rental households have "worst case housing needs," which means that they pay more than half their incomes for rent, live in severely substandard housing, or both. The primary source of income for 80% of these households is earnings from jobs. In 1998, this was the case for only 40% of households with worst case housing needs. This represents a 40% increase in working households with worst case housing needs from 1995 to 1999 (U.S. Housing and Urban Development, 2001).

8   The connection between impoverished workers and homelessness can be seen in homeless shelters, many of which house significant numbers of full-time wage earners. A survey of 27 U.S. cities found that over one in four people in homeless situations are employed, a significant increase from 1998 (U.S. Conference of Mayors, 2000). In a number of cities not surveyed by the U.S. Conference of Mayors—as well as in many states—the percentage is even higher (National Coalition for the Homeless, 1997).

9   The future of job growth does not appear promising for many workers: a 1998 study estimated that 46% of the jobs with the most growth between 1994 and 2005 pay less than $16,000 a year; these jobs will not lift families out of poverty (National Priorities Project, 1998).[2] Moreover, 74% of these jobs pay below a livable wage ($32,185 for a family of four).

10   Thus, for many Americans, work provides no escape from poverty. The benefits of economic growth have not been equally distributed; instead, they have been concentrated at the top of income and wealth distributions. A rising tide does not lift all boats, and in the United States today, many boats are struggling to stay afloat.

Decline in Public Assistance

11 The declining value and availability of public assistance is another source of increasing poverty and homelessness. Until its repeal in August 1996, the largest cash assistance program for poor families with children was the Aid to Families with Dependent Children (AFDC) program. Between 1970 and 1994, the typical state's AFDC benefits for a family of three fell 47%, after adjusting for inflation (Greenberg and Baumohl, 1996). The Personal Responsibility and Work Opportunity Reconciliation Act of 1996 (the federal

welfare reform law) repealed the AFDC program and replaced it with a block grant program called Temporary Assistance to Needy Families (TANF). Current TANF benefits and Food Stamps combined are below the poverty level in every state; in fact, the median TANF benefit for a family of three is approximately one-third of the poverty level. Thus, contrary to popular opinion, welfare does not provide relief from poverty.

12   Welfare caseloads have dropped sharply since the passage and implementation of welfare reform legislation. However, declining welfare rolls simply mean that fewer people are receiving benefits—not that they are employed or doing better financially. Early findings suggest that although more families are moving from welfare to work, many of them are faring poorly due to low wages and inadequate work supports. Only a small fraction of welfare recipients' new jobs pay above-poverty wages; most of the new jobs pay far below the poverty line (Children's Defense Fund and the National Coalition for the Homeless, 1998). These statistics from the Institute for Children and Poverty are particularly revealing:

> In the Institute for Children and Poverty study, 37% of homeless families had their welfare benefits reduced or cut in the last year. More strikingly, in Bucks Country and Philadelphia, PA, and Seattle, WA, more than 50% had their benefits reduced or cut. . . . Among those who lost their benefits, 20% said they became homeless as a direct result. Additionally, a second study of six states found that between 1997 and 1998, 25% of families who had stopped receiving welfare in the last six months doubled-up on housing to save money, and 23% moved because they could not pay rent. (Institute for Children and Poverty, 2001).

Moreover, extreme poverty is growing more common for children, especially those in female-headed and working families. This increase can be traced directly to the declining number of children lifted above one-half of the poverty line by government cash assistance for the poor (Children's Defense Fund and the National Coalition for the Homeless, 1998).

13   As a result of loss of benefits, low wages, and unstable employment, many families leaving welfare struggle to get medical care, food, and housing. Many lose health insurance, despite continued Medicaid eligibility: a recent study found that 675,000 people lost health insurance in 1997 as a result of the federal welfare reform legislation, including 400,000 children (Families USA, 1999). Moreover, over 725,000 workers, laid off from their jobs due to the recession this past year, lost their health insurance. (Families USA, 2001).

14   In addition, housing is rarely affordable for families leaving welfare for low wages, yet subsidized housing is so limited that fewer than one in four TANF families nationwide lives in public housing or receives a housing voucher to help them rent a private unit. For most families leaving the rolls, housing subsidies are not an option. In some communities, former welfare families appear to be experiencing homelessness in increasing numbers (Children's Defense Fund and the National Coalition for the Homeless, 1998).

©2007 Pearson Education, Inc.

15   In addition to the reduction in the value and availability of welfare benefits for families, recent policy changes have reduced or eliminated public assistance for poor single individuals. Several states have cut or eliminated General Assistance (GA) benefits for single impoverished people, despite evidence that the availability of GA reduces the prevalence of homelessness (Greenberg and Baumohl, 1996).

16   People with disabilities, too, must struggle to obtain and maintain stable housing. In 1998, on a national average, a person receiving Supplemental Security Income (SSI) benefits had to spend 69% of his or her SSI monthly income to rent a one-bedroom apartment at Fair Market Rent; in more than 125 housing market areas, the cost of a one-bedroom apartment at Fair Market Rent was more than a person's total monthly SSI income (Technical Assistance Collaborative & the Consortium for Citizens with Disabilities Housing Task Force, 1999).

17   Presently, most states have not replaced the old welfare system with an alternative that enables families and individuals to obtain above-poverty employment and to sustain themselves when work is not available or possible.

Housing

18 A lack of affordable housing and the limited scale of housing assistance programs have contributed to the current housing crisis and to homelessness.

19   The gap between the number of affordable housing units and the number of people needing them has created a housing crisis for poor people. Between 1973 and 1993, 2.2 million low-rent units disappeared from the market. These units were either abandoned, converted into condominiums or expensive apartments, or became unaffordable because of cost increases. Between 1991 and 1995, median rental costs paid by low-income renters rose 21%; at the same time, the number of low-income renters increased. Over these years, despite an improving economy, the affordable housing gap grew by one million (Daskal, 1998). Between 1970 and 1995, the gap between the number of low-income renters and the amount of affordable housing units skyrocketed from a nonexistent gap to a shortage of 4.4 million affordable housing units—the largest shortfall on record (Institute for Children and Poverty, 2001).

20   More recently, the strong economy has caused rents to soar, putting housing out of reach for the poorest Americans. Between 1995 and 1997, rents increased faster than income for the 20% of American households with the lowest incomes (U.S. Department of Housing and Urban Development, 1999). This same study found that the number of housing units that rent for less than $300, adjusted for inflation, declined from 6.8 million in 1996 to 5.5 million in 1998, a 19 % drop of 1.3 million units. The loss of affordable housing puts even greater numbers of people at risk of homelessness.

21   The lack of affordable housing has lead to high rent burdens (rents which absorb a high proportion of income), overcrowding, and substandard housing. These phenomena, in turn, have not only forced many people to become homeless; they have put a large and growing number of people at risk of becoming homeless. A recent Housing and Urban Development

(HUD) study found that 4.9 million unassisted, very low-income house-holds—this is 10.9 million people, 3.6 million of whom are children—had "worst case needs" for housing assistance in 1999 (U.S. Department of Housing and Urban Development, 2001).[3] Although this figure seems to be a decrease from 1997, it is misleading since, in the same two-year span, "the number of units affordable to extremely low income renters dropped between 1997 and 1999 at an accelerated rate, and shortages of housing both affordable and available to these renters actually worsened (HUD Report on Worst Case Housing Needs, 1999).

22   Housing assistance can make the difference between stable housing, precarious housing, or no housing at all. However, the demand for assisted housing clearly exceeds the supply: only about one-third of poor renter households receive a housing subsidy from the federal, state, or a local government (Daskal, 1998). The limited level of housing assistance means that most poor families and individuals seeking housing assistance are placed on long waiting lists. From 1996 to 1998, the time households spent on waiting lists for HUD housing assistance grew dramatically. For the largest public housing authorities, a family's average time on a waiting list rose from 22 to 33 months from 1996 to 1998—a 50% increase (U.S. Department of Housing and Urban Development, 1999). The average waiting period for a Section 8 rental assistance voucher rose from 26 months to 28 months between 1996 and 1998.[4]

23   Excessive waiting lists for public housing mean that people must remain in shelters or inadequate housing arrangements longer. For instance, in the mid-1990s in New York, families stayed in a shelter an average of five months before moving on to permanent housing. Today, the average stay is nearly a year (Santos, 2002). Consequently, there is less shelter space available for other homeless people, who must find shelter elsewhere or live on the streets.

24   A housing trend with a particularly severe impact on homelessness is the loss of single room occupancy (SRO) housing. In the past, SRO housing served to house many poor individuals, including poor persons suffering from mental illness or substance abuse. From 1970 to the mid-1980s, an estimated one million SRO units were demolished (Dolbeare, 1996). The demolition of SRO housing was most notable in large cities: between 1970 and 1982, New York City lost 87% of its $200 per month or less SRO stock; Chicago experienced the total elimination of cubicle hotels; and by 1985, Los Angeles had lost more than half of its downtown SRO housing (Koegel, et al., 1996). From 1975 to 1988, San Francisco lost 43% of its stock of low-cost residential hotels; from 1970 to 1986, Portland, Oregon lost 59% of its residential hotels; and from 1971 to 1981, Denver lost 64% of its SRO hotels (Wright and Rubin, 1997). Thus the destruction of SRO housing is a major factor in the growth of homelessness in many cities.

25   Finally, it should be noted that the largest federal housing assistance program is the entitlement to deduct mortgage interest from income for tax purposes. In fact, for every one dollar spent on low income housing programs, the federal treasury loses four dollars to housing-related tax expenditures, 75% of which benefit households in the top fifth of income

©2007 Pearson Education, Inc.

distribution (Dolbeare, 1996). Moreover, in 1994 the top fifth of households received 61% of all federal housing benefits (tax and direct), while the bottom fifth received only 18%. Thus, federal housing policy has not responded to the needs of low-income households, while disproportionately benefitting the wealthiest Americans.

Conclusion

26 Homelessness results from a complex set of circumstances which require people to choose between food, shelter, and other basic needs. Only a concerted effort to ensure jobs that pay a living wage, adequate support for those who cannot work, and affordable housing . . . will bring an end to homelessness.

Notes

1. FMRs are the monthly amounts "needed to rent privately owned, decent, safe, and sanitary rental housing of a modest (nonluxury) nature with suitable amenities." Federal Register. The U.S. Department of Housing and Urban Development determines FMRs for localities in all 50 states.

2. The poverty line for a family of three is $12,750; for a family of four, the poverty line is $16,813. See http://www.census.gov/hhes/www/poverty.html for details.

3. "Worst case needs" refers to those renters with incomes below 50% of the area median income who are involuntarily displaced, pay more than half of their income for rent and utilities, or live in substandard housing.

4. The Section 8 Program is a federal housing assistance program that provides housing subsidies for families and individuals to live in existing rental housing or in designated housing projects.

NATIONAL COALITION FOR THE HOMELESS, "Why Are People Homeless?"

Exercise 20   Work with Words

The following sentences appear in Reading 3, "Why Are People Homeless," by the National Coalition for the Homeless. Use context clues, your knowledge of word parts, and if necessary, your dictionary skills to determine the meaning of each italicized word in the sentences. Write the meaning of the word on the lines provided. The paragraph number is provided in case you want to check the context.

1. Two factors help account for increasing poverty: *eroding* employment opportunities for large segments of the workforce, and the declining value and availability of public assistance. (par. 4)

    Eroding: _____

2. These reasons [for homelessness] include *stagnant* or falling incomes and less secure jobs which offer fewer benefits. (par. 5)

    Stagnant: _____

3. In addition, housing is rarely affordable for families leaving welfare for low wages, yet *subsidized housing* is so limited that fewer than one in four TANF families nationwide lives in public housing or receives a housing voucher to help them rent a private unit. (par. 14)

Subsidized housing: _____

4. Between 1970 and 1995, the gap between the number of low-income renters and the amount of affordable housing units skyrocketed from a nonexistent gap to a shortage of 4.4 million affordable housing units—the largest *shortfall* on record (Institute for Children and Poverty, 2001). (par. 19)

Shortfall: _____

5. Finally, it should be noted that the largest federal housing assistance program is the *entitlement* to deduct mortgage interest from income for tax purposes. (par. 25)

Entitlement: _____

Exercise 21 ## Check Your Understanding

Based on Reading 3, write your answers to the following questions.

1. What is the topic of this reading? _____

2. What is the main idea (thesis) of this reading?

_____

_____

_____

3. What are the two major factors that explain the "eroding work opportunities"?

a. _____

b. _____

4. What are the five major supporting points that the authors give for their assertion of a "decline in public assistance"?

a. _____

b. _____

_____

c. _____

d. _____

e. _____

©2007 Pearson Education, Inc.

5. What is the solution to homelessness, according to the author?

_____

_____

_____

Exercise 22   Identify Patterns of Organization

Based on Reading 3, choose the best answer to each of the following multiple-choice questions.

1. What is the dominant pattern of organization used in Reading 3?
   a. Cause and effect
   b. Chronological order
   c. Definition

2. What are the patterns of organization for paragraph 6?
   a. Exemplification and description
   b. Chronological order, and cause and effect
   c. Definition, and problem and solution

3. What is the dominant pattern of organization for paragraph 8?
   a. Chronological order
   b. Problem and solution
   c. Exemplification

4. What are the patterns of organization for paragraph 10?
   a. Cause and effect, and argument
   b. Chronological order, and comparison and contrast
   c. Comparison, and contrast and definition

5. What are the patterns of organization for paragraph 26?
   a. Cause and effect, and problem and solution
   b. Chronological order, and definition
   c. Problem and solution, and exemplification

Exercise 23   Outline

On a separate sheet of paper, prepare an outline of Reading 3. Include only the major supporting points.

Exercise 24   Reflect

Think about what you read in Reading 3 and what you already know about homelessness. What do you think is the best way to deal with the problem of homelessness?

_____

_____

_____

CHAPTER REVIEW

✔ Reader's Checklist

Check (✔) the patterns of organization introduced in this chapter that you are confident you understand and can now recognize to help you organize to learn. Also check the additional key terms that follow. If you are not sure about any pattern or term (1) go back to the explanations in the text, (2) study and review with other members of your college learning community, (3) ask your instructor for help, (4) check out the Web site for this textbook at **www.ablongman.com/alexandercommunity4e** for additional exercises on understanding patterns of organization and to take the chapter quiz, or (5) complete additional practices in the *Reading Road Trip*.

❏ Chronological order and narration
❏ Definition and classification
❏ Exemplification
❏ Cause and effect
❏ Comparison and contrast
❏ Process
❏ Problem and solution
❏ Argument

❏ Patterns of organization
❏ Transitions
❏ Time Line
❏ Analogy
❏ Mapping
❏ Causal analysis
❏ Flowchart

When you are confident that you have mastered these concepts and skills, test yourself with Mastery Tests 5A and 5B (pp. 275–285).

Critical Reflections

Answer the following questions, and be prepared to discuss them with your classmates.

1. List three things in your neighborhood or college community that you think make living there enjoyable and pleasant.

   a. _____
   b. _____
   c. _____

2. List three things in your neighborhood or college community that make living there difficult.

   a. _____
   b. _____
   c. _____

3. List three things that you think would contribute to making your neighborhood or college community a better place.

   a. _____
   b. _____
   c. _____

©2007 Pearson Education, Inc.

Writing Activity

Write a paragraph or short essay explaining the positive and negative aspects of your neighborhood or college community.

Classroom Community

As a group, discuss the strengths and weaknesses of your neighborhood or college community. Propose some changes that could strengthen your community. Outline a plan to put your proposals in motion.

Extend Your Thinking

For another reading related to the problems of urbanization, see "Working with Our Hands," by Jimmy Carter and Rosalynn Carter, in "Extend Your Thinking," (pp.485–489).

Work the Web

Now that you have examined some issues related to place, take this time to use the Internet as a tool to understand more about where you live. One site to locate for statistics on your city and state is the U.S. Census Bureau.

Go to the U.S. Census Bureau (http://www.census.gov) and explore the information available to you. Once you've done a preview of the site, look for information about the city, county, and state you live in. You can check out statistics about things like the cost of housing, family income, and the ethnic background of people living there. You can compare some of those statistics with nationwide statistics. You can also see how certain things have changed over time. Find five facts that you find interesting. Write your information in the form of complete sentences. Your answers will often be in the comparison-and-contrast or chronological order pattern of organization.

1. _____

_____

2. _____

_____

3. _____

_____

4. _____

_____

5. _____

_____

Go to **www.ablongman.com/alexandercommunity4e** for additional Web-based activities.

Mastery Test **5A**

Life and Death in an Indian City

Joan Ferrante

The following reading from the college textbook Sociology: A Global Perspective *describes conditions in Bhopal, India, after one of the most disastrous industrial accidents in history took place in 1984. The fate of the poor people who lived in that city raises questions of how where we live affects the quality of our lives, affects our health, and can even be the cause of death. As you read, try to identify the various patterns of organization used to present this information.*

An Industrial Accident

1   On December 3, 1984, approximately 40 tons of methylisocyanate (MIC), a highly toxic, <u>volatile</u>, flammable chemical used in making <u>pesticides</u>, escaped from a Union Carbide storage tank and blanketed the densely populated city of Bhopal, India. Investigators determined that between 120 and 140 gallons of water somehow had entered the storage tank containing MIC. The combination <u>triggered</u> a violent chemical reaction that could not be contained. As a result, approximately 800,000 residents awoke coughing, vomiting, and with eyes burning and watering. They opened their doors and joined the "largest unplanned human <u>exodus</u> of the industrial age":

2   Those able to board a bicycle, moped, bullock car, bus, or vehicle of any kind did. But for most of the poor, their feet were the only form of transportation available. Many dropped along the way, gasping for breath, choking on their own vomit and, finally, drowning in their own fluids. Families were separated; whole groups were wiped out at a time. Those strong enough to keep going ran three, six, up to twelve miles before they stopped. Most ran until they dropped. (Weir 1984, p. 17)

3   Although exact numbers are not known, the most conservative estimates are that the chemical accident killed at least 2,500 people immediately and injured another 250,000. Since the accident, 22,149 deaths related to it have been officially registered. More than 17 years later, 10 to 15 people continue[d] to die each month from accident-related injuries, and most of the injured (an estimated 200,000 people) live with the long-term and <u>chronic</u> side effects of their exposure, which include lung and kidney damage, visual impairment, skin diseases and eruptions, neurological disorders, and gynecological damage (Everest 1986; Sharma 2000). Survivors also include a generation of Bhopal residents born around the time of the disaster, many of whom suffer lung and liver-related problems (Sharma 2000). These injuries have affected their capacity to earn a living.

© 2007 Pearson Education, Inc.

4   In 1989, Union Carbide agreed to pay $470 million to the Indian government as <u>compensation</u> to the victims and their families. The victims of Union Carbide were prevented by law from suing Union Carbide in U.S. courts (*The Economist* 1994). Depending on how one determines victim status, the <u>settlement</u> breaks down to about $3,000 per family affected. However, legal complications have delayed these payments. It also appears that government initiatives aimed at vocational rehabilitation of accident victims have failed. Only a few thousand survivors have received such services.

India's Problem of Urbanization

5   In India, the problem of urbanization is compounded by the fact that many migrants who come to the cities depart from some of the most economically <u>precarious</u> sections of India. In fact, most rural-to-urban migrants are not pulled into the cities by employment opportunities, but rather are forced to move there because they have no alternatives. When these migrants come to the cities, they face not only unemployment, but also a shortage of housing and a lack of services (electricity, running water, waste disposal). One distinguishing characteristic of cities in labor-intensive poor countries is the <u>prevalence</u> of slums and squatter settlements, which are much poorer and larger than even the worst slums in core economies.

6   One vivid and dramatic example concerns the city of Bhopal, India. . . . The population of Bhopal stood at 102,000 in 1966. After Union Carbide and other industries settled there in the 1960s, the population grew to 385,000 in 1971, 670,000 in 1981, and 800,000 in 1984.[1] At the time of the accident, approximately 20 percent of Bhopal's 800,000 residents lived in squatter settlements. The location of two of these squatter camps—directly across from the Union Carbide plant—explains why the deaths occurred <u>disproportionately</u> among the poorer residents. The people who lived in these camps were paid poverty-level wages, which prevented them from acquiring decent living quarters.[2]

Notes

[1] In 2001, Bhopal's population was 1.6 million. It has doubled in size in less than 20 years.

[2] Only a small percentage of people who lived in the camps were employees of Union Carbide.

FERRANTE, *SOCIOLOGY*

Exercise 1   **Work with Words**

Use context clues, dictionary skills, and your knowledge of word parts to choose the best definition for each of the following words underlined in the reading. The paragraph number is provided in case you want to check the context.

1. *Volatile* (par. 1)
   a. characterized by violence
   b. stable
   c. easily turning into vapor

2. *Pesticide* (par. 1)
   a. chemical to control pests
   b. chemical to kill pests
   c. free of pests

3. *Triggered* (par. 1)
   a. fired
   b. started
   c. shot

4. *Exodus* (par. 1)
   a. departure, flight
   b. departure of Israelites from Egypt
   c. second book of the Bible

5. *Chronic* (par. 3)
   a. habitual
   b. weakness and disability
   c. continuing and recurring

6. *Compensation* (par. 4)
   a. psychological mechanism to overcome a personal
      deficiency
   b. something received to pay for a loss or injury
   c. improvement of a defect by overusing something else

7. *Settlement* (par. 4)
   a. neighborhood of squatters
   b. legal agreement
   c. colony in its early stages

8. *Precarious* (par. 5)
   a. violently dangerous
   b. stable
   c. insecure

9. *Prevalence* (par. 5)
   a. superiority
   b. inferiority
   c. condition of being widespread

10. *Disproportionately* (par. 6)
    a. out of proportion, more often
    b. in small numbers, less often
    c. wrong shape, size, and figure

Check Your Understanding and Patterns of Organization

Based on the reading, Ferrante's "Life and Death in an Indian City," choose the best answer to each of the following multiple-choice questions.

1. Which of the following is the best topic for the reading?
   a. Bhopal, India: an example of urban growth, poverty, and disaster
   b. compensation for victims of the accident at Bhopal, India
   c. the largest human exodus of the industrial age

2. Which of the following is the best statement of the main idea of the reading?
   a. On December 3, 1984, approximately 40 tones of methyliso-cyanate (MIC), a highly toxic, volatile, flammable chemical used in making pesticides, escaped from a Union Carbide storage tank and blanketed the densely populated city of Bhopal, India.
   b. Poor people who migrate to the cities in poor countries frequently end up living in slums, which sometimes, as in the case of Bhopal, India, has disastrous consequences.
   c. Very few victims (or their relatives) of the accident in Bhopal have received any compensation for the damage to their health or for the loss of lives.

3. This reading provides
   a. the medical causes of the problems resulting from the Bhopal spill.
   b. an extended example of the possible disastrous consequences of urban poverty in poor countries.
   c. the problems and possible solutions for urban poverty in poor countries.

4. What is the dominant pattern of organization for paragraph 1?
   a. Narration
   b. Cause and effect
   c. Comparison and contrast

5. What is the dominant pattern of organization for paragraph 2?
   a. Cause and effect
   b. Narration
   c. Problem and solution

6. What is the dominant pattern of organization for paragraph 3?
   a. Comparison and contrast
   b. Definition
   c. Cause and effect

7. Which of the following sentences best expresses the main idea of paragraph 4?
   a. The victims of the Bhopal accident have not received fair compensation.
   b. The Indian government failed in its goal of providing vocational rehabilitation for the victims of the accident.

    c. Union Carbide agreed to pay $470 million to the Indian government as compensation to the victims and their families.

8. What is the dominant pattern of organization for paragraph 5?
   a. Exemplification
   b. Narration
   c. Cause and effect

9. Which of the following is the best main idea statement for paragraphs 5 and 6?
   a. One vivid and dramatic example concerns the city of Bhopal, India.
   b. What happened to the victims of the accident in Bhopal, India is an example of the consequences of poverty and the growth of slums in poor countries.
   c. Union Carbide should have provided greater compensation to the victims of the accident.

10. The author
    a. presents clear solutions to the problem of poverty and slums.
    b. probably sympathizes with the victims at Bhopal.
    c. probably sympathizes with the difficulties that Union Carbide faced because of the accident.

Exercise 3   **Organize to Learn and Write a Summary**

Review the reading and complete the following activities on a separate sheet of paper.

1. Organize the information in paragraph 4 in a way that demonstrates the dominant pattern of organization used in the paragraph as support for the main idea.

2. Write a summary of the reading.

Exercise 4   **Reflect**

Think about what you read in "Life and Death in an Indian City" and what you already know about the health consequences of different kinds of neighborhoods and living conditions. Then answer the following questions.

1. What kind of neighborhood do you live in? Are there any health dangers there? Explain.

   _____

   _____

   _____

2. What do you think are some of the things that could have prevented the deaths and injuries in Bhopal, India? Explain your answer.

   _____

   _____

   _____

©2007 Pearson Education, Inc.

Mastery Test

5B

Sociological Perspectives on Urbanization and City Life
Alex Thio

The following reading from the textbook Sociology: A Brief Introduction *explains the three basic approaches that sociologists use when analyzing social developments. In this reading, you will learn how sociologists analyze urbanization and city life using the functionalist perspective, conflict perspective, and symbolic interactionist perspective. As you read, try to identify the various patterns of organization used to present this information.*

1 Both the functionalist and conflict perspectives can be used to explain the forces behind the <u>urbanization</u> of U.S. society. To functionalists, the masses of ordinary people seek and benefit from urbanization as a way of adapting to their changing environment. To conflict theorists, the driving force and beneficiary of urbanization is really big business. Symbolic interactionists, however, are more interested in explaining city life by focusing on how people interact with one another in the city.

Functionalist Perspective: Urbanization Driven by the Masses

2 According to the functionalist perspective, the masses of ordinary people are the primary driving force behind urbanization, or urbanization reflects what the masses want when faced with changes in their environment (Rybczynski, 1995). Let's take a close look at the role of the masses in urbanization.

3   First, technology increases agricultural production so much that considerably fewer people are needed to work on farms. So, seeking better job opportunities, throngs of people leave the farms for the cities, which leads to explosive urban growth. Since these former farmers are mostly manual laborers, their influx to the cities helps to expand the manufacturing industry, allowing the mass production of everything from shoes to clothes to cars and computers. Next, as cities become crowded, increasing numbers of people move to the outskirts to live. They can continue to work in the inner cities, however, thanks to the mass production of cars. Then, as the suburbs become increasingly populated, various businesses emerge to cater to the shopping needs of suburbanites, eventually leading to the <u>proliferation</u> of shopping malls. Finally, a cornucopia of jobs is created in the suburbs, so that suburbanites do not need to commute to the central cities to work. At this late stage of urbanization, metropolises and megalopolises begin to emerge. Functionalists assume that all these social changes brought about by urbanization and suburbanization reflect what the masses need and seek to have a comfortable life.

Table 5.2	**Urbanization and City Life**	
Perspective	**Focus**	**Insights**
Functionalist	How the masses drive urbanization	People leave farms to seek better opportunities and lives in the cities and then the suburbs.
Conflict	How big business fuels urbanization	Large corporations pursue profit by starting agri-business that forces farmers to leave for the cities and then building homes, factories, and businesses in urban and suburban areas.
Symbolic Interactionist	How city people interact	City people tend to interact superficially, with civil inattention but with tolerance for others' lifestyles.

Conflict Perspective: Urbanization Fueled by Big Business

4 The conflict perspective, provides a different picture of urbanization, one that stresses the role played by big business in the growth and expansion of cities (Gottdiener, 1994, 1985).

5 First, in the pursuit of profit, large corporations bought up huge tracts of farmland and mass-produced food, driving many small family farms into bankruptcy and forcing huge numbers of farmers to leave for the city. In doing so, big business received considerable assistance from big government as a partner of the ruling elite. The assistance included direct subsidies to businesses, grants for research and development, low-interest loans, and support of farm-related education.

6 Second, the expansion of cities into suburbs has resulted from big business making a killing in the real estate, construction, and banking industries. Again, with considerable government subsidies and tax deductions, numerous single-family homes were built in the suburbs in the 1950s and 1960s. To induce people to buy these houses, the government guaranteed mortgages and provided tax deductions for interest payments. The result was massive suburbanization.

7 Third, from the 1970s to today, large corporations have helped turn many suburbs into edge cities by moving their businesses and factories there from central cities. This move has been motivated by profit. By building new plants in the suburbs, corporations have intended to avoid problems in central cities such as labor unrest, high city taxes, and other financial costs—or have expected to receive such benefits from the suburbs as cheap land, lower taxes, a local industry-friendly government, and the lack of organized labor.

Symbolic Interactionist Perspective: How Urbanites Interact

8 We can learn much from symbolic interactionists about how strangers interact in cities (Karp et al., 1991).

9 First, city people tend to interact with one another in a superficial, impersonal way. Given the density of the urban population and hence the

281

huge number of potential interpersonal contacts, urbanites have learned to protect themselves from *psychic overload* by shutting out as many sensations as possible, maybe even the call of a neighbor for help. Thus, most interactions with strangers are brief. An example is one person asking another for a street direction and the second person responding by pointing at a street and saying "over there."

10   Second, city people tend to interact through *civil inattention* as a way of respecting others' desire for privacy in public places. This involves avoiding eye or physical contact in an elevator, a bus, or some other public place. Conversations with strangers do occur but often under unusual circumstances, as when people are stuck in a stalled elevator or a traffic jam.

11   Third, city people tend to be tolerant of others' lifestyles, such as different sexual orientations and religious practices. When such people interact, they usually refrain from imposing their values on others or showing disapproval of others' behavior.

THIO, *SOCIOLOGY: A BRIEF INTRODUCTION*

Exercise 1   **Work with Words**

Use context clues, dictionary skills, and your knowledge of word parts to choose the best definition for each of the following words underlined in the reading. The paragraph number is provided in case you want to go back to check the context.

1. *Urbanization* (par. 1)
   a. growth and expansion of cities
   b. reflection of what the masses want
   c. driving force and beneficiary

2. *Proliferation* (par. 3)
   a. rapid spread
   b. slow destruction
   c. regular renewal

3. *Elite* (par. 5)
   a. group of the most skilled
   b. group of the most powerful
   c. group of the most critical

4. *Subsidies* (par. 5)
   a. complications
   b. financial assistance
   c. reductions

5. *Making a killing* (par. 6)
   a. making huge profits
   b. murdering
   c. losing money

6. *Induce* (par. 6)
   a. prevent
   b. infer
   c. influence

7. *Psychic overload* (par. 9)
   a. stressed mental condition caused by too many potential interpersonal contacts
   b. stressed mental condition caused by too much psychic power
   c. stressed mental condition caused by shutting down all sensations

8. *Civil inattention* (par. 10)
   a. pretending not to pay attention
   b. paying careful attention
   c. politely not paying attention

9. *Refrain* (par. 11)
   a. avoid
   b. insist on
   c. try to

10. *Imposing* (par. 11)
    a. reducing
    b. explaining
    c. forcing

Exercise 2   **Check Your Understanding and Patterns of Organization**

Based on the reading, Thio's "Sociological Perspectives on Urbanization and City Life," choose the best answer to each of the following multiple-choice questions.

1. Which of the following is the best topic for the reading?
   a. causes of urbanization
   b. sociological perspectives on urbanization and city life
   c. functionalist, conflict, and symbolic interactionist perspectives on how urbanites relate to each other

2. Which of the following sentences best states the main idea for paragraphs 1 through 7?
   a. The functionalist perspective asserts that urbanization takes place to benefit people, while the conflict perspective argues that it has been driven by big businesses.
   b. The masses of ordinary people are the primary driving force behind urbanization, which reflects the changes that the people want.
   c. The conflict perspective, unlike the functionalist perspective, stresses the role played by big business in the growth and expansion of cities.

© 2007 Pearson Education, Inc.

3. Which of the following is the best topic for paragraphs 2 and 3?
   a. technology and urbanization
   b. functionalist perspective: urbanization driven by the masses
   c. the role of business in urbanization

4. Which of the following is the best topic for paragraphs 8 through 11?
   a. how urbanites interact
   b. psychic overload
   c. civil inattention

5. Which of the following is the best main idea statement for paragraphs 8 through 11?
   a. City people tend to interact with one another in superficial ways.
   b. City people tend to be inattentive as a way to respect others' rights for privacy.
   c. City people tend to interact superficially, briefly, and with tolerance.

6. According to the conflict perspective, what is the fundamental motivation of big business?
   a. Serving the people
   b. Reducing costs
   c. Making profits

7. What is the dominant pattern of organization for paragraph 1?
   a. Chronological order
   b. Comparison and contrast
   c. Process

8. What is the dominant pattern of organization for paragraph 3?
   a. Process, and cause and effect
   b. Definition, and comparison and contrast
   c. Exemplification and definition

9. What is the dominant pattern of organization for paragraph 4?
   a. Definition
   b. Chronological order
   c. Exemplification

10. What is the dominant pattern of organization for paragraphs 5 through 7?
    a. Definition and chronological order
    b. Cause and effect, and chronological order
    c. Exemplification and narration

Exercise 3   Create an Outline or Map and Flowchart

Complete the following activities on a separate piece of paper.

1. Make a list of the ways that urbanites interact according to the symbolic interactionist perspective in paragraphs 8 through 11.

2. Create a map or a flowchart of the information in paragraphs 2 and 3.

3. Create an outline of the information in paragraphs 4 through 7.

4. Summarize the reading "Sociological Perspectives on Urbanization and City Life."

Exercise 4   **Reflect**

Think about what you read in "Sociological Perspectives on Urbanization and City Life" and what you already know about the topic. Then answer the following questions.

1. How does the table on page 281 assist you in understanding the text? Explain your answer.

_____

_____

_____

_____

2. The reading presents the functionalist perspective, the conflict perspective, and the symbolic interactionist perspective. Which of the three perspectives do you agree with? Explain your reasons.

_____

_____

_____

_____

_____

©2007 Pearson Education, Inc.

Chapter 6

Inferences and Reading Literature

Dealing with Gender

It is fatal for anyone to be a man or a woman pure and simple; one must be woman-manly or man-womanly.

—Virginia Woolf

● What do you notice about the way the people in the picture are dressed? When do you think this photograph was taken?

● What does the quotation mean?

● Do you think the photo illustrates the ideas of the quotation? Why or why not?

© 2007 Pearson Education, Inc.

PREPARE TO READ

The man and woman in the picture on page 287 are dressed almost identically. Do you think their roles in society are also identical? Should they be? Such fashions are described as *androgynous,* which means that they are appropriate for both males and females. Some people advocate androgyny in other areas of our lives to reduce social and economic inequality based on sex and gender. Is this blending of male and female identities and roles the solution to conflicts between the sexes? How can we ensure a more equitable and happier coexistence for men and women in the future?

Purpose

In this chapter, you will learn to

- Infer meaning from text and illustrations
- Recognize connotative meanings of words
- Interpret irony and imagery
- Practice reading poetry and fiction

In the process of acquiring these skills, you will read about concepts of gender and how they influence our lives.

Previous Knowledge

Answer these questions and prepare to discuss them in class.

1. Using your own judgment, mark the following sentences true or false.

   _____ Men are more aggressive than women.
   _____ Women are more nurturing than men.
   _____ Men are more mechanically minded than women.
   _____ Women are more emotional than men.

2. What would your grandparents think of as the appropriate roles for men and women in society?

   _____

   _____

Preview and Predict

Preview Chapter 6. Based on your preview, predict two things you think you will learn in this chapter.

1. _____

2. _____

Write two questions that you think will be answered in this chapter.

1. _____

2. _____

©2007 Pearson Education, Inc.

Reading 1 *Sex and Gender*

William E. Thompson and Joseph V. Hickey

William E. Thompson and Joseph V. Hickey discuss sex and gender in their sociology textbook, Society in Focus. *They describe gender roles and how they have evolved.*

1 Women and men are different. This undeniable fact has contributed to innumerable myths, stereotypes, and arguments concerning precisely what these differences mean. How much of the difference is based on genetics, biology, and physiology and how much is based on cultural values and social practices? Sociologists pursue answers to these questions when they attempt to differentiate between *sex* and *gender.*

2 Much of the debate over the differences between women and men stems from people's confusing the terms *sex* and *gender. Sex* is based on biological and physical differences between females and males; *gender* refers to a cultural understanding of what constitutes masculinity and femininity in a society.

Sex: Biological Differentiation

3 While there is no scientific evidence to support claims that women are unfit for military combat or that men are biologically driven to hunt large animals, at least part of the difference between females and males must be attributed to genetics and biology. Humans have 23 pairs of chromosomes. Two of these are the sex chromosomes, X and Y. The normal chromosomal pattern in females is XX; in males it is XY. During prenatal development, different hormones trigger physical changes in the male and female genitalia and reproductive systems. . . .

4 Later in life, people develop sex-linked disparities in height, weight, body and facial hair, physical strength, and endurance. And, although research suggests that the brains of females and males may be both structurally and operationally different, most researchers acknowledge that women and men are far more alike than they are different (Phillips, 1990; Shapiro, 1990; Begley, 1995). Since we cannot see peoples' chromosomes, hormones, or brains, all sex-linked differences are of far less consequence than the cultural and social expectations linked to them. . . .

Gender: Social and Cultural Differentiation

5 A popular nineteenth-century nursery rhyme tells us that little girls are made of "sugar and spice and everything nice," while little boys are made of "frogs and snails and puppy dogs' tails." Newborn baby boys are often described as "bouncing," while baby girls are "beautiful." Why do we make these distinctions between boys and girls? Males and females are biologically and physiologically distinct at birth; these differences become more pronounced as humans develop to maturity, but they do not explain the important social and cultural distinctions that are made on the basis of sex. . . .

the most important differences between the sexes are acquired through socialization as we all learn to fulfill our *gender roles,* the social and cultural expectations associated with a person's sex. These gender roles affect virtually every aspect of our lives, from our eating behavior and the type of neighbor we are likely to be, to how long we live and our cause of death—in short, the way we think about and live life itself (Gilligan, 1982; Campbell and Lee, 1990; Morgan et al., 1990; Slevin and Aday, 1993; Lott, 1994; Walzer, 1994).

Masculinity and Femininity

6 *Masculinity* refers to attributes considered appropriate for males. In American society, these traditionally include being aggressive, athletic, physically active, logical, and dominant in social relationships with females. Conversely, *femininity* refers to attributes traditionally associated with appropriate behavior for females, which in America include passivity, docility, fragility, emotionality, and subordination to males. Research conducted by Carol Gilligan and her students at Harvard's Gender Studies Department indicate that children are acutely aware of and feel pressure to conform to these powerful gender stereotypes by the age of 4 (Kantrowitz and Kalb, 1998). Some people insist that gender traits such as male aggressiveness are innate characteristics linked to sex and do not depend on cultural definitions (Maccoby, 1980). However, the preponderance of research indicates that females and males can be equally aggressive under different social and cultural conditions and that levels of aggression vary as widely within the sexes as between them (e.g., Fry, 1988; Melson and Fogel, 1988; Butler, 1990). . . .

Androgyny: Redefining Gender

7 Have you ever wondered why we place so much emphasis on distinctive gender identities and gender roles? Many people do, and in an effort to reduce social differentiation and inequality based on sex and gender some people advocate *androgyny,* a blending of masculine and feminine attributes. Androgyny is not role reversal, where boys are taught to act feminine and girls to behave more masculinely. It embraces the full range of human emotions and behaviors rather than only those traditionally considered appropriate to a specific sex. This involves redefining gender roles and attaching new meanings to the concepts of masculinity and femininity. Boys are taught that it is okay to cry and that it is perfectly natural to display their emotions and sensitivity when circumstances warrant. Likewise, girls are taught to be aggressive and assertive when social situations call for such behavior.

8   In the world of androgyny, children are not chastised for being tomboys or sissies, and there are no such things as "boys' toys" and "girls' toys." Similarly there is neither "women's work" nor "men's work"; whatever its nature, work is performed by whoever is capable, regardless of sex. Ideally, in a culture where androgyny is the norm, human potential would not be limited by narrow cultural stereotypes.

9   Despite more androgynous views of gender and the weakening of some gender stereotypes . . . powerful cultural distinctions between masculinity and femininity persist. Today, women must "prove" that they are capable of performing traditional "men's work" in the military and in the fields of law, medicine, science, and politics. Similarly, social and cultural attitudes often discourage or ridicule men who pursue "feminine roles" such as home-maker, secretary, nurse, flight attendant, and housekeeper. From a function-alist perspective, distinctive and complementary gender roles are important to preserving social structure and ensuring that society functions properly.

THOMPSON AND HICKEY, *SOCIETY IN FOCUS*

| Exercise 1 |

Recall and Discuss

Based on Reading 1, Thompson and Hickey's "Sex and Gender," answer the following questions in your own words and prepare to discuss them with your classmates.

1. What is the difference between *sex* and *gender*?

   _____

   _____

2. From your own observations and experience, how do you think a child develops gender identity?

   _____

   _____

3. Do you think it's a good idea to teach children to be androgynous? Explain your answer.

   _____

   _____

4. What have been some of the major influences for your own identifi-cation of men and women's roles in society?

   _____

   _____

INFERENCES

When we meet someone for the first time, we form much of our first im-pression about that person's adherence to conventional masculine or fem-inine roles, based on what we observe about his or her dress and appear-ance. We do this by making inferences based on our previous knowledge

©2007 Pearson Education, Inc.

inference A reasonable assumption based on the information we have

about how our culture understands "appropriate" gender roles; sometimes we do this based on stereotypes that are not always accurate. An **inference** is a reasonable assumption based on the information we have about an event, a person, or a written passage. Another way to think of making inferences, or inferring, is "reading between the lines." When reading, if you use the information you already have about the world (your previous knowledge) and the information provided to you by the author, you can often come to well-founded conclusions, which are probably accurate.

In your daily life, you make inferences from the signals you get from other people. Say, for example, that you are having a conversation with a friend, and your friend turns her back to you and opens a book. What can you infer from her action? You will probably infer that your friend does not want to talk to you anymore; she wants to end the conversation. You might also infer that your friend is not being sensitive to your feelings.

For another example, imagine that one day your boss, normally a very friendly guy, gets to work late and stomps into his office without talking to anybody. You know that he has been having trouble with his car, and you notice that he took a taxi to work. From these observations, you could reasonably infer that your boss had trouble with his car again this morning and that he is upset about the inconvenience, about being late for work, and perhaps about the expense of fixing it. You can also infer that he is most likely not directly angry at any of the people at work, even though his failure to greet people was impolite.

The inferences you make about your boss in this example would be based on a great deal of background information and accumulated experience. To correctly infer the cause of your boss's response would require that you already know him quite well. You would have worked with him for some time and would have seen his reactions under many conditions. You would, for example, know that he never treats his employees with anger, so he is unlikely to start now. Therefore, you can reason that his anger must be due to external events, and the taxi and yesterday's car trouble support your inference.

Inferences are *reasonable* assumptions and conclusions about what you see, hear, experience, or read. They are not immediate responses; you arrive at them after careful thought. The pictures and readings in this chapter, on the sometimes controversial issue of gender, will challenge you to exercise caution in drawing inferences.

Inferences from Visual Aids

Many inferences in everyday life and reading are based on visual clues. Visual aids provide a great deal of important information (see "Reading Visual Aids" in "A Reader's Toolkit," pages 529 through 576). They can also assist us in making inferences. For example, examine Figure 6.1, a 1924 German lithograph titled *Brot!* (*"Bread!"*) by Käthe Kollwitz. Now circle the inferences that are probably true based on what you observed in the picture. (You can choose more than one.)

Figure 6.1   Brot!
("Bread!") Käthe Kollwitz, 1924. Lithograph. Staaliche Museen Preussicher Kulturbesitz, Kupferstichkabinett, Berlin.

a. The woman in the picture is the mother of the two children.
b. The children are hungry, but the mother doesn't have food for them.
c. The woman has no husband.
d. The woman is proud of her family and of their accomplishments.

You should have chosen "a" and "b" as reasonable inferences you can make based on the picture. The size of the children and their close, clinging appearance reasonably support assumption "a," that the woman is their mother. She seems to be responding to their pleas, and she is not sending them away for hanging on her. The title of the print, *Bread!;* the sad, imploring eyes of the younger child; the clinging of the bigger child; and the woman's humped form seem to support assumption "b," that she cannot give her children the bread they want.

On the other hand, we cannot reasonably infer assumption "c," "The woman has no husband." She could have a husband, but he could be unemployed, in prison, or off at war and not able to help his family. We do not have enough information to assume that she is not married. Also, answer "d" is clearly incorrect: The woman does not appear to be "proud of her family and of their accomplishments." Rather, she seems, from her hunched posture and hidden face, to be overwhelmed by her inability to feed her hungry children.

©2007 Pearson Education, Inc.

Exercise 2   ## Make Inferences from Visual Clues

Look at the following cartoons (Figures 6.2 and 6.3) and read the dialogue. Then circle the letters of all the inferences that are probably true. You can choose more than one inference for each cartoon.

Figure 6.2
© Lynn Johnston Productions, Inc. Distributed by United Feature Syndicate.

For Better or For Worse   **by Lynn Johnston**

1. a. Elly is the dentist's wife.
   b. The dentist supports Elly's finding a job.
   c. The dentist is married to his dental assistant.
   d. The patient in the chair is not listening to the conversation.
   e. Michael is probably finishing college.

Figure 6.3
CATHY © Cathy Guisewite. Reprinted with permission of Universal Press Syndicate. All rights reserved.

Cathy   **by Cathy Guisewite**

2. a. The two people having coffee have known one another a long time.
   b. The two people having coffee are just getting to know one another.
   c. They are both nervous and a little embarrassed.
   d. They don't know how to act with each other.
   e. They will definitely get together again.

Exercise 3   ## Make Inferences from Visual Clues

Look at the following photographs (Figures 6.4 and 6.5). They depict two people in relation to one another. Study their "body language"—what their poses, gestures, and facial expressions tell you about their relationship. Then circle the letters of all the inferences you can make that are probably true. You can choose more than one inference for each photograph.

Figure 6.4

a. The two people in the picture have equal positions at work.
b. The two people teach in college.
c. The two people have known one another for a very long time.
d. The woman is interested in pleasing the man.
e. The man has more power in this relationship than the woman.

Figure 6.5

a. The man has more power in this relationship than the woman.
b. The man and woman in the photo are married.
c. The woman has more power in this relationship than the man.
d. The man is interested in pleasing the woman.
e. The two people are brother and sister.

Inferences in Textbooks

Writers of textbooks use inference in at least two ways: (1) they report on their own inferences, or conclusions, about data and concepts, and (2) they provide data and insights from which readers can make further

©2007 Pearson Education, Inc.

inferences. For example, read the following paragraph from a sociology textbook by William E. Thompson and Joseph V. Hickey. This is a concluding paragraph from their chapter on sex and gender, in which they draw some conclusions and make some predictions. (We have added the numbers appearing in parentheses.)

> (1) Will there be increased freedom, equality, and tolerance for those who violate traditional gender roles? (2) Or will a conservative backlash and a renewed emphasis on genetics and biology attempt to reestablish traditional masculine and feminine roles? (3) While these questions cannot be answered with any certainty, a 1996 survey shows that attitudes about women's and men's roles have become much more flexible since the 1970s (Teegardin, 1996). (4) From a sociological perspective it is indisputable that changing attitudes toward sex and gender will continue to have an impact on people's daily lives—in America and throughout the world. (Thompson and Hickey, *Society in Focus*)

Sentences 1 and 2 ask questions about gender roles in the future. Readers are asked to speculate about what the changes of the twentieth century mean for gender roles in the twenty-first century. Then the authors provide more information: sentence 3 reports on a study about gender roles completed by researcher Teegardin in 1996. The authors end with sentence 4, their vision of the future. Now circle the inference(s) that you can reasonably make about the information you read in this paragraph.

a.   There will definitely be more tolerance in the future for those who violate traditional gender roles.
b.   We cannot predict the impact that changing attitudes toward sex and gender will have on the future.
c.   Attitudes about men and women's roles have become more flexible.

You should have chosen "b" as the only reasonable inference from this paragraph. Statement "a" assumes too positive a response to gender issues; this is only one possible response, raised as a question in sentence 1. Statement "c" is not an inference; it simply repeats the findings of Teegardin's 1996 study.

Inferences in Autobiographies

autobiography A story of one's own life experience

Another type of writing we will consider in our discussion of inferences is autobiographical writing, or personal narrative. An **autobiography** is the story of the author's life experience. Often, to make a point, a writer will tell a story, or narrative, about his or her experience that reveals an aspect of personality. The writer does not state this personality trait but expects you, the reader, to infer it. You make a reasonable assumption based on the information the author gives you.

For example, read the following autobiographical paragraph from Carol Tavris's essay, "Love Story."

As a child, I was nuts about cowboys, guns, and palomino ponies, and so when I first saw the musical *Annie Get Your Gun* I was in heaven. Annie Oakley was a woman who could ride, wear cowgirl outfits, and shoot. She became my hero at once. She sang, "Anything you can do, I can do better," and she outshot her rival, Frank Butler. I loved Annie Oakley so much that I entirely blocked out the end of the musical when she realizes that "You can't get a man with a gun." Annie deliberately blows her next competition with Butler, who of course then realizes he loves her after all. I couldn't understand why a woman would give up being the world's best sharpshooter (even for Frank Butler, who was definitely terrific), or why Frank Butler could love Annie only if she gave up sharpshooting. (Tavris, "Love Story")

Which of the following statements are reasonable inferences you can make from this paragraph?

a.   Tavris admired Annie Oakley.
b.   Tavris was troubled by Annie's deliberate loss in the competition.
c.   The sure way to get a man is to let him win; don't beat him in any competition, even if you are more skilled.

You should have chosen statements "a" and "b" as reasonable inferences. Annie Oakley was a hero in Tavris's eyes, and Tavris was disturbed by Oakley's method of winning Butler's affection. (Actually, Tavris goes on in her essay to report that, in real life, Butler was attracted to Annie Oakley precisely because she was such a good shot, and they were happily married for more than 50 years.) Statement "c" might be an assumption some people would make from viewing *Annie Get Your Gun*, but Tavris implies in her response to this story that we should definitely question this strategy.

Exercise 4   ## Make Inferences in Passages from Written Texts

Carefully read the following passages, and then circle the letters of all the reasonable inferences you can make from the stated information in the passage.

1. When I was a young boy—before puberty, before girls, before feeling embarrassed when seen with my parents—I thought of myself as strong and athletic. I never doubted my sex and never thought about my ability or inability to attract a mate. But let me tell you, things changed. As a teenager beginning high school, I started noticing the size of other boys around me. I started noticing that even though I was great at sports, I was smaller than most boys my age, in both height and breadth. I started believing I wasn't even a man and never would be at the rate I was going. So I stayed at the school gym late every day, working out, pumping iron. I invested in special protein shakes and powders. I overate. Soon I started to grow and found myself constantly flexing and posturing like a

©2007 Pearson Education, Inc.

rooster about to get into a fight. Whenever I passed a mirror, I glanced at my reflection to make sure I wasn't that short, skinny boy any more. But even though I had grown thick and muscular, had gained over 50 pounds, I saw a puny runt in the mirror, and to this day, especially when my confidence gets shattered, I still do. (Wong, "The Runt")

a. The author had questions about his sexual orientation.
b. The author started to believe that to be a real man, he would need to increase in size.
c. The author is a man by now looking back on his experience as a teen.

2. Mainstream American culture determines that there are only two genders. A person is either male or female and must behave according to his/her biological sex. However, not all cultures within the United States have the same gender regulations. In fact, this country along with others, has had a third gender. Many North American Indian tribes accepted and respected men and women known as *berdache.* The *berdache* mixed characteristics of both genders and were often regarded as blessed and holy. To have a *berdache* as a family member was often considered a sign of good fortune. European conquest and conversion of native peoples virtually annihilated the *berdache* or forced them to live underground. Today, though, many *berdache* do still live in the American Southwest and other regions of the world. (McDermott, "Third Gender")

a. Mainstream American culture would not be very accepting of *berdache.*
b. *Berdache* have always been revered within their own tribes.
c. Settlers probably accepted the *berdache* shortly after the conquest and conversion of Native American peoples.

3. The controversy over the extent to which biological and physiological differences in the sexes determine gender differences continues to attract widespread attention. Sociobiological research in the field is likely to expand. An interesting technological development. . . is the ability of parents not only to know the sex of an infant before its birth but to choose the baby's sex. This choice is medically possible today. What if it were to become a widely accepted cultural practice in the future? The world of genetic engineering, human cloning, and other technological developments offers fascinating and even frightening possibilities. (Thompson and Hickey, *Society in Focus*)

a. Genetic engineering will lead to frightening results.
b. Parents' ability to choose a baby's sex could cause an imbalance of males and females in some cultures.
c. Choosing your baby's sex will be a widely accepted practice in the future.

4. I lay in bed with my eyes closed. I visualize the make-up sitting on my dresser, and my mother lying in her bed visualizing the make-up and wishing it were on my face instead of the dresser. I open my eyes and see the square blue eye shadow box and the triangular tube of pink lipstick. My parents! They buy me a pink lipstick and think it will hide my sexual feelings toward other women if I put it on my lips.

I lay back on my back glancing occasionally at the ceiling and the make-up. I really thought it would make my life easier if I told them how I was feeling. So instead of hiding my true self, I announced that I thought I might be a lesbian. I was grappling with this issue for four years and was wondering what my future would be like as a homosexual. What is life like when you are thirty, or forty? And what will my neighbors think? I hope they are not as hostile as my parents are; if so, I had better continue suppressing my feelings, I thought. (Watnick, "Triangular Tube of Pink Lipstick")

a. Watnick's feelings were hurt by her parents' response to her revelation.
b. Watnick's parents do not want to accept her sense of her sexual orientation.
c. Wearing pink lipstick will change Watnick's sexual feelings toward other women.

5. For travelers in parts of the developing world, the sight is a familiar one: barefoot women trudging for miles with enormous loads of firewood or water balanced on their heads. Scientists at the University of Nairobi in Africa, studying human energy expenditure, recently recruited women from the Kikuyu and Luo tribes to carry heavy loads on their heads while walking on a motorized treadmill (*New York Times,* 1986). Since oxygen use accurately reflects energy use, the researchers prepared to monitor carefully the extra amounts of oxygen that carrying loads of various sizes would require.

To the scientists' amazement, the women were able to carry loads weighing up to 20 percent of their body weights without any increase in their use of oxygen at all, which meant that loads of this size did not result in any increased expenditure of energy. Carrying an astounding 70 percent of their body weight increased the women's oxygen use by only 50 percent. In contrast, males carrying backpacks equaling 20 percent of their body weight increased their oxygen use by 13 percent; loads equal to 70 percent of the carrier's weight increased males' oxygen consumption by nearly 100 percent. (Hicks and Gwynne, *Cultural Anthropology*)

a. The men who were tested were probably not in the habit of carrying weight in backpacks.
b. The women who were tested were in excellent physical condition.
c. African women are probably stronger than African men in other ways as well.

©2007 Pearson Education, Inc.

Reading 2   *Sex, Lies, and Conversation*   Deborah Tannen

Deborah Tannen is a professor of linguistics at Georgetown University. She has published several books on the differences in communication styles between men and women. This article appeared in the Washington Post *in 1990. As you read, pay close attention to the misunderstandings that arise between men and women because each makes inferences based on wrong assumptions about the other.*

1   I was addressing a small gathering in a suburban Virginia living room—a women's group that had invited men to join them. Throughout the evening, one man had been particularly talkative, frequently offering ideas and anecdotes, while his wife sat silently beside him on the couch. Toward the end of the evening, I commented that women frequently complain that their husbands don't talk to them. This man quickly concurred. He gestured toward his wife and said, "She's the talker in our family." The room burst into laughter; the man looked puzzled and hurt. "It's true," he explained. "When I come home from work I have nothing to say. If she didn't keep the conversation going, we'd spend the whole evening in silence."

2   This episode crystallizes the irony that although American men tend to talk more than women in public situations, they often talk less at home. And this pattern is wreaking havoc with marriage.

3   The pattern was observed by political scientist Andrew Hacker in the late '70s. Sociologist Catherine Kohler Reissman reports in her new book *Divorce Talk* that most of the women she interviewed—but only a few of the men—gave lack of communication as the reason for their divorces. Given the current divorce rate of nearly 50 percent, that amounts to millions of cases in the United States every year—a virtual epidemic of failed conversation.

4   In my own research, complaints from women about their husbands most often focused not on tangible inequities such as having given up the chance for a career to accompany a husband to his, or doing far more than their share of daily life—support work like cleaning, cooking, social arrangements and errands. Instead, they focused on communication: "He doesn't listen to me," "He doesn't talk to me." I found, as Hacker observed years before, that most wives want their husbands to be, first and foremost, conversational partners, but few husbands share this expectation of their wives.

5   In short, the image that best represents the current crisis is the stereotypical cartoon scene of a man sitting at the breakfast table with a newspaper held up in front of his face while a woman glares at the back of it, wanting to talk.

Linguistic Battle of the Sexes

6   How can women and men have such different impressions of communication in marriage? Why the widespread imbalance in their interests and expectations?

7   In the April issue of *American Psychologist,* Stanford University's Eleanor Macoby reports the results of her own and others' research show-

ing that children's development is most influenced by the social structure of peer interactions. Boys and girls tend to play with children of their own gender, and their sex-separate groups have different organizational structures and interactive norms.

8   I believe these systematic differences in childhood socialization make talk between women and men like cross-cultural communication, heir to all the attraction and pitfalls of that enticing but difficult enterprise. My research on men's and women's conversations uncovered patterns similar to those described for children's groups.

9   For women, as for girls, intimacy is the fabric of relationships, and talk is the thread from which it is woven. Little girls create and maintain friendships by exchanging secrets; similarly, women regard conversation as the cornerstone of friendship. So a woman expects her husband to be a new and improved version of a best friend. What is important is not the individual subjects that are discussed but the sense of closeness, of a life shared, that emerges when people tell their thoughts, feelings, and impressions.

10   Bonds between boys can be as intense as girls', but they are based less on talking, more on doing things together. Since they don't assume talk is the cement that binds a relationship, men don't know what kind of talk women want, and they don't miss it when it isn't there.

11   Boys' groups are larger, more inclusive, and more hierarchical, so boys must struggle to avoid the subordinate position in the group. This may play a role in women's complaints that men don't listen to them. Some men really don't like to listen, because being the listener makes them feel one-down, like a child listening to adults or an employee to a boss.

12   But often when women tell men, "You aren't listening," and the men protest, "I am," the men are right. The impression of not listening results from misalignments in the mechanics of conversation. The misalignment begins as soon as a man and a woman take physical positions. This became clear when I studied videotapes made by psychologist Bruce Dorval of children and adults talking to their same-sex best friends. I found that at every age, the girls and women faced each other directly, their eyes anchored on each other's faces. At every age, the boys and men sat at angles to each other and looked elsewhere in the room, periodically glancing at each other. They were obviously attuned to each other, often mirroring each other's movements. But the tendency of men to face away can give women the impression they aren't listening even when they are. A young woman in college was frustrated: Whenever she told her boyfriend she wanted to talk to him, he would lie down on the floor, close his eyes, and put his arm over his face. This signaled to her "He's taking a nap." But he insisted he was listening extra-hard. Normally, he looks around the room, so he is easily distracted. Lying down and covering his eyes helped him concentrate on what she was saying.

13   Analogous to the physical alignment that women and men take in conversation is their topical alignment. The girls in my study tended to talk at length about one topic, but the boys tended to jump from topic to topic. The second-grade girls exchanged stories about people they knew. The

©2007 Pearson Education, Inc.

second-grade boys teased, told jokes, noticed things in the room and talked about finding games to play. The sixth-grade girls talked about problems with a mutual friend. The sixth-grade boys talked about 55 different topics, none of which extended over more than a few turns.

Listening to Body Language

14 Switching topics is another habit that gives women the impression men aren't listening, especially if they switch to a topic about themselves. But the evidence of the 10th-grade boys in my study indicates otherwise. The 10th-grade boys sprawled across their chairs with bodies parallel and eyes straight ahead, rarely looking at each other. They looked as if they were riding in a car, staring out the windshield. But they were talking about their feelings. One boy was upset because a girl had told him he had a drinking problem, and the other was feeling alienated from all his friends.

15 Now, when a girl told a friend about a problem, the friend responded by asking probing questions and expressing agreement and understanding. But the boys dismissed each other's problems. Todd assured Richard that his drinking was "no big problem" because "sometimes you're funny when you're off your butt." And when Todd said he felt left out, Richard responded, "Why should you? You know more people than me."

16 Women perceive such responses as belittling and unsupportive. But the boys seemed satisfied with them. Whereas women reassure each other by implying, "You shouldn't feel bad because I've had similar experiences," men do so by implying, "You shouldn't feel bad because your problems aren't so bad."

17 There are even simpler reasons for women's impression that men don't listen. Linguist Lynette Hirschman found that women make more listener-noise, such as "mhm," "uhuh," and "yeah," to show "I'm with you." Men, she found, more often give silent attention. Women who expect a stream of listener-noise interpret silent attention as no attention at all.

18 Women's conversational habits are as frustrating to men as men's are to women. Men who expect silent attention interpret a stream of listener-noise as overreaction or impatience. Also, when women talk to each other in a close, comfortable setting, they often overlap, finish each other's sentences and anticipate what the other is about to say. This practice, which I call "participatory listenership," is often perceived by men as interruption, intrusion and lack of attention.

19 A parallel difference caused a man to complain about his wife, "She just wants to talk about her own point of view. If I show her another view, she gets mad at me: When most women talk to each other, they assume a conversationalist's job is to express agreement and support. But many men see their conversational duty as pointing out the other side of an argument. This is heard as disloyalty by women, and refusal to offer the requisite support. It is not that women don't want to see other points of view, but that they prefer them phrased as suggestions and inquiries rather than as direct challenges.

20   In his book *Fighting for Life,* Walter Ong points out that men use "ago-nistic" or warlike, oppositional formats to do almost anything; thus discussion becomes debate, and conversation a competitive sport. In contrast, women see conversation as a ritual means of establishing rapport. If Jane tells a problem and June says she has a similar one, they walk away feeling closer to each other. But this attempt at establishing rapport can backfire when used with men. Men take too literally women's ritual "troubles talk," just as women mistake men's ritual challenges for real attack.

The Sounds of Silence

21   These differences begin to clarify why women and men have such different expectations about communication in marriage. For women, talk creates intimacy. Marriage is an orgy of closeness: you can tell your feelings and thoughts, and still be loved. Their greatest fear is being pushed away. But men live in a hierarchical world, where talk maintains independence and status. They are on guard to protect themselves from being put down and pushed around.

22   This explains the paradox of the talkative man who said of his silent wife, "She's the talker." In the public setting of a guest lecture, he felt challenged to show his intelligence and display his understanding of the lecture. But at home, where he has nothing to prove and no one to defend against, he is free to remain silent. For his wife, being home means she is free from the worry that something she says might offend someone, or spark disagreement, or appear to be showing off; at home she is free to talk.

23   The communication problems that endanger marriage can't be fixed by mechanical engineering. They require a new conceptual framework about the role of talk in human relationships. Many of the psychological explanations that have become second nature may not be helpful, because they tend to blame either women (for not being assertive enough) or men (for not being in touch with their feelings). A sociolinguistic approach by which male-female conversation is seen as cross-cultural communication allows us to understand the problem and forge solutions without blaming either party.

24   Once the problem is understood, improvement comes naturally, as it did to the young woman and her boyfriend who seemed to want to go to sleep when she wanted to talk. Previously, she had accused him of not listening, and he had refused to change his behavior, since that would be admitting fault. But then she learned about and explained to him the differences in women's and men's habitual ways of aligning themselves in conversation. The next time she told him she wanted to talk, he began, as usual, by lying down and covering his eyes. When the familiar negative reaction bubbled up, she reassured herself that he really was listening. But then he sat up and looked at her. Thrilled, she asked why. He said, "You like me to look at you when we talk, so I'll try to do it." Once he saw their differences as cross-cultural rather than right and wrong, he independently altered his behavior.

©2007 Pearson Education, Inc.

25   Women who feel abandoned and deprived when their husbands won't listen to or report daily news may be happy to discover their husbands trying to adapt once they understand the place of small talk in women's relationships. But if their husbands don't adapt, the women may still be comforted that for men, this is not a failure of intimacy. Accepting the difference, the wives may look to their friends or family for that kind of talk. And husbands who can't provide it shouldn't feel their wives have made unreasonable demands. Some couples will still decide to divorce, but at least their decisions will be based on realistic expectations.

26   In these times of resurgent ethnic conflicts, the world desperately needs cross-cultural understanding. Like charity, successful cross-cultural communication should begin at home.

TANNEN, "Sex, Lies, and Conversation"

Exercise 5   ## Work with Words

The following sentences appear in Reading 2, Tannen's "Sex, Lies, and Conversation." Use context clues, dictionary skills, and your knowledge of word parts to determine the meaning of each italicized word in the sentences. Write the meaning of the word on the lines provided. The paragraph number is provided in case you want to check the context.

1. Throughout the evening, one man had been particularly talkative, frequently offering ideas and anecdotes, while his wife sat silently beside him on the couch. Toward the end of the evening, I commented that women frequently complain that their husbands don't talk to them. This man quickly *concurred*. (par. 1)

   Concurred: _____

2. This episode crystallizes the *irony* that although American men tend to talk more than women in public situations, they often talk less at home. And this pattern is *wreaking havoc* with marriage. (par. 2)

   Irony: _____

3. *Wreaking havoc*: destroying

4. Boys and girls tend to play with children of their own gender, and their sex-separate groups have different organizational structures and interactive *norms*. (par. 7)

   Norms: _____

5. Boys' groups are larger, more inclusive, and more hierarchical, so boys must struggle to avoid the *subordinate* position in the group. (par. 11)

   Subordinate: _____

6. Also, when women talk to each other in a close, comfortable setting, they often overlap, finish each other's sentences and anticipate what the other is about to say. This practice, which I call *"participatory listenership,"* is often perceived by men as interruption, *intrusion* and lack of attention. (par. 18)

Participatory listenership: _____

_____

7. *Intrusion:* _____

8. In his book *Fighting for Life,* Walter Ong points out that men use *"agonistic"* or warlike, oppositional formats to do almost anything; thus discussion becomes debate, and conversation a competitive sport. (par. 20)

Agonistic: _____

9. This explains the *paradox* of the talkative man who said of his silent wife, "She's the talker." (par. 22)

Paradox: _____

10. Many of the psychological explanations that have become second nature may not be helpful, because they tend to blame either women (for not being *assertive* enough) or men (for not being in touch with their feelings). (par. 23)

Assertive: _____

Exercise 6   ## Check Your Understanding

Based on Reading 2, write your answers to the following questions.

1. According to Riessman's book *Divorce Talk,* what did most women say was the reason for their divorce?

_____

2. According to Tannen, what is the cornerstone of a friendship for women?

_____

3. According to Tannen, what is the basis of friendship for men?

_____

4. What kind of physical misalignments impede communication between men and women?

_____

©2007 Pearson Education, Inc.

5. What solution does Tannen suggest for the problems men and women have in communicating with each other?

_____

_____

Exercise 7 Evaluate Inferences

Based on Reading 2, put a check next to each of the following statements that is a reasonable inference.

_____ 1. Tannen was invited to give a talk to the women's group because of her expertise in language.

_____ 2. People laughed at the man who said that his wife was the "talker" because he was the one who was doing all the talking that evening.

_____ 3. Men's body language proves that men are not listening to their wives.

_____ 4. Poor communication is the only reason marriages don't last.

_____ 5. For many women, men's responses to them in conversation seem unsatisfying and simplistic.

_____ 6. If men and women just understood their different conversation styles, the divorce rate would go down drastically.

_____ 7. Women's conversational habits are probably superior because they are more communicative.

_____ 8. Men's conversational habits are more frustrating to men than women's conversational habits are to men.

_____ 9. Finishing someone else's sentence is considered rude by both men and women.

_____ 10. Tannen believes that ethnic conflicts could be more easily resolved with cross-cultural understanding.

Exercise 8 Organize to Learn: Create a Chart or Diagram

On a separate sheet of paper, design a chart or diagram that compares and contrasts men's and women's communication styles, based on Reading 2.

Exercise 9   **Reflect**

Think about what you read in Reading 2 and what you already know about men's and women's conversation styles. Answer the following questions, and prepare to discuss them with your classmates.

1. Which of the points of analysis of men's and women's communication styles in Tannen's article were new to you?

_____

_____

_____

2. What situations described in the reading are familiar to you? Explain.

_____

_____

_____

3. Having read about differences in women's and men's conversational styles, will you now infer different meanings when you communicate with someone of the opposite sex? Explain and give examples.

_____

_____

_____

INFERENCES FROM WORDS

The assumptions you make about information given in textbooks or personal narratives presented in autobiographies are based on paragraphs or longer passages. But these inferences are influenced by the author's choice of words, so careful reading also requires paying attention to the inferences from words.

Connotations

connotation
Positive or negative feelings suggested by a word

denotation The dictionary or literal meaning of a word

Some words have many possible effects on the reader. The positive or negative feelings evoked by a word are its **connotations.** By contrast, the precise meaning of a word, its literal meaning, is its **denotation,** or dictionary definition. If, for example, you think only of the denotative meaning of the word *family,* you might think of "people related by blood

©2007 Pearson Education, Inc.

or marriage" or "relatives." This definition of *family* is straightforward; it does not carry a lot of emotion. However, if you think of *family* as a group of caring and loving relatives, it has a positive connotation. Not all people have this reaction to the word *family*. Consider the saying, "You can choose your friends but not your family." Here the word *family* has a negative connotation, conveying the idea that there may be members of your family you would rather not associate with.

Good writers often use words that are rich in connotative meaning. As a reader, you need to be aware of the connotations of the words you (or others) use when discussing gender issues, because many people are particularly sensitive about it. Most writers try to use language that will not offend anyone.

Maya Angelou, prize-winning poet and author, addresses the issue of gender and language in her book *Wouldn't Take Nothing for My Journey Now*. Read the following passage and look for three adjectives that have strong connotations.

> In my young years I took pride in the fact that luck was called a lady. In fact, there were so few public acknowledgments of the female presence that I felt personally honored whenever nature and large ships were referred to as feminine. But as I matured, I began to resent being considered a sister to a changeling as fickle as luck, as aloof as an ocean, and as frivolous as nature. (Angelou, *Wouldn't Take Nothing for My Journey Now*)

Did you pick out *fickle, aloof,* and *frivolous*? These words have strong negative connotations. Something or someone who is *fickle* changes unpredictably; thus, fickle luck is not something you can depend on. *Aloof* means "removed or distant in interest or feeling." This definition is commonly extended to mean uncaring or unconcerned. And the definition of *frivolous*, "lacking in seriousness," usually has a negative connotation. Maya Angelou deliberately chose words with negative connotations to strengthen her criticism of the custom of referring to luck, ships, and nature as feminine.

Exercise 10   Evaluate Connotations and Inferences

Listed in the following columns under "Masculine" and "Feminine" are a number of adjectives commonly used to describe characteristics of each gender. Add any adjectives you often hear used to describe men or women to the appropriate lists. Then, in the "Connotation" column, indicate what kind of connotation each adjective usually has, positive (+) or negative (–). The first pair has been done for you.

Remember that this is a list of generalizations and stereotypes of the traditional gender roles in our society. Clearly, this list of adjectives cannot be accurate for all men or for all women.

Masculine	Connotation	Feminine	Connotation
strong	+	weak	−
decisive	_____	indecisive	_____
unemotional	_____	emotional	_____
distant	_____	nurturing	_____
hard	_____	soft	_____
direct	_____	indirect	_____
insensitive	_____	sensitive	_____
not gossipy	_____	gossipy	_____
mechanically inclined	_____	not mechanically inclined	_____
independent	_____	dependent	_____
_____	_____	_____	_____
_____	_____	_____	_____

Exercise 11   ## Reflect

Based on Exercise 10, answer the following questions in your own words.

1. How many positive or negative connotations are there for the words in each column? Which column has more negative connotations?

_____

2. Why do you think one side of a list of traditional gender roles has more negative connotations? What conclusions can you draw from this observation?

_____

_____

3. Do you think the connotations of a word might be different depending on who is interpreting the word and what the situation was at the time? Explain your answer.

_____

_____

◆

Irony

irony Writer says one thing and means another

Sometimes a writer wants you, the reader, to infer the opposite of what he or she writes. The writer is then using a device called **irony.** This device should be familiar to you. For example, if you crawl out from under your car where you've been changing the oil on a hot and muggy day and your friend says, "You look terrific!" you know you actually look a mess.

©2007 Pearson Education, Inc.

Or a writer may write about an ironic situation. For example, after a devastating flood, people often have no water to drink. Even though there is too much water, it's contaminated. Ironically, there's not a drop to drink.

Irony can often be humorous. At the least, it alerts the reader to look for other layers of meaning in a message. In an ironic statement, things are not what they seem to be. That is because the writer has stepped back from the subject and views it from a distance.

Exercise 12   ## Recognize Irony

Read the following scenarios, and choose the sentence that makes an ironic statement about or gives an ironic conclusion to the situation.

1. Johnny was voted the student "most likely to succeed" in his high school class.
   a. Now he has a nice family and a fulfilling job that pays well.
   b. Now he is divorced, unemployed, and lonely.
   c. Now he's cheerful and happy but definitely not wealthy.

2. At one time, Zimbabwe exported food to all of Africa.
   a. Today Zimbabwe has a famine and can't feed its own people.
   b. Today Zimbabwe is blaming its problems on the white former colonialists who still live there.
   c. Today Zimbabwe needs to reexamine its use of land.

3. Erica didn't respect her advanced placement biology teacher and ended up with an F in the class.
   a. None of the students passed the Advanced Placement Biology test because the teacher was bad.
   b. All of the students passed the Advanced Placement Biology test in spite of the teacher.
   c. Erica got the highest grade of all the students on the Advanced Placement Biology test.

4. The president of a wealthy country said that corruption would not be tolerated among top executives of corporations.
   a. The president himself had always been a crusader against corrupt practices of businesses, especially when he was on the board of directors.
   b. The president followed up on his position, saying that executives are responsible for what their corporations do and that if they do anything illegal, they should be sent to jail like any other criminal.
   c. The president himself had benefited from insider information and used it to make millions of dollars when he was on the board of directors of a corporation.

5. An American from one of the western states was visiting Denmark on New Year's Eve. When the family she was staying with prepared their fireworks for the evening's festivities, she told them, "Fireworks are illegal in my state because they're too dangerous." The Danes asked her what people did instead. She responded:
   a. "They go to big fireworks shows."
   b. "They don't do anything."
   c. "They shoot guns in the air."

Reading 3 | *Why I Want a Wife* | Judy Brady

The following essay, first published in Ms. *magazine in 1971, is now considered a classic ironic portrayal of what our society considers, or considered, a wife's proper role. The author of this essay, Judy Brady, was born in San Francisco in 1937. She graduated from the University of Iowa. This essay was first published under her married name, Judy Syfers, but she was later divorced. Ms. Brady is a professional writer and a feminist.*

As you read, attempt to infer what Brady presents as the role of the ideal wife. Does she mean that this is what a wife of a busy college student should really do? Or is she suggesting an alternative?

1   I belong to that classification of people known as wives. I am A Wife. And, not altogether incidentally, I am a mother.

2   Not too long ago a male friend of mine appeared on the scene fresh from a recent divorce. He had one child, who is, of course, with his ex-wife. He is looking for another wife. As I thought about him while I was ironing one evening, it suddenly occurred to me that I, too, would like to have a wife. Why do I want a wife?

3   I would like to go back to school so that I can become economically independent, support myself, and if need be, support those dependent upon me. I want a wife who will work and send me to school. And while I am going to school I want a wife to take care of my children. I want a wife to keep track of the children's doctor and dentist appointments. And to keep track of mine, too. I want a wife to make sure my children eat properly and are kept clean. I want a wife who will wash the children's clothes and keep them mended. I want a wife who is a good nurturant attendant to my children, who arranges for their schooling, makes sure that they have an adequate social life with their peers, takes them to the park, the zoo, etc. I want a wife who takes care of the children when they are sick, a wife who arranges to be around when the children need special care, because of course, I cannot miss classes at school. My wife must arrange to lose time at work and not lose the job. It may mean a small cut in my wife's income from time to time, but I guess I can tolerate that. Needless to say, my wife will arrange and pay for the care of the children while my wife is working.

4   I want a wife who will take care of *my* physical needs. I want a wife who will keep my house clean. A wife who will pick up after my children, a

©2007 Pearson Education, Inc.

wife who will pick up after me. I want a wife who will keep my clothes clean, ironed, mended, replaced when need be, and who will see to it that my personal things are kept in their proper place so that I can find what I need the minute I need it. I want a wife who cooks the meals, a wife who is a *good* cook. I want a wife who will plan the menus, do the necessary grocery shopping, prepare the meals, serve them pleasantly, and then do the cleaning up while I do my studying. I want a wife who will care for me when I am sick and sympathize with my pain and loss of time from school. I want a wife to go along when our family takes a vacation so that someone can continue to care for me and my children when I need a rest and change of scene.

5   I want a wife who will not bother me with rambling complaints about a wife's duties. But I want a wife who will listen to me when I feel the need to explain a rather difficult point I have come across in my course of studies. And I want a wife who will type my papers for me when I have written them.

6   I want a wife who will take care of the details of my social life. When my wife and I are invited out by my friends, I want a wife who will take care of the babysitting arrangements. When I meet people at school that I like and want to entertain, I want a wife who will have the house clean, will prepare a special meal, serve it to me and my friends, and not interrupt when I talk about things that interest me and my friends. I want a wife who will have arranged that the children are fed and ready for bed before my guests arrive so that the children do not bother us. I want a wife who takes care of the needs of my guests so that they feel comfortable, who makes sure that they have an ashtray, that they are passed the hors d'oeuvres, that they are offered a second helping of the food, that their wine glasses are replenished when necessary, that their coffee is served to them as they like it. And I want a wife who knows that sometimes I need a night out by myself.

7   I want a wife who is sensitive to my sexual needs, a wife who makes love passionately and eagerly when I feel like it, a wife who makes sure that I am satisfied. And, of course, I want a wife who will not demand sexual attention when I am not in the mood for it. I want a wife who assumes the complete responsibility for birth control, because I do not want more children. I want a wife who will remain sexually faithful to me so that I do not have to clutter up my intellectual life with jealousies. And I want a wife who understands that *my* sexual needs may entail more than strict adherence to monogamy. I must, after all, be able to relate to people as fully as possible.

8   If, by chance, I find another person more suitable as a wife than the wife I already have, I want the liberty to replace my present wife with another one. Naturally, I will expect a fresh, new life; my wife will take the children and be solely responsible for them so that I am left free.

9   When I am through with school and have a job, I want my wife to quit working and remain at home so that my wife can more fully and completely take care of a wife's duties.

10   My God, who *wouldn't* want a wife?

BRADY, "Why I Want a Wife"

Exercise 13 **Organize to Learn: List**

On a separate paper, list all the reasons for wanting a wife that Brady gives in Reading 3, "Why I Want a Wife."

Exercise 14 **Evaluate Inferences**

Based on Reading 3, check each of the following statements that is a reasonable inference.

_____ 1. The author believes there is a double standard—completely different expectations for wives and husbands.

_____ 2. The "husband" in this essay is a full-time student; he doesn't have a job.

_____ 3. This essay exaggerates what is expected of a wife, but it is somewhat accurate.

_____ 4. The author wrote this essay because her husband divorced her, so she is angry.

_____ 5. The author thinks that men and women should share the housework more equally.

_____ 6. Judy Brady meant this essay to be ironic; she obviously doesn't really want a wife, but she points out humorously that, considering all the things wives do, everybody would want one.

_____ 7. The author will never get married again.

_____ 8. The author is a wife and a mother.

_____ 9. Judy Brady wrote this essay because she thought it would convince husbands to be more helpful around the house.

_____ 10. The author believes that the expectations of wives are unfair.

Exercise 15 **Recognize Irony**

Based on Reading 3, answer the following questions in your own words.

1. What makes this reading ironic?

_____

_____

_____

_____

©2007 Pearson Education, Inc.

2. Write a sentence or two of your own that demonstrate irony.

_____

_____

_____

_____

Exercise 16   **Reflect**

Think about what you read in Reading 3 and what you already know about marriage. Answer the following questions, and prepare to discuss them with your classmates.

1. How is Brady's description of a marriage similar to the marriages that you are familiar with today?

_____

_____

2. How is Brady's description of a marriage different from the marriages that you are familiar with today?

_____

_____

READING LITERATURE

Reading literature—a category that includes fiction, poetry, and drama, as well as essays and autobiography—requires considerable skill in making inferences. Sometimes inferences are based not only on the usual reasonable assumptions but also on the interpretation of imagery.

Imagery

image A "sense picture" that uses words to describe something in terms of sight, taste, hearing, touch, and smell

An **image** in literature is a "sense picture" made up of words that describe something in terms of sight, taste, hearing, touch, and smell. Images can be descriptions of what the author has observed. For example, Scott Russell Sanders, in his essay "The Men We Carry in Our Minds" (see pages 343–345), uses descriptive words to create images of the men he knew: "The bodies of the men I knew were twisted and maimed in ways visible and invisible. The nails of their hands were black and split, the hands tattooed with scars. Some had lost fingers." When you read this description, it is easy to form a picture of the men and to think about how they were twisted in visible and invisible ways.

An author may also use figurative language to create images. **Figurative language** usually creates images by making direct or implied comparisons between two unlike things. For example, Sanders describes the faces of the men he knew, with their skin "creased *like the leather of old work gloves.*" In other words, their faces had so many wrinkles and lines from hard work that their skin looked like the fabric of cracked, worn-out leather gloves. When writers use these kinds of comparisons, they can make us understand what they are trying to communicate more clearly, with more imagination and fewer words. They expect us, as readers, to use these creative images to make inferences about their meanings.

figurative language
Direct or implied comparisons made to create an image

Although textbook authors and essay writers do use figurative language, writers of literature—fiction, poetry, drama, and autobiography—use it even more frequently. *Similes* and *metaphors,* two important examples of figurative language, are imaginative comparisons that convey a writer's attitude about characters, events, or ideas.

Similes

simile A comparison between unlike things, using *like* or *as*

A **simile** makes a comparison between two unlike things, using the words *like* or *as*. The phrase "like the leather of old work gloves" is an example of a simile. It provides an exceptionally vivid image of the skin of these old men who had worked hard all their lives. The film *Forrest Gump* included a memorable simile: "Mama always said, 'Life is like a box of chocolates. You never know what you're going to get.'" Here the unpredictability of life is compared to the chance selection of flavors—some you like, some you don't—in a box of chocolates.

Similes in literature are often a bit more complicated. For example: "Women are like pictures; of no value in the hands of a fool till he hears men of sense bid high for their purchase" (Farquhar, *The Beaux*, Act II, sc. 1). What can you infer from this statement? To understand this simile, you have to understand that the author is referring to an art auction, where people bid on paintings and other pieces. As long as someone is willing to pay more for the piece, the price continues to go up. Sometimes people go to an auction thinking that a particular picture is not very interesting and not worth much, but they may change their minds if other people are interested in it and are bidding high. Farquhar, then, is implying that some men (the "fools") do not value their women as highly as they should until they realize that other men are interested in them.

Exercise 17 **Identify Similes**

Read the following well-known poem by Robert Burns, and notice how he uses similes. (Some words are spelled differently because the poem was written 200 years ago in a Scottish dialect.) Then list the similes Burns used in this poem, and explain what you can infer from them about his lover.

©2007 Pearson Education, Inc.

My Luve Is Like a Red, Red Rose
O, My Luve is like a red, red rose,
   That's newly sprung in June;
O My Luve is like a melodie
   That's sweetly play'd in tune.

As fair art thou, my bonnie lass,
   So deep in luve am I:
And I will luve thee still, my dear,
   Till a' the seas gang dry.

Till a' the seas gang dry, my dear,
   And the rocks melt wi' the sun:
O I will luve thee still, my dear,
   While the sands o' life shall run.

And fare thee weel, my only luve,
   And fare thee weel awhile!
And I will come again, my luve,
   Tho' it were ten thousand mile!

         (Burns, "My Luve Is Like a Red, Red Rose")

Simile   **Inference**

1. _____   _____

2. _____   _____

                                                               ♦

Metaphors

metaphor An
implied comparison

A **metaphor** compares two things without using the words *like* or *as*. Often something unknown is compared to something known to make it easier to understand. For example, poet-songwriter Paul Simon wrote, in the song by the same name, "I am a rock." This line is a simple metaphor that compares the qualities of the singer—the narrator—to those of an inanimate object, a rock. Another metaphor is presented in the next line, "I am an island." Simon is explaining how the character in the song feels about his relationship to other people. He feels isolated and unable to make contact with others, "cold," distant, unbending, and inflexible. The song continues, "I touch no one/and no one touches me." These lines confirm the sense of isolation that the metaphors in the first two lines introduced.

Exercise 18   ## Identify Metaphors

Read the following lyrics from the song "The Rose," by Amanda Mc-Broom, and notice how she uses metaphors. Then list five metaphors that McBroom uses in this song and explain what you think she is inferring.

The Rose
Some say love it is a river that drowns the tender reed.
Some say love it is a razor that leaves your soul to bleed.
Some say love it is a hunger, an endless aching need.
I say love it is a flower and you its only seed.

(McBroom, "The Rose")

Metaphor	**Inferences**
1. _____	_____
2. _____	_____
3. _____	_____
4. _____	_____
5. _____	_____

Exercise 19   Recognize and Interpret Figurative Language

Read the following examples of figurative language. For each quotation, answer the questions that follow. Then write the meaning of the quotation in your own words.

1. They say love is a two-way street. But I don't believe it, because the one I've been on for the last two years was a dirt road." (McMillan, *Waiting to Exhale*)

   a. What is love compared to? _____

   _____

   b. Are the comparisons similes or metaphors? _____

   c. Write the meaning of this quotation in your own words.

   _____

   _____

2. Beauty without virtue is a flower without perfume. (Anonymous, French proverb)

   a. Is this a simile or a metaphor? _____

   b. What two things are being compared?

   _____

   _____

   _____

©2007 Pearson Education, Inc.

c. Write the meaning of this quotation in your own words.

_____

_____

3. Love is blind (William Shakespeare, *Merchant of Venice*)

a. What image does Shakespeare's words bring into your mind?

_____

b. What two things are being compared?

_____

c. Write the meaning of this quotation in your own words.

_____

_____

_____

4. The prolonged slavery of women is the darkest page in human history. (Elizabeth Cady Stanton, *History of Woman Suffrage*)

a. Is this a simile or a metaphor? _____

b. What two things are being compared?

_____

c. Write the meaning of this quotation in your own words.

_____

_____

5. Our hours in love have wings; in absence, crutches. (Colley Cibber, "Xerxes IV")

a. Is this a simile or a metaphor? _____

b. What two things are being compared?

_____

c. Write the meaning of this quotation in your own words.

_____

_____

_____

6. Love comforteth like sunshine after rain. (William Shakespeare, *Venus and Adonis*)

   a. Is this a simile or a metaphor? _____

   b. What two things are being compared?

   _____

   c. Write the meaning of this quotation in your own words.

   _____

   _____

7. Marriage . . . a fever in reverse: it starts with heat and ends with cold. (Anonymous, German proverb)

   a. Is this a simile or a metaphor? _____

   b. What two things are being compared?

   _____

   c. Write the meaning of the quotation in your own words.

   _____

   _____

8. A woman needs a man like a fish needs a bicycle. (Feminist slogan often attributed to Gloria Steinem)

   a. Is this a simile or a metaphor? _____

   b. What two things are being compared?

   _____

   c. Write the meaning of the quotation in your own words.

   _____

   _____

9. He has a heart of stone. (Common English expression)

   a. Is this a simile or a metaphor? _____

   b. What two things are being compared?

   _____

   c. Write the meaning of the quotation in your own words.

   _____

©2007 Pearson Education, Inc.

10. Love is the master key that opens the gates of happiness, of hatred, of jealousy, and, most easily of all, the gate of fear. (Oliver Wendell Holmes, *The Autocrat of the Breakfast Table*)

a. Is this a simile or a metaphor? _____

b. What two things are being compared?

_____

_____

c. Write the meaning of the quotation in your own words.

_____

_____

◆

Poetry

A poem is a combination of images, rhythm, and sometimes rhyme that creates meaning for the reader. Determining the meaning, or message, of a poem is similar to the process of selecting a thesis statement that you learned about in Chapter 3. But often the message is implied, not stated outright. As a reader, you need to add up the visual imagery, the way the poem sounds, and other impressions of the poem to infer the most accurate interpretation. Like making inferences, interpreting poetry requires you to reach reasonable conclusions about meaning based on the evidence provided.

To practice finding the meaning, read the following poem by Christine Huynh.

> The dryline between us
> Thickens every time we fight.
> We don't understand each other's needs,
> But the need to correct is stronger
> Than steel plates in heads
> And on torn up streets.
>
> (Huynh, "Corrections")

What metaphors does Huynh use in this poem, and what does each represent?

The dryline represents the communication problem that happens when the speaker and her/his lover fight. When this dryline thickens, the communications get worse.

The "steel plates in heads and on torn up streets" represent each person's need to correct the other, to be the person who is right, or who wins the argument. Steel plates are very hard, practically impossible to break or wear down.

What is the message or meaning of the poem?

The message is pessimistic because the comparisons of the dryline and steel plates

to communication and the need to be right are not hopeful. There is a barrier

to compromise.

Exercise 20   **Interpret Poetry**

Read each of the following poems. Answer the questions that follow.

1.   The summer came too fast,
      stayed too long,
      like an unwanted man
      you keep around
      because being alone
      makes you feel fatter than you really are.
                          (Gómez, "Chocolate Confessions")

   a. What two things is Gómez comparing and why?

   _____

   _____

   b. Explain why Gómez writes "being alone makes you feel fatter
      than you really are." What does feeling fat represent?

   _____

   _____

   c. What is the message or meaning of the poem?

   _____

   _____

2.   Our lives shall not be sweated from birth until life closes.
      Hearts starve as well as bodies;
      Give us bread, but give us roses.
              (James Oppenheimer, lyrics to the song, "Bread and Roses,"
                  inspired by the picket signs of women on strike at the
                          mills in Lawrence, Massachusetts, in 1912)

   a. The writer uses four images—hearts, bodies, bread, roses—that
      can be grouped into two connected pairs. What are the two pairs
      of connected images?

   _____

   b. What does the writer mean with the words, "Hearts starve as well
      as bodies?"

   _____

©2007 Pearson Education, Inc.

    c. What is the message or meaning of the poem?

_____

_____

3.   For courting's a pleasure,
        But parting is grief,
        And a false-hearted lover,
        Is worse than a thief.
               (From "On Top of Old Smokey," author unknown)

    a. What two things are being compared in the last two lines?

_____

    b. Is it a metaphor or a simile? _____

    c. What does the writer mean by making this comparison?

_____

_____

4.   Although I conquer all the earth,
        yet for me there is only one city.
        In that city there is for me only one house;
        And in that house, one room only;
        And in that room, a bed.
        And one woman sleeps there,
        The shining joy and jewel of all my kingdom.
            (Sanskrit poem, "Although I Conquer All the Earth")

    a. What is the woman sleeping in the bed compared to? Does the author use a metaphor or a simile?

_____

_____

    b. How do the images progress from the beginning of the poem to the end?

_____

    c. What is the message or meaning of the poem?

_____

5.   For us a handshake was a duel:
        two boys in a friendly clasp
        of greeting were fighting the test
        of power. Who squeezed first might have

an advantage, unless the cold
tendons got strained, and the grip,
so big and cruel at once would
weaken from the quick exertion
as the other built up a grasp
that overrode and then melted
the opposing hand, while we both
kept grinning hello. But the best
defense was to cup your palm so
knuckles weren't aligned for grinding
but curled under the hostile force.
It was the feint of giving in,
while the rival bore down and thought
himself near victory that was
the last strategy. And when he
crunched you toward acquiescence and
withdrawal from the lethal shake,
you put everything, your whole weight
and blood and warmth and thought, pumped down
through shoulder and elbow and wrist
on the opponent's paw as his
smile registered surprise and pain
and you broke down his control in
the vise of your own gesture of
reciprocation, serious welcome.

(Robert Morgan, "Shaking")

a. What metaphor does the author use for a handshake between the boys?

_____

_____

b. How do the following references reinforce the main metaphor of the poem: "test of power," "the grip, so big and cruel," "the opposing hand," "hostile force," and "lethal shake"?

_____

_____

c. What is the message or meaning of the poem?

_____

_____

_____

©2007 Pearson Education, Inc.

Fiction

Understanding inferences and the language of images is also important in reading the other forms of literature, such as short stories and novels. But imagery is only one element in fiction. Character, plot, setting, point of view, and theme are other elements. After you read a short story, ask yourself some of the questions in Table 6.1 to help you understand and organize the information.

Table 6.1	Key Questions for Reading Fiction

characters The people in a story

Characters—The People in the Story
- Who is the main character in the story? That is, who is the story primarily about? Who do we learn the most about?
- How does the main character change from the beginning to the end of the story? What causes this character to change?
- Describe each of the important people in the story. What kind of person is he or she? Base your answer on what the people do, what they say, and what other people say about them in the story.

plot The action of a story

Plot—The Action of the Story
- What happens to the main character(s) in the story?
- What is the most exciting part or turning point of the story? (This is called the climax, or crisis, of the plot.)
- List or map the main events in the story in the order in which they happen.

setting The time and place of a story

Setting—The Time and Place of the Story
- When does the story take place?
- Where does the story take place?
- What influence does the setting have on the other parts of the story?

point of view The perspective from which the story is told

Point of View—The Perspective from Which the Story Is Told
- Through whose eyes do we see the action of the story?
- Does the point of view change in the story, or is it consistent?
- How would the story be different if it were seen through another character's eyes?

theme Interpretation of life experience based on the outcome of the story

Theme—An Interpretation of Life Experience Based on the Outcome of the Story
- What is the meaning of the story? Can we learn something about life from the story?
- What general statement can you make about human experience based on the experience of the characters in this story?

Reading 4

The Chase

Alberto Moravia

Translated by Angus Davidson

The following short story is about relationships between men and women, and how those relationships can change. It is rich in the use of figurative language. As you read, think about the author's use of metaphor and the effect that it has on you as a reader.

1   I have never been a sportsman—or, rather, I have been a sportsman only once, and that was the first and last time. I was a child, and one day, for some reason or other, I found myself together with my father, who was holding a gun in his hand, behind a bush, watching a bird that had perched on a branch not very far away. It was a large, gray bird—or perhaps it was brown—with a long—or perhaps a short—beak; I don't remember. I only remember what I felt at that moment as I looked at it. It was like watching an animal whose vitality was rendered more intense by the very fact of my watching it and of the animal's not knowing that I was watching it.

2   At that moment, I say, the notion of wildness entered my mind, never again to leave it: everything is wild which is autonomous and unpredictable and does not depend upon us. Then all of a sudden there was an explosion; I could no longer see the bird and I thought it had flown away. But my father was leading the way, walking in front of me through the undergrowth. Finally he stooped down, picked up something and put it in my hand. I was aware of something warm and soft and I lowered my eyes: there was a bird in the palm of my hand, its dangling, shattered head crowned with a plume of already-thickening blood. I burst into tears and dropped the corpse on the ground, and that was the end of my shooting experience.

3   I thought again of this remote episode in my life this very day after watching my wife, for the first and also the last time, as she was walking through the streets of the city. But let us take things in order.

4   What had my wife been like; what was she like now? She once had been, to put it briefly, "wild"—that is, entirely autonomous and unpredictable; latterly she had become "tame"—that is, predictable and dependent. For a long time she had been like the bird that, on that far-off morning in my childhood, I had seen perching on the bough; latterly, I am sorry to say, she had become like a hen about which one knows everything in advance—how it moves, how it eats, how it lays eggs, how it sleeps, and so on.

5   Nevertheless I would not wish anyone to think that my wife's wildness consisted of an uncouth, rough, rebellious character. Apart from being extremely beautiful, she is the gentlest, politest, most discreet person in the world. Rather her wildness consisted of the air of charming unpredictability, of independence in her way of living, with which during the first years of our marriage she acted in my presence, both at home and abroad. Wildness signified intimacy, privacy, secrecy. Yes, my wife as she sat in front of her dressing table, her eyes fixed on the looking glass, passing the hairbrush with a repeated motion over her long, loose hair, was just as wild as the solitary quail hopping forward along a sun-filled furrow or the furtive fox coming out into a clearing and stopping to look around before running on. She was wild because I, as I looked at her, could never manage to foresee when she would give a last stroke with the hairbrush and rise and come toward me; wild to such a degree that sometimes when I went into our bedroom the smell of her, floating in the air, would have something of the acrid quality of a wild beast's lair.

6   Gradually she became less wild, tamer, I had had a fox, a quail, in the house, as I have said; then one day I realized that I had a hen. What effect

©2007 Pearson Education, Inc.

does a hen have on someone who watches it? It has the effect of being, so to speak, an automaton in the form of a bird; automatic are the brief, rapid steps with which it moves about; automatic its hard, terse pecking; automatic the glance of the round eyes in its head that nods and turns; automatic its ready crouching down under the cock; automatic the dropping of the egg wherever it may be and the cry with which it announces that the egg has been laid. Good-bye to the fox; good-bye to the quail. And her smell—this no longer brought to my mind, in any way, the innocent odor of a wild animal; rather I detected in it the chemical suavity of some ordinary French perfume.

7   Our flat is on the first floor of a big building in a modern quarter of the town; our windows look out on a square in which there is a small public garden, the haunt of nurses and children and dogs. One day I was standing at the window, looking in a melancholy way at the garden. My wife, shortly before, had dressed to go out; and once again, watching her, I had noticed the irrevocable and, so to speak, invisible character of her gestures and personality: something which gave one the feeling of a thing already seen and already done and which therefore evaded even the most determined observation. And now, as I stood looking at the garden and at the same time wondering why the adorable wildness of former times had so completely disappeared, suddenly my wife came into my range of vision as she walked quickly across the garden in the direction of the bus stop. I watched her and then I almost jumped for joy; in a movement she was making to pull down a fold of her narrow skirt and smooth it over her thigh with the tips of her long, sharp nails, in this movement I recognized the wildness that in the past had made me love her. It was only an instant, but in that instant I said to myself: She's become wild again because she's convinced that I am not there and am not watching her. Then I left the window and rushed out.

8   But I did not join her at the bus stop; I felt that I must not allow myself to be seen. Instead I hurried to my car, which was standing nearby, got in and waited. A bus came and she got in together with some other people: the bus started off again and I began following it. Then there came back to me the memory of that one shooting expedition in which I had taken part as a child, and I saw that the bus was the undergrowth with its bushes and trees, my wife the bird perching on the bough while I, unseen, watched it living before my eyes. And the whole town, during this pursuit, became, as though by magic, a fact of nature like the countryside: the houses were hills, the streets valleys, the vehicles hedges and woods, and even the passers-by on the pavements had something unpredictable and autonomous—that is, wild—about them. And in my mouth, behind my clenched teeth, there was the acrid, metallic taste of gunfire; and my eyes, usually listless and wandering, had become sharp, watchful, attentive.

9   These eyes were fixed intently upon the exit door when the bus came to the end of its run. A number of people got out, and then I saw my wife getting out. Once again I recognized, in the manner in which she broke free of the crowd and started off toward a neighboring street, the wildness that pleased me so much. I jumped out of the car and started following her.

10   She was walking in front of me, ignorant of my presence, a tall woman with an elegant figure, long-legged, narrow-hipped, broad-backed, her brown hair falling on her shoulders.

11   Men turned around as she went past; perhaps they were aware of what I myself was now sensing with an intensity that quickened the beating of my heart and took my breath away: the unrestricted, steadily increasing, ir-resistible character of her mysterious wildness.

12   She walked hurriedly, having evidently some purpose in view, and even the fact that she had a purpose of which I was ignorant added to her wild-ness; I did not know where she was going, just as on that far-off morning I had not known what the bird perching on the bough was about to do. Moreover I thought the gradual, steady increase in this quality of wildness came partly from the fact that as she drew nearer to the object of this mys-terious walk there was an increase in her—how shall I express it?—of biolog-ical tension, of existential excitement, of vital effervescence. Then, unexpect-edly, with the suddenness of a film, her purpose was revealed.

13   A fair-haired young man in a leather jacket and a pair of corduroy trousers was leaning against the wall of a house in that ancient, narrow street. He was idly smoking as he looked in front of him. But as my wife passed close to him, he threw away his cigarette with a decisive gesture, took a step forward and seized her arm. I was expecting her to rebuff him, to move away from him, but nothing happened: evidently obeying the rules of some exotic ritual, she went on walking beside the young man. Then af-ter a few steps, with a movement that confirmed her own complicity, she put her arm around her companion's waist and he put his around her.

14   I understood then that this unknown man who took such liberties with my wife was also attracted by wildness. And so, instead of making a con-ventional appointment with her, instead of meeting in a café with a hand-shake, a falsely friendly and respectful welcome, he had preferred, by agree-ment with her, to take her by surprise—or, rather, to pretend to do so—while she was apparently taking a walk on her own account. All this I perceived by intuition, noticing that at the very moment when he stepped forward and took her arm her wildness had, so to speak, given an upward bound. It was years since I had seen my wife so alive, but alas, the source of this life could not be traced to me.

15   They walked on thus entwined and then, without any preliminaries, just like two wild animals, they did an unexpected thing: they went into one of the dark doorways in order to kiss. I stopped and watched them from a dis-tance, peering into the darkness of the entrance. My wife was turned away from me and was bending back with the pressure of his body, her hair hanging free. I looked at that long, thick mane of brown hair, which as she leaned back fell free of her shoulders, and I felt at that moment her vitality reached its diapason, just as happens with wild animals when they couple and their customary wildness is redoubled by the violence of love. I watched for a long time and then, since this kiss went on and on and in fact seemed to be prolonged beyond the limits of my power of endurance, I saw that I would have to intervene.

©2007 Pearson Education, Inc.

16   I would have to go forward, seize my wife by the arm—or actually by that hair, which hung down and conveyed so well the feeling of feminine passivity—then hurl myself with clenched fists upon the blond young man. After this encounter I would carry off my wife, weeping, mortified, ashamed, while I was raging and broken-hearted, upbraiding her and pouring scorn upon her.

17   But what else would this intervention amount to but the shot my father fired at that free, unknowing bird as it perched on the bough? The disorder and confusion, the mortification, the shame, that would follow would irreparably destroy the rare and precious moment of wildness that I was witnessing inside the dark doorway. It was true that this wildness was directed against me: but I had to remember that wildness, always and everywhere, is directed against everything and everybody. After the scene of my intervention it might be possible for me to regain control of my wife, but I should find her shattered and lifeless in my arms like the bird that my father placed in my hand so that I might throw it into the shooting bag.

18   The kiss went on and on: well, it was a kiss of passion—that could not be denied. I waited until they finished, until they came out of the doorway, until they walked on again still linked together. Then I turned back.

MORAVIA, "The Chase"

Exercise 21   Work with Words

The following sentences appear in Reading 4, Moravia's "The Chase." Use the context clues, your knowledge of word parts, your understanding of connotations, and your dictionary skills to determine the meaning of each italicized word in the sentences. Write the meaning of the word on the lines provided. The paragraph number is provided in case you want to check the context.

1. I was aware of something warm and soft and I lowered my eyes: there was a bird in the palm of my hand, its dangling, shattered head crowned with a *plume* of already-thickening blood. (par. 2)

   Plume: _____

2. She once had been, to put it briefly, "wild"—that is, entirely *autonomous* and unpredictable. (par. 4)

   Autonomous: _____

3. Nevertheless I would not wish anyone to think that my wife's wildness consisted of an *uncouth*, rough, rebellious character. (par. 5)

   Uncouth: _____

4. I was expecting her to *rebuff* him, to move away from him, but nothing happened: evidently obeying the rules of some exotic ritual, she went on walking beside the young man. (par. 13)

   Rebuff: _____

5. The disorder and confusion, the *mortification*, the shame, that would follow would irreparably destroy the rare and precious moment of wildness that I was witnessing inside the dark doorway. (par. 17)

   Mortification: _____

Exercise 22   ## Check Your Understanding

Based on Reading 4, write your answers to the following questions.

1. What happened when the boy first went hunting with his father?

   _____

   _____

2. How, in his opinion, had his wife changed since they married?

   _____

3. Why did he start following her?

   _____

   _____

4. What did his wife do when she went out?

   _____

5. What did he do when he saw them kissing?

   _____

Exercise 23   ## Organize to Learn: Analyze Fiction

Use the questions in Table 6.1 (p. 324) to organize this story and understand it.

1. Character
   a. What kind of person is the main character (the "I" who is telling the story)?

   _____

   _____

   b. What kind of person is his wife?

   _____

   _____

   c. What kind of person is her lover?

   _____

©2007 Pearson Education, Inc.

d. How does the main character change in this story?

_____

_____

_____

2. Plot: List the main events of the story in order.

a. _____

b. _____

c. _____

d. _____

e. _____

f. _____

3. Setting
   a. How much can you tell about where and when the story takes place?

   _____

   _____

   b. How is the setting of the first paragraph different from the setting of the rest of the story?

   _____

   _____

   _____

4. Viewpoint
   a. Through whose eyes is the story told?

   _____

   b. How would the story be different if it were told through his wife's eyes?

   _____

   _____

   _____

   _____

5. Theme
   a. What happened in the marriage that might have caused the wife to have a secret affair?

   _____

   b. What does he mean when he says, "After the scene of my intervention it might be possible for me to regain control of my wife, but I should find her shattered and lifeless in my arms like the bird that my father placed in my hand"? (par. 17)

   _____

   _____

Exercise 24 **Identify Images and Metaphors**

Based on Reading 4, answer the following questions in your own words.

1. What are the main metaphors of "The Chase"? To whom are these metaphors applied?

   _____

   _____

2. What does the narrator mean when he says in paragraph 4 his wife was "wild" but became "tame"?

   _____

   _____

3. Find the metaphors in paragraph 6. Then explain how they deepen your understanding of "wild" and "tame"?

   _____

   _____

   _____

4. In paragraph 17, what does the writer (narrator) say is like the "shot my father fired"? What does he equate to the "free, unknowing bird"? How do these comparisons help you understand his decision?

   _____

   _____

   _____

   _____

©2007 Pearson Education, Inc.

5. What is the main metaphor embodied in the title, "The Chase"? (Perhaps the title refers to more than one aspect of the story.) Consider what is stated directly in the story, and then think about other possible levels of inference and interpretation.

_____

_____

Exercise 25 **Reflect**

Think about what you read in Reading 4 and what you already know about marriage. Answer the following questions, and prepare to discuss them with your classmates.

1. Why do you think the narrator's feelings toward his wife change again as he watches her through the window and then follows her to her rendezvous?

_____

_____

_____

2. What would you have done if you had been in the husband's place?

_____

_____

_____

3. What do you think will (or should) happen next?

_____

_____

_____

_____

4. Do you think it is inevitable that people who are married become "predictable" and "unexciting"?

_____

_____

_____

_____

CHAPTER REVIEW

✔ Reader's Checklist

Check (✔) the concepts and skills introduced in this chapter that you are confident you understand and can now use to help you interpret inferences and read literature effectively. If you are not sure about any items (1) go back to the explanations in the text, (2) study and review with other members of your college learning community, (3) ask your instructor for help, (4) check out the Web site for this book at **www.ablongman.com/alexander community4e** for additional exercises on understanding inferences and literature and to take the chapter quiz, or (5) complete additional practices in the *Reading Road Trip.*

❏ Inference
❏ Autobiography
❏ Irony
❏ Connotation
❏ Denotation
❏ Image
❏ Figurative language

❏ Simile
❏ Metaphor
❏ Characters
❏ Plot
❏ Setting
❏ Point of view
❏ Theme

When you are confident that you have mastered these concepts and skills, test yourself with Mastery Tests 6A and 6B (pp. 336–350).

Critical Reflections

Answer the following questions, and prepare to discuss them with your classmates.

1. Describe relationships between men and women in your college or workplace.

_____

_____

_____

_____

2. List how you think relationships between men and women are different today from relationships in your parents' or grandparents' generation?

_____

_____

_____

_____

©2007 Pearson Education, Inc.

3. What stereotypes do you think people have about men and women and their roles?

_____

_____

_____

_____

Writing Activity

1. Write a paragraph or short essay describing what you would consider to be an ideal relationship between a couple. Use your lists from "Critical Reflections" to develop your ideas.

2. Find a women's magazine, such as *Elle* or *Cosmopolitan,* and a magazine for men, such as *GQ* or *Esquire.* Compare the magazines. Write one or two paragraphs explaining how the magazines are similar and how they are different in their portrayal of women and men. For your paragraphs, focus on gender roles as portrayed in one of the following: the advertisements, an article or story in each, the photographs in each. What can you infer about gender roles from the visual and written contents of the magazines?

Classroom Community

1. Present your ideas about the "ideal relationship between a couple" to your class. With your classmates, prepare a list of the aspects of an "ideal relationship" on which you can all agree.

2. Present your findings about magazines directed at women and men. What can you conclude about gender roles today?

Extend Your Thinking

For more practice with understanding inferences and reading literature, read "Shame," by Dick Gregory, in "Extend Your Thinking," (pp.491–495).

Work the Web

As you have learned in Chapter 6, we use inferences to understand the meaning of a number of texts, including illustrations, poems, stories, and songs. The following exercise will give you further practice identifying imagery and figurative language and inferring meaning through analyzing song lyrics. A number of sites are devoted to providing the public with the lyrics of songs. For this exercise, find the lyrics to the following two songs, and then answer the questions below. (Go to http://www.google.com, type in the name of the song and the songwriter(s), and you'll get links to many sites.)

1. "Smoke Gets in Your Eyes," written by Jerome Kern and Otto Harbach, and performed by the Platters and others.

   a. What is love compared to in the song?

   _____

   _____

   b. Smoke is a central metaphor in this song. Explain the meaning of smoke and how it changes.

   _____

   _____

   _____

   _____

2. "A Boy Named Sue," written by Shel Silverstein and performed by Johnny Cash and others.

   a. What do we learn about the narrator of "A Boy Named Sue," the way he views his father, and their relationship based on the images Shel Silverstein uses and the plot of the song?

   _____

   _____

   _____

   _____

   b. What is the significance of the name Sue to the narrator of the song, and how has that name made him the man he is today?

   _____

   _____

   _____

   _____

   _____

Go to **www.ablongman.com/alexandercommunity4e** for additional Web-based activities.

©2007 Pearson Education, Inc.

Mastery Test   6A

Black Men and Public Space   Brent Staples

The following reading about how black men are perceived is based on the author's own experiences as a graduate student and as a journalist. The vocabulary he uses is quite difficult, but you will find that you can identify his thesis and supporting points even though you may not understand every word. As you read, compare Staples's experiences of being in public places to your own. Also, pay attention to his use of metaphors and descriptive language as he relates the incidents that support his thesis.

1   My first victim was a woman—white, well dressed, probably in her early twenties. I came upon her late one evening on a deserted street in Hyde Park, a relatively affluent neighborhood in an otherwise mean, impoverished section of Chicago. As I swung onto the avenue behind her, there seemed to be a discreet, uninflammatory distance between us. Not so. She cast back a worried glance. To her, the youngish black man—a broad six feet two inches with a beard and billowing hair, both hands shoved into the pockets of a bulky military jacket—seemed menacingly close. After a few more quick glimpses, she picked up her pace and was soon running in earnest. Within seconds she disappeared into a cross street.

2   That was more than a decade ago, I was twenty-two years old, a graduate student newly arrived at the University of Chicago. It was in the echo of that terrified woman's footfalls that I first began to know the unwieldy inheritance I'd come into—the ability to alter public space in ugly ways. It was clear that she thought herself the quarry of a mugger, a rapist, or worse. Suffering a bout of insomnia, however, I was stalking sleep, not defenseless wayfarers. As a softy who is scarcely able to take a knife to a raw chicken—let along hold one to a person's throat—I was surprised, embarrassed, and dismayed all at once. Her flight made me feel like an accomplice in tyranny. It also made it clear that I was indistinguishable from the muggers who occasionally seeped into the area from the surrounding ghetto. That first encounter, and those that followed, signified that a vast, unnerving gulf lay between nighttime pedestrians—particularly women—and me. And I soon gathered that being perceived as dangerous is a hazard in itself. I only needed to turn a corner into a dicey situation, or crowd some frightened, armed person in a foyer somewhere, or make an errant move after being pulled over by a policeman. Where fear and weapons meet—and they often do in urban America—there is always the possibility of death.

3   In that first year, my first away from my hometown, I was to become thoroughly familiar with the language of fear. At dark, shadowy intersections, I could cross in front of a car stopped at a traffic light and elicit the *thunk, thunk, thunk, thunk* of the driver—black, white, male, or female—hammering down the door locks. On less traveled streets after dark I grew accustomed to but never comfortable with people crossing to the other side of the street

rather than pass me. Then there were the standard unpleasantries with policemen, doormen, bouncers, cabdrivers, and others whose business it is to
screen out troublesome individuals *before* there is any nastiness. . . .

4   After dark, on the warrenlike streets of Brooklyn where I live, I often see
women who fear the worst from me. They seem to have set their faces on
neutral, and with their purse straps strung across their chests bandolier-
style, they forged ahead as though bracing themselves against being tack-
led. I understand, of course, that the danger they perceive is not a halluci-
nation. Women are particularly vulnerable to street violence, and young
black males are drastically overrepresented among the perpetrators of that
violence. Yet these truths are no <u>solace</u> against the kind of <u>alienation</u> that
comes of being ever the suspect, a fearsome entity with whom pedestrians
avoid making eye contact.

5   It is not altogether clear to me how I reached the ripe old age of twenty-
two without being conscious of the lethality nighttime pedestrians <u>attributed</u>
to me. Perhaps it was because in Chester, Pennsylvania, the small, angry industrial town where I came of age in the 1960s, I was scarcely noticeable
against a backdrop of gang warfare, street knifings, and murders. I grew up
one of the good boys, had perhaps a half-dozen fistfights. In retrospect, my
shyness of combat has clear sources.

6   As a boy, I saw countless tough guys locked away; I have since buried
several, too. They were babies, really—a teenage cousin, a brother of
twenty-two, a childhood friend in his mid-twenties—all gone down in
episodes of bravado played out in the streets. I came to doubt the virtues
of intimidation early on. I chose, perhaps unconsciously, to remain a
shadow—timid, but a survivor.

7   The fearsomeness mistakenly <u>attributed</u> to me in public places often
has a perilous flavor. The most frightening of these confusions occurred in
the late 1970s and early 1980s, when I worked as a journalist in Chicago.
One day, rushing into the office of a magazine I was writing for with a dead-
line story in hand, I was mistaken for a burglar. The office manager called
security and, with an <u>ad hoc</u> posse, pursued me through the labyrinthine
halls, nearly to my editor's door. I had no way of proving who I was. I could
only move briskly toward the company of someone who knew me.

8   Another time I was on assignment for a local paper and killing time before an interview. I entered a jewelry store on the city's affluent Near North
Side. The proprietor excused herself and returned with an enormous red
Doberman pinscher straining at the end of a leash. She stood, the dog extended toward me, silent to my questions, her eyes bulging nearly out of
her head. I took a cursory look around, nodded, and bade her good night.

9   Relatively speaking, however, I never fared as badly as another black
male journalist. He went to nearby Waukegan, Illinois, a couple of sum-
mers ago to work on a story about a murderer who was born there. Mis-
taking the reporter for the killer, police officers hauled him from his car at
gunpoint and but for his press credentials would probably have tried to
book him. Such episodes are not uncommon. Black men trade tales like
this all the time.

©2007 Pearson Education, Inc.

10   Over the years, I learned to smother the rage I felt at so often being taken for a criminal. Not to do so would surely have led to madness. I now take precautions to make myself less threatening. I move about with care, particularly late in the evening. I give wide <u>berth</u> to nervous people on subway platforms during the wee hours, particularly when I have exchanged business clothes for jeans. If I happen to be entering a building behind some people who appear skittish, I may walk by, letting them clear the lobby before I return, so as not to seem to be following them. I have been calm and extremely congenial on those rare occasions when I've been pulled over by the police.

11   And on late-evening <u>constitutionals</u> I employ what has proved to be an excellent tension-reducing measure: I whistle melodies from Beethoven and Vivaldi and the more popular classical composers. Even steely New Yorkers hunching toward nighttime destinations seem to relax, and occasionally they even join in the tune. Virtually everybody seems to sense that a mugger wouldn't be warbling bright, sunny selections from Vivaldi's *Four Seasons*. It is my equivalent of the cowbell that hikers wear when they know they are in bear country.

STAPLES, "Black Men and Public Space"

Exercise 1   **Work with Words**

Use context clues, your knowledge of word parts, and if necessary, your dictionary skills, to determine the meaning of the following words underlined in the reading. The paragraph number is provided in case you want to check the context.

1. *Uninflammatory* (par. 1)
   a. not causing excitement or anger
   b. not causing fire
   c. not causing inflammation

2. *Menacingly* (par. 1)
   a. in an extreme manner
   b. in a threatening manner
   c. in a comfortable manner

3. *Unwieldy* (par. 2)
   a. powerful
   b. predetermined
   c. difficult to manage

4. *Quarry* (par. 2)
   a. diamond shaped pane of glass
   b. game hunted with hawks
   c. something or someone being hunted

5. *Solace* (par. 4)
   a. source of relief
   b. source of additional worry
   c. certainty

6. *Alienation* (par. 4)
   a. feeling of self-worth
   b. isolation
   c. self-esteem

7. *Attributed* (par. 5 and par. 7)
   a. thought of as characteristic
   b. thought of as distinct
   c. thought of indifferently

8. *Ad hoc* (par. 7)
   a. improvised
   b. planned
   c. terrifying

9. *Berth* (par. 10)
   a. a place to sleep on a boat or train
   b. safe distance
   c. normal distance

10. *Constitutionals* (par. 11)
    a. things related to the Constitution
    b. things related to the government principles
    c. walks taken for one's health

| Exercise 2 | **Check Your Understanding** |

Based on the reading, Staples's "Black Men and Public Space," choose the best answer to the following multiple-choice questions.

1. Which of the following is the best topic for the reading?
   a. stereotypes about black men
   b. how best to exercise if you're a black man
   c. problems of black men

2. Which of the following sentences best states the main idea (thesis) of the reading?
   a. Black men are frequently guilty of crimes, and that's why people are afraid of them.
   b. Black men are frequently stereotyped as being criminals and dangerous.
   c. Educated black men are more likely to suffer from discrimination than any other group.

©2007 Pearson Education, Inc.

3. We can infer that Staples begins his essay by referring to his "first victim" to
   a. get our attention and recognition that he is seen as a criminal by people who don't know him.
   b. explain how he got into trouble with the law in the first place.
   c. make sure the reader knows that he is not a criminal.

4. When the author writes, "I was twenty-two years old, a graduate student newly arrived at the University of Chicago" we can infer that
   a. he was a poor student.
   b. he had a scholarship.
   c. he was not a criminal.

5. Staples supports his main idea (thesis) by
   a. providing personal examples and examples of acquaintances of people's fear of black men.
   b. demonstrating that he is a well-respected journalist and would therefore be a reliable source of information.
   c. explaining how it feels to be perceived as a dangerous person.

6. Although Staples had seen friends and family die young in the streets of Chester, Pennsylvania, he portrays himself as
   a. self-confident and tough.
   b. timid, but a survivor.
   c. a mere shadow.

7. Which of the following is *not* an example of Staples's "ability to alter public space in ugly ways"?
   a. People crossing the street when they see him.
   b. Shop owners getting their Doberman pinschers to scare him out of the store.
   c. Recognition he receives as an excellent journalist.

8. For Staples, knowing that he is perceived as a threat to others is
   a. not a major problem.
   b. extremely painful.
   c. simply a philosophical problem.

9. Why does Staples whistle melodies from classical music when he goes out at night?
   a. because he enjoys whistling.
   b. to make himself less threatening.
   c. to help him pace his walk.

10. In the last line of the essay, Staples writes that his whistling is his "equivalent of the cowbell that hikers wear when they know they are in bear country." We can infer that hikers wear cowbells
    a. so bears will hear them coming and stay out of their way.
    b. to make their hike more pleasant.
    c. so bears will come to them.

Exercise 3   **Interpret Figurative Language**

Based on the reading, answer the following questions about Staples's use of figurative language.

1. In paragraph 2, Staples reacts to the frightened woman's running from him by writing, "Suffering a bout of insomnia, however, I was stalking sleep, not defenseless wayfarers." What does the word *stalking* usually refer to? How does Staples use it here, and what is the effect?

   _____

   _____

   _____

   _____

2. In paragraph 3, Staples writes about "the language of fear." He is referring to things that people do when they are afraid. What examples does he give in the paragraph?

   _____

   _____

   _____

3. Staples writes that women who are afraid of him "seem to have set their faces on neutral" (par. 4). What image does this create, and what is its effect?

   _____

   _____

   _____

4. Staples writes "I chose, perhaps unconsciously, to remain a shadow—timid, but a survivor." (par. 6) What associations do you make with the word *shadow* and how does his use of this word affect our understanding?

   _____

   _____

   _____

5. In paragraph 10, Staples writes, "Over the years, I learned to smother the rage I felt at so often being taken for a criminal." What

does *smother* usually refer to? How does the use of *smother* make us understand his emotions?

_____

_____

_____

Exercise 4 **Reflect**

Think about what you read in "Black Men and Public Space" and what you already know about stereotypes. Then based on your reading and your previous knowledge answer the following questions.

1. In what ways do you think people's reactions would be different toward a black woman in a public space?

_____

_____

_____

2. How do you think a person's style of dress affects people's initial reactions? Explain your opinion with some examples.

_____

_____

_____

3. Have you ever been in a situation where you felt people made positive or negative assumptions about you on the basis of stereotypes of your gender or ethnicity?

_____

_____

_____

4. Have you ever avoided somebody you didn't know because of assumptions you made about that person? What were the circumstances, and what did you do? Why did you have those assumptions?

_____

_____

_____

Mastery Test

The Men We Carry in Our Minds

Scott Russell Sanders

In this essay, Scott Russell Sanders views relationships between men and women based on his childhood experiences of living in a poor, hardworking family. As you read, think about the differences between Sanders's background and assumptions, and how they compare to your own experiences.

1 "This must be a hard time for women," I say to my friend Anneke. "They have so many paths to choose from, and so many voices calling them."

2 "I think it's a lot harder for men," she replies.

3 "How do you figure that?"

4 "The women I know feel excited, innocent, like crusaders in a just cause. The men I know are eaten up with guilt."

5 "Women feel such pressure to be everything, do everything," I say. "Career, kids, art, politics. Have their babies and get back to the office a week later. It's as if they're trying to overcome a million years' worth of evolution in one lifetime."

6 "But we help one another. And we have this deep-down sense that we're in the *right*—we've been held back, passed over, used—while men feel they're in the wrong. Men are the ones who've been <u>discredited</u>, who have to search their souls."

7 I search my soul. I discover guilty feelings aplenty—toward the poor, the Vietnamese, Native Americans, the whales, an endless list of debts. But toward women I feel something more confused, a snarl of shame, envy, wary tenderness, and amazement. This muddle troubles me. To hide my <u>unease</u> I say, "You're right, it's tough being a man these days."

8 "Don't laugh," Anneke frowns at me. "I wouldn't be a man for anything. It's much easier being the victim. All the victim has to do is break free. The <u>persecutor</u> has to live with his past."

9 How deep is that past? I find myself wondering. How much of an inheritance do I have to throw off?

10 When I was a boy growing up on the back roads of Tennessee and Ohio, the men I knew labored with their bodies. They were <u>marginal</u> farmers, just scraping by, or welders, steelworkers, carpenters; they swept floors, dug ditches, mined coal, or drove trucks, their forearms ropy with muscle; they trained horses, stoked furnaces, made tires, stood on assembly lines wrestling parts onto cars and refrigerators. They got up before light, worked all day long whatever the weather, and when they came home at night they looked as though somebody had been whipping them. In the evenings and on weekends they worked on their own places, <u>tilling</u> gardens that were lumpy with clay, fixing broken-down cars, hammering on houses that were always too drafty, too leaky, too small.

©2007 Pearson Education, Inc.

11   The bodies of the men I knew were twisted and <u>maimed</u> in ways visible and invisible. The nails of their hands were black and split, the hands tattooed with scars. Some had lost fingers. Heavy lifting had given many of them finicky backs and guts weak from hernias. Racing against conveyor belts had given them ulcers. Their ankles and knees ached from years of standing on concrete. Anyone who had worked for long around machines was hard of hearing. They squinted, and the skin of their faces was creased like the leather of old work gloves. There were times, studying them, when I dreaded growing up. Most of them coughed, from dust or cigarettes, and most of them drank cheap wine or whiskey, so their eyes looked bloodshot and bruised. The fathers of my friends always seemed older than the mothers. Men wore out sooner. Only women lived into old age.

12   As a boy I also knew another sort of men, who did not sweat and break down like mules. They were soldiers, and so far as I could tell they scarcely worked at all. But when the shooting started, many of them would die. This was what soldiers were *for*, just as a hammer was for driving nails.

13   Warriors and <u>toilers</u>; those seemed, in my boyhood vision, to be the chief destinies for men. They weren't the only destinies, as I learned from having a few male teachers, from reading books, and from watching television. But the men on television—the politicians, the astronauts, the generals, the savvy lawyers, the philosophical doctors, the bosses who gave orders to both soldiers and laborers—seemed as <u>remote</u> and unreal to me as the figures in Renaissance tapestries. I could no more imagine growing up to become one of these cool, potent creatures than I could imagine becoming a prince.

14   A nearer and more hopeful example was that of my father, who had escaped from a red-dirt farm to a tire factory, and from the assembly line to the front office. Eventually he dressed in a white shirt and tie. He carried himself as if he had been born to work with his mind. But his body, remembering the earlier years of slogging work, began to give out on him in his fifties, and it quit on him entirely before he turned 65.

15   A scholarship <u>enabled</u> me not only to attend college, a rare enough <u>feat</u> in my circle, but even to study in a university meant for the children of the rich. Here I met for the first time young men who had assumed from birth that they would lead lives of comfort and power. And for the first time I met women who told me that men were guilty of having kept all the joys and privileges of the earth for themselves. I was baffled. What privileges? What joys? I thought about the maimed, <u>dismal</u> lives of most of the men back home. What had they stolen from their wives and daughters? The right to go five days a week, 12 months a year, for 30 or 40 years to a steel mill or a coal mine? The right to drop bombs and die in war? The right to feel every leak in the roof, every gap in the fence, every cough in the engine as a wound they must mend? The right to feel, when the layoff comes or the plant shuts down, not only afraid but ashamed?

16   I was slow to understand the deep grievances of women. This was because, as a boy, I had envied them. Before college, the only people I had ever known who were interested in art or music or literature, the only ones

who read books, the only ones who ever seemed to enjoy a sense of ease and grace were the mothers and daughters. Like the menfolk, they fretted about money, they scrimped and made do. But, when the pay stopped coming in, they were not the ones who had failed. Nor did they have to go to war, and that seemed to me a blessed fact. By comparison with the narrow, ironclad days of fathers, there was an expansiveness, I thought, in the days of mothers. They went to see neighbors, to shop in town, to run errands at school, at the library, at church. No doubt, had I looked harder at their lives, I would have envied them less. It was not my fate to become a woman, so it was easier for me to see the graces. I didn't see, then, what a prison a house could be, since houses seemed to me brighter, handsomer places than any factory. I did not realize—because such things were never spoken of—how often women suffered from men's bullying. Even then I could see how exhausting it was for a mother to cater all day to the needs of young children. But if I had been asked, as a boy, to choose between tending a baby and tending a machine, I think I would have chosen the baby. (Having now tended both, I know I would choose the baby.)

17   So I was baffled when the women at college accused me and my sex of having cornered the world's pleasures. I think something like my bafflement has been felt by other boys (and by girls as well) who grew up in dirt-poor farm country, in mining country, in black ghettos, in Hispanic barrios, in the shadows of factories, in Third World nations—any place where the fate of men is just as grim and bleak as the fate of women.

18   When the women I met at college thought about the joys and privileges of men, they did not carry in their minds the sort of men I had known in my childhood. They thought of their fathers, who were bankers, physicians, architects, stockbrokers, the big wheels of the big cities. They were never laid off, never short of cash at month's end, never lined up for welfare. These fathers made decisions that mattered. They ran the world.

19   The daughters of such men wanted to share in this power, this glory. So did I. They yearned for a say over their future, for jobs worthy of their abilities, for the right to live at peace, unmolested, whole. Yes, I thought, yes, yes. The difference between me and these daughters was that they saw me, because of my sex, as destined from birth to become like their fathers, and therefore as an enemy to their desires. But I knew better. I wasn't an enemy, in fact or in feeling. I was an ally. If I had known, then, how to tell them so, would they have believed me? Would they now?

SANDERS, "The Men We Carry in Our Minds"

Exercise 1   **Work with Words**

Use context clues, dictionary skills, and your knowledge of word parts to choose the best definition for each of the following words underlined in the reading. The paragraph number is provided in case you want to check the context.

© 2007 Pearson Education, Inc.

1. *Discredited* (par. 6)
   a. lacking believability
   b. being incredible
   c. not having economic credit

2. *Unease* (par. 7)
   a. not easy
   b. discomfort
   c. easy

3. *Persecutor* (par. 8)
   a. the victim
   b. the person who hurts the victim
   c. the person who grants the victim freedom

4. *Marginal* (par. 10)
   a. at the lower limits, poor
   b. situated on a border
   c. of or pertaining to the edge

5. *Tilling* (par. 10)
   a. breaking up the soil
   b. planting
   c. adding fertilizer

6. *Toilers* (par. 13)
   a. soldiers
   b. professionals
   c. workers

7. *Remote* (par. 13)
   a. close
   b. powerful
   c. distant

8. *Enabled* (par. 15)
   a. gave money
   b. made possible
   c. prevented

9. *Feat* (par. 15)
   a. great accomplishment
   b. grand plan
   c. ambitious goal

10. *Dismal* (par. 15)
    a. happy
    b. successful
    c. dreary

Exercise 2   **Check Your Understanding**

Based on the reading, Sanders's "The Men We Carry in Our Minds," choose the best answer to each of the following multiple-choice questions.

1. Which of the following sentences best states the main idea of the reading?
   a. Even though some women think that all men have a lot of power and an easy life, working-class men have very difficult lives.
   b. Women are the real victims of an unfair society.
   c. Women's lives, even working-class women's lives, are actually quite pleasant compared with the lives of men.

2. When Scott Russell Sanders wrote this essay,
   a. he was a student.
   b. he was not a student.
   c. he may or may not have been a student.

3. The author started thinking about the men in his life when he was growing up because
   a. his father passed away.
   b. a friend of his told him she thought men were persecutors.
   c. he was in the process of reconstructing his life.

4. The author grew up
   a. in the country.
   b. in the city.
   c. in the suburbs.

5. The author went to college because
   a. his parents scraped together enough money to send him.
   b. he worked his way through.
   c. he got a scholarship.

6. Sanders believed that women's lives were
   a. better than men's lives.
   b. easy.
   c. more difficult than men's lives.

7. Sanders admits that
   a. he was slow to understand the grievances of women.
   b. taking care of children is harder than taking care of a machine.
   c. he never was interested in sharing in the real power.

8. Sanders was confused when women at college accused him of being powerful because
   a. he didn't think there was anything wrong with being powerful.
   b. the men he had known in his life were not powerful.
   c. he thought that the really powerful people were educated women.

© 2007 Pearson Education, Inc.

9. Sanders felt like poor men were
   a. very different from women.
   b. in a position similar to women.
   c. in a position superior to women.

10. Sanders's essay, "The Men We Carry in Our Minds," discusses
    a. problems of social class.
    b. problems of power, gender, and social class.
    c. the problems of sexism for women who are trying to be successful.

Exercise 3   **Evaluate Inferences**

Based on the reading, put a check next to each of the following statements that is a reasonable inference.

_____ 1. Anneke, the woman Sanders refers to at the beginning of this essay, is probably from an upper-class family.

_____ 2. Sanders wants to follow his father's career path.

_____ 3. The author's understanding of gender roles was framed by his experiences and observations while he was growing up.

_____ 4. Depending on their economic status, people carry different men in their minds.

_____ 5. Sanders does agree that it is "tough" being a man because men have to live with guilt.

_____ 6. Anneke is planning to be a model housewife.

_____ 7. Sanders is not doing the kind of work his father did.

_____ 8. Sanders resents women for having it easier than men.

_____ 9. Sanders does not think that soldiers have it better than laborers.

_____ 10. Sanders likes to take care of children and would like to have a lot of them himself.

Exercise 4   **Interpret Figurative Language**

For each of the following sentences from "The Men We Carry in Our Minds," explain what Sanders is saying with his use of figurative language. Is he using a metaphor or a simile? How does the figurative language support the point the author wants to make?

1. As a boy I also knew another sort of men, who did not sweat and break down like mules. (par. 12)

_____

_____

2. But when the shooting started, many of them would die. This was what soldiers were *for*, just as a hammer was for driving nails. (par. 12)

_____

_____

3. The right to feel every leak in the roof, every gap in the fence, every cough in the engine as a wound they must mend? (par. 15)

_____

_____

4. I didn't see, then, what a prison a house could be. (par. 16)

_____

_____

5. They thought of their fathers, who were bankers, physicians, architects, stockbrokers, the big wheels of the cities. (par. 18)

_____

_____

_____

Exercise 5　　**Reflect**

Think about what you read in "Men We Carry in Our Minds" and what you already know about relationships and the lives of men and women. Then answer the following questions.

1. In your experience, who has more power, men or women? Give examples and explain what kind of power you mean (in the home, in the world, etc.).

_____

_____

_____

_____

© 2007 Pearson Education, Inc.

2. How do you think power should be divided in the home? at work? in society as a whole?

_____

_____

_____

_____

3. Thinking about the lives of the men and women you know, who do you think has it better and why? Explain your answer.

_____

_____

_____

_____

©2007 Pearson Education, Inc.

Chapter 7

Facts and Opinions

Living in a Diverse Society

We must learn to live together as brothers, or we are going to perish together as fools.

—DR. MARTIN LUTHER KING JR.

● What do you think is happening in this picture?

● What does the quotation mean? How does it relate to the picture?

PREPARE TO READ

Americans come from everywhere in the world. Even Native Americans are descendants of immigrants from Asia who crossed into North America some 20,000 years ago. After those immigrants came Europeans, Africans, and then Asians again, as well as people from Mexico and Central and South America. Today about 10 percent of the U.S. population was born elsewhere. Who is an American? What makes someone an American? How can those of us who live here—from so many different cultures and backgrounds—get along?

Purpose

In this chapter, you will learn to
- Recognize fact and opinion
- Understand the use and sources of facts
- Recognize an author's worldview, viewpoint, and purpose for writing
- Identify bias and tone

In the process of acquiring these skills, you will read about American diversity and its implications for our lives, regardless of our personal backgrounds.

Previous Knowledge

Answer the following questions and prepare to discuss them in class.

1. U.S. society is characterized by diversity—a variety of cultures, languages, national origins, and races. What is your ethnic background? List the different ethnic groups in your family.

   _____

2. Among the people you know, how many ethnic groups are represented? List them. Which ethnic groups are unfamiliar to you?

   _____

Preview and Predict

Preview Chapter 7. Based on your preview, predict two things you think you will learn in this chapter.

1. _____

2. _____

Write two questions that you think will be answered in this chapter.

1. _____

2. _____

©2007 Pearson Education, Inc.

Reading 1   *Identity in Transformation*   Yasmin Ahmed

Yasmin Ahmed was a student at San Diego City College when she wrote this essay. She was taking advanced courses in sciences but volunteered to write something about her experiences for A Community of Readers *because she wanted people to know what life is like for people like her— refugees from different parts of the world who have adopted the United States as their home.*

1   I spent the first years of my life growing up in East Africa. I was born in Somalia, but the civil war forced us to flee and live as refugees in Kenya and Ethiopia. When I was seven years old, I immigrated to the United States. At first, getting adjusted to a completely new culture was a shock, but I have since worked to integrate Western culture into the culture of my family and my heritage. I now lead a life with two different cultures wrapped around each other. But I am not the only one whose life is like this. There are many of us; we are East African Muslim girls struggling with the process of assimilation into American culture. Immigrating to the West has changed us for the better, but it has also introduced us to a puzzling, complex world.

2   Back home in East Africa, life for most young girls is much different from life for girls in the United States. The future of a girl in Somalia is determined by her family, culture, and religion. Girls are expected to grow up to fulfill their duties as mothers and wives and to remain disciplined, devout, respectful, and shy. From early childhood, girls are aware that their primary goal is to get married, and they are usually married by the time they

are sixteen. Families prepare their daughters for arranged marriages to older, already-established men, often men whom the girls have neither met nor seen. Once married, women are expected to cook, clean, bear children, and nurture the family, while men are expected to provide an income and the leadership for the family to survive. These roles limit the educational possibilities for girls. Education is scarce for most of the Somali population, especially those living in the countryside, but for citizens of the city, educational opportunities can, with effort, be pursued for boys. For girls, the paths are virtually closed.

3   The disparity between the way women and girls are viewed in Somalia and the opportunities they have in the United States made me appreciate the chance to come to the United States and share in the experiences of real American girls. Immigration to the United States provided me and my family with a life that was very different from anything we had ever known. As they incorporated the cultural and social expectations of the United States, my family changed their expectations for me. Equal opportunities were presented to me in ways that I had never dreamed before. I went to the same schools as my brothers, and my parents accepted the idea that I could be educated and even successful in a career. Marriage no longer became the first concern for girls, and I am so happy that I'm not at the moment being pressured to get married even though I'm already eighteen.

4   In spite of the changes in our families, though, we didn't forget who we are. Our social and cultural identity as Somali girls remained and at the same time was lost within the rushing of American crowds. We didn't picture ourselves different from anyone else, and in many ways we still don't. We watched the same television shows, listened to the same music, gossiped about the same celebrities, and bought magazines just to see the latest fashions. We led the same lives as other American children; nobody made us feel different. We were accepted as Somali Muslim girls living life with a Western flare. We were not discriminated against for who we were. At times we were asked curious questions, especially about how we dress, but nothing out of the ordinary.

5   Then, with the devastating attacks of September 11, everything changed for us, as well as for the country around us. Like our fellow Americans we lived life the next few days with our noses glued to the TV, fascinated by the reports, horror struck by the death tolls. Like all Americans, we mourned for the innocent dead, hated the terrorists who killed them, and decried the effects of this tragic day on our country and on our lives. We were reminded of the civil war taking place back home in Somalia, and we remembered how tragedy can corrupt daily life.

6   Though we endured the sadness of September 11 just like all Americans, the weeks, months, and even years that followed were no longer the same for us Muslim girls. None of the terrorists was Somali, but we began experiencing prejudice and discrimination as we had never known existed. People who never cared to look twice at us were now staring at us. The scarf that each of us wore on our head as an expression of our religious beliefs

became a center of attention and a symbol of terrorism. Our classmates began to whisper behind our backs, and some would go so far as to yell out "Terrorists!" or "Where is your Uncle Osama?" For those of us who wore black, kids would comment, "Here comes little Darth Vader." It was frustrating to hear such things out of the mouths of my friends and classmates; I can't even imagine where the idea of "Uncle Osama" or "little Darth Vader" came from. The most unbelievable change was that our teachers excluded us from the discussion of current and world events and looked at us suspiciously. Suddenly, we were less American because we chose to cover our heads, because we dressed like the women in the countries that our country was at war with. We were easier to identify, at least on the street, than Muslim men and therefore more likely to be discriminated against.

7   The ridicule and disdain we experienced were so hurtful that some of my friends chose to stay home from school. Others became more conservative in covering themselves just to show they were proud of their religion. The effect of the prejudice we endured in some ways parallels what we faced in East Africa—this time not because of our gender, but because of our religious affiliation. Now we speculate what people might be thinking about us when they see us: do they think of us as a threat ("Could she be a sister of a terrorist?") or as a victim ("Her husband or family must force her to wear that scarf, poor little thing")? Before we felt like American girls from another country. Now we feel we're first seen as Muslims (read terrorist), then as women, and last as human beings.

8   Muslim men have been more discriminated against by government agencies. Men older than sixteen from Muslim, Arab, and South Asian countries were required to report to the office of Immigration and Naturalization Services. Some were deported for visa violations, and some were detained for a long time, out of contact with the outside world, without knowing the charges against them and without having access to lawyers. Though the government has not revealed the total number of people detained since 9/11, the American Civil Liberties Union estimates that there were between three and five thousand Muslim, Arab, and South Asian detainees, none of whom had been charged with terrorist-related crimes.[1] It's just wrong to lump us all into one category. When Timothy McVeigh bombed the Oklahoma City Federal Building, nobody began rounding up white men or making stupid comments to their sisters. That would have been ridiculous, of course. So why don't people recognize that it's ridiculous to suspect all Muslims, or people who are Arab (and not necessarily Muslim), or people from South Asia?

9   At a time when Americans needed to lean on each other for support and comfort, we were leaning on empty space. We felt the pressure of being attacked from both sides: as Americans, we too had been attacked by the terrorists; as Muslims, we were now being attacked by our neighbors, harassed by people on the streets, and targeted by law enforcement agencies. In what is supposed to be a melting pot of various immigrant cultures that contributed to what is now America, we, as Muslims, are the ingredient

©2007 Pearson Education, Inc.

that causes suspicion. It is only those people who know the truth about who we are, the Americans who get to know us as individuals, who can get through this wall of prejudice. But my identity as a Muslim American has changed forever since the attacks of September 11, 2001.

Note

1. Many men from our mosque had to report to the immigration authorities, but not Somali men with refugee status in the United States. Other men have been interviewed by the Federal Bureau of Investigation.

AHMED, "Identity in Transformation"

Exercise 1   ## Recall and Discuss

Based on Reading 1, Ahmed's "Identity in Transformation," answer the following questions and prepare to discuss them with your classmates.

1. In what ways was Ahmed's life transformed when she came to the United States? How was her life different from what it would have been like had she remained in Somalia?

_____

_____

_____

2. How did Ahmed's life change after 9/11?

_____

_____

3. Why does Ahmed refer to Timothy McVeigh, the man convicted of bombing the Oklahoma City Federal Building?

_____

_____

4. At the end of her essay, what does Ahmed suggest would reduce the prejudice that she has experienced? Do you agree with her?

_____

_____

5. Now that you have read Ahmed's essay, look at the photograph of young Somali women on page 353. Has your reaction to the women changed from when you first saw them? What do you think about

the photo now that you know some of the experiences of these girls in the United States?

_____

_____

_____

FACT AND OPINION

As an active reader, you reflect on what you have read and you think critically about the information you have received. One important way to evaluate that information is by deciding whether it is based on fact or opinion—or both.

Fact

fact A piece of information that is verifiable

A **fact** is a piece of information that is verifiable, which means it can be checked. The easiest facts to identify are statements that include data such as dates, statistics, or numerical results of a study. Here is an example of a factual statement that includes data. "In 1905, the number of immigrants to the United States topped 1 million for the first time." If you read this sentence in an American history textbook, you would assume that it is correct because it is the kind of figure that could be obtained from immigration records. Statements of fact can also be easily checked for accuracy. For example, Yasmin Ahmed, in "Identity in Transformation" on pages 353 through 356, says that the civil war in Somalia "forced us to flee." We could verify information about the civil war and refugees leaving Somalia by checking in an encyclopedia or textbook or on a reputable site on the Web.

Opinion

opinion An interpretation of facts; an expression of beliefs or feelings

An **opinion** is an interpretation of information. It is also the expression of beliefs or feelings. Unlike statements of fact, statements of opinion do not usually provide data, or if they do, the data are used to support the opinion. The most obvious opinion statement includes language that acknowledges the opinion, such as "in my opinion," or "Ahmed thinks." An example of an opinion that Ahmed expresses in her essay is "Before we felt like American girls from another country. Now we feel we're first seen as Muslims (read terrorist), then as women, and last as human beings."

value words Words that indicate judgment

Another kind of opinion statement that is easy to recognize includes a value judgment, such as "Immigration is good for the United States" or Ahmed's statement, "Immigrating to the West has changed us for the better, but it has also introduced us to a puzzling, complex world." **Value words** indicate judgment. Examples such as _good, bad, detrimental, positive, negative, terrific,_ and _awful_ are usually good indicators that an opinion is being expressed (see Table 7.1, p. 358).

©2007 Pearson Education, Inc.

Table 7.1	Facts and Opinions

Facts	Opinions
Data	Interpretation of information
Statistics	Expression of beliefs, feelings, value judgments
Verifiable information	Language cues: acknowledge opinion, value words

Exercise 2   Report Facts and Opinions

In the columns below, write three facts and three opinions about your family.

Facts	Opinions
1.	1.
2.	2.
3.	3.

◆

Recognizing Fact and Opinion

Often a writer mixes facts and opinions or uses facts to support opinions. For example, in the following excerpt from Reading 1, Ahmed uses a combination of factual statements and opinions. (We added the numbers in parentheses and the italics.)

> (1) Muslim men have been more discriminated against by government agencies. (2) Men older than age sixteen from Muslim, Arab, and South Asian countries were required to report to the office of Immigration and Naturalization Services. (3) Some were deported for visa violations, and some were detained for a long time, out of contact with the outside world, without knowing the charges against them and without having access to lawyers. (4) Though the government has not revealed the total number of people detained since 9/11, the American Civil Liberties Union estimates that there are between three and five thousand Muslim, Arab, and South Asian detainees, none of whom have been charged with terrorist-related crimes.[1] (5) It's just *wrong* to lump us all into one category. When Timothy McVeigh bombed the Oklahoma City Federal Building, nobody began rounding up white men or making stupid comments to their sisters. (6) That would have been *ridiculous*, of course. (7) So why don't people recognize that it's *ridiculous* to suspect all Muslims, or people who are Arab (and not necessarily Muslim), or people from South Asia? (Ahmed, "Identity in Transformation")

The words we've italicized in this paragraph—*ridiculous* and *wrong*—provide judgments or opinions about the topic. These particular words reflect how Ahmed felt about some events in the post-9/11 world. Sentences 3 and 4 are predominantly factual because the information could be checked in newspaper articles reporting on the activities of the Immigration and Naturalization Services or statements of the American Civil Liberties Union. Sentences 5, 6, and 7 are predominantly opinion because they express how the author interprets the facts. As you read, you should be going through a natural filtering process to distinguish between the facts and the opinions.

Exercise 3   ### Recognize Fact and Opinion

Review these sentences from or based on Reading 1, and label them *F* if they are primarily factual and *O* if they are primarily opinion. Be aware of value words that influence your decision.

_____ 1. Back home in East Africa, life for most young girls is much different from life for girls in the United States.

_____ 2. Education is scarce for most of the Somali population, especially those living in the countryside, but for citizens of the city, educational opportunities can, with effort, be pursued for boys.

_____ 3. The opportunities women have in the United States made me appreciate the chance to come to the United States and share in the experiences of real American girls.

_____ 4. I am so happy that I'm not at the moment being pressured to get married, even though I'm already eighteen.

_____ 5. We didn't picture ourselves different from anyone else, and in many ways we still don't.

_____ 6. None of the terrorists was Somali.

_____ 7. Suddenly, we were less American because we chose to cover our heads, because we dressed like the women in the countries that our country was at war with.

_____ 8. Some of my friends chose to stay home from school.

_____ 9. No matter how anybody treated us, most of us became even more proud of our religion.

_____ 10. It is only those people who know the truth about who we are, the Americans who get to know us as individuals, who can get through this wall of prejudice.

Exercise 4   ### Recognize Fact and Opinion

The following statements from four American history textbooks deal with issues central to the American colonies—immigration and slavery.

©2007 Pearson Education, Inc.

Read each statement and indicate whether you think it is primarily fact or opinion.

_____ 1. Between 1700 and 1760 the colonial population mushroomed from 250,000 to 1.6 million persons—and 2.5 million by 1775. (Martin et al., *America and Its Peoples*)

_____ 2. "Pennsylvania, founded by the English, [will] become a colony of aliens, who will shortly be so numerous as to Germanize us, instead of our Anglifying them," since they "will never adopt our language or customs any more than they can acquire our complexion." (Benjamin Franklin, quoted in Martin et al., *America and Its Peoples*)

_____ 3. Many destitute Germans crossed the Atlantic as "redemptioners.". . . [F]amilies migrated together and shippers promised heads of households a few days' time, upon arrival in America, to find some person or group to pay for the family's passage in return for a set number of years of labor (usually three to six years per family member). (Martin et al., *America and Its Peoples*)

_____ 4. Slaves and indentured servants made up most of the incoming human tide after 1713. The traffic in servants became a regular part of the commerce linking Europe and America. (Nash et al., *The American People*)

_____ 5. Shipboard conditions for servants worsened in the eighteenth century and were hardly better than aboard the slave ships. Crammed between decks in stifling air, servants suffered from smallpox and fevers, rotten food, impure water, cold, and lice. (Nash et al., *The American People*)

_____ 6. Carolina's demand for slaves was so great that Charleston became the major port of entry for Africans brought to the American mainland from Africa and the Caribbean. By the time of the American Revolution almost one hundred thousand slaves had entered through Charleston harbor, most of them bound for the rice-growing regions of the colony. (Horton and Horton, *Hard Road to Freedom*)

_____ 7. Slavery made possible the existence of a gracious and cultured upper class that, with its leisure, guarded the highest refinements of human achievement. (Conlin, *American Past*)

_____ 8. "Men who emigrate are from the nature of their circumstances, the most active, hardy, daring, bold and resolute spirits, and probably the most mischievous also." (An Englishman quoted in Nash et al., *The American People*)

_____ 9. All told, as many as 21 million people were captured in West Africa between 1700 and 1850: some 9 million among them entered the Americas as slaves, but millions died before or during the Atlantic crossing. (Davidson et al., _Nation of Nations_)

_____ 10. Charles Woodmason, an Anglican missionary in the Carolina backcountry, lamented the arrival of "5 or 6000 Ignorant, mean, worthless, beggarly Irish Presbyterians, the Scum of the Earth, the Refuse of Mankind," who "delighted in a low, lazy, sluttish, heathenish, hellish life." (Quoted in Davidson et al., _Nation of Nations_)

EVALUATING FACTS

Although facts can be verified, they may not always tell the whole truth. The way facts are presented can sometimes distort the conclusions that you might draw from them. For example, public health officials know that the way risk statistics are presented makes a difference in how people react to them. Saying "0.7 percent of people will contract a certain disease" does not make an impact. But if the information is given as "7 out of 1,000 people will contract a certain disease," people regard the risk as much greater and take the warning more seriously—even though the information is the same.

Other questions to ask yourself in evaluating facts are: (1) What are the sources of the facts? and (2) Which facts are included and which are omitted?

What Are the Sources of the Facts?

In many types of readings, especially in scholarly works, you will find the sources of information in endnotes or references that appear in parentheses after a statement. Sometimes this information will be in a section of credits. In this textbook the bibliography, starting on page 577, gives complete information about the sources for readings used in this book, and you can look at the credits section, starting on page 580, to find out who gave permission to use this material.

Often the organization sponsoring the reading is a good indication of the source, and knowing its agenda can help you evaluate the facts. For example, when legislation is proposed to reduce greenhouse gases by improving the fuel efficiency of cars—important for reducing global warming—the auto industry responds by saying that the proposals are "costly and ineffective." An important question would be "Costly to

©2007 Pearson Education, Inc.

whom?" Increasing the fuel efficiency of cars, sport-utility vehicles, and trucks could very likely be a savings to owners, who would end up spending much less money on gas. These cars might be more costly, though, to manufacture (although some consumer advocates say this isn't true), and higher prices might reduce sales. Because the auto industry perceives emission controls and fuel efficiency to be against its interests, it will organize its research and use statistics to prove its position. Consumer advocacy groups, however, will counter the auto industry by asserting that vehicles have already been developed that are more fuel efficient, safer, and even less expensive to produce than what is on the market today. And these groups will also have studies and statistics to back up their assertions. As an alert and informed reader, it is up to you to evaluate the information you get. Recognizing the source of the information can be a clue to you that the facts are being presented to make you have a particular opinion—and only that opinion.

Exercise 5 — Consider the Source

Look through some newspapers and magazines. Select an advertisement that includes what appear to be statements of fact.

1. On a separate sheet of paper, make a list showing which facts are given and explaining how they might be presented in a certain way to influence your thinking.

2. Make a second list of what additional facts you might like to have.

3. Bring in the advertisement or a photocopy of it to share with classmates and to explain your lists.

◆

Which Facts Are Included?

Another important way to evaluate facts is to examine which facts are actually included. It is obviously impossible for an author to include every known detail about a specific topic. As a reader, you expect experts in various disciplines to select the most important information for you to learn. However, what information an author chooses to include, or exclude, strongly influences your understanding of what you read. **Inclusion** has become an important criteria for readers to consider when they begin to evaluate a text. Many school districts, for example, require that textbooks include information about people with disabilities, a group that has frequently gone unmentioned in history and social studies texts.

inclusion Which facts are included

Exercise 6 — Check for Inclusion

Read the following two excerpts from political science textbooks. Both cover U.S. population and immigration in roughly the same periods, but they do not present the same information. Examine what is included and what is excluded by each author. Then use the data supplied by each text to complete the table titled "The Origins of Immigrants" (p. 364). After the dates given in the table, write the types of immigrants that came into the United States at that time. The first row of the table has been done for you.

From *Government in America*

The United States has always been a nation of immigrants. As Lyndon Johnson said, America is "not merely a nation but a nation of nations." All Americans except for American Indians are either descended from immigrants or are immigrants themselves. Today federal law allows up to 630,000 new immigrants to be legally admitted every year. This is equivalent to adding a city with the population of Washington, D.C., every year.

There have been three great waves of immigration to the United States.

- Before the Civil War, northwestern Europeans (English, Irish, Germans, and Scandinavians) constituted the first wave of immigration.

- After the Civil War, southern and eastern Europeans (Italians, Jews, Poles, Russians, and others) made up the second wave. This immigration reached its high point in the first decade of the twentieth century, with almost all of these immigrants passing through Ellis Island in New York (now a popular museum) as their first stop in the new world.

- After World War II, Hispanics (from Cuba, Puerto Rico, Central America, and Mexico) and Asians (from Vietnam, Korea, the Philippines, and elsewhere) made up the third wave. The 1980s saw the second largest number of immigrants of any decade in American history. (Edwards et al. *Government in America*)

From *Struggle for Democracy*

Ours is an ethnically, religiously, and racially diverse society. The white European Protestants, black slaves, and Native Americans who made up the bulk of the U.S. population when the first census was taken in 1790 were joined by Catholic immigrants from Germany and Ireland in the 1840s and 1850s. In the 1870s, large numbers of Chinese migrated to America, drawn by jobs in railroad construction. Around the turn of the century, most immigration was from eastern, central, and southern Europe, with its diverse ethnic, language, and religious groups. Today, most immigration is from Asia and Latin America. The most recent immigration, like all the previous ones, has both added to the rich language, cultural, and religious diversity of our nation and created significant political and social tensions. (Greenberg and Page, *The Struggle for Democracy*)

©2007 Pearson Education, Inc.

Table 7.2	The Origins of Immigrants

Government in America	The Struggle for Democracy
Before Civil War (to 1861) *Northwestern European. English, Irish, Germans, Scandinavians*	1790 census *European Protestants, black slaves, and Native Americans*
	1840s and 1850s
After Civil War (1865–)	1870s
First decade of the twentieth century (1900–1910)	Turn of century (1900)
After World War II (1946–)	Today

Exercise 7	Reflect

Based on Exercise 6, answer the following questions and prepare to discuss them with your classmates.

1. In what ways do the two sets of information differ?

———————————————————————————

———————————————————————————

2. Are these differences important? Explain your answer.

———————————————————————————

———————————————————————————

———————————————————————————

3. Later in the same section, the authors of *Government in America* describe the African Americans in the United States by saying, "These are the descendants of reluctant immigrants, namely Africans who were brought to America by force as slaves." What do you think about calling slaves "reluctant immigrants"?

———————————————————————————

———————————————————————————

———————————————————————————

©2007 Pearson Education, Inc.

Reading 2

Colorblind: When Blacks and Whites Can See No Gray
Alex Kotlowitz

The following reading first appeared in the New York Times Magazine *on January 11, 1998. Alex Kotlowitz is the author of* The Other Side of the River: A Story of Two Towns, a Death and America's Dilemma, *a detailed account of the atmosphere of racial tensions surrounding a young boy's death in southwestern Michigan.*

1   One Christmas day seven years ago, I'd gone over to the Henry Horner Homes in Chicago to visit with Lafeyette and Pharoah, the subjects of my book *There Are No Children Here.* I had brought presents for the boys, as well as a gift for their friend Rickey, who lived on the other side of the housing complex, an area controlled by a rival gang. Lafeyette and Pharoah insisted on walking over with me. It was eerily quiet, since most everyone was inside, and so, bundled from the cold, we strolled toward the other end in silence. As we neared Damen Avenue, a kind of demilitarized zone, a uniformed police officer, a white woman, approached us. She looked first at the two boys, neither of whom reached my shoulder, and then directly at me. "Are you O.K.?" she asked.

2   About a year later, I was with Pharoah on the city's North Side, shopping for high-tops. We were walking down the busy street, my hand on Pharoah's shoulder, when a middle-aged black man approached. He looked at me, and then at Pharoah. "Son," he asked, "are you O.K.?"

3   Both this white police officer and middle-aged black man seemed certain of what they witnessed. The white woman saw a white man possibly in trouble; the black man saw a black boy possibly in trouble. It's all about perspective—which has everything to do with our personal and collective experiences, which are consistently informed by race. From those experiences, from our histories, we build myths, legends that both guide us and constrain us, legends that include both fact and fiction. This is not to say the truth doesn't matter. It does, in a big way. It's just that getting there may not be easy, in part because everyone is so quick to choose sides, to refute the other's myths and to pass on their own. . . .

4   While myths help us make sense of the incomprehensible, they can also confine us, confuse us and leave us prey to historical laziness. Moreover, truth is not always easily discernible—and even when it is, the prism, depending on which side of the river you reside on, may create a wholly different illusion. . . . We—blacks and whites—need to examine and question our own perspectives. Only then can we grasp each other's myths and grapple with the truths.

5   In 1992, I came across the story of a 16-year-old black boy, Eric McGinnis, whose body had been found a year earlier floating in the St. Joseph River in southwestern Michigan. The river flows between Benton Harbor and St. Joseph, two small towns whose only connections are two bridges and a powerful undertow of contrasts.

6   St. Joseph is a town of 9,000, and, with its quaint downtown and brick-paved streets, resembles a New England tourist haunt. But for those in Benton Harbor, St. Joseph's most defining characteristic is its racial makeup: it is 95 percent white. Benton Harbor, a town of 12,000 on the other side of the river, is 92 percent black and dirt poor. For years, the municipality was so hurt for money that it could not afford to raze abandoned buildings.

7   Eric, a high-school sophomore whose passion was dancing, was last seen at the Club, a teen-age nightspot in St. Joseph, where weeks earlier he had met and started dating a white girl. The night Eric disappeared, a white man said he caught the boy trying to break into his car and chased him—away from the river, past an off-duty white deputy sheriff. That was the last known moment he was seen alive, and it was then that the myths began.

8   I became obsessed with Eric's death, and so for five years moved in and out of these two communities, searching for answers to both Eric's disappearance and to matters of race. People would often ask which side of the river I was staying on, wanting to gauge my allegiance. And they would often ask about the secrets of those across the way or, looking for affirmation, repeat myths passed on from one generation to the next.

9   Once, during an unusually bitter effort by white school-board members to fire Benton Harbor's black superintendent, one black woman asked me: "How do you know how to do this? Do you take lessons? How do you all stick together the way you do?" Of course, we don't. Neither community is as unified or monolithic as the other believes. Indeed, contrary to the impression of those in St. Joseph, the black community itself was deeply divided in its support for the superintendent, who was eventually fired.

10   On occasion, whites in St. Joseph would regale me with tales of families migrating to Benton Harbor from nearby states for the high welfare benefits. It is, they would tell me, the reason for the town's economic decline. While some single mothers indeed moved to Benton Harbor and other Michigan cities in the early '80s to receive public assistance, the truth is that in the '30s and '40s, factories recruited blacks from the South, and when those factories shut down, unemployment, particularly among blacks, skyrocketed.

11   But the question most often asked was: "Why us? Why write about St. Joseph and Benton Harbor?" I would tell them that while the contrasts between the towns seem unusually stark, they are, I believe, typical of how most of us live: physically and spiritually isolated from one another.

12   It's not that I didn't find individuals who crossed the river to spend time with their neighbors. One St. Joseph woman, Amy Johnson, devotes her waking hours to a Benton Harbor community center. And Eric McGinnis himself was among a handful of black teen-agers who spent weekend nights at the Club in St. Joseph. Nor is it that I didn't find racial animosity. One St. Joseph resident informed me that Eric got what he deserved: "That nigger came on the wrong side of the bridge," he said. And Benton Harbor's former schools superintendent, Sherwin Allen, made no effort to hide his contempt for the white power structure.

13   What I found in the main, though, were people who would like to do right but don't know where to begin. As was said of the South's politicians

during Jim Crow, race diminishes us. It incites us to act as we wouldn't in other arenas: clumsily, cowardly and sometimes cruelly. We circle the wagons, watching out for our own.

14   That's what happened in the response to Eric's death. Most everyone in St. Joseph came to believe that Eric, knowing the police were looking for him, tried to swim the river to get home and drowned. Most everyone in Benton Harbor, with equal certitude, believes that Eric was killed—most likely by whites, most likely because he dated a white girl. I was struck by the disparity in perspective, the competing realities, but I was equally taken aback by the distance between the two towns—which, of course, accounts for the myths. Jim Reeves, the police lieutenant who headed the investigation into Eric's death, once confided that this teen-ager he'd never met had more impact on him than any other black person.

15   I'm often asked by whites, with some wonderment, how it is that I'm able to spend so much time in black communities without feeling misunderstood or unwelcomed or threatened. I find it much easier to talk to blacks about race than with fellow whites. While blacks often brave slights silently for fear that if they complain they won't be believed, when asked, they welcome the chance to relate their experiences. Among whites, there's a reluctance—or a lack of opportunity—to engage. Race for them poses no urgency; it does not impose on their daily routines. I once asked Ben Butzbaugh, a St. Joseph commissioner, how he felt the two towns got along. "I think we're pretty fair in this community," he said. "I don't know that I can say I know of any out-and-out racial-type things that occur. I just think people like their own better than others. I think that's pretty universal. Don't you? . . . We're not a bunch of racists. We're not anything America isn't." Butzbaugh proudly pointed to his friendship with Renée Williams, Benton Harbor's new schools superintendent. "Renée was in our home three, four, five days a week," he noted. "Nice gal. Put herself through school. We'd talk all the time." Williams used to clean for Butzbaugh's family.

16   As I learned during the years in and out of these towns, the room for day-to-day dialogue doesn't present itself. We become buried in our myths, certain of our truths—and refuse to acknowledge what the historian Allan Nevins calls "the grains of stony reality" embedded in most legends. A quarter-century ago, race was part of everyday public discourse; today it haunts us quietly, though on occasion—the Rodney King beating or the Simpson trial or Eric McGinnis's death—it erupts with jarring urgency. At these moments of crisis, during these squalls, we flail about, trying to find moral ballast. By then it is usually too late. The lines are drawn. Accusations are hurled across the river like cannon fire. And the cease-fires, when they occur, are just that, cease-fires, temporary and fragile. Even the best of people have already chosen sides.

Kotlowitz, "Colorblind"

Exercise 8   ## Work with Words

The following sentences appear in Reading 2, Kotlowitz's "Colorblind." Use context clues, dictionary skills, and your knowledge of word parts to

©2007 Pearson Education, Inc.

determine the meaning of each italicized word or phrase. Write the meaning of the word on the lines provided. The paragraph number is provided in case you want to check the context.

1. Both this white police officer and middle-aged black man seemed certain of what they witnessed. The white woman saw a white man possibly in trouble; the black man saw a black boy possibly in trouble. It's all about *perspective*—which has everything to do with our personal and collective experiences, which are consistently informed by race. (par. 3)

   Perspective: _____

2. From those experiences, from our histories, we build myths, legends that both guide us and *constrain* us, legends that include both fact and fiction. (par. 3)

   Constrain: _____

3. This is not to say the truth doesn't matter. It does, in a big way. It's just that getting there may not be easy, in part because everyone is so quick to choose sides, to *refute* the other's myths and to pass on their own. (par. 3)

   Refute: _____

4. While myths help us make sense of the incomprehensible, they can also confine us, confuse us and leave us *prey to* historical laziness. (par. 4)

   Prey to: _____

5. Moreover, truth is not always easily *discernible*—and even when it is, the *prism*, depending on which side of the river you reside on, may create a wholly different illusion. (par. 4)

   Discernible: _____

6. *Prism:* _____

7. And they would often ask about the secrets of those across the way or, looking for *affirmation*, repeat myths passed on from one generation to the next. (par. 8)

   Affirmation: _____

8. Neither community is as unified or *monolithic* as the other believes. (par. 9)

   Monolithic: _____

9. As was said of the South's politicians during *Jim Crow*, race diminishes us. (par. 13)

   Jim Crow: _____

10. Most everyone in Benton Harbor, with equal *certitude,* believes that Eric was killed—most likely by whites, most likely because he dated a white girl. (par. 14)

   Certitude: _____

| Exercise 9 | **Check Your Understanding** |

Based on Reading 2, answer the following questions in your own words.

1. Write the thesis of Reading 2.

   _____

   _____

   _____

2. Paragraphs 1 through 3 are organized around two examples. What are the examples, and what point is Kotlowitz making by using those examples?

   _____

   _____

   _____

   _____

3. How did people on each side of the river decide that Eric McGinnis died?

   _____

   _____

   _____

4. Why was Kotlowitz interested in writing about St. Joseph and Benton Harbor?

   _____

   _____

   _____

5. Why does Kotlowitz say that black people talk to him about race more than white people do?

   _____

   _____

   _____

©2007 Pearson Education, Inc.

Exercise 10 ## Recognize Fact and Opinion

The following sentences appear in or are based on Reading 2. For each sentence, write *F* on the blank if the statement is primarily factual and *O* if it is primarily opinion.

_____ 1. St. Joseph is a town of 9,000.

_____ 2. But for those in Benton Harbor, St. Joseph's most defining characteristic is its racial makeup.

_____ 3. Eric, a high-school sophomore whose passion was dancing, was last seen at the Club, a teen-age nightspot in St. Joseph, where weeks earlier he had met and started dating a white girl.

_____ 4. Eric was trying to steal a car.

_____ 5. A man "caught the boy trying to break into his car."

_____ 6. Eric drowned because he tried to swim across the river to get away from the police.

_____ 7. Eric was murdered because he was dating a white girl.

_____ 8. Eric got what he deserved.

_____ 9. Benton Harbor was in economic decline because families moved there for the generous welfare benefits.

_____ 10. In the '30s and '40s, factories recruited blacks from the South, and when those factories shut down, unemployment, particularly among blacks, skyrocketed.

Exercise 11 ## Recognize and Interpret Figurative Language

Answer the following questions in your own words.

1. In paragraph 5, Kotlowitz writes, "The river flows between Benton Harbor and St. Joseph, two small towns whose only connections are two bridges and a powerful undertow of contrasts." What is he comparing? What does he mean?

_____

_____

_____

2. In paragraph 13, Kotlowitz writes, "We circle the wagons, watching out for our own." What is he comparing? What does he mean?

_____

_____

_____

3. At the end of paragraph 16, Kotlowitz writes, "The lines are drawn. Accusations are hurled across the river like cannon fire. And the cease-fires, when they occur, are just that, cease-fires, temporary and fragile." Explain the metaphor. What does he mean?

_____

_____

_____

_____

Exercise 12   **Reflect**

Think about what you read in Reading 2 and what you already know about race relations in the United States. Answer the following questions, and prepare to discuss them with your classmates.

1. Why do you think Kotlowitz never tells us what really happened to Eric McGinnis?

_____

_____

_____

_____

2. What myths do people in your neighborhood or people you know have about other people? Explain.

_____

_____

_____

_____

EVALUATING OPINIONS

Evaluating facts—knowing how to consider their source as well as what they include and what they omit—helps in understanding and eventually in evaluating opinions. If you recognize that the source of a set of facts has an agenda and that the facts have been selected to promote that agenda, then you are in a better position to place the author's opinions in the right context.

©2007 Pearson Education, Inc.

It is also important to recognize an author's worldview and viewpoint, purpose for writing, bias, and tone.

What Are the Author's Worldview and Viewpoint?

In "Colorblind," Alex Kotlowitz describes two towns, each with its own perspective. The way the white people of St. Joseph view the world is different from the way the black people of Benton Harbor view the world—though only a river separates them. Race and economics make the difference.

worldview
Perspective on the world

Each of us has a **worldview,** or perspective on the world. Like the people of St. Joseph and Benton Harbor, we interpret events based on that perspective. How are our worldviews formed? What influences our beliefs? Here are some of the factors that influence our belief systems or worldviews:

- Our economic position in society, such as wealthy, poor, middle class, on welfare, in a high tax bracket, or unemployed
- Our sex
- Where we come from: the inner city, the suburbs, or a rural area
- Our ethnicity or religion, such as African American, Hispanic, or Anglo-Saxon, Catholic, Jewish, Hindu, Protestant, Muslim
- Our experiences in life
- Our friends and families and their opinions
- The media we read, watch, or listen to

Authors, too, have worldviews that have been formed by background and experience. It's clear from the first paragraph of Yasmin Ahmed's essay on pages 353 through 356 that she is a young woman from Somalia, she is an immigrant to the United States, and she is Muslim. Clearly, each of these characteristics influence her world view.

viewpoint An attitude or a position about an issue or event

Each of us has a worldview, but when we take an attitude or a position about an issue or event, we express a **viewpoint.** Viewpoint refers to much more specific concerns, but our viewpoint is almost always influenced by our worldview. Because of her worldview as a Somali girl and an immigrant, Ahmed believes that she and other Somalis have been unfairly discriminated against by Americans who, since September 11, have assumed they are terrorists.

What Is the Author's Purpose?

purpose Reason for writing

Related to the author's viewpoint is **purpose**—the reason for writing. Ahmed's purpose is to convince readers that they must move beyond assumptions and stereotypes and get to know people as individuals. Then they will know that she and young women like her are not terrorists but Muslim Americans.

A textbook author's purpose for writing is primarily to inform. How the writer approaches the task is influenced by his or her worldview. For example, one history book author might emphasize dates and devote a good deal of space to the "important people" in history about whom we have a written record. Another author might feel that history is more meaningful if it attempts to show what the life of a regular person was like at that time. Yet another author might decide to emphasize relationships between countries or diplomatic history. If you pick up four American history textbooks, you might find that one talks about the day-to-day lives of the slaves as well as about the plantation owners, one emphasizes women's roles in the family or in the economy, one has thorough coverage of the Native Americans, and one barely mentions minority groups or women but focuses on the stories of political campaigns, elections, and wars. In the latter book—the most common type of history textbook until the 1970s—the major focus would be on influential and powerful white men. Although the writers of all these textbooks might present what we consider to be facts, which facts they choose to present can make a lot of difference. You need to be aware that every writer makes these choices, and as a reader, you can form your own opinions about both the facts and the writer.

Often a textbook writer will explain his or her viewpoint or approach to the subject at the beginning of the book, in the preface or the introduction to the text. For example, read the following from the introduction to a world history text.

> This is a real *world* history text. It deals seriously with the Western tradition, but does not allocate extra space to it that might blur the distinction between a Western civilization text and a world history text. Correspondingly, civilizations or societies sometimes slighted [omitted] in world texts—such as the nomadic societies of Asia, Latin American societies, and nations and states of the Pacific Rim—receive additional attention here. This global orientation makes *World Civilizations: The Global Experience* the first of a logical new generation, one that will decide coverage in terms of international criteria, giving the West its respectful due but not pride of place. (Stearns et al., *World Civilizations*)

In this portion of the introduction, Stearns and his coauthors try to explain their approach to teaching world history. Their purpose is to be as inclusive as possible in the choice of cultures they cover. It is their intention to give the civilizations of the Western world their "respectful due" but also to cover other cultures, to provide the balanced coverage the authors feel is most appropriate.

Exercise 13 ## Check for Author's Worldview, Viewpoint, and Purpose

Read carefully the following paragraphs from the preface to the history text *Liberty, Equality, Power: A History of the American People,* by John M. Murrin and his coauthors. Then answer the questions that follow.

Global Emphasis in Early and Most Recent Chapters

1 The focus is global in chapters covering the early and most recent periods; in between, it is continental. We begin where the human

©2007 Pearson Education, Inc.

story began, with the Indian settlement of the Americas. The typical United States history textbook opens with a snapshot of Indian cultures on the East coast around 1600. This type of presentation suggests that these societies were stagnant and unchanging; that they are of more interest as curiosities than as participants in history; that history is something that Europeans did for themselves and to others; and that only their arrival brings focus and purposeful change to the Americas. We have rejected this formula. Native Americans had their own long and highly complex history before 1492, and much of that story is now being recovered. We incorporate it. We also alert readers to parallel or contrasting Canadian events, from the beginnings of New France through the adoption of Canadian Confederation in 1867. And, we have moved the Spanish borderlands much closer to the center of American history in the century and a half before the Mexican war.

Integration of Social, Cultural, and Political History

2   Because of our desire to integrate social, cultural, and political history, we have made efforts not to isolate the concerns and achievements of women, Native Americans, African Americans, Hispanics, Asians, and other minorities. We believe that the larger story of what is now the United States simply will not make sense unless the potent influence of race and gender is made clear. To give a simple but important example, the rise of capitalism in the 18th and 19th centuries depended on specific assumptions about gender among European settlers. Women rarely owned property, but they lived in fixed households where goods could be accumulated, and an acquisitive ethic could take hold among both men and women. By contrast, most Native American women in the eastern woodlands had to move twice a year. They had no interest in acquiring any more goods than they could carry on their backs. For them, an ethic of accumulation made no sense, even though their husbands, as hunters and trappers, played an active role as producers for a global market. (Murrin et al., *Liberty, Equality, Power*)

1. What perspective, or worldview, do the authors identify as their focus?

   _____

   _____

   _____

2. What is the authors' purpose for using their particular focus?

   _____

   _____

   _____

3. When they state in paragraph 1, "We have rejected this formula," what formula are the authors referring to?

_____

_____

_____

Exercise 14   ## Reflect

Based on the reading in Exercise 13, answer the following questions.

1. Murrin and his coauthors assert that their text is very different from other American history texts. Based on the history textbooks you have read, do you think the focus of their text would be very different? Why or why not?

_____

_____

_____

2. Do you think you would like the focus that Murrin and his coauthors emphasize? Why or why not?

_____

_____

_____

3. What has the focus been of history textbooks you have read or are reading this semester?

_____

_____

_____

◆

Is the Author Biased?

objective Presents facts without attempting to influence readers' opinions

subjective Presents primarily the author's perspective

Most textbook writers attempt primarily to present **objective** information about their topics; that is, they try to present the facts without influencing our opinions about the material. They also try to present both sides of an issue fairly so that we can form our own opinions based on the information. For example, a historian whose book includes the accomplishments of both men and women is trying to represent everyone's achievements in a society. However, if an author writes only from one perspective and does not include other viewpoints, his or her work might be called **subjective.** A subjective textbook reflects the writer's unique worldview from every perspective—religiously, socially, racially, ethni-

©2007 Pearson Education, Inc.

cally, economically. Literature, such as poetry, drama, and fiction, is expected to be highly subjective. Textbooks, on the other hand, are expected to be primarily objective.

If an author presents information subjectively and does not try to present both sides of an issue, readers should identify the writing as **biased.** The writer may be trying to influence our opinions without presenting all the information needed to arrive at a reasonable conclusion. Checking for bias is an important critical reading skill, and we examine it and other critical reading skills more thoroughly in Chapter 8. Frequently, an author will be straightforward about his or her bias and will state it very clearly. The following statements from the Web pages of Ralph Nader, a militant consumer advocate, and the Center for the Moral Defense of Capitalism, a pro-business organization, make very clear the bias of the writers.

biased Does not fairly present both sides of an issue

From the Ralph Nader Web Site

The nation's financial industry—banks, insurance companies and securities firms—often has consumers over a barrel. Financial industry titans, lax regulators and pro-industry legislators regularly work together to advance business interests. Unfortunately, consumers and taxpayers are rarely as organized or well represented in Congress, state legislatures, before regulatory agencies or in the courts. (Nader, from the Web site for the Center of the Moral Defense of Capitalism http://www.nader.org/ nader_letter/ feas.html accessed September 13, 2005)

From the Web Site for the Center for the Moral Defense of Capitalism
The mission of the Center for the Moral Defense of Capitalism is to present a moral defense of business, profit-making, and economic freedom based on a morality of rational self-interest. (http://moraldefense.com/ About accessed July 23, 2002)

The bias of each statement is clearly announced. We can see that the viewpoints are pretty much the opposite of each other. Nader states openly his opposition to big business and its overwhelming influence on government; the Center for the Moral Defense of Capitalism, in contrast, states openly its position in support of business, profit making, and economic freedom based on self-interest.

Often, however, bias is presented in much more subtle forms. For example, consider the reactions to a coal-mining accident that took place in July 2002. Nine coal miners were trapped in a mine in Pennsylvania. The accident happened when they inadvertently broke into a mine shaft that had been previously flooded. The map of the mine they were using had not been updated to show that the shaft was full of water. Thousands of gallons of water rushed in on them, blocking the exits. Finally, after being trapped for more than three full days, the miners were saved. All nine of them said they would never go down in the mines again. One news reporter covering the story introduced the news of the miners' rescue by saying, "Finally, something good and right has happened in our country. The nine miners who were trapped have been saved." A union spokesman, on the other hand, said, "Hopefully this tragic event will help us to make the mine owners follow more stringent safety guidelines and to always use the correct maps of the mines." The facts of the event are the same, but different worldviews result in very different biases in reporting them. As a reader, you need to be alert to worldviews and purposes that will help you detect bias.

Exercise 15   Work with Bias

Pick two topics from Table 7.3, or think of your own topics. Then, on a separate piece of paper, write two or three sentences about each topic from different points of view—that is, with a different bias. Here is an example:

Topic: Parking on campus

Student: The campus needs to provide more parking places for students because buying a parking permit at this school is really just buying a hunting permit. There are 1,000 parking spaces and 12,000 students. It hurts our educational possibilities to have to spend so much time looking for parking every day.

Administrator: We are in a period of restricted financing, so, while we recognize the very serious parking problem on campus, it is important to look at the larger picture. First, there are not enough classrooms on campus, and construction of classroom space should have priority. Second, our part-time teachers and clerical employees don't have medical insurance. If we spend money on parking, these people will be justifiably upset. And finally, there is convenient public transportation to our campus that students should use.

Table 7.3

Possible Topics and Biases	Possible Points of View
Immigrant workers who do not have papers to be in the United States	Police officer Auto insurance company spokesperson Immigrant official Son or daughter of undocumented immigrants
High prices of college textbooks	Consumer advocate for cheaper textbooks College bookstore manage Public relations person for a textbook publishing company Student
Uniforms on a high school campus	High school student who opposes uniforms High school student who supports uniforms High school administrator Parent
Establishment of police review board to review police brutality	Public relations officer for the police department Community member Mother of a teenager beaten by the police
Affirmative action programs for college admissions	Student who agrees Student who opposes State legislator
An existing curfew at 10:00 p.m. or all people under 16	Police officer 16-year-old Parent of 16-year-old

©2007 Pearson Education, Inc.

What Is the Author's Tone?

tone Indication of the author's emotional response to a topic

An author's viewpoint and purpose for writing naturally affect the emotional content of the writing. The author's **tone**, or emotional response to the topic, reveals how he or she feels. Our understanding of tone is influenced by the inferences we can make from the author's choice of vocabulary (see Chapter 6). For example, about the problems of population growth, one author might write, "The rate of world population growth is a problem that needs to be addressed." Another author might write, "If we don't do something to stop the worldwide population explosion, we are surely doomed." The first writer's tone is concerned, and the word *growth* doesn't carry either a positive or negative connotation. The second writer's tone is alarming and pessimistic. The words *explosion* and *doomed* carry heavy connotations—*explosion* makes us think of something that's very powerful and impossible to control, and *doomed* makes us think that there is no way to prevent the terrible things that will come to pass. Although this example is purposely extreme to show the differences in tone, it makes clear that recognizing the author's tone enhances our understanding.

The variety of tones authors can use is as wide ranging as human emotions. But an author usually uses a single, consistent tone throughout a piece of writing, based on the content of the piece. The tone can be matter-of-fact when the author simply provides factual information. Textbooks are usually written objectively, and the objective tone helps establish that the author is an expert. But tone can also be playful, and then the reader does not take the writer too seriously. A hopeful tone can keep the reader from becoming discouraged by negative or normally disheartening information. A sarcastic tone or irony lets the reader see that the writer is criticizing what is presented. A good example of the use of ironic tone is the reading "Why I Want a Wife" (Chapter 6, pp. 311–312). Here is a list of just some of the many possible tones writers use:

alarming	indifferent	positive
authoritative	ironic	regretful
cautious	matter-of-fact	resigned
concerned	moral	romantic
confessional	negative	sarcastic
dark	nostalgic	self-righteous
exuberant	objective	thoughtful
formal	optimistic	tongue-in-cheek
hopeful	pessimistic	

Exercise 16   **Work with Tone**

Write one sentence about each of the topics below. Choose one of the tones in the parentheses to use in your sentence.

1. The need for the city to put a stop sign at a street corner where a child was killed on the way to school. (alarming or pessimistic tone)

   _____

   _____

2. Congratulations to a newlywed couple. (positive or romantic tone)

   _____

   _____

3. Your friend got A's in all his classes. (exuberant or tongue-in-cheek tone)

   _____

   _____

4. Your instructor gives you extra homework at the last minute. (sarcastic or angry tone)

   _____

   _____

5. You are asking your boss for a raise. (humble or confident tone)

   _____

   _____

Reading 3

Signing for a Revolution: Gallaudet University and Deaf Culture
Heather Eudy

Heather Eudy has a background in cultural studies and teaches English as a Second Language as well as English classes of all levels at various community colleges in Southern California. She has worked with an extremely diverse population of students. Her contact with deaf students in many of her classes led to her interest in deaf culture and the history of deaf education. As you read her article, think about her presentation of facts and opinions, her worldview and viewpoint.

> *"The problem is not that the students do not hear; the problem is that the hearing world does not listen."*
>
> —JESSE JACKSON

1 In March 1988, deaf students started a revolution. When yet another hearing person was chosen as president of Gallaudet University in Washington,

©2007 Pearson Education, Inc.

DC, the first facility to offer college degrees for the deaf in the United States, the students had had enough. Since opening in 1864 the university had never had a deaf president. Yet there were qualified deaf candidates. The students marched, protested, organized rallies, pressured for better education, and demanded: first, that the newly picked hearing president be replaced with a deaf administrator; second, that the chair of the board resign; third, that deaf membership on the board rise to 51 percent; and finally, that there be no reprisals against the protesters. After days of rallying, media coverage, and nationwide support, the students' demands were met.

2   This was not the first battle deaf people have faced. The deaf have been discriminated against for centuries. Even religious leaders, philosophers, educators, and medical professionals have considered them inferior spiritually, mentally, intellectually, physically, and psychologically. The Greek philosopher Aristotle believed deaf people could not learn. The Christian leader Saint Augustine claimed deafness in a person was a sign of God's anger and served as punishment for sin. Struggles regarding how and what a deaf person should be taught continue today, as do the assumptions that deaf people are disabled or impaired.

3   The struggle over education methods for deaf students has lasted more than a century. The deaf community has fought to keep sign language in the schools, but it has not yet won. More than one hundred years ago, the Milan Conference endorsed oral education as opposed to education in sign, with the consequence that signing in the schools disappeared. Deaf students ended up leaving schools illiterate, with few opportunities available to them. This discrimination was one of the reasons that Gallaudet University was founded. The National Association of the Deaf also sought to keep sign language alive. Today bilingual education is provided in many states for students whose first language is not English, but American Sign Language (ASL) has not been granted the same status as Spanish, Vietnamese, or Navajo, even though as many as two million people use it.

4   There are two ways to view deafness. The Medical Model sets up a framework in which hearing is the norm. That makes deaf people different or wrong. Deaf people are viewed as though they have a disability or an impairment that needs to be fixed. On the other hand, the Cultural Model recognizes that deaf people have their own distinct culture and common language.

5   Unfortunately, the Medical Model is predominant in the hearing world. The hearing world tends to stigmatize deaf people, defining them as physically defective. Because they cannot communicate orally, deaf people are assumed to be simpleminded. Hearing parents of a deaf child are often pressured by medical professionals into a "solution" for their child's "problem" that involves testing, hearing aids, and even surgery. In *The Mask of Benevolence*, Harlan Lane presents evidence of the ways in which psychiatrists and educators, in professional journals and academic studies, brand

deaf people as mentally limited and lacking insight, as socially irresponsible and morally underdeveloped, as behaviorally aggressive and impulsive, and as emotionally disturbed. Lane calls these assessments symptomatic of "hearing paternalism" and "audism." Paternalism is evident in the assumption by hearing people that they should help deaf people be a part of hearing society. Audism is like racism but takes the form of hearing people's domination of the deaf community by enforcing the idea that the deaf are infirm, or ill, and by controlling deaf education.

6   The Cultural Model belongs to the deaf community. Here culture is not connected to ethnicity or race. If *culture* is defined as shared language, shared experiences, shared identifiable characteristics, and shared values and norms, then there is also a deaf culture. The deaf community has its own language, its own shared experiences, its own identifiable characteristics, and its own shared values and norms. Indeed, the deaf community sees itself as having a culture, distinct from any other and rightly so.

7   First, let's examine the deaf community's shared language. Be aware that language does not depend on the ability to speak or hear. The deaf community communicates through sign language, a manual and visual language with a distinct grammar. Not much is known about the development of sign language until the 1800s. However, we do know that in the 1500s Pedro Ponce de León of Spain created a system of gestures to educate the deaf, and in the late 1700s Jacob Rodríguez Pereira spread an adapted version of León's gestures across Europe. Soon after, Abbé de l'Épée founded the French institute for deaf students using Old French Sign Language (OFSL), followed by Ambroise Cucurron Sicard, who compiled a dictionary of signs. At the same time a very large deaf community on the island of Martha's Vineyard, in the United States, was using a version of sign language that contributed to modern day American Sign Language. In 1817 Laurent Clerc and Thomas Gallaudet founded the first permanent public American school for the deaf incorporating OFSL into the curriculum. OFSL constitutes 60 percent of today's American Sign Language. Sign Language is a language like other foreign languages, and it is estimated to be the fourth most used language in the United States today.

8   The deaf community also has its own literature. Deaf people have their own plays, poems, stories, newspapers, and magazines. They highly value mastery of their language and storytelling with clear communication. They excel in the arts, in mime, dance, sculpture, video, theater, television, and film. They engage in activities within cultural institutions such as residential schools, deaf clubs, political organizations, and athletic teams. They value deaf identity and see themselves as part of a unique heritage with pride. They usually marry other deaf people. In fact, nine out of ten deaf people marry a deaf person and hope for deaf children. Other deaf people are viewed as family, so there is intense group loyalty. Some even consider those who choose to talk or think like hearing people to be traitors. Bobby Jo Duffy, a teacher's aide at the Lexington School for the Deaf in New York, says, "I value our own culture, our own lan-

©2007 Pearson Education, Inc.

guage. It used to be that many people didn't realize that deaf people have a language. They felt sorry for deaf people. There's really no pity needed. Deaf people can do anything, except hear. That's all. . . . Everything that I am, how I express myself, my education, everything, it's with the deaf community."

9   Not all deaf people feel the same as Duffy, however. Some really do want to assimilate into the hearing mainstream and choose to invest in hearing aid technology and to learn to speak. The most recent technology that has stirred up controversy is the cochlear implant designed by Cochlear Corporation. This prosthesis puts electrodes into the inner ear, or cochlea, where sound waves get absorbed and interpreted. The controversy is twofold. First, are these implants effective enough to make them worth the risks? Second, are they even desirable for the deaf community? While some believe cochlear implants have enriched lives, others see the use of cochlear implants as another example of the assumption that deafness is an impairment in need of repair. Marvin Miller, a deaf man who is planning a town centered around deaf people's needs, expresses his view on these implants: "I do not want one for myself. I am very happy being deaf. To me, this is like asking a black or Asian person if he or she would take a pill to turn into a white person." Is this what we are asking of deaf people? To abandon their culture, their identity?

10   As the Gallaudet Revolution indicates, what's most important to the deaf community today is not finding ways to end deafness but finding ways to end educational and social injustice. Deaf culture wants the recognition and respect due every minority. Deaf people want equal rights.

Sources

Davey, Monica. "As Town for Deaf Takes Shape, Debate on Isolation Re-emerges." *New York Times,* March 21, 2005.

Lane, Harlan. *Masks of Benevolence.* San Diego, CA: DawnSign Press, 1999.

"Perspectives on Deaf People." Sign Media, Inc. http://www.signmedia.com/info/adc.htm

Public Broadcasting Service. "Sound and Fury." http://www.pbs.org/wnet/soundandfury/culture/index.html

Wilcox, Sherman, and Phyllis Wilcox. *Learning to See: American Sign Language as a Second Language.* Englewood Cliffs, NJ: Prentice-Hall, 1991.

EUDY, "Signing for a Revolution"

Exercise 17   Work with Words

The following sentences appear in Reading 3, Eudy's "Signing for a Revolution." Use context clues, dictionary skills, and your knowledge of word parts to determine the meaning of each italicized word. Write the meaning of the word on the lines provided. The paragraph number is provided in case you want to go back to the reading to check the context.

1. The students marched, protested, organized rallies, pressured for better education, and demanded: first, that the newly picked hearing president be replaced with a deaf administrator; second, that the chair of the board resign; third, that deaf membership on the board rise to 51 percent; and finally, that there be no *reprisals* against the protesters. (par. 1)

   Reprisals: _____

2. Struggles regarding how and what a deaf person should be taught continue today, as do the assumptions that deaf people are disabled or *impaired*. (par. 2)

   Impaired: _____

3. The *Medical Model* sets up a framework in which hearing is the norm. (par. 4)

   Medical Model: _____

   _____

4. On the other hand, the *Cultural Model* recognizes that deaf people have their own distinct culture and common language. (par. 4)

   Cultural Model: _____

5. The hearing world tends to *stigmatize* deaf people, defining them physically defective. (par. 5)

   Stigmatize: _____

6. In *The Mask of Benevolence,* Harlan Lane presents evidence of the ways in which psychiatrists and educators, in professional journals and academic studies, *brand* deaf people as mentally limited and lacking insight, as socially irresponsible and morally underdeveloped, as behaviorally aggressive and impulsive, and as emotionally disturbed. (par. 5)

   Brand: _____

7. *Paternalism* is evident in the assumption by hearing people that they should help deaf people be a part of hearing society. (par. 5)

   Paternalism: _____

©2007 Pearson Education, Inc.

8. *Audism* is like racism but takes the form of hearing people's domination of deaf community by enforcing the idea that the deaf are infirm, or ill, and by controlling deaf education. (par. 5)

Audism: _____

9. The most recent technology that has stirred up controversy is the cochlear implant designed by Cochlear Corporation. This *prosthesis* puts electrodes into the inner ear, or *cochlea,* where sound waves get absorbed and interpreted. (par. 9)

Prosthesis: _____

10. *Cochlea:* _____

Exercise 18   Check Your Understanding

Based on Reading 3, answer the following questions in your own words.

1. What are some of the ways deaf people have been discriminated against?

_____

_____

_____

_____

2. What is the difference between the Medical Model and the Cultural Model, and who has typically followed each model?

_____

_____

_____

_____

3. What are some of the things that deaf people have in common and lead the author to state that they have their own culture?

_____

_____

_____

_____

Exercise 19   Recognize Author's Viewpoint, Purpose, and Bias

Based on Reading 3, answer the following questions in your own words. Develop your answers as fully as possible.

1. What is Eudy's worldview or perspective that influences her opinion in this reading?

_____

_____

_____

_____

_____

2. What do you think is Eudy's purpose for writing this article? What do you think she wants to achieve?

_____

_____

_____

_____

_____

3. Could you describe Eudy as "objective"? Explain your answer.

_____

_____

_____

_____

_____

Exercise 20   ## Distinguish Fact from Opinion

List three sentences from Reading 3 that you think are clearly facts, and then list three opinions that Eudy presents.

Facts

1. _____

_____

_____

_____

_____

©2007 Pearson Education, Inc.

2. _____

_____

_____

_____

3. _____

_____

_____

_____

_____

Opinions

1. _____

_____

2. _____

_____

3. _____

_____

4. _____

_____

_____

Exercise 21   Reflect

Think about what you read in Reading 3 and what you already know about deaf people and deaf culture. Answer the following questions, and prepare to discuss them with your classmates.

1. Why does Eudy use the quotation from Jesse Jackson at the beginning of her essay?

_____

_____

_____

_____

_____

2. Eudy quotes Marvin Miller as saying that he doesn't want a cochlear implant. "I am very happy being deaf. To me, this is like asking a black or Asian person if he or she would take a pill to turn into a white person." (par. 9) What does Miller mean by this statement? In what ways do you think the circumstances of deaf people are similar or different from the circumstances of black or Asian people in this country?

_____

_____

_____

_____

3. Do you know any deaf people, or have you seen deaf people signing? What kind of relationship do you have with them, or what has your reaction been when you see people signing?

_____

_____

_____

_____

CHAPTER REVIEW

✔ Reader's Checklist

Check (✔) the terms introduced in this chapter that you are confident you understand and can now use to think critically about the various aspects of facts and opinions in what you read. If you are not sure about an item, (1) go back to the explanations in the text, (2) study and review with other members of your college learning community, (3) ask your instructor for help, (4) check out the Web site for this textbook at **www.ablongman.com/ alexandercommunity4e** for additional exercises on facts, opinions, worldview, viewpoint, and author's purpose and to take the chapter quiz, or (5) complete additional practices in the *Reading Road Trip*.

❏ Fact   ❏ Purpose
❏ Opinion   ❏ Objective
❏ Value words   ❏ Subjective
❏ Inclusion   ❏ Biased
❏ Worldview   ❏ Tone
❏ Viewpoint

When you are confident that you have mastered these concepts and skills, test yourself with Mastery Tests 7A and 7B (pp. 390–404).

©2007 Pearson Education, Inc.

Critical Reflections

Answer the following questions, and prepare to discuss them with your classmates.

1. Do you think that racism and other forms of prejudice are problems in American society today? Give examples from your experience and reading to support your answer. _____

_____

_____

_____

2. What have you learned from the readings in this chapter that you weren't aware of or hadn't thought about. What new perspective(s) have you gained? _____

_____

_____

_____

3. How can we, as people from a variety of cultural backgrounds, avoid prejudice based on race, nationality, gender, sexual orientation, class, religion, ability, or any other differences? _____

_____

_____

_____

Writing Activity

Write a paragraph or short essay in answer to one of the questions in "Critical Reflections."

Classroom Community

1. Check your college catalog to find out what your college does to prevent discrimination on campus. What speech or behavior codes are in place to guarantee that students are respectful to one another? Present your results to your class group. Discuss the advantages and disadvantages of these codes.

2. Present your thoughts about the ideal interactions between people within a diverse society to your class group. On which aspects of the ideal interactions can you all agree?

Extend Your Thinking

For further reading related to cultural diversity, see "The War Prayer" by Mark Twain, in "Extend Your Thinking," (pp.497–500).

Work the Web

In "A Reader's Toolkit" on pages 429 through 576, you will find a set of guidelines for evaluating Web sites. Although you can discover useful resources on the Internet, you must also be careful not to believe everything you read there. To avoid being unduly persuaded by inaccurate or biased sites, you need to ask certain questions to determine the legitimacy of a site.

1. Read pages 552 through 557 and familiarize yourself with how to evaluate a Web site.

2. Write a Web site evaluation based on the instructions and the sample Web site evaluations for the following site of an organization devoted to civil liberties: http://www.aclu.org

Go to **www.ablongman.com/alexandercommunity4e** for additional Web-based activities.

©2007 Pearson Education, Inc.

Mastery Test

7A

Rage

Martín Espada

Martín Espada is a prominent Puerto Rican poet. Formerly a lawyer, he eventually became a professor of literature at the University of Massachusetts–Amherst. Much of Espada's work deals with the lives and struggles of poor people and immigrants in the United States. In the following essay, he discusses some of the reasons that Latino men feel "rage," the different ways of handling anger, stereotypes of Latino men, his memories of his father, and his hopes for his son. As you read, think about Espada's viewpoint on anger.

1   My father has good reason for rage. A brown-skinned man, he learned rage when he was arrested in Biloxi, Mississippi, in 1950, and spent a week in jail for refusing to go to the back of the bus. He learned rage when he was denied a college education and instead struggled for years working for an electrical contractor, hating his work and yearning for so much more. He learned rage as the political triumphs of the 1960s he helped to achieve were attacked from without and betrayed from within. My father externalized his rage. He raged at his enemies and he raged at us. A tremendous ethical and cultural influence for us nonetheless, he must have considered himself a failure by the male career-obsessed standards of the decade into which I was born: the 1950s.

2   By adolescence, I had learned to <u>internalize</u> my rage. I learned to do this, not so much in response to my father, but more in response to my own growing awareness of <u>bigotry</u>. Having left my Brooklyn birthplace for the town Valley Stream, Long Island, I was dubbed a spic in an endless torrent of taunting, bullying, and brawling. To defend myself against a few people would have been feasible; to defend my self against dozens and dozens of people deeply in love with their own racism was a practical impossibility. So I told no one, no parent or counselor or teacher or friend, about the constant racial hostility. Instead, I punched a lamp, not once but twice, and watched the blood ooze between my knuckles as if somehow I could leech the poison from my body. My evolving manhood was defined by how well I could take punishment, and <u>paradoxically</u> I punished myself for not being man enough to end my own humiliation. Later in life, I would <u>emulate</u> my father and rage openly. Rarely, however, was the real enemy within earshot, or even visible.

3   Someday, my son will be called a spic for the first time; this is as much a part of the Puerto Rican experience as the music he gleefully dances to. I hope he will tell me. I hope that I can help him handle the glowing toxic waste of his rage. I hope that I can explain clearly why there are those waiting for him to explode, to confirm their stereotypes of the hot-blooded, bad-tempered Latino male who has, without provocation, injured the Anglo innocents. His anger—and that anger must come—has to be controlled,

directed, creatively channeled, <u>articulated</u>—but not all-consuming nor self-destructive. I keep it between the covers of the books I write.

4   The anger will continue to <u>manifest</u> itself as he matures and discovers the utter resourcefulness of bigotry, the ability of racism to change shape and survive all attempts to snuff it out. "<u>Spic</u>" is a crude expression of certain sentiments that become subtle and sophisticated and insidious at other levels. Speaking of crudity, I am reminded of a group organized by white ethnics in New York during the 1960s under the acronym of SPONGE: The Society for the Prevention of the Niggers Getting Everything. . . .

5   Violence is the first cousin to rage. If learning to confront rage is an important element of developing Latino manhood, then the question of violence must be addressed with equal urgency. Violence is terribly <u>seductive</u>; all of us, especially males, are trained to gaze upon violence until it becomes beautiful. Beautiful violence is not only the way to victory for armies and football teams; this becomes the solution to everyday problems as well. For many characters on the movie or television screen, problems are solved by *shooting* them. This is certainly the most emphatic way to win an argument.

6   Katherine and I try to minimize the seductiveness of violence for Clemente. No guns, no soldiers, and so on. But his dinosaurs still eat each other with great relish. His trains still crash, to their delight. He is experimenting with power and control, with action and reaction, which brings him to an imitation of violence. Needless to say, there is a vast difference between stegosaurus and Desert Storm [the U.S. military invasion of Iraq in 1990].

7   Again, all I can do is call upon my own experience as an example. I not only found violence seductive; at some point, I found myself enjoying it. I remember one brawl in Valley Stream when I snatched a chain away from an assailant, knocked him down, and needlessly lashed the chain across his knees as he lay sobbing in the street. That I was now the assailant with the chain did not occur to me.

8   I also remember the day I stopped enjoying the act of fistfighting. I was working as a bouncer in a bar, and found myself struggling with a man who was so drunk that he appeared numb to the blows bounding off his cranium. Suddenly, I heard my fist echo: *thok*. I was sickened by the sound. Later, I learned that I had broken my right ring finger with the punch, but all I could recall was the headache I must have caused him. I never had a fistfight again. Parenthetically, that job ended another romance: the one with alcohol. Too much of my job consisted of ministering to people who had passed out at the bar, finding their hats and coats, calling a cab, dragging them in their stupor down the stairs. Years later, I channeled those instincts cultivated as a bouncer into my work as a legal services lawyer, representing Latino tenants, finding landlords who forgot to heat buildings in winter or exterminate rats to be more deserving targets of my wrath. . . .

9   Will I urge my son to be a <u>pacifist</u>, thereby gutting one of the foundations of traditional manhood, the pleasure taken in violence and the power derived from it? That is an ideal state. I hope that he lives a life that permits him pacifism. I hope that the world around him evolves in such a way that pacifism is a viable choice. Still, I would not deny him the option of physical

391

©2007 Pearson Education, Inc.

self-defense. I would not deny him, on philosophical grounds, the right to resistance in any form that resistance must take to be effective. Nor would I have him deny that right to others, with the luxury of distance. Too many people in this world still need a revolution.

10   When he is old enough, Clemente and I will talk about matters of justification, which must be carefully and narrowly defined. He must understand that abstractions like "patriotism" and "country" are not reasons to fight on the battlefield. He must understand that violence against women is not acceptable, a message which will have to be somehow repeated every time another movie trailer blazes the art of <u>misogyny</u> across his subconscious mind. Rather than sloganizing, however, the best way I can communicate that message is by the way I treat his mother. How else will he know that jealousy is not love, that a lover is not property?

11   Clemente was born on December 28, 1991. This was a difficult birth. Katherine's coccyx, or tailbone, broken in childhood [by her abusive father], would break again during delivery. Yet only with the birth could we move from gesture to fulfillment, from generous moments to real giving. The extraordinary healing that took place was not only physical but emotional and spiritual as well. After years of constant pain, her coccyx bone set properly, as if a living metaphor for the new opportunity represented by the birth of this child. . . .

12   The behavior we collectively refer to as "macho" [usually thought of as a tough man] has deep historical roots, but the trigger is often a profound insecurity, a sense of being threatened. Clemente will be as secure as possible, and that security will stem in large part from self-knowledge. He will know the meaning of his name.

13   Clemente Soto Vélez was a great Puerto Rican poet, a fighter for the independence of Puerto Rico who spent years in prison as a result. He was also our good friend. The two Clementes met once, when the elder Clemente was eighty-seven years old and the younger Clemente was nine months. Fittingly, it was Columbus Day, 1992, the five-hundredth anniversary of the conquest. We passed the day with a man who devoted his life and his art to battling the very colonialism personified by Columbus. The two Clementes traced the topography of one another's faces. Even from his sickbed, the elder Clemente was gentle and generous. We took photographs, signed books. Clemente Soto Vélez died the following spring, and eventually my family and I visited the grave in the mountains of Puerto Rico. We found the grave unmarked but for a stick with a number and letter, so we bought a gravestone and gave the poet his name back. My son still asks to see the framed photograph of the two Clementes, still asks about the man with the long white hair who gave him *his* name. This will be family legend, family ritual, the origins of the name explained in greater and greater detail as the years pass, a source of knowledge and power as meaningful as the Book of Genesis.

14   Thankfully, Clemente also has a literal meaning: "merciful." Every time my son asks about his name, an opportunity presents itself to teach the power of mercy, the power of compassion. When Clemente, in later years consciously acts out these qualities, he does so knowing that he is doing

what his very name expects of him. His name gives him the beginnings of a moral code, a goal to which he can aspire. "Merciful": Not the first word scrawled on the mental blackboard next to the phrase "Puerto Rican male."

ESPADA, "Rage"

Exercise 1   Work with Words

Use context clues, dictionary skills, and your knowledge of word parts to choose the best definition for each of the following words underlined in the reading. The paragraph number is provided in case you want to check the context.

1. *Internalize* (par. 2)
   a. control
   b. keep inside
   c. deal with

2. *Bigotry* (par. 2)
   a. objectivity
   b. disillusionment
   c. prejudice

3. *Paradoxically* (par. 2)
   a. unexpectedly
   b. logically
   c. indifferently

4. *Emulate* (par. 2)
   a. accept
   b. respect
   c. copy

5. *Articulated* (par. 3)
   a. suppressed
   b. restricted
   c. expressed

6. *Manifest* (par. 4)
   a. show
   b. multiply
   c. fortify

7. *"Spic"* (par. 4)
   a. crude expression for Puerto Rican
   b. an objective expression for Puerto Rican
   c. a term only used by Puerto Ricans among themselves

8. *Seductive* (par. 5)
   a. tempting
   b. irritating
   c. pathetic and compulsive

9. *Pacifist* (par. 9)
   a. someone who promotes war
   b. someone who promotes peace
   c. someone who promotes violence

10. *Misogyny* (par. 10)
    a. self-love
    b. violent response
    c. hatred of women

Exercise 2   Check Your Understanding

Based on the reading, Espada's "Rage," choose the best answer to each of the following multiple-choice questions.

1. Which of the following best states the topic of "Rage"?
   a. Relationships between men and women in Latino culture
   b. Rage, violence, and hope for alternatives for Puerto Rican men
   c. Poetry, revolution, and the Puerto Rican independence movement

©2007 Pearson Education, Inc.

2. Which of the following best states the thesis of "Rage"?
   a. We can only hope that future generations of Latino (Puerto Rican) men will live in a world where violence is not necessary for self-defense or to feel good about oneself.
   b. We can only hope that future generations of Puerto Rican men will fight for the respect they deserve.
   c. It is never right for men to allow their anger—their rage—to take the form of violence against anyone.

3. In paragraph 2, Espada mentions moving to a town called Valley Stream, where he became aware of bigotry. From this paragraph, we can reasonably infer that
   a. the family was doing well so they moved to a more comfortable neighborhood.
   b. the new neighborhood was predominantly white.
   c. he was dubbed a spic and faced taunting, bullying, and brawling.

4. Espada writes in paragraph 2, "By adolescence, I had learned to internalize my rage." We can infer that Espada thinks that internalizing rage
   a. is probably not a good way to deal with anger.
   b. is a good solution and a healthy approach to anger management.
   c. is wrong and that it is much better to rage openly as his father did.

5. In paragraph 5, Espada assumes that his son will be tempted to be violent when he faces racism, but he hopes his son
   a. will respond to force with force.
   b. will live up to the reputation of the hot-blooded Latino man.
   c. will be able to channel and articulate his anger without resorting to violence.

6. According to Espada, violence is "terribly seductive." To support this statement, he gives examples of
   a. not buying toy guns or soldiers for his son.
   b. his own acts of violence, how he enjoyed it.
   c. how he learned to leave violence behind.

7. In which of the following cases does Espada say violence may be justified?
   a. For self-defense
   b. To defend one's respect and honor
   c. For patriotic reasons

8. In this essay, it is clear that Espada wanted to be a father who
   a. maintained a certain manly distance from his son.
   b. did not reveal his emotions to his son.
   c. was close to his son and able to discuss many things with him.

9. Espada believes that the best way to teach his son that violence against women is not acceptable is by
   a. not taking him to misogynistic movies.
   b. explaining to him that one must never be violent toward women.
   c. always treating Clemente's mother with respect.

10. Which of the following is not a reason that Espada named his son Clemente?
   a. He was named after Clemente Soto Vélez.
   b. *Clemente* means "merciful" in Spanish.
   c. His wife, Katherine, had always loved that name.

Exercise 3 **Recognize Figurative Language and Author's Worldview, Viewpoint, and Tone**

Based on the reading, briefly answer the following questions in your own words.

1. In paragraph 2, Espada writes, "Instead, I punched a lamp, not once but twice, and watched the blood ooze between my knuckles as if somehow I could leech the poison from my body." What does *poison* represent in this sentence. What does it mean to "leech the poison" out of his body? What is the impression that this metaphor establishes? _____

_____

_____

2. Espada writes in paragraph 3, "I hope that I can help him [Clemente, his son] handle the glowing toxic waste of his rage." What two things are being compared? What impression does this comparison make? _____

_____

3. How would you describe the tone of paragraph 3? Use two or three adjectives. _____

_____

4. What are some of the things you know from reading this essay and the introduction that shaped Espada's worldview? _____

_____

_____

5. How would you characterize Espada's viewpoint toward rage and violence in your own words? _____

_____

_____

©2007 Pearson Education, Inc.

Exercise 4   **Reflect**

Think about what you read in "Rage" and what you already know about bigotry and racial violence. Then answer the following questions.

1. In paragraph 14, Espada writes, "His name gives him the beginnings of a moral code, a goal to which he can aspire. 'Merciful': Not the first word scrawled on the mental blackboard next to the phrase 'Puerto Rican male.'" What do you think this passage means? Why is the passage so important to this essay? _____

   _____

   _____

   _____

2. What kinds of prejudices have you faced in your life? (Remember, people are prejudiced about many different things, not only race or ethnicity.) Explain your experiences. _____

   _____

   _____

   _____

3. Have you ever felt discriminated against? How did you react? Do you think you acted in a "directed, creatively channeled" way? What could you have done to improve the way you reacted?

   _____

   _____

   _____

   _____

Mastery Test

Can We All Get Along?

Al Martínez

The following essay was written by Al Martínez, a long-time columnist for papers like the Oakland Tribune *and the* Los Angeles Times, *and author of* Ashes in the Rain *(1989),* Dancing Under the Moon *(1992), and* City of Angels: A Drive-by Portrait of Los Angeles *(1996). In this essay, written for the* California Journal *in 1998, Martínez discusses the ethnic tensions that separate many Americans, and he suggests that the very diversity that creates those tensions can be a positive force in our lives. As you read, notice statements of fact and opinion, as well as the tone that Martínez uses in this reading.*

1   I was walking by an elementary school in the San Fernando Valley when I stopped to watch a group of children at play. As I stood staring through the mesh fence that surrounded the schoolyard, it occurred to me how lovely their world must be. No rage fueled their competitive spirits, no jealousies fired their energies. Gender wasn't a question in their games, nor were race or cultural history. A clean wind blew through their lives as they ran from and toward each other, and at the end of their play they fell in a heap of unrestricted laughter, their happiness isolated for a moment in a world fenced off from hatred.

2   Then they went home.

3   What they faced at home, what they heard there, what was <u>infused</u> into their souls there, were elements of the internal structure that will make them what they will be once memories of the schoolyard fade and the world beyond the fence becomes the world they occupy for the remainder of their lives. Will the joyful entanglements of their play emerge later as an easy respect for one another, or will forces yet to be applied alter their perceptions and cause a retreat from the closeness they knew at play?

4   The children I watched that day represented all the major races and cultures intermixing in California as we move toward a new millennium: blacks, whites, Asians, and Hispanics, a microcosm of what the future holds in a state that has not always welcomed diversity with parades and banners. Hatreds rooted in economics and cultural beliefs have tarnished the gleam in the Golden State since, and prior to, its <u>inception</u>.

5   The Chinese, at first welcomed in the 1840s because of their energy and their willingness to work for low pay in the gold mines and on the railroads, became the objects of hate-engendered legislation for those very traits. As their numbers grew and their ambitions thrived, the state responded with an ugliness difficult to forgive. The Chinese were taxed by race, barred from testifying in court against whites, excluded from certain jobs, and prohibited from marrying Caucasians. They were beaten, robbed, and murdered, their bodies left to rot in the cultural <u>debris</u> of our past.

©2007 Pearson Education, Inc.

6   A similar fate awaited the influx of Latinos at the turn of the century. Welcomed at first as cheap farm labor, they were deported by the thousands during the Great Depression, welcomed back in the state's brief Bracero program, then ousted again by Immigration and Naturalization Service agents responding to "Operation Wetback" and, later, to the termination of the Bracero program. Then in 1994, Proposition 187, supposedly aimed at illegal immigrants, created a new burst of xenophobia directed toward not the Danes or the British but those from south of the border whose millions still hunger for a better life beyond the Golden Door.

7   Two years later, Proposition 209 took aim at affirmative action and further widened the gap.

8   History reveals that laws, however crudely applied, can never stem the flow of immigrants yearning for betterment. A human instinct to improve has populated the world and will someday populate the stars. California is the proof of immigration's mighty force. Despite measures to keep foreigners out, a quarter of California's population, eight million, are foreign born, mostly from Latin America (51 percent) and Asia (33 percent). More than eighty languages are spoken in the state. By the year 2010, according to one estimate, the white population will be California's new minority.

9   One issue therefore becomes clear: we'd better take a lesson from those kids in the schoolyard and start getting along. Diversity is the word on which our future spins. Diversity of culture, diversity of color, diversity of language, diversity of religions, and diversity of dreams. Existing in a single political climate, elements of the differences between us can either lead to wars bloodier than any we've ever seen or to a rainbowed paradise more glorious than any we've ever imagined.

10   In multiculturalism exist the seeds of both. Former Governor Jerry Brown, now . . . [mayor of Oakland], senses danger in the emerging identity of minority groups if they don't expand beyond their clusters. He sees the clustering as a reaction to the state and the nation's racist history.

11   "What we have," he said to me, "is an identity perspective, a crisis. Each minority group feels it has to represent itself for protection against the outside world. It becomes a bundle of attitudes within itself, as opposed to citizens concerned with the total good. They are people looking at the world from the point of view of their own ethnic identity."

12   Brown sees a revival of civic life as a way of assuring that diversity will create the kind of California most of us want. "That's why I've come to Oakland," he said. "We're equally balanced among whites, blacks, Asians and Hispanics, and we're talking to each other. Oakland is an early warning portrait of California. There's no reason why it shouldn't succeed as a multicultural state. It will have to. If not, Bosnia."[1]

13   Brown's point is well taken. A people suppressed is a people enraged because hatred hurts and not forever will the oppressed tolerate its pain. In my house growing up in East Oakland lived a stepfather of German descent whose very soul seethed with a multitude of antipathies. He entered my life before I ever set foot in a school, and I learned from him how terrible hatred can be. He spewed it on blacks, Jews, Asians, and Latinos, saving a special

vitriol for me. I was a "spic" in his eyes, and he used physical force to establish his dominance over me. When, as he lay dying, I asked why he had hated me so, he only shook his head. There is no logical explanation for racial or ethnic hatred, no justification for its existence. We are molded by our <u>progenitors</u>, even those who assume the role by marriage and not blood, despite early realizations of how wrong that can be. I used the word *nigger* once in a rage when, during teenage, I found myself becoming my stepfather's son. The moment burns in memory with the heat of magnesium and no amount of later apologies, or subsequent years of fighting racism, will ever damp its fire. There is no <u>atonement</u> for the pain deliberately caused others. I never forgave my stepfather. Why should a young black boy at whom my ugly <u>epithet</u> was thoughtlessly hurled ever forgive me? . . .

14   A U.S. Census Bureau study points out that today, as in our past, the new immigrants to America demonstrate the same willingness to work as did their forebearers. Once it was building railroads and working the mines until those immigrants established footholds in an often hostile environment. Today, for the time being, it's cleaning tables and pulling weeds for minimum pay until the same energy that powered our ancestors elevates their social heirs into better jobs.

15   Meanwhile, the Census Bureau points out, unemployment among our current immigrants is just under 5 percent nationally, compared to about 4 percent among the native-born population. The difference is minimal. The same <u>quest</u> that fires our spirit fires theirs. Work, not the public dole, is the ladder that will get them to where they want to be. . . .

16   The question that awaits to be answered—"Can't we all just get along?"—was asked by police-beating victim Rodney King at the height of the 1992 riots in South-Central Los Angeles, the worst social uprising in U.S. history. The riots, in fact, began after a jury in Simi Valley acquitted four Los Angeles policemen in the videotaped beating that showed King, who is black, on the ground being <u>pummeled</u> by the white cops. It was later, pressed to comment on the riots, that King, an unlikely philosopher, asked the one question that remains a central factor in looking toward California's future: can we get along? I think we can because I think we must. There is growing evidence that the surge of history is on the side of those who march together away from an often violent and dismal past. There is hope.

Note

1. Bosnia, a country in Eastern Europe is used as an example of a place where ethnic hatred led to massacres based on ethnic and religious affiliation.

Martínez, "Can We All Get Along?"

Exercise 1   **Work with Words**

Use context clues, dictionary skills, and your knowledge of word parts to choose the best definition for each of the following words underlined in the reading. The paragraph number is provided in case you want to check the context.

© 2007 Pearson Education, Inc.

1. *Infused* (par. 3)
   a. demanded
   b. permeated
   c. brewed

2. *Inception* (par. 4)
   a. beginning
   b. initiation
   c. racism

3. *Debris* (par. 5)
   a. ruins
   b. enrichment
   c. garbage

4. *Xenophobia* (par. 6)
   a. friendliness
   b. fear of anything foreign
   c. close-mindedness

5. *Antipathies* (par. 13)
   a. empathies
   b. aversions
   c. oppressions

6. *Progenitors* (par. 13)
   a. ancestors
   b. friends
   c. relatives

7. *Atonement* (par. 13)
   a. resentment
   b. repercussion
   c. reconciliation

8. *Epithet* (par. 13)
   a. insult
   b. advice
   c. refusal

9. *Quest* (par. 15)
   a. question
   b. result
   c. search

10. *Pummeled* (par. 16)
    a. subdued
    b. restrained
    c. beaten

Exercise 2   **Check Your Understanding**

Based on the reading, Martínez's "Can We All Get Along?" choose the best answer to each of the following multiple-choice questions.

1. Which of the following best states the topic of "Can We All Get Along?"?
   a. The problems and promises of multiculturalism
   b. Race discrimination in California
   c. Solutions for ethnic conflict for the twenty-first century

2. Which of the following best states the main idea of "Can We All Get Along?"?
   a. I was walking by an elementary school in the San Fernando Valley when I stopped to watch a group of children at play.
   b. Hatreds rooted in economics and cultural beliefs have tarnished the gleam in the Golden State since, and prior to, its inception.
   c. If we're not blinded by old prejudices, diversity can lead to strength.

3. What is the dominant pattern of organization for paragraph 1?
   a. Problem and solution
   b. Narration
   c. Chronological order

4. Which of the following best states the main idea of paragraphs 5, 6, and 7?
   a. A similar fate awaited the influx of Latinos at the turn of the century.
   b. Latinos have been systematically discriminated against.
   c. Hatreds have tarnished the gleam of California since its beginnings.

5. What is the dominant pattern of organization for paragraphs 6 and 7?
   a. Problem and solution and exemplification
   b. Exemplification
   c. Chronological order and exemplification

6. Which of the following best states the main idea of paragraph 8?
   a. History reveals that laws, however crudely applied, can never stem the flow of immigrants yearning for betterment.
   b. Despite measures to keep foreigners out, a quarter of California's population, 8 million people, are foreign born.
   c. By the year 2010, according to one estimate, the white population will be California's new minority.

7. What is the dominant pattern of organization for paragraph 8?
   a. Narration
   b. Chronological order
   c. Exemplification

8. What is the dominant pattern of organization for paragraphs 11 and 12?
   a. Chronological order
   b. Definition
   c. Problem and solution

9. In paragraph 13, Martínez writes "I used the word *nigger* once in a rage when, during teenage, I found myself becoming my stepfather's son. The moment burns in memory with the heat of magnesium and no amount of later apologies, or subsequent years of fighting racism, will ever damp its fire." Which of the following is a reasonable inference about how the author feels about this incident?
   a. He will forgive his stepfather for being a racist because now he understands its basis.
   b. He feels that he did something terribly wrong, and he will not forget it.
   c. He thinks he can make up for his stepfather's racism by fighting for equality for all.

© 2007 Pearson Education, Inc.

10. In the first paragraph of "Can We All Get Along?" Martínez writes, "A clean wind blew through their lives as they ran from and toward each other, and at the end of their play they fell in a heap of unrestricted laughter, their happiness isolated for a moment in a world fenced off from hatred." In this sentence "A clean wind" probably represents
    a. the fact that it is often windy in that part of the city.
    b. the refreshing and invigorating nature of children playing together, without prejudices.
    c. the life that the students find when they leave the schoolyard and return to their homes.

Exercise 3 **Recognize Fact and Opinion**

Based on your reading, indicate whether each of the following statements is fact or opinion.

_____ 1. Each minority group feels it has to represent itself for protection against the outside world.

_____ 2. Despite measures to keep foreigners out, a quarter of California's population, eight million, are foreign born, mostly from Latin America (51 percent) and Asia (33 percent).

_____ 3. A people suppressed is a people enraged because hatred hurts and not forever will the oppressed tolerate its pain.

_____ 4. We'd better take a lesson from those kids in the schoolyard and start getting along.

_____ 5. Meanwhile, the Census Bureau points out, unemployment among our current immigrants is just under 5 percent nationally, compared to about 4 percent among the native-born population.

Exercise 4 **Identify Tone**

Based on the reading, choose the best answer to each of the following multiple-choice questions.

1. Which of the following best describes the tone of "Can We All Get Along?"?
   a. Sarcastic
   b. Fundamentally pessimistic
   c. Cautiously optimistic

2. Which of the following best describes the tone of paragraph 1?
   a. Appreciative
   b. Ostentatious
   c. Combative

3. Which of the following best describes the tone of paragraph 12?
   a. Cautiously optimistic
   b. Cautiously pessimistic
   c. Negative

4. Which of the following best describes the tone of the last half of paragraph 13?
   a. Confessional
   b. Condescending
   c. Nostalgic

5. Which of the following best describes the tone of paragraph 16?
   a. Worried and concerned
   b. Matter-of-fact
   c. Concerned but optimistic

Exercise 5 **Reflect**

Think about what you read in "Can We All Get Along?" and what you already know about ethnic tension. Then answer the following questions.

1. Why does Martínez describe children at an elementary school in the first paragraph of his essay and then write, "Then they went home."

   _____

   _____

   _____

   _____

2. Why do you think Martínez discusses his own childhood experiences in this essay?

   _____

   _____

   _____

   _____

3. In this essay, Martínez focuses on ethnic diversity. What other kinds of diversity do you think it might be important to consider?

   _____

   _____

   _____

   _____

©2007 Pearson Education, Inc.

4. Why do you think Martínez uses several examples from history?

_____

_____

_____

_____

Chapter 8

Critical Thinking

Science, Society, and Disease

**Of all the forms of inequality, injustice in healthcare
is the most shocking and inhumane.**

—DR. MARTIN LUTHER KING JR.

- What difficult decisions about disease and its treatment do we face in the twenty-first century?

- What do you think Dr. King meant when he referred to "injustice in healthcare"?

- What is the situation in the photo, and how does it relate to the quotation?

© 2007 Pearson Education, Inc.

PREPARE TO READ

There have been a great many advances in medicine in recent years—new drugs and new technologies for prevention and treatment. But there have also been new diseases, such as AIDS, which was first identified in 1981. And some diseases, such as skin cancer, are skyrocketing. How does science explain disease? And how do societies deal with diseases, particularly those that reach epidemic proportions? Are treatments for disease equally available to all? Can—or should—they be?

Purpose

In this chapter, you will
- Practice thinking critically—analyzing, synthesizing, and evaluating
- Consider how science and ethics are applied in decision making
- Evaluate arguments by examining their evidence, structure, weaknesses, and values

In the process, you will read and use information about disease in the past, present, and future and the way we make decisions about treatment.

Previous Knowledge

Answer these questions and prepare to discuss them in class.

1. What diseases do you think are most threatening to you personally? to the nation and to the world as a whole?

_____

_____

_____

2. How can medical science confront the challenges of disease in the twenty-first century? Who should be responsible?

_____

_____

_____

Preview and Predict

Preview Chapter 8. Based on your preview, predict two things you will learn in this chapter.

1. _____

2. _____

"This Is the End of the World":
The Black Death   Barbara Tuchman

In the fourteenth century, the Black Death struck Europe. The actual number of dead from the *atra mors* or "dreadful death," as the people called it at the time, is unknown. It is estimated that at least one-third of the population of Europe died over a 20-year period. The following reading, by noted historian Barbara Tuchman, provides an account of the Black Death.

1   In October 1347, two months after the fall of Calais, Genoese trading ships put into the harbor of Messina in Sicily with dead and dying men at the oars. The ships had come from the Black Sea port of Caffa (now Feodosiya) in the Crimea, where the Genoese maintained a trading post. The diseased sailors showed strange black swellings about the size of an egg or an apple in the armpits and groin. The swellings oozed blood and pus and were followed by spreading boils and black blotches on the skin from internal bleeding. The sick suffered severe pain and died quickly within five days of the first symptoms. As the disease spread, other symptoms of continuous fever and spitting of blood appeared instead of the swellings or buboes. These victims coughed and sweated heavily and died even more quickly, within three days or less, sometimes in 24 hours. In both types everything that issued from the body—breath, sweat, blood from the buboes and lungs, bloody urine, and blood-blackened excrement—smelled foul. Depression and despair accompanied the physical symptoms, and before the end "death is seen seated on the face."

2   The disease was bubonic plague, present in two forms: one that infected the bloodstream, causing the buboes and internal bleeding, and was spread by contact; and a second, more virulent pneumonic type that infected the lungs and was spread by respiratory infection. The presence of both at once caused the high mortality and speed of contagion. So lethal was the disease that cases were known of persons going to bed well and dying before they woke, of doctors catching the illness at a bedside and dying before the patient. So rapidly did it spread from one to another that to a French physician, Simon de Covino, it seemed as if one sick person "could infect the whole world." The malignity of the pestilence appeared more terrible because its victims knew no prevention and no remedy.

3   The physical suffering of the disease and its aspects of evil mystery were expressed in a strange Welsh lament which saw "death coming into our midst like black smoke, a plague which cuts off the young, a rootless phantom which has no mercy for fair countenance. Woe is me of the shilling in the armpit! It is seething, terrible . . . a head that gives pain and causes a loud cry . . . a painful angry knob . . . Great is its seething like a burning cinder . . . a grievous thing of ashy color." Its eruption is ugly like the "seeds of black peas, broken fragments of brittle sea-coal . . . the early ornaments of black death, cinders of the peelings of the cockle weed, a mixed multitude, a black plague like half-pence, like berries. . . ."

4   Rumors of a terrible plague supposedly arising in China and spreading through Tartary (Central Asia) to India and Persia, Mesopotamia, Syria,

©2007 Pearson Education, Inc.

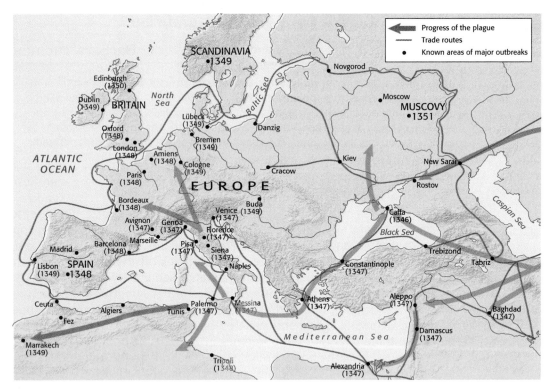

Figure 8.1

Egypt, and all of Asia Minor had reached Europe in 1346. They told of a death toll so devastating that all of India was said to be depopulated, whole territories covered by dead bodies, other areas with no one left alive. As added up by Pope Clement VI at Avignon, the total of reported dead reached 23,840,000. In the absence of a concept of contagion, no serious alarm was felt in Europe until the trading ships brought their black burden of pestilence into Messina while other infected ships from the Levant carried it to Genoa and Venice.

5   By January 1348 it penetrated France via Marseille, and North Africa via Tunis. Shipborne along coasts and navigable rivers, it spread westward from Marseille through the ports of Languedoc to Spain and northward up the Rhône to Avignon, where it arrived in March. It reached Narbonne, Montpellier, Carcassonne, and Toulouse between February and May, and at the same time in Italy spread to Rome and Florence and their hinterlands. Between June and August it reached Bordeaux, Lyon, and Paris, spread to Burgundy and Normandy, and crossed the Channel from Normandy into southern England. From Italy during the same summer it crossed the Alps into Switzerland and reached eastward to Hungary.

6   In a given area the plague accomplished its kill within four to six months and then faded, except in the larger cities, where, rooting into the close-quartered population, it abated during the winter, only to reappear in spring and rage for another six months.

7   In 1349 it resumed in Paris, spread to Picardy, Flanders, and the Low Countries, and from England to Scotland and Ireland as well as to Norway, where a ghost ship with a cargo of wool and a dead crew drifted offshore until it ran aground near Bergen. From there the plague passed into Sweden, Denmark, Prussia, Iceland, and as far as Greenland. Leaving a strange pocket of immunity in Bohemia, and Russia unattacked until 1351, it had passed from most of Europe by mid-1350. Although the mortality rate was erratic, ranging from one fifth in some places to nine tenths or almost total elimination in others, the overall estimate of modern demographers has settled—for the area extending from India to Iceland—around the same figure expressed in Froissart's casual words: "a third of the world died." His estimate, the common one at the time, was not an inspired guess but a borrowing of St. John's figure for mortality from plague in Revelation, the favorite guide to human affairs of the Middle Ages.

8   A third of Europe would have meant about 20 million deaths. No one knows in truth how many died. Contemporary reports were an awed impression, not an accurate count. In crowded Avignon, it was said, 400 died daily; 7,000 houses emptied by death were shut up; a single graveyard received 11,000 corpses in six weeks; half the city's inhabitants reportedly died, including 9 cardinals or one-third of the total, and 70 lesser prelates. Watching the endlessly passing death carts, chroniclers let normal exaggeration take wings and put the Avignon death toll at 62,000 and even at 120,000, although the city's total population was probably less than 50,000.

9   When graveyards filled up, bodies at Avignon were thrown into the Rhône until mass burial pits were dug for dumping the corpses. In London in such pits corpses piled up in layers until they overflowed. Everywhere reports speak of the sick dying too fast for the living to bury. Corpses were dragged out of homes and left in front of doorways. Morning light revealed new piles of bodies. In Florence the dead were gathered up by the Compagnia della Misericordia—founded in 1244 to care for the sick—whose members wore red robes and hoods masking the face except for the eyes. When their efforts failed, the dead lay putrid in the streets for days at a time. When no coffins were to be had, the bodies were laid on boards, two or three at once, to be carried to graveyards or common pits. Families dumped their own relatives into the pits, or buried them so hastily and thinly "that dogs dragged them forth and devoured their bodies."

10   Amid accumulating death and fear of contagion, people died without last rites and were buried without prayers, a prospect that terrified the last hours of the stricken. A bishop in England gave permission to laymen to make confession to each other as was done by the Apostles, "or if no man is present then even to a woman," and if no priest could be found to administer extreme unction, "then faith must suffice." Clement VI found it necessary to grant remissions of sin to all who died of the plague because so many were unattended by priests. "And no bells tolled," wrote a chronicler of Siena, "and nobody wept no matter what his loss because almost everyone expected death.

11   . . . And people said and believed, 'This is the end of the world.'"

TUCHMAN, *A DISTANT MIRROR*

©2007 Pearson Education, Inc.

Exercise 1   **Recall and Discuss**

Based on Reading 1, Tuchman's "'This Is the End of the World,'" answer the following questions and prepare to discuss them with your classmates.

1. What were the two types of the Black Death that arrived in Europe in 1347?

_____

_____

_____

2. Describe the symptoms of each type of the Black Death.

_____

_____

_____

_____

_____

3. Why weren't Europeans frightened when they heard estimates of 23,840,000 people having died in China and other areas of the East from a terrible plague?

_____

_____

_____

4. According to Tuchman's account and Figure 8.1 how was the Black Death carried to and through Europe? How would a highly contagious disease like the Black Death spread today? Explain.

_____

_____

_____

5. Tuchman says of the dead in Europe, "Contemporary reports were an awed impression, not an accurate count." What does this statement imply?

_____

_____

_____

6. This excerpt from Tuchman's history ends, "And people said and believed, 'This is the end of the world.'" Why do you think people said this?

_____

_____

_____

_____

CRITICAL THINKING

critical thinking
Effectively evaluating what you read using analysis, synthesis, and/or evaluation

There are many ways to think critically about what you read. In Chapter 7, for example, you learned to think critically by distinguishing fact from opinion and examining the author's use and selection of facts, worldview, viewpoint, purpose, bias, and tone. Analysis, synthesis, and evaluation are **critical thinking** skills that readers find useful, even essential. These thinking skills are used in all the disciplines, and you have already practiced using many critical thinking skills throughout this text. For example, students are often asked to complete a *causal analysis*, examining the causes of a certain event or series of events, or a *process analysis*, examining how a situation developed in a certain way. In this chapter, you will focus on using your critical thinking skills in *problem solving*. You will read about ways people have solved problems in the past and consider the challenges of solving the problems of the future.

Analysis

analysis Breaking any topic, item, or event into parts and examining the relationships among the parts

Analysis is a way of examining what you've read, what you've experienced, and what you know about any topic, item, or event. To analyze something means (1) to break it into its constituent parts (the parts that make it up) and then (2) to determine the relationships among the various parts. For example, if you want to analyze the performance of a football team such as the Minnesota Vikings, you might examine it from a variety of angles. You might choose to break one game into parts by examining each play the team made in the game. Or you might analyze the team's performance player by player. Whichever parts you choose to examine, you also need to examine the relationships among the parts. So even if you carefully examine the performance of each player, you still need to look at how each player related to every other player on the offense or defense and to the team as a whole. You might also examine how each individual performed in relationship to particular opponents on other teams, in night games versus day games, in home games versus road games, in third-down situations, and under various weather conditions.

©2007 Pearson Education, Inc.

It is often necessary to analyze aspects of our lives, our health in particular. For example, imagine you are having trouble sleeping at night and are considering seeing a doctor to remedy your problem with insomnia. To find the cause and propose possible solutions, your doctor will ask you questions regarding all the possible factors in need of analysis. Certain factors she might ask about would be your caffeine intake, the amount of exercise you do, the time you go to bed, the amount of stress you are under, and any environmental factors that might interrupt your sleep.

Synthesis

synthesis Drawing parts together to create a whole

Synthesis is putting ideas together. It involves drawing on facts, opinions, and observations from a variety of sources to create a new whole. For example, a coach who analyzed the Minnesota Vikings' performance might synthesize the results of that analysis and present a new game plan for the team. Of course, the plan wouldn't be entirely new; it would build on the team's and coach's prior knowledge and experience, but it would probably be a new combination of all the plays they'd made before. In another example, the doctor analyzing your insomnia would put together all your statements about the problem to come up with its root cause.

All kinds of information can be analyzed and synthesized. Literature students analyze poems, plays, and novels. Then they synthesize the knowledge they've gained in an interpretive essay. Political science students analyze the results of an election, the passage of a bill in Congress, or the attempts of lobbyists to promote special interests. Then they might arrive at a synthesis that proposes a better strategy for campaigning or a way to control the effects of lobbyists. Throughout history, men and women have used analysis to help them understand problem situations. Then they attempted to synthesize what they learned to come up with solutions.

Evaluation

evaluation Judging the effectiveness of something based on standards of reasoning

In Chapter 7, you learned to evaluate facts and opinions. More generally, **evaluation** involves judging the effectiveness of something—a plan, solution, argument, or idea—based on standards of reasoning. New solutions must be evaluated, or judged, before they are used. A critical thinker asks, "Is this the best possible solution? What kind of reasoning is this judgment based on? What are the advantages of this solution? Why is this solution better than any of the other possibilities? Do most of the people best qualified to make this decision agree?" For example, the Minnesota Vikings coach will try many ways to evaluate his new game plan before he uses it. He won't make the decision all on his own; he'll seek the advice of other people whose judgment he values. Once he reaches a conclusion about how to solve the problem, the coach plans how to implement his plan. After he uses the new game plan, more evaluation will be necessary. Did the game plan work as intended? How did each player perform? How might they improve the play for the next game? Why were they (or weren't they) able to score?

Similarly, once the doctor treating your insomnia problem determines the cause, and proposes a solution, you will evaluate its effectiveness after a few weeks or months. Did reducing caffeine intake and exercising in the morning help? Or, are further changes, or perhaps medication, needed?

Using Critical Thinking to Solve Problems

The rest of this chapter examines the ways in which people have historically used critical thinking skills as tools to solve problems and how we will be challenged to use these skills in the future. The process of **problem solving** requires us to follow these steps:

problem solving
Identifying the parts of a problem and following a process to reach a reasonable conclusion

1. Clearly *identify* the nature of the problem.
2. Use *analysis* and *synthesis* to move toward a solution.
3. *Evaluate* the possible solutions.
4. *Choose* and *implement* the solution.
5. *Evaluate* the effectiveness of the solution.

In the readings in this chapter, you'll see how people have attempted to analyze and solve the problems of the Black Death and other infectious diseases in their own time. You'll see that sometimes the information people had on which to base their conclusions was incomplete or faulty, or their reasoning in putting the information together was faulty, and thus their conclusions and solutions were wrong, or at least ineffective. This was true five centuries ago, and, of course, five centuries into the future people will be able to see how to solve problems, such as finding a cure for the AIDS epidemic, that we are struggling with today.

| Exercise 2 | ## Use Critical Thinking

As you read the following paragraphs on the Black Death, keep in mind the five-step problem-solving process. Then answer the questions that follow.

1. The diseased sailors showed strange black swellings about the size of an egg or an apple in the armpits and groin. The swellings oozed blood and pus and were followed by spreading boils and black blotches on the skin from internal bleeding. The sick suffered severe pain and died quickly within five days of the first symptoms. (Tuchman, "'This Is the End of the World'")

   a. What problem did the people identify?

   _____

©2007 Pearson Education, Inc.

b. Based on this information, what might people have thought was the cause of death?

_____

_____

c. What difficulties do you think people faced in trying to solve this problem through observation?

_____

_____

2. No one knows in truth how many died. Contemporary reports were an awed impression, not an accurate count. In crowded Avignon, it was said, 400 died daily; 7,000 houses emptied by death were shut up; a single graveyard received 11,000 corpses in six weeks; half the city's inhabitants reportedly died, including 9 cardinals or one-third of the total, and 70 lesser prelates. Watching the endlessly passing death carts, chroniclers let normal exaggeration take wings and put the Avignon death toll at 62,000 and even at 120,000, although the city's total population was probably less than 50,000. (Tuchman, "'This Is the End of the World'")

a. How accurately were the people who lived at the time able to count the number of people who died?

_____

_____

_____

b. Which details explain some of the reasons why the death counts were inaccurate?

_____

_____

_____

3. Froissart said "a third of the world" died from the Black Death. Tuchman, however, explained, "His estimate, the common one at the time, was not an inspired guess but a borrowing of St. John's figure for mortality from plague in Revelation, the favorite guide to human affairs of the Middle Ages." Revelation is the last book in the Bible.

a. Why do you think Revelation was a favorite source of guidance in the Middle Ages?

_____

_____

b. Why would people accept this estimate for the number of deaths?

_____

_____

4. Amid accumulating death and fear of contagion, people died without last rites and were buried without prayers, a prospect that terrified the last hours of the stricken. A bishop in England gave permission to lay-men to make confession to each other as was done by the Apostles, "or if no man is present then even to a woman," and if no priest could be found to administer extreme unction, "then faith must suffice." Clement VI found it necessary to grant remissions of sin to all who died of the plague because so many were unattended by priests. "And no bells tolled," wrote a chronicler of Siena, "and nobody wept no matter what his loss because almost everyone expected death." (Tuchman, "'This Is the End of the World'")

a. What did church authorities do as increasing numbers of people died?

_____

_____

_____

b. How effective do you think these actions were in alleviating suffering?

_____

_____

Reading 2   *Pathology of the Black Death*

John P. McKay, Bennett D. Hill, and John Buckler

An analysis of the actual causes of the Black Death, or bubonic plague, was not successful until 500 years later. The bacteriologists who are cred-ited with identifying the causes had a great deal more scientific and medical knowledge on which to base their conclusions than did the ex-perts of the Middle Ages. Read the following explanation from a current world history text.

1 Modern understanding of the bubonic plague rests on the research of two bacteriologists, one French and one Japanese, who in 1894 independently identified the bacillus that causes the plague, *Pasteurella pestis* (so labeled after the French scientist's teacher, Louis Pasteur). The bacillus liked to live in the bloodstream of an animal or, ideally, in the stomach of a flea. The flea in turn resided in the hair of a rodent, sometimes a squirrel but preferably

©2007 Pearson Education, Inc.

the hardy, nimble, and vagabond black rat. Why the host black rat moved so much, scientists still do not know, but it often traveled by ship. There the black rat could feast for months on a cargo of grain or live snugly among bales of cloth. Fleas bearing the bacillus also had no trouble nesting in saddlebags. Comfortable, well fed, and often having greatly multiplied, the black rats ended their ocean voyage and descended on the great cities of Europe.

2   Although by the fourteenth century urban authorities from London to Paris to Rome had begun to try to achieve a primitive level of sanitation, urban conditions remained ideal for the spread of disease. Narrow streets filled with mud, refuse, and human excrement were as much cesspools as thoroughfares. Dead animals and sore-covered beggars greeted the traveler. Houses whose upper stories projected over the lower ones eliminated light and air. And extreme overcrowding was commonplace. When all members of an aristocratic family lived and slept in one room, it should not be surprising that six or eight persons in a middle-class or poor household slept in one bed—if they had one. Closeness, after all, provided warmth. Houses were beginning to be constructed of brick, but many remained of wood, clay, and mud. A determined rat had little trouble entering such a home.

3   Standards of personal hygiene remained frightfully low. Since water was considered dangerous, partly for good reasons, people rarely bathed. Skin infections, consequently, were common. Lack of personal cleanliness, combined with any number of temporary ailments such as diarrhea and the common cold, naturally weakened the body's resistance to serious disease. Fleas and body lice were universal afflictions: everyone from peasants to archbishops had them. One more bite did not cause much alarm. But if that nibble came from a bacillus-bearing flea, an entire household or area was doomed.

MCKAY ET AL., *A HISTORY OF WORLD SOCIETIES*

Exercise 3   ## Work with Words

Identify words in Reading 2 that are unfamiliar to you and are important for understanding the reading. Choose three to five of these words to add to your personal vocabulary. On a separate sheet of paper, or on 3 × 5 cards, write each word and its appropriate meaning, the original sentence in which it appeared, and your own sentence using the word.

Exercise 4   ## Check Your Understanding

Based on Reading 2, McKay, Hill, and Buckler's "Pathology of the Black Death," answer the following questions in your own words.

1. What specific problem did the researchers identify?

_____

_____

2. The researchers were able to analyze the steps in the process by which the Black Death was spread. List the steps they identified in that process.

_____

_____

_____

_____

_____

3. The researchers were also able to analyze the causes for the easy spread of the plague. List three of the causes they found.

_____

_____

_____

_____

Exercise 5   **Reflect**

Think about what you read in Reading 2 and what you already know about the Black Death. Answer the following questions, and prepare to discuss them with your classmates.

1. Why do you think it took so long for scientists to understand what actually happened in the case of the Black Death?

_____

_____

2. If an outbreak of the Black Death were to occur today, how would medical experts respond, based on the researchers' solutions?

_____

_____

3. Do you think there are any similarities between people's responses to the AIDS epidemic today and people's response to the Black Death 600 years ago? What are the similarities? What are the differences?

_____

_____

©2007 Pearson Education, Inc.

Scientific Method

scientific method
A system for solving problems based on inquiry, observation, and experimentation

The **scientific method** is a problem-solving technique based on inquiry, observation, and experimentation. Scientists today consider this a most powerful problem-solving system, but it is a relatively recent approach to the interpretation of experience. In fourteenth-century Europe, learned men believed truth was revealed in scripture. Not until the sixteenth and seventeenth centuries did people begin to search for truth through observation and experimentation. Today, all branches of science adhere to some form of the scientific method. Physical scientists, such as biologists, chemists, and physicists use observation and experimentation to develop theories about the natural world around us. Social scientists, such as sociologists, psychologists, and political scientists, use techniques such as surveys, observation, and case studies, as well as experiments, to study human behavior and the human condition.

The following explanation from a college biology textbook introduces the scientific method through a visual aid (flowchart) and an example from daily life. Notice the steps shown in the flowchart and how they are applied to the case study involving a flashlight. First, you observe the situation, or problem. In this case, a flashlight fails during a camping trip. You inquire about the problem's cause. You then make an educated guess or **hypothesis**, based on past experience. You recall that in the past, when your flashlight no longer worked, your batteries were usually dead. So you predict the result based on your hypothesis and replace the batteries. This is the experiment, or test. If the flashlight now works, the result tells you your hypothesis was correct. If the flashlight does not work, you need to make further observations and come up with

hypothesis A system for solving problems based on inquiry, observation, and experimentation

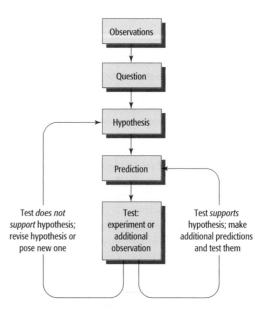

Figure 8.2   Source: Neil A. Campbell, Lawrence G. Mitchell, and Jane B. Reese, *Biology: Concept and Connections,* 4th ed. (San Francisco: Benjamin Cummings, 2003).

another hypothesis, repeating all the steps until you solve the problem. Using the terminology of the scientific method, this thinking process might look like this:

Observation: My flashlight doesn't work.

Question: What's wrong with my flashlight?

Hypothesis: The flashlight batteries are dead.

Prediction: <u>If</u> this hypothesis is correct,

Experiment: and I replace the batteries with new ones,

Predicted result: <u>then</u> the flashlight should work.

(Campbell et al., *Biology*)

<table>
<tr><td>**Exercise 6**</td><td></td></tr>
</table>

Use the Scientific Method

Read the following excerpt from a college biology textbook about the use and effectiveness of antibiotics to treat disease. Relate your knowledge of the scientific method to the reading, and then answer the questions that follow.

Antibiotic Resistance in Bacteria

1   Antibiotics are drugs that disable or kill infectious microorganisms. Most antibiotics are naturally occurring chemicals derived from other microorganisms. Penicillin, for example, was originally isolated from a mold and has been widely prescribed since the 1940s. A revolution in human health rapidly followed its introduction, rendering many previously fatal diseases easily curable (such as strep throat and surgical infections). During the 1950s, some doctors even predicted the end of human infectious disease.

2   Why hasn't this optimistic prediction come true? Because it did not take into account the force of evolution. . . . For nearly every antibiotic that has been developed, a resistant strain of bacteria has appeared within a few decades. For example, some strains of the tuberculosis-causing bacterium are now resistant to all three of the antibiotics commonly used to treat the disease.

3   In what ways do we contribute to the problem of antibiotic resistance? Livestock producers add antibiotics to animal feed as a growth promoter. As a result, much of the packaged meat for sale in supermarkets contains bacteria that are resistant to standard antibiotics. Doctors contribute to the problem by overprescribing antibiotics—for example, to patients with viral infections, which do not respond to antibiotic treatment. And patients contribute to this problem through the misuse of prescribed antibiotics—for example, by prematurely stopping the medication because they feel better. This allows mutant bacteria that may be killed more slowly by the drug to survive and multiply. Subsequent mutations in such bacteria may lead to full-blown antibiotic resistance. During the anthrax crisis of 2001, public health officials urged panicked citizens to avoid unnecessarily taking ciprofloxacin, the drug

©2007 Pearson Education, Inc.

used to treat the deadliest form of anthrax infection, because doing so could select for resistant bacteria.

4   Difficulty in treating common human infections is a serious public health concern. Penicillin was effective against nearly all bacterial infections in the 1940s but is virtually useless today in its original form. Increasingly powerful drugs have since been developed, but they continue to be rendered ineffective as resistant bacteria evolve. The medical community and pharmaceutical companies are engaged in an ongoing race against the powerful force of bacterial evolution. (Campbell et al., *Biology*)

1. State the hypothesis (prediction) that was made in the 1950s about antibiotics and their effectiveness in the treatment of disease. What factors led to the prediction?

_____

_____

_____

2. What has experience with antibiotics demonstrated?

_____

_____

_____

3. What information do scientists have about tuberculosis-causing bacterium?

_____

_____

_____

4. What three factors contribute to the problem of antibiotic-resistant bacteria?

_____

_____

_____

5. What hypothesis would be reasonable to make based on what you know from this reading about the future of antibiotics?

_____

_____

_____

◆

Ethics

Science has proven itself to be a highly effective problem-solving method. However, progress requires that we ask ourselves some difficult questions. How will the solutions that scientists reach be used? What part does ethics play in determining the use of this knowledge? **Ethics** is a set of moral values, our standards for good or bad, right or wrong. Many of the ethical questions involving science arise when technology, as physicist Paul Hewitt says, develops the "tools, techniques, and procedures for putting the findings of science to use."

ethics A set of standards for distinguishing right from wrong

To carefully evaluate the solutions science provides, we must understand the impact of technology on the world around us. Might some scientific advances actually do more harm than good to people and the environment? For example, modern technology, in the form of insecticides, was promoted in India to improve their agricultural production. But in 1984, history's worst industrial accident occurred when a deadly gas leaked from a Union Carbide insecticide plant at Bhopal, India. Author David Watson, in an article in *The Fifth Estate* in 1985, attacked the underlying failure of ethics he perceived in this disaster.

> The cinders of the funeral pyres at Bhopal were still warm, and the mass graves still fresh, but the media prostitutes of the corporations have already begun their homilies in defense of industrialism and its uncounted horrors. Some 3,000 people were slaughtered in the wake of the deadly gas cloud, and 20,000 will remain permanently disabled. The poison gas left a 25-square-mile swath of dead and dying, people and animals, as it drifted southeast away from the Union Carbide factory. "We thought it was a plague," said one victim. Indeed it was: a chemical plague, an *industrial plague.*
>
> *Ashes, ashes, all fall down!*
>
> A terrible, unfortunate "accident," we are assured by the propaganda apparatus for Progress, for History, for "Our Modern Way of Life." A price, of course, has to be paid—since the risks are necessary to ensure a Higher Standard of Living, a Better Way of Life. (Watson, "We All Live in Bhopal")

Watson concludes the article by stating, "The corporate vampires are guilty of greed, plunder, murder, slavery, extermination and devastation," and describing "the chemical factories and the chemical way of life" as "nothing but death." Clearly, Watson believed the tragedy of Bhopal was due to corporate greed, which led to corporate disregard for the safety of the people working in and living near the factory. His use of a series of words with extremely negative meanings and connotations—*plunder, murder, slavery*—reinforces his condemnation of the events that led to the tragedy and establishes a tone of outrage. On the other hand, Watson quotes an editorial printed in the *Wall Street Journal* on December 13, 1984: "It is worthwhile to remember that the Union Carbide insecticide

©2007 Pearson Education, Inc.

plant and the people surrounding it were where they were for compelling reasons. India's agriculture is thriving, bringing a better life to millions of rural people, and partly because of the use of modern agricultural technology that includes applications of insect killers." Union Carbide officials concluded that, regardless of the disaster, "the benefits outweigh the costs."

Other ethical issues regarding science and technology produce questions like these:

■ Who should pay scientists to do their work? How does the source of the funds affect their choice of problems to consider? Should any part or all of their funds come from corporations?

■ What is the best way to spend money for scientific research, especially if the amount is limited? Should researchers study breast cancer, AIDS, human DNA, how to clean up the carcinogens in the environment, how to prevent environmental pollution in the first place, or how to colonize the moon?

■ Who should benefit from the profits of scientific discoveries—business or the public?

■ How should medical resources be spent? Is it right for some people to have access to excellent health care while others have none? or poor care?

■ What responsibilities, if any, do wealthy nations have toward poor nations for helping them with health care problems?

■ Are there any things that science should not do?

Can you think of other ethical issues related to science? As you continue to read in this chapter, keep in mind some of the bioethical issues that you are familiar with as well as the ones listed here.

Reading 3   *AIDS: The Long War*   *The Economist*

The following reading about the threat of the AIDS epidemic to our world as we know it appeared as an editorial in the prestigious British journal The Economist in July 2002. AIDS is the twenty-first century's equivalent to the fourteenth century's plague. Significant differences to take into consideration, however, are how long it takes to succumb to the illness, the advances of science, the medical treatments available, and who has access to them, as well as the tendency for individuals and governments to make moral judgments or to avoid the subject of AIDS, since it is a sexually transmitted disease. As you read, consider how convincingly the author uses statistics and the author's point of view toward the AIDS crisis.

1   Just a reminder. Some 40 million people are infected with HIV, the AIDS virus. Another 20 million have died of it already. Around 3 million more will do so over the next 12 months. That is nearly 9,000 a day—three times as many people as died in the terrorist attack on the World Trade Center last September [2001]. Every day, 15,000 more people are infected. Unless

things change a lot for the better, almost all of them will die of it, too. And most of those people will be young. AIDS is a disease that takes people in the prime of life, rather than in decrepit old age.

2   It is much easier to notice, deplore and act against deaths caused by human wickedness than deaths caused by nature. But if all men are created equal, all avoidable deaths should be regarded as equally sad. And AIDS is the one cause of such deaths that is rising, not declining. AIDS kills predominantly in poor countries, compounding the problem. Poor-country governments must do whatever is in their power to save their citizens from this scourge before waving a collecting tin at the rich. But common decency suggests that the rich world should do whatever it can to help. For, despite the availability of drugs that can keep the disease at bay in those who can afford them (or whose governments can), AIDS has not gone away. Indeed, it is getting much worse.

Digging Deep

3   At the moment, the worst affected countries are in Africa. Some places have infection rates that are above 30%, or even 40%, of the adult population—and still rising. Cynics in the West might write Africa off. Are China, India, Indonesia and Russia to be written off as well?

4   All these countries (two of them the world's most populous nations) are threatened. The Chinese government admits to one million infections—widely regarded as an underestimate. India admits to four million. Indonesia's case load is still tiny but, after years of stability, an epidemic is raging through the country's prostitutes. Elsewhere, that has been an early sign of trouble. In Russia, the catalyst is intravenous drug use, rather than prostitution, but the result may be the same. A projection by Imperial College, London, suggests Russia may have 5 million people infected with HIV in five years' time, 4 million of them suffering the symptoms of AIDS.

5   The first task for such countries is to own up to the scale of the problem. Too many governments still feel shy about discussing this horror in public. Then, they need to spend wisely the money from the recently created Global Fund—to use it to best effect, and to encourage donors to keep donations coming. As for rich countries, America can do most. Already, America makes a contribution that, as a proportion of the rich-world total, is roughly in line with its share of its GDP (Gross Domestic Product). But as Stephen Lewis, the United Nations' special envoy on AIDS to Africa, pointed out to the recent International AIDS Conference in Barcelona [July 2002], that is because other countries align their contributions with the American benchmark. If America gave more, the rest would probably follow.

6   If properly supervised, such extra aid could be well spent. Even something as simple as more condoms would help. Better education, including sex education, is essential, especially for girls, since more women than men die from AIDS. Women also need stronger legal protection against sexual violence. Testing programs should be particularly encouraged, as prevention

©2007 Pearson Education, Inc.

is better than cure. Spending is needed on health-care infrastructure, including clinics, equipment, and doctors. Infrastructure to deliver a vaccine also needs to be planned, so that it can be quickly put to use when a vaccine is eventually invented. And poor countries need to copy the example of Brazil, which has made good use of the fact that anti-AIDS drugs can now be bought fairly cheaply outside the rich world, thanks to a liberal interpretation of international treaties on patent law (and also to decent behavior on the part of many drug companies).

7   The Global Fund for AIDS, tuberculosis and malaria hopes to raise about $10 billion a year, more than half of it for AIDS. That is a large sum, but an affordable one. Already 3 million people a year are dying; without renewed effort, the figure will rise. Surely, a toll so dreadful demands the utmost urgency.

THE ECONOMIST, "AIDS: The Long War"

Exercise 7   ## Work with Words

Identify words in Reading 3 that are unfamiliar to you and are important for understanding the reading. Choose three to five of these words to add to your personal vocabulary. On a separate sheet of paper, or on 3 × 5 cards, write each word and its appropriate meaning, the original sentence in which it appeared, and your own sentence using the word.

Exercise 8   ## Check Your Understanding

Based on Reading 3, "AIDS: The Long War," choose the best answer for each of the following multiple-choice questions.

1. Which of the following is the best thesis statement for the reading?
   a. The AIDS epidemic worldwide is at crisis proportions and growing, and both rich and poor countries must increase attention and resources to stopping its spread.
   b. Some 40 million people are infected with HIV and the AIDS virus, and already 20 million people have died of it.
   c. The first task of countries threatened by an explosion of AIDS cases is to acknowledge the immensity of the problem.

2. Which of the following best describes the tone of paragraph 1?
   a. Matter-of-fact
   b. Cautious
   c. Alarming

3. Which of the following is a reasonable inference we can make from reading paragraph 3?
   a. People in the West have written off Africa.
   b. Some areas of Africa have infection rates of 30 percent, 40 percent, and even higher.
   c. China, India, Indonesia, and Russia are soon to be among the countries with epidemics that are out of control.

4. According to the author, the United States is
    a. already giving a sufficient amount of money to the Global Fund.
    b. giving its proportionate amount of money to the Global Fund but should give more and set an example for the rest of the world.
    c. giving too much to a fund that is not properly supervised.

5. We can infer that the author believes that
    a. it is unethical for countries to shy away from discussing the AIDS epidemic in public.
    b. the United States should double its contributions to AIDS research and prevention internationally.
    c. it is ethical for countries to shy away from discussing the AIDS epidemic because governments should not get involved in making moral judgments for their citizens.

6. The author's purpose in writing this editorial is to
    a. inform readers of the current status of the AIDS epidemic.
    b. inform readers of the status of the worldwide AIDS epidemic and to propose solutions.
    c. propose detailed solutions to the worldwide AIDS epidemic.

Exercise 9   **Think Critically and Reflect**

Think about what you read in Reading 3 and what you already know about the AIDS epidemic. Answer the following questions, and prepare to discuss them with your classmates.

1. What are the author's predictions about the future of the AIDS epidemic? What are these predictions based on? Why, in your opinion, are these predictions reasonable?

_____

_____

_____

_____

_____

2. What is the dominant pattern of organization used in Reading 3? (Choose from chronological order, problem and solution, and comparison and contrast.) In what ways is this organizational pattern effective for the author's purpose in writing the article?

_____

_____

_____

_____

©2007 Pearson Education, Inc.

3. Why do you think the author compares the number of people dying from AIDS each day to the number of deaths at the World Trade Center (on September 11, 2001)? How does making this comparison strengthen the author's thesis?

_____

_____

_____

4. What is the author's ethical position on how we should react to people dying of human-inflicted violence in comparison to those dying of "natural causes"?

_____

_____

_____

5. What is the author's viewpoint regarding resources going to help prevent the spread of AIDS? Do you agree with his point of view? Why? Who do you think might disagree with him? Explain some possible reasons for this disagreement.

_____

_____

_____

_____

_____

6. What do you think is the ethical response to the AIDS epidemic that governments of countries with high infection rates should have?

_____

_____

_____

EVALUATING ARGUMENTS

When we read about epidemics such as the Black Death in the fourteenth century and AIDS in the twenty-first century, or about industrial accidents such as the gas cloud at Bhopal, we quickly become aware that there can be very different opinions about an event or a problem. Especially in our "information age," with so much data available, writers who have very different, even opposite, points of view can seem convincing. We are challenged to think critically about many significant issues—health, politics, the environment, the economy. How do we decide whom to believe and whether to be convinced or persuaded to agree with a certain position a writer might take? The reading skills you've already developed by working through this textbook will help you evaluate arguments. Here are four guidelines you can use to evaluate arguments that you read. The guidelines are summarized in Table 8.1 on page 429.

Examine the Evidence

To examine the evidence, you need to use the skills you have developed in recognizing main ideas and supporting points (Chapters 3 and 4) and recognizing facts, the sources of facts, and whether important facts have been omitted (Chapter 7). Other considerations are the author's authority and the type of publication the reading is from, whether the information is documented, and whether it is current (Chapter 7).

Consider the Structure

When you look at the structure of a reading, you will want to use the skills you have developed to determine if the thesis is clearly stated (Chapter 3) and if the supporting points (Chapter 4) and patterns of organization (Chapter 5) are appropriate. For example, if a comparison-and-contrast organizational pattern is used, you must determine if similar things are being compared. In exemplification, you need to consider whether the examples are appropriate and relevant. If a process is described, you need to determine if the steps are logical.

Check for Fallacies

fallacies Errors or weaknesses in reasoning in an argument

Fallacies are errors or weaknesses in reasoning in an argument that can lead to incorrect conclusions. When evaluating arguments, it is important to be aware of any and all fallacies. The following are common fallacies:

- *Ad hominem* involves attacking the opponent rather than the idea the opponent is discussing. For example, "When he was president, Bill Clinton initially denied having an affair with a White House aide, so how could we trust what he said about health care."
- *Appeal to emotions* takes advantage of the reader's emotions and sways the reader from evaluating the argument logically. For example, "If you have a heart, you will find the money to support this cause."
- *Bandwagon* attempts to convince the reader based on the popularity of the thing being proposed. Often you are meant to feel you will miss out on what everyone else is doing if you don't participate or believe. For example, "All the other parents have bought their kids cars, so why don't you?"

©2007 Pearson Education, Inc.

- *Overgeneralization* assumes that what is true under certain conditions is true under all conditions or what fits certain members of a group applies to all members. For example, "Workers can't get health insurance through jobs anymore."
- *Oversimplification* describes a complex idea or situation in terms that are so simple that they ignore the complexity and distort the idea or situation. For example, "If a child is having problems, the parent is to blame."
- *Slippery slope* claims that an action ought to be avoided because it will invariably lead to a series of unpleasant consequences for similar situations. For example, "If you let one student leave the room to get a drink of water during a test, then you'll have to let all students leave for all kinds of made-up reasons."
- *Testimonial* uses famous people as representatives of authority on issues for which they have no expertise. Television commercials, for example, often hire actors to promote services or products they know nothing about.

Make Ethical Decisions

Making ethical decisions may be the most important consideration in evaluating an argument. First, you must consider if the potential benefits and risks of a position have been taken into consideration. Then, question whether all the ethical issues have been considered. Finally, you must consider whether or not you agree with the writer's system of values. Do you share the author's worldview—as a mother, employer, patient, child, philosopher, scientist, minister, businessperson—so that you might share the same viewpoint or value system?

Exercise 10 ## Check for Fallacies

Examine the following statements and determine which fallacies are used. Circle the best answer.

1. How can you deny a human being the right to health and happiness?
   a. Slippery slope
   b. Ad hominem
   c. Appeal to emotions

2. My doctor told me I should lose weight, but that's ridiculous. He's fat himself.
   a. Oversimplification
   b. Bandwagon
   c. Ad hominem

3. If the government controls drug prices, next thing you know they'll be controlling everything you do.
   a. Slippery slope
   b. Testimonial
   c. Appeal to emotions

4. Poverty would end if people stopped having so many babies.
   a. Bandwagon
   b. Oversimplification
   c. Slippery slope

5. This is the most popular pain reliever on the market.
   a. Testimonial
   b. Bandwagon
   c. Appeal to emotions

6. If that lipstick is good enough for Jennifer Lopez, it's good enough for me.
   a. Slippery slope
   b. Testimonial
   c. Ad hominem

7. If you're not part of the solution, you're part of the problem.
   a. Appeal to emotions
   b. Slippery slope
   c. Oversimplification

8. Give my daughter a fighting chance to survive and support the scientific research on stem cells.
   a. Bandwagon
   b. Appeal to emotions
   c. Overgeneralization

9. I would never go to that marriage counselor. She has been divorced twice already.
   a. Ad hominem
   b. Overgeneralization
   c. Testimonial

10. People who contract sexually transmitted diseases are irresponsible.
    a. Slippery slope
    b. Appeal to emotions
    c. Overgeneralization

Table 8.1	**Guidelines and Key Questions for Evaluating Arguments**

Examine the Evidence
- Is there enough evidence to support the argument? Are the appropriate facts included, and are they documented?
- Is the writer an authority in the field or knowledgeable enough to write with authority? Is the publication or the publisher reputable?
- Is the information current, or is it outdated? Does the date of publication matter?

(continued)

©2007 Pearson Education, Inc.

Table 8.1	Guidelines and Key Questions for Evaluating Arguments (continued)

Consider the Structure
- Is the thesis clearly stated, and are the supporting points appropriate and convincing?
- Is the organizational pattern appropriate?

Check for Fallacies
- Does the writer attack people rather than the issues? Is the writer appealing to emotions?
- Does the writer attempt to sway the reader by focusing on the popularity of the subject or by using a testimonial from a celebrity rather than from an expert?
- Does the writer oversimplify a complex issue or overgeneralize from just a few samples?
- Has the writer attempted to convince the reader that something must be avoided to prevent even further exaggerated undesirable consequences?

Make Ethical Decisions
- Have all potential benefits and risks been weighed? Have social, legal, and environmental effects, for example, been fully explored?
- Have all ethical issues been considered?
- Do you agree with the writer's system of values? On what basis?

Reading 4   *As Sick As It Gets*   Rudolph Mueller, MD

Rudolph Mueller, MD, practices internal medicine and geriatrics in upstate New York, and he is professor of medicine at the State University of New York at Buffalo. In his book As Sick As It Gets, *he criticizes the American health care system and proposes what he sees as the only solution to its inadequacies. The following reading is the introduction to that book.*

> *"Of all of the forms of inequality, injustice in healthcare is the most shocking and inhumane."*
>
> —DR MARTIN LUTHER KING JR.

1   There is ill will and controversy among America's healthcare professionals. In nursing, fewer students are entering the field while experienced nurses retire prematurely or leave patient care altogether.[1] Surveys show that a third or more of senior physicians plan early retirement or a change in career in the next three years.[2] Many other practitioners consider the American system to be sick and in need of major reform and restructuring. A recent CBS News poll has reported the American people feel the same way.[3] Many caregivers are disgusted with the greed, waste, and excesses they see daily. For individual Americans, healthcare costs continue to rise, creating economic hardship and concerns over access to proper care for themselves and their families. Corporations and businesses feel the same cost increases

and continually face decisions regarding insurance benefits for their employees.

2   Except for the United States, all democratic, industrialized nations of the Organization for Economic Cooperation and Development (OECD), and in some developing nations, healthcare is considered a human right.[4] Those societies validate that right by providing all people with access to healthcare. This is woefully not true in the United States. In this country medical care is not a right; rather it is a service based on market-driven principles.

3   The healthcare industry and its lobbying organizations and many caregivers fiercely maintain that the American delivery system is the very best in the world because it is based on market-driven principles. They continually criticize other nations' health programs, which are essentially publicly financed and government guaranteed. They want Americans to believe that any change in their health system that includes more government involvement would court disaster, deprive Americans of quality medical care and constrain choice. They allege that government involvement will interfere with research and technology advances. This perception has been established by what is possibly the most extensive and costly combination in American history of a long-term public affairs program and government lobbies at the national and state levels. Elements of the industry oppose any universal program that would provide quality, affordable, accessible healthcare for all Americans. Through its influence, long cultivated in state legislatures and in Washington, the healthcare industry has garnered political control of issues relating to it.

4   The apparent motives are singularly related to the mammoth cash flow that streams toward the insurance companies, HMOs, pharmaceutical companies, and for-profit hospitals and providers. Healthcare is now the largest industry in every developed nation. In the United States, revenues reached $1,077.1 billion in 1998, the last year for which comprehensive data are available.[5] In 1998 Americans paid $4,178 per capita for healthcare or nearly 40% more than the next most expensive country, Switzerland, where it was $2,794 per capita. The American total expenditure on healthcare was 13.6% of Gross Domestic Product (GDP) in 1998. The next nine largest industrialized democracies spent a weighted average of 8.43% of their GDP. The excess paid by Americans was $428 billion, 43% more than the U.S. defense budget.[6] This raises a huge question: Where does this excess money go? Americans are not healthier than the Germans, Canadians or French. They are notably less healthy. In terms of total results, the U.S. health system ranks 37th in the world, as measured by the World Health Organization, the worst performance of any affluent democratic nation.[7]

5   This mediocre performance and high cost raise another question: Does a profit-motivated or market-driven system deliver high-quality care for every American, or does it deliver high profits for those in the industry who seek profit? The market-driven concept, in fact, brings inherent injustices to the people of the United States, allowing 43 million Americans to live without health insurance.[8] Nearly the same number of people are underinsured, creating a healthcare "underclass" in this nation. This underclass comprises real people with feelings, hopes, dreams, joys and sorrows. Those individuals

©2007 Pearson Education, Inc.

must struggle to maintain their health or cope with illness without adequate resources to do so.[9] Nearly 11 million children are being raised without health insurance, and many will fail to obtain even basic health needs.[10] Uninsured children and adults pass in and out of the system, and in the end, some of them become needlessly sick.

6   When people of any age lack access to preventive or even basic health-care, diseases can progress unabated, leading to more costly emergency hospitalizations, and to premature disability and death. In the case of diabetes, cardiovascular diseases and cancer, early treatment prevents disability and saves lives. Prevention can be dramatically less expensive than later-stage interventions. This system failure also inflicts large indirect costs on families and society. The only way to save money by not providing basic healthcare to all people in this nation is to not treat the consequent diseases and let patients in the underclass die quickly and quietly outside the hospital and the system. In the United States over 200,000 people die annually without seeing a doctor during the previous year.[11]

7   [T]he American healthcare system is sick, *As Sick As It Gets.* It is a system with a confused purpose and mission, contaminated by its focus on money and its exploitation of the massive cash flow that modern medical technology has created. Its mission should be to maximize the well-being and health of every individual and our society as a whole, as well as to prevent illness and to relieve pain. . . .

8   The United States is carrying the burden of an unnecessary number of sick people, a burden that could have been prevented with a universal health system. . . . [T]he cost of treatment for Americans who are sick and who should not be sick represents a significant portion of the cost excess between the United States and other OECD nations. It is on the twin pillars of human need and cost savings that I base my call for universal, quality, affordable healthcare for the people in America with the freedom to choose their own doctor, hospital, or other provider. It will prove to be a monumental controversy.

Notes

1. Stephanie Stapleton, "Where's the Nurse?" *American Medical News*, June 18, 2001, 50.

2. Jeff Forster, "Reality Check: Which Doctors Are Heading for the Exits," *Medical Economics*, August 21, 2000; and "And Then There Were None: The Coming Physician Supply Problem," California Medical Association, July 2001, http://www.cmanet.org/publicdoc.cfm/574/1.

3. CBS News Poll, July 13–14, 2001, http://www.pollingreport.com/health.

4. World Health Organization (WHO), *Center for Health Economics Research* 18 (1993): 6.

5. Organisation for Economic Co-operation and Development (OECD), *Health Data 2000*, and Health Care Financing Administration, *Healthcare Financing*

Review (Winter 1999), "Statistical Abstract of the United States 2000," tables 151, 152.

6. OECD, *Health Data 2000*.

7. WHO, *World Health Organization Report 2000*, http://www.pollingreport.com/health.

8. G. Aston, "Number of Uninsured Down, But Struggle Continues," *AMNews*, October 16, 2000.

9. OECD, *Health Data 2000*.

10. Kaiser Family Foundation, http://www.statehealthfacts.kff.org (accessed June 1, 2001).

11. National Center for Health Statistics, "New Study of Patterns of Death in U.S.," February 23, 1998.

MUELLER, *As Sick As It Gets*

Exercise 11   Work with Words

Identify words in Reading 4 that are unfamiliar to you and are important for understanding the reading. Choose three to five of these words to add to your personal vocabulary. On a separate sheet of paper, or on 3 × 5 cards, write each word, its appropriate meaning, the original sentence in which it appeared, and your own sentence using the word.

Exercise 12   Check Your Understanding

Based on Reading 4, Mueller's introduction to *As Sick As It Gets*, choose the best answer for each of the following multiple-choice questions.

1. Which of the following best describes the tone of the reading?
   a. Optimistic
   b. Positive
   c. Alarming

2. Which of the following is not an operating principle for the American health care industry according to Mueller?
   a. Quality, affordable care for all patients
   b. Maximization of profits
   c. Maintenance of case flow

3. Mueller titles his book *As Sick As It Gets* because his major assertion is that
   a. the American people are more sickly than any other people worldwide.
   b. the American health care system is sick because there are not enough quality doctors and researchers.
   c. the American health care system is sick because it focuses on profits rather than quality, affordable care for all citizens.

©2007 Pearson Education, Inc.

4. By citing Martin Luther King Jr. at the beginning of this reading, the author is appealing to
   a. a carefully reasoned analysis of the health care problem.
   b. the hypocritical position taken by the health care industry in its lobbying and marketing efforts.
   c. a general admiration of Dr. King, known for his ethical belief in equality for all people.

5. Which of the following best states the thesis of the reading?
   a. The mission of health care in the United States should be to promote the well-being and health of every individual in our society, not to maximize the profits of private industry.
   b. Prevention of disease is much less expensive than later-stage interventions; therefore, the health care industry should focus on prevention above all else.
   c. There is ill will and controversy among health care professionals.

| Exercise 13 | **Evaluate the Argument**

Answer the following questions as fully as you can in your own words.

1. What does Mueller intend to accomplish with the first paragraph of this reading?

   _____

   _____

   _____

   _____

2. What do we know about the author's worldview that might influence his viewpoint on health care in the United States?

   _____

   _____

   _____

   _____

3. Explain Mueller's purpose in writing this book. What are his motives?

   _____

   _____

   _____

   _____

4. Examine the evidence Mueller uses to convince the reader of his viewpoint. List the evidence.

_____

_____

_____

_____

_____

5. How does Mueller document the data that he presents to support his argument. What are the sources of his information?

_____

_____

_____

_____

6. Mueller wants to convince the reader of his view about medical care in the United States. As a critical reader, what evidence might you find that would counter Mueller's position?

_____

_____

_____

_____

7. What sources would provide evidence that counter Mueller's viewpoint?

_____

_____

_____

8. Check the reading for logical fallacies. Are there any errors in Mueller's reasoning?

_____

_____

_____

_____

©2007 Pearson Education, Inc.

9. Analyze the possible advantages and disadvantages of a universal health care system that is publicly financed and government guaranteed (like those in other countries, as described by Mueller)?

_____

_____

_____

_____

10. Analyze the problems of a market-driven health care system that Mueller presents. What are some possible solutions to those problems that would leave the basic market-driven structure in place?

_____

_____

_____

_____

_____

_____

Exercise 14   **Reflect**

Think about what you read in Mueller's introduction to *As Sick As It Gets* and what you already know about health care in the United States. Then answer the following questions.

1. What experience do you or people you know have with the cost and quality of health care? How did this information influence your reading?

_____

_____

_____

2. In what ways is Mueller's argument most convincing to you? In what ways do you think his argument could be strengthened?

_____

_____

_____

_____

3. Do you agree with Mueller's proposal for "a universal health system" that is not based on profit? How does your perspective, as a potential patient, influence your position?

_____

_____

_____

_____

CHAPTER REVIEW

✔ Reader's Checklist

Check (✔) the concepts and skills introduced in this chapter that you are confident you understand and can now use to think critically about what you read. If you are not sure about any items, (1) go back to the explanations in the text, (2) study and review with other members of your college learning community, (3) ask your instructor for help, (4) check out the Web site for this book at **www.ablongman.com/alexandercommunity4e** for additional exercises on critical thinking and to take the chapter quiz, or (5) complete additional practices in the _Reading Road Trip._

- ❏ Critical thinking
- ❏ Analysis
- ❏ Synthesis
- ❏ Evaluation
- ❏ Problem solving
- ❏ Scientific method
- ❏ Hypothesis
- ❏ Ethics
- ❏ Fallacies

When you are confident that you have mastered these concepts and skills, test yourself with Mastery Tests 8A and 8B (pp. 440–458).

Critical Reflections

Answer the following questions, and prepare to discuss them with your classmates.

1. What do you think are the most important health challenges facing you and your family today? Identify them and briefly explain.

_____

_____

_____

_____

©2007 Pearson Education, Inc.

2. What do you think are the most serious health challenges facing the United States and the world community today? Identify them and briefly explain.

_____

_____

_____

_____

3. How can both scientific reasoning and ethical standards be brought to bear on the treatment of disease—at your local doctor's office or hospital? around the world?

_____

_____

_____

_____

Writing Activity

1. Find a recent article about AIDS or strange new outbreaks of disease (e.g., avian flu in Asia or Ebola in Africa). Write out the steps that should be taken to control or eliminate the disease and to help the people who are sick.

2. Find a newspaper, magazine, or Web page advertisement for a drug. Analyze the purpose, audience, effectiveness, and consequences of the advertisement. Be sure to discuss the fine-print warnings that are included. Comment on the difference between reporting data (as required by law) and reporting data and information to persuade.

Classroom Community

Bring to class the article or advertisement you wrote about in the "Writing Activity." Share it and your analysis with your classmates.

Extend Your Thinking

For another reading related to disease and health care in the twenty-first century, read "Ethical Issues Surrounding Death," by John Macionis, in "Extend Your Thinking," (pp.503–504).

Work the Web

Access the Web site of a pharmaceutical company such as Merck or Pfizer. What impression does the site intend to make on the general public? What are the elements of the site that contribute to this impression? Find the company mission statement. Does the pharmaceutical company claim that its main mission is to help people by curing disease and relieving pain? Does the company's mission statement seem complete and truthful? If so, why? If not, what do you think is omitted or misrepresented? How effective is the Web site at representing the pharmaceutical company the way it wants to be seen by the public?

Finally, write a short paper analyzing some of the parts of the Web site and evaluating its effectiveness. Consult "Evaluating and Navigating Web Sites" in "A Reader's Toolkit," pages 529 through 576, for guidance.

Go to **www.ablongman.com/alexandercommunity4e** for additional Web-based activities.

©2007 Pearson Education, Inc.

Mastery Test   8A

The Emergency Room and the Uninsured
Rudolph Mueller, MD

The following reading is from Dr. Rudolph Mueller's book As Sick As It Gets. *Here he examines the predicament facing Americans who don't have health insurance. The problem identified in this reading deals with our country's policies regarding disease and wellness at the beginning of the twenty-first century. The author charges that there are ethical and practical problems with the U.S. policy. As you read, consider Dr. Mueller's thesis and whether his support is convincing. Do you agree with Dr. Mueller? How do your worldview and ethical beliefs influence you to agree or disagree with him?*

> *Suppose a man comes into your meeting wearing a gold ring and fine clothes, and a poor man in shabby clothes also comes in. If you show special attention to the man wearing fine clothes and say, 'Here's a good seat for you,' but say to the poor man, 'You stand there' or 'Sit on the floor by my feet,' have you not discriminated among yourselves and become judges with evil thoughts?*
> —JAMES 2:2–4, (NEW INTERNATIONAL VERSION)

1 By census estimates in 1999, the United States had nearly 43 million people who were living without health insurance.[1] Who are these uninsured millions? Over 75% of America's uninsured have full-time jobs or live in a household where at least one person is working full time.[2] One-fifth of the uninsured reside in homes where two or more employed adults live. Nearly one-third of the poor, one-third of Hispanics, and one-fifth of African-Americans are uninsured. Being uninsured is clearly related to household income, as 24% of households with incomes of less than $25,000 are uninsured compared to 8% of households with incomes over $75,000.[3] . . .

2 Over one hundred different medical studies document that uninsured patients suffer worse medical outcomes compared to the insured.[4] Nearly four of ten uninsured working-age adults failed to see any doctor in the previous year compared to less than one out of ten insured people. The chronically uninsured people in poor health fared even worse, with seven out of ten failing to see any doctor in the previous year.[5] As a practicing physician, I believe this is just plain bad medicine and exactly opposite of what any rational health system should provide. With our current system, patients in poor health see a doctor less often than those in good health.

3 When hospitalized, the uninsured are two to three times more likely to die than the insured because they seek and receive care later in the course of their illnesses, unlike "the more fortunate" insured patients.[6] The uninsured also undergo fewer cancer screening tests, including Pap smears, mammograms, or sigmoidoscopies, each shown to increase early detection

and reduce cancer mortality rates.[7] But these are only medical studies and statistics of the uninsured. The poignant reality is revealed in their stories.

Terminal Cervical Cancer

4 I met Emily, a patient in the emergency room when she <u>presented</u> critically ill. She was emaciated and yellow with <u>jaundice</u>. When I saw her I thought immediately of concentration camp victims. I found a large mass in her low abdomen and suspected it was cancer. Further tests confirmed this, and showed the cancer was advanced and untreatable.

5 In the hospital I talked with Emily and told her what I had found. She then told me about how she had been uninsured for nearly ten years. She had left her employment to remain at home and care for her ailing father who later died. When I listened to her talk about him, it was obvious how much she loved her father. Unfortunately, Emily failed to see a doctor during her years of being uninsured, and sadly, now it was too late. A simple Pap smear a few years earlier could have saved her life.

6 "Why didn't you see a doctor sooner?" I asked her. Uninsured, Emily had two reasons why she delayed seeking care earlier—her fear of cancer and her fear of medical bills. She told me she would have seen a doctor sooner if she had insurance. She died only three days after admission to the hospital. Premature death is a common occurrence for the uninsured who present late in the course of their illness.

A Hypertensive Diabetic

7 Sam, a rugged working farmer, arrived in the emergency room by ambulance late one evening. The emergency room doctor consulted me for further management of this patient. Sam was self-employed, married and uninsured. He knew he had high blood pressure and possible "sugar" but had been treating it with herbs. He had not seen a doctor in nearly two years.

8 After working in the barn, Sam suddenly started coughing up pinkish phlegm and gasping for air. He thought it was merely a cold. Sam's <u>vital</u> signs were critically unstable. His skin was a dark blue in color from inadequate oxygen entering his bloodstream as a result of fluid-filled lungs. He nearly died from heart failure that night, but intravenous medications took hold and turned the precarious situation around. The untreated high blood pressure and diabetes, however, had already done considerable damage. Urgent cardiac testing at a larger medical center was required. I spent considerable time convincing Sam and his family of the necessity for additional tests and hospital treatments. I know they were concerned about the costs and possible need for cardiac surgery. . . .

Chronic Hypertension and Diabetes

9 Lois was a middle-aged health aid who worked part time for many years at a for-profit or "investor-owned" nursing home. She had a career in the health industry, yet was uninsured and could not afford doctor visits or her

441

prescriptions. It is incredible to me that any health industry employer would deny health insurance benefits to its employees. There is no employer in the healthcare profession who does not know the risks and consequences employees face if they are uninsured. Some employers I know consider health insurance to be too expensive and potentially a penalty to their company's profits. However, I believe companies may benefit if they would invest in the health of their employees. Healthy employees are more productive and may enhance company profits.

10   Part-time employees are much less likely to be insured than full-time employees. Lois told me that she tried to obtain Medicaid and was turned down because her family's yearly income of $12,200 was too high. Lois suffers from chronic high blood pressure and diabetes, but without health insurance, she did not see her physician for over a year. Having had trouble affording her medications, she went without some. She told me, "I borrowed insulin from my sister who has insurance." Lois had stopped working one year earlier, explaining that she hadn't felt well and couldn't see. Her son's old toy binoculars soon became her means of watching TV. I wondered how she could inject herself with insulin.

11   No one was surprised when Lois was later admitted to the intensive care unit with a major stroke, severe hypertension and uncontrolled diabetes. Incredibly, she had even stayed at home for three days with her stroke symptoms before coming to the emergency room. Maybe she thought the symptoms would go away. To me, this delay again exemplifies the often unnoticed and unmentioned underclass of uninsured Americans who stand in an interminable "waiting line" for healthcare in this country. The following day, after considerable improvement, she thanked me for not "yelling" at her. Obviously she was feeling guilty for "noncompliance," but how was she to comply? I admit that I may have "yelled" at a similar patient, years earlier, but I have gained more understanding of the human predicament in our country.

12   I saw Lois in the office after her discharge from the hospital, and she was now compliant, checking her sugars and taking her medications. Sadly however, she had not qualified for Medicaid yet. Her husband still made "too much money," $100 per month over the minimum Medicaid threshold. Her monthly medications easily cost more than that. Her husband said to me, "We have worked all our lives, and we have never asked for handouts. Now we need help and can't get it." Her son thanked me for helping his mother. He told me how he had sent money to her for her prescriptions, but she spent it on food and rent.

13   Unfortunately, Lois' lack of insurance and her sporadic treatment for diabetes contributed to her inability to work more than a year earlier. Now unable to work or even see, she deals with the physical impairments and suffers. I am certain that her hypertension and elevated cholesterol were also under treated.

14   There are estimates of the number of people between the ages of eighteen and sixty-five with various diseases who are uninsured for at least one entire year: 528,000 with diabetes, 1.8 million with high blood pressure, and

1.5 million with high cholesterol.[8] How many preventable disabling strokes will other doctors treat next year? How many will I treat? One is too many.

15   Months later, Lois finally did qualify for Medicaid and was seen by an eye specialist. Her diabetes is now under better control, and her eye specialist eventually operated on her cataracts. I know that her lack of affordable healthcare significantly affected her overall health and contributed to her inability to be gainfully employed. For many years Lois contributed to society. Now she is an early long-term cost. I doubt that she ever will return to even part-time work.

16   Too many uninsured patients show up too late and too sick. Despite the growth of managed care, emergency room visits keep climbing. There are many reasons for this increase including lack of access to primary care doctors, especially among the poorest urban and rural communities, and uninsured patients. The Common Wealth Fund, a private philanthropic organization, found 75% of all emergency room visits in New York City were for non-emergencies. A spokesman for the American College of Emergency Physicians stated, "The situation is grave. We are a symptom of the disease that is the healthcare system."[9] In the United States, the only places where patients have universal healthcare and guaranteed medical treatments are the emergency rooms. Unfortunately, these are also the most expensive and the least able to provide continuity of care or adequate follow-up.

17   These true stories demonstrate how the uninsured show up in our emergency rooms suffering the consequences of delayed access to care for serious conditions. Some of these uninsured patients have no regular physician and use the emergency room for their ongoing care. This is probably a more expensive choice of healthcare provider and definitely lacks significant continuity. Other patients delay seeking care because of the cost and fear of mounting medical bills. Unfortunately, I see them wait too long, sometimes needlessly suffering additional morbidity and mortality. Frequently, these additional problems could have been avoided or lessened with earlier treatment. . . .

18   There is also a key issue of justice and humanity, as well as an issue of cost. Many of these stories conclude with treatments that are probably more expensive than prevention. The terrible outcomes only lead to further costs. Families drop into public assistance; welfare picks up nursing home costs; loved ones are lost; family structures are destabilized; children lose love and care. In human terms, the cost of being uninsured is staggering. Why do all of the other OECD [Organisation for Economic Co-operation and Development] nations provide universal care? Most likely they know it is less expensive to prevent diseases than to treat them. All Americans share in paying the costs of the human tragedy of our current healthcare system.

Notes

1. G. Aston, "Number of Uninsured Down, But Struggle Continues," *American Medical News*, October 16, 2000.

2. Kaiser Commission Report, "Uninsured in America," May 2000.

3. U.S. Census Bureau, Health Insurance Data.

4. American College of Physicians/American Society of Internal Medicine (ACP/ASIM), http://www.acponline.org/uninsured/index.html (accessed August 31, 2001).

5. John Z. Ayanian, Joel S. Weissman, Eric C. Schneider, Jack A. Ginsburg, and Alan M. Zaslavsky, "Unmet Health Needs of Uninsured Adults in the United States," *Journal of the American Medical Association* 284 (October 25, 2000):2061–2069.

6. *Journal of the American Medical Association* 265 (1991):374.

7. American College of Physicians/American Society of Internal Medicine ACP/ASIM, http://www.acponline.org/uninsured/index.html (accessed August 31, 2002).

8. Jennifer Steinhauer, *New York Times*, October 25, 2000.

9. http://www.statehealthfacts.kff.org (accessed June 1, 2001).

MUELLER, *As Sick As It Gets*

Exercise 1 **Work with Words**

Use context clues, dictionary skills, and your knowledge of word parts to choose the best definition for each of the following words underlined in the reading. The paragraph number is provided in case you want to check the context.

1. *Chronically* (par. 2)
   a. unfrequently
   b. continually
   c. inconsequentially

2. *Rational* (par. 2)
   a. balanced
   b. cost effective
   c. organized in a reasonable way

3. *Presented* (par. 4)
   a. came forward
   b. gave
   c. introduced

4. *Jaundice* (par. 4)
   a. a yellowish condition that is a sign of illness
   b. a distasteful attitude
   c. a yellowish condition that is normal

5. *Vital* (par. 8)
   a. extremely important
   b. full of life and vigor
   c. essential for the maintenance of life

6. *Interminable* (par. 11)
   a. crowded
   b. seeming to have no end
   c. in between

7. *Noncompliance* (par. 11)
   a. not following the doctor's directions
   b. not understanding the doctor's directions
   c. not listening to the doctor's directions

8. *Threshold* (par. 12)
   a. boundary
   b. entrance
   c. cut-off

9. *Sporadic* (par. 13)
   a. regular
   b. cost effective
   c. inconsistent

10. *Impairments* (par. 13)
    a. improvements
    b. interventions
    c. disabilities

Exercise 2   **Check Your Understanding**

Based on the reading, Mueller's "The Emergency Room and the Uninsured," choose the best answer to each of the following questions.

1. Which of the following best states the topic of the reading?
   a. The emergency room
   b. Americans without health insurance
   c. The human and financial cost of being uninsured

2. Which of the following best states the thesis of the reading?
   a. People without health insurance have worse health and are more likely to die because they wait too long to go to emergency rooms, are often too late, and must undergo treatment that is more expensive than prevention.
   b. Nearly 43 million people did not have health insurance in the United States in 1999.
   c. When hospitalized, the uninsured are much more likely to die than the insured because they receive their care later in the course of their illness.

3. Most people without health insurance are
   a. unemployed.
   b. diagnosed with serious illnesses.
   c. employed full time or live with someone who is.

4. Which of the following is the best main idea statement for paragraph 2?
   a. Nearly four of ten uninsured working-age adults failed to see any doctor in the previous year compared with fewer than one out of ten insured people.
   b. Over one hundred different medical studies document that uninsured patients suffer worse medical outcomes compared with the insured.
   c. People who need to be seeing a doctor more often are not doing so and are suffering poorer health because they don't have insurance.

5. What is the dominant pattern of organization for paragraphs 4 through 15?
   a. Process and definition
   b. Chronological order
   c. Cause and effect, and exemplification

6. Mueller uses the examples of Emily, Sam, and Lois to
   a. statistically demonstrate the size of the problem of people not having health insurance.
   b. give a human dimension to the problem of so many people not having health insurance.
   c. depress us with the personal stories of people who do not have health insurance.

© 2007 Pearson Education, Inc.

7. The cases of Emily, Sam, and Lois illustrate
   a. the terrible effects of waiting for treatment or of not taking the proper medication.
   b. the importance of people understanding the treatment they need to follow.
   c. the effectiveness of using the emergency room, even in cases where the emergency might have been prevented.

8. Which of the following best describes the tone of paragraph 5?
   a. Sad
   b. Cautious
   c. Cynical

9. In paragraph 16, Mueller quotes a spokesman for the American College of Emergency Physicians as saying, "We are a symptom of the disease that is the health care system." What does this statement mean?
   a. The speaker is comparing the problems of emergency rooms to the symptoms of a disease (the health care system) because he believes that something is wrong and it needs to be fixed (cured).
   b. The speaker believes that emergency rooms are a good place to detect disease.
   c. The speaker recognizes problems with the health care system but believes that it functions satisfactorily overall.

10. We can reasonably infer that Dr. Mueller is
    a. slightly fed up with health care in the United States.
    b. very upset with the inequalities of health care in the United States.
    c. critical of the emergency room staffing.

Exercise 3   Evaluate the Argument

Based on the reading, choose the best answer to each of the following multiple-choice questions.

1. Mueller begins with a quotation from the Bible to
   a. alienate people who are not Christians.
   b. lend weight to his moral position that health care should be available to all Americans.
   c. distract the reader from the inconsistencies in his argument.

2. What can we guess is the background of Rudolph Mueller from this reading?
   a. He is a medical doctor who has worked in emergency rooms.
   b. He is a science writer who focuses on medical issues.
   c. He is an informed citizen who is concerned about medical issues.

3. What kind of publication did this reading appear in?
   a. A medical journal
   b. A book
   c. A magazine that advocates for patients' rights

4. This reading was probably written for
   a. other physicians.
   b. health insurance companies.
   c. the general public.

5. The sources of Mueller's information are
   a. not given.
   b. documented in endnotes.
   c. impossible to verify.

6. Mueller bases his argument in paragraphs 1 through 3 on
   a. studies and statistics collected on the uninsured.
   b. anecdotal information based on his own experiences.
   c. personal impressions.

7. Mueller bases his argument in paragraphs 4 through 15 on
   a. studies conducted by the medical establishment.
   b. personal examples of patients he has treated.
   c. his family experience with health care.

8. Health insurance companies would probably
   a. completely agree with Mueller.
   b. completely disagree with Mueller.
   c. be indifferent to Mueller's discussion of health care.

9. Which of the following does Mueller not use in the reading?
   a. Appeals to the readers' emotions
   b. Reasoned argument
   c. Appeals to the readers' guilt

10. Which of the following does Mueller not do in the reading?
   a. Present statistics
   b. Present the position of someone who opposes his position on health care.
   c. Present convincing examples to support his thesis

Exercise 4   **Reflect**

Think about what you read in "The Emergency Room and the Uninsured" and what you already know about the medical system in the United States. Then answer the following questions.

1. Have you or anyone you know had to go to an emergency room? Describe the circumstances and the care received. How much did it cost, and who paid?

   _____

   _____

   _____

   _____

©2007 Pearson Education, Inc.

2. What kind of health insurance do you have, and how confident are you that your insurance is adequate to meet your needs? Explain your answer.

_____

_____

_____

_____

3. How do you think the situation of the uninsured affects everyone else? If you are insured, why or in what way should you be concerned about the uninsured?

_____

_____

_____

_____

Mastery Test

Making Well People "Better" Pat Mooney

The following reading appeared in the July/August 2002 edition of World Watch. *This nonprofit magazine is the publication of the World Watch Institute, which is a widely respected research organization that studies "key indicators of the Earth's well-being." The journal receives support from a wide variety of nonprofit foundations as well as from the United Nations Environment Program. This article is about drug companies' profit motive and how it affects their research. It is important to understand that certain pharmaceutical companies make most of their money from patents that usually last for 20 years and, for that period, guarantee them a monopoly on a drug that they have developed. In this way, they are able to dominate the market and control prices. While the vocabulary in this reading is fairly difficult, most words are explained in context, and you can get the most important point the author is making without having to memorize some of the more technical terms. As you read, consider the ethical issues surrounding medicines (pharmaceuticals), their development, whom they are for, and what they are designed to treat.*

The Poor Are No One's Market

1 When heads of state gathered for the Earth Summit in Rio de Janeiro 10 years ago, biotechnology was the buzzword miracle cure for world hunger and disease. A decade later, biotech has brought the poor no closer to the dinner table or better health. The reason is obvious: as ever, the poor are no one's market. Not that progress in biopharmaceuticals has lagged; advances in mapping the human genome have spawned new opportunities, and the prospects for human cloning and stem cell therapies have made headlines. However, the companies involved are actually pursuing more strategic agendas. Reproductive cloning might never be more than a niche market that the industry is happy to leave to quacks. The real money is in human performance enhancement drugs (call them "HyPEs"). And whether the focus is on pharmaceuticals developed the old-fashioned way or those that are linked via research or function to biotechnologies, they employ the same self-serving strategies.

Healthy Markets

2 The pharmaceutical industry has always suffered from a seemingly incurable marketing problem. Its customers are sick, and sick people are unreliable. If they die or get well, they stop buying drugs. If they remain sick, they tend to become unemployable. Unemployable sick people either can't afford drugs or (worse) they elicit sympathy and threaten prices. In the mid-1970s, pharmaceutical companies saw that the solution to the uncertainty of an ill clientele was to develop drugs for well people, who not only remain

©2007 Pearson Education, Inc.

employed but never get "better." Best of all, well customers don't create sympathy and threaten price margins and profits. Now, biotechnology and the map of the human genome are making the task of creating new drugs for well people much easier.

3   Although the birth of biotech a quarter-century ago inspired the drive for a brave new market in well-people products, the industry has always been open to the opportunities. Morphine was purified from opium at the outset of the nineteenth century and first commercialized by Merck in Germany in 1827. Bayer was an early proponent of amphetamines and brought the world two blockbuster commercial winners, aspirin and heroin. In 1892, a Parke-Davis publication for doctors provided 240 pages of documentation extolling coca and cocaine, its two leading products; only three of the 240 pages discussed the drugs' unfortunate side effects.[1] Following World War II, the industry routinely blended barbiturates with amphetamines in diet drugs in order to encourage consumers to stay on the regime (and keep buying).[2] Sandoz (now Novartis) invented LSD, though the company was horrified by its abuses.[3]

4   The industry's view of "recreational" drugs has always been ambiguous. The annual global pharmaceutical market is worth roughly $300 billion, and the illicit narcotics market, valued at $400 billion in 1995,[4] is hugely inviting. New HyPE drugs could allow the industry to claim a share of this market by offering a battery of well-people products without the stigma society attaches to addictive drugs.

Drug Ethics

5 Originally "ethical drugs" were defined as drugs advertised only to doctors and pharmacists, but not to potential patients. Now the industry is advertising on television in the United States and elsewhere and has gone so far as to blend Internet advertising and medical research studies on websites targeting doctors. . . .

6   The industry's selective ethical concern for the sick is also clear. For example, of the 1,223 drugs brought to market between 1975 and 1996, only 13 targeted the deadly tropical diseases that afflict millions of the world's poor, and just four of those drugs came from the private sector.[5] The nature of private pharmaceutical companies' commitment to patients was underscored in a 1993 study by the federal Office of Technology Assessment showing that 97 percent of the 348 ethical drugs brought to the market by the 25 leading U.S. drug companies between 1981 and 1988 were copies of existing medications. Of the 3 percent offering genuine therapeutic advances, 70 percent resulted from public research. . . .

Working HyPEs

7 Making "well" people "better" could have significant benefits for employers. Try as we will to automate every kind of work, people are likely to remain the most versatile and efficient tool of production for many jobs. But we do have our defects, and the pharmaceutical industry is working on developing

performance enhancement drugs to turn workers into superhumans. Employers (and governments) are lining up to try the new drugs. Here are some examples of recent genome-inspired innovations and some old drugs being given new, augmented lives through genetic research:

8   *8 Days a Week:* Cephalon Inc. has developed a drug called Provigil for the treatment of narcolepsy (a neurological disease that causes irrepressible sleep attacks). Because Provigil is not an amphetamine, it is attracting attention as a possible alertness aid for healthy people.

9   *Rhythm and blues:* Northwestern University has patented the circadian rhythm gene. The circadian clock regulates 24-hour rhythms in physiological systems. The patent covers the gene's uses for sleep-related problems, jet lag, alertness, stress response, diet, and sexual function, and could be exploited to enhance mood in intensive care units.

10   *Stringed-out quartets:* A "beta-blocker" drug meant for treatment of congestive cardiac failure is best known as "the musicians' underground drug" because of its effect on musical performance. (The drug blocks stage fright.) Twenty-seven percent of symphony orchestra musicians take beta-blockers.[6] A drug therapy capable of blocking anxiety would have major workplace applications. . . .

11   Our new understanding of genomics and the neurosciences is also making possible a generation of HyPE medicines that could be used in more sinister ways, e.g., to control dissent. Mood-altering drugs that dispel discontent might be individually prescribed, pressed upon workers, or even hosed into crowds. Enhancement technologies could also become disabling technologies in military or police hands. Those refusing to take HyPEs could be punished by their teachers, employers, or governments because they are refusing to maximize their potential. And if it is possible to "enhance" an infantryman's performance with a drug that turns off the brain's fear mechanism, for example, then it is also possible to switch on irrational fear in the enemy. Drugs that target hearing, memory, or alertness could be mirrored by drugs that weaken those qualities.

Optional Equipment

12 *Brain Viagra?* In 1995, Cold Spring Harbor Laboratory created a fruit fly with an apparently photographic memory. The lab then partnered with Hoffman-La Roche to see if the human mind could be similarly modified. Roche Pharmaceuticals later announced a break-through in learning and memory that could lead to treatment for cognitive deficit diseases such as Alzheimer's, depression, schizophrenia, or aging. Several drugs are readily available and widely used as memory enhancers, though they are not proven, tested, or approved for such uses.

13   *Trauma tamers:* After demonstrating that the fruit fly's ability to learn could also be abolished by subtle genetic alterations, Cold Spring Harbor researchers launched Helicon Therapeutics Inc. to make drugs aimed at different brain molecules. They see lucrative markets in products for boosting failing memory and medicines for blocking trauma recollection.

451

©2007 Pearson Education, Inc.

14   *Learning too much?* Scientists have genetically engineered mice with enhanced memory that persists until researchers use genetic trait control technology to switch off a key memory-governing enzyme.[7]

15   *Social IQ:* Those who exhibit "anti-social" behavior could be subjected to genetic therapies to "cure" them of conditions such as depression, obsessive behavior, and hyperactivity. Even shyness is now being treated with the drug Seratox, originally developed as an anti-depressant. It is believed that a gene inherited from the father might act to fine-tune a part of the brain involved in social abilities.

HyPES: Hope for the Poor?

16 The choice between developing drugs to make ill people well or well people better is best manifested in the enormous corporate investment in diet-related medicine. Research on new forms of proteins, and on old woes like obesity and diabetes, suggests that it may be possible to develop drugs that could help people utilize food and energy more effectively.

17   It's clear, however, that the world's roughly 820 million malnourished poor are suffering most from a political failure to have their basic needs and human rights met by a world that is richer in food than in justice. Drug companies could at least collaborate with plant breeders to develop nutriceuticals that would enable the poor to make better use of the food they have. Instead, the pharmaceutical industry is hard at work at developing drugs that allow people to eat <u>gluttonously</u> without getting fat. With obesity a major health problem in industrialized countries, companies are in hot pursuit of "uncoupling protein" (UCP) molecules that interfere with the conversion of food calories into metabolic energy and release them instead as waste heat. Of course the logical solution is to eat less and exercise more. But there is a multi-billion-dollar market waiting for any pharmaceutical company that can turn UCP molecules into drugs that let people stuff their faces without losing their figures. . . .

From HyPE to Health

18 If we continue to rely upon the world's giant pharmaceutical corporations to determine research goals, our societies will remain unhealthy and become unhealthily dependent. We need to strengthen socially oriented public research and public health initiatives and, simultaneously, eliminate the patent incentive that distorts medical innovation and dictates profiteering. Until we dispel the myth that the biotech and pharmaceutical industries are working on our behalf, the prognosis is poor.

Notes

1. David T. Courtwright, *Forces of Habit: Drugs and the Making of the Modern World* (Cambridge: Harvard University Press, 2001), 86.

2. Courtwright, 105.

3. Courtwright, 89.

4. United Nations Development Program (UNDP). *Human Development Report 2001—Making New Technologies Work for Human Development* (New York: UNDP/Oxford University Press, 2001), 13.

5. UNDP, 3.

6. Karla Harby et al., "Beta Blockers and Performance Anxiety in Musicians," A Report by the beta blocker study committee of FLUTE, March 17, 1997.

7. Deborah L. Stull, "Better Mouse Memory Comes at a Price," *The Scientist* 15 (April 2, 2001):21

MOONEY, "Making Well People 'Better'"

Exercise 1   **Work with Words**

Use context clues, dictionary skills, and your knowledge of word parts to choose the best definition for each of the following words underlined in the reading. The paragraph number is provided in case you want to check the context.

1. *Genome* (par. 1)
   a. genetic material
   b. eugenic material
   c. pharmaceutical material

2. *Niche* (par. 1)
   a. small and specialized
   b. large and profitable
   c. unprofitable

3. *HyPEs* (par. 1)
   a. a class of drugs designed to help people who are sick
   b. a class of drugs designed to perform well in humans
   c. a class of drugs designed for human performance enhancement

4. *Illicit* (par. 4)
   a. recreational
   b. illegal
   c. global

5. *Battery* (par. 4)
   a. assault
   b. large number
   c. demand

6. *Irrepressible* (par. 8)
   a. unstoppable
   b. uncomfortable
   c. dangerous

7. *Sinister* (par. 11)
   a. productive
   b. profitable
   c. evil

8. *Dispel* (par. 11)
   a. drive away
   b. augment
   c. improve

9. *Lucrative* (par. 13)
   a. hidden
   b. huge
   c. profitable

10. *Gluttonously* (par. 17)
    a. unjustly
    b. greedily
    c. hungrily

© 2007 Pearson Education, Inc.

Check Your Understanding

Based on the reading, Mooney's "Making Well People 'Better,'" choose the best answer to the following multiple-choice questions.

1. Which of the following is the best topic for the reading?
   a. Treatment breakthroughs for common illnesses
   b. The dangers of biotechnology and genetic engineering
   c. The motivation and practices of the pharmaceutical industry

2. Which of the following is the best thesis statement for the entire reading?
   a. Pharmaceutical corporations do not function to help the most people possible to be healthy; rather, their emphasis is increasingly on making profits from people who can afford to buy drugs even though they may not be that sick.
   b. Drug companies have been incredibly successful at developing human performance enhancement drugs that will be very helpful to all Americans sooner or later.
   c. The pharmaceutical industry is interested in figuring out how to profit from the "illicit" drug market, and history demonstrates that they were initially involved in the marketing of opium and cocaine.

3. What is the marketing problem that pharmaceutical industries face?
   a. Their biotechnological research is complex and expensive.
   b. Sick people who get better don't need drugs, but people who stay sick frequently can't afford them.
   c. People who remain sick tend to become unemployable.

4. What is the primary pattern of organization for paragraph 3?
   a. Cause and effect
   b. Definition
   c. Chronological order

5. Which of the following is not an ethical issue described in paragraph 5?
   a. Pharmaceutical companies do most of their advertising in the United States.
   b. Pharmaceutical companies are now advertising to patients directly as well as to doctors and pharmacists.
   c. Pharmaceutical companies blend their advertising with medical research studies on Internet sites for doctors.

6. Which of the following best describes the tone of paragraph 6?
   a. Sarcastic and pessimistic
   b. Optimistic
   c. Matter-of-fact and objective

7. What is the primary pattern of organization for paragraphs 8 through 10?
   a. Cause and effect
   b. Exemplification
   c. Problem and solution

8. What is the main idea of paragraph 11?
   a. HyPE medicines may have sinister applications in the future.
   b. We should stop all research on HyPE medicines immediately.
   c. Controlling dissent is a worthwhile use for HyPE medicines.

9. The overall tone of the reading is
   a. alternately sensational and objective.
   b. extremely shocked and condemnatory.
   c. seriously concerned and sometimes sarcastic.

10. The author advocates
   a. abolishing or severely limiting the for-profit pharmaceuticals.
   b. strengthening socially oriented public research and health initiatives and eliminating the patent incentive for profiteering.
   c. recognizing that biotech and pharmaceutical industries are working on everyone's behalf, and spending billions of dollars in the process.

Exercise 3   **Evaluate the Argument**

Based on the reading, choose the best answer to each of the following multiple-choice questions.

1. This article was probably written for
   a. people who are already interested in this issue and are somewhat inclined to agree with Mooney.
   b. executives and researchers at pharmaceutical companies to persuade them to change the focus of their research.
   c. people who are taking any of the drugs described in this article and the doctors who prescribe them.

2. Which of the following is likely to have been Mooney's motivation for writing the article?
   a. He wants to get more money for publicly funded pharmaceutical research.
   b. He is writing an informative article about recent medical advances.
   c. He is critical of certain pharmaceutical industry practices and wants to expose them.

© 2007 Pearson Education, Inc.

3. A reasonable inference that can be made from paragraph 7 is that the author thinks
   a. employers would like a wider range of drugs available for sick employees, because they want them to be able to return to work.
   b. employers would be interested in performance-enhancing drugs, because they could make employees more alert, efficient, and productive.
   c. employers need to make sure their health insurance plans make these new drugs available to all employees.

4. A reasonable inference that can be made from paragraph 17 is that the author thinks
   a. pharmaceutical companies could help prevent malnutrition.
   b. technology can't help solve the problem of malnutrition, because that issue requires a political solution.
   c. advances in biotechnology and pharmaceuticals benefit everyone eventually.

5. Which of the following counterarguments is not addressed in this reading?
   a. The market for pharmaceuticals is not very large.
   b. Drug companies help people by constantly developing and patenting an important array of new and important drugs.
   c. There is no objective dividing line between "well" and "unwell," and some of the things Mooney calls "enhancers" are really treatments for serious conditions like anxiety, obesity, and cognitive deficit diseases.

6. Mooney bases most of his arguments in this reading on
   a. finding arguments against his position and rebutting them.
   b. facts and statistics about drugs and the pharmaceutical industry, and informed speculation about their future direction.
   c. insider knowledge of the pharmaceutical industry and how those companies work.

7. The sources of Mooney's information are
   a. impossible to verify.
   b. not given.
   c. documented in endnotes.

8. What is the problem (as identified by Mooney) with pharmaceutical research, and how does he propose the problem be solved?
   a. Research is too expensive for companies to develop drugs that won't make a profit. It could be solved by government subsidies to the pharmaceutical industry.
   b. Research is based on making a profit instead of healing sick people. It could be solved by having research done by public, socially oriented institutions.
   c. Research is not innovative enough. It could be solved by only granting patents for genuine medical advances.

9. Why is Mooney concerned about some of the drugs currently being developed?
   a. They can manipulate people's feelings and abilities.
   b. They have not yet been proven to be effective.
   c. They might have dangerous side effects.

10. How would an opponent probably characterize Mooney's predictions about the future in paragraphs 7 ("the pharmaceutical industry is working on developing performance enhancement drugs to turn workers into superhumans") and 11 (the new "generation of HyPE medicines . . . could be used in more sinister ways")?
   a. Impossible
   b. Possible but unlikely
   c. Valid concerns

Exercise 4   **Reflect**

Think about wht you read in "Making Well People 'Better'" and what you already know about the marketing practices of large drug companies. Then answer the following questions.

1. How do you think someone undergoing successful drug treatment for an anxiety disorder would react to Mooney's title, "Making Well People 'Better'"? Explain.

   _____

   _____

   _____

   _____

   _____

   _____

2. Why might Mooney's definition of *well* be considered limited? What are some of the factors that enter into the idea of "wellness"?

   _____

   _____

   _____

   _____

   _____

   _____

©2007 Pearson Education, Inc.

3. Do you think everyone in a pharmaceutical company shares the same goals and motivation? How might the goals of a scientific researcher differ from the goals of a CEO? Explain.

_____

_____

_____

_____

_____

_____

4. How do you think pharmaceutical companies would justify advertising prescription medicines to the general public?

_____

_____

_____

_____

_____

5. Why is the practice of advertising prescription drugs to the general public an ethical issue?

_____

_____

_____

_____

_____

Extend Your Thinking

Additional Readings and Exercises

©2007 Pearson Education, Inc.

For Chapter 1, **THE READING PROCESS**

How We Learn   Ricki Linksman

Ricki Linksman, M.Ed., is an expert in the field of learning. She is also the founder of the National Reading Diagnostic Institute and its educational training divisions. In the following reading from How to Learn Anything Quickly, *she explains that we each have a preferred style of learning new material, and we each use one side of the brain more than the other.*

Learning Styles

1   Research has identified that people learn in different ways. We rely on all our senses to receive information from the outside world, yet, over time, many people develop one sense more than others and find it easier to rely on that one for learning new material. This is how we develop a preference for one type of learning style. If we want to learn something rapidly, the material needs to be presented to us in our most developed pathway to the brain—our learning style. There are four main learning styles: visual, auditory, tactile, and kinesthetic.

2   **Visual learners** learn by seeing.

3   **Auditory learners** learn by listening, hearing themselves talk, and discussing their thoughts with others.

4   **Tactile learners** learn by touching or feeling sensation on their skin, by using their hands and fingers, and connecting what they learn to their sense of touch or their emotions.

5   **Kinesthetic learners** learn by moving their large, or gross, muscles in space, and by getting actively involved in the learning process through simulations, role-play, experimentation, exploration, and movement, and participating in real-life activities.

6   **Learners who use other senses:** Though they are rare, there are also some learners who rely on their sense of taste and smell. Although they are not addressed in the assessment, these learners have an acute sense of smell or taste, are sensitive to odors or tastes, and can learn well by involving these senses.

Learning Style and the Brain

7   Brain research has advanced enough that we have at least a *limited* understanding of how the brain works. Although there is still much to learn, we do know some basic principles that are relevant to understanding how we learn. As our brains are exposed to stimuli, new interconnections between nerve cells are created; this quality is known as plasticity. The more stimuli we receive, the more interconnections and learning patterns are formed. Thus, as certain learning patterns become more rapid, easier, and automatic, we learn more quickly, developing our best learning style. This is the essence of accelerated learning.

8   We have pathways between our senses and our brains. If, over time, we have relied more upon our eyes, then the passageways between the nerves in our eyes and the part of the brain that interprets visual stimuli were developed more than passageways between the brain and other senses. As a result, we find it easier to rely upon our eyes. For some people, the neural connections between the ears and the part of the brain that interprets auditory stimuli are stronger; thus, they find it easier and quicker to learn through the ears. For others the neural passages between the skin, hands, and fingers and the part of the brain that interprets tactile stimuli of feeling physical sensation and physical responses to emotion has been used more and those people find it easier to learn through the sense of touch. Some have made more use of their large motor muscles, so the neural pathways from their muscles to the part of the brain that senses body motion have become stronger. Thus, we have people with increased ability to learn kinesthetically.

9   When learning something new, we need to concentrate on assimilating the new information, process, or skill. We do not want to be encumbered by trying to learn through a weak sensory modality, so to accelerate learning, new information should be presented in our best learning style. If you want to develop other learning styles, you can do so when you are *not* trying to learn new material. The basic rule of thumb is: If you want to learn something quickly, learn it through your preferred learning style.

How Learning Styles Develop

10 Learning styles are a combination of nature and nurture. Some tendencies are genetically inherited, some are a result of exposure to certain stimuli over a long period of time, and some develop due to one's reliance on that particular sense for survival. These repeated stimuli strengthen certain passageways between one or more senses and the brain.

11   There are men and women who fall into each of the learning style categories. There are visual men and visual women. Similarly, there are auditory men and auditory women, tactile men and tactile women, kinesthetic men and kinesthetic women. While certain learning styles—like the kinesthetic, or movement-oriented learning style—seem to be attributed in our society more to men, and others—like the tactile, or emotionally-oriented learning style—seem to be attributed more to women, these stereotypes do not hold true in reality. Cultural pressures may have influenced numbers of each gender to exhibit certain behaviors. As a result, people may have been forced to suppress their natural way of learning to conform to social expectations. However, over the past decade people of both genders have been given more opportunities to engage in a wider range of experiences, allowing them to develop along the lines of their natural way of learning. Thus, we find people of both sexes developing all of the learning styles. I hope that, with this newfound knowledge of learning styles, parents and teachers will realize the importance of exposing the young to stimuli that develop *all* their senses, giving them an opportunity to develop their whole brain and make better use of their natural talents.

©2007 Pearson Education, Inc.

12   A question frequently raised is: Since traditional schools teach people mostly through the visual and auditory senses, wouldn't all learners develop into visual and auditory learners? The answer can best be understood by a similar question: If you are right-handed, would you become left-handed if you were forced to use only the left hand in school? Think of what that would be like. you could *force* yourself to use your left hand but you would be slower, more conscious of the motions of writing than the actual work, and it might take you years to become as proficient with your left hand as you are with your right. (The same situation would be applicable if we were to make left-handed people write with their right hand.) It may take you the same number of years to develop your nondominant hand as it took to become automatic with your dominant hand, putting you several years back in development of skills that require writing ability. Similarly, if you were a visual, tactile, or kinesthetic learner you could force yourself to develop your auditory sense, but during the years you are developing it you would struggle with material presented auditorily, putting you at a disadvantage in that environment. The same holds true for forcing auditory, tactile, or kinesthetic learners into a visual environment. When learning something new, you naturally want to use your most comfortable sense to accelerate progress. At other times you can strengthen your weaker senses, and over time they will become stronger, but they will not equal your ability in your strongest sense unless you stop using it for a part of that time.

Brain Hemispheric Preference

13 The brain is divided into two hemispheres, or halves—the right and the left. While we all use both sides of the brain, many people process and store information using one side more than the other, exhibiting a *brain hemispheric preference.* A preference for one side of the brain develops when we use particular neural pathways more, developing them to a higher degree; we become more skilled in using that hemisphere. It is not that we are incapable of using the other side of the brain, but when we use one half more, over time it feels more comfortable and natural to use.

14   When people receive instruction in a way that does not match their brain hemispheric preference they may take longer to learn, they may struggle, or even fail. But when we communicate in the way that matches our brain hemispheric preference, we learn more easily and quickly.

15   Scientists have helped us understand some of the characteristics of the right and left sides of the brain. Each side looks at life differently. Thus, someone who processes mostly through the right side of the brain will experience an event or situation differently from one who processes mostly through the left side of the brain.

16   Our brain hemispheric preference is not a conscious choice, but we grow up mostly using one side for many tasks. As children we may have been exposed to many linear tasks, so our brain had enough stimuli to

develop neural pathways that support left-brain thinking. Or, we may have been exposed to many wholistic and global experiences, stimulating the development of right-brain thinking.

17   Neither side of the brain is superior to the other; they merely do different tasks important for survival. Ideally, people should be able to use both sides of their brains equally well. Unfortunately, this information on brain hemispheric preference has only recently become public knowledge. Left to chance, people often end up using one side more than the other and rely on that side for all tasks, even those more appropriately handled by the other side. This is why many people have difficulty learning or find it takes them a long time to learn. While we are waiting for the educational system to catch up and use the new teaching methods that engage both hemispheres of the brain, we need to find ways to deal with the limitations we inherited. Thus, if you have favored one side of the brain for most tasks, you will learn techniques to adapt any learning situation to be compatible with your brain preference.

18   Can we develop the other side of our brain if we have a preference? Yes, we can, but it takes time. Everyone has spent a certain number of years learning through one side of the brain, and you can calculate how long it may take to balance that by developing the other side. In the meantime, if you have a preference, you can use it to your advantage to accelerate learning by having material presented to you in a way that is compatible with the way your brain works. The rule is: Learn something new through your preferred side. When not learning, develop the undeveloped side of the brain.

19   While scientists are still mapping the brain and have not yet completed work that will give us a full understanding of how the entire brain works, we currently know a great deal and can apply these findings to the field of accelerated learning.

Learning Style and Brain Hemispheric Preference

20 Learning style relates to the different ways of receiving material from the world and conveying those messages from the senses to the brain. Brain hemispheric preference deals with what we do with data—how we process, or think about it, and store it once it reaches the brain.

21   The sensory data received from our eyes, ears, sense of touch, or the muscles of our body can be channeled to the right or left side of the brain. These process and store the information in different ways. It is essential to know these differences to learn anything quickly.

22   Some educators focus only on using learning styles when teaching, while others focus only on using brain hemispheric preference. To have a total picture of the way people need to learn, a blending of both is required; thus the development of the concept of a superlink: learning style *plus* brain hemispheric preference. It is necessary to know our best learning style and our brain hemispheric preference to accelerate learning.

©2007 Pearson Education, Inc.

Differences Between the Left and Right Hemispheres

Processing Information: Symbolically versus Sensorially

23 One difference in the way the side of the brain processes is that the left side processes data symbolically in the form of letters, numbers, words, and abstract ideas, and the right side processes data in a sensory way, perceiving the world through the senses, without words.

24   The left hemisphere allows human beings to have a gift of language. Without it, we would only perceive what we see, hear, taste, smell, and touch, and our movements—without words. We would not be able to talk about our experiences or communicate them to others. In most people, the left side of the brain handles language, although there are exceptions. . . . Think of the hemisphere in which our speech and language center is located as a built-in translator that takes whatever happens and puts words or numbers to it.

25   The right side of the brain processes information without language. It perceives sensations of sight, touch, smell, taste, movement, music, the sounds of the human voice and of nature without putting words or labels to the experience. It perceives life as a movie without words.

26   Although everyone processes language, the difference is that some people first process everything into words and language, while other people first perceive the event as a pure sensory experience without words. As the material is processed in someone's mind, they can "think" about it either in words, as if a dialogue were going on in their head, or can "think" about it in sensory images full of sight, sound, smell, taste, and touch, as well as movement, without words. If you wonder how this is possible, think of a time when you saw someone you knew but could not remember his or her name. You tried so hard to remember but drew a blank—yet you were sure you knew the person. This is an example of how the right brain functions—without words.

27   This information is critical in terms of accelerated learning. Why? If someone processes information in symbols such as words, he or she will respond to being taught in terms of words and language. If someone processes information in sensory images, he or she will respond to being taught in terms of sensory images and experiences. When we match the presentation of new material to our brain hemispheric preference learning is assured. When we do not do this, we struggle with learning new material and may not understand the material at all.

28   This does not mean that none of us use both sides of the brain to process information. Everyone is capable of speaking and receiving sensory images; we blend the two together to learn and to perform different tasks. The difference is that when we are learning something new for the first time we need to process the new material through our preferred brain hemisphere. If we receive data through our preferred side of the brain it is more automatic, natural, and easier for us to accelerate our learning.

Storing Information: Step-by-Step or Simultaneously

29 When we learn something new, we also find it easier if the material is presented in a way that matches the way we *store* information. The left side of the brain stores it in a sequential, step-by-step order. The left side absorbs information in a linear order, bit by bit, one piece at a time. It has difficulty getting the big picture unless information is presented sequentially. The right side of the brain stores information in a simultaneous, global way; it sees the whole picture at once. It has difficulty receiving information in a step-by-step way unless it gets the big picture. Both sides of the brain are equally important, have their role to play in human life, and must work together.

30   Are there people who can store information both ways? Yes. These people have developed the use of both sides of the brain. They are equally comfortable with both left-brain linear thinking and right-brain global thinking. Those who do not use both sides of the brain, who favor one side, need to know their preference in order to find out how to learn more rapidly.

31   Although intuition has been traditionally assigned to the right side of the brain, research has not confirmed this. What is perceived as intuition could actually be a function of reading nonverbal communication, synthesizing unrelated material and events into a whole, or using imagination or inventiveness. Both right-brain and left-brain people may have intuition. Future studies may reveal that intuition may be beyond the scope of the right or left hemispheres of the brain.

LINKSMAN, *HOW TO LEARN ANYTHING QUICKLY*

Exercise 1   ## Work with Words

Use context clues, dictionary skills, and your knowledge of word parts to choose the best definition for each italicized word in the following sentences from the reading. The paragraph number is provided in case you want to check the context.

1. *Auditory* learners learn by listening, hearing themselves talk, and discussing their thoughts with others. (par. 3)

   Auditory
   a. having to do with hearing, listening, and talking
   b. having to do with learning
   c. having to do with discussing thoughts

2. *Tactile* learners learn by touching or feeling sensation on their skin, by using their hands and fingers, and connecting what they learn to their sense of touch or their emotions. (par. 4)

   Tactile
   a. having to do with the sense of sight and sound
   b. having to do with the sense of touch
   c. related to learning styles

©2007 Pearson Education, Inc.

3. Kinesthetic learners learn by moving their large, or *gross,* muscles in space, and by getting actively involved in the learning process through simulations, role-play, experimentation, exploration, and movement, and participating in real-life activities. (par. 5)

Gross
a. muscled
b. real-life
c. large

4. As our brains are exposed to stimuli, new interconnections between nerve cells are created; this quality is known as *plasticity.* (par. 7)

Plasticity
a. being made of plastic
b. exposed to stimuli
c. the ability to create interconnections between nerve cells

5. The brain is divided into two hemispheres, or halves—the right and the left. While we all use both sides of the brain, many people process and store information using one side more than the other, exhibiting a *brain hemispheric preference.* (par. 13)

Brain hemispheric preference
a. the preferred two hemispheres of the brain
b. the tendency to process and store information using one side of the brain more than the other
c. the exhibition of the processing and storing of information

Exercise 2   Check Your Understanding

Based on the reading, Linksman's "How We Learn," choose the best answer to each of the following multiple-choice questions.

1. Which of the following sentences best expresses the most important idea of the reading?
   a. People learn best in different ways and usually prefer to use one hemisphere of the brain more than the other.
   b. The four most important learning styles are visual, auditory, tactile, and kinesthetic.
   c. Scientists are still learning more about how the brain works.

2. It is good to know what your preferred learning style is because
   a. it's always interesting to know more information about yourself.
   b. you can learn new information faster if you consciously use your preferred learning style.
   c. you should always try to learn new material with different learning styles to maximize your performance.

3. Traditional schools teach mostly through
   a. the tactile senses.
   b. the kinesthetic senses.
   c. the visual and auditory senses.

4. Educators need to be able to focus on
   a. students' learning styles.
   b. students' brain hemispheric preferences.
   c. both learning styles and brain hemispheric preferences.

5. Which of the following describes the way that the right side of the brain stores information? (par. 29)
   a. Simultaneously and globally
   b. Linearly, in a step-by-step fashion
   c. Through language

| Exercise 3 | ## Reflect |

Think about what you read in "How We Learn" and what you already know about learning and the brain. Then answer the following questions in your own words.

1. How do you best learn new information? What do you think your learning style is?

   _____

   _____

   _____

   _____

2. What is your brain hemispheric preference? Why do you think so?

   _____

   _____

   _____

   _____

3. How can you use the information about learning styles and brain hemispheric preference to help you study?

   _____

   _____

   _____

   _____

©2007 Pearson Education, Inc.

For Chapter 2, WORKING WITH WORDS

Social and Ethical Issues of Computer Technology

George Beekman

In the following reading from the computer science textbook Computer Confluence, *George Beekman discusses some of the broader issues we need to think about—the implications, or unforeseen ethical problems that our technology creates. As you read, consider how these implications affect you directly now or how they affect our society more broadly.*

> *True computer literacy is not just knowing how to make use of computers and computational ideas. It is knowing when it is appropriate to do so.*
> —SEYMOUR PAPERT, IN *MINDSTORMS*

1 Computers and networks are transforming the world rapidly and irreversibly. Jobs that existed for hundreds of years are eliminated by automation while new careers are built on emerging technology. Start-up businesses create new markets overnight while older companies struggle to keep pace with "Internet time." Instant worldwide communication changes the way businesses work and challenges the role of governments. Computers routinely save lives in hospitals, keep space flights on course, and predict the weekend weather.

2 More than any other recent technology, the computer is responsible for profound changes in our society; we just need to imagine a world without computers to recognize their impact. Of course, computer scientists and computer engineers are not responsible for all the technological turbulence. Developments in fields as diverse as telecommunications, genetic engineering, medicine, and atomic physics contribute to the ever-increasing rate of social change. But researchers in all these fields depend on computers to produce their work.

3 While it's exciting to consider the opportunities arising from advances in artificial intelligence, multimedia, robotics, and other cutting-edge technologies of the electronic revolution, it's just as important to pay attention to the potential risks. . . .

4 • *The threat to personal privacy posed by large databases and computer networks.* When you use a credit card, buy an airline ticket, place a phone call, visit your doctor, send an email message, or explore the Web, you are leaving a trail of personal information in one or more computers. Who owns that information? Is it okay for the business or organization that collected the information to share it with others or make it public? Do you have the right to check its accuracy and change it if it's wrong? Do laws protecting individual privacy rights place undue burdens on businesses and governments?

5 • *The hazards of high-tech crime and the difficulty of keeping data secure.* Even if you trust the institutions and businesses that collect data about you, you can't be sure that data will remain secure in their computer systems. Computer crime is at an all-time high, and law enforcement officials are having a difficult time keeping it under control. How can society protect itself from information thieves and high-tech vandals? How can lawmakers write laws about technology that they are just beginning to understand? What kinds of personal risk do you face as a result of computer crime?

6 • *The difficulty of defining and protecting intellectual property in an all-digital age.* Software programs, musical recordings, videos, and books can be difficult and expensive to create. But in our digital age, all of these can easily be copied. What rights do the creators of intellectual property have? Is a teenager who copies music files from the Web a computer criminal? What about a shopkeeper who sells pirated copies of Microsoft Office for $10? Or a student who posts a clip from *The Matrix* on his Web site? Or a musician who uses a two-second sample from a Beatles song in an electronic composition?

7 • *The risks of failure of computer systems.* Computer software is difficult to write, because it is incredibly complex. As a result, no computer system is completely fail-safe. Computer failures routinely cause communication problems, billing errors, lost data, and other inconveniences. But they also occasionally result in power blackouts, telephone system meltdowns, weapons failure, and other potentially deadly problems. Who is responsible for loss of income—or loss of life—caused by software errors? What rights do we have when buying and using software? How can we, as a society, protect ourselves from software disasters?

8 • *The threat of automation and the dehumanization of work.* Computers and the Internet fueled unprecedented economic growth in the last decade of the twentieth century, producing plenty of new jobs for workers with the right skills. But the new information-based economy has cost many workers—especially older workers—their jobs and their dignity. And many workers today find that their jobs involve little more than tending to machines—and being monitored by bosses with high-tech surveillance devices. As machines replace people in the workplace, what rights do the displaced workers have? Does a worker's right to privacy outweigh an employer's right to read employee email or monitor worker actions? What is the government's role in the protection of worker rights in the high-tech workplace?

9 • *The abuse of information as a tool of political and economic power.* The computer age has produced an explosion of information, and most of that information is concentrated in corporate and government computers. The emergence of low-cost personal computers and the Internet makes it possible for more people to access information and the power

©2007 Pearson Education, Inc.

that comes with that information. But the majority of the people on the planet have never made a phone call, let alone used a computer. Will the information revolution leave them behind? Do information-rich people and countries have a responsibility to share technology and information with the information-poor?

10 • *The dangers of dependence on complex technology.* One of the biggest news stories of 1999 was the impending threat of massive problems caused by the so-called Y2K bug—the failure of some computer programs on January 1, 2000, because those systems represented the year with only two digits. People stockpiled food and fuel, hid cash and jewels, and prepared for the possibility that the power grid would fail, leaving much of the world's population helpless and hungry. Businesses and governments spent billions of dollars repairing and replacing computer systems, and the Y2K crisis never materialized. But the Y2K scare reminded us how much we have come to depend on this far-from-foolproof technology. Are we, as a society, addicted to computer technology? Should we question technological innovations before we embrace them? Can we build a future in which technology never takes precedence over humanity?

Beekman, *Computer Confluence*

| Exercise 1 | Work with Words

Use context clues, dictionary skills, and your knowledge of word parts to choose the best definition for each italicized word in the following sentences from the reading. The paragraph number is provided in case you want to check the context.

1. Computers and networks are transforming the world rapidly and *irreversibly*. (par. 1)

   Irreversibly
   a. able to go into reverse
   b. able to go back
   c. unable to go back

2. While it's exciting to consider the opportunities arising from advances in artificial intelligence, multimedia, robotics, and other *cutting-edge* technologies of the electronic revolution, it's just as important to pay attention to the potential risks. (par. 3)

   Cutting-edge
   a. most established
   b. most reliable
   c. newest

3. Computer software is difficult to write, because it is incredibly complex. As a result, no computer system is completely *fail-safe.* (par. 7)

   Fail-safe
   a. safe from accidents
   b. guaranteed to always work
   c. identical

4. Does a worker's right to privacy *outweigh* an employer's right to read employee email or monitor worker actions? (par. 8)

   Outweigh
   a. have more importance than
   b. have less importance than
   c. weigh more than

5. Should we question new technological innovations before we *embrace* them? (par. 10)

   Embrace
   a. hug fervently
   b. relate to
   c. accept

| Exercise 2 | ## Check Your Understanding

Based on the reading, Beekman's "Social and Ethical Issues of Computer Technology," choose the best answer to each of the following multiple-choice questions.

1. Which of the following sentences best expresses the most important idea of the reading?
   a. Computers and networks are transforming the world rapidly and irreversibly.
   b. More than any other recent technology, the computer is responsible for profound changes in our society; we just need to imagine a world without computers to recognize their impact.
   c. It's important to pay attention to the potential risks of the advances in computer technology.

2. In this reading, Beekman basically
   a. makes some constructive suggestions about how we should deal with the implications of recent advances in computer technology.
   b. asks questions about some of the risks involved in advanced computer technology.
   c. recognizes that solving all the concerns we have about advances in computer technology is unrealistic.

©2007 Pearson Education, Inc.

3. Intellectual property refers to
   a. the books, software programs, videos, and musical recordings that you have in your house.
   b. ideas and creations that are produced by a person's mind or intellect and owned by that person as property.
   c. the freedom to think without anybody being able to control your thoughts.

4. Which of the following is an example of the dehumanization of work that Beekman mentions in this reading?
   a. Workers finding the satisfaction of being able to do more than ever with the help of computers
   b. Workers being monitored with high-tech surveillance devices
   c. Workers losing their jobs to computers

5. Why is Beekman worried about our becoming dependent on complex technology?
   a. Because of the disastrous consequences of Y2K
   b. Because the technology is far too complicated for one person to understand
   c. Because of the possibility that this technology can fail to work

| Exercise 3 | **Reflect** |

Think about what you read in "Social and Ethical Issues of Computer Technology" and what you already know about the risks of advanced technology. Then answer the following questions in your own words.

1. Which of the concerns about advanced computer technology listed in this reading do you believe will affect you most personally? Explain your answer.

   _____

   _____

   _____

   _____

2. What are some examples of computer crime that have happened recently? Have you or anybody you know been the victim of computer crime? Be as specific as you can in your answers.

   _____

   _____

   _____

   _____

   _____

For Chapter 3, TOPICS AND MAIN IDEAS

Table Rituals Laurie Tarkan

The following article by Laurie Tarkan appeared in the New York Times *in May 2005. In it, Tarkan discusses studies that support the importance of families eating together. As you read, consider your personal experience of eating meals with members of your family.*

1   The family dinner has long been an example of family togetherness. But recently, scientists have been coming up with compelling reasons—including a lowered risk of smoking, drinking and doing illicit drugs among teenagers—for families to pull up a chair around the table.

2   The interest in the ritual may have been spurred by concerns that the number of families who do not dine together is increasing. According to several surveys, 30 to 40 percent of families do not eat dinner together five to seven nights a week, though most families eat dinner together some days a week. Families with older teenagers eat fewer dinners together than those with younger children. The two most common obstacles, parents say, are late working hours and activities that overlap with mealtime, like soccer games and Girl Scout meetings.

3   Many families that do dine together make a concerted effort to carve out the time. Some spend Sundays cooking meals for the week, some do prep work the evening before, some use takeout a couple of nights a week, and many parents of young children guiltily admit that they could not prepare a dinner if it were not for the TV, which gets turned on for 30 to 60 minutes while they cook. . . .

4   Childhood memories often influence people's opinion about the importance of family dinners. Isabel Wurgaft, a member of a group for working mothers in Millburn, N.J., said: "Growing up, my father got home late, at 8 p.m., but my mother always made us wait to eat as a family no matter how much we complained. Now that my father has passed away over 10 years ago, dinner conversations are the strongest and best memories for me and my sisters." For others, though, the struggle is apparent. "I feel guilty because it's supposed to be very important for families to eat together, but it just doesn't work with our schedule," said Janette Pazer, another member of the working mothers' group. "I'd have to leave work an hour early, and try to cook while they're hanging on me for attention and asking for homework help, rather than getting my full attention when I get home."

5   In past eras, the family meal was more of a practicality—people had to eat, and they turned up at the table, where food was being served. "In the contemporary world, we've made an icon of the dinner hour as a way to hold on to something, otherwise people would go off in different directions and never get together," said Barbara Haber, the author of *From Hardtack to Home Fries: An Uncommon History of American Cooks and Meals.*

©2007 Pearson Education, Inc.

6   Recent studies have begun to shore up the idea that family dinners can have an effect. For example, a 2004 study of 4,746 children 11 to 18 years old, published in the *Archives of Pediatrics and Adolescent Medicine,* found that frequent family meals were associated with a lower risk of smoking, drinking and using marijuana; with a lower incidence of depressive symptoms and suicidal thoughts; and with better grades. Another study last year, a survey of 12- to 17-year-olds by the National Center on Addiction and Substance Abuse at Columbia University, found that teenagers who reported eating two or fewer dinners a week with family members were more than one and a half times as likely to smoke, drink or use illegal substances than were teenagers who had five to seven family dinners. "We also noticed that the more often teens had dinner with their parents, the less likely they were to have sexually active friends, less likely girls were to have boyfriends two years older, and the less time teens spent with boyfriends or girlfriends," said Joseph A. Califano Jr., the center's chairman and president. A study from the University of Minnesota published last year found that adolescent girls who reported having more frequent family meals and a positive atmosphere during those meals were less likely to have eating disorders.

7   "The family dinner is an important time for families to be together and talk, it's important for family bonds having time together that's not stressful, enjoying each other's company and being around food," said Dr. Karen Weber Cullen, a behavioral nutritionist at the Children's Nutrition Research Center at Baylor College of Medicine in Houston. Family meals, experts say, also offer a predictable routine and an opportunity for parents to monitor their children's behavior. "That monitoring has been related to a host of positive physical and mental health outcomes in children and adolescents," said Dr. Barbara Fiese, who studies family routines and rituals at Syracuse University. She added that regular family meals also provide an opportunity to establish a sense of belonging to a family unit.

8   According to one study, family dinners may help improve the vocabulary of younger children. Researchers at Harvard in 1996 looked at the types of activities that promoted language development. Family dinners were more important than play, story time and other family events. And those families that engaged in extended discourse at the dinner table, like story telling and explanations, rather than one-phrase comments, like "eat your vegetables," had children with better language skills, said Dr. Catherine Snow, professor of education at Harvard and the researcher of the study. "When there is more than one adult at the table, it tends to make talk richer, topics are established by adult interest and can be extremely valuable opportunities for children to learn," Dr. Snow said.

9   A handful of studies have also suggested that eating as a family improves children's consumption of fruits and vegetables, grains, fiber and vitamins and minerals. Children who have family meals also eat less fried food, saturated fat, and soda, studies suggest.

TARKAN, "Families That Dine Together Reap Benefits"

Exercise 1   Work with Words

Use context clues, dictionary skills, and your knowledge of word parts to choose the best definition for each italicized word in the following sentences from the reading. The paragraph number is provided in case you want to check the context.

1. But recently, scientists have been coming up with *compelling* reasons—including a lowered risk of smoking, drinking and doing illicit drugs among teenagers—for families to pull up a chair around the table. (par. 1)

   Compelling
   a. unconvincing
   b. forceful
   c. disagreeable

2. Many families that do dine together make a *concerted* effort to carve out the time. (par. 3)

   Concerted
   a. planned
   b. arbitrary
   c. spontaneous

3. "In the contemporary world, we've made an *icon* of the dinner hour as a way to hold on to something, otherwise people would go off in different directions and never get together." (par. 5)

   Icon
   a. painting
   b. drawing
   c. symbol

4. Recent studies have begun to *shore up* the idea that family dinners can have an effect. (par. 6)

   Shore up
   a. reinforce
   b. duplicate
   c. contradict

5. And those families that engaged in extended *discourse* at the dinner table, like story telling and explanations, rather than one-phrase comments, like "eat your vegetables," had children with better language skills, said Dr. Catherine Snow, professor of education at Harvard and the researcher of the study. (par. 8)

   Discourse
   a. conversation
   b. argument
   c. fun

©2007 Pearson Education, Inc.

Exercise 2   Check Your Understanding

Based on the reading, Tarkan's "Table Rituals," choose the best answer to each of the following multiple-choice questions.

1. Which of the following best states the main idea of the reading?
    a. Many families make a special effort to eat together at least a few times a week.
    b. In the past, the family meal was more of a practicality—people had to eat, and they turned up at the table, where food was being served.
    c. Recent studies have been demonstrating some important reasons for families to eat meals together, especially for the benefit of teenagers.

2. What is the best statement of the main idea of paragraph 4?
    a. Childhood memories influence people's opinions about the importance of family dinners.
    b. Some people just can't manage to get things organized to have meals together, even though for many people childhood meals are among their most important memories.
    c. It simply does not work out for people with small children to try to have meals together in the evening because the children need so much attention and homework help.

3. Which of the following behaviors of teenagers seems to be encouraged when the family has meals together?
    a. Performing well in athletics
    b. Smoking
    c. Getting good grades

4. Family meals—with good interaction and conversation—tend to improve which of the following for young children?
    a. Language skills
    b. Math skills
    c. Skills for getting along with people

5. It's important to remember that for family meals to have so many good effects,
    a. the food should be nutritious.
    b. the atmosphere should not be stressful.
    c. the interaction should be exciting.

Exercise 3   Reflect

Think about what you read in "Table Rituals" and what you already know about families eating together. Then answer the following questions in your own words.

1. Why do you think that families sharing a meal together seems to be such a good thing to do? List the qualities you think these families would have.

_____

_____

_____

2. What eating habits does/did your family have? Do/did you eat together? Is/was it a pleasant experience? Explain. If you don't eat together, explain why not.

_____

_____

_____

For Chapter 4, SUPPORT FOR MAIN IDEAS

Creativity and Longevity   Norman Cousins

The following passage is a chapter from Anatomy of an Illness *by Norman Cousins (1912–1990). In this book, Cousins discusses his recovery from a serious disease that doctors considered nearly impossible to cure. Cousins decided that he would not simply give up, but if the doctors couldn't cure him, he would take responsibility for his own health and figure out a way to get better on his own. Cousins began to think about the connections between positive attitudes and longevity, and he proceeded to heal himself through a combination of vitamins, laughter, and a positive attitude. In this reading, Cousins writes about his personal experiences with Pablo Casals (1876–1973), a world-famous Spanish cellist and musician, and Albert Schweitzer (1875–1965), a physician, musician, missionary, and philosopher who received the Nobel Peace Prize in 1952. Both were very talented people who had lived long lives and who were an inspiration to Cousins during his illness.*

1   What started me thinking about creativity and longevity, and the connection between the two, were examples of two men who were very much alike in vital respects: Pablo Casals and Albert Schweitzer.

2   Both were octogenarians when I met them for the first time. Both were fully creative—almost explosively so. Both were committed to personal undertakings that were of value to other human beings. What I learned from these two men had a profound effect on my life—especially during the period of my illness. I learned that a highly developed purpose and the will to live are among the

©2007 Pearson Education, Inc.

prime raw materials of human existence. I became convinced that these materials may well represent the most potent force within human reach.

3   First, some observations about Pablo Casals.

4   I met him for the first time at his home in Puerto Rico just a few weeks before his ninetieth birthday. I was fascinated by his daily routine. About 8 a.m. his lovely young wife Marta would help him to start the day. His various infirmities made it difficult for him to dress himself. Judging from his difficulty in walking and from the way he held his arms, I guessed he was suffering from rheumatoid arthritis. His emphysema was evident in his labored breathing. He came into the living room on Marta's arm. He was badly stooped. His head was pitched forward and he walked with a shuffle. His hands were swollen and his fingers were clenched.

5   Even before going to the breakfast table, Don Pablo went to the piano—which, I learned, was a daily ritual. He arranged himself with some difficulty on the piano bench, then with discernible effort raised his swollen and clenched fingers above the keyboard.

6   I was not prepared for the miracle that was about to happen. The fingers slowly unlocked and reached towards the keys like the buds of a plant toward the sunlight. His back straightened. He seemed to breathe more freely. Now his fingers settled on the keys. Then came the opening bars of Bach's *Wohltemperierte Klavier,* played with great sensitivity and control. I had forgotten that Don Pablo had achieved proficiency on several musical instruments before he took up the cello. He hummed as he played, then said that Bach spoke to him here—and he placed his hand over his heart.

7   Then he plunged into a Brahms concerto and his fingers, now agile and powerful, raced across the keyboard with dazzling speed. His entire body seemed fused with the music; it was no longer stiff and shrunken but supple and graceful and completely freed of its arthritic coils.

8   Having finished the piece, he stood up by himself, far straighter and taller than when he had come into the room. He walked to the breakfast table with no trace of a shuffle, ate heartily, talked animatedly, finished the meal, then went for a walk on the beach.

9   After an hour or so, he came back to the house and worked on his correspondence until lunch. Then he napped. When he rose, the stoop and the shuffle and the clenched hands were back again. On this particular day, a camera and recording crew from public television were scheduled to arrive in mid-afternoon. Anticipating the visit, Don Pablo said he wished some way could be found to call it off; he didn't feel up to the exertion of the filming, with its innumerable and inexplicable retakes and the extreme heat of the bright lights.

10   Marta, having been through these reluctances before, reassured Don Pablo, saying she was certain he would be stimulated by the meeting. She reminded him that he liked the young people who did the last filming and that they would probably be back again. In particular, she called his attention to the lovely young lady who directed the recording.

11   Don Pablo brightened. "Yes, of course," he said, "it will be good to see them again."

12   As before, he stretched his arms in front of him and extended his fingers. Then the spine straightened and he stood up and went to his cello. He began to play. His fingers, hands, and arms were in sublime coordination as they responded to the demands of his brain for the controlled beauty of movement and tone. Any cellist thirty years his junior would have been proud to have such extraordinary physical command.

13   Twice in one day I had seen the miracle. A man almost ninety, beset with the infirmities of old age, was able to cast off his afflictions, at least temporarily, because he knew he had something of overriding importance to do. There was no mystery about the way it worked, for it happened every day. Creativity for Pablo Casals was the source of his own cortisone. It is doubtful whether any antiinflammatory medication he would have taken would have been as powerful or as safe as the substances produced by the interaction of his mind and body.

14   The process is not strange. If he had been caught up in an emotional storm, the effects would have been manifested in an increased flow of hydrochloric acid to the stomach, in an upsurge of adrenal activity, in the production of corticoids, in the increase of blood pressure, and a faster heart beat.

15   But he was caught up in something else. He was caught up in his own creativity, in his own desire to accomplish a specific purpose, and the effect was both genuine and observable. And the effects of his body chemistry were no less pronounced—albeit in a positive way—than they would have been if he had been through an emotional wringer.

16   Don Pablo played it [the piano]. His fingers were thin and the skin was pale but they belonged to the most extraordinary hands I had ever seen. They seemed to have a wisdom and a grace of their own. When he played Mozart, he was clearly the interpreter and not just the performer; yet it was difficult to imagine how the piece could be played in any other way.

17   After he got up from the piano he apologized for having taken up so much time in our talk with music, instead of discussing the affairs of the world. I told him I had the impression that what he had been saying and doing were most relevant in terms of the world's affairs. In the discussion that followed there seemed to be agreement on the proposition that the most serious part of the problem of world peace was that the individual felt helpless.

18   "The answer to helplessness is not so very complicated." Don Pablo said. "A man can do something for peace without having to jump into politics. Each man has inside him a basic decency and goodness. If he listens to it and acts on it, he is giving a great deal of what it is the world needs most. It is not complicated but it takes courage. It takes courage for a man to listen to his own goodness and act on it. Do we dare to be ourselves? This is the question that counts."

19   The decency and goodness within Don Pablo were clearly evident. But there were other resources—purpose, the will to live, faith, and good humor—that enabled him to cope with his infirmities and to perform as cellist and conductor well into his nineties.

©2007 Pearson Education, Inc.

20 Albert Schweitzer always believed that the best medicine for any illness he might have was the knowledge that he had a job to do, plus a good sense of humor. He once said that disease tended to leave him rather rapidly because it found so little hospitality inside his body.

21 The essence of Dr. Schweitzer was purpose and creativity. All his multiple skills and interests were energized by a torrential drive to use his mind and body. To observe him at work at his hospital in Lambarene was to see human purpose bordering on the supernatural. During an average day at the hospital, even after he turned ninety, he would attend to his duties at the clinic and make his rounds, do strenuous carpentry, move heavy crates of medicine, work on his correspondence (innumerable letters each day), give time to his unfinished manuscripts, and play the piano.

22 "I have no intention of dying," he once told his staff, "so long as I can do things. And if I do things, there is no need to die. So I will live a long, long time."

23 And he did—until he was ninety-five.

24 Like his friend Pablo Casals, Albert Schweitzer would not allow a single day to pass without playing Bach. . . .

25 In an earlier book, I wrote about my experience at the Lambarene hospital when, one night, long after most the of oil lamps had been turned out, I walked down toward the river. It was a sticky night and I couldn't sleep. As I passed the compound near Dr. Schweitzer's quarters, I could hear the rapid piano movement of a Bach toccata.

26 I approached the doctor's bungalow and stood for perhaps five minutes outside the latticed window, through which I could see his silhouette at the piano in the dimly lit room. His powerful hands were in total control of the composition and he met Bach's demands for complete definition of each note—each with its own weight and value, yet all of them intimately interlaced to create an ordered whole.

27 I had a stronger sense of listening to a great console than if I had been in the world's largest cathedral. The yearning for an architectured beauty in music; the disciplined artistry and the palpable desire to keep alive a towering part of his past; the need for outpouring and catharsis—all these things inside Albert Schweitzer spoke in his playing.

28 And when he was through he sat with his hands resting lightly on the keys, his great head bent forward as though to catch the lingering echoes. Johann Sebastian Bach had made it possible for him to free himself of the pressures and tensions of the hospital, with its forms to fill out in triplicate. He was now restored to the world of creative and ordered splendor that he had always found in music.

29 The effect of the music was much the same on Schweitzer as it had been on Casals. He felt restored, regenerated, enhanced. When he stood up, there was no trace of a stoop. Music was his medicine.

30 But not the only medicine. There was also humor.

31 Albert Schweitzer employed humor as a form of equatorial therapy, a way of reducing the temperatures and the humidity and the tensions. His use of humor, in fact, was so artistic that one had the feeling he almost regarded it as a musical instrument.

©2007 Pearson Education, Inc.

32   Life for the young doctors and nurses was not easy at the Schweitzer Hospital. Dr. Schweitzer knew it and gave himself the task of supplying nutrients for their spirits. At mealtimes, when the staff came together, Schweitzer always had an amusing story or two to go with the meal. Laughter at the dinner hour was probably the most important course. It was fascinating to see the way the staff members seemed to be rejuvenated by the wryness of his humor. At one meal, for example, Dr. Schweitzer reported to the staff that, "as everyone knows, there are only two automobiles within seventy-five miles of the hospital. This afternoon, the inevitable happened; the cars collided. We have treated the drivers for their superficial wounds. Anyone who has reverence for machines may treat the cars."

33   The next evening, he passed along the news that six baby chicks had been born to Edna the hen, who made her home near the dock. "It was a great surprise to me," he said solemnly. "I didn't even know she was that way."

34   One night at the dinner table, after a particularly trying day, he related to the staff an account of his visit to the Royal Palace in Copenhagen some years earlier. The invitation was for dinner, the first course of which was Danish herring. Schweitzer didn't happen to like herring. When no one was looking he deftly slipped the herring off the plate and into his jacket pocket. The next day, one of the local newspapers, reporting on the life at the Royal Palace, told of the visit of the jungle doctor and of the strange eating habits he had picked up in Africa. Not only did Dr. Schweitzer eat the meat of the fish, the newspaper reported; he ate the bones, head, eyes and all.

35   I noticed that when the young doctors and nurses got up from the table that evening, they were in a fine mood, refreshed as much by the spirit of the occasion as by the food. Dr. Schweitzer's fatigue, so palpable when he first came into the dining room, now gave way to anticipations of things that had to be done. Humor at Lambarene was vital nourishment.

36   The Bible tells us that a merry heart works like a doctor. Exactly what happens inside the human mind and body as the result of humor is difficult to say. But the evidence that it works has stimulated the speculations not just of physicians but of philosophers and scholars over the centuries. Sir Francis Bacon called attention to the physiological characteristics of mirth. Robert Burton, in his *Anatomy of Melancholy*, almost four hundred years ago, cited authorities for his observation that "humor purges the blood, making the body young, lively, and fit for any manner of employment." In general, Burton said, mirth is the "principal engine for battering the walls of melancholy . . . and a sufficient cure in itself." Hobbes described laughter as a "passion of sudden glory."

37   Immanuel Kant, in his *Critique of Pure Reason,* wrote that laughter produces a "feeling of health through the furtherance of the vital bodily processes, the affection that moves the intestines and the diaphragms; in a word, the feeling of health that makes up the gratification felt by us; so that we can thus reach the body through the soul and use the latter as the physician of the former." If Kant was intimating in these remarks that he never

knew a man who possessed the gift of hearty laughter to be burdened by constipation, I can readily agree with him. It has always seemed to me that hearty laughter is a good way to jog internally without having to go outdoors.

38   Sigmund Freud's fascination with the human mind was not confined to its malfunctioning or its torments. His researches were directed to the supremely mysterious station occupied by the brain in the universe. Wit and humor to him were highly differentiated manifestations of the uniqueness of the mind. He believed that mirth was a highly useful way of counteracting nervous tension, and that humor could be used as effective therapy.

39   Sir William Osler regarded laughter as the "music of life." His biographer, Harvey Cushing, quoted Osler as having advised doctors who are spiritually and physically depleted at the end of a long day to find their own medicine in mirth. "There is the happy possibility," Osler wrote, "that like Lionel in, I think, one of Shelley's poems, he may keep himself young with laughter."

40   Current scientific research in the physiological benefits of laughter may not be abundant but is significant nonetheless. William Fry, of Stanford University, has written a highly illuminating paper, "The Respiratory Components of Mirthful Laughter." I assume he is referring to what is commonly known as belly laughter. Like Immanuel Kant, Fry finds that the entire process of respiration is benevolently engaged by laughter. Another paper worth consulting on the subject is "Effect of Laughter on Muscle Tone," written by H. Paskind in the *Archives of Neurology and Psychiatry* in 1932.

41   Some people, in the grip of uncontrollable laughter, say their ribs are hurting. The expression is probably accurate, but it is a delightful "hurt" that leaves the individual relaxed almost to the point of an open sprawl. It is the kind of "pain," too, that most people would do well to experience every day of their lives. It is as specific and tangible as any other form of physical exercise. Though its biochemical manifestations have yet to be as explicitly charted and understood as the effects of fear or frustration or rage, they are real enough.

42   Increasingly, in the medical press, articles are being published about the high cost of the negative emotions. Cancer, in particular, has been connected to intensive states of grief or anger or fear. It makes little sense to suppose that emotions exact only penalties and confer no benefits. At any rate, long before my own serious illness, I became convinced that creativity, the will to live, hope, faith, and love have biochemical significance and contribute strongly to healing and to well-being. The positive emotions are life-giving experiences.

COUSINS, *ANATOMY OF AN ILLNESS*

Exercise 1   ## Work with Words

Use context clues, dictionary skills, and your knowledge of word parts to choose the best definition for each italicized word in the following sentences from the reading. The paragraph number is provided in case you want to check the context.

1. His *emphysema* was evident in his labored breathing. (par. 4)

   Emphysema
   a. lung disease
   b. speaking disability
   c. difficulty in singing

2. Anticipating the visit, Don Pablo said he wished some way could be found to call it off; he didn't feel up to the exertion of the filming, with its innumerable and *inexplicable* retakes and the extreme heat of the bright lights. (par. 9)

   Inexplicable
   a. not surprising
   b. not explainable
   c. not memorable

3. It is doubtful whether any *antiinflammatory* medication he [Pablo Casals] would have taken would have been as powerful or as safe as the substances produced by the interaction of his mind and body. (par. 13)

   Antiinflammatory
   a. causing sleep
   b. stopping bleeding
   c. stopping swelling

4. He [Sigmund Freud] believed that *mirth* was a highly useful way of counteracting nervous tension, and that humor could be used as effective therapy. (par. 38)

   Mirth
   a. sorrow
   b. fear
   c. laughter

5. It makes little sense to suppose that emotions exact only penalties and *confer* no benefits. (par. 42)

   Confer
   a. eliminate
   b. go against
   c. give

Exercise 2 ## Check Your Understanding

Based on the reading, Cousins's "Creativity and Longevity," choose the best answer to each of the following multiple-choice questions.

©2007 Pearson Education, Inc.

1. What is the main idea of this reading?
   a. We must study the lives of people who live for a long time.
   b. Purpose, creativity, and humor help us to live long and healthy lives.
   c. Freud, Schweitzer, and Casals each had a strong sense of humor.

2. The major supporting examples that Cousins gives to support his position are
   a. Fry and Kant.
   b. Freud and Osler.
   c. Casals and Schweitzer.

3. Which of the following sentences from paragraph 4 contains a major supporting point?
   a. His various infirmities made it difficult for him to dress himself.
   b. About 8 a.m. his lovely young wife Marta would help him to start the day.
   c. I was fascinated by his daily routine.

4. Which of the following best explains the process that Casals was "caught up in"? (pars. 12 through 15)
   a. An emotional process that increased his blood pressure and adrenal activity
   b. A creative process with a specific purpose
   c. A medical process for people with arthritis

5. For William Fry of Stanford University, laughter
   a. releases toxins damaging to respiration.
   b. is a healthy way to stimulate respiration.
   c. creates better muscle tone.

| Exercise 3 | **Reflect**

Think about what you read in "Creativity and Longevity" and what you already know about creativity, humor, and health. Then answer the following questions in your own words.

1. Has humor ever been useful to you in reducing stress? Describe your experience with humor.

   _____

   _____

   _____

   _____

2. Are you involved in any creative activity such as playing an instrument, painting, writing, or dancing, that helps you reduce stress? Describe your experience.

_____

_____

_____

_____

3. Besides creativity and humor, what other factors do you know about that can lead to a long, healthy, and productive life?

_____

_____

_____

_____

For Chapter 5, PATTERNS OF ORGANIZATION

Working with Our Hands

Jimmy Carter and Rosalynn Carter

"Working with Our Hands," from the book Everything to Gain, _is former President Jimmy Carter and his wife Rosalynn's first-person account of their volunteer work with such groups as Habitat for Humanity, which builds housing for homeless people. In this segment, the Carters discuss the circumstances that led to their decision to work with Habitat for Humanity and what they learned from their experiences about the problems of housing for poor people. The paragraphs that begin with "J" are Jimmy Carter's comments, and those that begin with "R" are Rosalynn Carter's._

When it comes to giving, some folks will stop at nothing.
—JIMMY TOWNSEND

1   **J.** We planned to leave home on the Saturday before Labor Day, 1984, ride all night on the bus, and arrive in New York City Sunday afternoon. Under a program called Habitat for Humanity we were going to help renovate an old, dilapidated building in the Lower East Side and turn it into nineteen apartments for poor families.

2   On a previous trip to New York I had gone to the building on Sixth Street with a group of young Habitat volunteers. We had to push our way inside through piles of trash and debris and climb laboriously from one floor to another where stairs would one day be built. The place was a haven for drifters, drug dealers and addicts, some of whom had been

©2007 Pearson Education, Inc.

building fires on top of the trash for warmth and cooking. Many of the ceiling joists were burned in two, and the floors had collapsed in places. From the top three stories we could look up and see the clouds and the blue sky.

3   My heart went out to the few young people responsible for the project. They were ambitious and determined, but I learned that they had very few specific plans and no means in sight to achieve the goals they had set for themselves. On the spur of the moment and half in jest I said, "I'll have to come back and do some volunteer carpenter work."

4   By the time I returned home, Millard Fuller, the president and founder of Habitat, had already heard about my offer, and he called to thank me! He suggested that a few others might be willing to go with me and Rosalynn sometime during the summer. Rosalynn, too? I hadn't volunteered her for the task, and I didn't know whether I really wanted to go or not.

5   A trip to the big city to work for a week in the sweltering heat of July was not a very attractive proposition. And volunteers, if we could get them, would have to pay for their own transportation and food, carry their own tools, and stay in crowded bunk rooms that had been offered by an old church near the Lincoln Tunnel. There was no information about what our specific tasks would be, and most of the group that we might recruit probably would never have used a saw, mixed mortar, laid a brick, put up a stud, or used a hammer except to hang a picture on the wall.

6   However, after a few weeks we thought we might have enough prospects to fill a small van—including several professional carpenters, a member of the Americus City Council, a motel owner, a college professor and his new bride—and the list kept growing. It wasn't long before we had enough volunteers to fill a large bus, and we even turned down additional people who wanted to make the trip. Rosalynn's reaction had been: "I don't want to ride a bus all the way to New York!" She seemed to be excited about the trip, though. It would be an adventure of a different type for us, involving no speeches, no letters to write, no major problems to solve, no deep thinking—it would be only manual labor, which might be fun for a change and, she said, a real challenge.

7   So now the volunteers and I were on our way. the first day of work would be Monday, on which Rosalynn already had a long-standing speaking engagement for the morning. She would have to fly to New York and join us late in the afternoon. The truth is that if she had not had a previous engagement, I think she would have invented one. She felt that strongly about the long bus ride, which was necessary because many of the volunteers couldn't afford to take a week off from work and also spend the money required for airfare.

8   The trip turned out to be quite an experience. It was a tiring twenty-five-hour journey, with stops only for meals and a Sunday-morning worship service—but it was an exhilarating twenty-five hours. We sang and told stories, and there developed among us a camaraderie that comes from being somewhat set apart from others, joined together in a common and, we were sure, worthwhile cause. Many in the bus had never visited New York or seen any city larger than Atlanta, and the newness, excitement, and uncertainty about what lay ahead gave us a feeling of adventure.

©2007 Pearson Education, Inc.

9   When we arrived at the site on Sunday afternoon, one look at the bare shell of a building—six stories high with no windows, no doors, no roof, and burned and collapsing floors and ceilings—instantly dampened our spirits. It looked much worse and more fragile now with the structure more fully exposed than it had been in April, when it was full of trash. Our hearts sank. And the loudest dissents were from the few professional builders in the group. "It can't be done," they said in chorus. "If this building has been purchased already, we need to tear it down and start from scratch. There is no way it can ever be made livable." To describe their reaction as despair would be an understatement. They were discouraged almost to the point of resentment that anyone—they all looked at me—could have thought of bringing them so far to be part of an absolute fiasco. There was almost total silence as we made the trip to the church where we would be staying.

10   During supper I invited the most experienced carpenters to sit with me, and asked each of them to describe a possible approach to be followed *if* we should go on with the job. Soon they were competing with each other to outline the best plan for how our group could be divided into teams, which tasks had to be performed first, what additional materials we would need, and how much might be accomplished while we were in New York. Finally, exhausted from the trip and still mostly discouraged, we all went to bed—for the first time in two days.

11   Even the narrow and cramped bunk beds didn't prevent our getting a good night's sleep, and early the next morning we piled into the bus again and drove to the old building. Everyone was grim as doubts returned, but no one expressed them. Instead, we all did our best to maintain an atmosphere of confidence. Seven or eight workers were assigned to each floor and the roof, each group under the supervision of someone with experience in construction. Then, donning hard hats, we went to work.

12   It was dirty, dusty, gritty work, and dangerous for those attempting to rebuild the roof and replace the large structural timbers in the upper floors. Soon we had to put on goggles and masks because of the thick dust that was sifting down from above and billowing up from below, where the remaining debris was being loaded into wheelbarrows and hauled away. It was a long, hard day, but we went back to the church in the late afternoon with a sense of fulfillment, for after only one day with fifty of us there we could begin to see that we could make a difference.

13   **R.** There is great satisfaction in being able to "make a difference" for someone who needs help. The tiredness that comes from any physical activity is all worthwhile, and the spirit sometimes soars. Working with Habitat has been that kind of experience for us. Of all the activities we have undertaken since leaving the White House, it is certainly one of the most inspiring. To help build a home for people who have never lived in a decent place and never dreamed of owning a home of their own can bring both a lot of joy and an emotional response. One has only to have had the experience to know what it means—to the one who is giving time and energy and to the one who is receiving the new home. Soon after we began our work with Habitat, we asked Tom Hall, who had come to the international headquarters for brief volunteer service and had already

stayed five years, "Why do you keep on staying?" His answer was, "I see the faces of those who receive the homes." We have seen the faces too.

14   Habitat for Humanity is only one of many worthwhile programs in which anyone with a little time and inclination can perform challenging and useful work. There are so many people in trouble, so many needs right around us. We can find programs to help the poor, the elderly, the handicapped, the imprisoned, the mentally ill, alcoholics, and drug addicts, to name a few. So many of our young people need a helping hand, as do our hospitals, our libraries, art museums, and schools. There is something that every single one of us can do, even the busiest of younger people, but we in the "second half" of our lives often have more time for getting involved. And especially with our life span lengthening and the chances of good health so great, there is an additional stage of life after work when we can devote more of our time to voluntary service. And when we do, as one speaker at a national conference for retirees said, "Everyone benefits. The talents, wisdom and energy of our retirees are badly needed by our communities . . . and retirees who are active and involved have a new sense of self-worth, a source of daily enrichment. The aging process is slowed." That, we think, appeals to all of us!

15   Helping others can be surprisingly easy, since there is so much that needs to be done. The hard part comes in choosing what to do and getting started, making the first effort at something different. Once the initiative is taken we often find that we can do things we never thought we could.

16   **J.** Even Rosalynn, who often ventures into the unknown, was sure she would only be cleaning up around the work site on our Habitat trip to New York, or carrying tools and light supplies, or maybe even helping with meals for the other volunteers. To her amazement, she was soon doing a multitude of carpenter's jobs, and doing them well!

17   **R.** I arrived in New York somewhat anxious about what I would be doing. I went first to the church and everyone was there, having returned from the first full day of work. I was taken to the fourth floor and shown a bottom bunk in a dormitory-type room that I would be sharing with six other women. Though dinner was being served in the basement, many of the women were still upstairs. I soon learned why. There was one bathroom and more than twenty women! Some still had on their dirty work clothes, and their hair was stiff with plaster dust. Listening to them relate the stories of the day and the disbelief at the work conditions, I was even less sure about what I was in for.

18   Next morning I put on jeans and a Habitat T-shirt and prepared for my first day on the job. When we arrived at the site, I was assigned to the second story. Jimmy was the foreman of this level and had decided that the best thing we could do during the week would be to get down a good solid floor. It was a tall order. Many of the joists had to be replaced or shored up, and most of the floor was gone. To do any work we had to walk on plywood laid across what supporting beams were left.

19   I was first assigned, along with two other women, to clean up the floor that still remained in one corner of the back section. We scraped up layers of old glue and paint and patches of linoleum that were stuck to it,

removed nails that were sticking up, and had made it perfectly smooth, when one of the men came over with a sheet of plywood and said, "Nail it down." Nail it down: Before we left home I had told Jimmy that I would do anything but hammer. I didn't think I could use a hammer and I didn't want to use a hammer. We nailed it down! At first it took me fifteen or twenty strokes for each nail, but before the week was over I could drive one in with only four or five strokes!

20   The next day Jimmy made me foreman of the back half of the second floor, which would eventually be two apartments. And with three other women and an occasional male volunteer, before the week was over we had laid the subfloor and the floor in our entire section—and with a great feeling of accomplishment. We had learned to leave a nail's width of space between the sheets of plywood we put down so that they could expand without buckling, to measure the spaces accurately, and to use a power saw to cut the plywood to fit the spaces. We were pleased and proud. The last day when we were racing against the clock to get our section finished, we had one piece of flooring left to put in place. It was in an awkward spot that fit around a brick chimney and tapered off at one end. We measured it, sawed the wood, held our breath, and dropped it in place. It was perfect! "A perfect fit!" We screamed, "We did it! We did it!"

21   Jimmy came running from the front of the building: "What's the matter? Who's hurt?" When he saw what we had done, even he was impressed—and we all signed our names to that one piece of flooring on the second floor in a new apartment in a New York City slum.

CARTER AND CARTER, *EVERYTHING TO GAIN*

Exercise 1   ## Work with Words

Use context clues, dictionary skills, and your knowledge of word parts to choose the best definition for each italicized word in the following sentences from the reading. The paragraph number is provided in case you want to check the context.

1. We had to push our way inside through piles of trash and debris and climb *laboriously* from one floor to another where stairs would one day be built. (par. 2)

   Laboriously
   a. with a lot of effort
   b. with a lot of speed
   c. with a lot of planning

2. A trip to the big city to work for a week in the *sweltering* heat of July was not a very attractive proposition. (par. 5)

   Sweltering
   a. risky and deadly
   b. unusual and surprising
   c. hot and humid

©2007 Pearson Education, Inc.

3. When we arrived at the site on Sunday afternoon, one look at the bare *shell* of a building—six stories high with no windows, no doors, no roof, and burned and collapsing floors and ceilings—instantly dampened our spirits. (par. 9)

Shell
a. foundation
b. disaster
c. outer structure

4. Habitat for Humanity is only one of many worthwhile programs in which anyone with a little time and *inclination* can perform challenging and useful work. (par. 14)

Inclination
a. willingness
b. money
c. ideas

5. Listening to them *relate* the stories of the day and the disbelief at the work conditions, I was even less sure about what I was in for. (par. 17)

Relate
a. improvise
b. improve
c. tell

Exercise 2   ## Check Your Understanding

Based on the reading, Carter and Carter's "Working with Our Hands," choose the best answer to each of the following multiple-choice questions.

1. What is the most important point Jimmy and Rosalynn Carter make?
   a. It takes a lot of time and hard work to volunteer for an organization.
   b. Many people in the world need reasonably affordable housing.
   c. When you give your time as a volunteer, you learn many important lessons.

2. Why was Jimmy Carter reluctant to volunteer for the New York project at first?
   a. He had a speaking engagement and couldn't take time off from work.
   b. He was unclear about the tasks he'd have to do and whether he could find enough volunteers.
   c. He didn't want to work with professional carpenters.

3. What is the dominant organizational pattern for paragraphs 9 and 10?
   a. Comparison and contrast
   b. Chronological order
   c. Problem and solution

4. What is the dominant pattern of organization in paragraphs 19 and 20?
   a. Cause and effect
   b. Definition and classification
   c. Narration

5. What is the primary purpose of Habitat for Humanity?
   a. To lend money to people in other countries so that they can buy a house
   b. To renovate old houses and build new ones to provide housing for poor people
   c. To recruit and provide jobs for volunteers and expert carpenters

Exercise 3   Reflect

Think about what you read in "Working with Our Hands" and what you already know about volunteer work. Then answer the following questions in your own words.

1. Have you ever had the opportunity to volunteer or to help someone? Have you ever changed the way you thought about a person or a group of people as a result of your experience? Describe what happened and how you changed.

   _____

   _____

   _____

2. Besides poverty and homelessness, what other issues affect the way people live in your community? Discuss these problems, and brainstorm about possible solutions.

   _____

   _____

   _____

For Chapter 6, INFERENCES AND READING LITERATURE

Shame
Dick Gregory

Dick Gregory is a well-known African-American comedian, social commentator, and activist for justice and equality. The following reading is from his

©2007 Pearson Education, Inc.

autobiography, Nigger: An Autobiography, *published in 1964. In this excerpt, he discusses the pain he experienced from feeling different from the other children while he was growing up, and how his pain was intensified because he was infatuated with a young girl in his class.*

1   I never learned hate at home, or shame. I had to go to school for that. I was about seven years old when I got my first big lesson. I was in love with a little girl named Helene Tucker, a light-complected little girl with pigtails and nice manners. She was always clean and she was smart in school. I think I went to school then mostly to look at her. I brushed my hair and even got me a little old handkerchief. It was a lady's handkerchief, but I didn't want Helene to see me wipe my nose on my hand. The pipes were frozen again, there was no water in the house, but I washed my socks and shirt every night. I'd get a pot, and go over to Mister Ben's grocery store, and stick my pot down into his soda machine. Scoop out some chopped ice. By evening the ice melted to water for washing. I got sick a lot that winter because the fire would go out at night before the clothes were dry. In the morning I'd put them on, wet or dry, because they were the only clothes I had.

2   Everybody's got a Helene Tucker, a symbol of everything you want. I loved her for her goodness, her cleanness, her popularity. She'd walk down my street and my brothers and sisters would yell, "Here comes Helene," and I'd rub my tennis sneakers on the back of my pants and wish my hair wasn't so nappy and the white folks' shirt fit me better. I'd run out on the street. If I knew my place and didn't come too close, she'd wink at me and say hello. That was a good feeling. Sometimes I'd follow her all the way home, and shovel the snow off her walk and try to make friends with her Momma and her aunts. I'd drop money on her stoop late at night on my way back from shining shoes in the taverns. And she had a Daddy, and he had a good job. He was a paper hanger.

3   I guess I would have gotten over Helene by summertime, but something happened in that classroom that made her face hang in front of me for the next twenty-two years. When I played the drums in high school it was for Helene and when I broke track records in college it was for Helene and when I started standing behind microphones and heard applause I wished Helene could hear it, too. It wasn't until I was twenty-nine years old and married and making money that I finally got her out of my system. Helene was sitting in that classroom when I learned to be ashamed of myself.

4   It was on a Thursday. I was sitting in the back of the room, in a seat with a chalk circle drawn around it. The idiot's seat, the troublemaker's seat.

5   The teacher thought I was stupid. Couldn't spell, couldn't read, couldn't do arithmetic. Just stupid. Teachers were never interested in finding out that you couldn't concentrate because you were so hungry, because you hadn't had any breakfast. All you could think about was noontime, would it ever come? Maybe you could sneak into the cloakroom and steal a bite of some kid's lunch out of a coat pocket. A bite of something. Paste. You can't really make a meal of paste, or put it on bread for a sandwich, but sometimes I'd scoop a few spoonfuls out of the big paste jar in the back of the room. Pregnant people get strange tastes. I was pregnant with poverty. Pregnant

with dirt and pregnant with smells that made people turn away, pregnant with cold and pregnant with shoes that were never bought for me, pregnant with five other people in my bed and no Daddy in the next room, and pregnant with hunger. Paste doesn't taste too bad when you're hungry.

6   The teacher thought I was a troublemaker. All she saw from the front of the room was a little black boy who squirmed in his idiot's seat and made noises and poked the kids around him. I guess she couldn't see a kid who made noises because he wanted someone to know he was there.

7   It was on a Thursday, the day before the Negro payday. The eagle always flew on Friday. The teacher was asking each student how much his father would give to the Community Chest. On Friday night, each kid would get the money from his father, and on Monday he would bring it to the school. I decided I was going to buy a Daddy right then. I had money in my pocket from shining shoes and selling papers, and whatever Helene Tucker pledged for her Daddy I was going to top it. And I'd hand the money right in. I wasn't going to wait until Monday to buy me a Daddy.

8   I was shaking, scared to death. The teacher opened her book and started calling out names alphabetically.

9   "Helene Tucker?"

10   "My Daddy said he'd give two dollars and fifty cents."

11   "That's very nice, Helene. Very, very nice indeed."

12   That made me feel pretty good. It wouldn't take too much to top that. I had almost three dollars in dimes and quarters in my pocket. I stuck my hand in my pocket and held onto the money, waiting for her to call my name. But the teacher closed her book after she called everybody else in the class.

13   I stood up and raised my hand.

14   "What is it now?"

15   "You forgot me."

16   She turned toward the blackboard. "I don't have time to be playing with you, Richard."

17   "My Daddy said he'd . . . "

18   "Sit down, Richard, you're disturbing the class."

19   "My Daddy said he'd give . . . fifteen dollars."

20   She turned around and looked mad. "We are collecting this money for you and your kind, Richard Gregory. If your Daddy can give fifteen dollars you have no business being on relief."

21   "I got it right now, I got it right now, my Daddy gave it to me to turn in today, my Daddy said . . . "

22   "And furthermore," she said, looking right at me, her nostrils getting big and her lips getting thin and her eyes opening wide, "we know you don't have a Daddy."

23   Helene Tucker turned around, her eyes full of tears. She felt sorry for me. Then I couldn't see her too well because I was crying, too.

24   "Sit down, Richard."

25   And I always thought the teacher kind of liked me. She always picked me to wash the blackboard on Friday, after school. That was a big thrill, it made me feel important. If I didn't wash it, come Monday the school might not function right.

©2007 Pearson Education, Inc.

26   "Where are you going, Richard!"

27   I walked out of school that day, and for a long time I didn't go back very often. There was shame there.

28   Now there was shame everywhere. It seemed like the whole world had been inside that classroom, everyone had heard what the teacher had said, everyone had turned around and felt sorry for me. There was shame in going to the Worthy Boys Annual Christmas Dinner for you and your kind, because everybody knew what a worthy boy was. Why couldn't they just call it the Boys Annual Dinner, why'd they have to give it a name? There was shame in wearing the brown and orange and white plaid mackinaw the welfare gave to three thousand boys. Why'd it have to be the same for everybody so when you walked down the street the people could see you were on relief? It was a nice warm mackinaw and it had a hood, and my Momma beat me and called me a little rat when she found out I stuffed it in the bottom of a pail full of garbage way over on Cottage Street. There was shame in running over to Mister Ben's at the end of the day and asking for his rotten peaches, there was shame in asking Mrs. Simmons for a spoonful of sugar, there was shame in running out to meet the relief truck. I hated that truck, full of food for you and your kind. I ran into the house and hid when it came. And then I started to sneak through alleys, to take the long way home so the people going into White's Eat Shop wouldn't see me. Yeah, the whole world heard the teacher that day, we all know you don't have a Daddy.

29   It lasted for a while, this kind of numbness. I spent a lot of time feeling sorry for myself. And then one day I met this wino in a restaurant. I'd been out hustling all day, shining shoes, selling newspapers, and I had googobs of money in my pocket. Bought me a bowl of chili for fifteen cents, and a cheeseburger for fifteen cents, and a Pepsi for five cents, and a piece of chocolate cake for ten cents. That was a good meal. I was eating when this old wino came in. I love winos because they never hurt anyone but themselves.

30   The old wino sat down at the counter and ordered twenty-six cents worth of food. He ate it like he really enjoyed it. When the owner, Mister Williams, asked him to pay the check, the old wino didn't lie or go through his pocket like he suddenly found a hole.

31   He just said: "Don't have no money."

32   The owner yelled: "Why in hell you come in here and eat my food if you don't have no money? That food cost me money."

33   Mister Williams jumped over the counter and knocked the wino off his stool and beat him over the head with a pop bottle. Then he stepped back and watched the wino bleed. Then he kicked him. And he kicked him again.

34   I looked at the wino with blood all over his face and I went over. "Leave him alone, Mister Williams. I'll pay the twenty-six cents."

35   The wino got up, slowly, pulling himself up to the stool, then up to the counter, holding on for a minute until his legs stopped shaking so bad. He looked at me with pure hate. "Keep your twenty-six cents. You don't have to pay, not now. I just finished paying for it."

36   He started to walk out, and as he passed me, he reached down and touched my shoulder. "Thanks, sonny, but it's too late now. Why didn't you pay it before?"

37   I was pretty sick about that. I waited too long to help another man.

GREGORY, *NIGGER: AN AUTOBIOGRAPHY*

Exercise 1   ## Work with Words

Use context clues and dictionary skills to answer the following questions about each of the italicized words in the sentences.

1. What does *pregnant* mean in paragraph 5? What is the effect of his repeated use of *pregnant*? Explain.

   _____

   _____

   _____

   _____

   _____

2. What do you think *Community Chest* refers to in paragraph 7? In which paragraph do you find out the meaning?

   _____

   _____

3. What would being "on relief" be called today? (par. 20 and par. 28)

   _____

4. What does *worthy* mean? (par. 28) Why does Gregory wish that they would leave out the word *worthy* from the name of the Christmas dinner?

   _____

   _____

   _____

   _____

   _____

5. What is a *mackinaw*? (par. 28)

   _____

©2007 Pearson Education, Inc.

| Exercise 2 | **Check Your Understanding**

Based on the reading, Gregory's "Shame," choose the best answer to each of the following multiple-choice questions.

1. Gregory learned shame for the first time when
   a. he had to sleep in the same bed with five brothers and sisters.
   b. his teacher pointed out to the whole class that his family was poor.
   c. he ate paste because he was hungry in school.

2. Helene Tucker was important to Gregory while he was growing up so he
   a. imagined himself through her eyes, based on what she would think of him.
   b. talked to her.
   c. remained infatuated with her, even after he was happily married.

3. Why did Gregory do poorly as a student?
   a. He couldn't spell.
   b. He couldn't sit still.
   c. He was hungry.

4. Richard thought that his teacher liked him because
   a. she was always kind to him.
   b. she was careful not to embarrass him.
   c. she picked him to wash the blackboard.

5. We can reasonably infer that
   a. the rest of the children were also African American.
   b. many of the children lived in single-parent families.
   c. Gregory's family was poorer than the families of the other children.

| Exercise 3 | **Reflect**

Think about what you read in "Shame" and what you already know about the experience of children when they feel different to answer the following questions in your own words.

1. How did Helene Tucker influence Gregory's decision to tell the teacher that he could contribute to the Community Chest? What was he trying to prove?

   _____

   _____

   _____

   _____

2. Why does Gregory tell two stories—about his experience in school and his experience with the wino—in "Shame"?

_____

_____

_____

_____

3. What feelings did the wino have toward Gregory?

_____

_____

_____

_____

4. Based on this reading, what do you think Gregory was most worried about as a child—his poverty and not having a father or how other people (children) thought of him? Explain.

_____

_____

_____

_____

For Chapter 7, FACTS AND OPINIONS

The War Prayer   Mark Twain

Samuel Clemens (1835–1910), known best by his pen name, Mark Twain, was one of the most important American writers of the nineteenth and twentieth centuries. His most famous novels are Tom Sawyer *and* Huckleberry Finn. *But he also wrote satirical novels and shorter pieces of fiction that were satires about injustice and the oppression and exploitation of the poor by the rich. Late in his life he traveled around the world and became aware of the negative effects of U.S. expansion and control of other countries, especially for the native inhabitants of those countries. As you read, consider how the theme fits into a larger concept of understanding how those who are different from you experience life. In this case, those who are different are a hypothetical enemy population from another country with whom the United States is at war.*

1 It was a time of great and exalting excitement. The country was up in arms, the war was on, in every breast burned the holy fire of patriotism; the drums

©2007 Pearson Education, Inc.

were beating, the bands playing, the toy pistols popping, the bunched fire-crackers hissing and spluttering; on every hand and far down the receding and fading spread of roofs and balconies a fluttering wilderness of flags flashed in the sun; daily the young volunteers marched down the wide avenue gay and fine in their new uniforms, the proud fathers and mothers and sisters and sweethearts cheering them with voices choked with happy emotion as they swung by; nightly the packed mass meetings listened, panting, to patriot oratory which stirred the deepest deeps of their hearts, and which they interrupted at briefest intervals with cyclones of applause, the tears running down their cheeks the while; in the churches the pastors preached devotion to flag and country, and invoked the God of Battles, beseeching His aid in our good cause in outpouring of fervid eloquence which moved every listener. It was indeed a glad and gracious time, and the half dozen rash spirits that ventured to disapprove of the war and cast a doubt upon its righteousness straightway got such a stern and angry warning that for their personal safety's sake they quickly shrank out of sight and offended no more in that way.

2   Sunday morning came—next day the battalions would leave for the front; the church was filled; the volunteers were there, their young faces alight with martial dreams—visions of the stern advance, the gathering momentum, the rushing charge, the flashing sabers, the flight of the foe, the tumult, the enveloping smoke, the fierce pursuit, and surrender!—then home from the war, bronzed heroes, welcomed, adored, submerged in golden seas of glory! With the volunteers sat their dear ones; proud, happy, and envied by the neighbors and friends who had no sons and brothers to send forth to the field of honor, there to win for the flag, or, failing, die the noblest of noble deaths. The service proceeded; a war chapter from the Old Testament was read; the first prayer was said; it was followed by an organ burst that shook the building, and with one impulse the house rose, with glowing eyes and beating hearts, and poured out that tremendous invocation—

> "God the all-terrible! Thou who ordainest,
> Thunder thy clarion and lightning thy sword!"

Then came the "long" prayer. None could remember the like of it for passionate pleading and moving and beautiful language. The burden of its supplication was, that an ever-merciful and benignant Father of us all would watch over our noble young soldiers, and aid, comfort, and encourage them in their patriotic work; bless them, shield them in the day of battle and the hour of peril, bear them in His mighty hand, make them strong and confident, invincible in the bloody onset; help them to crush the foe, grant to them and to their flag and country imperishable honor and glory—

3   An aged stranger entered and moved with slow and noiseless step up the main aisle, his eyes fixed upon the minister, his long body clothed in a robe that reached to his feet, his head bare, his white hair descending in a frothy cataract to his shoulders, his seamy face unnaturally pale, pale even to ghastliness. With all eyes following him and wondering, he made his

silent way; without pausing, he ascended to the preacher's side and stood there, waiting. With shut lids the preacher, unconscious of his presence, continued his moving prayer, and at last finished it with the words, uttered in fervent appeal, "Bless our arms, grant us the victory, O Lord our God, Father and Protector of our land and flag!"

4   The stranger touched his arm, motioned him to step aside—which the startled minister did—and took his place. During some moments he surveyed the spell-bound audience with solemn eyes, in which burned an uncanny light; then in a deep voice he said:

5   "I come from the Throne—bearing a message from Almighty God!" The words smote the house with a shock; if the stranger perceived it he gave no attention. "He has heard the prayer of His servant your shepherd, and will grant it if such shall be your desire after I, His messenger, shall have explained to you its import—that is to say, its full import. For it is like unto many of the prayers of men, in that it asks for more than he who utters it is aware of—except he pause and think.

6   "God's servant and yours has prayed his prayer. Has he paused and taken thought? Is it one prayer? No, it is two—one uttered, the other not. Both have reached the ear of Him Who heareth all supplications, the spoken and the unspoken. Ponder this—keep it in mind. If you would beseech a blessing upon yourself, beware! lest without intent you invoke a curse upon a neighbor at the same time. If you pray for the blessing of rain upon your crop which needs it, by that act you are possibly praying for a curse upon some neighbor's crop which may not need rain and can be injured by it.

7   "You have heard your servant's prayer—the uttered part of it. I am commissioned of God to put into words the other part of it—that part which the pastor—and also you in your hearts—fervently prayed silently. And ignorantly and unthinkingly? God grant that it was so! You heard these words: 'Grant us the victory, O Lord our God!' That is sufficient. The *whole* of the uttered prayer is compact into those pregnant words. Elaborations were not necessary. When you have prayed for victory you have prayed for many unmentioned results which follow victory—*must* follow it, cannot help but follow it. Upon the listening spirit of God the Father fell also the unspoken part of the prayer. He commandeth me to put it into words. Listen!

8   "O Lord our Father, our young patriots, idols of our hearts, go forth to battle—be Thou near them! With them—in spirit—we also go forth from the sweet peace of our beloved firesides to smite the foe. O Lord our God, help us to tear their soldiers to bloody shreds with our shells; help us to cover their smiling fields with the pale forms of their patriot dead; help us to drown the thunder of the guns with the shrieks of their wounded, writhing in pain; help us to lay waste their humble homes with a hurricane of fire; help us to wring the hearts of their unoffending widows with unavailing grief; help us to turn them out roofless with their little children to wander unfriended the wastes of their desolated land in rags and hunger and thirst, sports of the sun flames of summer and the icy winds of winter, broken in spirit, worn with travail, imploring Thee for

©2007 Pearson Education, Inc.

the refuge of the grave and denied it—for our sakes who adore Thee, Lord, blast their hopes, blight their lives, protract their bitter pilgrimage, make heavy their steps, water their way with their tears, stain the white snow with the blood of their wounded feet! We ask it, in the spirit of love, or Him Who is the Source of Love, and Who is the ever-faithful refuge and friend of all that are sore beset and seek His aid with humble and contrite hearts. Amen."

9   *(After a pause.)* "Ye have prayed it; if ye still desire it, speak! The messenger of the Most High waits."

10   It was believed afterward that the man was a lunatic, because there was no sense in what he said.

Twain, "The War Prayer"

Exercise 1   ## Work with Words

Use context clues, dictionary skills, and your knowledge of word parts to choose the best definition for each italicized word in the following sentences from the reading. The paragraph number is provided in case you want to check the context.

1. In the churches the pastors preached devotion to flag and country, and *invoked* the God of Battles, *beseeching* His aid in our good cause in outpourings of fervid eloquence which moved every listener. (par. 1)

   Invoked
   a. criticized
   b. eliminated
   c. called upon

2. *Beseeching*
   a. urgently requesting
   b. refusing
   c. forcefully demanding

3. The burden of its *supplication* was, that an ever-merciful and *benignant* Father of us all would watch over our noble young soldiers, and aid, comfort, and encourage them in their patriotic work; bless them, shield them in the day of battle and the hour of *peril*, bear them in His mighty hand, make them strong and confident, invincible in the bloody onset; help them to crush the foe, grant to them and to their flag and country imperishable honor and glory—. (par. 2)

   Supplication
   a. the act of humbly praying for something
   b. the act of begging for something
   c. the act of denying something

4. *Benignant*
   a. strong and invincible
   b. gracious and good
   c. indifferent but kind

5. *Peril*
   a. bravery
   b. cowardice
   c. danger

Check Your Understanding

Based on the reading, Twain's "The War Prayer," choose the best answer to each of the following multiple-choice questions.

1. What is the point of view about the war expressed in the first three paragraphs?
   a. Acceptance and enthusiasm
   b. Cautious optimism
   c. Criticism

2. Which of the following most accurately describes the tone and content of paragraphs 1 through 3?
   a. Thoughtful
   b. Cautious
   c. Self-righteous

3. What does the "aged stranger" say he is doing?
   a. Representing the government
   b. Preaching
   c. Bearing a message from God

4. What does the "aged stranger" mean when he says "God's servant and yours has prayed his prayer. Has he paused and taken thought? Is it one prayer? No, it is two—one uttered, the other not."
   a. He means that God tries to answer every prayer.
   b. He means that the prayer has two sides to it: victory and glory for one side will mean pain, suffering, defeat, and humiliation for the other side.
   c. He means that they may not realize all the consequences that the prayer will have for them.

5. Which of the following most accurately describes the tone and content of paragraph 8?
   a. Peaceful and calm
   b. Resigned but indifferent
   c. Dark and violent

©2007 Pearson Education, Inc.

| Exercise 3 | **Reflect**

Think about what you read in "The War Prayer" and what you already know about the meaning and experience of war. Then answer the following questions in your own words.

1. Write the moral of this reading in your own words.

   _____

   _____

   _____

2. Think of examples of other prayers or wishes that really involve a second prayer or wish. Explain your example and how it implies yet a different prayer or wish.

   _____

   _____

   _____

   _____

3. What can you infer is Mark Twain's view of war? What wars would he have experienced or been aware of during his lifetime?

   _____

   _____

   _____

4. Mark Twain submitted "The War Prayer" to *Harper's Bazaar,* which refused to publish it. Why do think the magazine would have refused? Explain your answer.

   _____

   _____

   _____

5. Why do you think the message of "The War Prayer" is important in a society as diverse as ours?

   _____

   _____

   _____

   _____

For Chapter 8, CRITICAL THINKING

Ethical Issues Surrounding Death

John J. Macionis

The following reading is from a sociology textbook. It is not an argument but rather a sociologist's objective analysis of a social problem created by scientific advances. The author does not offer answers to the difficult questions of how we handle death in a time when medical technology can keep people alive artificially. Rather, the reading presents a survey of practice and opinion.

1   Now that technological advances give human beings the power to draw the line separating life and death, we must decide how and when to do so.

When Does Death Occur?

2   Common sense suggests that life ceases when breathing and heartbeat stop. But the ability to replace a heart and artificially sustain respiration makes such a definition of death obsolete. Medical and legal experts in the United States now define death as an *irreversible* state involving no response to stimulation, no movement or breathing, no reflexes, and no indication of brain activity (Ladd, 1979: Wall, 1980).

Do People Have a Right to Die?

3   Today, medical personnel, family members, and patients themselves face the agonizing burden of deciding when a terminally ill person should die. Among the most difficult cases are the roughly 10,000 people in the United States in a permanent vegetative state who cannot express their desires about life and death. Generally speaking, the first duty of physicians and hospitals is to protect a patient's life. Even so, a mentally competent person in the process of dying may refuse medical treatment and even nutrition. Moreover, federal law requires hospitals, nursing homes, and other medical facilities to honor a patient's desire if spelled out in advance in a document called a "living will."

What about Mercy Killing?

4   *Mercy killing* is the common term for *euthanasia, assisting in the death of a person suffering from an incurable disease.* Euthanasia (from the Greek term meaning "a good death") poses an ethical dilemma, being at the same time an act of kindness and a form of killing.

5   Whether there is a "right to die" is one of today's most difficult questions. All people with incurable diseases have a right to forgo treatment that might prolong their lives. But whether a doctor should be allowed to

©2007 Pearson Education, Inc.

help bring about death is the heart of the debate. In 1994, two states— Washington and California—placed before voters propositions that stated physicians should be able to help people who wanted to die; in both cases, the initiatives were defeated. The same year, however, voters in Oregon approved such a measure. This law remained tied up in state court until 1997, when voters again endorsed it. Since then, Oregon doctors have legally assisted in the death of terminally ill patients. In 1997, however, the U.S. Supreme Court decided that under the U.S. Constitution, there is no "right to die," and this has slowed the spread of such laws. Moreover, in 1999 Congress began debating whether to pass a law that would prohibit states from adopting laws similar to the one in Oregon.

6   Supporters of *active* euthanasia—allowing a dying person to enlist the services of a physician to bring on a quick death—argue that there are circumstances (such as when a dying person suffers from great pain) that make death preferable to life. However, critics counter that permitting active euthanasia invites abuse. They fear that patients will be pressured to end their lives in order to spare family members the burden of caring for them or the high cost of hospitalization. Furthermore, research in the Netherlands, where physician-assisted suicide is legal, indicates that about one-fifth of all deaths occurred without a patient explicitly requesting to die (Gillon, 1999).

7   In the United States, a majority of adults express support for giving dying people the right to choose to die with a doctor's help (Rosenbaum, 1997; NORC, 2001). Therefore, the "right to die" debate is sure to continue.

MACIONIS, *SOCIOLOGY*

Exercise 1   ## Work with Words

Use context clues, dictionary skills, and your knowledge of word parts to choose the best definition for each italicized word in the following sentences from the reading. The paragraph number is provided in case you want to check the context.

1. Among the most difficult cases are the roughly 10,000 people in the United States in a permanent *vegetative* state who cannot express their desires about life and death. (par. 3)

   Vegetative
   a. looking like a vegetable
   b. unable to move, talk, or communicate
   c. characteristic of plants

2. Moreover, federal law requires hospitals, nursing homes, and other medical facilities to honor a patient's desire if spelled out in advance in a document called a *"living will."* (par. 3)

Living will
a. a legal document that expresses an individual's decision on the use of artificial life support systems.
b. a legal declaration of how a person wants to have possessions dispersed after his or her death.
c. the mental capacity to choose what one wants to do

3. In 1994, two states—Washington and California—placed before voters propositions that stated physicians should be able to help people who wanted to die; in both cases, the *initiatives* were defeated. The same year, however, voters in Oregon approved such a measure. (par. 5)

Initiatives
a. abilities to begin and follow through with a plan
b. proposed laws introduced by citizens after obtaining enough signatures on a petition
c. abilities to begin something new and interesting

4. This law remained tied up in state court until 1997, when voters again *endorsed* it. (par. 5)

Endorsed
a. rejected
b. released
c. approved

5. However, critics *counter* that permitting active euthanasia invites abuse. (par. 6)

Counter
a. respond in support
b. explain in detail
c. respond in opposition

Exercise 2   ## Check Your Understanding

Based on the reading, Macionis's "Ethical Issues Surrounding Death," choose the best answer to each of the following multiple-choice questions.

1. According to the reading, death
   a. cannot be defined.
   b. is difficult to determine now that doctors can often bring people back to life.
   c. is defined by medical experts as an irreversible state involving no response to stimulation, no movement, and no indication of brain activity.

©2007 Pearson Education, Inc.

2. Today medical personnel, family members, and patients themselves have to
   a. decide when a terminally ill person should die.
   b. guarantee that a terminally ill patient will be allowed to die comfortably.
   c. accept euthanasia as the most humane way to deal with the end of life.

3. Euthanasia
   a. is not a complicated issue.
   b. poses an ethical dilemma.
   c. is legal in two states.

4. Even though voters in Oregon voted in favor of euthanasia twice,
   a. the Supreme Court decided that there is no "right to die" expressed in the U.S. Constitution.
   b. the law was never put into effect because it was so controversial.
   c. Congress passed a law to prohibit states from adopting laws like the one in Oregon.

5. The author of this reading
   a. clearly supports euthanasia.
   b. provides various points of view about euthanasia.
   c. argues forcefully for his own opinion.

Exercise 3   Reflect

Think about what you read in "Ethical Issues Surrounding Death" and what you already know about death and dying. Then answer the following questions in your own words.

1. What are the arguments that the author provides in support of euthanasia, and what arguments does he provide against euthanasia?

   _____

   _____

   _____

   _____

2. Are there any circumstances under which a person should be able to request euthanasia to assist his or her own death? What should be taken into consideration before this kind of decision is necessary?

   _____

   _____

   _____

   _____

3. Do you think the government should be able to decide issues about your "right to die"? Explain your answer.

_____

_____

_____

_____

4. What are some other ethical dilemmas that advances in science and technology pose?

_____

_____

_____

_____

©2007 Pearson Education, Inc.

Cumulative Mastery Tests

©2007 Pearson Education, Inc.

Cumulative Mastery Test   1A

Workers Feel Like Suckers   Ralph Frammolino

The following reading appeared in the Los Angeles Times *on March 20, 2002. It gives the stories of real people who lose their jobs when factories relocate in other countries to maximize profits. As you read, think about the importance of jobs. What do they mean to people besides the income they provide? How do they affect people's lives for better or for worse?*

Life Savers Is Moving Its Factory from Michigan to Canada

1   As factory jobs go, Stan Rewa always thought his was pretty neat. The work is steady and the pay good, and there's the added satisfaction of producing something special, a piece of Americana that has delighted—and hushed—generations of rambunctious kids. Rewa doesn't make electric trains, or yo-yos. He makes Life Savers. "We are a part of America," said Rewa, who cooks and flavors the candy at the Life Savers factory here. "I don't know anybody who didn't grow up eating them, to see if you could get a whole roll in your mouth."

2   The memories will <u>endure</u>, but the factory that turns out 46 billion Life Savers each year won't. Kraft Foods Inc. is closing the plant and moving its operations to Canada, where sugar is half the price and its work force will be nonunion. The move will wipe out 600 union jobs that pay an average of $15.50 an hour.

3   For 35 years, the Life Savers plant was a symbol of stability and financial security for 115,000 residents living in and around this western Michigan town. Layoffs at factories that make office furniture and car interiors are <u>cyclical</u> in this region. But a job at Life Savers was considered a job for life. Employees <u>lobbied</u> to get their relatives hired, and many families drew two or more Life Savers paychecks. Brad and Brenda Morris and their extended family have put in a collective 105 years there. "A lot of our lives went into Life Savers," said Brenda Morris, 38, who earns $16 an hour at a spinning machine that forms the candy rings. "When we got hired there, we thought we were going to retire from there," said Morris, whose 56-year-old mother also works at the plant.

4   To city officials like Mayor Al McGeehan, the closing is a painful lesson in international economics—the story of an all-American city that tried to put out the welcome mat to business, got whipsawed by forces beyond its control and lost a major taxpayer and civic symbol. "It's been an <u>icon</u>. I can't find a better word to describe it," say McGeehan. "That traditional candy, with a hole in the middle—every one of them for the last 35 years has come from Holland, Michigan."

Figure 1.1   Between them, Sallie and Stan Rewa have worked more than 40 years at the Life Savers plant. They met while making lollipops. Photos by Adam Bird/For the *Los Angeles Times*.

5   The treats were invented in 1912 by Cleveland candy-maker Clarence Crane. Eager to find a sweet that wouldn't melt during summer, he asked a pill maker to produce round, flat mints with a hole in the middle. Crane named them for the life preservers that ships began stocking after that year's *Titanic* disaster. His slogan: "For that Stormy Breath." Crane sold the franchise, and Life Savers evolved. Hard-candy fruit rings were introduced in 1929. The popular five-flavor pack—lemon, lime, orange, pineapple and cherry—<u>debuted</u> in 1935. During World War II, about 23 million boxes of Life Savers were packed into military field rations, allowing G.I.s to introduce the candy to foreign lands.

6   Over the years, flavors were added and dropped. Of the current 33 flavors, cherry is the most popular, lemon the least. But the most intriguing is Wint-o-green, which emits flashes of light when smashed or bitten vigorously in the dark. The reason: The oil of wintergreen flavoring turns ultraviolet light from crunched nitrogen molecules into blue sparks. Today, there are Gummi Life Savers, sugar-free Life Savers and Life Savers fruit slices. They're made in Chattanooga, Tenn., Oklahoma City, and Des Plaines, Ill., respectively.

200 Million Rolls a Year

7   But for more than three decades, all of the traditional hard-candy Life Savers sold in the United States have originated here, 170 miles west of

©2007 Pearson Education, Inc.

Detroit in a community founded 250 years ago by Dutch Protestants and now known for its annual tulip festival. The Holland plant belches steam under a giant <u>replica</u> of a Life Saver that turns the colors of the original fruit flavors at night. It produces 200 million rolls a year. Laid end to end, they would stretch from Los Angeles to New York nearly 10 times over.

8   Hired out of high school, Stan and Sallie Rewa fell in love working side-by-side in the lollipop division. Sallie, 38, stayed through the birth of two kids. Stan, 42, found fishing and hunting buddies at work. The Rewas also hoped to retire from the mechanized candyland. Stan Rewa's job inspired a certain pride, especially when someone unwrapped a Life Savers lollipop. "When you see someone eating one, you know you made it," said Rewa, who earns $16.43 an hour. "It is a pretty good feeling."

9   The atmosphere at work began to change a few years ago under former owner Nabisco Holdings Corp. The bosses convened labor-management meetings to talk abut cutting costs and waste. Before Nabisco could sell to Kraft Foods, federal <u>antitrust</u> regulators required the divestiture of the Bubble Yum and Life Savers breath mints. They were afraid Kraft, which owns Altoids, might corner the "intense mint market," said a Kraft spokes-woman.

City Hall Helps Out

10 That led to 180 layoffs. Part of the plant was left idle. When Kraft took over in December 2000, it laid off a dozen more employees, then set a goal of reducing production costs from $1.28 per pound to about 95 cents over the next several years. The current rate is $1.18, right on target, say union officials. Meanwhile, local plant executives asked Holland City Hall to help cut an additional $2 million in expenses. The municipal utility offered an annual $200,000 reduction in electric rates. Economic development officials found $1.8 million in savings with a plan to have Life Savers buy liquid sugar from a Michigan mill, rather than ship it by rail from North Dakota and Minnesota. "We were pleased with ourselves and the responses we were getting from the company were very positive—until we received "The Fax," said Chris Byrnes, president of the Holland Economic Development Corp.

11   On January 7, Kraft's corporate headquarters sent out a news release announcing the closing. The same day the workers were called to a meet-ing. "I was pretty bummed out about it," said Sallie Rewa. "I mean, nobody wants to have to work forever but it's a good place to work. We've got a lot of good friends down there and we're going to miss that. Not to mention the pay and benefits."

12   Officials of the Northfield, Ill.–based food conglomerate say cost-cutting didn't make up for the fact the plant was "significantly <u>underutilized.</u>" They also said it made economic sense to <u>consolidate</u> Life Savers production in a facility in Mount Royal, Canada, on the outskirts of Montreal. Lower labor costs, they said, were not the "driving factor" behind the move.

Table 1.1   Trade-Related Job Losses by State, 1994–2000

State	Jobs Lost	State	Jobs Lost
Alabama	63,239	Montana	7,521
Alaska	6,972	Nebraska	15,312
Arizona	32,461	Nevada	16,493
Arkansas	37,469	New Hampshire	12,936
California	309,762	New Jersey	84,749
Colorado	34,992	New Mexico	16,733
Connecticut	31,431	New York	179,288
Delaware	6,467	North Carolina	133,219
District of Columbia	6,558	North Dakota	5,788
Florida	100,047	Ohio	135,139
Georgia	89,736	Oklahoma	42,266
Hawaii	7,116	Oregon	41,124
Idaho	11,021	Pennsylvania	142,221
Illinois	139,537	Rhode Island	29,164
Indiana	102,873	South Carolina	54,233
Iowa	31,770	South Dakota	8,458
Kansas	23,248	Tennessee	96,355
Kentucky	50,948	Texas	227,559
Louisiana	44,940	Utah	22,523
Maine	22,357	Vermont	6,283
Maryland	31,057	Virginia	66,083
Massachusetts	64,434	Washington	45,739
Michigan	152,061	West Virginia	14,458
Minnesota	49,927	Wisconsin	73,476
Mississippi	41,338	Wyoming	6,977
Missouri	68,392	**Total**	**3,044,241**

Source: Robert E. Scott, "Fast Track to Lost Jobs," Economic Policy Institute, October 2001, based on U.S. Census Bureau, Bureau of Labor Statistics.

13   John Boyd, president of a Princeton, New Jersey, consulting firm that helps companies select plant locations, said payroll savings are a "fundamental" reason that companies like Kraft move production abroad. Boyd said a recent survey by his firm indicates Life Savers will pay nonunion workers in Mount Royal about $12.50 an hour—$3 less than their counterparts in Holland. With the Canadian government picking up the tab for health coverage, the savings come to about $6.5 million a year. "Labor costs dominate the equation," Boyd said. "They account for at least 70% of all operating costs. . . . That's the real driver in the site selection process."

14   Workers and city officials remain convinced that the culprit is sugar. They blame the closing on a combination of federal tariffs, trade quotas and loans that benefit U.S. sugar beet and sugar cane farmers by keeping the price of <u>domestic</u> bulk sugar at 21 cents a pound, compared to 6 cents on the international market. That makes a big difference to Life Savers, which uses 113 tons of sugar a day. Each Life Savers candy is 95% sugar.

©2007 Pearson Education, Inc.

Last year, Brachs candy cited high domestic sugar prices in announcing that it would close its 77-year-old west Chicago plant and move 1,100 jobs overseas, one of several candy-makers to do so. Kraft isn't saying how much it will save on the crucial ingredient. State and local officials estimate it will be $6 million a year. Mark Davis, an international representative for the Retail, Wholesale and Department Store Union, said that fact, combined with other savings on materials like cardboard, meant there was nothing the union could do.

15   "We could have gone to the table and agreed to work for nothing and they still would have saved money by moving to Canada," Davis said. Michigan Governor John Engler wrote Kraft CEO Betsy Holden on January 15, offering to give the plant a $25.5 million tax break over 15 years. It wasn't enough. . . .

16   Stan Rewa says he's nervously optimistic he'll get a job, even in Holland's current down market, but hopes to avoid the swing shift so he can watch his son play high school football. Sallie Rewa wants to remake herself into a medical office assistant, but the thought of such a change in midlife has given her stress headaches. And while she understands that corporate America has the right to save money, she said it especially hurts in the case of Life Savers. "It's sad that they started in the United States and now they're going to be gone from here," she said. "A lot of people say they're not going to buy them anymore."

FRAMMOLINO, "Workers Feel Like Suckers"

| Exercise 1 | **Work with Words** |

Use context clues, dictionary skills, and your knowledge of word parts to choose the best definition for each of the following words underlined in the reading. The paragraph number is provided in case you want to check the context.

1. *Endure* (par. 2)
   a. undergo hardship
   b. undergo without giving in
   c. remain firm

2. *Cyclical* (par. 3)
   a. in spirals
   b. at intervals of time
   c. permanent

3. *Lobbied* (par. 3)
   a. attempted to influence
   b. bribed
   c. flattered

4. *Icon* (par. 4)
   a. religious image

    b. respected civic symbol

    c. object of devotion

5. *Debuted* (par. 5)

    a. appeared for the first time

    b. entered into society

    c. was first tasted

6. *Replica* (par. 7)

    a. copy

    b. factory

    c. newer version

7. *Antitrust* (par. 9)

    a. against having confidence

    b. on credit

    c. against unfair monopolies in business

8. *Underutilized* (par. 12)

    a. used adequately

    b. not used enough

    c. used beyond capacity

9. *Consolidate* (par. 12)

    a. simplify

    b. bring together in one location

    c. make solid

10. *Domestic* (par. 14)

    a. in the home

    b. in the country

    c. out of the country

Exercise 2   ## Check Your Understanding

Based on the reading, Frammolino's "Workers Feel Like Suckers," choose the best answer to each of the following multiple-choice questions.

1. Which of the following is the best main idea statement for the reading?

    a. The Life Savers plant moved to Canada because sugar is cheaper there.

    b. Workers should never assume that their jobs are permanent because while it may have been the case 50 years ago for some jobs, it is no longer the case today.

    c. It is difficult if not impossible to stop an industry from relocating to a place where it can increase its profits, even if it means suffering for many people and for whole regions of the country.

2. Frammolino, the author of this article, provides us mostly with information from which points of view regarding the moving of the Life Savers factory?

    a. the workers and city officials

©2007 Pearson Education, Inc.

    b. Kraft foods and the union

    c. Canadian workers and government officials

3. Which of the following is the best main idea sentence for paragraph 8?
   a. Working at the Life Saver factory gave people a sense of community and pride.
   b. When you see someone eating a lollipop, you know you made it.
   c. Workers assumed they had a good job for life when they started working at the Life Saver factory.

4. The Life Savers plant in Holland, Michigan, was
   a. the biggest employer in town.
   b. a symbol of stability and financial security in town.
   c. operated on a cyclical basis.

5. The main patterns of organization for paragraph 5 are
   a. narration and chronological order.
   b. problem and solution.
   c. definition and description.

6. The city government
   a. did nothing to keep the Life Savers plant in town.
   b. did everything possible to keep the Life Savers plant in town.
   c. was not aware of the problem of losing the Life Savers plant.

7. Which of the following statements is true?
   a. Everyone agrees on the reasons the plant is moving.
   b. There is disagreement on why the plant is moving; some say it's the cost of labor, others say it's the cost of sugar.
   c. The workers are not terribly worried about their futures because the economy of Holland is healthy.

8. Sugar is cheaper in Canada because
   a. it is easier to produce there.
   b. the United States has protected domestic sugar producers with high tariffs.
   c. Brachs candy buys sugar there, so it keeps the prices down.

9. Which of the following is a reasonable inference?
   a. Stan and Sallie Rewa are confident in their possibilities for the future.
   b. Stan and Sallie Rewa are devastated by losing their jobs.
   c. The workers at the plant believe that the company was completely honest with them.

10. Which of the following is a reasonable inference?
    a. Frammolino talked to the president of a Princeton, New Jersey, consulting firm because he was not convinced by the reasons Kraft gave for moving the factory.
    b. Representatives from Kraft refused to talk to Frammolino when he was working on this story.
    c. Frammolino relied on interviews with Kraft management for the information in the article because he clearly assumed that the

corporation itself would have the most accurate information regarding the reasons for moving the factory.

Exercise 3 **Evaluate the Argument**

Answer the following questions as fully as you can in your own words.

1. Frammolino writes "It produces 200 million rolls a year. Laid end to end, they would stretch from Los Angeles to New York nearly 10 times over." What is the effect of his using this image?

_____

_____

2. What is the effect of including the photo of Stan and Sallie Rewa with the article about the Life Savers factory moving?

_____

_____

_____

_____

3. To analyze, synthesize, and evaluate the solutions to the problem in this reading, answer the following questions:

a. List the factors that contributed to the profitability problem of the Life Saver factory.

_____

_____

b. What was the first solution to the problem?

_____

_____

c. Kraft decided not to stick to the first solution and chose a different solution. (1) What was the second solution? (2) What reasons did the company give for it? (3) What did the workers think about this company decision? (4) What did John Boyd, the consultant, say? (5) What is John Boyd's position, and how might it make his comment more or less believable?

_____

_____

_____

_____

_____

© 2007 Pearson Education, Inc.

d. Who were the "winners" and "losers" in this situation?

_____

_____

_____

e. Do you think the company will stay in Canada? Explain your answer.

_____

_____

_____

Exercise 4   ## Reflect

Think about what you read in "Workers Feel Like Suckers" and what you already know about businesses relocating. Then answer the following questions.

1. What is another possible solution to the Life Savers profitability problem?

_____

_____

_____

_____

2. What do you think workers can do to protect their jobs and their futures? What do you think government can do?

_____

_____

_____

_____

3. What do jobs mean to people besides being a source of income? What do you think employees mean to corporations? Explain your answer.

_____

_____

_____

_____

Cumulative Mastery Test — **1B**

Criminals at Work

Hugh D. Barlow and David Kauzlarich

Both authors are professors of criminology at Southern Illinois University in Edwardsville. Their text, Introduction to Criminology, *is renowned as a comprehensive introduction to crime, criminality, and society's responses from a sociological perspective. In the following reading, they discuss a type of crime for which people rarely go to jail: corporate crime.*

1 Robbery, burglary, assault, and rape may be called traditional crimes but this does not mean they are the most common forms of crime or that they create the most victims, the highest economic costs, or the greatest damage to social institutions. The crimes discussed in this chapter have a far greater impact on society, and often on individual victims as well. A closer look at occupational and organizational crimes will show that "crimes in the suites" deserve far more attention than they commonly receive in the press, and in criminology.

Types of White-Collar Crime

2 The term *white-collar crime* was coined in 1939 by Edwin H. Sutherland. He defined it as crimes committed by people of respectability and high social status in the course of their occupations. Sutherland also observed that criminologists had virtually ignored the illegal activities of those in business, politics, and the professions, concentrating instead on the world of lower-class criminality emphasized in crime statistics and in the criminal justice system. Lawbreaking, he argued, goes on in all social <u>strata</u>. Restraint of trade, <u>misrepresentation</u> in advertising, violations of labor laws, violations of copyright and patent laws, and financial manipulations were a part of what Sutherland called white-collar crime.

3 Over the years since Sutherland's groundbreaking work, other criminologists have refined the definition of white-collar crime. One of the earliest of these was Clinard and Quinney's (1973) effort to define white-collar crime in more operational terms. They split the concept of white-collar crime into *corporate crime*—crimes organizationally based and directed toward reaching corporate goals—and *occupational crime*, crimes committed by individuals in the course of their occupation for their own personal gain. . . .

Corporate Violence

4 While many corporate crimes result in economic harms, a sizeable amount of corporate crimes are violent. It is clearly a myth that white-collar crimes can be correctly called "economic crimes." Here we review several instances

© 2007 Pearson Education, Inc.

519

of violent corporate crimes committed as a part of a company's pursuit of profit, a major cause of most forms of corporate crime.

5 ***Violence Against Consumers***   Most of us rely on corporations to provide us with the <u>commodities</u> we use in our daily lives. We assume these products will not expose us to unreasonable threats to our life and safety. Unfortunately, this assumption can be in serious error, as we shall see in the following illustration.

6   Ford Motor Company's Pinto was designed in the late 1960s to compete in the "small car for a small price market," which was at the time controlled by Volkswagen. Ford president Lee Iacocca and other executives directed the Pinto to be produced quickly, weigh under 2,000 pounds, and cost less than $2,000. While the Pinto was being tested prior to its release into the marketplace, a major problem in the fuel system was discovered. When rear-ended, the Pinto's gas tank often ruptured. The problem could be fixed by placing a rubber bladder or flak within and/or around the tank or by locating the tank in a safer area. Ford executives rejected these <u>avenues</u> because the assembly line was already tooled for production, and it would cost the company several millions of dollars to redesign and produce a safer car. As a direct result of the deadly design of the Pinto, dozens of drivers and passengers of the vehicle were killed or seriously burned in rear-end collisions over the next several years (Cullen, Maakestad, and Cavender, 1987).

7   In the course of several successful civil suits against Ford and one unsuccessful criminal prosecution, it came to light that the company had made a conscious decision to risk the lives of consumers in order to make a profit. Ford calculated that a burn death would result in an average $200,000 loss and any injury less than death would cost them $67,000. Ford officials also calculated that the cost of fixing the problem with the Pinto's fuel tank placement would be a paltry $11 per vehicle. But with 11 million cars to fix, paying the estimated $49.5 million it would cost in lawsuits for deaths and injuries would be a better business deal for the corporation. Ford was eventually forced to recall the Pinto after several successful product <u>liability</u> lawsuits (Mokhiber, 1988). No one was ever sentenced to prison for the deaths.

8   Two widely publicized cases of corporate violence against consumers are also crimes against women and children (Fox and Szockyj, 1996; Rynbrandt and Kramer, 1995). First, the Dalkon Shield, an intrauterine birth control device, was marketed by the A. H. Robins Company in the 1960s. The device was popular in part because it supposedly did not have negative side effects like the "pill." It was also marketed as an extremely effective way of blocking pregnancy (Mokhiber, 1988). But because the shield was poorly designed (and poorly tested), it often caused severe pelvic infections, sterility, poor pregnancy protection, and the spontaneous abortions of fetuses. Twelve women also died from using this device. The Robins company, which knew of many of the problems with the Shield but

did nothing to protect consumers, has escaped criminal charges but has paid nearly $1 billion in lawsuits.

9   Another corporate crime against women and children involved the sale and distribution of the drug *thalidomide*. Many women were given prescriptions for thalidomide as a tranquilizer and to combat morning sickness while pregnant. The producer of the drug, the German company Chemie Grunenthal, had information that the drug could cause major health problems, including severe disturbances of the nervous system. This information was ignored and then <u>downplayed</u> by Grunenthal for years, but the company was finally forced to come clean after overwhelming evidence of the drug's horrible side effects on fetuses. At least 8,000 children, the "thalidomide babies," were born with deformed genitals, eyes, and ears, brain damage, and shortened limbs. While Grunenthal escaped criminal fines, Distillers Ltd., a company later distributing thalidomide under the name of Distaval in Britain, was forced to pay millions of dollars to British and German victims of this drug (Mokhiber, 1988).

10   ***Violence Against Workers*** According to the Occupational Safety and Health Administration (OSHA, 2000), there were 5.9 million work-related injuries and illnesses in 1999. OSHA also estimates that 6,026 workers died on the job that year. However, these statistics are <u>conservative estimates</u> of the risks involved in work. There is strong evidence that up to 100,000 workers in the United States lose their lives each year in the context of work (Friedrichs, 1996). Many illnesses and injuries are simply not reported to the authorities, whether that authority is the company, OSHA, or the U.S. Department of Labor. Some workers also know that whistle blowing to agencies like OSHA could cost them their jobs (OSHA, 2000).

11   A study of mining disasters in five countries concluded that most of them were related to violations of workplace safety laws (Braithwaite, 1985). Some of the violations were a cause of the disasters and others made the disasters worse than they should have been. Workers are not the only ones at risk in the mining industry. In 1972 in Buffalo Creek, West Virginia, an entire community was virtually destroyed by a dam break (Erikson, 1976).

12   During the twentieth century, at least 100,000 U.S. miners were killed and 1.5 million injured (Mokhiber, 1988). Black lung disease, which took the life of one of this text's authors' (Kauzlarich) great-grandfathers, is still a major problem today. It is now called "coal workers' pneumoconiosis," and usually results from the inhalation of and exposure to assorted coal dusts and silica (U.S. Department of Labor, 2000). There is no doubt that many coal companies knew of the dangers of black lung but did nothing to prevent worker exposure to dangerous coal dust (Mokhiber, 1988). Even today a few companies do not adequately protect their workers from <u>contracting</u> the disease (OSHA, 2000).

13   Even if we use the conservative OSHA statistics, we get some sense of how routine violations of worker safety laws actually are in the United States. Federal and state OSHA agencies conducted 89,331 inspections in 1999.

©2007 Pearson Education, Inc.

521

These inspections uncovered 280,158 violations of worker safety laws and resulted in over $159 million worth of fines (OSHA, 2000). Here are some examples of these violations, most of which were classed as serious or <u>willful</u>:

14 • Four companies were fined a total of $410,900 for safety violations during the attempted repair of a tunnel beneath Boston Harbor. On July 21, 1999, two workers died attempting to remove underwater bulkheads on the tunnel (OSHA 2000b).

15 • Three companies were fined over $500,000 for safety violations that resulted in the deaths of three workers involved in the construction of Miller Park, home of the Milwaukee Brewers baseball team. The companies violated numerous regulations relating to maximum crane loads, operations in poor weather conditions, and the physical placement of crews too close to a crane lift operation (OSHA, 2000c).

16 • Dozens of companies have been fined for not providing protection to workers who perform duties while elevated. In one case, a worker fell to his death from a 600-foot-tall radio tower (OSHA, 2000d, 2000e).

17 Other examples of corporate violence against workers could be detailed here. For example, the owners and managers of the Imperial Food Products company in Hamlet, North Carolina, routinely locked fire doors to prevent employees from stealing chickens. When a fire erupted in the plant on September 3, 1991, the workers were trapped—twenty-five were killed and another fifty-six were injured (Aulette and Michalowski, 1993). Another case centers around the Johns Manville company's refusal to protect workers and others from exposure to asbestos. Even with the knowledge that the substance was harmful, Johns Manville allowed the product to be manufactured across the country. The company declared bankruptcy in the wake of a <u>deluge</u> of lawsuits (Friedrichs 1996; Mokhiber, 1988).

BARLOW AND KAUZLARICH, *INTRODUCTION TO CRIMINOLOGY*

Exercise 1   Work with Words

Use context clues, dictionary skills, and your knowledge of word parts to choose the best definition for each italicized word in the following sentences from the reading. The paragraph number is provided in case you want to check the context.

1. *Strata* (par. 2)
   a. get togethers
   b. complications
   c. class levels

2. *Misrepresentation* (par. 2)
   a. factual information
   b. false presentation
   c. precise presentation

3. *Commodities* (par. 5)
   a. everyday consumer products
   b. safety standards
   c. unsafe food products

4. *Avenues* (par. 6)
   a. ways to solve a problem
   b. streets
   c. costs of doing business

5. *Liability* (par. 7)
   a. legal responsibility
   b. money owed
   c. criminal action

6. *Downplayed* (par. 9)
   a. made to look more important
   b. made to look unimportant
   c. made to look downward

7. *Conservative estimates* (par. 10)
   a. wild guesses
   b. statistics that are slanted to be probusiness
   c. educated guesses that make cautious claims

8. *Contracting* (par. 12)
   a. paying someone to do dangerous work
   b. developing an illness over a period of time
   c. taking action to counteract health hazards

9. *Willful* (par. 13)
   a. overly stubborn
   b. foolish
   c. deliberate

10. *Deluge* (par. 17)
    a. substance toxic to human beings
    b. complicated legal case
    c. overwhelming number; flood

Exercise 2 **Check Your Understanding**

Based on the reading, Barlow and Kauzlarich's "Criminals at Work," choose the best answer to each of the following multiple-choice questions.

1. What is the main idea of this reading?
   a. The government needs to make sure everyone has safe working conditions and to force corporations to stop making unsafe products.
   b. Corporate pursuit of profit sometimes leads to violence against consumers and workers, although this violence is not usually thought of as "crime," and the perpetrators almost never go to jail.

©2007 Pearson Education, Inc.

c. When businesses provide unsafe working conditions or faulty products, they usually face stiff criminal penalties, and the decision makers are punished appropriately.

2. After reading paragraph 1 of "Criminals at Work," you can reasonably infer the authors believe that
   a. all criminology textbooks have chapters about occupational and organizational crimes.
   b. it's important to place more emphasis on traditional crimes.
   c. many criminology textbooks don't pay as much attention as they should to "crimes in the suites."

3. What are the primary patterns of organization the authors use in this reading?
   a. Definition and classification
   b. Comparison and contrast
   c. Exemplification, and cause and effect

4. What are the primary patterns of organization in paragraph 2?
   a. Chronological order and process
   b. Definition and exemplification
   c. Cause and effect, and chronological order

5. In this excerpt, which of the following are not included in the authors' categories for corporate violence?
   a. Violence against the environment
   b. Violence against consumers
   c. Violence against workers

6. Violence against consumers takes the form of
   a. overcharging consumers for commodities and services.
   b. failing to provide consumers with the goods they need in a timely fashion.
   c. selling consumers unsafe commodities.

7. The company Chemie Grunenthal had known for years that the drug thalidomide could cause major health problems,
   a. so it listed side effects in small print on the packaging.
   b. so it was never able to put it on the market.
   c. but it ignored and then downplayed that information.

8. Based on the information we learn in paragraph 12, we can reasonably infer that
   a. the worldview of one of the authors was influenced by the experience of his great grandfather.
   b. the authors will focus on giving "both sides" of the story of coal workers' exposure to dangers on the job.

    c. one of the authors had direct experience with coal mining.

9. Which of the following sentences from or based on the reading is primarily a statement of opinion or an interpretation of facts?
   a. "Crimes in the suites" deserve far more attention than they commonly receive in the press or among criminologists.
   b. Clinard and Quinney divided white-collar crimes into two types: corporate crime and occupational crime.
   c. According to the Occupational Safety and Health Administration (OSHA, 2000), there were 5.9 million work-related injuries and illnesses in 1999.

10. Which of the following sentences from or based on the reading is primarily a statement of fact?
    a. Even if we use the conservative OSHA statistics, we get some sense of how routine violations of worker safety laws actually are in the United States.
    b. In general, corporations have shown that their bottom line is to make profits and if that means occasionally putting their workers or the public in danger, so be it.
    c. Ford Motor Company calculated that a burn death would result in an average $200,000 loss, and any injury less than death would cost them $67,000.

Exercise 3   Evaluate the Argument

Answer the following questions as fully as you can in your own words.

1. According to the authors, why did Ford produce the Pinto even after tests proved it was unsafe?

   _____

   _____

   _____

2. What are the reasons given for the low estimates of risks involved in work, according to the authors? (par. 10)

   _____

   _____

3. According to the authors, what is a major cause of workplace accidents? (pars. 11 through 17)

   _____

   _____

   _____

© 2007 Pearson Education, Inc.

4. What was the authors' purpose in including corporate crime in their textbook on criminology?

_____

_____

_____

Exercise 4   **Reflect**

Think about what you read in "Criminals at Work" and what you already know about corporate crime. Then answer the following questions in your own words.

1. Besides the examples in this reading, what other kinds of corporate crime can you think of? Give examples.

_____

_____

_____

_____

_____

2. What are some of the things that some companies do to give full information to consumers about the safety of their products?

_____

_____

_____

_____

3. What are the similarities and differences between direct violence against people (like assault and murder) and corporate decisions that do violence to workers or consumers (like knowingly selling medicine that will make some people sick, or causing accidents and/or death at work by willfully not following safety regulations)? Should the penalties be the same? Explain your answer.

_____

_____

_____

_____

4. Do you think Sutherland's concept of white-collar crime (as both economic and violent) is valid, or a useful way for us to understand such crime? Explain your answer.

_____

_____

_____

_____

5. What, in your opinion, can be done to reduce or eliminate corporate crime?

_____

_____

_____

_____

© 2007 Pearson Education, Inc.

PART II

A Reader's Toolkit

©2007 Pearson Education, Inc.

1. NOTE TAKING: THE CORNELL NOTE-TAKING SYSTEM

One of the most important ways college students acquire knowledge is through the process of taking notes during lectures. Although collaborative learning, discussion groups, and individualized learning are important sources of information, lectures by scholars and experts will continue to be a major means of instruction. Even if innovations such as distance learning and multimedia computer/video presentations enhance these lectures in the future, you will still need some basic note-taking techniques to organize and use the information you receive.

The **Cornell Note-Taking System,** which originated at Cornell University in New York, is one of the most popular note-taking systems among college students. To make the system easy to remember, it breaks the process into steps, called the **5Rs:**

1. **R**ecord

2. **R**educe

3. **R**eflect

4. **R**ecite

5. **R**eview

To begin the Cornell Note-Taking System, you need to draw a new left margin on a standard 8½ by 11 piece of notebook paper. Draw the left margin about 3 inches from the left edge of the paper. This space is for the *reduce* column, which you will fill in after recording your notes in the space at the right. Leave about a 2-inch space at the bottom of the page to record your reflections on the lecture sometime after the class session. (To see what this setup looks like, turn to the example on page 533.) You can buy notebooks at some college bookstores that already have the correct margins printed for the Cornell Note-Taking System.

Record

Before you begin recording notes for a class lecture, write the date at the top of the paper. Keep the notes for each course in a separate notebook, or at least in a clearly divided portion of a notebook.

Be on time for the lecture, or even a little early, so you don't miss introductory comments or directions. *Read* assigned textbook material. Before you get to class, *review* the reading as well as your lecture notes from recent classes. This review process enables you to easily recognize the context, or framework, of this day's lecture presentation.

Record all the essential information you need to remember from the lecture. How do you choose the right information? First, you need to *listen* carefully and *select* the important points. Don't try to be a human tape recorder, writing down every word that the lecturer says. You will be frustrated, and you won't have time to think about what is being said. Record points such as the following:

©2007 Pearson Education, Inc.

- Main ideas, major supporting points
- Patterns of organization (recognizing the pattern of the lecturer's organization will help you to order your notes accordingly)
- Major transitions (to help you recognize the relationships between ideas)
- Information written on the board or presented on an overhead or with computer graphics
- Points that the lecturer obviously stresses by introducing with phrases such as "you need to know," "this will be on the test," "remember this point," and "it is most important to consider"
- Emphasized information (watch for lecturer's style: raising or lowering the voice, gesturing, pacing, or other movements may indicate emphasis)
- Repeated information

Check your notes at the end of class for any errors. If you missed an important point and didn't have a chance to ask about it during the lecture, ask the instructor or a classmate as soon as you can after class so you don't forget it.

Reduce

As soon as you have a chance to study your notes, you can *reduce* them. Read over the notes you have recorded in the right column. Select key words and phrases that summarize the main points of the lecture. List these points in the left-hand column.

Reflect

You already know that thinking about what you read is an important part of active reading. *Reflecting* on what you learn in lectures is also important. Consider how the concepts, facts, and interpretations you learned in the lecture relate to what you've read, what you've experienced, and what you already know about the topic. Does this information reinforce what you already know? Does it add new information or understanding? Does it contradict your previous knowledge? If so, how can you resolve the differences? What new questions or problems are raised that you need to explore? Record your reflections at the bottom of your notes.

Recite

As you already know from the PRO system, *recite* means to test yourself. In the Cornell Note-Taking System, you use the key words and phrases identified in the *reduce* section of your notes to assist you. Cover the recorded notes, and use the reduced notes to form questions. See if you can provide detailed definitions, explanations, comparisons, and so on, without looking back. Uncover the detailed notes to check your answers.

Review

The process of *reviewing* your notes is actually the same as reviewing your selected points in reading. Repeat the recite step periodically—within 24 hours, two to three days, a week, two to three weeks, and over increasingly spaced intervals—to retain the essential information and understanding you will need for tests and for work.

You can take notes from what you read as well as from lectures. You could then use the Cornell Note-Taking System to organize these reading notes for reciting and review.

Use the Cornell Method

If you had used the Cornell Note-Taking system to take notes on the information you just read, it would look something like the following. First the important ideas are recorded on the right. Then that information is reduced to key terms in the left-hand column. At the end are some reflections on the information.

The Cornell Note-Taking System   January 5, 2007

Reduce	Record
Set up	Set up paper with 3-inch margin from left side of the paper and a 2-inch margin at the bottom.
Record	Record all essential information on the right side of the paper. Listen carefully and select important points, main ideas, patterns, information on the board, and emphasized information. If you missed something, ask a classmate or the professor.
Reduce key words and phrases	After the lecture, select key words and phrases that summarize main points. List these in the left column.
Reflect	Think about how concepts, facts, and information from the lecture relate to what you know and to your reading. What observations can you make? What questions can you ask? Write your thoughts at the bottom of the paper as soon as you can at the end of the lecture.
Recite	Test yourself. Ask yourself questions from the key words and phrases in the left column, and try to fill in the rest of the information, keeping the right column covered. Uncover your detailed notes to check your answers.

©2007 Pearson Education, Inc.

| Review | Repeat the recite step periodically—after one day, a few days later, two to three weeks later. |
| Reflections | This seems like a good method of note taking. The hardest part will be to take the time to reduce my notes, write my reflections, and then recite and review them. If I do all these things on a regular basis, studying from my notes for tests will be pretty easy. |

2. READING VISUAL AIDS

Visual aids are images that assist the reader in understanding text, whether that text is on a book page or a computer screen. A visual aid can be a picture, map, cartoon, graph, table, pie chart, flowchart, or diagram as well as a figure, time line, or illustration in a story, article, or text selection. The chapters of this book offer you instruction and practice in reading many types of visual aids (pictures, p. 294; cartoons, p. 294; flowcharts, p. 251; diagrams, p. 248, time lines, p. 236). This brief section offers you further instruction and practice. The answers to the practices are on page 543.

When you read a chapter in a textbook, an article in a magazine, or a page on a Web site, always look at the visual aids as you prepare to read. Study them again while you are reading. You will need to "read" each visual aid actively.

- *Decide* what you think is the purpose of the visual aid. Why is this visual aid included? What does it mean in relation to the reading?
- *Compare* items in different parts of the visual aid. What is the relationship between the parts? What is being compared? What is the result of the comparison?
- *Think* about what conclusions you can reach or what trends you can predict based on the information the visual aid provides. In some ways, you can consider this step as finding the *main idea* of the visual aid.

When you examine a visual aid, especially one in a textbook, be sure to read the caption and the credit line. The caption, a brief explanation that appears immediately above or below the image, will help you determine the purpose of the visual aid and reach some conclusions about the information it provides. The credit line identifies who created or supplied the image. Together they will help you understand and evaluate the image. For examples, see Figure II.1 (opposite).

Maps

Maps convey geographical information and can help you understand distance relationships (through mileage legends) and the influence of physical features such as rivers, oceans, and mountains. Often maps show the location of specific populations or trends related to them. For example, Figure II.1 shows how much money per hour people earn working in the garment industry in different parts of the world. Notice that the title for the map is "Hourly Wage Estimates for Garment Industry Workers in the United States and Selected Countries." It's important to understand that the numbers shown on the map are not exact but pretty close. Also, notice that the date in the credit line is 1997, so the numbers are not completely up-to-date, either. Nevertheless, the numbers graphically illustrate the reason that garment manufacturers are moving their factories

©2007 Pearson Education, Inc.

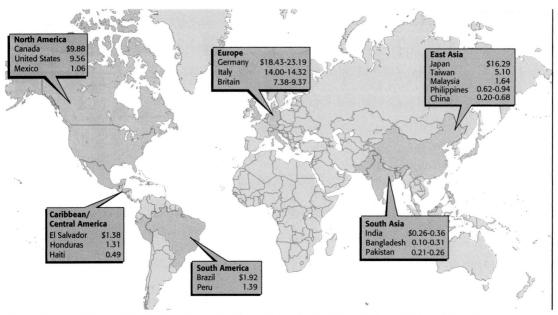

Figure II.1 **Hourly Wage Estimates for Garment Industry Workers in the United States and Selected Countries** *SOURCE:* Werner International as reported by Greenhouse (1997) and Sweatshop Watch (1997), in Joan Ferrante, *Sociology: A Global Perspective,* 5th ed. (Belmont, CA: Thomson/Wadsworth, 2003).

from the United States and Europe to other parts of the world. Rather than pay about $9.56 per hour to a worker in the United States, some corporations move their operations to, for example, El Salvador, where the workers make the equivalent of about $1.38 per hour, or to Bangladesh, where people work for between 10 cents and 31 cents per hour.

Practice II.1 **Interpret a Map**

Study the map in Figure II.2. Then answer the following questions.

1. Which states have a dropout rate of 41 percent or more?

_____

_____

2. Which state has the highest dropout rate and what is it?

_____

3. Which state has the lowest dropout rate and what is it?

_____

4. What is the dropout rate of your state?

_____

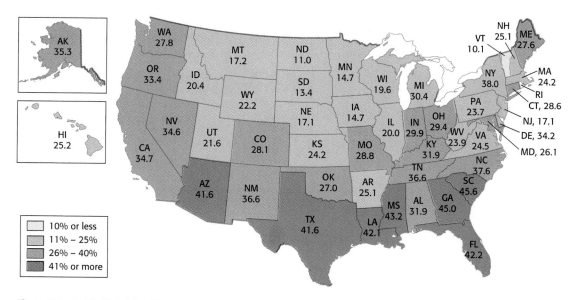

Figure II.2   Public High School Dropout Rates in the United States *NOTE:* The data points are placed at the midpoints of the respective years.
SOURCE: Joan Ferrante, *Sociology: A Global Perspective,* 5th ed. (Belmont, CA: Thomson/Wadsworth, 2003).

5. What regional trends do you see?

_____

_____

_____

6. What factors do you think contribute to high dropout rates?

_____

_____

_____

7. What do you think these dropout rates mean for the future of the American workforce?

_____

_____

_____

(See answers on page 543.)

Graphs

Graphs are diagrams that present data using dots, lines, or bars to show the relationship between two things. Often one element is time, shown on the horizontal line, and the other element is a figure that changes

©2007 Pearson Education, Inc.

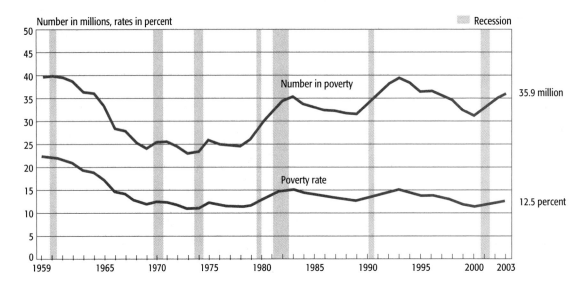

Figure II.3   Number in Poverty and Poverty Rate: 1959 to 2003 *NOTE:* The data points are placed at the midpoints of the respective years.

SOURCE: U.S. Census Bureau, *Income, Poverty, and Health Insurance Coverage in the United States, 2003,* http://www.census.gov/prod/2004pubs/p60-226.pdf.

with time, such as the number of people in poverty. To understand graphs, ask yourself the following questions:

■ What does the horizontal line or bar indicate?
■ What does the vertical line or bar indicate?
■ What is the relationship between the information on each line or bar?
■ What does the overall graph demonstrate? (In other words, what is the main idea?)

For example, as its title suggests, Figure II.3 shows the number of people living in poverty and the poverty rate (percentage of people living in poverty) between 1959 and 2003. The graph gives the reader a visual representation of the increases and decreases in poverty. It allows us to understand that a much higher percentage of Americans were poor in 1959 (22%) than in 2003 (12.5%) but that because the U.S. population is greater now, almost the same number of people were poor in 2003 (35.9 million) as were poor in 1959 (40 million).

Exercise II.2   Interpret a Graph

Study the graph in Figure II.4. Then answer the following questions.

1. In which age categories are men and women's median weekly earnings closest to being the same?

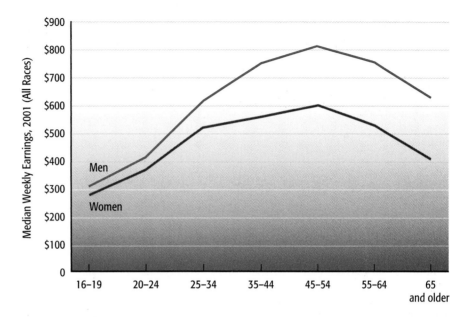

Figure II.4   **The Wage Gap, 2001** *SOURCE:* Unpublished tabulations, Bureau of Labor Statistics, *Current Population Survey.*

2. In which age categories are men and women's median weekly earnings most dissimilar?

_____

3. What does this graph show us overall? (That is, what is its main idea?)

_____

_____

(See answers on page 543.)

◆

Tables

Tables provide information in list form. For example, Table II.1 presents information similar to Figure II.4 but in a different way. The information is organized into three columns: "Race," "Median Annual Earnings" for "Men," and "Median Annual Earnings" for "Women." Even a quick look at this table shows that men earn considerably more (a median of $37,339) than women (a median of $27,355). This disparity is even more extreme if you also consider race. White men earn about $14,000 per year more than Hispanic men and $18,000 per year more than Hispanic women.

©2007 Pearson Education, Inc.

| Table II.1 | **Median Annual Earnings of Year-Round, Full-Time Workers by Race and Gender, 2000** | |

Race	**Median Annual Earnings**	
	Men	**Women**
White	$38,869	$28,080
African American	$30,409	$25,117
Asian and Pacific Islander*	$40,946	$31,156*
Hispanic	$24,638	$20,527
	All Men: $37,339 (100%)	All Women: $27,355 (73%)

*Due to the small size of the survey sample, these data may not be representative

SOURCE: National Committee on Pay Equity, based on U.S. Census Bureau, *Current Population Reports*, Series P60, *Income Statistics* (Washington, DC: Government Printing Office, 2001).

| Practice II.3 | Interpret a Table

Study Table II.2. Then answer the following questions.

1. How much more does the average man earn annually if he has completed a bachelor's degree rather than just a high school diploma?

2. What's the average annual salary for a male professional? For a female professional?

3. What year's earnings is this analysis based on, and what is the source?

4. Why do you think men and women's average salaries are so different when they have the same educational levels?

5. Frequently, a person with the education level indicated in the table earns far less than is indicated. Why might this happen?

(See answers on page 543.)

Table II.2	Median Annual Incomes of Men and Women, Year-Round, Full-Time Workers, Ages 25-64, by Education Level, 2000	

Education Level	Medium Income	
	Men	**Women**
Less than 9th grade	$20,464	$15,428
9th to 12th grade, nongraduate	$24,478	$17,190
High school graduate/GED	$32,544	$23,777
Some college, no degree	$38,804	$27,186
Associate's degree	$41,184	$30,189
Bachelor's degree	$53,855	$38,442
Master's degree	$65,183	$47,108
Professional degree	$91,855	$55,850
Doctorate degree	$74,163	$55,969

SOURCE: U.S. Census Bureau, *Annual Demographic Survey,* December 14, 2001.

Pie Charts

A pie chart shows the relationships of parts to a whole. The whole is the contents of a circle, or a pie, and divisions are appropriately sized portions, or slices. For example, look at Figure II.5. One circle represents the U.S. population in 1999, and the divisions of the pie or circle indicate the racial distribution of that population. The other circle shows the same information as it is projected for 2050. You can readily see that the most notable change will be in the proportion of the population that is of Hispanic origin: up from 11.5 percent in 1999 to 24 percent in 2050.

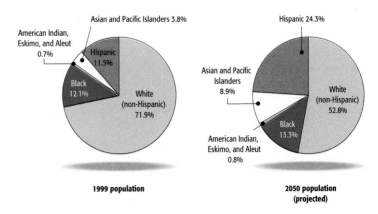

1999 population

2050 population (projected)

Figure II.5 **Percentage Distribution of Population by Race and Hispanic Origin, 1999 and 2050**

Note: Racial categories exclude those of Hispanic origin. Source: U.S. Census Bureau, News Release, March 21, 2001.

©2007 Pearson Education, Inc.

Practice II.4   Interpret Pie Charts

Study the pie charts in Figure II.6. Then answer the following questions.

1. How did the percentage of income that Americans spent on food change between 1919 and 1998? Why do you think this change occurred?

_____

_____

_____

2. How did the percentage of income that Americans spent on housing change between 1919 and 1998? Why do you think this change occurred?

_____

_____

_____

3. How did the amount Americans spent on clothing change? Explain why you think it changed so much.

_____

_____

_____

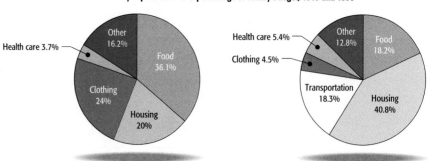

Figure II.6   Family Expenditures as a Percentage of an Average Family Budget, 1919 and 1998
SOURCE: Bureau of Labor Statistics, 2001.

4. What expense did Americans have in 1998 that they didn't have in 1919? Explain why this happened.

_____

_____

_____

(See answers on page 544.)

◆

Practice Answers

Practice II.1

1. Arizona, Texas, Louisiana, Mississippi, Georgia, Florida, and South Carolina
2. South Carolina; 45.6 percent
3. Vermont; 10.1 percent
4. Answers will vary.
5. Dropout rates are higher in the southern and western states.
6. Answers will vary. Possible answers: Students have to learn English as a Second Language; students have to go to work; they don't like going to school; some of the girls get pregnant.
7. Answers will vary. Possible answer: It means the American workforce will be less educated and possibly less competitive in the global market.

Practice II.2

1. 16–19 and 20–24
2. 45–54 and 55–64
3. Overall, it shows that men earn more money than women, especially during the peak earning years.

Practice II.3

1. A man with a bachelor's degree earns approximately $21,000 more per year than a man with a high school diploma.
2. Male, $91,855; female, $55,850
3. 2000, U.S. Census Bureau
4. Answers will vary. Possible answers: Women take time off work for childbearing and child raising, reducing their chances of advancement; there is some discrimination against women.
5. Answers will vary. Possible answers: Frequently, people work part time; the table is for full-time, year-round employment.

©2007 Pearson Education, Inc.

Practice II.4

1. In 1919, Americans spent 36 percent of their income on food, but in 1998, they spent only 18.2 percent of their income on food. Perhaps the cost of food dropped as it became cheaper to produce because of mechanization and very cheap farm labor.

2. In 1919, Americans spent 20.0 percent of their income on housing, but in 1998, they spent 40.8 percent of their income on housing. The cost of renting or owning a home became very high by 1998 and has continued to rise.

3. Americans spent only 4.5 percent of their income on clothing in 1998 compared with 24.0 percent in 1919. Maybe clothing became much less expensive because by 1998 it was being mass produced and the cost of labor in some places was very cheap.

4. In 1998, Americans had transportation expenses, which are not listed for 1919. Transportation expenses constituted 18.3 percent of Americans' expenditures in 1998, reflecting modern Americans' tendency to live far from the places they have to go and their reliance on cars for transportation, which, including purchase price, insurance, gas, and upkeep, are very expensive.

3. TEST TAKING

Being confident and well prepared are the basic essentials for successful test taking. Regular exams are part of the requirements of college courses. Some employers give new or potential employees tests to measure knowledge and aptitude. Entry into certain professions, such as nursing, cosmetology, accounting, insurance, and teaching, require special tests for certification or licensing. Whatever the testing situation, careful preparation is the key to confidence.

Overcome Test Anxiety

Preparing for tests in college courses is simplified by using a system for reading and studying such as PRO. With conscientious study and review, test taking becomes a less anxious experience. If you tend to be overly stressed about tests, try *overlearning* the material—learning it so well that you could "recite it in your sleep." Even when you are confident about what you know, test taking is still a challenge, but you should be able to approach it positively. Your stress at this point should be *eustress*, which helps you to do your very best, instead of *distress*. Visualize yourself arriving for the test a little early, with time to relax, and then calmly and confidently answering even the most difficult questions. Know that you are well prepared and can answer any objective or essay questions that arise.

Anticipate Test Questions

A helpful way to prepare for tests is to anticipate what the questions will be and then *recite,* to test yourself on those questions. Use your knowledge of the course objectives from the syllabus, the professor's suggestions and clues in lectures, and your own identification of what is important in both the textbook and in lectures through the application of the PRO Reading System and the Cornell Note-Taking System. Ask yourself, "What are the essential pieces of information, relationships among data, and understandings I have mastered so far in the course?" Do you know how you will be tested—objective questions, essay questions, or a combination of both?

Write possible test items. Practice answering them yourself and in study groups. If you review in a study group, you might divide writing and answering the practice questions. The advantages of a study group, of course, are that together you have a better chance of covering all the essentials, you can cover them more quickly and completely, and you can test each other.

Follow Directions

Students and job applicants frequently lose points on tests because they simply don't follow directions. Read *all* the directions on a test before you do anything else. Take note of any changes in directions or corrections to

©2007 Pearson Education, Inc.

test items that the professor may announce or write on the board at the beginning of class. Be sure you know how many points each portion of the test is worth, decide how much time you will spend on each section accordingly, and *budget your time* so you can complete the entire test.

Understand the Types of Questions

Objective Questions Objective questions on tests are usually multiple choice, true/false, or matching. Objective questions may be perceived as relatively easy because they don't appear to require complete recall of the content, only recognition of a correct answer. However, it is possible to be overconfident when approaching objective tests and thus lose points unnecessarily. Read carefully the directions for the scoring of objective questions. Sometimes there is a definite penalty for guessing; you may, for example, lose double points for a wrong answer. Here are some additional hints that can help you become more accurate in answering objective questions.

- In matching exercises, how many choices will be used? How useful will the process of elimination be in making your choices?
- Watch for qualifying words and negative words that will strongly influence your answer.
- For multiple-choice questions, always read all the choices before making a decision. Check each choice as if it were a true/false statement. Then choose the best answer for the question. Remember that "none of the above" or "all of the above" is sometimes the right answer. Again, read the directions carefully; you may be asked to choose all the correct answers, not just one.

Essay Questions Essay test questions require answers of various lengths, from one paragraph to two or three pages or more. The first requirement for answering an essay question effectively is to read the question carefully. Be sure you understand the requirements. What exactly is the question asking you to do? Essay directions usually include terms that you should now associate with patterns of organization (as discussed in Chapter 5). You may, for example, be asked to *define, compare* and *contrast, analyze,* give *examples,* or explain *causes or effects.* Each of these directions gives you a specific task. See pages 547 and 548 for more vocabulary clues for essay questions.

Before you begin writing an essay exam, take a few minutes to outline your answer. This step helps you organize your ideas. Begin with a thesis statement that answers the question directly. List all the supporting points you want to include; that way, you won't forget any of them, and you'll be able to present them in the best possible order.

Begin your essay by answering the question directly. Choose key words from the question itself to begin your answer so it is obvious that you are answering the question and not straying. For example, if a question on a history test is "Discuss the immediate cause for the beginning of the American Revolutionary War," your answer might begin something like this: "Although many incidents led up to the outbreak of the Revolutionary War, *the immediate cause for the beginning of the American Revolutionary War* was the firing of arms at Lexington and Concord." The italicized words show that you have answered the question at the very beginning and that you will go on to develop the points to support your answer.

Divide the time allowed for the test to be sure you can include all the supporting points you noted in your preliminary outline. Your goal in an essay test is to let the instructor know how much you know about the topic and how well you can organize and express your knowledge in a limited amount of time.

Vocabulary Clues for Test Taking

There are a number of ways that your vocabulary skills can assist you in successful test taking.

In Objective Questions   For true/false questions, identify the *qualifying words* used, such as *most, some, all, none,* and *few.* These words often make the difference between a true and a false statement. Obviously, absolutes such as *all* or *none* seldom exist, so statements containing them may well be false. For example, in the sentence "All dogs have fleas," the word *all* obviously makes the statement false.

For both true/false and multiple-choice questions, be aware of *negative words,* such as *no, not, never;* one word can reverse the meaning of the entire sentence. Always be careful of *except.* Sometimes a multiple-choice question is worded something like, "all of the following are true, except." In this case, you are looking for the choice that is *not* true.

In Essay Questions   Read the directions for essay questions very carefully, and distinguish between the various parts of answers required. Use the following key words in the directions to help you plan an answer.

- *Discuss:* Write about various aspects of the topic; you decide how to limit the scope or provide a focus.
- *Define:* Provide a definition; that is, place an item in a category and then explain the specific characteristics that distinguish it from other items in that category.
- *Effect:* Write about the consequences or the results of a previous action or event.
- *Compare:* Write about the similarities and differences between two items, persons, concepts, and so on.
- *Contrast:* Write about the differences between two items, persons, concepts, and so on.
- *Cause:* Write about the reasons why something is the way it is. You may be asked to identify and analyze both immediate causes and underlying causes.

©2007 Pearson Education, Inc.

- *Analyze:* Write about the parts of a whole and discuss how the parts are related to each other. You might be asked to analyze a process, a cause-effect relationship, a character in literature, or any complex concept.
- *Summarize:* State concisely, usually in a paragraph or essay, the main ideas and major supporting points in the original reading or lecture.
- *Evaluate:* Write a reasoned response about the effectiveness or worth of a process, solution, argument, or product. Evaluating goes beyond stating an opinion—a simple like or dislike. It is based on thorough knowledge and careful analysis.

4. WRITING TIPS FOR READERS

Many college writing assignments ask you to write about what you have read. These assignments vary from short answers on tests to longer critiques, reflections, essays, and research papers. In this text, for example, each chapter ends with a writing activity that asks you to write a paragraph or short essay. Here are some tips on how to complete such assignments.

- *Read* thoroughly all the information on which the assignment is based. As you read, think about the question(s) you will be writing about.
- *Write* notes for your answer to the question.
- *Decide* what the main point is you want to make about the topic. In one sentence, state your answer to the question. (This is similar to finding the main idea as a reader. Now, as a writer, you are deciding what the main idea will be for your readers. Clearly answering the question will make it easier for your readers to comprehend what you write.)
- *Organize* what you want to say in an outline so you don't forget any points you want to include and your points will be presented in a clear and logical order.
- *Write* a rough draft of your answer.
- *Get feedback* on what you have written. Have classmates or friends read your paper, and see what questions they have about what you have written. If your campus has a writing center, ask a writing tutor to review your paper with you.
- *Revise* what you have written, and write your final draft. (As you review what you wrote, check to see if you have answered all parts of the question. Did you include enough supporting points to fully explain your ideas? Then proofread to ensure that all your sentences make sense and all words are spelled correctly.)
- *Keep your completed writing assignments* for the semester in a portfolio. Your instructor may want to evaluate your semester's progress by reviewing your work in this format. Many students find it useful to save what they have learned and to monitor their own writing and learning from semester to semester by keeping a portfolio. Some colleges ask for a portfolio of student work for admission into certain programs.

©2007 Pearson Education, Inc.

5. READER RESPONSE JOURNALS

Often readers are asked to reflect on what they have read. Throughout this text, you have been asked to answer questions about your reflections on readings from all types of sources. Sometimes instructors ask students to organize their reflections in a *reader response journal.* Reader response journals are assigned in various kinds of courses, from math and biology to philosophy and English literature. If you read an additional book, besides your text, for this reading course, a reader response journal would be a good way to record your reflections on what you read.

The most common kind of reader response journal is organized like the one shown on the opposite page, with a quotation from the text recorded on the left and the reader's reflections recorded on the right. Other times, the quotation is simply recorded first and the reflections follow. Regardless of the format, instructors are usually looking for certain types of responses in journal entries. They will probably request some of the following types of entries:

- Connections between new knowledge and previously acquired understandings
- Responses to the ease or difficulty of mastering new concepts or processes
- Evaluations of the significance of new concepts
- Personal responses to new concepts; comments on the value of the reading to your own life
- Questions that arise from the new ideas
- Ethical considerations that need to be added
- Comments on logical fallacies or other errors in reasoning
- New ideas that the recently learned information stimulated
- Recognition of relationships between ideas
- Applications of new concepts to other areas of knowledge
- Specific assignments, such as a list of quotations and reflections that lead to an analysis of a character in a literary text

Quote from Text	Response
Computer Science	
"Artificial intelligence is the branch of computer science that explores the use of computers in tasks that require intelligence, imagination, and insight— tasks that have traditionally been performed by people rather than machines." (Beekman, Computer Confluence)	What kinds of "human" activities can be done by machines? How could a computer possibly show imagination? This seems like a uniquely human trait. Perhaps Beekman defines imagination differently than I do!
Sociology	
"Paycheck inequality has grown so much that the top 4 percent of Americans make more in wages and salaries than the entire bottom half." (Sklar, Chaos or Community?)	Wow! That isn't fair! How can they even spend all that money? I'm working 40 hours a week besides going to school and barely making it. Maybe there should be laws that regulate how much profit individuals can take out of a company.
Psychology	
"Although machines are likely to break down, humans will continue to work even when they are overloaded." (Smither, The Psychology of Work and Human Performance)	This idea of human advantage contradicts what we read in computer science by Beekman. I'm not sure that working when you're "overloaded" is really an advantage though. Consider all the injuries studies that show what happens when workers are fatigued.
Literature	
"It is fatal for anyone to be a man or a woman pure and simple; one must be woman-manly or man-womanly." (Virginia Woolf, A Room of One's Own)	Virginia Woolf was certainly ahead of her time; this statement probably wasn't very popular when she was alive. A lot of people even today would feel threatened by it. (My brother would!) I think it's a good idea, though. Men and women shouldn't emphasize their differences; they should realize how similar they are. We can learn from each other.
Literature	
"Gradually she became less wild, tamer, I had had a fox, a quail, in the house, as I have said, then one day I realized I had a hen." (Moravia, "The Chase")	The image of a hen is certainly negative. It tells a lot about the narrator's (husband's) changed attitude toward his wife. He now sees her as ordinary, dowdy, uninteresting. Does this really describe her character at this time, or is it just his perspective? Would she still see herself as a quail? This is a good example of how perspective influences the telling of a story.

©2007 Pearson Education, Inc.

6. EVALUATING AND NAVIGATING WEB SITES

You can find all kinds of information on the Internet. It can be an invaluable resource for researching topics ranging from diseases, drugs, and diets to history, literature, and technological advances. But the Web also has lots of inaccurate, misleading, and even slanderous "information." So it is essential for you to develop the ability to evaluate Web sites. To use the information on a Web site, you should familiarize yourself with ways to judge its reliability. How do you judge whether the information on a Web site is true and reliable? To do so effectively, you will use many of the skills you've learned: prereading (scanning the site home page), reading, organizing, and critical thinking. To provide a structure for your evaluation, you should answer the following questions.

Source

Who is giving you the information? Should you trust the author? One way to evaluate a site's author is by looking at the address, or URL (uniform resource locator). Part of the URL, called the domain name, tells you who originated the site. For instance, the URL for the Web site for this book is www.ablongman.com/alexandercommunity4e. The domain name for this URL is .com. As shown in Table II.3, the .com domain name indicates that the main purpose of the site is to sell products—in this case, books. The table lists other common domain names and what they mean.

Many sites have an "About" section that gives you a little background information on the author and/or the purpose of the site so you can judge his or her qualifications as well as the agenda of the site. Is this person an expert? Is his or her resumé on the site? Is there a list of the author's print media publications?

If the Web site includes information from outside printed sources, such as newspapers or magazines, does it properly document them? A Web site author who makes it easy for you to check sources and get background information is probably more reliable than one who states "facts" without saying where they come from.

Finally, take into account who can put information on the site. To post a comment on some Web sites, such as discussion boards, a person need only register an e-mail address. The authors of these posts are not held responsible for the information they contain, and the Web site owners usually put a disclaimer that they are not liable for any misinformation. Avoid using this sort of Web site in your research.

Currency

How current is the site—that is, is the information kept up-to-date?
Many sites tell you when the last update occurred, and articles are usually dated. If there isn't a date on the page, try going to the View menu in

Table II.3	**Domain Names and Reliability**	

Domain Name	Reliability of Sponsor	Possible Purposes
.edu	Educational institution (college, university, or research institution). Information found here is usually reliable. But a person affiliated with the institution (a student, for example) may have a page on the site that reflects only that individual's viewpoint. The URL for this kind of Web page usually ends with the person's name in the form of http://www.university.edu/~*name*.	• Disseminate information about the institution • Disseminate research • Make useful information available to the public
.com	Anyone can buy a .com Web address, and there are few or no restrictions on the content that can go on the site. Usually, the purpose of a .com site is to sell things. Most businesses have .com sites.	• Sell a product • Promote the public image of a private company
.org	Like .com, the .org domain name is available for anyone to purchase. Most nonprofit organizations have .org addresses. While the information is probably reliable, it usually has a bias. Many .org addresses promote a particular viewpoint.	• Promote a position (i.e., defending the rights of children, protecting the environment, etc.) • Advocate that readers do something to support the position of the group • Announce events • Disseminate information
.gov	Official site maintained by the U.S. government. This kind of site should be reliable but can be political, reflecting and promoting the views of the politicians or party that controls the particular government agency.	• Provide information (regulations, statistics reports, etc.) • Provide resources for the public (how to apply for unemployment insurance, etc.) • Promote the political position of the current administration

your browser and selecting Page Info, Source, or whatever option is available to provide the information you need.

Usefulness

How useful is the site?   Even reliable information is useless if you can't find it. An established, reliable Web site usually has a home page, which is the first document you see when you enter the site and serves as an introduction to the site. A home page includes links to other parts of the site and frequently links to other Web sites that have related information. Sometimes the home pages are well organized, but sometimes they are not. In any case, "reading" a home page is not a linear process. You do not necessarily start at the top of the page and read down. Often you will find yourself "looking all around" the page to get an idea of what is available. You will need to scan the page, not read it word for word. You are acting as a detective, searching until you find what you want and using clues to guide your search.

©2007 Pearson Education, Inc.

The Elements of a Web Site

For practice, examine Figure II.7, the home page for the U.S. Department of Labor's Web site (http://www.dol.gov). If you examine the Find It column on the left, you will see that you can look for information by topic. If you have a specific question about wages, for example, you can click on Wages. You can also look for information by audience. Here you can find information important to workers or employers. For example, if you are looking for a job, you would first click on Workers. This takes you to a new Web page with several sections, including one titled Information for Job Seekers.

Figure II.7   U.S. Department of Labor Home Page
SOURCE: http://www.dol.gov
September 30, 2005

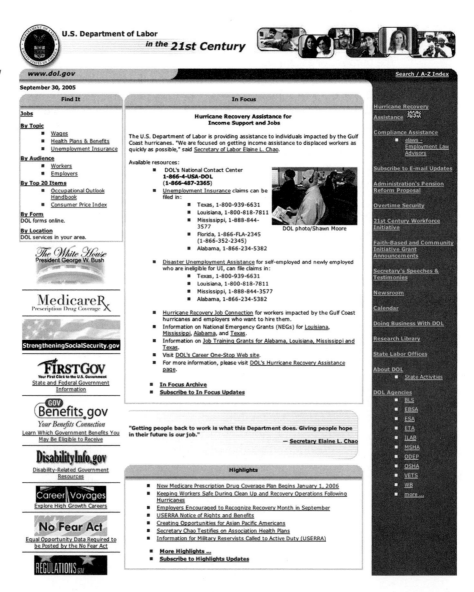

There are many other interesting features on this Web site, and you could easily spend hours exploring them all. For example, the In Focus section of the home page includes recent news items or bulletins that the Department of Labor would like you to see; and the right column of the home page lists more topics you might want to check.

It is important to remember that most active Web sites do not remain the same. They are constantly updated, and even the home page may change, so the picture you see here for the Department of Labor Web site dated September 30, 2005 may not be the same when you go to the site yourself.

Notice the links on the Department of Labor's Web site. You can click on them to go directly to other sites. Some Web sites get information from other sources and provide links to those outside sites. A site may also provide links to other sites with a similar viewpoint, even if those sites are not sources of information. Both types of links help expand the amount of information you can gain from one site. Be aware, however, that you'll need to evaluate each link just as you did the original site.

Most Web sites provide e-mail addresses you can write to if you have questions or comments. If you find a piece of information you really want to use, but you're not sure whether it's accurate, try writing to the author of the page to ask for the source.

Practice II.5 Evaluate a Web Site

Go to the Web site for the Centers for Disease Control and Prevention (http://www.cdc.gov), and then fill out the following evaluation form. (Answers for Practice II.5 are on page 556.)

1. Site address: _____ Date accessed: _____

2. Who created the site? What are the qualifications and affiliations of the site? For whom is the site written? What is the purpose of the site?

   _____

   _____

   _____

3. When was the site last updated?

   _____

4. What is the content of the site?

   _____

   _____

   _____

©2007 Pearson Education, Inc.

5. Where can you find the information you need from this site?

_____

_____

_____

_____

_____

6. How can you use the information on this site? Would you recommend this site to another student? Remember to use your reading and critical thinking skills to evaluate the content of the site. (See the discussions in Chapter 7 on worldview, viewpoint, and bias on pages 372 through 377, and in Chapter 8 on evaluating arguments, especially Table 8.1 on page 429.)

_____

_____

_____

_____

_____

_____

◆

Practice Answers

Practice II.5

1. Site address: *http://www.cdc.gov*   Date accessed *July 7, 2005*

2. Who created the site? What are the qualifications and affiliations of the site? For whom is the site written? What is the purpose of the site?

   This site is created by the Centers for Disease Control and Prevention, an agency

   of the U.S. Department of Health and Human Services. Because it is a

   government site (with a .gov domain name), the information is probably accurate,

   although it is possible that it reflects the political bias of the current

   administration. The site is written for health professionals but also for anybody who wants to research health issues. The site's purpose is to make information about health widely available.

3. When was the site last updated?

It has announcements for events in September 2005; at the bottom of some of the linked sites, it says when those sites were last reviewed, but each has a different date.

4. What is the content of the site?

The site has interesting information on hurricane season and summer health. (This part is current, so it will definitely be different if you look at this site in the winter.) It also has links to health and safety topics, and a section on health statistics that includes data such as adolescent mortality by state and race. In addition, there is a section on training opportunities in public health.

5. Where can you find the information you need from this site?

The home page includes links to several sections of the site that provide specific information, including an A–Z index of health topics and a search box. The site also has links to other federal government agencies and to some independent and private agencies that deal with health care.

6. How can you use the information on this site? Would you recommend this site to another student? Remember to use your reading and critical thinking skills to evaluate the content of the site. (See the discussions in Chapter 7 on worldview, viewpoint, and bias on pages 372 through 377 and in Chapter 8, on evaluating arguments, especially Table 8.1 on page 429.

7. This site is a good source for information on health issues in the United States. It has lots of well-documented data, and the CDC itself is an authoritative source. The information in this site can be used in a research paper about various health subjects. It can also be used by people who might be interested in going into a health-related career or by somebody who just wants to find out more about a specific disease or health condition. The links it provides are also excellent for finding additional information about specific subjects.

©2007 Pearson Education, Inc.

7. READING CIRCLES

Reading circles provide a student-centered format that empowers students to work in groups independently of direct instructor involvement. At the same time, reading circles provide a system that enables the instructor to know exactly who is doing the work and what each member is contributing to the group. The following guidelines are adapted from Harvey Daniels's *Literature Circles* (1994), where the technique was first explained. They will help you make your reading circle a success.

Get Organized

1. In class, preview and choose a book you wish to read from a list of about four to six books your instructor provides.
2. Form a reading circle with other students who chose the same book you chose. Your instructor will help in this process to ensure that the groups are about the right size. Usually, each reading circle has three to five students.
3. Groups meet during class time to get organized. At the first meeting, members of your reading group should
   a. introduce yourselves and exchange contact information.
   b. decide how you will divide up reading the book. If your group has four meetings, for example, and your chosen book has 16 chapters, you might decide to prepare 4 chapters for each meeting.
   c. Develop a calendar. If your instructor has assigned a presentation at the end of the reading circle project, plan on using your last meeting or two, and possibly a meeting scheduled outside of class time, to prepare and practice the presentation.
   d. Assign each member a role for the next meeting. (See the role guidelines on the assignment sheets that follow.) If you don't have enough members to fill all the roles, some people can fill more than one. The assignments for the first three roles must be done each time you meet, however. The roles are summarizer, discussion leader, passage selector, researcher/connector, illustrator, and vocabulary finder.

Reading Circle Meetings

1. Read the assignment ahead of time and complete your role assignment sheet. Bring the book and *two copies* of the role assignment sheet to the meeting.
2. Turn in one copy of the completed assignment sheet to your instructor.
3. Share your role assignment preparations, starting with the summarizer. *Everyone* is expected to participate in all parts of the discussion.

4. Assign new roles for the next meeting, paying attention to what would be best for your book and for the interests of the members.
5. Anonymously, each member of the reading circle evaluates the group's work, answering the questions on page 566 (Anonymous Reading Circle Evaluation).

Final Presentation (optional)

Your presentation should communicate to the class important information about your book without "giving everything away."

1. Everyone in the reading circle needs to be involved in the presentation and to speak. The presentation should stay within the time allotted by your instructor (usually 5 to 10 minutes).
2. As a group, decide what you want to present about your book. You might decide to summarize the most important information or to give a few highlights about the best and most interesting parts of your book. You might also present some of the research done by some members of your group. Or you could even act out a scene from the book. Your presentation should have a beginning, or introduction, a middle, and an end, or conclusion.
3. Use visual aids to reinforce the content of your presentation. They can be realia (stuff), a poster (see pages 567–568 for suggestions on how to prepare a poster), a video clip, music, or even food. But make sure that all the aids you use relate to the content of your presentation.
4. In your group, practice your presentation. Help each other with presentation skills (see page 569 for suggestions). Make sure your presentation is clearly coordinated and flows well.

Role Assignment Sheets

The following role assignment sheets will help you think about, organize, and record your assignments for your reading circle meetings.

©2007 Pearson Education, Inc.

Summarizer

Name: _____   Meeting Date: _____

Book: _____   Assignment: Page _____ to _____

Summarize the reading for today's meeting. The group discussion will start with your statement, covering the main ideas and/or key points of today's reading assignment. Use the spaces below or a separate piece of paper to write your summary and list the key points. Be prepared to read them to the group.

Summary:

_____

_____

_____

_____

_____

_____

_____

_____

Key Points:

1. _____

2. _____

3. _____

4. _____

Discussion Leader

Name: _____   Meeting Date: _____

Book: _____   Assignment: Page _____ to _____

Develop five or six discussion questions (not short answer or yes/no questions) that will stimulate discussion in your group. To write good questions, try answering your question yourself. Is there a correct answer? If there is, then it's not a good discussion question. To answer the question, do you have to think and organize your thoughts? If so, then it's a good discussion question. Use a separate piece of paper if necessary.

Discussion questions:

1. _____

2. _____

3. _____

4. _____

5. _____

6. _____

Sample questions:

Why do you think the author _____?

What is/are the central theme(s) of the book so far? Why do you think so?

Did you find anything disturbing about _____? Why?

What questions did you have about _____?

Remember: Apply your questions to the assigned portion of the book.

©2007 Pearson Education, Inc.

Passage Selector

Name: _____   Meeting Date: _____

Book: _____   Assignment: Page _____ to _____

Find and record four to six especially important passages from the read-ing assignment. You can pick passages for many different reasons: (1) the writing is particularly beautiful or has powerful language; (2) it's funny; (3) it's a turning point in the plot; (4) it reveals how a character really thinks; (5) it captures the theme of the reading.

   Use the chart below or create a chart on a separate piece of paper to record your passages. At the meeting, you will read your passages out loud to your reading group (members of your group might choose to fol-low along in their books), explain why you picked them, and get other members' ideas about them.

Page and paragraph	The passage	Reason for picking

Researcher/Connector

Name: _____   Meeting Date: _____

Book: _____   Assignment: Page _____ to _____

Research background information on the author and other relevant information such as (1) the historical period dealt with in the book, (2) the geographical location, or (3) some of the issues or events in the book. You may do your research on the Web, but don't just download information. Rather, choose information to share that will be helpful for understanding the book. Record the information below or on a separate piece of paper, and record where the information came from—the name of the Web site or the book title and author. Finally, make connections between the reading assignment and what you already know—your life experiences, other books you are familiar with, or other events and issues.

Author's background:

_____

_____

_____

Source(s):

_____

Other relevant information:

_____

_____

_____

Source(s):

_____

Connections:

_____

_____

_____

©2007 Pearson Education, Inc.

Illustrator

Name: _____   Meeting Date: _____

Book: _____   Assignment: Page _____ to _____

Illustrate an important event or idea in the reading assignment by drawing and/or finding a photo or other image that relates to it. You can make
a sketch or a diagram or flowchart, or even draw stick figures. You can
also do research in the library or on the Internet for a photo, drawing, or
other type of illustration. Be sure to *give credit* to the source of your illustration. Put your illustration in the box below or on a separate piece
of paper. When you share the illustration with your group, explain how
it relates to the reading.

Source(s):

_____

_____

Vocabulary Finder

Name: _____   Meeting Date: _____

Book: _____   Assignment: Page _____ to _____

Choose about five terms or vocabulary words from the reading assignment to discuss with your group. You can pick words that are particularly
interesting, appear often, or are not familiar to you but seem important.
Use the chart below or a separate piece of paper to record the words,
where you found them in the book, and why you picked them. If it's a
word you don't know, write down the definition that is most appropriate
for its context.

Word	Page number	Definition and/or why you picked it.
1.		
2.		
3.		
4.		
5.		

©2007 Pearson Education, Inc.

Anonymous Reading Circle Evaluations (Sample)

Answer the following questions, and be sure to *explain* your answers.

1. How did your reading circle work at this meeting?

_____

_____

_____

2. Was everyone in your reading circle prepared? Did everyone do his or her role assignments?

_____

_____

_____

3. Did you participate constructively in the group? Did you talk enough? Did you talk too much?

_____

_____

_____

4. Did everyone participate in the discussion? Were quiet students encouraged to speak up?

_____

_____

_____

5. What can you do to improve how your group functions?

_____

_____

_____

6. What can the instructor do to improve how your group functions?

_____

_____

_____

8. POSTER SESSIONS

A poster session allows you to make a presentation in a comfortable environment that encourages the "listeners" to be active. Poster sessions can be used for book reports or other reading projects that you do independently.

Your instructor will set aside at least one day for poster sessions. Each student will prepare a poster and an oral presentation. At the beginning of class, about one-third or one-half of the students (depending on the class size and time available) will set up their posters around the room. The other students and your instructor will circulate around the room, visiting each presenter.

For your presentation, you will give a prepared talk (usually 3 to 5 minutes) about the book or reading for which you prepared the poster. During your talk, you will refer to various parts of the poster as a visual aid for your oral presentation. Your classmates will ask you questions, and a lively interchange of ideas will probably take place.

Students observing your presentation will fill out an evaluation sheet and move on to the next presentation until they've seen them all. Then another group of students will set up their posters, and the process will continue until all students make their presentations.

The following guidelines will help you make your poster presentation a success.

Preparing Your Topic

To make a presentation about an article, research you have done, or a book you have read, follow these steps:

1. Complete your reading carefully, giving yourself enough time to finish your reading and research well in advance. Allow several days to prepare the entire poster session.
2. Decide on the most important points or information you want to share with your audience. Remember, you have a limited amount of time. If you are presenting a book you have read, you need to distill the story or information to make it understandable for your listeners. You may be able to prepare a brief summary or just give some highlights.
3. Make an outline of what you want to "say."
4. Think about the best way to put what you want to "say" in a visual format.

Preparing Your Poster

Content   When you know what you want to "say" in the poster, you need to decide how to handle its three major components.

©2007 Pearson Education, Inc.

1. *Title.* Decide on a title that is catchy and will attract the attention of your audience as well as accurately represent the information in your poster. If your poster is about a book you have read, the title of the book with the author's name is satisfactory.
2. *Visual elements.* Remember, your poster is above all supposed to explain your information *visually*, so decide what the visual aids will be. They can include graphs, charts, maps, photos, or art.
3. *Text.* Decide what written information you want to include on your poster. Keep the amount of text very small because your audience will not have time to read a lot of information on your poster. Their role is to listen to your presentation and look at the poster to better understand what you say.

   Remember! This is *your* poster project. Everything you write on your poster must be *your own ideas and your own words.* If you use *anything* written by somebody else, you *must* give credit to the author and use quotation marks.

Visual Appearance

1. *Neatness.* Make your poster neat to demonstrate the thought and care you put into it.
2. *Visibility.* Everything on your poster should be large enough for observers to see 4 to 8 feet away.
3. *Organization.* Think about how people will be looking at your poster. Do you need arrows to show cause-and-effect relationships or to direct people's eyes as they look at your poster? Do you need to number its various parts?
4. *Lettering and written text.* Here you have a choice. Some people can write the title very well by hand, but if you use a computer, follow these suggestions:
   a. Use only one font style for your poster. A standard font like Times or Times New Roman is best.
   b. Make the title a very large font (at least 72 points). The subtitles can be smaller (36 points). Any other text can be smaller, but still should be easy to read (14 to 18 point).
5. *Color.* Using color will improve the visual impact. Some experts recommend that light items be mounted on darker contrasting colors and dark items be mounted on lighter paper. Leave a border of ¼ to 1 inch around any artwork or text.
6. *Sources.* If you get any visual aids from the Internet or from a published book, be sure to provide the name of the Web site or the title and author of the book at the bottom of the visual aid itself. For this you can use a small font.

Preparing Your Oral Presentation

1. Decide what you want to say. Organize your presentation into three sections:
   a. A brief *introduction,* in which you explain the purpose of your presentation and get your audience's attention.
   b. A *body* in which you make the points that you have decided are most important for others to know about your book, reading, or research.
   c. A *conclusion,* in which you sum up what you have said, with a recommendation about the topic or book you are presenting.
2. Make notes on 3 × 5 cards or on a piece of paper so you can remember what you want to say.
3. Practice your presentation by delivering your talk just as if students were listening to you. (It's a good idea to get a friend to listen to your presentation.)
   a. Time yourself. You don't want to be too long or too brief. Be sure you stay within the time limits that your instructor gives you.
   b. Remember to refer to your poster. You want your listeners to look at the poster for at least part of the time during your presentation. You also want them to understand the relation between the poster and your talk.

Giving Your Presentation

1. Be on time, and be prepared.
2. Dress appropriately.
3. Make eye contact.
4. Speak clearly and slowly enough so people can easily understand you. Speak loudly enough so people can hear you.
5. Finally, be enthusiastic about your subject.

©2007 Pearson Education, Inc.

Poster Session Peer Evaluations

Name of the Presenter: _____

Title of the Presentation: _____

Poster

   1. What I liked best:

     _____

     _____

     _____

     _____

   2. Suggestions for improvement:

     _____

     _____

     _____

     _____

Oral Presentation

   1. What I liked best:

     _____

     _____

     _____

     _____

   2. Suggestions for improvement:

     _____

     _____

     _____

     _____

How Poster Sessions Are Graded

These are the things your instructor will consider in grading your poster presentation.

1. Reading assignment
   a. Completeness
   b. Evidence that you've read and understood the assignment (the entire book or all the articles)
   c. Evidence that you've done the appropriate research
2. Poster
   a. Thoughtfulness
   b. Illustration helpful for oral presentation
   c. Neatness
   d. Creativity
   e. Appropriate size of art and lettering
   f. Clarity
3. Oral presentation
   a. Evidence of preparation and practice
   b. Good organization and appropriate level of information
   c. Within the time limit
   d. Good eye contact
   e. Clear speech, appropriate speed of speech
   f. Good use of poster to support points

©2007 Pearson Education, Inc.

SUGGESTED READING FOR BOOK REPORTS

Increasing your reading skills as quickly as possible requires considerable practice. Many teachers assign an extra book for students to read and discuss along with their text. This section lists books that relate to the themes presented in this textbook, and other books in the list were chosen by students and teachers. You have already read excerpts from some of the books as you completed your work in this textbook. The list includes books of various lengths and levels of difficulty. After each author and title is a short description of the book.

Achebe, Chinua. *Things Fall Apart.* The acclaimed first novel by Achebe tells the story of Okonkwo, an Ibo tribesman in Nigeria, before and after the coming of colonialism.

Alvarez, Julia. *How the García Girls Lost Their Accents.* Yolanda and her three sisters tell their family's story after they immigrated from the Dominican Republic to the United States.

Anaya, Rudolfo. *Bless Me Última.* Now a classic, this Chicano coming-of-age novel tells of a young boy who faces the conflicts in his life with the help of Última, a magic healer.

Baldacci, David. *Wish You Well.* This legal thriller, set in rural Appalachia, is a coming-of-age novel dealing with the struggles of the people of Appalachia during the Great Depression.

Bortner, M. A., and Linda M. Williams. *Youth in Prison: We the People of Unit Four.* This book deals with crime, youth, drugs, schools, gangs, and violence by looking at the lives of young people before, during, and after their incarceration.

Brooks, Geraldine. *Year of Wonders: A Novel of the Plague.* A housemaid tells the story of the struggles of villagers in England in 1666 as they quarantine themselves to avoid spreading the plague that has stricken their village when it is transmitted by a bolt of cloth.

Brumbert, Joan Jacobs. *The Body Project: An Intimate History of American Girls.* This book explores the issues of appearance for teenage girls and how insecurity is exploited for profit.

Butler, Octavia. *Kindred.* In this story of time travel, a woman from the twentieth century is repeatedly pulled back in time by her slave-owning ancestor, Rufus, when his life is endangered. She chooses to save him because she discovers that one of his slaves will eventually become her grandmother.

Butler, Octavia. *Parable of the Sower.* This science fiction tale is about a teenage girl's life in a barricaded village in Southern California amid the rapid socioeconomic decay of the early twenty-first century.

Canada, Geoffrey. *Fist Stick Knife Gun.* The author tells his own story of growing up in a violent South Bronx neighborhood. Canada has spent most of his life working with young people and communities at risk.

Carter, Jimmy, and Rosalynn Carter. *Everything to Gain: Making the Most of the Rest of Your Life.* The former president and first lady describe their post–White House careers, including their volunteer work with Habitat for Humanity.

Chevalier, Tracy. *Girl with a Pearl Earring.* A servant girl in the household of the great Dutch painter Vermeer tells her story of growing up in the rigid class and gender structure of seventeenth-century Holland. At the same time, the story explores the gift of artistic vision.

Cisneros, Sandra. *The House on Mango Street.* This book describes Esperanza's childhood among family, friends, and neighbors in a Spanish-speaking neighborhood of Chicago.

Cofer, Judy Ortiz. *The Latin Deli.* An anthology of short stories about Puerto Rican life in New Jersey by an important contemporary writer.

Conway, Jill Ker. *The Road from Coorain: An Autobiography.* Conway describes her life from her childhood in Australia until the age of 23, when she leaves home for graduate school at Harvard University.

Cook, Robin. *Contagion.* Cook's novel is a medical thriller about three extremely rare diseases that start killing patients at a New York hospital. A pathologist suspects that the deaths may have been caused deliberately.

Courtenay, Bryce. *Power of One.* This is the moving story of struggle and triumph of an orphaned boy of English descent growing up in racially and ethnically torn South Africa.

Cousins, Norman. *Anatomy of an Illness.* Faced with a life-threatening illness and long hospital stay, respected journalist and editor Norman Cousins figures out ways to use humor and creativity to regain his health.

Dangarembga, Tsitsi. *Nervous Conditions.* Tambu, a young African, faces oppression as a woman in her native Zimbabwe and in the colonial British school where she seeks an education.

Ehrenreich, Barbara. *Nickel and Dimed.* Essayist and cultural critic Ehrenreich sets out to determine if it's possible to support herself as an unskilled worker. She recounts her experiences with jobs in restaurants, retail stores, and hotels in different parts of the country.

Esquivel, Laura. *Like Water for Chocolate.* Esquivel's popular novel intersperses recipes with a story of thwarted love in Mexico at the beginning of the twentieth century.

Ferris, Susan, Ricardo Sandoval, and Diana Hembree. *The Fight in the Fields: César Chavez and the Farmworkers' Movement.* This book is the story of César Chavez and the many farmworkers—often, but not always, immigrants—who organized a struggle for decent wages and working conditions for the people working to bring food to our tables.

Grealy, Lucy. *Autobiography of a Face.* At age 9, Lucy Grealy had a third of her jaw removed because of bone cancer. She then underwent years of treatment and operations, as well as cruel taunts from her classmates because of her appearance.

Haley, Alex. *The Autobiography of Malcom X.* Based on a series of interviews the author did with Malcolm X, this book relates the story of Malcolm's childhood, youth, trouble with the law, and conversion to Islam.

©2007 Pearson Education, Inc.

Hayden, Torey. *Murphy's Boy*. Hayden tells the moving story of a young boy who must struggle to overcome his disabilities.

Hillerman, Tony. *Talking God*. This suspenseful story of a grave robber and a corpse features Officer Jim Chee, who solves the mystery surrounding the two.

Houston, Jeanne Wakatsuki. *Farewell to Manzanar*. This is a true story of one spirited Japanese-American family's survival of the indignities of forced detention at Manzanar interment camp during World War II.

Johnson, Louanne. *Dangerous Minds*. A female ex-Marine teaches a class of inner-city high school students about self-respect, courage, and success.

Jordan, Barbara. *Barbara Jordan: A Self-Portrait*. In her memoir, Barbara Jordan tells how she broke down barriers of race and gender to become a successful lawyer and politician and one of the ten most influential women in Texas.

Keller, Helen. *The Story of My Life*. Helen Keller became deaf and blind at 19 months due to scarlet fever. She learned to read (in several languages) and even speak, eventually graduating with honors from Radcliffe College in 1904. She wrote this autobiography while she was a student.

Keyes, Daniel. *Flowers for Algernon*. This science fiction novel tells the story of a semiliterate young man with a limited IQ who undergoes experimental brain surgery and becomes a genius.

Kingsolver, Barbara. *The Bean Trees*. Kingsolver's novel tells the story of a spirited young woman who grew up poor in rural Kentucky and headed West to escape. It is a story of love and friendship, abandonment and belonging.

Kotlowitz, Alex. *The Other Side of the River: A Story of Two Towns, a Death, and America's Dilemma*. Exploring how two towns—one mostly black, the other white—react to the death of an African American teenaged boy, Kotlowitz reveals a deep understanding of the racial divide in this country.

Kotlowitz, Alex. *There Are No Children Living Here*. The true story of brothers faced with the horrors of growing up in a Chicago public housing project.

Martel, Yann. *The Life of Pi*. This is the story of how a boy, stranded on a lifeboat with a tiger, crosses the Pacific Ocean—facing storms, hunger, and all manner of disasters. In the end, he actually becomes comfortable with himself, the tiger, and the ocean.

McBride, James. *The Color of Water*. A black man, McBride tells the story of his white mother's remarkable battle against racism and poverty to raise 12 children.

Meléndez, Mickey (Miguel). *We Took the Streets: Fighting for Latino Rights with the Young Lords*. Meléndez tells the story of the Young Lords, a mostly Puerto Rican group of militant activists who, in the 1960s and 1970s, dedicated themselves to fighting for social and political justice of the Latino community in the Bronx and Harlem.

Mohr, Nicholasa. *In Nueva York.* This book is a collection of stories of New York's Puerto Rican immigrants growing up in the South Bronx from 1946 to 1956.

Morrison, Toni. *The Bluest Eye.* This is the story of an 11-year-old black girl who is abused by her father. Because of the difficult conditions of her life, she yearns to be her exact opposite: a blonde, blue-eyed white girl.

Mueller, Rudolph. *As Sick As It Gets.* In this accessible book, Mueller describes the problems of the medical system in the United States and offers his own solutions to the medical crisis.

Obama, Barack. *Dreams from My Father: A Story of Race and Inheritance.* Obama, currently a senator from Illinois, deals with his childhood experiences as well as his experiences as a young adult. It explores in detail what it's like to be a mixed-race child: his father was African, his mother white American.

Rodriguez, Luis. *Always Running: La Vida Loca: Gang Days in LA.* This book explores the motivation of gang life and cautions against the death and destruction that inevitably claim its participants. Rodriguez himself is a veteran of East L.A. gang warfare, but he successfully broke free and became an award-winning Chicano poet.

Santiago, Esmeralda. *When I Was Puerto Rican.* Essentially autobiographical, this book recounts the struggles of a teenage girl whose family moves to New York from Puerto Rico when she is 14 years old, her determination to succeed against the odds in her new environment, and her successes.

Schlosser, Eric. *Fast Food Nation.* Investigative reporter Schlosser relates the story behind the fast-food industry: the history, the raw materials (potatoes and cattle), the processing, the food, the workers, the problems, and some of the consequences—cultural, environmental, and economic—of the global popularity of fast food.

Tan, Amy. *The Joy Luck Club.* Four mothers and four daughters tell their family stories as Chinese immigrants living in San Francisco.

Tannen, Deborah. *You Just Don't Understand: Women and Men in Conversation.* In this book, Tannen explains the different conversational styles of women and men and some of the problems of misunderstanding that these styles create.

Viramontes, Helena María. *Under the Feet of Jesus.* This novel tells about the dangers and challenges Estrella and her Mexican-American migrant family face during a summer working in the fields.

Villasenor, Victor. *Macho.* Roberto García, a 17-year-old Mexican, crosses the border into California, where he experiences considerable culture shock and comes of age.

Waitley, Denis. *The Psychology of Winning.* Waitley is one of this country's best-known and respected motivational psychologists. In this book, he emphasizes that being a winner is an attitude, a way of life, a self-concept.

©2007 Pearson Education, Inc.

Weisel, Eli. *Night.* A Jewish teenager struggles with the guilt he feels at surviving the Holocaust in which the rest of his family died. Although fictional, the story strongly parallels Weisel's experiences in the death camps.

Welch, James. *Winter in the Blood.* This novel is about a young Native American in Montana coming to terms with his heritage and his dreams.

YenMah, Adeline. *Falling Leaves.* The author tells her own story of growing up in China, where she suffers nonstop emotional abuse from her wealthy father and his cruel second wife. She escapes to America, where she begins a medical career and enters a happy marriage.

BIBLIOGRAPHY

Ahmed, Yasmin, "Identity in Transformation." Written for *A Community of Readers.*

"AIDS: The Long War." *The Economist,* July 13–19, 2002, 16.

American Heritage Talking Dictionary. CD-ROM, version 3.0. Softkey, 1998.

American Heritage Dictionary of the English Language: New College Edition. Boston: Houghton Mifflin, 1979.

Angelou, Maya. *Wouldn't Take Nothing for My Journey Now.* New York: Random House, 1993.

"Although I Conquer All the Earth." In *Poems from the Sanskrit.* Translated by John Brough. Harmondsworth, UK: Penguin Classics, 1968.

Barlow, Hugh D., and David Kauzlarich. *Introduction to Criminology.* Upper Saddle River, NJ: Prentice Hall, 2001.

Baron, Robert A. *Psychology: Course Compass Edition.* 5th ed. Boston: Allyn and Bacon, 2001.

Beekman, George. *Computer Confluence: Exploring Tomorrow's Technology.* 4th ed. Upper Saddle River, NJ: Prentice Hall, 2001.

—*Computer Confluence: Exploring Tomorrow's Technology.* 6th ed. Upper Saddle River, NJ: Prentice Hall, 2005.

Brady, Judy. "Why I Want a Wife." *Ms.,* December 1971.

Brunn, Stanley D., and Jack F. Williams. *Cities of the World.* New York: HarperCollins, 1993.

Burns, Robert. "My Luve Is Like a Red, Red Rose." In *English Romantic Poetry and Prose.* Edited by Russell Noyes. New York: Oxford University Press, 1956.

Byer, Curtis, and Louis Shainberg. *Living Well: Health in Your Hands.* 2nd ed. New York: HarperCollins, 1995.

Campbell, Neil A., Lawrence G. Mitchell, and Jane B. Reece. *Biology: Concepts and Connections.* 3rd ed. San Francisco: Addison Wesley Longman, 2000.

—*Biology: Concepts and Connections.* 4th ed. San Francisco: Benjamin Cummins, 2003.

Capron, H. L. *Computers: Tools for an Information Age.* 5th ed. Reading, MA: Addison Wesley Longman, 1998.

Carter, Jimmy, and Rosalynn Carter. *Everything to Gain.* New York: Random House, 1987.

Coleman, James W., and Donald R. Cressey. *Social Problems.* New York: Addison Wesley, 1999.

Conlin, Joseph Robert. *American Past.* San Diego, CA: Harcourt Brace Jovanovich, 1991.

Cousins, Norman. *Anatomy of an Illness.* New York: Norton, 1979.

Cunningham, Jesse. "Use the Tools for College Success!" Written for *A Community of Readers.*

Daniels, Harvey. *Literature Circles: Voice and Choice in the Student-Centered Classroom.* Portland, ME: Stenhouse Publishers, 1994.

Dávalos, Enrique. "Tijuana and San Diego: Contrasting Neighbors." Written for *A Community of Readers.*

Davidson, James West, Christine Leigh Heyrman, Mark H. Lytle, Michael B. Stoff, and William E. Gienapp. *Nation of Nations: A Narrative History of the American Republic.* Vol. 2, *Since 1865.* 4th ed. Boston: McGraw-Hill, 2001.

Divine, Robert A., T. H. Breen, George M. Fredrickson, R. Hal Williams, *America, Past and Present.* 7th ed. New York: Longman, 2002.

Donatelle, Rebecca. *Access to Health.* 7th ed. San Francisco: Benjamin Cummings, 2001.

Edwards, George C., Martin P. Wattenberg, and Robert L. Lineberry. *Government in America.* Brief 4th ed. New York: Addison Wesley Longman, 1999.

Espada, Martín. "The Puerto Rican Dummy and the Merciful Son" (original title of "Rage"). In *Muy Macho: Latino Men Confront Their Manhood.* Edited by Ray González. New York: Anchor, 1996.

Eudy, Heather. "Gated Developments: Fortresses or Communities?" Written for *A Community of Readers.*

—"Signing for a Revolution: Gallaudet University and Deaf Culture." Written for *A Community of Readers.*

©2007 Pearson Education, Inc.

Ferrante, Joan. *Sociology: A Global Perspective*. 5th ed. Belmont, CA: Thomson/Wadsworth, 2003.

Frammolino, Ralph. "Workers Feel Like Suckers." *Los Angeles Times*, March 20, 2002.

Garland, Hamlin. "Up the Coulé." In *The Heath Anthology of American Literature*. Vol. 2. 3rd ed. Edited by Paul Lauter. Boston: Houghton Mifflin, 1998.

Garrett, Rachel M. "Reading the Labels." Written for *A Community of Readers*.

Gómez, Magdalena. "Chocolate Confessions." In *Puerto Rican Writers at Home in the USA: An Anthology*. Edited by Faythe Turner. Seattle, WA: Open Hand, 1991.

Greenberg, Edward S., and Benjamin I. Page. *The Struggle for Democracy*. 4th ed. New York: Addison Wesley Longman, 1999.

Gregory, Dick, with Robert Lipsyte. *Nigger: An Autobiography*. New York: Dutton, 1964.

Hales, Dianne. *An Invitation to Health*. 8th ed. Pacific Grove, CA: Brooks/Cole, 1999.

Haring-Smith, Toni. *Writing Together: Collaborative Learning in the Writing Classroom*. New York: HarperCollins, 1994.

Henslin, James M. *Sociology: A Down-to-Earth Approach*. 7th ed. Boston: Pearson, 2005.

Hicks, David, and Margaret A. Gwynne. *Cultural Anthropology*. New York: HarperCollins, 1996.

Horton, James Oliver, and Lois E. Horton. *Hard Road to Freedom*. New Brunswick, NJ: Rutgers University Press, 2001.

Hursel, Paul. "Food Pyramids: For Profit or Health?" Written for *A Community of Readers*.

Huynh, Christine. "Corrections." Unpublished MS, 2002.

Insel, Paul M., Walton T. Roth, L. McKay Rollins, and Ray A. Peterson. *Core Concepts in Health*. Brief 8th ed. Mountain View, CA: Mayfield, 1998.

Johnson, Khalid. "Peppers." Unpublished MS, 2005.

Jordan, Barbara, and Shelby Hearon. *Barbara Jordan: A Self-Portrait*. Garden City, NY: Doubleday, 1978.

Jordan-Bychkov, Terry G., and Mona Domosh. *Human Mosaic*. 8th ed. New York: Addison Wesley Longman, 1999.

Kotlowitz, Alex. "Colorblind: How Can You Have a Dialogue about Race When Blacks and Whites Can See No Gray?" In *Dialogues: An Argument Rhetoric and Reader*. Edited by Gary Goshgarian, Kathleen Krueger, and Janet Barnett Minc. 3rd ed. New York: Addison Wesley Longman, 2000.

Kotulak, Ronald. "Cyberthought." *Chicago Tribune*, February 16, 2005.

Linksman, Ricki. *How to Learn Anything Quickly*. Secaucus, NJ: Carol Publishing Group, 1997.

Lyman, Howard F., with Glen Merzer. *Mad Cowboy*. New York: Touchstone, 1998.

Ma, Lora Elise. "How Stressed Out Are You?" *Health*, October 1994, 47–48.

Macionis, John J. *Sociology*. 9th ed. Upper Saddle River, NJ: Prentice Hall, 2003.

Martin, James K., Randy Roberts, Steven Mintz, Linda O. McMurry, and James H. Jones. *America and its Peoples: A Mosaic in the Making*. 3rd ed. New York: Addison Wesley Longman, 1997.

Martínez, Al. "Can We All Get Along?" *California Journal*, January 1998.

Mayhew, Kelly. "Easy Bake Ovens and Fashion Magazines: Women's Complex Relationships to Food and Eating." Written for *A Community of Readers*.

McBroom, Amanda. "The Rose." Warner Brothers, 1977.

McDermott, Beverly. "Third Gender." Written for *A Community of Readers*.

McKay, John P., Bennett D. Hill, and John Buckler. *A History of World Societies*. 2nd ed. Boston: Houghton Mifflin, 1988.

Meyer, Ruby Lynn. "Dust Bowl Days." Unpublished MS, 2005.

Mintz, Sidney W. "Pleasure, Profit, and Satiation." In *Seeds of Change*. Edited by Herman J. Viola and Carolyn Margolis. Washington, DC: Smithsonian Institution Press, 1991.

Mooney, Pat. "Making Well People 'Better.'" *World Watch*, July/August 2002, 13–16, 43.

Moravia, Alberto. "The Chase." In *Command and I Will Obey You*. Translated by Angus Davidson. New York: Farrar, Straus and Giroux, 1969.

Morgan, Robert. "Shaking." In *Men of Our Time: An Anthology of Male Poetry in Contemporary America*. Edited by Frank Moramarco and Al Zolynas. Athens: University of Georgia Press, 1992.

Mueller, Rudolph. *As Sick As It Gets*. Dunkirk, NY: Olin Frederick, 2001.

Murrin, John M., Paul E. Johnson, James M. McPherson, Gary Gerstle, Emily S. Rosenberg, and Norman L. Rosenberg. *Liberty, Equality, Power: A History of the American People.* 2nd ed. Fort Worth, TX: Harcourt Brace, 1999.

Nader, Ralph. "The Nader Page." *The Nader Letter.* http://www.nader.org/ nader_letter.

Nash, Gary B., Julie Roy Jeffrey, John R. Howe, Peter J. Frederick, Allen F. Davis, and Allan M. Winkler. *The American People: Creating a Nation and a Society.* 4th ed. New York: Addison Wesley Longman, 1998.

National Coalition for the Homeless. "Why Are People Homeless?" NCH Fact Sheet 1. September, 2002. http://www.nationalhomeless.org/ causes.html.

Oppenheimer, James. "Bread and Roses." http://www.hartford-hwp.com/archives/26/141.html.

Peifer, Marley. "Suburb High, USA: School or Prison?" Written for *A Community of Readers.*

Perry, John, and Erna Perry. *Contemporary Society.* New York: Addison Wesley Longman, 1994.

Roberts, Paul. "How Americans Eat: The New Food Anxiety." *Psychology Today,* March/April 1998.

Sanders, Scott Russell. "The Men We Carry in Our Minds." In *Crossfire: An Argument Rhetoric and Reader.* Edited by Gary Goshgarian and Kathleen Krueger. New York: Longman, 1997.

Schlosser, Eric. *Fast Food Nation.* Boston: Houghton Mifflin, 2001.

Schnetzer, Amanda Watson, "The World in a Grain of Salt: A Review of *Salt* by Mark Kurlansky." *Insight on the News,* March 11, 2002.

Spadaccina, Jim. "The Sweet Lure of Chocolate." Exploring Online. http://www.exploratorium.edu/exploring/exploring_chocolate/choc_8.html.

Staples, Brent. "Just Walk on By." *Ms.,* September 1986.

Stearns, Peter N., Michael Adas, and Stuart B. Schwartz. *World Civilizations: The Global Experience.* New York: Harper Collins, 1992.

Tannen, Deborah. "Sex, Lies, and Conversation." In *Essays from Contemporary Culture.* 3rd ed. Edited by Katherine Anne Ackley. Fort Worth, TX: Harcourt Brace, 1998.

Tarkan, Laurie. "Families That Dine Together Reap Benefits." *New York Times,* May 9, 2005.

Tavris, Carol. "Love Story." In *Essays from Contemporary Culture.* 3rd ed. Edited by Katherine Anne Ackley. Fort Worth, TX: Harcourt Brace, 1998.

Thio, Alex. *Sociology: A Brief Introduction.* 6th ed. Boston: Pearson, 2005.

Thompson, William E., and Joseph V. Hickey. *Society in Focus: An Introduction to Sociology.* 4th ed. Boston: Allyn and Bacon, 2002.

Tuan, Yi-Fu. "American Space, Chinese Place." *Harper's,* July 1974.

Tuchman, Barbara. *A Distant Mirror: The Calamitous Fourteenth Century.* New York: Random House, 1978.

Twain, Mark. "The War Prayer" (1905). In *Heath Anthology of American Literature.* 2nd ed. Edited by Paul Lauter. Lexington, MA: D. C. Heath, 1994.

U.S. Census Bureau. Income, Poverty, and Health Insurance coverage in the United States, 2003. http://www.census.gov/prod/2004pubs/p60-226.pdf (accessed September 20, 2005).

U.S. Department of Health and Human Services. *A Systematic Approach to Health Improvement: Healthy People 2010 Goals.* http://www.health.gov/healthypeople/Document/html/uih/uih_2.htm#goals.

U.S. Department of Housing and Urban Development. *The State of the Cities, 1999.* Washington, DC: U.S. Department of Housing and Urban Development, June 1999.

Wade, Carole, and Carol Tavris. *Invitation to Psychology.* New York: Addison Wesley Longman, 1999.

Wade, Carole, and Carol Tavris. *Psychology.* New York: Addison Wesley Longman, 1998.

Watnick, Gail. "Triangular Tube of Pink Lipstick." In *Race, Class, and Gender in the United States: An Integrated Study.* 4th ed. Edited by Paula S. Rothenberg. New York: St. Martin's Press, 1998.

Watson, David. "We All Live in Bhopal." In *Business as Ethical and Business as Usual: Text, Readings, and Cases.* Edited by Sterling Harwood. Boston: Jones and Bartlett, 1996.

Weiner, Tim. "A New Model Army Soldier Rolls Closer to the Battlefield." *New York Times,* February 2005.

Williams, Bryan, and Sharon Knight. *Healthy for Life: Wellness and the Art of Living.* Pacific Grove, CA: Brooks/Cole, 1994.

Wong, Kevin. "The Runt." Unpublished MS, 2005.

©2007 Pearson Education, Inc.

TEXT CREDITS

Yasmin Ahmed. "Identity in Transformation" by Yasmin Ahmed. Reprinted with permission.

Hugh Barlow and David Kauzlarich. *Introduction to Criminology*, 8th Edtion, Copyright © 2002, pp. 116, 132-134. Reprinted by permission of Pearson Education, Inc., Upper Saddle River, NJ.

Robert A. Baron. "Eating Disorders" from *Psychology, Course Compass Edition, 5E* by Robert A. Baron. Published by Allyn and Bacon, Boston, MA. Copyright © 2001 by Pearson Education. Reprinted by permission of the publisher.

George Beekman. *Computer Confluence Comprehensive Edition*, Sixth Edition, Copyright © 2005. Reprinted by permission of Pearson Education, Inc., Upper Saddle River, NJ.

George Beekman. *Computer Confluence: Exploring Tomorrow's Technology*, Fourth Edition, Copyright © 2001. Reprinted by permission of Pearson Education, Inc., Upper Saddle River, NJ.

George Beekman. *Computer Confluence*, Stand Alone Version, ® 1999 Addison Wesley Longman, Inc. Reprinted by permission of Pearson Education, Inc. Publishing as Pearson Addison Wesley.

Judy Brady. "Why I Want a Wife" by Judy Brady as appeared in *Ms. Magazine*. Copyright © 1970 by Judy Brady.

Stanley D. Brunn and Jack F. Williams. *Cities of the World: World Regional Urban Development, 2E*, Copyright © 2003.

New York: HarperCollins Publishers.

Curtis O. Byer and Louis W. Shainberg. *Living Well, Health in Your Hands*, Copyright © 1995. New York: HarperCollins Publishers.

Neil A. Campbell, et. al. "Plant Autotrophs" and excerpts from *Biology: Concepts and Connections*, Third Edition by Neil A. Campbell, Jane B. Reese, and Lawrence G. Mitchell, Copyright © 1997. Reprinted by permission of Pearson Education, Inc.

Neil A. Campbell, et. al. "The Hypothesis-driven scientific method-Figure 1.3A" from *Biology: Concepts and Connections*, Fourth Ed. by Campbell, Reese, and Mitchell.

H.L. Capron. *Computers: Tools for an Information Age, 5E* by H.L. Capron, pp. 26 and 239, Copyright © 1998 Addison Wesley Longman. Reprinted by permission of Pearson Education, Inc.

Jimmy Carter. "Working with Our Hands" by Jimmy Carter from *Everything to Gain*. Reprinted by permission of the University of Arkansas Press. Copyright © 1995 by Jimmy Carter.

James William Coleman and Donald R. Cressey. From *Social Problems* by Coleman/ Cressey, Copyright © 1998. Reprinted by permission of Prentice-Hall, Inc. Upper Saddle River, NJ.

Norman Cousins. From *Anatomy of an Illness as Perceived by the Patient: Reflections on Healing and Regeneration* by Norman Cousins. Copyright © 1979 by W. W. Norton & Com-

pany, Inc. Used by permission of W. W. Norton & Company, Inc.

Jesse Cunningham. "Use the Tools for College Success!" by Jesse Cunningham. Reprinted with permission.

Divine, et. al. From "Toward an Urban Society, 1877-1900, pp. 549-550 from *America, Past and Present*, Sixth Edition, by Divine, etal. Copyright © 2002 Addison Wesley Longman. Reprinted by Pearson Education, Inc.

Rebecca Donatelle. "Calcium" from *Access to Health*, 7th Edition, by Rebecca Donatelle. Copyright © 2002 Pearson Education, Inc. publishing as Benjamin Cummings. Reprinted by permission of Pearson Education, Inc.

Rebecca Donatelle. "Self-Esteem" from *Access to Health*, 7th Edition, by Rebecca Donatelle. Copyright © 2002 Pearson Education, Inc. publishing as Benjamin Cummings. Reprinted by permission of Pearson Education, Inc.

Martín Espada. From *The Puerto Rican Dummy and the Merciful Son* by Marín Espada. Copyright © 1998 by Martín Espada. Reprinted by permission of the author.

Heather Eudy. "Gated Developments: Fortresses or Communities" by Heather Eudy. Reprinted with permission.

Heather Eudy. "Signing for a Revolution: Gallaudet University and Deaf Culture" by Heather Eudy. Used with permission of the author.

Joan Ferrante. "Corn", and excerpts from *Sociology: A Global Perspective*, 5th Edition by Joan Ferrante. Copyright © 2003.

Thomson/Wadsworth. Reprinted by permission.

Ralph Frammolino. From "Workers Feel Like Suckers" by Ralph Frammolino, *Los Angeles Times*, March 20, 2002. Reprinted by permission of TMS Reprints.

Hamlin Garland. "Up the Coule" from *The Health Anthology of American Literature, Vol. 2*, 3rd Edition, edited by Paul Lauter. Copyright © 1998 Houghton Mifflin Company. Reprinted by permission.

Rachel Garrett. From "Reading the Labels" by Rachel Garrett. Used by permission.

Magdalena Gomez. Excerpt from "Chocolate Confessions" by Magdalena Gomez as appeared in *Puerto Rican Writers At Home in the USA*. Reprinted by permission of the author.

Edward S. Greenberg and Benjamin I. Page. *The Struggle for Democracy*, Copyright © 1997. New York: Longman, 1997.

Dick Gregory. "Shame" from *Nigger: An Autobiography* by Dick Gregory. Copyright © 1964 by Dick Gregory Enterprises, Inc. Used by permission of Dutton, a division of Penguin Group (USA) Inc.

Dianne Hales. *From An Invitation to Health (with InfoTrac), Eighth Edition*, by Dianne Hales, Copyright © 1999. Reprinted with permission of Brooks/Cole, a division of Thomson Learning: http://www.thomsonrights.com. Fax 800-730-2215.

Toni Haring-Smith. From *Writing Together: Collaborative Learning in the Writing Classroom* by Toni Haring-Smith. Copyright © 1994 Addison Wesley Longman. Reprinted by permission of Pearson Education, Inc.

Gardiner Harris and Eric Koli. "Lucrative Drug, Danger Signals and the F.D.A." by Gardiner Harris and Eric Koli. Copyright © 2005 by The New York Times Co. Reprinted with permission.

Shelby Hearon and Barbara Jordan. Excerpt from *Barbara Jordan: A Self Portrait* by Shelby Hearon and Barbara Jordan. Reprinted by permission of The Wendy Weil Agency, Inc. First published by Doubleday & Co., Inc. Copyright © 1978, 1979 by Barbara Jordan and Shelby Hearon.

James M. Henslin. Excerpts from *Sociology: A Down to Earth Approach,* Seventh Edition, James M. Henslin.

Christine Huynh. "Corrections" by Christine Huynh. Copyright © 2001 by Christine Huynh. Reprinted by permission.

Paul M. Insel and Walton T. Roth. From *Core Concepts in Health*, Ninth Edition by P. Insel and W. Roth, Copyright © 2002. Reprinted by permission of The McGraw-Hill Companies.

Terry G. Jordan-Bychkov and Mona Domosh. From *The Human Mosaic: A Thematic Introduction to Cultural Geography*, by Terry G. Jordan- Bychkov and Mona Domosh. Copyright © 2003 by W. H. Freeman and Company. Used with permission.

Robert D. Kaplan. From *An Empire's Wilderness: Travels into America's Future* by Robert D. Kaplan. Reprinted by permission of Random House, Inc.

Alex Kotiowitz. "Colorblind: How Can You Have A Dialogue about Race When Blacks and Whites Can See No Gray?" by Alex Kotiowitz, *New York Times Magazine*. Copyright © 1998, Alex Kotiowitz. Reprinted by permission.

Ronald Kotulak. "Cyberthought" by Ronald Kotulak, *The Chicago Tribune*. March 2004.

Robert Lineberry. *Government in America*, Copyright © 1994. New York: HarperCollins Publishers.

Ricki Linksman. From *How to Learn Anything Quickly* by Ricki Linksman. Copyright © 1997 by Ricki Linksman. Reprinted by permission of Citadel Press. All Rights Reserved.

Howard F. Lyman. Reprinted with the permission of Scribner, an imprint of Simon & Schuster Adult Publishing Group, from *Mad Cowboy* by Howard Lyman with Glen Merzer. Copyright © 1998 by Howard Lyman and Glen Merzer.

Lora Elise Ma. "How Stressed out Are You?" by Lora Elise Ma, *Health*, October 1994. Reprinted by permission.

John J. Macionis. *Sociology*, Ninth Edition, Copyright © 2003, pp. 552-553. Reprinted by permission of Pearson Education, Inc., Upper Saddle River, NJ.

Al Martinez. "Can We All Get Along" by Al Martinez from *California Journal*, January 1998. Reprinted with permission of California Journal Magazine.

Kelly Mayhew. "Easy Bake Ovens and Fashion Magazines" by Kelly Mayhew. Reprinted by permission.

Amanda McBroom. "The Rose" by Amanda McBroom, Copyright © 1977 (Renewed) Warner-Tamerlane Publishing Corp. (BMI) and Third Story Music, Inc. (ASCAP). All rights administered by Warner-Tamerland Publishing Corp. All Rights Reserved. Used by permission of Warner Bros. Publications U.S., Inc., Miami, FL 33014.

©2007 by Pearson Education, Inc.

John P. McKay, Bennett D. Hill, and John Buckler. *A History of World Societies*, Second Edition. Copyright © 1988 by Houghton Mifflin Company. Reprinted with permission.

Pat Mooney. From "Making Well People Better" by Pat Mooney, *World Watch Magazine*, Vol. 15, No. 4, www.world-watch.org.

Alberto Moravia. "La Caccia" (The Chase) from *Una Cosa e' una Cosa* by Alberto Moravia. Copyright © R.C.S. Libri SpA-Milano, Bompiani 1967. Reprinted by permission.

Morris. *American Heritage Dictionary of the English Language*, third edition. Dictionary definitions, copyright 1979.

Rudolph Mueller. From *As Sick As It Gets* by Rudolph Mueller. Reprinted by permission of Olin Frederick, Inc.

John Murrin. From Liberty, Equality, Power, A History of the American People, Concise Edition (Non-Info Trac Version), Second Edition, by Murrin. Copyright © 2001. Reprinted with permission of Wadsworth, a division of Thomson Learning: http://www.thomsonrights.com. Fax (800) 730-2215.

National Coalition for the Homeless. "Why Are People Homeless?" National Coalition for the Homeless, Fact Sheet #1, 2002, p. 1-9. Used by permission.

Timothy J. O'Leary and Linda L. O'Leary. From *Computing Essentials 1999-2000* by Timothy and Linda O'Leary. Reprinted by permission of The McGraw-Hill Companies.

Marley Peifer. "Suburb High, USA" by Marley Peifer. Reprinted by permission.

John Perry and Erna Perry. *Contemporary Society: An Introduction to Social Science*, Copyright © 1997. New York: Longman.

Malvina Reynolds. "Little Boxes" by Malvina Reynolds.

Paul Roberts. From "How Americans Eat: The New Food Anxiety" by Paul Roberts, *Psychology Today*, March/April 1998. Reprinted with permission from Psychology Today Magazine, Copyright © 1998 Sussex Publishers, Inc.

Scott Russell Sanders. "The Men We Carry in Our Minds" by Scott Russell Sanders. Copyright © 1984 by Scott Russell Sanders; first appeared in *Milkweed Chronicle* from *The Paradise of Bombs*, reprinted by permission of the author and the Virginia Kidd Agency, Inc.

Eric Schlosser. Excerpts from *Fast Food Nation: The Dark Side of the All-American Meal* by Eric Schlosser. Copyright © 2001 by Eric Schlosser. Reprinted by permission of Houghton Mifflin Company. All rights reserved.

Jim Spadaccina. From "The Sweet Lure of Chocolate" by Jim Spadaccina, *Exploratorium Magazine*. Reprinted by permission of Exploratorium.

Brent Staples. From "Black Men and Public Space" by Brent Staples. Reprinted by permission of the author.

Peter N. Stearns, et al. *World Civilizations*, Copyright © 1996. New York: HarperCollins Publishers.

Deborah Tannen. "Sex, Lies, and Conversation" by Deborah Tannen, *The Washington Post*, June 24, 1990, copyright Deborah Tannen. Reprinted by permission of the author.

Laurie Tarkan. "Benefits of the Dinner Table Rituas" by Laurie Tarkan, Copyright © 2005 by The New York Times Co. Reprinted with permission.

Carol Tavris and Carole Wade. From *Psychology, 5E* by Tavris/Wade, Copyright © 1997. Reprinted by permission of Prentice-Hall, Inc., Upper Saddle River, NJ.

Alex Thio. From *Sociology: A Brief Introduction*, Third Edition, by Alex Thio. Published by Allyn and Bacon, Boston, MA Copyright © 2002 by Pearson Education. Reprinted/adapted by permission of the Publisher.

William E. Thompson and Joseph V. Hickey. From *Society in Focus, 4E* by William E. Thompson and Joseph V. Hickey. Published by Allyn and Bacon, Boston, MA. Copyright © 2002 by Pearson Education. Reprinted/adapted by per mission of the publisher.

Yi-Fu Tuan. "American Space, Chinese Place" by Yi-Fu Tuan. Copyright © 1974 by Harper's Magazine. All rights reserved. Reproduced from the July issue by special permission.

Barbara Tuchman. From *A Distant Mirror* by Barbara Tuchman, Copyright © 1978 by Barbara W. Tuchman. Used by permission of Alfred A. Knopf, a division of Random House, Inc.

U.S. Department of Health and Human Services. *A Systematic Approach to Health Improvement: Healthy People 2010 Goals*.

U.S. Department of Housing and Urban Development. "State of the Cities". 1999.

Herman J. Viola and Carolyn Margolis. *Seeds of Change*, Copyright © 1991. Washington: Smithsonian Institution Press.

Carole Wade and Carol Tavris. From *Invitation to Psychology* by Wade/Tavris,

Tim Weiner. From "A New Model Army Soldier Rolls

Closer to Battle" by Tim Weiner, *The New York Times*, February 16, 2005. Copyright © 2005 by The New York Times Co. Reprinted with permission.

Brian K. Williams and Sharon M. Knight. From *Healthy for Life: Wellness and the Art of Living*, First Edition by

Williams/Knight. Copyright © 1994. Reprinted with permission of Brooks/Cole, a division of Thomson Learning: http://www.thomsonrights.com. Fax 800 730-2215.

PHOTO AND ART CREDITS

p. 3 Gary Conner/Photo Edit

p. 51 Wayne R. Bilenduke/ Getty Images

p. 107 Tom Stewart/CORBIS

p.169 © Photodisc/Inmagine

p.227 Jim Wark/Lonely Planet/Getty Images

p. 286 *Women's Wear Daily* © Fairchild Publications Inc.

p. 291 Bildarchiv Preussischer Kulturbesitz/Art Resource, NY. Photo: Joerg P. Anders

p. 293 *(top and bottom)* Janet Lee Mills

p. 349 Berringer/Dratch/The Image Works

p. 351 Christoph Grandt

p. 403 Michael Newman/ PhotoEdit

p. 507 Adam Bird/*Los Angeles Times*

©2007 by Pearson Education, Inc.

INDEX

©2007 Pearson Education, Inc.

©2007 Pearson Education, Inc.